W9-CEU-540

Speaker's
Lifetime
Library

Also by the authors

Instant Almanac of Events, Anniversaries, Observances,
Quotations, and Birthdays for Every Day of the Year

Treasury of Great American Sayings

Speaker's Lifetime Library

Leonard and Thelma Spinrad

Parker Publishing Company, Inc.
West Nyack, New York

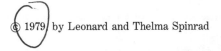
Library of Congress Cataloging in Publication Data

Spinrad, Leonard
  Speaker's lifetime library.

  Includes index.
  CONTENTS: v. 1. The speaker's reference guide.—
v. 2. Apt comparisons.—v. 3. The day and date book.—
v. 4. The special occasion book.
  1. Public speaking—Handbooks, manuals, etc.
I. Spinrad, Thelma, joint author. II. Title.
PN4193.I5S64   080   78-31291
ISBN 0-13-824557-6

A Resource For All The Days of Your Life

If all the wisdom of the world were contained in a single room, what would be the most important thing to have? The answer, of course, is the key to the room.

Think of this single volume, *Speaker's Lifetime Library*, as that kind of key. It unlocks a treasure-trove of wisdom that can give you the basis for a successful public speech every day of every year for the rest of your life.

For the first time, in a single book, conveniently arranged for easy reference, can be found the wise comments of the ages, the anecdotes, the historical facts, the figures of speech, the "jumping-off" or introductory gambits for speeches on every kind of subject.

"The power of eloquence," said St. Augustine, "is open to all." It is timeless, it is simple and it is here in these pages for the taking. You do not have to be an accomplished orator to make a good speech. You need to have good tools.

Speeches that seem to flow spontaneously, orations that appear to be off the cuff, usually aren't quite that simple. They come from careful preparation and backgrounding. They come from knowing what you want to say, understanding how to get into it gracefully, and how to make it memorable with an appropriate anecdote or wise quotation.

These are the various aspects of public speaking which *Speaker's Lifetime Library* is designed to make easier. The several volumes of this book are for use by everyone who is called upon to speak in public.

A speech has the same first problem as an automobile. It has to be started. Even though you know exactly what message you want to leave with your audience, you've got to figure out how you can grab their attention at the outset. Audiences are generally eager to be your friends; they don't want to be bored or antagonized any more than you do. Whether they expect to enjoy your speech or not, they *hope* to.

And even if they know you well, they still have to be led attractively and interestingly into the nitty-gritty of your remarks. It is sometimes helpful to be introduced by someone else who, so to speak, warms up the audience for you. Even gifted entertainers on television like to have somebody warm up the audience for them. But when you step up to speak, you are stepping into a situation that always represents a challenge—a challenge to establish your own quick and clear claim to be worth listening to. Like the farmer who hits a stubborn mule over the head simply "to get the critter's attention," you have to use your opening words—since you can't hit the audience over the head—to get its attention.

But the attention of the audience, even when won, has to be held. Even the audience that greets a speaker with tremendous enthusiasm at the outset won't hold on to that enthusiasm if it is being bored to tears.

Few speeches are remembered for their lengthy oratory. Most of those that live are remembered for a sentence, a paragraph, a turn of phrase here or there. William Jennings Bryan's great "Cross of Gold" oration, which captured the 1896 Democratic Presidential nomination for him, generally has the same three sentences quoted from it, because these relatively few words say so much so well.

Every great speaker in modern times has used these notable piths from speakers of earlier vintage. Sometimes quotations are employed directly. Sometimes the wisdom of previous speakers is studied to suggest new approaches or new directions in which a point can be developed. The wise speaker, in preparing a speech, looks for everything from quips and epigrams to scholarly citations. Accordingly, **Volume 1** of *Speaker's Lifetime Library* is a **Speaker's Reference Guide** containing, under more than 150 different subject headings, several thousand individual quotations, definitions, anecdotes, witticisms and epigrams for use in constructing, enlivening and elucidating the points the speaker wishes to make. In this same volume are capsules of basic facts about most subjects and suggested additional sources of information. For the conscientious speaker, this volume combines research and preparatory functions which, until now, have required any number of separate areas of research.

Most great speeches depend to a large extent upon metaphorical allusions such as Bryan's cross of gold, Churchill's iron curtain or FDR's forgotten man. **Volume 2** of *Speaker's Lifetime Library* is a collection of **Apt Comparisons.** This is meant to be a quick and convenient guide to similes, metaphors, symbols and opposites that can be used to make a speaker's word picture more effective. Some of these comparisons in the present compilation are drawn from literature, some from mythology, some from comedy routines. All are there to help the speaker say what is to be said in terms most graphic for the audience.

When two people are introduced by a mutual friend, their first words are usually small talk, as they try to find a common interest or simply feel each other out. This getting to know one another has its parallel at the outset of a speech. Once the speaker has been introduced to the audience, there is still that initial tentativeness, that need to find a way to get started toward the business at hand. The best speech in the world still will need some kind of opening tailored to the particular audience. Simply having the speaker express delight at being present in this town on this occasion is not enough. A good speech can get off to a better start than that. Taking note of a timely anniversary, or of some reason why this day or this location happens to be appropriate for the appearance of the speaker, is always effective as part of the opening "small talk." It helps to let the audience know that the speaker has taken the trouble to find a special link with them.

Volume 3 of *Speaker's Lifetime Library* is **The Day and Date Book,** listing past events for each day of the year, quotations of particular dates, holidays and other observances. **The Day and Date Book** also includes, for each day of the year, various suggested "lead-ins" for speeches appropriate to that day, based on the events, quotations and anniversaries of the day. The lead-ins can be used as ways to introduce the speaker of the day, or as opening gambits for the principal speaker.

Very often, of course, there is a specific reason for a speaking engagement to which the speaker must refer at the outset. If you are asked to speak at a golden wedding anniversary dinner, certainly recognition of that occasion should be offered early in your remarks. **Volume 4** of *Speaker's Lifetime Library* is **The Special Occasion Book.** It is a compilation of special speech material for various occasions, ranging, in alphabetical order, from acceptance of a nomination to welcoming a distinguished visitor. The entries for each occasion are arranged in sequential paragraphs. Every paragraph contains a separate speech angle; they can be used independently or combined into a single speech if desired.

What we offer in the following pages, then, is a series of reference books for all the vital elements of a good speech. The uses to which these various elements can be put are infinite, in terms of the number of different combinations and in terms of the brilliance with which each speaker develops thoughts of his or her own arising from this assembled wisdom.

For, above all, every single entry can and should be used to lead into the speaker's own thoughts and words. What is contained in this library is a collection of the precious bricks of a speech's outer walls—the furniture and the warmth of heart must be the speaker's own.

Leonard and Thelma Spinrad

Contents

Volume 1

The
Speaker's
Reference
Guide

List of Subjects

Accounting
Achievement
Adolescence (see also Teenagers, Youth)
Advertising
Age (see also Longevity, Youth)
Agriculture
Alibis
Alumni (see also College)
Ambition
America
Ancestry
Aristocracy
Armed Forces
Art
Athletics (see also individual sports)
Automobiles
Aviation
Babies (see also Children, Parents)
Baseball
Basketball
Blacks (see also Minorities, Prejudice, Race)
Books (see also Literature)
Boxing
Building
Business
Candidates (see also Elections, Political Parties, Voting)
Censorship (see also Books, Journalism, Liberty, Motion Pictures, Radio, Television)
Charity
Children (see also Babies, Parents)
Citizenship
City Life
Civilization (see also Society)
Clubs (see also Fraternities)
College (see also Alumni, Education, School)
Constitution (see also Government)
Conventions
Cooking (see also Dieting, Food)
Courage
Courts (see also Justice, Law)
Creativity
Crime (see also Law and Order, Violence)
Criticism

Death
Dieting (see also Food, Health)
Drama (see also Theater)
Dreams
Drink
Drugs (see also Medicine)
Economics
Education (see also College, School)
Elections (see also Candidates, Voting)
Ethics
Ethnicity (see also Immigration, Minorities, Race)
Experience
Exploration (see also Space)
Family
Fashion
Feminism (see also Women)
Flag
Food (see also Cooking, Dieting)
Football
Foreign Affairs
Fraternities (see also Clubs)
Friendship
Gambling
Geography
Golf
Government (see also Constitution)
Graduation
Gratitude
Happiness
Health (see also Dieting, Food, Medicine)
History
Hobbies (see also Leisure)
Horseracing
Hospitality
Housing
Humanity
Humor
Immigration (see also Ethnicity, Minorities)
Individualism
Inspiration
Invention
Jobs (see also Labor, Opportunity)
Journalism (see also Radio, Television)
Justice (see also Courts, Law)
Knowledge

Labor (see also Jobs)
Language
Law (see also Courts, Justice, Law and Order)
Law and Order (see also Crime, Justice, Law, Violence)
Leadership
Leisure (see also Hobbies and various Sports)
Liberty
Life (see also Nature)
Lincoln
Literature (see also Books)
Longevity (see also Age)
Love (see also Marriage, Sex)
Loyalty
Luck
Mail
Manners
Marriage (see also Love, Sex)
Medicine (see also Drugs, Health)
Memory
Men
Midwest
Minorities (see also Blacks, Ethnicity, Immigration, Prejudice, Race)
Motion Pictures (See also Censorship)
Music
Nature (see also Life)
Neighbors
New England
Nuclear Energy
Opportunity (see also Jobs)
Parents (see also Adolescence, Babies, Children, Family, Marriage)
Peace (see also Armed Forces, War)
Political Parties (see also Candidates, Elections, Government, Voting)

Population (see also Children, Family)
Poverty
Prejudice (see also Blacks, Minorities, Race)
Privacy
Psychology
Public Opinion
Public Relations
Public Speaking
Race (see also Blacks, Ethnicity, Prejudice)
Radio (see also Journalism, Television)
Religion
School (see also College, Education)
Science
Seasons
Sex (see also Love, Marriage)
Society (see also Civilization)
South
Space (see also Exploration)
Taxes
Teenagers (see also Adolescence, Youth)
Television (see also Journalism, Radio)
Tennis
Theater (see also Drama)
Time
Violence (see also Crime, Law and Order)
Voting (see also Candidates, Elections, Political Parties
War (see also Peace)
Washington, D.C.
Washington, George
Wealth
West
Women (see also Feminism)
Worry
Youth (see also Adolescence, Teenagers)

ACCOUNTING

Definitions: method or system of keeping records; the language of business; the world's greatest balancing act.

Quotations:

Facts and Figures! Put 'em down! *Charles Dickens,* **The Chimes,** *1844.*

Figures won't lie, but liars will figure. *Attributed to many, notably Ohio's Charles H. Grosvenor at the end of the 19th century.*

Statistics are like alienists—they will testify for either side. *New York Representative Fiorello H. LaGuardia, 1933.*

. . . give an account of thy stewardship. **Luke,** *16.2*

Don't tell me of facts, I never believe facts; you know Canning said nothing was as fallacious as facts, except figures. *Reverend Sydney Smith, quoted by his daughter, Lady Holland, 1855.*

. . . keep your accounts on your thumb-nail. *Henry D. Thoreau,* **Walden,** *1854.*

Anonymous aphorisms:

The difference between an accountant and a bookkeeper is a sizeable figure.

There are three kinds of lies—lies, damned lies and statistics. *Authorship unknown, though credited by Mark Twain to Benjamin Disraeli.*

Accounting is ledger de main.

When things look black to an accountant, it means the account is in the red.

CPA stands for Constantly Proposing Audits.

Julius Caesar's motto as a soldier was veni, vidi, vici. If he had been an accountant it would have been aught, ought to, audit.

Anecdotage:

A journalist and an accountant were riding together and passed a flock of sheep. "Look," said the journalist, "the sheep have all been shorn." "On this side, at least," said the accountant.

Facts:

The keeping of financial records has been traced back to the 23rd century B.C., but it took a long time for accountants to gain full professional recognition. Accounting was recognized officially as a profession in England in 1854 and in the United States in the 1890s, not long after the formation of the American Association of Public Accountants. The first certified public accountants were accredited by New York State in 1896. As taxes and methods of financing business have become more complicated, accounting education and professional standards have grown more rigorous.

The American Institute of Certified Public Accountants is located at 1211 Avenue of the Americas, New York, N.Y. 10036.

ACHIEVEMENT

Definitions: the result of effort or toil when successful; feat; deed; accomplishment; being able to look back and see how far you've come.

Quotations:

The toughest thing about success is that you've got to keep on being a success. *Irving Berlin, 1958.*

We succeed only as we identify in life, or in war, or in anything else, a single overriding objective, and make all other considerations bend to that one objective. *President Dwight D. Eisenhower, speech, April 2, 1957.*

The reward of a thing well done is to have done it. *Ralph Waldo Emerson,* **Essays, Second Series:** *New England Reformers, 1844.*

What we call results are beginnings. *Ralph Waldo Emerson,* **The Conduct of Life:** *Fate, 1860.*

Death comes to all/ But great achievements raise a monument/ Which shall endure until the sun grows cold. *George Fabricius,* **In Praise of Georgius Agricola,** *16th century.*

Well done is better than well said. *Benjamin Franklin,* **Poor Richard's Almanac,** *1737.*

My object all sublime I shall achieve in time . . . *W. S. Gilbert,* **The Mikado,** *1885.*

The heights by great men reached and kept/ Were not attained by sudden flight,/ But they, while their companions slept,/ Were toiling upward in the night. *Henry Wadsworth Longfellow,* **The Ladder of Saint Augustine,** *1858.*

The difficult we do immediately; the impossible takes a little longer. *Attributed variously, including, in slightly different wording, to George Santayana, Fridtjof Nansen and the U.S. Army Corps of Engineers.*

Anonymous aphorisms:

Getting something done is an accomplishment; getting something done right is an achievement.

They said it couldn't be done, but we did it.

Those who dare, do; those who dare not, do not.

Anecdotage:

At the end of a year out in the world, a young man came home and told his father he was worth $100. His father simply smiled. The following year he reported he was worth $1,000; his father still merely smiled. Year after year, as he came home and reported how much more he was worth, his father merely smiled. Then one year the son came home and said, "Father, this year, in order to keep the business going, I had to borrow a million dollars." His father clapped him on the back and said, "Now *that* is an achievement."

Facts:

Achievement is one of the things that divides humanity from the beasts. It is one of the things that humanity recognizes: we have Halls of Fame, Emmies, Oscars, Nobel and Pulitzer Prizes and thousands of other formal types of recognition of outstanding achievement. *Who's Who in America* grows larger with every edition. The number of new products available and the new inventions which make life easier from generation to generation all testify to mankind's thirst for more achievement. No matter what kind of society or political system a country may have, it seeks to provide recognition for what it regards as achievement. For a current assessment of outstanding achievement see lists of awards in various almanacs.

ADOLESCENCE
(See also Teenagers, Youth)

Definitions: the process of going from childhood to maturity; the age between childhood and adulthood; a way of passing the time; "a kind of emotional sea-sickness" (*Arthur Koestler*).

Quotations:

Young people are in a condition like permanent intoxication, because youth is sweet and they are growing. *Aristotle,* **Nicomachean Ethics,** *4th century B.C.*

A boy becomes an adult three years before his parents think he does, and about two years after he thinks he does. *Major General Lewis B. Hershey, Director of Selective Service, December 30, 1951.*

Young people are usually thoughtless. *Homer,* **The Odyssey,** *about 9th century B.C.*

The imagination of a boy is healthy, and the mature imagination of a man is healthy, but there is a space of life between, in which the soul is in a ferment, the character undecided, the way of life uncertain, the ambition thicksighted. *John Keats, preface to* **Endymion,** *1818.*

Anonymous aphorisms:

Adolescence does not accentuate the last syllable.

They're either too young or too old—depending on what you want them to do.

You can always tell an adolescent, but you can't tell her much.

Adolescents like to rebel against conformity by all dressing exactly the same.

Addle essence.

An adolescent is a new dog learning old tricks.

The question is not how you tell an adolescent but what you tell.

Adolescence is when young people finally break the unbilical cord. They trade it for a telephone cord.

An adolescent is a person whose vice is changing.

First adolescent, then obsolescent.

Anecdotage:

A civic leader brought a group of adolescent boys together and asked them what particularly interested them. "Girls," they all said as one.

After the adolescent party, the young host was seen raiding the refrigerator. His father asked, "How can you do that when you're spent the whole afternoon eating hamburgers and popcorn and drinking soda pop?" "Well," said the adolescent, "eating gives me an appetite."

A short-tempered man was offended by the giggling of a group of adolescent girls who passed him. "What's so funny?" he demanded. "Nothing," said one of the girls, "we were just laughing."

Facts:

Adolescence is part of teenage (which is a separate section in this volume), at the younger half of the teens, but adolescence has its own separate status. Adolescent offenders are treated differently at law than older teenagers. U.S. awkward age or adolescent population is going down; in 1970 there were 52,500,000 Americans between 5 and 17 years of age, but there were slightly less five years later; by the year 2000 most estimates say the proportion of adolescents in the population will be lower than now, although the overall population will be higher because of better health conditions.

For informed analysis of adolescent behavior patterns see *Youth–The Years from 10 to 16,* by Gesell, Ilg and Ames.

ADVERTISING

Definitions: a public notice intended to call attention to something; the art of making something more attractive by saying it is; getting people to buy things they hadn't previously known they wanted; promises,, promises; selling by suggestion; "the public face of business" *(Neal W. O'Connor).*

Quotations:

Advertise, or the sheriff may do it for you. *P.T. Barnum, attributed.*

The advertisements in a newspaper are more full of knowledge in respect to what is going on in a state or community than the editorial columns are. *Rev. Henry Ward Beecher,* **Proverbs from Plymouth Pulpit,** *1887.*

. . . we've got to know what we've got a choice of. This is the function of advertising. *Tom Dillon, Chairman, BBD&O, July 1, 1976*

You can tell the ideals of a nation by its advertisements. *(George) Norman Douglas,* **South Wind,** *1917.*

Advertisements contain the only truths to be relied on in a newspaper. *Thomas Jefferson, letter to Senator Nathaniel Macon, 1819.*

Advertisements are now so numerous that they are very negligently perused, and it is therefore become necessary to gain attention by magnificence of promises, and by eloquences sometimes sublime and sometimes pathetic. Promise—large promise—is the soul of advertising. *Dr. Samuel Johnson,* **The Idler,** *No. 40, 1759.*

Half the money I spend on advertising is wasted; the trouble is I don't know which half. *Attributed to John Wanamaker.*

Anonymous aphorisms:

Advertising is the art form that introduces itself by saying buy, buy.

You always buy familiar names, the ones you recognize, that's why the adman always claims it pays to advertise.

Advertising is sell service.

When business is good, it pays to advertise. When business isn't good, you've got to advertise.

Advertising moves the goods—if it's good advertising. Bad advertising doesn't move the goods because it doesn't move the buyers.

Events being what they are these days, advertising is the good news amid the bad news.

Advertisers are merchants of dreams.

Anecdotage:

A friend said to a man who had a frankfurter stand by the side of the road, "If you put up a sign advertising your stand a mile up the road so people see it before they get here, they might be influenced to stop." He put up the sign and it worked; so as time went on he put up more signs further and further away on the road, and more and more people bought the frankfurters and the owner was able to send his son to the finest university. When the son returned he said "You're spending too much money on your advertising. You don't need *all* those signs." So the father took down some of the signs; the business went down a little, but so did the expense for advertising. With less business, they decided to cut down a little more on the advertising, and the business went down a little more, until finally they were back to a little frankfurter stand without any signs on the road at all. The moral of this story is that if you don't advertise your product, if you are quiet about your business, your business is apt to be quiet, too.

"Anybody can advertise," said the skeptic to the ad man, "and get the same results." They agreed to test this by both advertising the same offer in the same paper on the same day. The skeptic's ad read, "Free trip to Disneyland. Driver needed to deliver new car from New York." He got three responses. But the advertising man got 103 answers to *his* ad, which consisted of the same number of words: "Drive free from New York to Disneyland delivering new air conditioned Cadillac." It isn't always what you advertise, it's how you advertise it.

Facts:

Many people think advertising is purely a capitalistic enterprise, but it is not. Even in state owned economies without a profit system, there is advertising directed at consumers and potential customers, as well as advertising of political ideas. In profit oriented societies, advertising is a competitive tool. Since 1960, advertising expenditures in the U.S. have more than tripled in dollar totals. In the past half-century, advertising has been included in university curricula. Advertising has financed the radio and television broadcasting industries in the U.S. as well as most newspapers and magazines. It has been estimated that the average adult is the target of at least 565 ads a day.

The American Association of Advertising Agencies is at 200 Park Avenue, New York, N.Y. 10017.

AGE

(See also Longevity, Youth)

Definitions: the length of time a person or thing has existed; the time of your life; a woman's secret and a man's fear; the opposite of youth; the inevitable aftermath of youth.

Quotations:

To me, old age is always 15 years older than I am. *Bernard M. Baruch, 1940s.*

Behold, thou has made my days as an handbreadth; and mine age is as nothing before thee: verily every man at his best state is altogether vanity.**The Book of Psalms,** *Psalm 39.*

Grow old along with me!/ The best is yet to be,/ The last of life, for which he first was made . . . *Robert Browning,* **Dramatis Personae,** *Rabbi Ben Ezra, 1864.*

. . . anecdotage. . . *Benjamin Disraeli,* **Lothair,** *1870.*

At twenty years of age, the will reigns; at thirty the wit; at forty the judgment. *Benjamin Franklin,* **Poor Richard's Almanac,** *1741.*

Gather ye rosebuds while ye may/ Old Time is still a-flying:/ And this same flower that smiles today/ Tomorrow will be dying.*Robert Herrick, "To Virgins, To Make Much of Time," 1648.*

. . . there's nothing that keeps its youth,/ So far as I know, but a tree and truth. *Oliver Wendell Holmes, "The Deacon's Masterpiece," 1858.*

Youth longs and manhood strives, but age remembers . . . *Oliver Wendell Holmes, "The Iron Gate," 1880.*

The riders in a race do not stop short when they reach the goal. There is a little finishing canter before coming to a standstill. There is time to hear the kind voices of friends and to say to one's self, "the work is done." *Oliver Wendell Holmes, Jr., speech on his 91st birthday, March 8, 1932.*

My only fear is that I may live too long. *Thomas Jefferson, letter to Philip Mazzei, 1801.*

It makes me shudder to think that I graduated from college thirty years ago and how doddering and venerable the thirtieth reunion class looked to me then. *Adlai E. Stevenson, October 8, 1952. Madison, Wis.*

It is better to be a young June bug than an old bird of paradise. *Mark Twain,* **The Tragedy of Pudd'nhead Wilson,** *1894.*

Anonymous aphorisms:

Old age is no bar to men chasing women; they just have trouble remembering why.

We grow too soon old and too late smart. *Pennsylvania Dutch saying.*

A man is as old as he feels, a woman is as old as she looks.

In life, it's always later than you think.

Age is a relative thing; you're young as long as you have a relative who's older.

Human beings are like steak: a little aging helps, but it can go too far.

Anecdotage:

An actress told Bob Hope she was "approaching 30," and he wondered "from which direction."

Supreme Court Justice Oliver Wendell Holmes, Jr., ninetyish, was out for a stroll with a friend when a pretty young girl walked by. "Oh," said the Justice to his friend, "what I'd give to be 70 again!"

Half a dozen years after he had been her cameraman, a Hollywood cinematographer worked on another film with a glamorous Hollywood beauty, and she was very upset with the results. "When you filmed me before, I looked much more beautiful," she complained. "Well," said the diplomatic cameraman, "I was six years younger then."

Facts:

Of all the privileges and restrictions applied to human beings, more have been based on age than on anything else. There are age qualifications for various public offices (35 for the Presidency, 30 for the Senate, 25 for the House, for example), for marriage, for retirement, for enlistment in the armed forces, for voting. Some of these age requirements have changed over the years; some have remained constant. The vote for 18-year-olds came after the draft of 18-year-olds. Mandatory retirement at 65 was born of the depression of the 1930s to produce more jobs for younger people; it began to fade in the late 1970s. In earlier times, retirement was less of a problem because not as many people lived long enough to retire. Male life expectancy in the U.S. in 1920 was 53.6 years; in 1940 it was 60.8 years and in 1974 it was 68.2. For women, expectancy has lengthened from 54.6 years in 1920 to an age of 75.9 in 1974.

Information: Statistical Abstract of the U.S.

AGRICULTURE

Definitions: farming; tilling the soil; raising crops or cattle; the original growth business; down-to-earth America; plant you now and dig you later.

Quotations:

Burn down your cities and leave our farms, and your cities will spring up again as if by magic; but destroy our farms and the grass will grow in the streets of every city in the country. *William Jennings Bryan, "Cross of Gold" speech to the Democratic national convention, July 8, 1896.*

Farming looks mighty easy when your plow is a pencil, and you're a thousand miles from the corn field. *President Dwight D. Eisenhower, September 11, 1956.*

The first farmer was the first man, and all historic nobility rests on possession and use of land. *Ralph Waldo Emerson,* **Society and Solitude,** *Farming, 1870.*

A Plowman on his legs is higher than a Gentleman on his Knees. *Benjamin Franklin,* **Poor Richard's Almanac,** *1746.*

Those who labor in the earth are the chosen people of God, if ever He had a chosen people, whose breasts He has made His peculiar deposit for substantial and genuine virtue. *Thomas Jefferson,* **Notes on Virginia,** *1781.*

Farmers are farmers in the first place because they have the deep-seated instinct to raise crops, not to cut them back, not to leave the land unproductive. *President Lyndon B. Johnson, October 7, 1964.*

One American farmer now feeds and clothes himself and 32 others besides—an achievement unmatched anywhere on earth. One man on the farm today does all the work that was performed by four in 1939. *President Lyndon B. Johnson, November 4, 1965.*

I know of no pursuit in which more real and important services can be rendered to any country, than by improving its agriculture—its breed of useful animals—and other branches of a husbandman's cares. *President George Washington, July 20, 1794.*

It will not be doubted that with reference either to individual or national welfare agriculture is of primary importance. In proportion as nations advance in population and other circumstances of maturity this truth becomes more apparent, and renders the cultivation of the soil more and more an object of public patronage. Institutions for promoting it grow up, supported by the public purse; and to what object can it be dedicated with greater propriety. *President George Washington, address to Congress, December 7, 1796.*

Let us never forget that the cultivation of the earth is the most important labor of man. *Daniel Webster, January 13, 1840.*

Anonymous aphorisms:

Agriculture is what happens when people go to seed.

Forty acres can be ruined by one wise acre.

Agriculture is a good field to work in.

Agriculture is people waiting to see what comes up.

The farmer and the manufacturer agree that prosperity comes from thriving plants.

Anecdotage:

The farmer's son said, "Goodbye, Dad, I'm off to the big city so my talents can flower." "Same reason the corn stays here," said the farmer.

Farmer Brown was being paid not to plant crops on several of his fields one year, and he thought he had figured out a way to make more money. He asked the government how much they would pay him not to dig for oil.

Facts:

People think of agriculture as America's first preoccupation, but the Indians were not farmers and the first European colonists came here as traders and trappers and fishermen; they began growing food simply for subsistence, and then to sell their crops to others. At one time a majority of Americans were farmers. The proportion of farmland is still higher in the U.S. than in the world as a whole, even though the number of U.S. farmers has shrunk tremendously. About a fifth of the land in the entire world could be used to grow food, but less than half that amount is actually cultivated. In the United States, more than 40 percent of the land area is farmland. The average farm size in the mid-1970s was 385 acres and less than 5 percent of the population was on farms.

ALIBIS

Definitions: excuses; evidence to disprove allegations; slip covers: provable absence from the scene at the time of the crime.

Quotations:

Bad excuses are worse than none. *Thomas Fuller,* **Gnomologia,** *1732.*

The absent are always in the wrong. *George Herbert,* **Jacula Prudentum,** *1640.*

"Alibi Ike": Title of a Ring Lardner story about a ball player who had an excuse for everything, 1924.

Hence with denial vain, and coy excuse. *John Milton,* **Lycidas,** *1637.*

It is better to offer no excuse than a bad one. *George Washington, letter to his niece Harriet Washington, October 30, 1791.*

Anonymous aphorisms:

There may be a bible in every hotel room, but the register can be an alibible.

Too often a successful alibi depends on finding someone else who will do what the word says—a lie buy.

Absence is usually easier to explain than presence.

The purpose of an alibi is to get away with something by getting away from it.

The accused protests innocence by saying, "Who, me?" and tries to prove it by saying "Me, where?"

An alibi is something else again.

An alibi is like a good shot in tennis—a matter of placement.

An alibi is like a compression chamber; if it isn't airtight it doesn't work.

A bad alibi is a poor excuse for an answer.

The perfect alibi is not a claim of innocence; it is a proof.

Anecdotage:

A man claiming not to have been at the scene of the crime was nevertheless accused because his car had been seen the night of the crime parked for hours outside the home of the victim. While he was out on bail he parked his car overnight outside a monastery. "If you believe I committed the crime," he said the next day, "then you have equal proof that I have repented."

Facts:

The word alibi comes from the Latin, meaning elsewhere. In law an alibi is a defense through proving that the accused was someplace else when the crime was committed. In modern times the meaning of the word has been broadened to cover all sorts of excuses. Ring Lardner's Alibi Ike was a baseball player who had an excuse for everything. The word excuse, like alibi, comes from the Latin and originally had a legal meaning, namely to take out of or remove from a lawsuit. People in law enforcement find that the same situation gives rise, time after time, to the same excuses or alibis. Those accused of crimes stemming from drunkenness are apt to say they "just had a couple of beers" and those who come late say it was because "my watch was slow."

ALUMNI

(see also College)

Definitions: graduates or former attendees of a particular school, college or institution; members of a permanent class; the Monday morning quarterbacks of the groves of academe; refugees from the good old days.

Quotation:

I find that the three major administrative problems on a campus are sex for the students, athletics for the alumni and parking for the faculty. *President Clark Kerr of the University of California, 1958.*

Anonymous aphorisms:

The alumni of an educational institution are like the wake of a ship; they spread out and ultimately disappear, but not until they have made a few waves.

Alumni graduate from the university, but the university never graduates from its alumni.

Everybody belongs to an alumni group, even if it is the School of Hard Knocks.

The students ask why, the faculty asks how, and the alumni ask how much.

An alumni reunion is living history in the process of being rewritten.

A student becomes an alumnus when he stops thinking of class as a side in a revolution and starts thinking of class as something that has a reunion.

Students and alumni are like acorns and oaks; there's a lot more bark to the oak and a lot more nuttiness to the acorn.

The difference between an alumnus and an alumna is what they studied the most while they were students.

A student keeps trying to win a letter at college; an alumnus keeps getting letters from the college.

Alumni homecoming brings out the youth in all the old alumni.

Many alumni believe there should be more recognition of the most important of all conspicuous alumni achievements—survival.

Anecdotage:

"The old school isn't what it used to be," sighed the alumnus to the college president. "No," said the president tactfully, "but then, neither are we."

Trying to find words of comfort for the pitifully few members of the class at its fiftieth reunion, the class president said, "As we look at our ranks today and compare them to the long roster of classmates when we were at school and the grades were posted, let us remember that by now a lot more of us have passed."

Facts:

More than 40 million living Americans have spent time in college and thus constitute alumni. In terms of high school alumni, the figures of course are considerably higher. College and university alumni are not a cohesive or class group in the U.S. and their role is different from one institution to another. In some cases, they elect trustees to help govern the institution; in some places they have an automatic voice in the university family, while in others they have to pay dues to qualify. Except for the American Association of University Women, alumni associations and organizations are generally separate for individual schools, colleges and universities. A number of large alumni groups maintain clubs in larger cities, and in some cities there are also university clubs serving alumni of different institutions in one facility.

AMBITION

Definitions: desire and enthusiastic effort for advancement, power or success; high hopes combined with goal tending; "avarice on stilts and masked" *(Walter Savage Landor,* **Imaginary Conversations:** *Brooke and Sidney);* "the glorious fault of angels and of gods" *(Alexander Pope, "Elegy to the Memory of an Unfortunate Lady").*

Quotations:

Hitch your wagon to a star. *Ralph Waldo Emerson,* **Society and Solitude: Civilization,** *1870.*

Nothing is so commonplace as to wish to be remarkable. *Oliver Wendell Holmes,* **The Autocrat of the Breakfast-Table,** *1858.*

I would sooner fail than not be among the greatest. *John Keats, letter to James Hessey, 1818.*

One often goes from love to ambition, but one rarely returns from ambition to love. *Duc François de La Rochefoucauld,* **Maxims,** *17th century.*

Most people would succeed in small things if they were not troubled with great ambitions. *Henry Wadsworth Longfellow,* **Driftwood;** *Table Talk, 1857.*

Not failure, but low aim, is crime. *James Russell Lowell,* **Under the Willows and Other Poems,** *For an Autograph, 1868.*

Ambition should be made of sterner stuff. *William Shakespeare,* **Julius Caesar,** *1599.*

I charge thee, fling away ambition./ By that sin fell the angels; how can man then,/The image of his Maker, hope to win by it? *William Shakespeare,* **Henry VIII,** *1613 (possibly by John Fletcher or a collaboration).*

Ambition often puts men upon doing the meanest offices; so climbing is performed in the same posture with creeping. *Jonathan Swift,* **Miscellanies,** *1711.*

Ambition/Is like the sea wave, which the more you drink/ The more you thirst—yea—drink too much, as men/ Have done on rafts of wreck—it drives you mad. *Alfred Tennyson,* **The Cup,** *1880.*

If you think you're a second-class citizen, you are. *Ted Turner, 1977.*

Anonymous aphorisms:

Ambition is hard work.

Ambition lubricates the mind.

Onward and upward.

There's always room at the top.

Keep your sights high—and your powder dry.

Most people want to improve themselves, but not too many work at it.

Where there's a will there's a way.

Where there's a will, there's a beneficiary.

The way to go from rags to riches is to start by getting a decent set of rags.

Ambition looks up; failure looks down.

Anecdotage:

The brash young man barged into the boss's office and explained, "Ambition makes its own opportunities." "Yes," said the boss, "but opportunity knocks."

Then there's the story of the man who was so busy climbing the ladder of success he forgot to watch his step.

In high school and college everybody knew how anxious Johnny Brown was for success. The college year book tabbed him as the class's most ambitious member. But 20 years later he hadn't gotten anyplace. He had a ready explanation. "Everybody thought I would be a success because I talked about it. So I was a success already. I was a successful talker. I had realized my ambition before I understood that it was my ambition. Ambition, in the last analysis, is to do well what you like doing best. And I like to talk."

Facts:

In rigid class societies, there are not as many outlets for ambition as in a society that is upwardly mobile. In open societies there is more room for inventiveness, new business ideas, new arts. The best qualification for a politician for so long was to have been born of a humble family in a log cabin on the American frontier. America was settled by generations of immigrants who came here with a burning ambition to make something of themselves and something better of their children. With the highest salary levels, the greatest variety of creature comforts and the broadest range of opportunity in the world, it is logical that ambition should flourish in America. Ambition, essentially, is the desire to fulfill what the Declaration of Independence described as "the pursuit of happiness."

AMERICA

Definitions: name generally given to the North American continent and usually to the U.S. portion; "a country where anything can happen" (*George and*

Helen Papashvily, **Anything Can Happen**); "the land of the free and the home of the brave" (*Francis Scott Key, "The Star Spangled Banner"*); "a nation of many nationalities, many races, many religions—bound together by a single unity, the unity of freedom and equality" (*President Franklin D. Roosevelt, 1940*); "the melting pot of the world" (*Israel Zangwill,* **The Melting Pot,** *1908*); melting pot turned pressure cooker; "Columbia, the gem of the ocean,/ The home of the brave and the free" (*Thomas Becket or David T. Shaw, 1843*) "sweet land of liberty" (*Rev. Samuel F. Smith, "America," 1831*).

Quotations:

The American is a new man, who acts upon new principles; he must therefore entertain new ideas, and form new opinions. . . . It is in consequence of that change, that he becomes an American. *Michel-Guillaume de Crevecoeur,* **Letters from an American Farmer,** *1782.*

Whatever America hopes to bring to pass in the world must first come to pass in the hearts of America. *President Dwight D. Eisenhower, Inaugural Address, January 20, 1953.*

Here in America we are descended in blood and in spirit from revolutionists and rebels—men and women who dared to dissent from accepted doctrine. *President Dwight D. Eisenhower, May 31, 1954.*

Now, we Americans understand freedom. We have earned it, we have lived for it, and we have died for it. This nation and its people are freedom's models in a searching world. We can be freedom's missionaries in a doubting world. *Senator Barry M. Goldwater of Arizona, accepting Republican Presidential nomination, July 16, 1964.*

. . . not merely a nation but a nation of nations. *President Lyndon B. Johnson, 1965.*

Give me your tired, your poor,/ Your huddled masses yearning to breathe free,/ The wretched refuse of your teeming shore./ Send these, the homeless, tempest-tost to me,/ I lift my lamp beside the golden door! *Emma Lazarus. "The New Colossus," written about and inscribed upon the base of the Statue of Liberty, written in 1883.*

I believe in the United States of America as a government of the people, by the people, for the people, whose just powers are derived from the consent of the governed; a democracy in a republic; a sovereign nation of many sovereign states; a perfect union, one and inseparable; established upon those principles of freedom, equality, justice and humanity for which Americans sacrificed their lives and their fortunes. I therefore believe it is my duty to my country to love it, to support its Constitution, to obey its laws, to respect its flag and to defend it against all enemies. *William Tyler Page, "The American's Creed," adopted by the U.S. House of Representatives April 3, 1918.*

The American idea . . . a democracy—that is, a government of all the people, by all the people, for all the people . . . *Reverend Theodore Parker, speech in*

Boston, May 29, 1850 (later used in Abraham Lincoln's Gettysburg Address in 1863).

Since the days when the fleet of Columbus sailed into the waters of the New World, America has been another name for opportunity . . . *Frederick Jackson Turner, "The Significance of the Frontier in American History," 1893.*

In America the President reigns for four years, and Journalism governs for ever and ever. *Oscar Wilde,* **The Soul of Man Under Socialism,** *1891.*

The youth of America is their oldest tradition. *Oscar Wilde,* **A Woman of No Importance,** *1893.*

Just what is it that America stands for? If she stands for one thing more than another, it is for the sovereignty of self-governing people. *President Woodrow Wilson, January 20, 1916.*

Anonymous aphorisms:

Baseball, hot dogs and apple pie.

America is the land of opportunity.

America is fast foods, fast cars and fast friends.

An American believes more than anything else in the last four letters of that title—I can.

America is still the New World.

America is a mobile civilization that some day will rediscover walking.

America is wide open spaces and traffic jams, sometimes in the same place.

The colossus of the north.

America is still the promised land.

America is a nation on the move.

When the going gets tough in America, the tough get going.

Anecdotage:

A Frenchman, an Austrian and an American were discussing national traits of character. "We French are quick to see others' faults," said the Frenchman, "while you Austrians always sit and wonder what's behind a remark and you Americans think you know it all." "I know," said the American.

The pessimist said gloomily, "America just isn't what it used to be." The optimist answered, "It never was. We always have room here for improvement."

Q. What's the difference between the American Dream and everybody else's dream?

A. Everybody else's dream is to come to America.

Facts:

What is unique about America is not its wealth, its size, its natural resources, its democratic government, its ethnic diversity or the popularity of its arts. What is unique is to have all these in a single country. No nation has ever contributed more inventions to the world or accepted more immigrants from the rest of the world. No nation educates as high a proportion of its citizenry through high school, college and higher professional and graduate schools. No nation has freedom of movement through more thousands of miles of its territory. No nation has longer peaceful and unarmed borders. No nation has an older political party than the Democrats. But not all the superlatives are necessarily signs of health. No nation has more psychiatrists. No nation has more good food—or more junk food. No nation's scientists have probed more of the universe. Some countries, it has been said, are punctuated by a question mark. For America, the best punctuation is an exclamation point.

ANCESTRY

Definitions: line of descent; parents, grandparents and on back into history; the bloodlines you were born with; family tree; pedigree.

Quotations:

People will not look forward to posterity who never look backward to their ancestors. *Edmund Burke*, **Reflections on the Revolution in France**, *1790*.

The pride of ancestry increases in the ratio of distance. *George W. Curtis*, **Prue and I**, *1856*.

Men resemble their contemporaries even more than their progenitors. *Ralph Waldo Emerson*, **Representative Men:** *On the Uses of Great Men, 1850.*

I can trace my ancestry back to a protoplasmal primordial atomic globule. Consequently my family pride is something inconceivable. I can't help it. I was born sneering. *W. S. Gilbert*, **The Mikado,** *1885.*

A child's education should begin at least one hundred years before he was born. *Oliver Wendell Holmes*, **The Autocrat of the Breakfast-Table,** *1858.*

We are all omnibuses in which our ancestors ride, and every now and then one of them sticks his head out and embarrasses us. *Oliver Wendell Holmes*, **The Guardian Angel,** *1867.*

Men have their intellectual ancestry, and the likeness of some one of them is forever unexpectedly flashing out in the features of a descendant, it may be after a gap of several generations. In the parliament of the present every man represents a constituency of the past. *James Russell Lowell, "Keats," 1854.*

It is certainly desirable to be well descended, but the glory belongs to our ancestors. *Plutarch, "Morals," about 1st century.*

He who boasts of his ancestry is praising the deeds of another. *Seneca, "Hercules Furens," 1st century.*

Our ancestors are very good kind of folks; but they are the last people I should choose to have a visiting acquaintance with. *Richard Brinsley Sheridan,* **The Rivals,** *1775.*

Whoever serves his country well has no need of ancestors. *Voltaire,* **Merope,** *1743.*

Anonymous aphorisms:

Good birth in your lineage is apt to lead to a good berth in life.

Nobody got here without ancestors.

People who prate of their ancestry should go climb a family tree.

Ancestry is a hereditary condition.

You can't choose your ancestors, and neither can your descendants.

People are generally prouder of their ancestors—or pretend to be—than their ancestors would be of them.

Ancestry tells us where we come from, and posterity is apt to tell us where to get off.

Ancedotage:

A snob and an egalitarian were arguing. "My people," said the snob, "go back to the Mayflower," "I wish they would," said the egalitarian.

Asked about his family's coat of arms, the mechanic said, "We never had a coat of arms. We were lucky to have a coat of grease."

He was always describing himself as coming from one of "the first families." He explained that his was one of the first families to come to the New Land. The trouble with that, someone observed, was that you never knew whether it was a spirit of adventure that was responsible or whether the family had been thrown out of the old world they came from.

I can trace my ancestors back 23 generations, said the haughty dowager. I never felt the need, said her friend.

Facts:

Ancestor worship is one of humanity's oldest devotions—almost as old as the tendency to scoff at other people's ancestry. We have upwards of 100 generations of ancestors, which offers plenty of latitude and longitude. Associations based on ancestry are numerous: for example, the Society of Mayflower Descendants, the Daughters of the American Revolution, the Sons of Union Veterans of the Civil War, the Ancient Order of Hibernians. General family groups can be large. There are well over two million people in the U.S. named Smith and 1,700,000 named Johnson. Even before Alex Haley's book, *Roots*, and its television triumph captured popular attention, the genealogy business was a thriving field of commercial enterprise, as was the sale of family crests. In a relatively classless or fluid society, ancestry still has importance beyond pride of antecedents, in establishing claims to legal inheritances and in tracing genes and physical characteristics.

The National Genealogical Society is located at 1921 Sunderland Place NW, Washington, D.C. 20036.

ARISTOCRACY

Definitions: a privileged class; government by a select elite; a state with a privileged class; upperclass; the better people.

Quotations:

What is Aristocracy? A corporation of the best, of the bravest. *Thomas Carlyle,* **Chartism,** *1839.*

I was told that the Privileged and the People formed two nations. *Benjamin Disraeli,* **Sybil,** *1845.*

The aristocrat is the democrat ripe and gone to seed. *Ralph Waldo Emerson,* **Representative Men:** *Napoleon, 1850.*

All communities divide themselves into the few and the many. *Alexander Hamilton, at the Constitutional Convention in Philadelphia, 1787.*

He comes of the Brahmin caste of New England. This is the harmless, inoffensive, untitled aristocracy. *Oliver Wendell Holmes in The Atlantic Monthly, 1860.*

. . . I agree with you that there is a natural aristocracy among men. The grounds of this are virtue and talents. . . . There is also an artificial aristocracy, founded on wealth and birth, without either virtue or talents; for with these it would belong to the first class. *Thomas Jefferson, letter to John Adams, October 28, 1813.*

Thus our democracy was, from an early period, the most aristocratic, and our aristocracy the most democratic in the world. *Thomas Babington Macaulay,* **History of England,** *1849.*

Aristocracy is always cruel. *Wendell Phillips,* "Toussaint L'Ouverture," 1861.

It is an interesting question how far men would retain their relative rank if they were divested of their clothes. *Henry D. Thoreau,* **Walden,** *1854.*

Anonymous aphorisms:

Some aristocrats are born and others simply cannot be borne.

In a democracy it can be said that when it comes to aristocrats many are culled and few are chosen.

The best people always know who they are—or always think they know.

The true aristocrat is not merely a descendant of previous generations, but more particularly an improvement.

In a free country, the aristocracy are the people who are more free than the rest.

Facts:

There is no country without a privileged class, and no country where such privilege does not "rub off" on the children of its aristocracy. U.S. aristocracy has various components—first families, elected officials, the wealthy—but ancestry is less important than wealth or power. Throughout the world, the hereditary nature of aristocracy is in decline, except where hereditary wealth accompanies it. The most ancient of thrones, in Iran, has been occupied by the son of a onetime Army sergeant who made himself an aristocrat by taking power. The collateral descendants of George Washington cover the full spectrum of U.S. life without any hereditary aristocratic overtones. The pace of modern life has so quickened that not even the inheritance of wealth can last as long as it once did.

ARMED FORCES

Definitions: Army, Navy, Air Force and Marine Corps; the military, naval and aviation uniformed organizations and installations of the nation; the military; the GIs; the dogfaces; our national defense; the defense establishment; our boys.

Quotations:

I am convinced that the best service a retired general can perform is to turn in his tongue along with his suit, and to mothball his opinions. *General of the Army Omar N. Bradley, Armed Forces Day address, May 16, 1959.*

Our country has long been remarkable for utilizing officers of the army and the navy in works of peace. *Andrew Carnegie, March 5, 1914.*

Before we cast away the solid assurances of national armaments for self-preservation, we must be certain that our temple is built, not upon shifting sands or quagmires, but upon the rock. *Winston Churchill, speech in Fulton, Mo., March 5, 1946.*

No nation ever had an army large enough to guarantee it against attack in time of peace or insure it victory in time of war. *President Calvin Coolidge, October 6, 1925.*

In the councils of government, we must guard against the acquisition of unwarranted influence, whether sought or unsought, by the military-industrial complex. *President Dwight D. Eisenhower, Farewell Address, January 17, 1961.*

Praise the Lord and pass the ammunition. *Chaplain Howell M. Forgy of the U.S.S. New Orleans at Pearl Harbor, December 7, 1941.*

There is a kind of valorous spleen which, like wind, is apt to grow unruly in the stomachs of newly made soldiers, compelling them to box-lobby brawls and brokenheaded quarrels, unless there can be found some more harmless way to give it vent. *Washington Irving,* **A History of New York by Diedrich Knickerbocker,** *1809.*

Then it's Tommy this, an' Tommy that, an' "Tommy, 'ow's yer soul?"/ But it's "Thin red line of 'eroes" when the drums begin to roll . . . For it's Tommy this, an' Tommy that, an' "Chuck him out, the brute!"/ But it's "Saviour of 'is country," when the guns begin to shoot . . . *Rudyard Kipling, "Tommy," 1892.*

Old soldiers never die; they just fade away. *Recalled from the words of an old "barracks ballad," as he described it, by General of the Army Douglas MacArthur in speech to joint session of Congress, April 19, 1951.*

. . . the soldier above all other people prays for peace, for he must suffer and bear the deepest wounds, and scars of war . . . *General of the Army Douglas MacArthur, speech at West Point, May 12, 1962.*

. . we've got the enemy on our right flank, our left flank, in front of us and behind us. They won't get away this time. *Marine General Lewis (Chesty) Puller, discussing the position of a Marine division in the Korean War, 1950.*

The Army and Navy forever/ Three cheers for the red, white and blue. *Adapted as "Columbia, the Gem of the Ocean" from "Britannia, the Pride of the Ocean," an 1843 British song by David T. Shaw and/or Thomas Becket.*

Retreat Hell! We're just advancing in another direction. *Marine General O. P. Smith, widely quoted remark in autumn of 1950 when counterattack hit United Nations lines in Korean War.*

When we assumed the soldier, we did not lay aside the citizen. *George Washington, speech in New York, June 26, 1775.*

To be prepared for war is one of the most effectual means of preserving peace. *President George Washington, message to Congress, January 8, 1790.*

Anonymous aphorisms:

Join the Navy and see the world.

He isn't old enough to be a sergeant. He must be an officer. *World War II joke about Air Force personnel.*

Uncle Sam wants you. *World War I recruiting motto.*

Military procurement and streetwalking have many things in common—the business is interestingly solicited, it does its best when your defenses are down and one side or the other is always being taken advantage of.

There are three ways of doing it—the right way, the wrong way and the Army way.

They used to say all officers were gentlemen, but that wasn't even true before women joined the services.

Rank has its privileges, and privileges have their rank.

Anecdotage:

During an uprising in a primitive land, a single U.S. Marine was sent in, only to be greeted by a furious local governor. "Why did they just send one man?" the governor roared. "Well," said the Marine, "they figured there was only one uprising."

After completing all but one day of his enlistment, Tim was bawled out furiously by the same familiar non-commissioned officer for the 1000th time for failing to fall in line. "When I'm out of service tomorrow with the rest of the guys," Tim said, "I'm going to bust him in the nose." "Well," said his friend, "you'll have to stand in line to do it."

"Tomorrow's wars will be fought by pushbutton," said the young scientist to the wounded veteran. "By the way, where were you wounded?" "On the button," said the veteran.

Q. Why do you salute officers? A. To make them salute back.

Facts:

Service with the U.S. armed forces, for most of the time other than major wars, has been on a voluntary basis, with growing numbers of women now taking part. The U.S. service academies began admitting women in the mid-1970s. Although active military service rolls declined after the Vietnam War, the military budget continued to be huge, not only because of the increasing cost of armament but also because of higher pay for the armed forces, including retired military personnel. In the mid-1970s it was estimated that the world as a whole and the United States were spending about 6 percent of their total gross product on defense costs. Although the U.S. and Russia are commonly supposed to be the wellsprings of military rivalry, various other countries have had higher percentages of their population serving in the armed forces. More and more, however, it is firepower rather than numbers of soldiers, sailors and air personnel which provides the best comparison, and there the armaments rivalry is between Russia and America.

Information: Annual report on World Military Expenditures and Arms Trade, U.S. Arms Control and Disarmament Agency, Department of State, Washington, D.C.

ART

Definitions: skill used in the production or performance of an aesthetic object or impression; skillful graphic presentation; "silent poetry and speaking painting" *(Ralph Waldo Emerson,* **Society and Solitude:** *Art, 1870);* "surface and symbol" *(Oscar Wilde,* **The Picture of Dorian Gray,** *1891).*

Quotations:

Every artist dips his brush in his own soul, and paints his own nature into his pictures. *Rev. Henry Ward Beecher,* **Proverbs from Plymouth Pulpit,** *1887.*

New arts destroy the old. *Ralph Waldo Emerson,* **Essays, First Series:** *Circles, 1841.*

Art is a jealous mistress. *Ralph Waldo Emerson,* **The Conduct of Life:** *Wealth, 1860.*

Every artist was first an amateur. *Ralph Waldo Emerson,* **Letters and Social Aims:** *Progress of Culture, 1876.*

In art, as in life, instinct is enough. *Anatole France,* **The Garden of Epicurus,** *1894.*

Art is not a tender or fragile thing. It has kept alive in the habitations of cruelty and oppressions. It has struggled toward light from the manifold darkness of war and conflict and persecution. Yet it flourishes most abundantly when the artist can speak as he wishes and describe the world as he sees it without any official direction. *President Lyndon B. Johnson, June 14, 1965.*

We must never forget that art is not a form of propaganda; it is a form of truth. *President John F. Kennedy, Amherst, Mass., October 26, 1963.*

In free society art is not a weapon. *Ibid.*

The arts cannot thrive except where men are free to be themselves. . . . *President Franklin D. Roosevelt, New York, May 10, 1939.*

Great art is precisely that which never was nor will be taught; it is preeminently and finally the expression of the spirits of great men. *John Ruskin,* **Modern Painters,** *Vol. 3, 1856.*

Art should never try to be popular; the public should try to make itself artistic. *Oscar Wilde,* **The Soul of Man Under Socialism,** *1891.*

. . . the moment that an artist takes notice of what other people want, and tries to supply the demand, he ceases to be an artist, and becomes a dull or an amusing craftsman, an honest or dishonest tradesman. *Ibid.*

Anonymous aphorisms:

Great art is regarded as a luxury, but for the great artist, it is a necessity.

Even the greatest of art, if copied unduly, becomes less than great. Greatness is Titian; dullness is repetition.

Art is what separates man from beast.

Chimpanzees have painted interesting pictures; but they were interesting only to human beings, not to other chimpanzees.

Anecdotage:

Abraham Lincoln was once asked to look at a painting. His comment was that the artist was clearly a gifted and devout man—devout because he followed the commandment of the Good Book not to make "any likeness of any thing in heaven above, the earth beneath or the water under the earth."

"How will I ever get into the Metropolitan Museum of Art?" the aspiring young artist asked a great teacher. "You can either take the Fifth Avenue bus to 81st Street," said the teacher, "or work hard, be inspired, wait 20 years and have them come to you."

"I know great art when I see it," said the critic. "And I know great art when I feel it," said the artist.

Facts:

Ancient Greece divided the arts into three families—the fine arts for beauty, the liberal arts for useful knowledge and the arts of conduct or behavior for goodness. Today when we speak of art we think principally of the fine arts, but beauty is no longer the constant aim. Art today is often challenging and intellectual rather than beautiful; it is sometimes deliberately propagandistic and shocking. The fine arts today can be more rewarding than ever before; it has proven to be a good though highly speculative investment to buy art work, and the level of prices for art, sculpture, books, plays and music is rising, along with the number of people who either work or play at the arts.

The Art Information Center at 189 Lexington Avenue, New York, N.Y. 10016 serves as a clearing house for information on contemporary fine arts.

ATHLETICS

(see also individual sports)

Definitions: the organized and often competitive exercise of physical skills; sports; America's weekend madness; a lot of hit and run.

Quotations:

Exercise ferments the humors, casts them into their proper channels, throws off redundancies, and helps nature in those secret distributions, without which the body cannot subsist in its vigor, nor the soul act with cheerfulness. *Joseph Addison,* **The Spectator,** *July 12, 1711.*

The wise, for cure, on exercise depend;/ God never made his work for man to mend. *John Dryden, "Epistle to John Driden of Chesterton," 17th century.*

Winning isn't everything. It's the only thing. *Attributed to Vincent Lombardi when he was coaching the Green Bay Packers football team in the 1960s.*

I wish to preach, not the doctrine of ignoble ease, but the doctrine of the strenuous life. *Vice President Theodore Roosevelt, April 10, 1899.*

. . . I do not in the least object to a sport because it is rough. *President Theodore Roosevelt, February 23, 1907.*

The battle of Waterloo was won on the playing fields of Eton. *Attributed to Arthur Wellesley, Duke of Wellington, first half of the 19th century.*

Anonymous aphorisms:

You don't have to be athletic to have a case of athlete's foot.

Isn't it strange that a man can spend all week racing for his commuter train, walk up and down the station stairs and yearn for the weekend when he can get some exercise?

Athletics is America's favorite exercise—to sit and watch.

They keep saying that what really matters is not whether you win or lose, but how you played the game. The trouble is that the best way to determine how you played the game is by whether you won or lost.

Amateur athletics is part training, part physical ability, part will to win and part time.

The difference between amateur and professional athletics is what exercises a lot of people.

Running for your college team is athletics; running for a train is exercise; running for office is work.

Anecdotage:

The team had lost seventeen games in a row, so they tried both alternatives; first they tried to find some new players and when that failed, they fired the coach.

After examining the postures of all the customers in the health club, the visiting professor reached his diagnosis: "Americans are prone to exercise."

Facts:

Never in history have more people participated in athletics than now, and never have as many types of athletics been popular. Each new edition of the Olympic games includes more events, and this athletic explosion has been heightened by the great surge of women's participation in sports. Since 1963, the number of sporting goods stores and bicycle shops in the U.S. has doubled. The development of year-round, climate-proof facilities helped encourage booms in such sports as tennis; basketball proved to be a sport for which room could be found in the most crowded quarters; indoor pools proliferated and made participation in swimming and diving more easily available. The number of golf courses in the U.S. has doubled since 1950 and the number of golfers more than tripled.

Information: Amateur Athletic Union, 3400 West 86th Street, Indianapolis, Ind. 46268 or American Alliance for Health, Physical Education and Recreation, 1201 16th Street NW, D.C. 20036.

AUTOMOBILES

Definitions: self-propelled 3, 4 or more-wheeled vehicle; horseless carriage; highway horsepower; "The Insolent Chariots" *(John Keats, 1958);* wreck-creation; a traffic cop's moving target; motor car.

Quotations:

Except the American woman, nothing interests the eye of American man more than the automobile. . . . *Alfred H. Barr, Jr., 1963.*

. . . . For much too long, the man who owns and drives an automobile has been treated like a stepchild. We require him to pay for the highways he uses and we require him to pay in advance. We divert his taxes to other uses but we delay the building of the roads he deserves. We denounce him for getting snarled in traffic jams not of his making. We complain about what he costs us but we never thank him for what he adds to the worth and wealth of our economy. We could not get along without him, but we often talk as though we can't live with him. *President Lyndon B. Johnson, August 13, 1964.*

More than any country, ours is an automobile society. *President Lyndon B. Johnson, message to Congress, February 8, 1965.*

The automobile . . . created suburbia in America. *President Lyndon B. Johnson, October 15, 1966.*

This is the only country that ever went to the poorhouse in an automobile. *Will Rogers, early 1930s.*

Anonymous aphorisms:

Drivers careless may wind up carless.

Money makes the wheels go round.

The American automobile salesman waits to see who walks in; the American automobile customer waits to see what's thrown in.

America's favorite step is a step on the gas.

Drive carefully; the life you save may be your own.

Drive carefully; we love our children. *Highway sign in U.S. in 1930s and 1940s.*

The easiest way to determine a person's innermost character is to put that person behind the wheel of a high-powered car on a U.S. highway.

You can drive a car for less money a day in some cities than it costs to park it.

The most dangerous animal in the U.S.A. is the road hog.

Too many used car buyers drive a hard bargain.

Would you buy a used car from this man?

American automobile driving is highway roulette.

The only foolproof car is one without a driver.

Anecdotage:

Then there's the used car salesman who described his profession as auto-suggestion.

Mr. Jones watched his seventeen-year-old son labor over an old jalopy, keeping it in perfect mechanical condition, polishing its chrome, washing it down and fussing over it hour after hour. "Maybe," said Mr. Jones, "if we put his room on wheels he'd clean that too."

He had been hard put to keep up the payments on his nice, shiny new sports car, and finally he went to his boss for advice. "Well" said his boss, "you'll either have to stop eating or stop driving." The sports car owner didn't say a word. "I said you'll either have to stop eating or stop driving," the boss repeated. "Why don't you say something?" "It's a hard choice," said the sports car owner, "I'm thinking."

Facts:

The automobile may well be the single most important factor in modern American life. It is responsible for more employment, more movement, more pleasure and more business than any other American product. It sparked the expansion of surburban life, the worldwide appetite for oil, the air pollution problem, installment buying and travel. It is also a democratizing factor; used cars put transportation within easy reach for millions who in previous generations would have been confined to their own home areas. In the U.S. there are more than 110 million registered automobiles—enough to provide a seat in a car for every living American—plus 25 million trucks and buses and 5 million motorcycles. There are also more than 125 million Americans holding driving licenses.

The American Automobile Association is at 8111 Gatehouse Road, Falls Church, Va. 22042.

AVIATION

Definitions: the field and science and/or components of airplane transportation; flying; cloud hopping; riding on air.

Quotations:

Soon shall thy arm, unconquer'd steam! afar/ Drag the slow barge, or drive the rapid car;/ Or on wide-waving wings expanded bear/ The flying chariot through the field of air. *Erasmus Darwin*, **The Botanic Garden, 1795**.

In the space age, man will be able to go around the world in two hours—one hour for flying and the other to get to the airport. *Secretary of Defense Neil H. McElroy, 1958.*

For I dipt into the future far as human eyes could see—/ Saw the vision of the world, and all the wonders that would be—/ Saw the heavens fill with commerce, argosies of magic sails,/ Pilots of the purple twilight, dropping down with costly bales;/ Heard the heavens fill with shouting, and there rain'd a ghastly dew/ From the nations' airy navies grappling in the central blue. *Alfred Tennyson*, **Locksley Hall, 1842**.

Anonymous aphorisms:

A white-knuckle flier is one whose fears are groundless.

First-class air travel is a flight of fancy; cheap economy travel is fly-by-night.

Today's airport is three big parking lots—one for the planes, one for the autos and one for the passengers, waiting to get to the planes or the autos.

Anecdotage:

Mrs. Harris thought she could pick any plane she wanted because she heard they were stacked up at the airport.

Mr. Brown arrived at the airport one minute before the flight was due to leave. The check-in clerk asked him, "do you have a reservation?" "Well," he said, "I'm a little skeptical about flying."

The little old lady wanted to buy a ticket for a cross country flight, and the clerk said, "I'm sorry; we're full, but I can have you waitlisted." "My goodness," she said, "I didn't know you were that careful. My weight is 102 pounds."

Facts:

Aviation is perhaps our most truly international business. Every nation seems to insist on having its own airline, and air transportation has ended the isolation of some of the most remote countries on the face of the earth. In 1960 the number of U.S. airports almost doubled, the number of active civil aircraft in this country doubled, the hours flown more than doubled and air cargo ton-miles in domestic flights more than quadrupled. In more recent years, mergers reduced the number of U.S. scheduled airlines and, as a result of rising fuel costs and the increased size of planes, the number of flights was curtailed. Aviation in most countries is far more heavily subsidized than in the U.S. as a matter of both national pride and national defense.

The Air Transport Association of America is located at 1709 New York Avenue NW, Washington, D.C. 20006.

BABIES

(See also Children, Parents)

Definitions: New-born humans; young children; small fry; small change; the next generation; toothless tyrants.

Quotations:

There is no finer investment for any community than putting milk into babies. *British Prime Minister Winston Churchill, broadcast, March 21, 1943.*

Every baby born into the world is a finer one than the last. *Charles Dickens,* **Nicholas Nickleby,** *1838-1839.*

Infancy conforms to nobody; all conform to it. *Ralph Waldo Emerson,* **Essays, First Series:** *Self-Reliance, 1841.*

Who can tell what a baby thinks? *Josiah Gilbert Holland, "Cradle Song", c. 1860.*

O child! O new-born denizen/ Of life's great city! on thy head/ The glory of the morn is shed,/ Like a celestial benison. *Henry Wadsworth Longfellow, "To a Child," 1846.*

Who would not tremble and rather choose to die than to be a baby again, if given such a choice? *St. Augustine,* **The City of God,** *5th century.*

Sweetes' li'l feller—/ Everybody knows;/ Dunno what ter call 'im,/ But he's mighty lak' a rose! *Frank L. Stanton, "Mighty Lak' A Rose," 1901.*

Thrice happy state again to be/ The trustful infant on the knee,/ Who lets his rosy fingers play/ About his mother's neck and knows/ Nothing beyond his mother's eyes! *Alfred Tennyson, "Supposed Confessions," 1830.*

But what am I?/ An infant crying in the night;/ An infant crying for the light:/ And with no language but a cry. *Alfred Tennyson,* **In Memoriam,** *1850.*

Heaven lies about us in our infancy! *William Wordsworth, "Ode on Intimations of Immortality," 1807.*

Anonymous aphorisms:

A baby is the world's longest suspense story; you have to wait for a generation to see how it turns out.

A mother bears a baby for nine months; then the family has to bear the child for years.

Every adult lives in dread of his own old baby pictures.

Politicians woo adult votes by kissing babies; they'd get more parents' votes if they changed a few diapers.

Anecdotage:

"Now that you've got a baby, you have to plan ahead," said the proud father's boss. "That's how we got the baby," said the proud father.

"When the baby cries," said the pediatrician to the new parents," you have two alternatives—one at each end."

Facts:

Babies remain the focal points of two of the century's most bitter issues, population limitation and abortion. An increasing number of nations, including the U.S., are moving downward or leveling off in birthrate, but increases in the quality of obstetrical and pediatric care are giving more babies the chance to survive where in the past they would have been doomed. Science has helped to equip babies better for the rigors of life, and the state, in many capitalistic as well as socialist nations, is assuming greater responsibility for early childhood care. Since human babies are just about the most helpless living creatures, and the slowest to become self sufficient, they still are principal victims of both man's and nature's wars and cruelties.

The Child Welfare League of America, 67 Irving Place, New York, N.Y. 10003, is an organization of child care agencies.

BASEBALL

Definitions: a game played by two teams, usually of nine players each, with bat and ball; the ball used in the game; the national pastime; hardball.

Quotations:

A baseball club is part of the chemistry of the city. A game isn't just an athletic contest. It's a picnic, a kind of town meeting. *Michael Burke, then president of the New York Yankees, testifying before the New York City Council, 1971.*

You've got to be a man to play baseball for a living, but you've got to have a lot of little boy in you, too. *Roy Campanella, 1957.*

Why do I like baseball? The pay is good, it keeps you out in the fresh air and sunshine and you can't beat them hours. *Attributed to umpire Tim Hurst.*

Hit 'em where they ain't. *Willie Keeler, summarizing his batting tactics at the turn of the century.*

"Take Me Out to the Ball Game." *Title of song lyric by Jack Norworth, 1908.*

"Casey at the Bat." *Title of classic poem by Ernest L. Thayer, 1888.*

But there is no joy in Mudville—Mighty Casey has struck out. *Ernest L. Thayer, "Casey at the Bat," 1888.*

Anonymous aphorisms:

Kill the umpire!

Slide, Kelly, slide!

Three strikes, you're out.

The hit and run is on.

No hits, no runs, no errors.

Don't give him anything he can hit.

Anecdotage:

An American took a British friend to a baseball game. In the bottom of the ninth inning, with two out, the home team loaded the bases and the fans began to cheer. The Britisher, puzzled, asked why the fans were so excited. "There's a man on every base," said the American, "our team has a man on every base." "But," said the Britisher, "so does the other side."

Mr. and Mrs. Jones finally got into the ballpark an hour after the baseball game had started. It was a tight pitcher's battle, sixth inning, 0-0. "Good," said Mrs. Jones, "we haven't missed a thing."

Facts:

America's first successful professional team sport and amateur team pastime was dubbed the national pastime many years ago, but it is international. Latin America and Japan adopted it and Little League champions have come from as far away as Taiwan. U.S. professional baseball was racism's Maginot Line until Branch Rickey broke the color barrier by bringing Jackie Robinson to the Brooklyn Dodgers after World War II. Baseball was the first professional sport to be given exemption from various government regulations governing other businesses.

BASKETBALL

Definitions: game between two teams in which points are scored by throwing a large inflated ball through a basket hoop on the wall; a tall story; dribble, pass and shoot; the hoopsters.

Anonymous aphorisms:

When it comes to starting a basketball game, a lot of people jump at the chance.

Basketball is America's—and maybe the world's—second favorite indoor sport.

The play-by-play report of a basketball game is a running commentary, a passing phenomenon and a shooting sensation.

Basketball is a game in which nobody tries to hide his light under a basket.

Most professional sports in this country are on the up and up, but basketball is on the up and up and up and up and . . .

In basketball dribbling isn't a mess, it's a talent.

A highboy is either a traditional piece of furniture or a bright new basketball prospect.

Basketball players go back and forth a great deal, but the rules say you can't travel with the ball.

Anecdotage:

They asked the coach why Bill had left the basketball team. "Well," said the coach, "as a forward he was backward, as a center he was always out of position, and he thought the guards should be armed."

Where can you keep shooting and never be shot? On a basketball court.

Facts:

Basketball may well be the most universal of sports. Other sports are as international, but basketball can be played practically anyplace. It was invented in the YMCA in Springfield, Mass. and brought to the world as a sort of U.S. missionary effort. Because its squads are smaller in number than most other professional mass audience team sports, basketball has been one of the most lucrative sports for the general run of salaried players. As an amateur sport, it is within the economic and geographic reach of even the poorest young people. Professional basketball is largely confined to the U.S.

BLACKS

(See also Minorities, Prejudice, Race)

Definitions: members of the black race; Afro-Americans; formerly known as negroes; persons of dark-skinned race; colored people.

Quotations:

I believe the life of the Negro race has been a life of tragedy, of injustice, of oppression. The law has made him equal, but man has not. *Clarence Darrow, plea to a jury, 1926.*

Though the colored man is no longer subject to be bought and sold, he is still surrounded by an adverse sentiment which fetters all his movements. In his downward course he meets with no resistance, but his course upward is resisted at every stop of his progress. *Frederick Douglass, September 24, 1883.*

My hope for the Negro is largely based on his enduring qualities. No persecutions, no proscriptions, no hardships are able to extinguish him. He neither dies out, nor goes out. He is here to stay, and while here he will partake of the blessings of your education, your progress, your civilization and your Christian religion. His appeal to you today is for an equal chance in the race of life, and, dark and stormy as the present appears, his appeal will not go unanswered. *Frederick Douglass, 1894.*

The real hero of this struggle is the American Negro. His actions and protests, his courage to risk safety and even to risk his life, have awakened the conscience of this nation. *President Lyndon B. Johnson, March 15, 1965.*

The Negro baby born in America today, regardless of the section or the state in which he is born, has about one-half as much chance of completing a high school as a white baby, born in the same place, on the same day; one-third as much chance of completing college; one-third as much chance of becoming a professional man; twice as much chance of becoming unemployed; about one-seventh as much chance of earning $10,000 a year; a life expectancy which is seven years shorter and the prospects of earning only half as much. *President John F. Kennedy, June 11, 1963.*

There are no "white" or "colored" signs on the foxholes or graveyards of battle. *President John F. Kennedy, June 19, 1963*

I have a dream that one day in the red hills of Georgia, sons of former slaves and the sons of former slave-owners will be able to sit down together at the table of brotherhood. *Rev. Martin Luther King, Jr., address at the Lincoln Memorial in Washington, D.C., August 28, 1963.*

I want to be the white man's brother, not his brother-in-law. *Attributed to Rev. Martin Luther King, Jr. after his death.*

What a happy country this will be, if the whites will listen. *David Walker, Black abolitionist, September 28, 1829.*

Anonymous aphorisms:

Black is beautiful.

An Oreo is black outside and white inside.

Blacks created the blues because their life was so gray.

The real measure of Black progress will be when they can spurn professional sports careers as easily as whites.

Anecdotage:

The impatient white said, "You used to be called Negro, then you switched to Afro-American, then Black. Now what do you want to be called?" "Mister," said the Black.

Facts:

Optimists see how much the situation of the Blacks has improved; pessimists see how much remains to be done. Beginning in the 1960s, progress became notable in many parts of the world—voting and employment rights in the U.S., independence in most of Black Africa and more opportunities in athletics and on the campus. In 1969 there were 1,195 Black elected officials in the U.S; by 1975 the figure had tripled to 3,503. In 1960 the median number of school years for U.S. Blacks was 8.2, or just past the eighth grade. By 1975 the median was 10.9 years, or more than halfway through high school. And the number of Blacks with four or more years of college rose from 3.1 percent of the over-25 population in 1960 to 6.4 percent in 1975. But unemployment continued to be much higher for Blacks than for whites and in 1975 Black median family income was only 61 percent of the white median family income in the U.S.

The National Urban League is headquartered at 500 East 62 Street, New York, N.Y. 10021.

BOOKS

(See also Literature)

Definitions: Bound volumes of printed sheets of prose, poetry or visual reproductions; "sepulchers of thought" (*Henry Wadsworth Longfellow*); "the legacies that genius leaves to mankind, to be delivered down from generation to generation" (*Joseph Addison*); knowledge bound and shelved; "silent conversation" (*Walter Savage Landor*).

Quotations:

Some books are to be tasted, others to be swallowed, and some few to be chewed and digested: that is, some books are to be read only in parts, others to be read, but not curiously, and some few to be read wholly, and with diligence and attention. *Francis Bacon,* **Essays:** *Of Studies, 1625.*

Many books require no thought from those who read them, and for a very simple reason; they made no such demand upon those who wrote them. *Charles Caleb Colton,* **Lacon,** *1820s.*

Books are the quietest and most constant of friends; they are the most accessible and wisest of counsellors, and the most patient of teachers, *Charles W. Eliot,* **The Happy Life,** *1896.*

In the highest civilization, the book is still the highest delight. He who has once known its satisfactions is provided with a resource against calamity. *Ralph Waldo Emerson,* **Letters and Social Aims:** *Quotation and Originality, 1876.*

Who knows whether in retirement I shall be tempted to the last infirmity of mundane minds, which is to write a book. *Geoffrey Fisher, Archbishop of Canterbury, attributed in 1961.*

Books give not wisdom where was none before,/ But where some is, there reading makes it more. *Sir John Harington,* **Epigrams,** *1613.*

Old books, as you well know, are books of the world's youth, and new books are fruits of its age. *Oliver Wendell Holmes,* **The Professor at the Breakfast-Table,** *1860.*

I cannot live without books. *Thomas Jefferson, letter to John Adams, 1815.*

The love of learning, the sequestered nooks,/ And all the sweet serenity of books. *Henry Wadsworth Longfellow, "Morituri Salutamus," 1875.*

As good almost kill a man as kill a good book: who kills a man kills a reasonable creature, God's image; but he who destroys a good book, kills reason itself, kills the image of God, as it were, in the eye, *John Milton,* **Areopagitica,** *1644.*

All books are divisible into two classes: the books of the hour, and the books of all time. *John Ruskin,* **Sesame and Lilies,** *1865.*

Books are good enough in their way, but they are a mighty bloodless substitute for life. *Robert Louis Stevenson,* **Virginibus Puerisque,** *1881.*

How many a man has dated a new era in his life from the reading of a book. *Henry D. Thoreau,* **Walden:** *Reading, 1854.*

With books, as with men, a very small number play great parts, while the rest are lost in the crowd. *Voltaire,* **Philosophical Dictionary,** *1764.*

There is no such thing as a moral or an immoral book. Books are well written, or badly written. That is all. *Oscar Wilde,* **The Picture of Dorian Gray,** *preface, 1891.*

Anonymous aphorisms:

You can't tell a book by its cover.

Books produce more royalty than kings do.

A book is a constant friend.

A book is new until you have read it.

Anecdotage:

The book was a novel, preceded by a statement that any resemblance to any real person, living or dead, was purely coincidental. The reviewer said the book fully lived up to that statement.

"Enough about me," said the author to the interviewer. "Have you read my new book?"

Facts:

Although there were hand-produced books before there were printing presses, they were scarce, and so was the number of people who knew how to read. Literacy and mass production brought the age of books, which is now. In the heyday of radio and television, more books than ever are being published and more copies are being sold. The size of the book trade is due largely to several comparatively recent phenomena: the book club, which came into its own in the second quarter of the 20th century, and the inexpensive paperback reprint.

The American Booksellers Association is located at 122 East 42nd Street, New York, N.Y. 10017 and the Association of American Publishers is at One Park Avenue, New York, N.Y. 10016.

BOXING

Definitions: the pastime of fighting with the fists; the manly art of self defense; prizefighting; the fights; pugilism; cauliflower alley; the punch bowl.

Quotations:

The bigger they come, the harder they fall. *Bob Fitzsimmons, comment before his bout with heavyweight champion Jim Jeffries, 1902. (Jeffries, the bigger man, won by a knockout.)*

A boxing match is like a cowboy movie. There's got to be good guys and there's got to be bad guys. And that's what people pay for—to see the bad guys get beat. *Attributed to ex-heavyweight champion Sonny Liston in his obituary in* **The New York Times,** *1971.*

He can run but he can't hide. *Joe Louis, before his bout with Billy Conn, 1946.*

Don't bet on fights. *Sports page slogan in* **The New York Sun,** *1920s.*

Anonymous aphorisms:

When a Sunday punch lands, it gives its target a day of rest.

Here lies a fighter who ran out of gas;/ His fists were steel but his jaw was glass.

Boxing is an art with overtones of nobility—you put up your dukes, worry about taking the count and observe the Marquess of Queensberry rules.

Boxing is dueling with gloves on.

Boxing is a case of fist things first.

Prizefighting is a Punch and Judy show without Judy.

Years ago a fighter sometimes telegraphed a punch; now they televise the whole fight.

Anecdotage:

Mr. Jones claims that mugging is a direct descendant of prizefighting, because in both you find men fighting over purses.

"I am opposed to prize fighting," said the reformer, "because it involves brutal conflict." "What do you plan to do about it," asked the reporter. "I will fight it with every weapon at my command," said the reformer.

BUILDING

Definitions: the act of constructing or erecting a structure; construction; the edifice complex; a structure with walls and a roof.

Quotations:

Houses are built to live in, not to look on; therefore, let use be preferred before uniformity, except where both may be had. *Francis Bacon,* **Essays:** *Of Building, 1623.*

He builded better than he knew . . . *Ralph Waldo Emerson, "The Problem," 1840.*

A man builds a fine house; and now he has a master, and a task for life: he is to furnish, watch, show it, and keep it in repair, the rest of his days. *Ralph Waldo Emerson,* **Society and Solitude:** *Works and Days, 1870*

In Building, rather believe any man than an Artificer for matter of charges. Should they tell thee all the cost at the first, it would blast a young Builder in the budding. *Thomas Fuller,* **The Holy State and the Profane State,** *1642.*

Light, God's eldest daughter, is a principal beauty in a building. *Ibid.*

Build thee more stately mansions, O my soul. . . *Oliver Wendell Holmes, "The Chambered Nautilus," 1858.*

To build is to be robbed. *Samuel Johnson.* **The Idler,** *June 23, 1759.*

Ah, to build, to build!/ That is the noblest of all the arts. *Henry Wadsworth Longfellow,* **Michael Angelo,** *1882.*

When we build, let us think that we build for ever. *John Ruskin,* **Modern Painters,** *1843.*

We require from buildings, as from men, two kinds of goodness: first, doing their practical duty well; then that they be graceful and pleasing in doing it. *John Ruskin,* **The Stones of Venice,** *1851.*

Anonymous aphorisms:

A big city building is one story on top of another.

It isn't so much what you build as how well you build it.

A building is what you make of it.

They call it a high rise because that's what happens to its taxes.

Anecdotage:

Mr. Brown: I hear that you are planning to park a trailer here instead of putting up a building. Mr. Jones: That is without foundation.

A builder who was known for the shabby quality of his structures invited the city planning commission to inspect a plot of land that he had bought in a crowded area. He asked them what kind of building they felt would serve the community best in that location. Their answer was unanimous. They all suggested he build a park.

Facts:

Building is many businesses rolled into one; financed by dollars from savings institutions and commercial banks, with building materials whose manufacture and storage and transportation are basic industries in themselves. The value of buildings is directly related to the revenues of government, since so much of our local tax system is based on real estate and building taxes. Construction rates are also a leading measure of national prosperity. The U.S. Bureau of the Census issues regular Current Construction Reports and the Bureau of Domestic Commerce publishes a monthly Construction Review, as of the mid-1970s.

BUSINESS

Definitions: commercial or industrial enterprise; trade; commerce; manufacture, distribution, buying or selling of goods or services; the seeking of profit in other than professional capacities; the working day, as opposed to time devoted to leisure or pleasure; capitalism; what when you don't have any, you go out of.

Quotations:

Few people do business well who do nothing else. *Lord Chesterfield, letter to his son, August 7, 1749.*

Civilization and profits go hand in hand. *Vice President-elect Calvin Coolidge, November 27, 1920.*

The business of America is business. *President Calvin Coolidge, January 17, 1925.*

Keep thy shop and thy shop will keep thee. *Benjamin Franklin,* **Poor Richard's Almanac,** *1735.*

If you would have your business done, go; if not, send. *Benjamin Franklin,* **Poor Richard's Almanac,** *1758.*

The most sensible people to be met with in society are men of business and of the world, who argue from what they see and know, instead of spinning cobweb distinctions of what things ought to be. *William Hazlitt, "On the Ignorance of the Learned," 1821.*

It is just as important that business keep out of government as that government keep out of business. *Republican Presidential nominee Herbert Hoover, October 22, 1928.*

I hold it to be our duty to see that the wage-worker, the small producer, the ordinary consumer, shall get their fair share of the benefit of business prosperity. But it either is or ought to be evident to everyone that business has to prosper before anybody can get any benefit from it. *Theodore Roosevelt, February 1, 1912.*

To business that we love we rise betime./ And go to't with delight. *William Shakespeare,* **Antony and Cleopatra,** *1607.*

This world is a place of business. *Henry D. Thoreau, published after his death.*

In democracies, nothing is more great or brilliant than commerce; it attracts the attention of the public, and fills the imagination of the multitude; all passions of energy are directed towards it. *Alexis de Tocqueville,* **Democracy in America,** *Vol. 2, 1840.*

Put all your eggs in the one basket and—WATCH THAT BASKET. *Mark Twain,* **The Tragedy of Pudd'nhead Wilson,** *1894.*

Anonymous aphorisms:

Business is a two-way street.

The secret of business is simple: buy low and sell high.

Business before pleasure.

There's no room for sentiment in business.

The customer is always right.

Anecdotage:

Business is a matter of perspective, and I can illustrate it. A maker of backup lights is happy to meet reverses.

Then there was the man whose life was so tied up in his business that his family organized a union so he'd have to meet them around the table.

If business is hard work, asks the skeptic, then how come when businessmen relax what they do is sometimes described as monkey business?

Facts:

Business is an ancient occupation of mankind, but it deals more and more with new products and new services. In our own time these have included television, jet airplanes and computers. It has been estimated that about 10,000 different products each year enter or leave production. Since 1950 the trend has been toward more corporations and proprietorships, with much smaller growth in the number of partnerships, in the U.S. In the same span, the number of people owning shares in U.S. corporations has more than doubled, and total corporate receipts have grown faster than those of proprietorships or partnerships

For current information see the U.S. Department of Commerce periodical, Survey of Current Business; or consult the latest Statistical Abstract of the U.S.

CANDIDATES

(See also Elections, Political Parties, Voting)

Definitions: Those who seek or are proposed for a particular office or honor; those whose hats are in the ring; white knights and dark horses; running targets.

Quotations:

You can't beat somebody with nobody. *Attributed to longtime Speaker of the House of Representatives Joseph Cannon, early 20th century.*

I do not choose to run. *President Calvin Coolidge, August 2, 1927.*

Offices are acceptable here as elsewhere, and whenever a man has cast a longing eye on them, a rottenness begins in his conduct. *Vice President Thomas Jefferson, letter to Tench Coxe, May 21, 1799.*

For many are called but few are chosen. **Matthew,** *22:14.*

If nominated, I will not accept; if elected, I will not serve. *General William T. Sherman, telegram to Republican National Convention in Chicago, June 5, 1884. Sometimes reported in slightly different words.*

The idea that you can merchandise candidates for high office like breakfast cereal . . . is, I think, the ultimate indignity for the democratic process. *Illinois Governor Adlai E. Stevenson, accepting Democratic Presidential nomination in Chicago, August 18, 1956.*

Anonymous aphorisms:

Before the people raise their voice, how many are called "the people's choice."

Very few candidates are actually drafted; most are swept along by a lot of wind, but it's a wind, not a draft.

Running for office is often a primary consideration.

Nobody ever ran for office against his or her will. It takes only one word to say no to a nomination.

In this country they run for office and in England they stand for office. It doesn't matter as long as they don't lie for office.

A favorite son candidacy is more of a courtesy than a candidacy.

Anecdotage:

Early in the primary stages of the 1960 Presidential election, Senator John F. Kennedy told another Senator he had dreamed that the Lord above had told him he would be the nominee. The other Senator said it was strange because *he* had had the same dream and the Lord had told him *he* would be the nominee. The two Senators told their story of the matching dreams to a Senatorial colleague, Lyndon Johnson, and Senator Johnson, according to Senator Kennedy, remarked, "I can't remember tapping either of you for the job."

Facts:

One of America's favorite exercises is running for office. In the 1976 Presidential campaign, there were 125 candidates before the summer. While there are less than 600 elective posts in the federal government, there are some 80,000 state and local governments and governmental units, and the 50 largest U.S. cities have elected city boards or councils with more than 650 elected members in just that one particular category. An individual voter is called upon to choose among candidates for the Presidency (through choice of electors), the House, the Senate, the governor's chair, the state legislature, the city or town council, judges in various courts, school boards, district attorneys etc. And if that roster does not provide enough candidacies, there are also races for offices in associations, unions and all kinds of institutional governing boards.

CENSORSHIP

(See also Books, Journalism, Liberty, Motion Pictures, Radio, Television)

Definitions: prohibition of the publication or utterance of material; excision of passages from what is permitted to be published or uttered; suppress agentry; big brother.

Quotations:

Don't join the book burners. Don't think you are going to conceal thoughts by concealing evidence that they ever existed. *President Dwight D. Eisenhower, speech at Dartmouth College, June 14, 1953.*

. . . every burned book or house enlightens the world . . . *Ralph Waldo Emerson,* **Essays, First Series:** *Compensation, 1841.*

Every society has a right to preserve public peace and order, and therefore has a good right to prohibit the propagation of opinions which have a dangerous tendency. *Samuel Johnson, May 7, 1773 (from James Boswell's* **Life of Samuel Johnson).**

If all mankind, minus one, were of one opinion, and only one person were of the contrary opinion, mankind would be no more justified in silencing that one person, than he, if he had the power, would be justified in silencing mankind. *John Stuart Mill,* **On Liberty,** *1859.*

We can never be sure that the opinion we are endeavoring to stifle is a false opinion; and if we were sure, stifling it would be an evil still. *Ibid.*

And though all the winds of doctrine were let loose to play upon the earth, so truth be in the field, we do injuriously by licensing and prohibiting to misdoubt her strength. Let her and falsehood grapple; whoever knew truth put to the worse, in a free and open encounter? *John Milton,* **Areopagitica,** *1644.*

When indecent books no longer find a market, when pornographic films can no longer draw an audience, when obscene plays open to empty houses, then the tide will turn. Government can maintain the dikes against obscenity, but only people can turn back the tide. *President Richard M. Nixon, message to Congress, May 2, 1969.*

Tell it not in Gath, publish it not in the streets of Askelon; lest the daughters of the Philistines rejoice . . . **II Samuel,** *I: 20.*

The moment we begin to fear the opinions of others and hesitate to tell the truth that is in us, and from motives of policy are silent when we should speak, the divine floods of light and life no longer flow into our souls. *Elizabeth Cady Stanton, 1890.*

Once a government is committed to the principle of silencing the voice of opposition, it has only one way to go, and that is down the path of increasingly repressive measures, until it becomes a source of terror to all its citizens and creates a country where everyone lives in fear. *President Harry S. Truman, August 8, 1950.*

Anonymous aphorisms:

The non-controversial dies, but the banned plays on.

Blessed are the censors, for they shall inhibit the earth.

What you don't know *can* hurt you.

Given his choice, the censor will choose asterisks over other risks every time.

The almighty censor, good old Julius Scissor . . .

What the public is not permitted to see or hear or read, it generally imagines much more vividly. Why else would show business for so many years have been advertising happily that this or that presentation was banned in Boston or given an X rating? Forbidden fruit, as the story of Adam and Eve bears witness, is most inviting.

Anecdotage:

Johnny Carson demonstrates the way censorship can make things seem even more objectionable. He takes a familiar passage and removes words here and there. If you read or heard these lines and were told that the words removed were objectionable ones, what would you believe the original really said? Little Miss Muffet ____ on a ____, eating her ____ and ____; along came a ____ and ____ down ____ her and ____ Miss Muffet away.

Censorship in modern times has not merely included banning material; it has also included the forced inclusion of material or messages. This in turn has led to some really creative writing, such as the letter from an American who had gone to explore conditions in a total dictatorship and wrote back from there: What you have been reading about terror and fear here is absolutely untrue. Please be sure to tell what I have said to the editors and the broadcasters and above all tell it to the Marines.

Facts:

Official statistics on censorship are hard to come by, impossible to believe and rarely even issued. Many countries, while denying that they have official censorship, impose heavy penalties on those who speak or write against the official party line. Even in free countries there are ongoing censorship problems such as the so-called gag rules limiting news reports in connection with a trial, the imposition of secrecy classifications on government documents and the selection or refusal of shelf space for books in libraries. Many journalistic and civil liberties groups in the U.S. maintain current dossiers of pending censorship cases. Among key groups are the American Society of Newspaper Editors, the Reporters Committee for Freedom of the Press and the American Library Association.

CHARITY

Definitions: giving assistance to those in need; alms; a helping hand; poor comfort; "the sterilized milk of human kindness" *(Oliver Herford).*

Quotations:

In charity to all mankind, bearing no malice or ill-will to any human being . . . *Representative (and ex-President) John Quincy Adams, letter to A. Bronson Alcott, July 30, 1838.*

He that defers his charity until he is dead is, if a man weighs it rightly, rather liberal of another man's than of his own. *Francis Bacon, 17th century.*

Charity suffereth long, and is kind; charity envieth not; charity vaunteth not itself, is not puffed up. **I Corinthians,** *XIII, 1.*

And now abideth faith, hope, charity, these three; but the greatest of these is charity. **I Corinthians,** *XIII, 13.*

We do not quite forgive a giver. The hand that feeds us is in some danger of being bitten. *Ralph Waldo Emerson,* **Essays, Second Series:** *Gifts, 1844.*

He gives twice that gives soon; i.e., he will soon be called to give again. *Benjamin Franklin,* **Poor Richard's Almanac,** *1752.*

. . . charity must be built upon justice. *Henry George,* **The Condition of Labor,** *1891.*

It has been said that we feed the hungry, clothe the naked, bind up the wounds of the man beaten by thieves, pour oil and wine into them, set him on our own beast and bring him to the inn, because we receive ourselves pleasure from these acts. *Thomas Jefferson, letter to Thomas Law, June 13, 1814.*

With malice toward none; with charity for all; with firmness in the right, as God gives us to see the right . . . *President Abraham Lincoln, second Inaugural Address, March 4, 1865.*

. . . when thou doest alms, let not they left hand know what thy right hand doeth. **Matthew,** *IV, 3.*

As for charity, it is a matter in which the immediate effect on the persons directly concerned, and the ultimate consequence to the general good, are apt to be at complete war with one another. *John Stuart Mill,* **The Subjection of Women,** *1869.*

. . . charity shall cover the multitude of sins. **I Peter,** *IV, 8.*

He that hath pity upon the poor lendeth unto the Lord; and that which he hath given will he pay him again. **Proverbs,** *XIX, 17.*

Blessed is he that considereth the poor . . . **Psalms,** *XLI, 1.*

Anonymous aphorisms:

Charity begins at home.

He that has no charity deserves none.

He gives twice who gives quickly.

Giving honors the giver.

Thank the Lord that you can give, instead of depending on others to give to you.

Anecdotage:

The Jewish sage Moses Maimonides, in the 12th century, outlined eight grades of charity: The first is to give reluctantly; the second is to give cheerfully but not sufficiently; the third is to give cheerfully and sufficiently, but only after being asked; the fourth is to give cheerfully and sufficiently and without being asked, but to put it in the recipient's hand in such a way as to make him feel ashamed; the fifth grade of charity is to let the the recipient know who the donor is but not let the donor know the identity of those receiving the charity; the sixth grade of charity is to know who is getting your charity but to be unknown to them; the seventh is to have neither the donor nor the recipient aware of the other's identity; but the eighth and highest grade of charity is to forestall it by enabling your fellow humans to have the wherewithal to earn a livelihood.

The tightwad decided that instead of giving money to charity he would give of himself in good deeds. That morning, as he was headed for business, he saw an old lady all bent over, standing on a corner as the traffic walked by; so he came up to her, took her by the arm, and gently and firmly guided her across the street. "That," he said to her proudly, "was part of my pledge to give of myself by helping others." "Helping others!" said the old lady, "I was waiting for a bus and now I've missed it. Do you have a couple of dollars for a taxi?"

Facts:

In addition to the longstanding efforts of religious organizations in the U.S., there has recently been great growth in the concept of a United Fund or Community Chest as a single fund raising organization for a whole complex of community activities that are supported by voluntary contributions. Another growing source of charity has been the charitable foundations which have proliferated as a result of income and inheritance tax laws. It is estimated that foundation funds have tripled since 1960. Charitable bequests have also been stimulated by tax laws. The majority of private philanthropic contributions by far goes to religious institutions, with health second and education third..

The Foundation Center, an information center, is at 888 Seventh Avenue, New York, N.Y. 10019.

CHILDREN

(See also Babies, Parents)

Definitions: Young human beings, older than babies and younger than adults; small fry; the tomorrow generation; youngsters; creatures that are always halfway between their parents and the television set.

Quotations;

Backward, turn backward, O Time, in your flight,/ Make me a child again, just for tonight. *Elizabeth Chase Akers, "Rock Me To Sleep, Mother," 1860.*

Late children, early orphans. *Benjamin Franklin,* **Poor Richard's Almanac,** *1742.*

Children are without pity. *Jean de La Fontaine,* **Fables,** *17th century.*

Between the dark and the daylight,/ When the night is beginning to lower,/ Comes a pause in the day's occupations,/ That is known as the children's hour. *Henry Wadsworth Longfellow, "The Children's Hour," 1860.*

Suffer the little children to come unto me, and forbid them not: for of such is the kingdom of God. **Mark,** *X, 14.*

The childhood shows the man,/ As morning shows the day. *John Milton,* **Paradise Regained,** *1671.*

Train up a child in the way he should go: and when he is old, he will not depart from it. **Proverbs,** *XXII, 6.*

Give a little love to a child, and you get a great deal back. *John Ruskin,* **The Crown of Wild Olive,** *1866.*

A child should always say what's true,/ And speak when he is spoken to,/ And behave mannerly at table:/ At least as far as he is able. *Robert Louis Stevenson, "Whole Duty of Children," 1885.*

I have found the best way to give advice to your children is to find out what they want and then advise them to do it. *Harry S. Truman, May 27, 1955.*

Children begin by loving their parents. After a time, they judge them. Rarely, if ever, do they forgive them. *Oscar Wilde,* **A Woman of No Importance,** *1893.*

Anonymous aphorisms:

The two things children wear out are clothes and parents.

The worst children are always somebody else's.

The universal language of children is called gimme, otherwise known as I wanna.

Children should be seen and not heard.

Children are poor people's riches.

Anecdotage:

"Where do I come from," the little girl asked her mother. The mother launched a long explanation of the birds and the bees. "No," said the child impatiently. "My friend Susie comes from Boston. Where do I come from?"

The garrulous child kept pestering the distinguished houseguest and finally told the distracted adult, "Gee, you certainly know a lot." The adult said, "What am I supposed to say to that?" "You're supposed to say thank you," said the child.

Facts:

In 1860 about half the U.S. population was less than 20 years old; now, some 35 percent are teen-aged or younger. People are living longer and children are not quite as dominant in the composition of the total population. Today's child is part of a generally smaller family than heretofore, with fewer siblings, better nutrition and better medical care, as well as more years of education. But all is not bright. More children today, than at any time in the past, are confronted by broken homes. Illegitimacy is no longer the bar sinister of the past, but the rise in illegitimate births poses many problems about the psyches of children growing up with the knowledge of such parentage.

Statistics are available from U.S. Public Health Service and U.S. Census Bureau, as well as annual almanacs.

CITIZENSHIP

Definitions: the condition of owing allegiance to and/or being a participant in a governmental jurisdiction such as a city or nation; the attributes of participation in community activities; the only ship where everyone is expected to be a part of the crew; what everyone expects his neighbors to demonstrate.

Quotations:

Amongst the virtues of the good citizen are those of fortitude and patience. *William Cobbett,* **Advice to Young Men,** *1829.*

Presidents learn—perhaps sooner than others—that our destiny is fashioned by what all of us do, by the deeds and desires of each citizen, as one tiny drop of water after another ultimately makes a big river. *President Lyndon B. Johnson, September 5, 1966.*

Political activity is the highest responsibility of a citizen. *Massachusetts Senator John F. Kennedy, Democratic Presidential nominee, October 20, 1960.*

The first requisite of a good citizen in this republic of ours is that he shall be able and willing to pull his weight. *President Theodore Roosevelt, November 11, 1902.*

No man can be a good citizen unless he has a wage more than sufficient to cover the bare cost of living, and hours of labor short enough so that after his day's work is done he will have time and energy to bear his share in the management of the community, to help in carrying the general load. We keep countless men from being good citizens by the conditions of life with which we surround them. *Theodore Roosevelt, August 31, 1910.*

I am a citizen not of Athens or Greece, but of the world. *Socrates, as reported by later chroniclers.*

Who is the Forgotten Man? He is the clean, quiet, virtuous, domestic citizen who pays his debts and his taxes and is never heard of out of his little circle. *William Graham Sumner, "The Forgotten Man," 1883.*

Citizenship is man's basic right, for it is nothing less than the right to have rights. *Chief Justice Earl Warren, dissenting opinion in Perez v. Brownell, U.S. Supreme Court, 1958.*

Citizens by birth or choice of a common country, that country has a right to concentrate your affections. *President George Washington, Farewell Address, 1796.*

Anonymous aphorisms:

A good citizen doesn't rely on government. Government relies on him.

A good citizen is her own best friend.

Citizenship is a right for the native born and a goal for the foreign born.

Citizenship is apt to be more appreciated by those who earn it than by those born to it.

A good citizen is one who doesn't always keep his mouth shut.

The more you take part in government, the less government will take part of you.

Anecdotage:

When Mrs. Schultz got her citizenship papers, she had them framed and placed in the spot on the living room wall where previously she had kept a picture of her home town in the Old Country. "I know where I came from," she said, "but now I want to see what I stand for."

Mr. Brown was active in many different organizations, and he kept ringing his neighbors' doorbells trying to get them to take part in the various community activities. "He's a very good citizen," said one neighbor to another. "No," said the second neighbor, "he's just a guy looking for good citizens."

Facts:

Citizenship began as the privilege of participating in the affairs of the community. In ancient Greece citizens were those property owners entitled to vote. In feudal England there were gradations of citizenship ranging from the semi-serf with few rights to the barons who asserted for themselves what we would regard today as the normal rights of citizens, in the Magna Carta. In free societies such as the U.S., non-citizens are fully protected, but nevertheless subjected to requirements for entry or residence in the country which do not apply to citizens. In many foreign lands, non-citizens face discrimination in traveling rights, residence and business. Naturalization is a relatively simple process in the U.S., but in some other nations it is so difficult as to be virtually impossible. Citizenship entitles the citizen to the protection of his government when traveling abroad, although refugees can often travel as stateless persons under the protection of international agreements.

CITY LIFE

Definitions: living in a modern, high-population-density metropolitan community; modern multiple dwelling, mass transportation existence; the big apple; metropolitanism.

Quotations:

. . . a city of many people can rarely, if ever, be well governed . . . *Aristotle,* **Politics,** *4th century B.C.*

Burn down your cities and leave our farms, and your cities will spring up again; but destroy our farms and the grass will grow in the streets of every city in the country. *William Jennings Bryan, July 8, 1896.*

If you would be known, and not know, vegetate in a village; if you would know, and not be known, live in a city. *Charles Caleb Colton.* **Lacon,** *1820s.*

Cities degrade us by magnifying trifles. *Ralph Waldo Emerson,* **The Conduct of Life;** *Culture, 1860.*

The city is recruited from the country. *Ralph Waldo Emerson,* **Essays, Second Series:** *Manners, 1844.*

Great cities seldom rest; if there be none/ T'invade from far, they'll find worse foes at home. *Robert Herrick,* **Hesperides,** *1648.*

When we get piled upon one another in large cities, as in Europe, we shall become as corrupt as Europe . . . *Thomas Jefferson, letter to James Madison, December 20, 1787.*

To say the least, a town life makes one more tolerant and liberal in one's judgment of others. *Henry Wadsworth Longfellow,* **Hyperion,** *1839.*

We need help, and we need it yesterday. *Cleveland Mayor Carl Stokes, at Senate hearing, June 3, 1971.*

I love to see the other mayors; misery loves company. *Seattle Mayor Wesley C. Uhlman, April 21, 1971.*

A great city is that which has the greatest men and women . . . *Walt Whitman, "Song of the Broad-Axe," 1856.*

Anonymous aphorisms:

City people think they are the smartest, but that's where the population is the most dense.

A city is a large town made up of people being lonely together.

The modern city has skyscrapers reaching for the heavens because it has run out of room on earth.

In the country you live longer than in the city—or does it just seem longer?

In the cities these days they worry more about parking than about parks.

America is becoming one large urban community, in which the components are separated from each other by traffic jams.

Anecdotage:

"I prefer the country to the city, because you don't have to rush." "Maybe that's because there's nothing to rush to or from."

When people are young they leave the country to come to the city, and when they are old they leave the city to go to the country, but what do you think makes them old?

"I love the big city because I can do whatever I want to without anybody bothering me," said Mr. Brown. "Funny," said Mr. Black, "that's precisely why I moved out of the city."

Facts:

In the U.S., as in most of the world, the percentage of the total population living in urban as opposed to rural places went steadily up in the first 75 years of the 20th century. In 1975 about 75 percent of the U.S. population was urban. However, our cities and suburbs are spreading out, with less density. In 1960 the urban population was 3,113 per square mile; by 1970 this had gone down to 2,760 per square mile. Business as well as residency is shifting from central cities to suburban rings, prompted by rise in urban crime rates, mid-city transportation difficulties and new building.

The National League of Cities is at 1620 I Street NW, Washington, D.C. 20006.

CIVILIZATION

(See also Society)

Definitions: a developed culture and mode of life; man's "improvements" on nature; man's advance from pushing a plow to pushing a button; the triumph of the bathtub over the outdoor shower.

Quotations:

The beginning of civilization is marked by an intense legality; that legality is the very condition of its existence, the bond which ties it together; but that legality—that tendency to impose a settled customary yoke upon all men and all actions—if it goes on, kills out the variability implanted by nature, and makes different man and different ages facsimiles of other men and other ages, as we see them so often. *Walter Baqehot,* **Physics and Politics,** *1869.*

The whole history of civilization is strewn with creeds and institutions which were invaluable at first, and deadly afterwards. *Ibid.*

Civilization and profits go hand in hand. *Vice President-elect Calvin Coolidge, November 27, 1920.*

Increased means and increased leisure are the two civilizers of man. *Benjamin Disraeli, April 3, 1872.*

The civilized man has built a coach, but has lost the use of his feet. He is supported on crutches, but lacks so much support of muscle. He has a fine Geneva watch, but he fails of the skill to tell the hour by the sun. *Ralph Waldo Emerson,* **Essays, First Series:** *Self-Reliance, 1841.*

The true test of civilization is, not the census, nor the size of cities, nor the crops—no, but the kind of man the country turns out. *Ralph Waldo Emerson,* **Society and Solitude:** *Civilization, 1870.*

A sufficient measure of civilization is the influence of good women. *Ibid.*

A decent provision for the poor is the true test of civilization. *Samuel Johnson, 1770.*

A civilization without culture and art is no civilization. *New York Governor Nelson A. Rockefeller, August 1970.*

Civilization is the making of civil persons. *John Ruskin,* **The Crown of Wild Olive,** *1866.*

Anonymous aphorisms:

Civilization is what took the country away from the Indians.

Civilization, like beauty, is in the eye of the beholder.

Civilization is a process whereby those who have already experienced it impose it on others.

Civilization is always our way of doing things, compared to theirs.

Civilization is what separates human beings from the beasts.

Anecdotage:

The man wandered, alone in the trackless waste and past the towering mountainside gleaming with wildflowers, walking on and on, desperate. At last he came to a change in the landscape, a desolate little valley in which he saw an automobile junkyard. "Thank the Lord," he said, "I've finally reached civilization."

The upperclassman separated the two freshmen who were fighting each other. "Civilized people settle their differences across the table" he said. "Or under it," said a passing professor.

Facts:

Every tribe or human group regards itself as civilized, and sees the ways of the rest of the world as uncivilized. Westerners thought they were bringing civilization to the Far East, while Orientals felt they were being invaded by barbarians. American Indians had what they regarded as a civilized way of life, with its own culture, standards of conduct, morality and art; but the colonists from Europe thought that what they imposed on America, and the way they imposed it, was civilization. The entire course of human history has been marked by clashes between different civilizations and their rise and fall. See the writings of such historians as Arnold Toynbee, H. G. Wells and Oswald Spengler.

CLUBS

(See also Fraternities)

Definitions: groups of people associated for a common purpose; membership organizations which establish their own criteria for admission; places where members of an organization meet; home away from home; "an assembly of good fellows, meeting under certain conditions" *(Samuel Johnson).*

Quotations:

I don't want to belong to any club that will accept me as a member. *Attributed to Groucho Marx, perhaps as early as 1930s*

No place in England where everyone can go is considered respectable. This is the genesis of the club—out of the Housewife by Respectability. *George Moore,* **Confessions of a Young Man,** *1888.*

Good company and good discourse are the very sinews of virtue. *Izaak Walton,* **The Compleat Angler,** *1653.*

Anonymous aphorisms:

A club is a mutual association of people who like each other's society.

A country club is part park and part parking lot.

If you want to be a member of the club, you have to pay your dues.

A club has to have more than one person and it also has to exclude more than one person; if everybody's a member, it is no longer a club.

The more exclusive a club is, the more people want to get in.

Clubs used to be meeting places for like-minded people; now they are ways of getting chartered airline rates.

A club may be judged by its choice of members, and an individual by choice of clubs.

Anecdotage:

Do you have any problems with dues at the club? No, just with the don'ts.

This particular club, which shall be nameless, was notorious for the singleminded fervor with which it espoused the status quo. Indeed, said one observer, it wasn't just a club, it was a blunt instrument.

Facts:

The modern club is a lineal descendant of the British coffeehouse clubs where people met to dine and talk in the 17th and 18th centuries. Membership organizations also have a tradition which goes back to fraternal orders of rather ancient vintage as well as to the medieval crafts and trade guilds. The Gale Research Company's Encyclopaedia of Associations, confined to national organizations, lists 16,000 such groups and that number is far exceeded by local groups.

COLLEGE

(See also Alumni, Education, School)

Definitions: an institution of higher education, granting either a degree or a certificate of accomplishment beyond the high school level; the groves of academe; sheepskin alley; "places where pebbles are polished and diamonds are dimmed" (Robert Ingersoll).

Quotations:

A university should be a place of light, of liberty, and of learning. *Benjamin Disraeli, speech in House of Commons, 1873.*

Colleges, in like manner, have their indispensible office—to teach elements. But they can only highly serve us, when they aim not to drill, but to create; when they gather from far every ray of various genius to their hospitable halls, and, by the concentrated fires, set the hearts of their youth on flame. *Ralph Waldo Emerson, "The American Scholar," 1837.*

One of the benefits of a college education is to show the boy its little avail. *Ralph Waldo Emerson,* **The Conduct of Life:** *Culture, 1860.*

Learn to give/Money to colleges while you live./ Don't be silly and think you'll try/ To bother the colleges, when you die,/ with codicil this, and codicil that,/ That Knowledge may starve while Law grows fat . . . *Oliver Wendell Holmes, "Parson Turell's Legacy," 1857.*

The idea of a college education for all young people of capacity, provided at nominal cost by their own states, is very peculiarly American. We in America invented the idea. We in America have developed it with remarkable speed. *President Lyndon B. Johnson, August 13, 1964.*

It might be said that I have the best of both worlds: a Harvard education and a Yale degree. *President John F. Kennedy, a Harvard alumnus, upon receiving an honorary degree at Yale, June 11, 1962.*

The most conservative persons I ever met are college undergraduates. *Princeton University President Woodrow Wilson, November 19, 1905.*

The use of a university is to make young gentlemen as unlike their fathers as possible. *President Woodrow Wilson, October 24, 1914.*

Anonymous aphorisms:

A college diploma used to be a license to look for a job. Now it is a license to look for a higher degree.

There are two classes in every college—passers and flunkers.

College is a storehouse of learning because so little is taken away.

It says something about the popular attitude toward college that adults speak of their children having a choice—go to college or go to work. When did they become opposites?

For lots of students their college letter is X—the unknown quantity.

Anecdotage:

College professors are apt to be more subtle than secondary and primary school teachers in rebuking their students. A college professor was in the middle of an important point when the bell rang to end the period; the students began leaving immediately, without waiting for the point of the teacher's words of widsom. "One moment," said the professor, "I have a few more pearls to cast."

When Clark Kerr was President of the University of California he said that "the three major administrative problems on a campus are sex for the students, athletics for the alumni and parking for the faculty." But that was a college generation ago. Now, with the financial crisis for higher education, the problems are fees from the students, contributions from the alumni and berths for the faculty.

Facts:

In 1960, there were 3,227,000 undergraduate students in degree-granting U.S. colleges. Since then this figure has more than doubled, and for women it has almost tripled. The U.S. National Center for Education Statistics found that the percentage of persons 18-21 attending college had risen from 33.2 percent in 1960 to 48.4 percent in 1974 and was expected to go a bit higher, at least until 1984. In 1970 there were 50 public college students for every 18 private college students, and for 1984 the forecast is 76 public college students to 17 private. In public and private colleges, tuition and required fees have more than doubled since 1965. Public institutions, of course, are still charging less than private colleges.

CONSTITUTION
(See also Government)

Definitions: the basic law or statute of a governed community; "the soul of a state" (*Isocrates*); "the fundamental and paramount law of the nation" (*Chief Justice John Marshall*); "the night watchman of democratic representative government" (*Alfred E. Smith*).

Quotations:

The Constitution of the United States was made not merely for the generation that then existed, but for posterity—unlimited, undefined, endless, perpetual posterity. *Kentucky Senator Henry Clay, February 6, 1850.*

The Constitution of the United States is a law for rulers and people, equally in war and in peace, and covers with the shield of its protection all classes of men, at all times, and under all circumstances. *Associate Justice David Davis, Supreme Court decision in* **Ex Parte Milligan,** *December 1866.*

Our Constitution works. Our great republic is a government of laws and not of men. Here, the people rule. *President Gerald R. Ford. Inaugural Address, August 9, 1974.*

We are under a Constitution, but the Constitution is what the judges say it is. *New York Governor Charles Evans Hughes, May 3, 1907.*

Our peculiar security is in the possession of a written Constitution. Let us not make it a blank paper by construction. *President Thomas Jefferson, in letter to Wilson C. Nicholas, September 7, 1803.*

The government of the United States, then, though limited in its powers, is supreme; and its laws, when made in pursuance of the Constitution, form the supreme law of the land, "anything in the constitution or laws of any State to the contrary notwithstanding." *Chief Justice John Marshall, Supreme Court decision in* **McCulloch v. Maryland,** *March 6, 1819.*

A constitution is a thing antecedent to a government, and a government is only the creature of a constitution. The constitution of a country is not the act of its government, but of the people constituting a government. *Thomas Paine,* **The Rights of Man,** *1791.*

The United States Constitution has proven itself the most marvelously elastic compilation of rules of government ever written. *New York Governor Franklin D. Roosevelt, March 2, 1930.*

Keep your eye on the Constitution. This is the guarantee, that is the safeguard, that is the night watchman of democratic representative government . . . *Alfred E. Smith at Harvard University, June 22, 1933.*

Constitutions are checks upon the hasty action of a majority. They are the self-imposed restraints of a whole people upon a majority of them to secure sober action and a respect for the rights of the minority, and of the individual . . . *President William Howard Taft, veto message, August 22, 1911.*

The basis of our political systems is the right of the people to make and alter their constitutions of government. But the constitution which at any time exists, until changed by an explicit and authentic act of the whole people, is sacredly obligatory upon all. *President George Washington, Farewell Address, September 1796.*

Anonymous aphorisms:

A nation, like its citizens, needs a strong Constitution.

For some people the Constitution guarantees life, liberty and the pursuit of loopholes.

The Constitution is the Supreme Court law of the land.

The Constitution is the yardstick of the law.

What's the Constitution among friends?

Facts:

The idea of a written Constitution as we know it today, formulated by the designated representatives of the people, is an American original, though drawn from the philosophy of British thinkers. Constitutions existed long before those adopted by the rebellious British colonies in America, but they were either unwritten ones or an accumulation of generations of separate laws and institutions or agreements wrung from a monarch by privileged groups, such as the British peers did with King John when they forced him to sign the

Magna Carta. The uniqueness of the United States Constitution, which became a model for the modern democratic world, was that it was the supreme law of the land, as interpreted by the Supreme Court that the Constitution had established. It is the basic law, the provisions of which all further laws must satisfy.

CONVENTIONS

Definitions: groups of delegates or representatives meeting for a common purpose; gatherings of people of common interests; meetings of minds who don't mind meeting; billet and ballot.

Quotations:

A convention is a splendid place to study human nature. Man in a crowd is quite a different creature than man acting alone. *William Jennings Bryan, 1912.*

Of representative assemblies may not this good be said: That contending parties in a country do thereby ascertain one another's strength? They fight there, since fight they must, by petition, parliamentary eloquence, not by sword, bayonet and bursts of military cannon. *Thomas Carlyle,* **Chartism,** *1839.*

Observe any meeting of people, and you will always find their eagerness and impetuosity rise or fall in proportion to their numbers: when the numbers are very great, all sense and reason seem to subside, and one sudden frenzy to seize on all, even the coolest of them. *Lord Chesterfield, September 1748.*

More than a generation ago, there existed widespread disapproval of the kind of national convention which became merely a trading post for a handful of powerful leaders, and where the nomination itself had nothing to do with the popular choice of the rank and file of the party itself. . . . The rank and file should be heard. *New York Governor Franklin D. Roosevelt, comment some months before 1932 Democratic National Convention.*

Anonymous aphorisms:

Running a convention is the art of the passable.

A convention, particularly a Presidential nominating convention, is a rostrum for nostrums.

It is only natural that visiting firemen should look for a hot time in the old town tonight.

An individual starts off by facing his problem with resolution, but a convention saves the resolution for the end.

At a convention some delegates reach for the stars and others keep reaching for the floor.

Anecdotage:

William Jennings Bryan compared the way a convention feels about demonstrations to the feeling of a big man whose wife "was in the habit of beating him. When asked why he permitted it, he replied that it seemed to please her and did not hurt him."

"Since you regard conventions as a waste of time," the reporter asked the old convention-goer, "why do you keep going to them?" "If I didn't," answered the old convention-goer, "how could I be sure?"

Facts:

Political decisions in the U.S. have been made by selecting delegates to meet and vote since well before the American Revolution. Our Constitution was created by a Convention called for that purpose, and then submitted to the states. The first political party conventions, in a modern sense, on a national basis, for the purpose of nominating Presidential candidates, were for the 1832 election, when the Democrats nominated Andrew Jackson and two other parties also met (the national Republicans to nominate Henry Clay and the Anti-Masonic Party to name William Wirt). In our own time, the convention has become popular for trade and labor groups, learned societies, sales staffs and all kinds of social organizations.

COOKING

(See also Dieting, Food)

Definitions: preparation of food for eating through processes such as baking, boiling, frying, broiling, stewing etc.; the art of formulating recipes and processes for the preparation of tasty dishes; burnt offerings; kitchen mechanics; the culinary art.

Quotations:

The discovery of a new dish does more for human happiness than the discovery of a new star. *Anthelme Brillat-Savarin,* **Physiologie du Gout,** *1825.*

We may live without friends; we may live without books;/ But civilized man cannot live without cooks. *E. R. Bulwer-Lytton (Lord Lytton; Owen Meredith),* **Lucile,** *1860.*

Cookery is become an art, a nobel science; cooks are gentlemen. *Robert Burton,* **The Anatomy of Melancholy,** *1621.*

Meat so dressed and sauced and seasoned that you didn't know whether it was beef or mutton—flesh, fowl, or good red herring. *George du Maurier,* **Trilby,** *1894.*

What is food to one may be bitter poison to others. *Lucretius,* **De Rerum Natura,** *2nd century B.C.*

Kissing don't last; cookery do! *George Meredith,* **The Ordeal of Richard Feverel,** *1859. A similar saying is attributed to the Pennsylvania Dutch.*

Anonymous aphorisms:

Too many broths spoil the cook.

A good cook makes a delicacy out of what an ordinary cook makes hash.

Very few state secrets are guarded as fiercely as a great recipe.

The motto of most cooks is "come fry with me."

There is basically one season in the kitchen—a long hot simmer.

American cooking is 4F—fast, frozen and fat-free.

There are two kinds of food at the average American banquet—warmed over and wondered over.

She calls him her recipe, because he tells her what she can do with the food.

Anecdotage:

"I always feel like a god when I come home," said the dyspeptic diner, "because for dinner there is always a burnt offering."

Mrs. Brown was a fabulous cook, but her recipes, when she was asked for them, always were a little vague. Finally, someone said to her, "what do you mean by a pinch of this or a touch of that? Can't you give us exact quantities?" "Well," said Mrs. Brown, "it depends on what you're pinching—or how touched you are."

Facts:

The preparation of food is probably humanity's first skill—or art. Cookbooks are among the most widely published and read books of all time. In the U.S. Census Bureau's tabulation of various types of retail trade, the category of eating places has the largest number of establishments. The American concept of fast food cooking and merchandising, from the hamburger to frozen foods, has captured the imagination of the world. French cuisine remains recognized as the standard of elegance, but in food preparation, American appetites have made this country an international trend-setting culinary clearing house, from bagels to frankfurters to chow mein to pizza to sukiyaki. In this country, cookery truly provides a cook's tour of the world.

COURAGE

Definitions: the opposite of fear or the ability to conquer it; bravery; valor; standing up to danger; guts.

Quotations:

It is a brave act of valour to contemn death; but where life is more terrible than death, it is then the truest valour to dare to live. *Sir Thomas Browne,* **Religio Medici,** *1642.*

The Red Badge of Courage *Title of book by Stephen Crane, 1895.*

None but the brave deserves the fair. *John Dryden,* **Alexander's Feast,** *1697.*

Damn the torpedoes, full spead ahead! *Rear Admiral David G. Farragut, August 5, 1864, at the Battle of Mobile Bay.*

Some have been thought brave because they were afraid to run away. *Thomas Fuller,* **Gnomologia,** *1732.*

It is better to die on your feet than to live on your knees. *Dolores Ibarruri, September 3, 1936.*

. . . every submission to our fear enlarges its dominion . . . *Samuel Johnson,* **The Rambler,** *June 29, 1751.*

I have not yet begun to fight. (Sometimes quoted as I have just begun to fight.) *Captain John Paul Jones aboard the Bonhomme Richard, when asked whether he was ready to surrender to the British warship Serapis, September 23, 1779.*

No one can prove his courage when he has never been in danger. *Francois, Duc de La Rochefoucauld,* **Maxims,** *1665-1672.*

Don't give up the ship. *Captain James Lawrence (also attributed to others), 1813.*

What though the field be lost?/ All is not lost—th' unconquerable will,/ And study of revenge, immortal hate,/ And courage never to submit or yield;/ And what else is not to be overcome. *John Milton,* **Paradise Lost,** *1667.*

But screw your courage to the sticking place,/ And you'll not fail. *William Shakespeare* **Macbeth,** *1606.*

Cannon to right of them,/ Cannon to left of them,/ Cannon in front of them/ Volley'd and thunder'd;/ Storm'd at with shot and shell,/ Boldly they rod and well,/ Into the jaws of Death,/ Into the mouth of Hell,/ Rode the six hundred. *Alfred Tennyson, "The Charge of the Light Brigade," 1854.*

Bravery never goes out of fashion. *William M. Thackeray,* **The Four Georges,** *1860.*

Anonymous aphorisms:

When the going gets tough, the tough get going.

Those who dare not, do not.

If a thing is worth having, it's worth fighting for.

Stand up and fight.

Stand up and be counted.

Anecdotage:

"It took real courage to stand up to that gunman in the cocktail lounge." "Not really—I didn't know I was loaded."

An unlikely hero was being hailed for standing up to an attacker twice his size and asked how he could be so brave. "I was too scared to run," he said, "and too dumb to think of anything else." But his friends said, "No, you didn't have time to think. Courage is a natural instinct—if you have it."

Facts:

Throughout time, courage has been regarded as one of the major human virtues. Today, modern psychology has sought to make it possible for a greater portion of society to accept without condemnation an individual's admission of lacking courage; but collectively, on a nation by nation basis, courage still must always be proclaimed. Nations fear that giving up without a fight may mean having to give up more again tomorrow. On an individual basis, the traditional high regard for courage is sometimes counseled against by the most courageous of people, the police. Most police authorities, for example, council victims of armed robberies not to fight back, but rather to yield and leave the catching of the robbers to the authorities. Courage may be fine, say the police, but there are times when common sense calls for something else. Perhaps the best point to remember is that the courage to accept a difficult and disagreeable fact has often been demonstrated by gallant people.

COURTS

(See also Justice, Law)

Definitions: places where judgments and decisions of law are rendered; the machinery of justice, determining guilt or innocence; tribunals; the domain of judges; the bench; where a suit is pressed and a man can be taken to the cleaners.

Quotations:

Judges ought to remember that their office is Ius dicere and not Ius dare; to interpret law, and not to make law, or give law. *Francis Bacon, "Of Judicature," 1625.*

Agree, for the law is costly. *William Camden,* **Remains Concerning Britain,** *1605.*

. . . th' supreme court follows th' iliction returns. *Finley Peter Dunne,* **Mr. Dooley:** *"The Supreme Court's Decisions," 1900.*

When a judge puts on his robes he puts off his relations to any, and, like Melchisedech, becomes without pedigree. *Thomas Fuller,* **The Holy State and the Profane State,** *1642.*

A good and faithful judge prefers what is right to what is expedient. *Horace, "Carmina," 13 B.C.*

It is emphatically the province and duty of the judicial department to say what the law is. *Chief Justice John Marshall, Supreme Court decision in* **Marbury v. Madison,** *February 24, 1803.*

I have always thought, from my earliest youth till now, that the greatest scourge an angry Heaven ever inflicted upon an ungrateful and sinning people was an ignorant, a corrupt, or a dependent judiciary. *Chief Justice John Marshall, as recorded in the Debates of the Virginia (Constitutional) Convention of 1829-31.*

If one man sin against another, the judge shall judge him . . . **I Samuel,** *II:25.*

Anonymous aphorisms:

Sue now, settle later.

Court is the only place where the benchwarmer is the boss.

A court calendar has no pin-ups but lots of put-offs.

In court you present your briefs and run the risk of losing your shirt.

If at first you don't succeed, sue, sue again.

Everyone is entitled to his day in court—no matter how many days he has to wait.

Anecdotage:

A man asked to be excused from jury duty because he was needed where he worked. "Your business will have to get along without you," said the judge, "you're not indispensable." "That's what I'm afraid they'll find out," said the man.

When does a judge commit a public nuisance? When he sends a peeping Tom to jail.

Facts:

Never have the courts had more laws to interpret and apply or more litigants with whom to deal. The caseload has grown far more than the dimensions of the judicial system. In 1950, U.S. Courts of Appeals had 2,830 cases brought before them; since then the number has risen to more than 16,000, almost a sixfold increase. On the state and local level the figures have risen at least equally dramatically. Part of the increase is due to rising crime rates; part simply to the fact that there is a larger population and part to the fact that every legislative session seems to pass new laws defining new crimes or establishing new court remedies. Years ago, for example, courts had far fewer ecological or discrimination cases simply because there were fewer laws on these subjects.

CREATIVITY

Definition: originality in the arts; the talent or inspiration to conceive and express new ideas; inspiration; inventiveness combined with artfulness; making something out of nothing.

Quotations:

Men are like trees: each one must put forth the leaf that is created in him. *Rev. Henry Ward Beecher*, **Proverbs from Plymouth Pulpit**, *1887*.

No great thing is created suddenly, any more than a bunch of grapes or a fig. If you tell me that you desire a fig, I answer that there must be time. Let it first blossom, then bear fruit, then ripen. *Epictetus*, **Discourses**, *1st to 2nd Century*.

Thine was the prophet's vision, thine/ The exaltation, the divine/ Insanity of noble minds,/ That never falters nor abates,/ But labors and endures and waits,/ Till all that it foresees it finds,/ Or what it cannot find creates! *Henry Wadsworth Longfellow*, "Keramos," *1878*.

In creating, the only hard thing's to begin;/ A grass blade's no easier to make than an oak. *James Russell Lowell*, **A Fable for Critics**, *1848*.

Nothing can be created out of nothing. *Lucretius*, **De Rerum Natura**, *1st Century B.C.*

All good things which exist are the fruits of originality. *John Stuart Mill*, **On Liberty**, *1859*.

We want the creative faculty to imagine that which we know. *Percy Bysshe Shelley,* **A Defence of Poetry,** *1821.*

He or she is greatest who contributes the greatest original practical example. *Walt Whitman, "By Blue Ontario's Shores," 1856.*

Every great and original writer, in proportion as he is great and original, must himself create the taste by which he is to be relished. *William Wordsworth, May 21, 1807.*

Anonymous aphorisms:

Creativity has no precedents.

It is better to create than to cremate.

Brand new ideas are rare; good new ideas are even rarer.

Too many people think they are being creative when they are just being different.

Creativity has no script; it is inspired ad libbing.

Originality is not necessarily better than imitation, but it makes imitation possible.

Anecdotage:

Billy wasn't doing well at school, and his mother went to see his teacher. "I've asked Billy why he did so poorly in mathematics and reading and history," said she to the teacher, "and he seemed to have lots of excuses." The teacher, searching for soothing words of comfort, said, "Well, ma'am, he doesn't work very hard but he certainly shows a lot of creativity."

An art class was assigned to copy Michelangelo's "Creation of Adam." One student produced a confusing pattern of straight lines that bore no more resemblance to the Michelangelo painting than to a blank wall. "I felt I had to express my own instinctive spirit of creativity," said the student. "What you have created," said the teacher, "is a void."

Facts:

Human creativity has had its high and low eras in history. The Renaissance was one of the highest eras because greater creative freedom and increased support for creative people came together. Amid all the problems of the modern world, the combination of these same conditions encourages creativity today. Government policy, both through tax exemptions and through positive subsidy, is helping to establish and support places where creative talents can be nurtured and creativity displayed. These include theaters for the dramatic and concert arts, museums, professional groups and schools. The climate for creativity can be attested to by one admittedly incomplete statistic. Not all creative ideas can be copyrighted, but the number of copyrights can be considered at least partial evidence of creativity. Since 1960 the total number of copyrights in the U.S. filed annually rose about 65 percent; musical compositions increased about 75 percent and works of art over 100 percent.

CRIME

(See also Law and Order, Violence)

Definitions: violation of the law; offenses against legal standards of conduct; wrongdoing; a story told in sentences; the underworld; the rackets; wrongdoers.

Quotations:

The greatest incitement to crime is the hope of escaping punishment. *Cicero,* **Pro Milone,** *52 B.C.*

I hear much of people's calling out to punish the guilty, but very few are concerned to clear the innocent. *Daniel Defoe,* **An Appeal to Honor and Justice,** *1715.*

You cannot do wrong without suffering wrong. *Ralph Waldo Emerson,* **Essays, First Series:** *Compensation, 1841.*

The greater the man the greater the crime. *Thomas Fuller,* **Gnomologia,** *1732.*

My object all sublime,/I shall achieve in time—/To let the punishment fit the crime . . . *W. S. Gilbert,* **The Mikado,** *1885.*

. . . where legitimate opportunities are closed, illegitimate opportunities are seized. Whatever opens opportunity and hope will help to prevent crime and foster responsibility. *President Lyndon B. Johnson, March 9, 1966.*

All go free when many offend. *Lucan,* **Pharsalia,** *1st Century.*

Whoso diggeth a pit shall fall therein: and he that rolleth a stone, it will return upon him. **Proverbs,** *26:27.*

He who does not prevent a crime when he can, encourages it. *Seneca,* **Troades,** *1st Century.*

Anonymous aphorisms:

Crime doesn't pay.

Wrong never comes right.

Whoever profits from crime is part of it.

Temptation makes thieves, but some thieves make their own temptations.

There are black sheep in every flock.

Murder will out.

It takes a thief to catch a thief.

Give a thief enough rope to hang himself

Straight trees can have crooked roots.

Anecdotage:

They say Diogenes came to the big city to look for an honest man, but he didn't stay long. Someone stole his lantern.

A practical joker sent the same anonymous wire to ten leading citizens of the town, saying "Everything has been found out, but you still have time to leave town." Seven of the ten left.

Facts:

Crime is a growth industry in every part of the world. Its growth stems from various causes: more things are characterized as crimes today, it is increasingly difficult to control individuals through the family and other established institutions, and popular "direct action" has grown against governmental restraint in various parts of the world. Although crime statistics are reported differently in different countries, the U.S. appears to lead the modern nations of the world in the rise in crime rates. A homogeneous society generally has been found to have a lower crime rate, particularly as regards violent crimes, than a heterogeneous society. In the U.S., the murder, auto theft and assault rates have all risen dramatically in recent years.

CRITICISM

Definitions: expressions of judgment of a work of art; reviews; comments and observations; grandstand quarterbacking; first nighters and second guessers.

Quotations:

As soon/ Seek roses in December—ice in June;/ Hope constancy in wind, or corn in chaff,/ Believe a woman or an epitaph,/ Or any other thing that's false, before/ You trust in Critics. *George Gordon, Lord Byron,* **English Bards and Scotch Reviewers,** *1809.*

It is much easier to be critical than to be correct. *Benjamin Disraeli, January 24, 1860.*

You know who critics are?—the men who have failed in literature and art. *Benjamin Disraeli,* **Lothair,** *1870.*

Blame-all and praise-all are two blockheads. *Benjamin Franklin*, **Poor Richard's Almanac**, *1734*.

What a blessed thing it is, that Nature, when she invented, manufactured and patented her authors, contrived to make critics out of the chips that were left! *Oliver Wendell Holmes*, **The Professor at the Breakfast-Table**, *1860*.

Criticism is a study by which men grow important and formidable at very small expense. *Samuel Johnson*, **The Idler**, *June 9, 1759*.

Nature fits all her children with something to do,/ He who would write and can't write can surely review. *James Russell Lowell*, **A Fable for Critics**, *1848*.

A wise skepticism is the first attribute of a good critic. *James Russell Lowell*, **Among My Books**, *1870*.

Judge not, that ye be not judged. **Matthew**, *7:1*

You do not get a man's most effective criticism until you provoke him. Severe truth is expressed with some bitterness. *Henry D. Thoreau*, **Journal**, March 15, 1854.

If you can't stand the heat you better get out of the kitchen. *Attributed by President Harry S. Truman to an "old friend and colleague on the Jackson County Court" in speech December 17, 1952.*

Anonymous aphorisms:

One man's work is another man's target.

Those who can, do; those who can't, review.

Those who do well like criticism; those who do not do well resent it.

Anecdotage:

It was Eugene Field who reviewed a performance of "King Lear" by saying that the role of the King was played as though someone else was about to play the Ace.

It was said of one of the great Broadway theater critics that "he left no turn unstoned."

An art critic who got tired of being asked what he thought of this painting and that one now offers the same answer to all: "What a picture!"

Facts:

The Encyclopaedia Britannica names Plato as the first theater critic; criticism of the arts is thus almost as old as the arts themselves. Some critics, like John Ruskin and Matthew Arnold, have gained world stature alongside those whose work they reviewed. Criticism is a staple of most newspapers, magazines and broadcasting stations in the U.S., but even with the multitude of reviews available today, a handful of critics of a Broadway play can often make a significant difference in the play's box office success or failure. Until television, most of the audience depended on reviews in choosing what they would go to see or pick up to read, but, despite pre-reviewing by newspaper critics, most television broadcasts are seen by the public before detailed reviews of them are read. Excerpts from favorable reviews are still considered among the best ways of promoting interest in a book, movie or theater presentation. Indeed, some critics, who do not like to be quoted in advertising, go to considerable lengths to try to couch their reviews in language that cannot be easily excerpted.

DEATH

Definitions: the end of life; the opposite of life; the ultimate equality; the end; the way of all flesh; the final reward; the peace of the grave.

Quotations:

O death; where is thy sting? O grave, where is thy victory? **I Corinthians,** *15:55.*

Death, be not proud, though some have called thee/Mighty and dreadful, for thou art not so,/For those whom thou think'st thou dost overthrow/Die not, poor Death, nor yet canst thou kill me. *John Donne,* **Holy Sonnets,** *X, early 17th century.*

. . . in this world nothing is certain but death and taxes. *Benjamin Franklin, letter to Jean-Baptiste Leroy, November 13, 1789.*

Why fear death? It is the most beautiful adventure in life. *Charles Frohman, May 7, 1915; supposedly said as he was dying in the torpedoing of the S.S. Lusitania in World War I.*

. . . dust thou art, and unto dust shalt thou return. **Genesis,** *3:19.*

The paths of glory lead but to the grave. *Thomas Gray,* **Elegy Written in a Country Churchyard,** *1751.*

Dust thou art, to dust returnest,/Was not spoken of the soul. *Henry Wadsworth Longfellow, "A Psalm of Life," 1839.*

I have a rendezvous with Death/At some disputed barricade. *Alan Seeger. "I Have a Rendezvous with Death," 1916.*

. . . death—/The undiscover'd country, from whose bourne/No traveller returns. *William Shakespeare,* **Hamlet** *1601.*

. . . I hope to see my Pilot face to face/When I have crost the bar. *Alfred Lord Tennyson, "Crossing the Bar," 1889.*

. . . Adam, the first great benefactor of our race. He brought death into the world. *Mark Twain,* **The Tragedy of Pudd'nhead Wilson,** *1894.*

Nothing can happen more beautiful than death. *Walt Whitman, "Starting from Paumanok," 1860.*

Anonymous aphorisms:

Say nothing but good about the dead.

Life ends, but memory lives.

Death is the last great accomplishment of life.

Living is temporary; death is recorded in stone.

Death is another stage in the life of the soul.

Death, like life, is a gift of God.

There is no arguing with death.

Anecdotage:

When an uncle died and left him a substantial inheritance, the French writer Balzac commented that now both he and his uncle had passed on to a better life.

The fable is told of the man who lived in Bagdad and one day came rushing in to see the Grand Vizir to ask permission to go immediately to Samarra. When the Vizir asked him why he was in such a rush, he explained that in a dream he had seen the face of Death, who said they would meet that night. "But," said the man, "if I ride swiftly, I will not be here tonight. I will be safely far away in Samarra." And so he fled; and that night the Grand Vizir dreamed and saw the face of Death, and Death said to him, "Do not be afraid, for I am not concerned with you. Tonight I have an appointment in Samarra."

This story is told of Voltaire. When he was asked to comment about the death of a famous man, he said, "He was a man of character, of whom nothing but good should now be said—provided he's really dead."

Facts:

Probably humanity's oldest aspiration is the fight to conquer death. Because we are mortal, we never conquer it; but we have slowed it down. In 1976, the U. S. government was able to report that the nation's death rate was at the lowest point in our national history. For the first time, it had dropped below 9 for every 1,000 Americans. And as the lifespan increases, the attitude of humanity toward death has also showed signs of change. Euthanasia, and the idea of letting doomed people die in dignity rather than keeping them painfully alive, still create the most bitter arguments, but the concept of death as release, long a mark of all the major religions, is becoming a sociological concept as well. Death has always provided a rallying point for families and friends not merely to help the bereaved but to come together and reassert the eternal continuum of human life. In some primitive cultures, the old go off to die when they cease to be active. They do not think of this as a cruel practice, but rather as a sensible and inevitable one. In our society, however, the idea of a person's determining voluntarily the time of his own death remains contrary to our heritage of both law and custom.

DIETING

(See also Food, Health)

Definitions: eating less or eating selected foods with an eye toward losing or controlling weight; reducing; counting calories; weight watching; thinking thin.

Quotations:

To lengthen thy life, lessen thy meals. *Benjamin Franklin,* **Poor Richard's Almanac,** *1737.*

Kill no more pigeons than you can eat. *Benjamin Franklin, letter to Catherine Ray, October 16, 1755.*

A little with quiet is the only diet. *George Herbert,* **Outlandish Proverbs** *1640.*

Who ever hears of fat men heading a riot, or herding together in turbulent mobs? *Washington Irving,* **History of New York, by Diedrich Knickerbocker,** *1809.*

One must eat to live, not live to eat. *Moliere,* **The Miser,** *1668.*

What some people call health, if purchased by perpetual anxiety about diet, isn't much better than tedious disease. *George Dennison Prentice,* **Prenticeana,** *1860.*

The appetite grows by eating. *Francois Rabelais,* **Gargantua,** *1534.*

O, that this too too solid flesh would melt . . . *William Shakespeare,* **Hamlet,** *1601.*

Everything I like is either illegal, immoral or fattening. *Alexander Woollcott, attributed, 1920s or 1930s.*

Anonymous aphorisms:

Taste makes waistline.

Dieting is a losing battle.

Inside every fat person there's a thin person hoping to get out.

One exercise that is guaranteed to help you lose weight is pushing away from the table.

Dieting is a weighty problem.

If nothing at the table goes to waste it goes to somebody's waist.

Rich food is usually poor eating.

Anecdotage:

"I have the perfect diet," said Mr. Hopkins. "I eat my head off one day and starve the next." "And how do you feel?" he was asked. "Great," he said, "every other day."

An author approached a publisher with a manuscript called "The 100-year Diet." The publisher said it was a crazy idea, because the kind of book that sells is one telling how to lose a lot of pounds quickly. "Maybe so," said the author, "but my book tells you how long you have to stay on the diet to avoid getting the pounds back."

Facts:

There are almost as many weight-control diets extant as there are cookbooks. Indeed, more and more of the cookbooks today are diet cookbooks. That is one reason for the tremendous boom in sugar substitutes and fad foods. But no magic formulas are needed to explain the diet craze. One reason is the extent to which physical exercise through hard labor has disappeared in the age of electric power and automation. We ride where we used to walk; we push a button where we used to turn a hand-powered tool. And we eat "better" than we used to, with larger quantities on the plate. But there has been another change in our ways. A couple of generations ago, the fatter a baby was, the healthier we thought he was; in those years there was no thought that butter-fat might be harmful or eggs allergenic. The discovery that fat was not a harbinger of health is a relatively recent one. Even our ideas of feminine beauty have changed. The heartbreakers of the gay 90's all look rather too ample nowadays. It has been estimated that diet foods, whether for weight reduction or other health reasons, have become a multi-billion dollar industry in the United States. Since 1960, the number of dietitians in the U.S. has risen by well over 50 percent.

DRAMA

(see also Theater)

Definitions: theatrical presentation involving the enactment of a narrative; byplay between conflicting forces; what is usually more fun to watch than to be part of; an offering in acts and scenes, in return for an offering at the box office.

Quotations:

The business of plays is to recommend virtue, and discountenance vice; to show the uncertainty of human greatness, the sudden turns of fate, and the unhappy conclusions of violence and injustice; tis to expose the singularities of pride and fancy, to make folly and falsehood contemptible, and to bring everything that is ill under infamy and neglect. *Jeremy Collier,* **A Short View of the Immorality and Profaneness of the English Stage,** *1698.*

A play ought to be a just and lively image of human nature, representing its passions and humors, and the changes of fortune to which it is subject, for the delight and instruction of mankind. *John Dryden,* **An Essay of Dramatic Poesy,** *1668.*

The anomalous fact is that the theater, so called, can flourish in barbarism, but that any drama worth speaking of can develop but in the air of civilization. *Henry James, letter to C. E. Wheeler, April 9, 1911.*

The drama's laws, the drama's patrons give,/For we that live to please, must please to live. *Samuel Johnson, Prologue at opening of Drury Lane Theater, 1747.*

The business of the dramatist is to keep out of sight and let nothing appear but his characters. *Thomas B. Macaulay, "Essay on Milton," 1825.*

The play's the thing/Wherein I'll catch the conscience of the king. *William Shakespeare,* **Hamlet,** *1601.*

Through all the drama—whether damned or not—/Love gilds the scene, and women guide the plot. *Richard Brinsley Sheridan,* **The Rivals,** *1775.*

Anonymous aphorisms:

Too many dramas these days are in the hands of people who don't have any dramatic license.

Life is like a drama—they're both likely to have third act trouble.

The central idea of the drama is that you can escape from your own problems by watching somebody else's.

There is no play on the stage that isn't hard work.

Anecdotage:

Danny Kaye has noted that there is a clear difference in Russian drama between comedy and tragedy. In both, everybody dies; but in a comedy, they die happy.

It was Oscar Wilde who commented after a disastrous opening night that the play was a great success but the audience was a failure.

Facts:

When the novel had not yet been invented, the drama was already entertaining the multitudes. Of all the great forms of human representation, the drama has the longest history of effectiveness. The ancient Greek drama is as great in theatrical presentation today as it was three thousand years ago. The plays of Shakespeare have been translated and played in every corner of the world. Over the centuries, those connected with the drama have been alternately sneered at and idolized, but "play acting" has always been a part of community life. Today the drama is more widespread an art form than ever, and in a greater variety of formats than ever before, thanks to the miracles of motion pictures, radio and television.

DREAMS

Definitions: thoughts, experiences or emotions seen in the mind's eye during sleep; imagined things; optimistic visions; idealistic hopes; what you see clearly with your eyes closed; out of Morpheus by indigestion.

Quotations:

. . . your young men shall see visions, and your old men shall dream dreams. **Acts of the Apostles,** *2:17.*

I walked beside the evening sea/And dreamed a dream that could not be; The waves that plunged along the shore/Said only: "Dreamer, dream no more!" *George William Curtis, "Ebb and Flow," late 19th century.*

We need men who can dream of things that never were. *President John F. Kennedy, speech in Dublin, Ireland, June 28, 1963.*

. . . a dreamer lives forever,/And a toiler dies in a day. *John Boyle O'Reilly, "The Cry of the Dreamer," 1873.*

All that we see or seem/Is but a dream within a dream. *Edgar Allan Poe, "A Dream Within a Dream," 1827.*

Those who dream by day are cognizant of many things which escape those who dream by night. *Edgar Allan Poe, "Eleanora," 1842.*

I talk of dreams;/Which are the children of an idle brain,/Begot of nothing but vain fantasy. *William Shakespeare,* **Romeo and Juliet,** *1595.*

Men never cling to their dreams with such tenacity as at the moment when they are losing faith in them, and know it, but do not dare yet to confess it to themselves. *William Graham Sumner, "The Banquet of Life," 1887.*

. . . if one advances confidently in the direction of his dreams, and endeavors to live the life which he has imagined, he will meet with a success unexpected in common hours. *Henry D. Thoreau,* **Walden,** *1854.*

Anonymous aphorisms:

Unimaginative people dream in black and white, but poets dream in glorious color.

One man's dream is another man's dramamine.

Those who dream the night away wonder why throughout the day.

Young people dream dreams; old people dream memories.

A dream is a very exclusive production, played for an audience of one.

A dream is the subconscious at work; a daydreamer is the unconscious at work.

Dreams are the stuff of progress.

Anecdotage:

"I keep having this dream," said the patient, "that I am an Arab sheik with a magnificent harem, huge oilfields, a marvelous physique and the best cook in the world." "So what's your problem?" asked the doctor. "I keep waking up," said the patient.

"Every time I eat scallops," said Mr. Jones, "I dream I have struck oil. I suppose I should stop eating scallops, but then I wouldn't know any more what it's like to strike oil."

Facts:

Dreams have fascinated human beings since virtually the dawn of time. In ancient times, they were regarded as supernatural prophecies, and even to this day, dream interpreters offer to predict a customer's future by the portents of his dreams. But modern science prefers to regard dreams as mirrors of the subconscious, echoes of what has been thought, experienced or feared in the past. Sigmund Freud's book, *The Interpretation of Dreams,* published in 1900, gave great impetus to this view, with particular emphasis on the idea that dreams were expressions of secret desires. Many leading modern psychiatrists and psychologists disagree, but all are to some degree the heirs of what might be termed Freud's own dreams.

DRINK

Definitions: beverage; liquid refreshment; alcoholic beverages in particular; overconsumption of spirituous beverages; John Barleycorn; the demon rum; hard stuff.

Quotations:

A man will be eloquent if you give him good wine. *Ralph Waldo Emerson,* **Representative Men:** *Montaigne, 1850.*

He that drinks fast, pays slow. *Benjamin Franklin,* **Poor Richard's Almanac,** *1733.*

Bacchus hath drowned more men than Neptune. *Thomas Fuller,* **Gnomologia,** *1732.*

What doesn't drunkenness do? It unlocks secrets, confirms our hopes, pushes the lazy into battle, relieves the burdens of tense brains, teaches new wiles. *Horace,* **Epistles,** *Book 1, 5:16, about 16 B.C.*

Claret is the liquor for boys; port for men; but he who aspires to be a hero must drink brandy. *Samuel Johnson, April 7, 1779 (from James Boswell's* **Life of Samuel Johnson**).

I don't drink any more—just the same amount. *Joe E. Lewis, 1940s.*

Whether or not the world would be vastly benefited by a total banishment from it of all intoxicating drinks seems not now an open question. Three-fourths of mankind confess the affirmative with their tongues, and I believe all the rest acknowledge it in their hearts. *Abraham Lincoln, speech in Springfield, Ill., February 22, 1842 (for another Lincoln viewpoint see Anecdotage).*

The Elixir of Perpetual Youth,/Called Alcohol . . . *Henry Wadsworth Longfellow, "The Golden Legend," 1851.*

All experience shows that temperance, like other virtues, is not produced by lawmakers, but by the influences of education, morality and religion. Men may be persuaded—they cannot be compelled to adopt habits of temperance. *New York Governor Horatio Seymour, statement on vetoing state Prohibition Act, 1854.*

A bumper of good liquor/Will end a contest quicker/Than justice, judge or vicar. *Richard Brinsley Sheridan,* **The Duenna,** *1775.*

Anonymous aphorisms:

There are more old drunkards than old doctors.

Too much of here's mud in your eye can mean a face in the dirt.

Drink loosens a man up until he gets tight.

Work is the curse of the drinking classes.

He shot off his mouth because he didn't know he was loaded.

I would rather forget to drink than drink to forget.

The drunks are on the house.

Anecdotage:

During the Civil War, when someone complained to him that General Grant was a heavy drinker, President Lincoln is supposed to have said, "Find out what brand he drinks, so I can send some to my other generals," or words to that effect.

Not all drunks recognize their weakness. In one crowd of drinkers, Jones started to go wild, removing his clothes until, as he was down to his underwear, he collapsed and passed out. "Good old Jones," said one of his drinking buddies approvingly, "he always knows when to stop."

Fact:

Drink has been a problem for mankind as long as the processes of fermentation and distillation have existed. In this country the great Prohibition experiment failed, and the results since its repeal have not been much better. Alcohol is still regarded by crime and health authorities as creating more victims than drugs. At the same time, the values and pleasures of spirituous beverages in moderation, whether as refreshment or as cooking ingredients, have been recognized. The idea of drunkenness as a crime in itself seems to be declining, although there is greater recognition of the need to treat alcoholism as a disease.

The National Council on Alcoholism at 733 Third Avenue, New York, N.Y. 10017 is one of several active national groups working in this field.

DRUGS

(See also Medicine)

Definitions: medicines, stimulants or depressants that affect living creatures' moods, attitudes or conditions; habit-forming substances that are ingested, injected or smoked; the push-pill civilization; narcotics; the other meaning for hash, grass, pot, speed, acid etc.; addictives.

Quotations:

Opiate: An unlocked door in the prison of Identity. It leads into the jail yard. *Ambrose Bierce,* **The Devil's Dictionary** *1906.*

There is no dirtier or deadlier bullet than the illegal drug capsule. *U.S. delegate to the United Nations George Bush, 1971.*

The spirit of the world, the great calm presence of the Creator, comes not forth to the sorceries of opium or of wine. *Ralph Waldo Emerson,* **Essays, Second Series:** *The Poet, 1844.*

The young physician starts life with 20 drugs for each disease, and the old physician ends life with one drug for 20 diseases. *Dr. William Osler, early 20th century.*

Anonymous aphorisms:

Drugs are escapes from which there is no escape.

People who peddle drugs are called pushers, but they should be called clutchers.

A shot in the arm can indicate a hole in the head.

For every high the lows get lower.

Nobody ever solved a problem by giving it the needle.

Better a party-pooper than a pill-popper.

People who will try anything once may not get a second chance.

LSD is not the stuff of dreams; it is the stuff of nightmares.

Anecdotage:

"Once a person is addicted," said Dr. Jones, "it is better to switch him to something like methadone than to try to cure him, because the odds against cure are so great." "That," said Dr. Smith, "is like saying if you can't like them join them." "No," said Dr. Jones, "it's more like taking rat poison away from a baby and substituting a teething ring."

Facts:

Addiction to drugs and narcotics is an ancient vice, and one that has existed all over the world. In the era of easy global transportation, it has become a more pressing problem because the younger Western nations provided such a lucrative market. Government efforts to control the drug traffic began largely in this century, and no one would say they have been notably successful. Indeed, the milder of the drugs, such as marijuana, have gained increasing tolerance despite the law in the U.S. The U.S. Drug Enforcement Administration found that, as of the end of 1973, the average age of what they term "active addict/abusers" was 28.2 years and the number of new addict/abusers reported each year quadrupled between 1965 and 1972. In 1973 it began to go down.

ECONOMICS

Definitions: The function and relationship of the creation, production, distribution and consumption of resources, goods and services; the science of the cost of living; "the dismal science" (*Thomas Carlyle*).

Quotations:

. . . the age of chivalry is gone. That of sophisters, economists, and calculators, has succeeded; and the glory of Europe is extinguished for ever. *Edmund Burke,* **Reflections on the Revolution in France,** *1790.*

Annual income twenty pounds, annual expenditure nineteen nineteen six, result happiness. Annual income twenty pounds, annual expenditure twenty pound ought and six, result misery. *Charles Dickens,* **David Copperfield,** *1849.*

Our economy is the result of millions of decisions we all make every day about producing, earning, saving, investing, and spending. *President Dwight D. Eisenhower, May 20, 1958.*

If you would know the Value of Money, go and try to borrow some. *Benjamin Franklin,* **The Way to Wealth,** *1757.*

From an economic standpoint, I like to think of society as having two functions. First, it must direct its attention to the age-old problem of converting the earth's resources into goods and commodities. Second, it must direct its attention to placing those goods and commodities into the hands of the men, women, and children who use them. *President Lyndon B. Johnson, December 13, 1963.*

We have always known that heedless self-interest was bad morals; we know now that it is bad economics. *President Franklin D. Roosevelt, Second Inaugural Address, January 20, 1937.*

The number of useful and productive laborers is everywhere in proportion to the quantity of capital stock which is employed in setting them to work, and to the particular way in which it is so employed. *Adam Smith,* **The Wealth of Nations,** *1776.*

Anonymous aphorisms:

Bad money drives good money out of circulation. (Known as Gresham's Law, in the mistaken belief that it was originated by Sir Thomas Gresham.)

Competition is the life of trade.

Everyone, in the final analysis, is in business for himself.

Nobody has ever repealed the law of supply and demand.

Economics is nothing more nor less than keeping your head as far above water as you can.

Anecdotage:

. . . there was a farmer who planted some corn. He said to his neighbor, "I hope I break even this year. I really need the money." *Presidential candidate John F. Kennedy, speech in Grand View, Missouri, October 22, 1960.*

Facts:

Economics is a comparatively new science—and many contend it isn't a science at all. About a fourth of the doctorates conferred on American graduate students in the social sciences in the mid-1970s were in economics, but unlike anthropology or history, the economist operates in a field with less and less, rather than more and more, established truths. Economics, perhaps more than other fields of learning, depends on the ingenuity of science—the efficiency with which new oil deposits are found, or ways are devised to extract the wealth of the earth. The opposite poles of economic theory are laissez-faire, which critics find less than fair to the poorer multitudes, and the totally managed economy, which has yet to prove its ability to provide just and acceptable long-term efficiency. One unmistakable truth is that in modern times, for good or bad, the world of economics and the world of politics and of government have become more and more intertwined.

EDUCATION

(See also College, School)

Definitions: the field or process of teaching or learning; the teaching establishment; "that which discloses to the wise and disguises from the foolish their lack of understanding" (*Ambrose Bierce*); organized but sometimes synthetic experience.

Quotations:

Only the educated are free. *Epictetus,* **Discourses,** *1st century.*

Next in importance to freedom and justice is popular education, without which neither freedom nor justice can be permanently maintained. *Representative James A. Garfield, letter accepting Republican Presidential nomination, July 12, 1880.*

To the strongest and quickest mind it is far easier to learn than to invent. *Samuel Johnson,* **The Rambler,** *September 7, 1751.*

A child miseducated is a child lost. *President John F. Kennedy, message to Congress, January 11, 1962.*

. . . it was in making education not only common to all, but in some sense compulsory on all, that the destiny of the free republics of America was practically settled. *James Russell Lowell,* **Among My Books:** *New England Two Centuries Ago, 1870.*

'Tis education forms the common mind:/Just as the twig is bent the tree's inclined. *Alexander Pope,* **Moral Essays,** *1731.*

Learn to live, and live to learn. *Bayard Taylor, "To My Daughter," mid 19th century.*

Training is everything. The peach was once a bitter almond; cauliflower is nothing but cabbage with a college education. *Mark Twain,* **The Tragedy of Pudd'nhead Wilson,** *1894.*

Today, education is perhaps the most important function of state and local government. *Chief Justice Earl Warren, Supreme Court decision in* **Brown v. Board of Education of Topeka,** *May 17, 1954.*

Anonymous aphorisms:

School ends, but education doesn't.

Unlearning is harder than learning.

Education has moved from three R's to six: remedial reading, remedial 'riting and remedial 'rithmetic.

He was highly educated—his classroom was on the top floor.

It is hard to teach an old dog new tricks and easy to teach a new dog old tricks.

The only thing more expensive than education is ignorance.

It is more important to use an education than to show it.

Anecdotage:

Asked what he thought should be taught to children first, Samuel Johnson, according to Boswell, replied that "it is no matter what you teach them first, any more than what leg you shall put into your breeches first. Sir, you may stand disputing which is best to put in first, but in the mean time your breech is bare. Sir, while you are considering which of two things you should teach your child first, another boy has learnt them both."

"Before you get to the three R's," said Grandpa, "you've got to master the three L's—look, listen and learn."

Facts:

The percentage of the gross national product spent on education in the U.S. has more than doubled since 1950. In 1950, 1.3 percent of all college degrees conferred in the U.S. were doctorates; that percentage has since doubled. And the total number of college degrees of all kinds has increased from 499,000 in 1950 to more than 1,200,000. The trend is to devote more time and more money to education. This is not simply a matter of spontaneous enthusiasm for the learning process. It is largely a result of the increasingly complicated world in which we live, the development of new science and technology and the instinct of most parents to want more for their children than they themselves had as education. The baby boom after World War II sparked an explosion of educational needs, but even though that baby boom is over, the expansion of educational facilities has continued. Sophisticated teaching machines and the use of television and computers have all been part of the onward march of organized education, even while its costs pose increasing problems for both government and individuals. One notable aspect of the modern educational challenge is the growth of nursery schools and pre-school facilities to enable both parents to work. The result has been to lengthen the number of years of educational experience at both ends—pre-primary and post-secondary.

The Statistical Abstract of the United States and publications of the National Education Association, 1201 16th Street N.W., Washington, D.C. 20036, are excellent sources of information on the dimensions and growth of education.

ELECTIONS

(See also Candidates, Voting)

Definitions: acts or processes involved in electing, or casting ballots; going to the polls; where you decide what basket to put your X in; where we learn the public will and the public won't.

Quotations:

When annual elections end, there slavery begins. *John Adams,* **Thoughts on Government,** *1776.*

To govern according to the sense and agreeably to the interests of the people is a great and glorious object to government. This object cannot be obtained but through the medium of popular election, and popular election is a mighty evil. *Edmund Burke, Speech on the Duration of Parliaments, May 8, 1780.*

Turn the rascals out! *Charles A. Dana,* **New York Sun,** *1870s.*

Public confidence in the elective process is the foundation of public confidence in government. *President Lyndon B. Johnson, letter to Congressional leaders, May 26, 1966.*

. . . ballots are the rightful and peaceful successors of bullets . . . *President Abraham Lincoln, message to Congress, July 4, 1861.*

Democracy substitutes election by the incompetent many for appointment by the corrupt few. *George Bernard Shaw,* **Man and Superman,** *1903.*

You know how it is in an election year. They pick a President and then for four years they pick on him. *Adlai E. Stevenson. August 28, 1952.*

After the election's over I bear no malice or feel badly toward anyone because the fellow who lost feels badly enough without eating crow. *President Harry S. Truman, November 4, 1948.*

Anonymous aphorisms:

If you want your vote to register, be sure to register to vote.

The reason they have no electioneering at the polls is that you never find enough voters there

For every x on a ballot there is a why.

I care not who writes the nation's songs, as long as I can count the votes.

Elections are the way we find chosen people.

Anecdotage:

It was a crucial election and Mr. Jones had to stand on line for almost an hour to cast his vote. "I've heard the expression 'Stand up and be counted,' " he said, "but I didn't expect it to be taken literally."

Mr. Brown disliked both candidates but, like a good citizen, he voted anyway. He refused to say which candidate he had voted for, but when asked, he said, "I cast my pearls."

"I vote by proportional representation," said Mr. Green. "How can you do that when you have to choose between two candidates?" he was asked. "It's simple," he replied. "If I'm only 30% for one candidate, and 20% for the other, I vote for the top percentage."

Facts:

The two most important facts about elections are that they are losing popularity and that they are more important than ever. If these facts seem to be mutually contradictory, that is part of the problem of elections. Free elections are held in fewer countries than they used to be. In this country, a smaller proportion of the public is voting. In 1960, for example, well over 60 percent of the eligible voters cast their ballots in the Presidential election. In 1976, about 55 percent voted. With embarrassing regularity, the percentage of eligible voters who actually go to the polls in the U.S. falls far short of the democracies of Western Europe. This has happened even though the American electorate is now called upon to vote on more issues than ever before—ecological proposals, housing policies and many others as well as the selection of government officials. The history of the 20th century has been marked by the steady expansion of the franchise—woman suffrage, lowering of the voting age, abolition of the poll tax, passage of voting rights laws—and yet the challenge to get the people to the polls remains.

The Statistical Abstract of the United States annually includes a section devoted to elections and lists other sources of information about the size and nature of federal, state and local voting.

ETHICS

Definitions: principles of right or justice; morals; a science or set of moral principles; standards of conduct; whatever society decides is the right way.

Quotations:

Expedients are for the hour, but principles are for the ages. *Reverend Henry Ward Beecher,* **Proverbs from Plymouth Pulpit,** *1887.*

A people that values its privileges above its principles soon loses both. *President Dwight D. Eisenhower, Inaugural Address, January 20, 1953.*

The shield against the stingings of conscience is the universal practice of our contemporaries. *Ralph Waldo Emerson,* **Representative Men:** *On the Uses of Great Men, 1850.*

Everybody has a little bit of Watergate in him. *Reverend Billy Graham, February 3, 1974.*

The moral sense, or conscience, is as much a part of man as his leg or arm. *Thomas Jefferson, letter to his nephew, Peter Carr, August 10, 1787.*

We cannot divide ourselves between right and expedience. Policy must yield to morality. *Immanuel Kant,* **Critique of Pure Reason,** *1781.*

This above all: to thine own self be true,/And it must follow, as the night the day,/ Thou canst not then be false to any man. *William Shakespeare,* **Hamlet,** *1600.*

Goodness is the only investment that never fails. *Henry D. Thoreau,* **Walden;** *Higher Laws, 1854.*

There is only one morality, as there is only one geometry. *Voltaire,* **Philosophical Dictionary,** *1764.*

Anonymous aphorisms:

All's fair in love and war.

We live in a society where the sin is getting caught.

Honesty is the best policy, but sometimes it has a high premium.

Knowing what's right doesn't mean much unless you do what's right.

Do right or get left.

Anecdotage:

"The worst thing that can happen to a youngster starting school," said the lawyer, "is to be caught cheating." "Not at all," said the clergyman, "the worst thing at the start of a person's life is to cheat and not get caught."

Facts:

It is commonly accepted, on the heels of recurrent tales of corruption in every aspect of modern life, that ethics are what each of us thinks should govern the other fellow. But the fact is that life today is infinitely more ethical in many respects than any previous age. We have simply created more and higher ethical standards than in the past. For example, we no longer permit rich people to buy their way out of compulsory service in time of war, although this was once considered perfectly ethical and proper. Indeed, there is room to believe that what seems to be a decline in ethics is actually a rise in acceptable standards.

ETHNICITY

(See also Immigration, Minorities, Race)

Definitions: a word of debatable legitimacy, meaning: the subject of race, nationality, cultural heritage or customs maintained in common by a recogniz-able group of people, "background", "derivation," "the club you were born in."

Quotations:

It is true that Heaven's infinite wisdom grants a different genius to each people, but it is equally true that Heaven's law changes by time and place. *Pierre Corneille*, **Cinna,** *about 1640.*

We conceive distinctly enough the French, the Spanish, the German genius, and it is not the less real, that perhaps we should not meet in either of those nations a single individual who corresponded with the type. *Ralph Waldo Emerson*, **Essays, Second Series:** *Nominalist and Realist, 1844.*

We are a nation of many nationalities, many races, many religions—bound together by a single unity, the unity of freedom and equality. *President Franklin D. Roosevelt, November 1, 1940.*

Anonymous aphorisms:

A lot of those who talk fondly of the old country were either born here or only began to think of it fondly after they got out of it.

America is its own league of nations.

You can take a man out of a country, but you can't take that country out of the man.

We are all ethnics; some of us just work at it harder than others.

Some people are more concerned with where they sprung from than with where they are going.

Anecdotage:

When New York politicians used to refer to the Three-I League, they were not referring to an old-time middle Western baseball league. They were referring to the political trip that any aspiring candidate for Mayor of the melting pot city felt he had to make at the start of his campaign — a visit to Ireland, Italy and Israel.

"You can't tell anything by people's names any more," lamented Mr. Jones, "because all the foreigners take new ones." "On the contrary," said Mr. Smith, "you can tell the most important thing about them. They don't want to be foreigners."

Facts.

There are more than 140 nations holding membership in the United Nations. There are at least ten separate major religions, with innumerable sects and cultural or national divisions among them, just as so many nations have different languages and racial groups within their borders. The variety of ethnicity is almost infinite, and the richest and healthiest life is in those countries which have managed to blend and absorb a number of different ethnic heritages. The World Almanac lists some 150 different languages. It's a multiethnic world, and the U.S. is that world in miniature.

EXPERIENCE

Definitions: knowledge gained from having performed or been part of a specific event or function; an event or function that is remembered by those who participated; "the name everyone gives to their mistakes" (Oscar Wilde); what's left after everything else is gone.

Quotations:

Men are wise in proportion, not to their experience, but to their capacity for experience. *James Boswell,* **Life of Samuel Johnson,** *1791.*

The knowledge of the world is only to be acquired in the world, and not in a closet. *Lord Chesterfield,* **Letters to His Son,** *1746, published 1774.*

Experience keeps a dear school, yet fools will learn in no other. *Benjamin Franklin,* **Poor Richard's Almanac,** *1743.*

Measurement of life should be proportioned rather to the intensity of its experience than to its actual length. *Thomas Hardy,* **A Pair of Blue Eyes,** *1873.*

I have but one lamp by which my feet are guided, and that is the lamp of experience. I know of no way of judging of the future but by the past. *Patrick Henry, March 23, 1775.*

I know of no way of judging of the future but by the past. *Patrick Henry, March 23, 1775.*

Nothing ever becomes real till it is experienced. *John Keats, letter to George and Georgiana Keats, February 14-May 3, 1818.*

One thorn of experience is worth a whole wilderness of warning. *James Russell Lowell,* **Among My Books:** *Shakespeare Once More, 1870.*

A strong and secure man digests his experiences (deeds and misdeeds alike) just as he digests his meat, even when he has some bits to swallow. *Friedrich Wilhelm Nietsche,* **Genealogy of Morals,** *1887.*

I had rather have a fool to make me merry than experience to make me sad. *William Shakespeare,* **As You Like It,** *1600.*

Anonymous aphorisms:

A self-made man has no factory guarantee.

Experience is largely non-transferable.

The trouble with experience is that it sometimes teaches you too late.

Experience is the dividend you get from your mistakes.

Experience is good if not bought too dear.

Anecdotage:

"A gentleman who had been very unhappy in marriage, married immediately after his wife died: Johnson said, it was the triumph of hope over experience." *James Boswell,* **Life of Samuel Johnson,** *1791.*

The matchmaker arranged sight unseen for an opponent for the local boxing champion. He asked for an experienced fighter, and on the day of the fight a middle-aged man with a much broken nose, a punch-drunk manner and two huge cauliflower ears arrived to enter the ring. The matchmaker was aghast. "I asked for an experienced fighter, "he complained, "but not a damaged one."

EXPLORATION
(See also Space)

Definitions: traveling to or through unknown areas to determine their nature; finding out what you're in; going places and seeing things; getting to know the unknown.

Quotations:

Knowledge begets knowledge. The more I see, the more impressed I am — not with what we know — but with how tremendous the areas are that are as yet unexplored. *Lt. Col. John H. Glenn, Jr., speech to joint session of Congress, February 26, 1962.*

The future leaves no option. Responsible men must push forward in the exploration of space, near and far. Their voyages must be made in peace for purposes of peace on earth. *President Lyndon B. Johnson, message to Senate, February 7, 1967.*

Together let us explore the stars, conquer the deserts, eradicate disease, tap the ocean depths and encourage the arts and commerce. *President John F. Kennedy, Inaugural Address, January 20, 1961.*

Behind him lay the gray Azores,/Behind, the Gates of Hercules;/Before him not the ghost of shores;/Before him only shoreless seas./The good mate said: "Now must we pray,/For lo! the very stars are gone./Brave Admiral, speak; what shall I say."/"Why, say 'Sail on! Sail on! and on!'" *Joaquin Miller, "Columbus," 1896.*

The learn'd is happy Nature to explore,/The fool is happy that he knows no more . . . *Alexander Pope,* **Essay on Man,** *1734.*

Anonymous aphorisms:

One man's exploration is another man's home ground.

There is always someone who wants to see what's on the other side of the mountain, and there's always another mountain.

The more you explore, the more you find that needs exploring.

America was outer space to Christopher Columbus.

Exploration means going where the hand of man has never before set foot.

Anecdotage:

Explorers often prefer wild territory to the sophisticated civilization they have left behind. This has given rise to a new version of the dialogue when reporter Henry Stanley finally found Dr. Livingstone and uttered the words, "Dr. Livingstone, I presume?" "You certainly do," said the good doctor, some would have us believe, because he liked being where he had hoped to remain undiscovered.

Columbus set out to find a passage to the Indies and failed; he found America instead. Ponce de Leon looked for the fountain of youth and found Florida. The greatest explorers seem to find something other than what they are looking for.

Facts:

Terrestrial exploration, as opposed to that in outer space, is far from over. Indeed, there is more exploration today than at any time in the history of man. People centuries ago hunted for gold, new routes to the East, new lands. Today we seek oil, the secrets of the sea and earth.

The Society of Exploration Geophysicists, Box 3098, Tulsa, Oklahoma 74101, and the Explorers Club, 46 East 70th Street, New York, N.Y. 10021 span the range of modern exploration.

FAMILY

Definitions: a household composed of parents and children; a group of persons closely related by blood or marriage; a creation of nature which is never what it used to be; the original mom and pop enterprise; "the nucleus of civilization" (*Will and Ariel Durant*).

Quotations:

It is not observed in history that families improve with time. *George William Curtis*, **Prue and I,** *1856.*

Men are what their mothers made them. *Ralph Waldo Emerson*, **The Conduct of Life:** *Fate, 1860.*

Late children, early orphans. *Benjamin Franklin*, **Poor Richard's Almanac,** *1742.*

Back of every achievement is a proud wife and a surprised mother-in-law. *Brooks Hays, sworn in as aide to President Kennedy, December 1, 1961.*

. . .how convenient it would be to many of our great men and great families of doubtful origin, could they have the privilege of the heroes of yore, who, whenever their origin was involved in obscurity, modestly announced themselves descended from a god . . . *Washington Irving*, **A History of New York by Diedrich Knickerbocker,** *1809.*

. . . a family . . . is a little kingdom, torn with factions and exposed to revolutions. *Samuel Johnson*, **Rasselas,** *1759.*

The family is one of nature's masterpieces. *George Santayana*, **The Life of Reason, Vol. 2, Reason in Society,** *1905.*

. . . I do not condemn nepotism, provided the relatives really work. *Maine Senator Margaret Chase Smith, speech to National Women's Republican Conference, April 16, 1962.*

The family — that great conservator of national virtue and strength — how can you hope to build it up in the midst of violence, debauchery and excess? *Mrs.*

Elizabeth Cady Stanton, testimony to New York State Senate Judiciary Committee, 1861.

Anonymous aphorisms:

An ounce of blood is worth a pound of friendship.

Large family, quick help.

Blood will tell.

Blood is thicker than water.

You pick your friends, but not your family.

Anecdotage:

The salesman knocked at the front door and a young woman with two tykes clinging to her answered the door. "Oh," said the salesman, "I wanted to speak to the head of the family." "How about talking to the heart of the family," asked the young woman.

Some families, it has been said, look after each other, but others merely look like each other. When this was told to Mr. Brown, he disagreed. "What makes a family," he said, "isn't whether they look like or look after each other; it's that they share a common will—waiting for probate."

Facts:

It is apparently the habit of every generation to worry about the decline of the family. Currently, the doomsayers point to the tremendous rise in the divorce rate, the rise in unmarried couples living and having children together and the rise in the number of powerful social influences that "compete" with parental control of teenagers. They also point to the increased mobility of young people, even before they go off to college and careers. And they discern in the trend toward smaller families a decline in the number of uncles, aunts, cousins, sisters and brothers who comprise the larger family edifice. But there are some good prospects for the family of the future. For example, longer life expectancy gives hope that more young people will know their grandparents longer, and that older people will have more older relatives around too. The nature of family life continues to change, of course. In the 1940s, 20 percent of wives worked outside their homes. Thirty years later, that percentage has more than doubled and is increasing. In 1975 there were 56.7 million U.S. families. The expectation was that in 1985 there would be 66.3 million.

The publications of the U.S. Bureau of the Census provide basic information about various statistical aspects of U.S. family life. Many of these are summarized in the Statistical Abstract of the U.S.

FASHION

Definitions: the established style of the time; that which is considered the height of contemporary taste in clothing, homes, automobiles and lifestyles; keeping up with the Joneses; the look-of-the-month club.

Quotations:

If you are not in fashion, you are nobody. *Lord Chesterfield,* **Letters to His Son,** *April 30, 1750.*

Eat to please thyself, but dress to please others. *Benjamin Franklin,* **Poor Richard's Almanac,** *1738.*

Be not the first by whom the new are tried,/Nor yet the last to lay the old aside. *Alexander Pope,* **An Essay on Criticism,** *1711.*

On the whole, I think that it cannot be maintained that dressing has in this or any country risen to the dignity of an art. *Henry D. Thoreau,* **Walden:** *Economy, 1854.*

Every generation laughs at the old fashions, but follows religiously the new. *Ibid.*

When seen in the perspective of half-a-dozen years or more, the best of our fashions strike us as grotesque, if not unsightly. *Thorstein Veblen,* **The Theory of the Leisure Class,** *1899.*

Fashion is that by which the fantastic becomes for a moment universal. *Oscar Wilde,* **The Picture of Dorian Gray,** *1891.*

Anonymous aphorisms:

Fashion is just a more polite name for forced obsolescence.

There is no tyrant stronger than fashion.

Yesterday's fashion will probably be tomorrow's; but it isn't today's.

Those who follow the fashion never create it.

Fashion is one human being's inconquerable will to look just like all the others.

Anecdotage:

"This," said the salesman as he trotted out a new suit for Mr. Jones, "is what they are wearing." "In that case," came the reply, "I think I'd like to see something newer."

"I can't keep up with the hemlines," said Mrs. Jones. "The way they go up and down, with the fashions, they should call them hem and haw lines."

Facts:

Fashion becomes an important factor in the economy when there is sufficient prosperity so that a good deal of spending is discretionary. That is because fashion depends so much on the look of a product becoming out of date, rather than on the product wearing out. Fashions are not all dependent on forced obsolescence, however. Some arise from the desire of people to be accepted by those who adhere to a particular style. It is not accidental, in the view of some observers, that fashions in spoken English and in dress among teenagers generally have picked up characteristics from young Black Americans, in the same period that integration of the races was being advanced. Young people also tend to ape the styles of their entertainment heroes, and this seems to be true no matter what the social or political system of the particular place.

FEMINISM

(See also Women)

Definitions: theories or activities devoted to full and equal rights for women; the advancement of the interests of women as a group; women's lib (liberation).

Quotations:

You have to make more noise than anybody else, you have to make yourself more obtrusive than anybody else, you have to fill all the papers more than anybody else, in fact you have to be there all the time and see that they do not snow you under, if you are really going to get your reform realized. That is what we women have been doing, and in the course of our desperate struggle we have had to make a great many people very uncomfortable. *Emmeline Pankhurst, speech in Hartford, Conn., November 13, 1913.*

Feminism is a movement, which demands the removal of all social, political, economic, and other discriminations which are based upon sex, and the award of all rights and duties in all fields on the basis of individual capacity alone. *Henrietta Rodman, definition of the Feminist Alliance as reported in* **The New York Times,** *April 5, 1914.*

Too often the great decisions are originated and given form in bodies made up wholly of men, or so completely dominated by them that whatever of special value women have to offer is shunted aside without expression. *Mrs. Eleanor Roosevelt, U.S. Delegate to the United Nations, speech at the U.N. in December 1952.*

We hold these truths to be self-evident: that all men and women are created equal . . . *Seneca Falls Declaration of Sentiments and Resolutions at Women's Rights Convention, Seneca Falls, N.Y., July 19, 1848.*

The history of mankind is a history of repeated injuries and usurpations on the part of man toward woman, having in direct object the establishment of an absolute tyranny over her. *Ibid.*

Resolved, that woman is man's equal — was intended to be so by the Creator, and the highest good of the race demands that she should be recognized as such. *Ibid.*

. . . the deepest and most important revolution under way in the world today . . . *Gloria Steinem, remarks at meeting in support of Equal Rights Amendment in Washington, D.C., August 28, 1976.*

The world cannot afford the loss of the talents of half its people if we are to solve the many problems that beset us. *Dr. Rosalyn S. Yalow, at Nobel Prize dinner in Stockholm, December 10, 1977.*

Anonymous aphorisms:

What's sauce for the gander is sauce for the goose.

Feminism is the triumph of mind over mattress.

Women's rights became a movement because of man's wrongs.

Feminism is designed to give hens as well as roosters something to crow about.

Any woman's movement is bound to be watched attentively by men.

Anecdotage:

"Have faith in God," said the feminist to a friend. "She will protect you."

"Feminism," said the contented gentleman, "is just another form of women's work in the last analysis." "On the contrary," was the reply, "feminism is the work of men. Women are trying to do something about what men have done to them."

Facts:

Feminism has flowered in the modern era, because each new freedom makes it possible for more freedom to come. The long fight for women's suffrage in the United States was the first truly significant victory, and it was not as effective as its advocates had hoped in helping to remove economic and social discrimination against women for many years thereafter. In the 1960s the fight against discrimination of all kinds picked up steam, and the early 1970s were a period of discovery — for many women and many men as well — of the discriminations which still existed. Many Americans today have the impression that "women's lib" is a modern phenomenon, and that the militancy of our times — the bitter struggle to enact an Equal Rights Amendment to the Constitution, the mythology of the "bra burners" and the public disputes over sexual anatomy and functioning — is peculiar to our own era. But a look at the remarks of Emmeline Pankhurst in 1913 (see the first quotation in this section) or the life story of Elizabeth Cady Stanton shows how long and how deep the waters of righteous female rage have run. There are many different women's organizations and views involved.

The National Organization for Women and the General Federation of Women's Clubs — both of which have chapters or constituent groups throughout the country — are good sources of information.

FLAG

Definitions: usually a piece of cloth, apt to be oblong or square, bearing the distinctive arrangement of symbols and colors of a nation, or state, or having a meaning as a signal; in the U.S., "Old Glory" or "The Stars and Stripes" or "The Star Spangled Banner;" the colors; our national trademark.

Quotations:

I pledge allegiance to the flag of the United States of America and to the Republic for which it stands, One Nation under God, indivisible, with liberty and justice for all. *Pledge of Allegiance, initiated by the Reverend Francis Bellamy in 1892.*

The Republic never retreats. Its flag is the only flag that has never known defeat. Where that flag leads we follow, for we know that the hand that bears it onward is the unseen hand of God. *Albert J. Beveridge, speech in Philadelphia, February 15, 1899.*

"You're a Grand Old Flag," *George M. Cohan, song from* **George Washington, Jr.,** *1906.*

Oh, say, does that star-spangled banner yet wave/O'er the land of the free, and the home of the brave? *Francis Scott Key, "The Star-Spangled Banner," September 14, 1814.*

Yes, we'll rally 'round the flag, boys, we'll rally once again/Shouting the battle cry of Freedom...*George F. Root, "The Battle Cry of Freedom," 1863.*

"Shoot, if you must, this old gray head,/But spare your country's flag," she said. *John Greenleaf Whittier, "Barbara Frietchie," 1863.*

The flag is the embodiment, not of sentiment but of history. It represents the experiences made by men and women, the experiences of those who do and live under that flag. *President Woodrow Wilson, speech in New York, June 14, 1915.*

Anonymous aphorisms:

Show the flag.

Three cheers for the red, white and blue!

Show your colors,

As long as your flag is flying, your cause is still alive.

Show a little respect for the flag.

Anecdotage:

Nobody knows who devised the first flag, but there is a story about how it happened. Seems that one warrior got hurt in a fight between two tribes, and held up his bloody garment to show that he needed help, and everybody followed him. That's why so many flags use the color red, say the mythmakers.

"Why do you have such respect for the flag?" "Because it's so easy to follow."

Facts:

There is no reliable estimate of the number of flags flown every day in the United States, but the Elks and military and veterans groups have material about the history and etiquette of the U.S. flag that can be helpful.

FOOD

(See also Cooking, Dieting)

Definitions: that which is ingested by living organisms in solid form to sustain life (although food can also be in liquid form and drunk rather than eaten); nutrients; victuals; provisions; grub.

Quotations:

An army marches on its stomach. *Napoleon Bonaparte (attributed).*

Tell me what you eat, and I will tell you what you are. *Anthelme Brillat-Savarin,* **The Physiology of Taste,** *1825.*

A Book of Verses underneath the Bough,/A Jug of Wine, a Loaf of Bread — and Thou/Beside me singing in the Wilderness — /Oh, Wilderness were Paradise enow. *Edward Fitzgerald,* **Rubaiyat of Omar Khayyam** *(translation of 11th century Persian philosopher-poet), 1859-1872.*

Life, within doors, has few pleasanter prospects than a neatly arranged and well-provisioned breakfast table. *Nathaniel Hawthorne,* **The House of the Seven Gables,** *1851.*

Other circumstances being the same, it may be affirmed that countries are populous according to the quantity of human food which they produce or can acquire, and happy according to the liberality with which this food is divided, or the quantity which a day's labour will purchase. *Thomas R. Malthus,* **Essay on the Principle of Population,** *1798.*

Avoid fried meats, which angry the blood. *Leroy (Satchel) Paige, quoted in Collier's magazine, June 13, 1953.*

Upon what meat doth this our Caesar feed,/That he is grown so great. *William Shakespeare,* **Julius Caesar,** *1599.*

There is no love sincerer than the love of food. *George Bernard Shaw,* **Man and Superman,** *1903.*

Anonymous aphorisms:

One man's meat is another man's poison.

Eat to live, not live to eat. (Old saying used by Ben Franklin in *Poor Richard's Almanac* in 1733 but going back to the Latin.)

America is the home of fast food and slow burns.

Destiny may shape our ends, but it gets a lot of help from the food we eat.

The way to a man's heart is through his stomach. (Sometimes attributed to author Fanny Fern.)

Anecdotage:

A man was dying in the endless desert when suddenly he came across a bottle in the sand. It was empty but he rubbed it against his chest and as he did so there was a cloud of vapor and a huge genie popped out of the bottle, saying, "For three wishes, I am yours to command." The man did not make a wish immediately, because he realized that he had only three, so he thought carefully and said, "My first wish is to have the greatest riches of every kind in the world — food, drink, women, power." "It is done," said the genie, and with a snap of fingers the man was transported to a magnificent mansion, clothed in rich raiment, surrounded by adoring beauties who fed him and fondled him. "Now what is your second wish?" the genie asked. "To be once more in the absolute prime of life," said the man. Once again the genie snapped his fingers and there, in the same magnificent mansion, surrounded by the same beauties, the man became a magnificent physical specimen of young manhood. "You have one wish left," said the genie. The man thought to himself, "I have everything I have always wanted, but as long as I know there is one thing more — " and he said to the genie, "Make me a malted." And in another snap of the finger there was the mansion, there were the beautiful women, and there, on the couch where the man had been, there rested a soda fountain glass containing a chocolate malted. The moral of this story is that what you eat is always food for thought.

Facts:

The 20th century, particularly in recent years, has seen the burgeoning of the so-called green revolution — the development of hybrid and mutant forms of major foods like rice and wheat that resist the familiar ravages of nature better than ever before. As a result, the supply of food in the world has generally risen; but the big problem is that the supply of people in the world has gone up even more. Food and population conferences on the threshold of the last quarter of the 20th century agreed that with about 70 million people a year being added to the world's population, the collective appetite was growing faster than the crops to take care of it. The U.S. Department of Agriculture has issued quarterly reports on the National Food Situation, as well as annual crop estimates; and the Food and Agriculture Organization, an international group working with the United Nations, concerns itself with problems of world food supply.

FOOTBALL

Definitions: the name for several related games played on a rectangular field with a ball, the American game using an oval ball, and involving considerable physical contact; tackle, run, punt and pass; gridiron mayhem; week-end war.

Quotations:

Pro football is like nuclear warfare. There are no winners, only survivors. *Frank Gifford in* **Sports Illustrated,** *July 4, 1960.*

Football is really and truly an American institution. It embodies our highest ideals of character and courage. *President Lyndon B. Johnson, January 13, 1966.*

Football today is far too much a sport for the few who can play it well; the rest of us, and too many of our children, get our exercise from climbing up the seats in stadiums, or from walking across the room to turn on our television sets. *President John F. Kennedy, speech in New York, December 5, 1961.*

In short, in life, as in a football game, the principle to follow is: Hit the line hard; don't foul and don't shirk, but hit the line hard. *Theodore Roosevelt,* **The Strenuous Life,** *1910.*

. . . you base foot-ball player. *William Shakespeare,* **King Lear,** *1605.*

As concerning football, I protest unto you that it may rather be called a friendly kind of fight than a play or recreation . . . *Philip Stubbes,* **The Anatomie of Abuses,** *1583.*

Anonymous aphorisms:

Football is sport's battlefield, where they speak of quarterbacks throwing bombs, penalties, kicks, hits, blitzing and defense.

For every quarterback on the field, there are a thousand in the stands.

It's quite a game when you risk a foot to gain a yard.

Making the team is hard enough for a single player, but hardest for the coach.

The most wide open position in football is that of Monday morning quarterback.

Anecdotage:

When Mr. Brown went to the stadium to see his son play quarterback for the local team in the big game, he found himself surrounded by fans for the other team. When they yelled "offense" he screamed "defense"; when his son was playing and he yelled "pass" they yelled "intercept." It was a close game, and the clamor grew and grew. Finally, time came for the last play. Quarterback Brown threw a long pass and just as time ran out his teammate caught it and scored the winning touchdown. When the Browns got home, the son said, "I've got to go lie down. It's been a hard afternoon." "You had a hard afternoon," said his father. "It was nothing compared to what I went through in the stands."

Facts:

The modern American game of football is only a bit more than 100 years old, but its ancestors go back to the early savage tribes. Today it is perhaps the most American of the major sports. Most others have international scope, but only Canada has anything like the American sport. Rugby and soccer are international relatives, but they are different from the U.S. game. Like all U.S. sports, football has become big business, bigger than ever in the second half of the 20th century. It has also helped support educational institutions, provide television entertainment and build commercial sports enterprises in dozens of cities. Its advocates regard it as the ultimate team sport, requiring a degree of coordination more demanding than in any other team competition. Its critics say it is unnecessarily rough and risky to the players. These are points of view. The indisputable fact is that with an attendance of more than 40 million at college and professional games each year, it is surpassed only by horseracing in popularity as a spectator sport in the U.S.

Unlike some other sports, football has no single rule-making authority. The professional and college games are governed by their constituent associations — the principal ones being the National Football League, 410 Park Avenue, New York, N.Y. 10017, and the National Collegiate Athletic Association, Box 1906, Shawnee Mission, Kansas 66222.

FOREIGN AFFAIRS

Definitions: a government's conduct of its dealings with other nations; the whole subject of relations among nations; statesmanship; the function of diplomats; the striped pants set; diplomacy; us and them.

Quotations:

. . . the Constitution follows the flag . . . We warn the American people that imperialism abroad will lead quickly and inevitably to despotism at home . . . *Democratic Party platform, 1900.*

We live . . . in a sea of semantic disorder in which old labels no longer faithfully describe. Police states are called "people's democracies." Armed conquest of free people is called "liberation." *President Dwight D. Eisenhower, State of the Union message, January 7, 1960.*

Millions for defense but not a cent for tribute. *Robert Goodloe Harper, June 18, 1798.*

. . . peace, commerce and honest friendship, with all nations — entangling alliances with none. *President Thomas Jefferson, first Inaugural Address, March 4, 1801.*

Let us never negotiate out of fear. But let us never fear to negotiate. *President John F. Kennedy, Inaugural Address, January 20, 1961.*

The country is as strong abroad only as it's strong at home. *President John F. Kennedy, speech in St. Paul, October 6, 1962.*

Our policy is directed not against any country or doctrine but against hunger, poverty, desperation, and chaos. *Secretary of State George C. Marshall, introducing Marshall Plan at Harvard, June 5, 1947.*

We seek friendly relations with all nations. Any nation can be our friend without being any other nation's enemy. *President Richard M. Nixon, July 15, 1971.*

We must be the great arsenal of democracy. *President Franklin D. Roosevelt, December 29, 1940.*

There is a homely adage which runs, "Speak softly and carry a big stick; you will go far." If the American nation will speak softly and yet build and keep at a pitch of the highest training a thoroughly efficient navy, the Monroe Doctrine will go far. *Vice President Theodore Roosevelt, September 2, 1901.*

I believe that it must be the policy of the United States to support free peoples who are resisting attempted subjugation by armed minorities or by outside pressures. *President Harry S. Truman, speech to joint session of Congress, March 12, 1947.*

It is our true policy to steer clear of permanent alliances with any portion of the foreign world. *President George Washington, Farewell Address, September 1796.*

Anonymous aphorisms:

International relations are as difficult as any other in-laws.

The United States always seems to lose when it wears a diplomat's striped pants.

In international relations it isn't as important being right as not getting left.

The language of international relations, when you get down to it, is a language of signs, smoke signals and ultimatums; its actions speak louder than its words.

Diplomacy is the language of international relations, which can say one thing that has two absolutely opposite meanings for the two parties involved.

Anecdotage:

"How did you like your trip abroad?" "Well, it was all right, but all the people there are foreigners."

Who was the first person to settle in America? I don't know; undoubtedly some damned foreigner.

"The trouble with international relations," said the expert, "is that we have a whole new group of powers involved." "Not at all," said the other expert, "they're the same powers as before—the power of persuasion and the power of superior force."

Facts:

Even as Washington and Jefferson were counseling our infant nation against foreign alliances, America's ships were building international commerce and people from all over the world were beginning to come to our shores. Today, an American city is host to the people of the world in the United Nations, already the longest-lived attempt at any kind of international Parliament. In the old days, the U.S. thought of itself as self-sufficient, but today its own natural resources are not sufficient; it is both customer and supplier to the world. The United Nations began with 51 nations; by the mid-1970's it was approaching a membership of 150 nations. Some are very tiny, and some are huge, but in the General Assembly of the UN each is a member unto itself.

For a list of the currently operating international organizations and their particular subjects, see the latest World Almanac.

FRATERNITIES
(See also Clubs)

Definitions: social clubs of college or sometimes high school students, originally restricted to males, but now used collectively to embrace sororities as well, with Greek letters as their names; "the Greeks."

Quotations:

Man seeketh in society comfort, use, and protection. *Francis Bacon*, **The Advancement of Learning**, *1605*.

All men seek the society of those who think and act somewhat like themselves. *William Cobbett*, **Advice to Young Men**, *1829*.

Brothers all/In honor, as in one community,/Scholars and gentlemen. *William Wordsworth*, **The Prelude**, *1850*.

Anonymous aphorisms:

His college fraternity was Gotta Getta Gal.

College today is like a batch of French Revolutions—the students take liberties, the parents worry about fraternities and the government insists on equalities.

The basis of the fraternity system is that not all men are brothers.

Anecdotage:

After Johnny was invited to join a college fraternity, he had to undergo a rather arduous initiation. When it was over, he said to the fraternity head, "If this is what happens when you get tapped, what happens when they don't like you?"

"Remember," said the fraternity man to a prospective member, "when you join a fraternity you become part of a carefully selected group." "But," said the student, "that's what I was told my whole college class was — part of a carefully selected group." "Yes," said the fraternity man, "but our group is smaller and even more selective." "So am I," said the student.

Facts:

After a generation of decline, college fraternities seem to be holding their own. One reason is that they have broadened their base of potential member ship with the abandonment of the degree of racial and religious barriers which used to exist. Another reason is that, in many colleges, fraternity houses offer an interesting alternative to dormitory residence. The honorary scholastic fraternities, which have always been marks of accomplishment, have not had the problems that have faced the social ones. During the long drought, a number of the social fraternities and sororities have lost chapters to an unprecedented extent, and for a while the colleges themselves did nothing to help "the Greeks" because of the belief that modern egalitarianism frowned on exclusive clubs. But this has also become moderated with time, and the rigors of old-time fraternity hazing have also been moderated. "The Greeks," it appears, are here to stay on most modern campuses.

The National Interfraternity Conference, P.O. Box 40368, Indianapolis, Ind. 46240, includes many national fraternities.

FRIENDSHIP

Definitions: the bond of affection which exists between two unrelated individuals, or among more than two unrelated individuals; the state of being close to emotionally or through common interests with another or others; "a union of spirits" (*William Penn*); "a plant of slow growth" (*George Washington*); "a ship big enough to carry two in fair weather, but only one in foul" (*Ambrose Bierce*).

Quotations:

Friendship makes prosperity more shining and lessens adversity by dividing and sharing it. *Cicero,* **On Friendship,** *44 B.C.*

The only way to have a friend is to be one. *Ralph Waldo Emerson,* **Essays, First Series:** *Friendship, 1841.*

The ornament of a house is the friends who frequent it. *Ralph Waldo Emerson,* **Society and Solitude:** *Domestic Life, 1870.*

There are three faithful friends — an old wife, an old dog, and ready money. *Benjamin Franklin,* **Poor Richard's Almanac,** *1738.*

Friendship is seldom lasting but between equals, or where the superiority on one side is reduced by some equivalent advantage on the other. *Samuel Johnson,* **The Rambler,** *1750.*

Friendship is constant in all other things,/Save in the office and affairs of love. *William Shakespeare,* **Much Ado About Nothing,** *1599.*

A man cannot be said to succeed in this life who does not satisfy one friend. *Henry D. Thoreau,* **Journal,** *February 19, 1857.*

The holy passion of Friendship is of so sweet and steady and loyal and enduring a nature that it will last through a whole lifetime, if not asked to lend money. *Mark Twain,* **The Tragedy of Pudd'nhead Wilson,** *1894.*

You cannot be friends upon any other terms than upon the terms of equality. *President Woodrow Wilson, speech in Mobile, October 27, 1913.*

Anonymous aphorisms:

A friend to everybody is a friend to nobody.

You are born with your relatives, but you pick your friends.

A friend in need is a friend indeed.

Friendship is not a one-way street.

The surest bond of friendship is having enemies in common.

Anecdotage:

Half his friends left Mr. Jones after he lost his money. Most of the others left when they found out.

"Which," the philosopher was asked, "would you rather have — a gift of money or a gift of friendship?" "Friendship," said the philosopher, "because money is spent but friendship can last forever." "I shall think of that advice forever," said the questioner, "as a mark of your friendship." "Never mind that," said the philosopher, "my advice is not free. Pay me."

GAMBLING

Definitions: taking a chance; wagering, betting; playing a game with stakes of money; man's passion for getting nothing for something; everybody's ante; a chance encounter.

Quotations:

The gambling known as business looks with austere disfavor on the business known as gambling. *Ambrose Bierce, attributed to* **The Devil's Dictionary,** *1881-1906.*

Most men (till by losing rendered sager) /Will back their own opinions by a wager. *George Gordon, Lord Byron,* **Beppo,** *1818.*

Whoever plays deep must necessarily lose his money or his character. *Lord Chesterfield,* **Letters to His Godson,** *1776.*

No gambler was ever yet a happy man. *William Cobbett,* **Advice to Young Men,** *1829.*

Man is a gaming animal. *Charles Lamb, "Mrs. Battle's Opinions on Whist,"* *1820.*

The roulette table pays nobody except him who keeps it. *George Bernard Shaw,* **Man and Superman,** *1903.*

If there were two birds sitting on a fence, he would bet you which one would fly first. *Mark Twain, "The Celebrated Jumping Frog of Calaveras County,"* *1865.*

October. This is one of the peculiarly dangerous months to speculate in stocks in. The others are July, January, September, April, November, May, March, June, December, August and February. *Mark Twain,* **The Tragedy of Pudd'nhead Wilson,** *1894.*

. . . the child of avarice, the brother of iniquity, and the father of mischief. *General George Washington, in a letter to his nephew, Bushrod Washington, January 15, 1783.*

Anonymous aphorisms:

Giving up gambling is a four-to-one shot.

Winner take all, but not all are winners.

Bet me no bets.

A man who always plays the odds rarely ends up even.

When it comes to gambling, every country is a nation of losers.

Most of the time that you are asked to take a chance, chance ends up taking you.

Anecdotage:

The horse was a 1000-to-1 shot; never in the history of racing had there been so dismal a prospect. But Mr. Jones bet $10 on him and when asked why said, "At those odds, how could I resist?"

The devout young man went to his pastor to ask whether it was all right to take part in the office football pool. "Don't you know," said the pastor, "that such gambling is contrary to the views of the church, with our own bingo night coming up tomorrow?"

Facts:

The U.S. Committee on the Review of the National Policy Toward Gambling, reporting in 1976 on a three-year study, decided that gambling is here to stay, and the government might as well be in the business. Indeed, American government raised public funds in our nation's earliest days through lotteries. Today, more than 80 percent of Americans approve of some form of gambling and estimates of the volume of gambling annually go as high as $75 billion. Virtually everybody, it seems, wants a piece of the action.

GEOGRAPHY

Definitions: the science that deals with the natural appearance or climate of the earth, area by area; the nature of a region; faraway places with strange-sounding names; what on earth.

Quotations:

Mountains interposed/Make enemies of nations, who had else/Like kindred drops been mingled into one. *William Cowper*, **The Task**, *1785*.

In the world today, with air the means of communication, with time and space almost annihilated, geography still remains a fact. *Secretary of State John Foster Dulles, April 11, 1955.*

The difference between landscape and landscape is small, but there is a great difference in the beholders. *Ralph Waldo Emerson,* **Essays, Second Series:** *Nature, 1844.*

In America, the geography is sublime, but the men are not . . . *Ralph Waldo Emerson,* **The Conduct of Life:** *Considerations by the Way, 1860.*

All rivers do what they can for the sea. *Thomas Fuller,* **Gnomologia,** *1732.*

A mountain and a river are good neighbors. *George Herbert,* **Jacula Pruden-tum,** *1651.*

Oh, East is East, and West is West, and never the twain shall meet . . . *Rudyard Kipling, "The Ballad of East and West," 1889.*

There are No Islands Any More. *Edna St. Vincent Millay, book title, 1940.*

Anonymous aphorisms:

Geography is what's where in the world.

Where we live is environment; where everybody else lives is geography.

Geography is where they make history.

Nature is magnificent, which is why geography starts by saying, "Gee!"

Geography always sets the scene.

Anecdotage:

What's the difference between history and geography?" a child was asked. "Well," she said, "geography tells me where I am and history tells me how I got here."

"Geography," said the philosopher, "is the most important study of man, because it ends up telling him where he can go."

Facts:

Geography is a concern not only of explorers into the unknown but also of government. An entire section of the U.S. Statistical Abstract is devoted to the subject, and at least three separate national survey units work at geographical tasks — the Geological Survey, the National Ocean Survey and the U.S. National Oceanic and Atmospheric Administration. The search for oil and minerals pushes the world into ever more intensive examination, exploration and charting of its geography.

The National Geographic Society in Washington testifies to humankind's insatiable curiosity about what's where.

GOLF

Definitions: game played with variety of clubs and small hard ball on specially prepared grounds with nine or 18 holes; "cow pasture pool" (*O.K. Bovard*); a game in which the balls lie on the ground and the players lie in the clubhouse.

Quotations:

The golf links lie so near the mill/That almost every day/The laboring children can look out/And see the men at play. *Sarah Cleghorn, "The Golf Links," 1915.*

The dirty little pill . . . rolling down the hill . . . *Novelty song broadcast by Frank Crumit, 1930's.*

Houston, you might recognize what I have in my hand is the handle for the contingency sample return. It just so happens to have a genuine 6 iron on the bottom of it. In my left hand I have a little white pellet that's familiar to millions of Americans. I'll drop it down. Unfortunately, the suit is so stiff I can't do this with two hands but I'm going to try a little sand trap shot here. *Captain Alan B. Shepard, Jr., U.S.N., on the moon, February 6, 1971.*

Anonymous aphorisms:

As a game golf is full of holes.

Golf is for swingers.

A golfer never feels better than when he's below par.

At one time a very exclusive sport, golf now gives every player a choice of clubs.

When a golf ball lies poorly, the guy who hit it usually does too.

Anecdotage:

A golfer was being distracted by his noisy and contemptuous partner and finally said, "You are driving me out of my mind." "That," said his partner, "is not a drive; it's a putt."

A duffer was ruining the course with his bad strokes, digging up the turf with every shot. Finally, as he approached the ball, he said to his caddy, "What club do you think I should use?" "Why don't you try the one in the next county?" asked the caddy.

Facts:

The number of golfers in the U.S. has more than tripled since 1950, and the number of courses almost tripled. The costs of golfing, and the prizes for the professional, have gone much the same route. This has been accomplished in the face of the fact that land near population centers is much less available for golf courses than in the past. In 1949, the leading money maker of the Professional Golfers Association was Sam Snead, at $31,593; today the top prize in most tournaments exceeds that figure. Part of the upsurge is, of course, a reflection of inflation; part is the result of greater leisure time and more mobility for people, men and women alike. Golf as a spectator sport has also boomed in recent years.

The U.S. Golf Association is at Golf House, Far Hills, New Jersey 07931.

GOVERNMENT

(See also Constitution)

Definitions: the organization which exercises regulatory and civil authority over the population; the act of governing; the administration in office; the administration of public office; Uncle Sam; Washington; city hall; the establishment.

Quotations:

As the happiness of the people is the sole end of government, so the consent of the people is the only foundation of it. *John Adams*, **Thoughts on Government,** *1776.*

The worst thing in this world, next to anarchy, is government. *Reverend Henry Ward Beecher*, **Proverbs from Plymouth Pulpit,** *1887.*

. . . government is not an exact science . . . *Associate Justice Louis D. Brandeis, dissenting opinion in Supreme Court in* **Truax v. Corrigan,** *1921.*

Government is a contrivance of human wisdom to provide for human wants. *Edmund Burke*, **Reflections on the Revolution in France,** *1790.*

In the long run every Government is the exact symbol of its people, with their wisdom and unwisdom. *Thomas Carlyle*, **Past and Present,** *1843.*

Government is a trust, and the officers of the government are trustees; and both are created for the benefit of the people. *Henry Clay, 1829.*

While the people should patriotically and cheerfully support their Government, its functions do not include the support of the people. *President Grover Cleveland, veto message, February 16, 1887.*

Our best protection against bigger government in Washington is better government in the states. *Dwight D. Eisenhower, speech in Cleveland to National Governors Conference, June 8, 1964.*

A government that is big enough to give you all you want is big enough to take it all away. *Senator Barry M. Goldwater, October 21, 1964.*

The natural progress of things is for liberty to yield and government to gain ground. *Thomas Jefferson, letter to Col. Edward Carrington, May 27, 1788.*

. . . the republican is the only form of government which is not eternally at open or secret war with the rights of mankind. *Thomas Jefferson, letter to Mayor William Hunter of Alexandria, Va., March 11, 1790.*

A President's hardest task is not to do what is right, but to know what is right. *President Lyndon B. Johnson, State of the Union Message, January 4, 1965.*

The general story of mankind will evince, that lawful and settled authority is very seldom resisted when it is well employed. *Samuel Johnson,* **The Rambler,** *September 8, 1750.*

The basis of effective government is public confidence. *President John F. Kennedy, message to Congress, April 27, 1961.*

No man is good enough to govern another man without that other's consent. *Abraham Lincoln, October 16, 1854.*

. . . and that government of the people, by the people, for the people, shall not perish from the earth. *President Abraham Lincoln, Gettysburg Address, November 19, 1863. ((See Parker and Webster quotations in this section.)*

. . . a government of all the people, by all the people, for all the people. *Reverend Theodore Parker, speech in Boston, May 29, 1850.*

If men be good, government cannot be bad. *William Penn, "Fruits of Solitude," 1693.*

. . . government should do only those things the people cannot do for themselves. *California Governor Ronald Reagan, June 23, 1971.*

The government is us; we are the government you and I. *President Theodore Roosevelt, September 9, 1902.*

No government is perfect. One of the chief virtues of a democracy, however, is that its defects are always visible and under democratic processes can be pointed out and corrected. *President Harry S. Truman, address to Congress, March 12, 1947.*

The basis of our political systems is the right of the people to make and to alter the constitutions of government. But the constitution, which at any time exists, until changed by an explicit and authentic act of the whole people, is sacredly obligatory upon all. *President George Washington, Farewell Address, September 1796.*

I think every nation has a right to establish that form of government under which it conceives it shall live most happy; provided it infracts no right, or is not dangerous to others; and that no governments ought to interfere with the internal concerns of another, except for the security of what is due to themselves. *George Washington, letter to Lafayette, December 25, 1798.*

It is, Sir, the people's Constitution, the people's government, made by the people, and answerable to the people. *Massachusetts Senator Daniel Webster, reply to Hayne, January 26, 1830.*

Anonymous aphorisms:

Government never shrinks.

The people's government is always run by government people.

In business money makes the wheels go round. In government the wheels make the money go round.

Before you can govern people you've got to learn to govern your tongue.

Government gets the best people—one way or another.

Popular government is a collective enterprise for the common good.

American government is a system of checks and balances, as long as the checks don't bounce.

Anecdotage:

"Government," says the scholar, "is double taxation." "How do you mean?" "It not only taxes your income; it taxes your patience."

The Chaplain of the Senate was asked whether he prayed for the Senators. "No," he said, "I pray for the country."

"The American system of government," said the professor, "is a system of checks and balances. How would you say it is working?" A student answered: "The checks don't balance."

Why do they call our government Uncle Sam? Because it's always fiddling around with our ante.

Facts:

The biggest fact about government, here and abroad, is the way it has grown. Much of this growth has come from the assumption of new functions in many different fields—regulation, welfare, exploration, defense. Much has also come from the fact that people work shorter hours today than they did a century ago, so that more people are needed to do the work. But another sometimes neglected element of growth has been the simple fact that there are more people to be served by government. In the United States in 1960 there were 8.8 million federal, state and local government employees—other than the uniformed personnel of the armed forces of the U.S. This figure has almost doubled, with the greatest growth being in state and local public employment. Much of the increase in state and local public employment came as the result of taking over what had previously been private employment, as, for example, when a city's privately owned transport system is taken over by a government agency. Another growth area during that period was the expansion of higher education in public institutions, the growth of community colleges and the necessary staffing involved. The Statistical Abstract of the United States and the budgets of local governments provide details.

GRADUATION

Definitions: the bestowal of a degree or diploma in recognition of completion of a course of study; commencement; completion of school; the end of the beginning; ceremonies attendant on bestowal of a degree or diploma for completion of a phase of education.

Quotations:

I am not unmindful of the fact that countless middle-aged moralists like me are rising these days on countless platforms all over the world to tell thousands of helpless young captives the score — and I suspect that all of those commencement orators are almost as uncomfortable as I am. *Adlai E. Stevenson, Smith College commencement, June 6, 1955.*

. . . sweet girl-graduates in their golden hair . . . *Alfred Tennyson,* **The Princess,** *1847.*

. . . it's not at all hard for me to remember that vivid day of my own graduation. Strangely enough, the one thing about that day that I cannot remember is what the commencement speaker had to say. My thoughts, like yours, were targeted upon my family and my friends and my plans for the summer. But of one thing I'm sure: If the speaker made a short speech, I know I blessed him. *Thomas J. Watson, Jr., Brown University commencement, 1964.*

Anonymous aphorisms:

When they are supposed to be receiving their sheepskins, too many new graduates are wool-gathering.

Graduation is an academic ritual to the nth degree.

Graduation is the intermission between school and real life.

Too many graduates are really getting honorary degrees

When you graduate it's one for the books.

Graduation for a great many people is like jumping from the frying pan into the fire.

The greatest achievement of graduation is sitting through the commencement exercises.

Anecdotage:

"I'm building a new wall to show off the most expensive thing in the house," said Mr. Jones. "Come see it." It was his son's diploma.

"Are you going to the graduation exercises." "No, it took enough exercise to qualify for them."

A proud father presented to his son, on graduation day, his treasured "ruptured duck," the symbol of his own honorable discharge from the service. "I'm giving you this," he said, "because you too have finished something you won't have to go through again."

Facts:

Graduation ceremonies have probably changed less than any other custom in recent centuries, although what is worn under the cap and gown has changed considerably. Some people think the same is true of commencement speeches. But one change is notable. Instead of being reserved for higher education, graduation ceremonies are now held by schools at all levels. The average American today has gone through at least three formal graduation ceremonies, not including college. Even the supplying of "props" for graduations has become a viable business enterprise and paper gowns are available for institutions not wishing to become involved in rentals.

GRATITUDE

Definitions: thankfulness; appreciation; the memorial to good deeds; what some people consider payment in full.

Quotations:

Next to ingratitude, the most painful thing to bear is gratitude. *Reverend Henry Ward Beecher*, **Proverbs from Plymouth Pulpit**, *1887*.

Gratitude is not only the greatest of virtues, but the parent of all others. *Cicero, "Pro Plancio," 54 B.C.*

Revenge is profitable, gratitude is expensive. *Edward Gibbon*, **The Decline and Fall of the Roman Empire**, *Volume II, 1781*.

Every acknowledgment of gratitude is a circumstance of humiliation; and some are found to submit to frequent mortifications of this kind, proclaiming what obligations they owe, merely because they think it in some measure cancels the debt. *Oliver Goldsmith*, **The Citizen of the World**, *1762*.

I sincerely wish ingratitude was not so natural to the human heart as it is. *Alexander Hamilton, letter to George Washington, March 25, 1783*.

The public has neither shame nor gratitude. *William Hazlitt,* **Characteristics,** *1823.*

We seldom find people ungrateful as long as we are in a position to be helpful. *Francois, Duc de La Rochefoucauld,* **Maxims,** *1665.*

Evermore thanks, the exchequer of the poor. *William Shakespeare,* **Richard II,** *1596.*

How sharper than a serpent's tooth it is/ To have a thankless child! *William Shakespeare,* **King Lear,** *1605.*

Anonymous aphorisms:

Gratefulness is the poor man's payment.

Thanksgiving is the only kind of giving some people know.

Gratitude can only be given. It cannot be taken.

Thanks is a memory.

Gratitude begets more kindness.

Gratitude is sometimes more easily given than received.

Thanks is sometimes a mask for ingratitude. True gratitude is expressed in deeds rather than words.

Gratitude is an attitude.

Anecdotage:

A four-year-old actress was appearing in a movie with an aging crotchety star. One day the star came on the set made up to the nines, and the little girl said to her, "Gee, you look so nice." The actress made a pouty face and spoke: "What am I supposed to say to that?" The little girl immediately replied, "You're supposed to say thank you."

An old prospector wandering through the west came upon a little house in a clearing, surrounded by neat rows of growing vegetables, with chickens and cows in well-kept areas and the odor of good food cooking. The family invited him in and he had a delicious meal with them and their lovely children. "You must be very grateful for all this," he said. "Grateful!" they echoed. "How'd you like to live all alone with no neighbors?"

HAPPINESS

Definitions: state of contentment, joy and well-being; bliss; having it all together.

Quotations:

True happiness is of a retired nature, and an enemy to pomp and noise; it arises, in the first place, from the enjoyment of one's self, and in the next, from the friendship and conversation of a few select companions. *Joseph Addison,* **The Spectator,** *March 17, 1911.*

Happiness is speechless. *George William Curtis,* **Prue and I,** *1856.*

To fill the hour — that is happiness . . . *Ralph Waldo Emerson,* **Essays, Second Series:** *Experience, 1844.*

He is happy that knoweth not himself to be otherwise. *Thomas Fuller,* **Gnomologia,** *1732.*

Happiness is the only good./The time to be happy is now./The place to be happy is here./The way to be happy is to make others so. *Robert G. Ingersoll, "Creed," late 19th century.*

. . . the pursuit of happiness . . . *Thomas Jefferson, Declaration of Independence, July 4, 1776.*

A merry heart doeth good like a medicine . . . **Proverbs,** *17:22*

The happiest is the person who suffers the least pain; the most miserable who enjoys the least pleasure. *Jean Jacques Rousseau,* **Emile,** *1762.*

It is the inalienable right of all to be happy. *Elizabeth Cady Stanton, February 1861.*

Man is the artificer of his own happiness. *Henry D. Thoreau,* **Journal,** *January 21, 1838.*

Happy days are here again. *Jack Yellen song lyric title, 1929, used as Democratic Party motto in 1932 election.*

Anonymous aphorisms:

The pursuit of happiness is mankind's favorite sport.

People cannot be ordered to be happy.

It is better to enjoy happiness than to analyze it.

One man's happiness may be another man's hell.

Happiness sometimes comes from ignorance — not knowing how much better your life might be.

Some people are happy remembering the past, and some happy forgetting it.

Happiness can be contagious.

Anecdotage:

It was a poor family and overrun with children. The gracious lady came to visit their careworn mother, who kept complaining about all the work the children gave her and how hard it was to keep going. "My dear," said the gracious lady, "they now have all kinds of methods of birth control. Let me give you the money to go to an expert for guidance." "What," said the careworn mother, "are you trying to take away my only happiness?"

HEALTH

(See also Dieting, Food, Medicine)

Definitions: soundness of bodily functions; freedom from disease; physical and mental well-being; "the first wealth" *(Ralph Waldo Emerson)*.

Quotations:

Health is not a condition of matter, but of Mind . . . *Mary Baker Eddy*, **Science and Health,** *1908*.

Early to bed, and early to rise, makes a man healthy, wealthy and wise. *Benjamin Franklin*, **The Way to Wealth,** *1757*.

Health is not valued till sickness comes. *Thomas Fuller*, **Gnomologia,** *1732*.

If you mean to keep as well as possible, the less you think about your health the better. *Oliver Wendell Holmes*, **Over the Teacups,** *1891*.

. . . health is worth more than learning . . . *Thomas Jefferson, letter to his cousin John Garland Jefferson, June 11, 1790*.

. . . the world's "wealthiest nation" can never be satisfied until we are the world's healthiest. *President Lyndon B. Johnson, March 31, 1966*.

We should pray for a sound mind in a sound body. *Juvenal*, **Satires:** *10:356, about 115 A.D.*

The first medical right of all Americans is care within their means. *Maine Senator Edmund S. Muskie, May 27, 1971*.

Look to your health; and if you have it, praise God, and value it next to a good conscience; for health is the second blessing that we mortals are capable of; a blessing that money cannot buy. *Izaak Walton*, **The Compleat Angler,** *1653*.

Health that mocks the doctor's rules./Knowledge never learned of schools. *John Greenleaf Whittier, "The Barefoot Boy," 1855*.

Anonymous aphorisms:

Health doesn't insure happiness; but there's not much happiness without it.

People who enjoy good health should think of the doctor's bill as an amusement tax.

While there's health there's hope, and while there's hope at least there's healthy thinking.

You have to heal to have health.

Having a good constitution is as important for an individual as for a nation.

Health is better than wealth.

Money can't buy health, but can certainly make it easier to stay healthy.

Anecdotage:

"If you want to enjoy good health," said the doctor, "you must get eight hours sleep every day, don't burn the candle at both ends and practice moderation in all things." "In that case," said his patient," what am I being healthy for?"

"My bones ache," said Mr. Jones,"my feet hurt, I can't sleep at night and I am always short of breath." "Well," said his friend, "as long as you're healthy."

"I'm as strong as a horse," said eager Harry as he went out without a coat to shovel the snow off his walkway. "And just about as bright," said his wife.

Facts:

Health is, of course, primarily a scientific challenge, because it depends on how much we know or can find out about preventing disease, improving nutrition and curing ailments. But the major problem of public health is the problem of rising costs. Whether for the education of doctors, the provision of sufficient good food, the maintenance of preventive measures or care facilities, money is the root of concern. In the United States, according to the Council on Wage and Price Stability, it costs more than $2,000 a year for health care for the average four-person family. It is estimated that more than 10 percent of the average citizen's income is spent on health. Since 1950, private health expenditures in the U.S. have gone up sevenfold and government expenditures about tenfold. The U.S. Social Security Administration publishes helpful Social Security Bulletins on related statistics. Figures from the World Health Organization indicate great worldwide success in limiting, and in some instances eradicating, the threat of infectious and contagious diseases such as smallpox, which once were endemic.

HISTORY

Definitions: the record or study of events of the past; "clarified experience" *(James Russell Lowell);* "the propaganda of the victors" *(Ernst Toller),* what happened when, where and why; today's view of yesterday's dreams.

Quotations;

Histories make men wise; poets witty; the mathematics subtile; natural philosophy deep; moral grave; logic and rhetoric able to contend. *Sir Francis Bacon,* **Essays:** *Of Studies, 1625.*

Peoples and governments have never learned anything from history . . . *George Wilhelm Friedrich Hegel,* **Philosophy of History,** *published posthumously in 1832.*

. . . a page of history is worth a volume of logic. *Associate Justice Oliver Wendell Holmes, Jr., opinion in Supreme Court case of* **New York Trust Co. v. Eisner,** *1921.*

History fades into fable . . . *Washington Irving,* **The Sketch Book,** *Westminster Abbey, 1820.*

We can draw lessons from the past, but we cannot live in it. *President Lyndon B. Johnson, December 13, 1963.*

Thrice happy is the nation that has a glorious history. *Governor Theodore Roosevelt of New York, speech in Chicago, April 10, 1899.*

Those who cannot remember the past are condemned to repeat it. *George Santayana,* **The Life of Reason, Volume 1,** *1905.*

. . . the frontier has gone, and with its going has closed the first period of American history. *Frederick Jackson Turner, "The Significance of the Frontier in American History," 1893.*

It has been said that the only thing we learn from history is that we do not learn. *Chief Justice Earl Warren, eulogy of late President Kennedy, Washington, D.C., November 24, 1963.*

Anonymous aphorisms:

Some people make history and some make it up.

History doesn't repeat itself; men repeat history.

History is the rear view mirror on the road of life.

History is the past imperfect.

History is not simply what happened; it is the way what happened is remembered.

History is the way the present views the past.

Your life is your grandchildren's history.

Anecdotage:

"Winston Churchill once suggested . . . during World War II that history would deal gently with him. 'Because,' Mr. Churchill said, 'I intend to write it,' " *President John F. Kennedy, October 3, 1961.*

"I don't want to discuss the mark I got in history," said Johnny to his father, "because that's all in the past."

Facts:

The art and study of history is one of man's oldest preoccupations. It is not accidental that the most enduring lore of the world is contained in largely historical works of scripture. Unlike reading, writing and arithmetic, history did not require formal instruction to be handed down from generation to generation, in epic tales — where the fact has to be sorted out from the fiction. History is by far the most popular of the social sciences, in terms of the number of degrees granted, books written and tales told. One of the most interesting aspects of a world that prides itself on looking toward the future, in fact, is the degree to which that world is preoccupied with finding out more about the past. As the work of so-called revisionist historians and government committees alike bears witness, commonly accepted "facts" of history are constantly being re-examined. Such subjects as the Dead Sea Scrolls, the search for Noah's Ark, the challenge to the findings of the Warren Commission about the assassination of President Kennedy and the eagerness to open classified documents to public scrutiny, illustrate man's constant appetite for the study of and traffic in history.

The National Council for the Social Studies, though not an organization restricted to teachers of history, provides in its journals a continuing review of the latest historical thinking. The Council is located at 1515 Wilson Boulevard, Arlington, Virginia 22209.

HOBBIES

(See also Leisure)

Definitions: a field of endeavor or interest engaged in for relaxation and enjoyment rather than for a living; hard work you wouldn't do for a living; what you do to avoid doing nothing.

Quotations:

And now each man bestride his hobby, and dust away his bells to what tune he pleases. *Charles Lamb*, **Essays of Elia:** *All Fools' Day, 1823.*

Nothing is as certain as that the vices of leisure are gotten rid of by being busy. *Seneca*, **Moral Letters to Lucilius,** *64 A.D.*

So long as a man rides his hobby-horse peaceably and quietly along the king's highway, and neither compels you or me to get up behind him — pray, Sir, what have either you or I to do with it? *Laurence Sterne*, **Tristram Shandy,** *1759.*

Anonymous aphorisms:

Time is the factor in all hobbies: some are practiced to kill time, some have time set aside for them and all are intended to provide a good time for the hobbyist.

One man's work is another man's hobby.

Those who can, do; those who can't think they can.

If you spend money on it, it's a hobby; if you make money on it, it's a business.

Your hobby is none of your business.

Everyone to his hobby.

A hobby is what you love to do, rather than what you live to do.

Hobbies are fire escapes in the conflagration of life.

Anecdotage:

"My work is my hobby," the businessman said. "He only says that," remarked his wife, "because he doesn't make a living at it."

John Jones went to see the doctor because he was nervous, unable to relax. "You ought to take up a hobby," the doctor said. "I have a hobby," said Mr. Jones; "I make miniature furniture carved by hand to exact scale, and I love doing it." "And you don't find it relaxes you?" asked the doctor. "Not when my wife throws out a year's work by mistake," said Mr. Jones. "Her hobby is redecorating."

Facts:

In past generations, men and women, in order to live, had to work at the very things that have now gained the status of hobbies — needlecraft, carpentry, tinkering, metalwork, for example. And in past generations, working hours were so long for the average person and the comforts of life so much less than today that there was little if any time for hobbies. Do-it-yourself in those days was the necessity of the times, not a leisure craze. But in our age, shorter work weeks, convenience tools, electric power and pre-fabricated supplies have made it possible for millions upon millions to devote countless hours to doing things for no reward other than the fun of doing. The hobby industries today, as a result, are big business. Many, indeed, are not hobby industries essentially, but rather enterprises and sources which are principally suppliers to business. Stained glass, for example, comes from the same manufacturers who turn it out for church windows, so the dimensions of hobbies in the United States can't be measured simply by the number of hobby businesses. But every year more do-it-yourself stores open, more do-it-yourself supplies and kits are sold and more types of do-it-yourself books and courses are developed. One good illustration of the growth of hobbies is the field of photography, where, at first, all pictures were taken to the drug store to be developed and printed and now home equipment for the amateur photographer's darkroom fills stores and jingles cash registers all over the world. Your local library, under the heading of hobbies in the card catalogue, can probably tell you a good deal about the extent of interest in hobbies in your own community.

HORSERACING

Definitions: competitions at fixed distances and over specified courses among horses ridden by humans; the sport of kings; the horses; the flats and the trotters; the bangtails.

Quotations:

Gwine to run all night! Gwine to run all day! I'll bet my money on de bob-tail nag—/ Somebody bet on de bay. *Stephen Foster, "Camptown Races," about 1850.*

Hast thou given the horse strength? Hast thou clothed his neck with thunder? **Job,** *39:19.*

Spur a free horse, he'll run himself to death. *Ben Jonson,* **The Tale of a Tub,** *1633.*

The ways of a man with a maid be strange, yet simple and tame/ To the ways of a man with a horse, when selling or racing that same. *Rudyard Kipling, "Certain Maxims of Hafiz," 1886.*

Competition makes a horserace. *Ovid,* **The Art of Love,** *about 1 B.C.*

The spirited horse, which will try to win the race of its own accord, will run even faster if encouraged. *Ovid,* **Epistolae ex Ponto,** *about 9 A.D.*

I wish your horses swift and sure of foot . . . *William Shakespeare,* **Macbeth,** *1606.*

O for a horse with wings! *William Shakespeare,* **Cymbeline,** *1609.*

It is a good horse that never stumbles. *C. H. Spurgeon,* **John Ploughman's Talk,** *1869.*

Anonymous aphorisms:

Horseracing is the sport of kings and the trap of fools.

Can you ever imagine horses betting on people?

I got it right from the horse's mouth.

A racetrack is a place where the human race is secondary.

A horserace is where a horse performs for his bettors.

The race is to the swiftest.

Anecdotage:

"Never bet on a polite horse," said my friend the tout. "What's a polite horse?" I asked. "A horse that lets the others in first," said the tout.

"Do you follow the horses?" "Yes, with about the same results as the streetcleaners after a mounted parade."

"Today was my best day at the track," said an inveterate loser. "Did you win?" he was asked. "No," he said, "my horse was scratched before I could get to the window."

Facts:

In the United States there are more than 13,000 racing days per year. That is to say, the total number of days various race tracks are open during the year adds up to over 13,000. More than 80 million people yearly go to the track. And, from the parimutuel turnover, approximately $600 million goes in revenue to the states. In New York and other cities, the government itself is also in the offtrack betting business. Horseracing is not only one of America's favorite spectator sports, it is also, to a considerable extent, everybody's business. You can update the statistics above in the latest Statistical Abstract of the U.S.

HOSPITALITY

Definitions: cordial treatment as a guest in a home or resting place; enthusiastic welcome and courtesy from a host; "a little fire, a little food, and an immense quiet" (*Ralph Waldo Emerson*); the red carpet treatment; making people feel at home in your home even when you don't.

Quotations:

The ornament of a house is the friends who frequent it. *Ralph Waldo Emerson,* **Society and Solitude:** *Domestic Life, 1870.*

Fish and visitors smell in three days. *Benjamin Franklin,* **Poor Richard's Almanac,** *1736.*

True friendship's laws are by this rule express'd,/Welcome the coming, speed the parting guest. *Homer,* **The Odyssey,** *translated by Alexander Pope.*

If your house be like an inn, nobody cares for you. *Samuel Johnson, Boswell's* **Life of Samuel Johnson,** *May 15, 1783.*

I was hungered, and ye gave me meat: I was thirsty, and ye gave me drink: I was a stranger, and ye took me in. **Matthew,** *25:35*

. . . you are very welcome to our house:/ It must appear in ways other than words . . . *William Shakespeare,* **The Merchant of Venice,** *1597.*

Anonymous aphorisms:

When there is room in the heart there is room in the house.

A good host puts the first stain on the tablecloth.

The master of the house is the servant of the guest.

Hospitality is homemade.

My house is your house.

The acid test of hospitality is the uninvited guest.

Hospitality is tested by the quality of the guest.

The drinks are on the house.

Hospitality begins with the invitation.

Anecdotage:

Mrs. Brown always managed to come up with a delicious meal for unexpected guests. When asked how she did it, she said, "I simply add tomorrow's dinner to yesterday's leftovers."

"The secret of always seeming happy when you have guests," says the wise host, "is to go around smiling at the thought of how nice it will be when they leave."

HOUSING

Definitions: places of abode; dwelling places; dwellings; cover, protection or shelter; a roof over one's head; residences; pads; habitation; where you hang your hat.

Quotations:

He that builds a fair house upon an ill seat committeth himself to prison. *Sir Francis Bacon, "Of Building," 1625.*

A man's house is his castle. *Sir Edward Coke,* **Institutes,** *vol. III, 1644.*

A man builds a fine house; and now he has a master, and a task for life; he is to furnish, watch, show it, and keep it in repair the rest of his days. *Ralph Waldo Emerson,* **Society and Solitude:** *Works and Days, 1870.*

Let me live in my house by the side of the road/And be a friend of man. *Sam Walter Foss, "The House by the Side of the Road," 1897.*

The house shows the owner. *George Herbert,* **Jacula Prudentum,** *1651.*

From Plymouth Rock to Puget Sound, the first priority of the men and women who settled this vast and this blessed continent was to put a roof over the heads of their family. And that priority has never, and can never, change. *President Lyndon B. Johnson, signing the Housing and Urban Development Act, August 10, 1965.*

I suppose I've passed it a hundred times,/but I always stop for a minute/And look at the house, the tragic house,/the house with nobody in it. *Joyce Kilmer, "The House with Nobody In It," c. 1917.*

I see one-third of a nation ill-housed, ill-clad, and ill-nourished. *President Franklin D. Roosevelt, Second Inaugural Address, January 20, 1937.*

Our houses are such unwieldy property that we are often imprisoned rather than housed in them. *Henry D. Thoreau,* **Walden:** *Economy, 1854.*

Anonymous aphorisms:

A house divided is a multiple dwelling.

It takes a heap to make a house a home.

In housing there is always room for improvements.

America is a land of opportunity where anybody can owe his own home.

Fools build houses and wise men buy them.

High rise apartments don't get their name from the course of their rents — or do they?

A housing development is for the purpose of developing houses into homes.

Anecdotage:

"If a man's home is his castle," said the tax assessor, looking at Mr. Jones' badly neglected abode, "this one should have a moat around it."

How many stories does your house have? As many as there are people who have lived in it.

"My house is your house," said the tenant to the guest at the door. "You're darned right," said the man at the door, "I just bought the building."

Facts:

There has never been a time in the past two hundred years of American history when there was enough housing. Originally, the cause was the growth of population and the expansion into new lands. But then, as now, cost was also a factor. It is approximately a century since President Franklin D. Roosevelt asserted that one-third of the nation was ill-housed. In the years since then, there has been steady growth in low-rent public housing units and in subsidized housing construction. By way of example, in 1950, according to the Statistical Yearbook of the U.S. Department of Housing and Urban Development (a department whose founding in 1965 was evidence of the need), there was a total of 302,100 units already in existence or in planning or construction stages; a recent comparable figure was 1,314,000. The ambition to own your own home is common in every sector of the nation and every ethnic group. Housing is, by every measure, our most popular necessary expenditure. The number of housing units started each year is one of the measures of basic prosperity for the nation.

HUMANITY

Definitions: the state of being human; people in general; the study or learning related to general human culture; compassion; human understanding.

Quotations:

Love, hope, fear, faith—these makes humanity;/These are its sign and note and character. *Robert Browning,* **Paracelsus,** *1835.*

I come to speak to you in defense of a cause as holy as the cause of liberty — the cause of humanity. *William Jennings Bryan, speech to the Democratic convention in Chicago, July 8, 1896.*

There is but one law for all, namely, that law which governs all law, the law of our Creator, the law of humanity, justice, equity — the law of nature, and of nations. *Edmund Burke, May 28, 1794.*

No human ideal is ever perfectly attained, since humanity itself is not perfect. *Herbert Hoover, Presidential campaign speech in New York, October 22, 1928.*

We will be remembered not for the power of our weapons but for the power of our compassion, our dedication to human welfare. *Vice President Hubert H. Humphrey, September 15, 1966.*

. . . our similarities and our differences have been like separate rivers, flowing from a common lake of humanity. *President Lyndon B. Johnson, remarks in Bangkok, October 29, 1966.*

Be ashamed to die until you have won some victory for humanity. *Horace Mann, address at Antioch College, 1859.*

Know then theyself, presume not God to scan;/The proper study of mankind is man. *Alexander Pope, An Essay on Man, 1733.*

Rejoice with them that do rejoice, and weep with them that weep. **Romans,** *12:15.*

The still, sad music of humanity. *William Wordsworth, "Tintern Abbey," 1798.*

Anonymous aphorisms:

It's not the heat, it's the humanity.

Some people show their humanity by their mistakes; some by their accomplishments.

Humanity is the difference between being human and being humane.

Why is it we hear so little about man's humanity to man, when there is so much more of it than of man's inhumanity.

Humanity separates us from the beasts — which may be lucky for the beasts.

Anecdotage:

"When you study the humanities," said the professor to his college class, "what you are really studying is the stories of people. Or is it the people of stories?"

"Show a little humanity," the defense attorney pleaded with the jury. So they cried when they found the defendant guilty.

There was a tremendous fire, and the animals were fleeing before it; but when they came to the outskirts of the city, the king of the beasts let out a roar and said, "Go no further." "But the fire may come closer," said the animals. "First enemies first," said the lion. "And the first enemy is not the heat, it's the humanity."

HUMOR

Definitions: that which is designed to arouse laughter; wit; comedy; laughing matters.

Quotations:

Man is distinguished from all other creatures by the faculty of laughter. *Joseph Addison,* **The Spectator,** *September 26, 1712.*

Men will let you abuse them if only you will make them laugh. *Reverend Henry Ward Beecher,* **Proverbs from Plymouth Pulpit,** *1887.*

Wit is so shining a quality that everybody admires it; most people aim at it, all people fear it, and few love it unless in themselves. *Lord Chesterfield, letter to his godson, December 18, 1765.*

A difference of taste in jokes is a great strain on the affections. *George Eliot,* **Daniel Deronda,** *1876.*

Wit makes its own welcome, and levels all distinctions. No dignity, no learning, no force of character, can make any stand against good wit. *Ralph Waldo Emerson,* **Letters and Social Aims:** *The Comic, 1876.*

Thou canst not joke an enemy into a friend, but thou may'st a friend into an enemy. *Benjamin Franklin,* **Poor Richard's Almanac,** *1739.*

Men show their characters in nothing more clearly than in what they think laughable. *Johann Wolfgang von Goethe, undated maxim.*

That frolic which shakes one man with laughter will convulse another with indignation. *Samuel Johnson,* **The Rambler,** *September 28, 1751.*

Laugh at yourself first, before anyone else can. *Elsa Maxwell, September 28, 1958.*

All Human Race would fain be Wits,/And Millions miss, for one that hits. *Jonathan Swift, "On Poetry: A Rhapsody," 1733.*

Laugh and the world laughs with you;/Weep and you weep alone . . . *Ella Wheeler Wilcox, "Solitude," 1883.*

Anonymous aphorisms:

Being funny is no laughing matter.

A joke that has to be explained is at its wit's end.

Whether something is funny often depends on whom it is happening to.

Laughter is more contagious than tears.

He who laughs lasts.

People who can agree on what's funny can usually agree on other things.

Many friends have been lost by jest, but few have been gained.

Anecdotage:

"Laughter is God's gift to mankind," said the preacher. "And mankind," said the cynic, "is the proof that God has a sense of humor."

Every time Mr. Jones told a joke and joined in the laughter, Mrs. Jones would say disapprovingly, "I don't think that's funny." One day Mr. Jones told what he thought was an uproarious joke and, as he burst into a laugh at the end of it, he found he was laughing alone. Everybody else had a puzzled look. "Now that," said Mrs. Jones, "is funny."

Facts:

Humor is a most salable commodity in the market place. Popular comedians make more money than the President of the United States (but then of
course so do business executives and professional athletes, among others), and
situation comedies are the nation's favorite television viewing. Joke books have
been best sellers since the original edition of Joe Miller. On the college campus,
a humor magazine is as much a staple as the pretentious literary periodical.
Slapstick comedy was the keystone of Hollywood's movie success. Over the
years, Americans have laughed at many of the same things time after time —
pie in the face, irreverence toward government, the funny differences among
us. A sense of humor often seems to be the best sense of all.

IMMIGRATION

(See also Ethnicity, Minorities)

Definitions: the act or state of entering a strange or foreign land and settling
there; entering a country for the purpose of establishing permanent residence
there; the food for the melting pot; choosing your country rather than being
born in it.

Quotations:

We are the Romans of the modern world — the great assimilating people.
Oliver Wendell Holmes, **The Autocrat of the Breakfast-Table,** *1858.*

I think it fortunate for the United States to have become the asylum for so
many virtuous patriots of different denominations. *Thomas Jefferson, letter to
M. de Meusnier, April 29, 1795.*

The fundamental, longtime American attitude has been to ask not where a
person comes from but what are his personal qualities. On this basis men and
women migrated from every quarter of the globe. By their hard work and their
enormously varied talents they hewed a great nation out of a wilderness. By
their dedication to liberty and equality, they created a society reflecting man's
most cherished ideas. *President Lyndon B. Johnson, message to Congress,
January 13, 1965.*

A Nation of Immigrants. *John F. Kennedy, title of book, published posthumously, 1964.*

"Keep, ancient lands, your storied pomp!" cries she/With silent lips. "Give me
your tired, your poor,/Your huddled masses yearning to breathe free,/The
wretched refuse of your teeming shore./Send these, the homeless, tempest-
tost to me,/I lift my lamp beside the golden door!" *Emma Lazarus, "The
New Colossus," 1883, now affixed to the base of the Statue of Liberty.*

My folks didn't come over on the *Mayflower*, but they were there to meet the boat. *Will Rogers (part Indian), in the 1920s.*

Remember, remember always that all of us, and you and I especially, are descended from immigrants and revolutionists. *President Franklin D. Roosevelt, speech to the Daughters of the American Revolution, April 21, 1938.*

Some Americans need hyphens in their names because only part of them has come over. *President Woodrow Wilson, May 16, 1914.*

We may have come over on different ships, but we're all in the same boat now. *Whitney Young, Jr., speech in New York, May 7, 1970.*

America is God's Crucible, the great Melting Pot where all the races of Europe are melting and reforming! *Israel Zangwill,* **The Melting-Pot,** *1908.*

Anonymous aphorisms:

When the white man and the black man came to the land of the red man, they were all greenhorns.

In the history of the world, people have more often struggled to get out of a country than to get in; the country they have struggled to get into, however, is the U.S.

America is interested in the whole world because that's where most of us came from.

The most important ship for the immigrants who came here was citizenship.

An immigrant is here by choice, a native by chance.

Before things commingle in the melting pot, they have to get hot enough to melt.

Anecdotage:

The newly-arrived immigrant drove his host crazy by talking about how much better food was in the old country, and how much better the weather was and how much better everything was back where he came from. Finally his host said, "If everything was so much better there, why did you come here?" And the immigrant answered, "Because if I said over there that something was better elsewhere they would have shot me. The one thing that's better here is that now I can complain."

People like to think that I and millions of others came here because we thought the streets were paved with gold. Many of us were happy enough to find that the streets were paved at all.

"America," said the native son, proudly, " is the best place in the world to come from," "I don't know about that," said the immigrant, "but I do know it's the best place in the world to come to."

Facts:

Immigration over the centuries has been America's greatest asset. Immigrants opened the vast territory of the United States to civilization, planted and grew the crops, swelled the population and supported the ideals of independence. We may see immigration as a past page of American history, flourishing in the late 19th and early 20th centuries when millions of Europeans went through the portal at Ellis Island. But immigrants are part of today's mainstream as well. In one recent year, 395,000 immigrants were admitted to this country, a figure larger than the annual average in the 1890s. About 10 million people in this country are foreign-born and another 24 million are native-born of foreign parentage. To people all over the world, the United States is still the peerless sanctuary of freedom and opportunity.

The American Immigration and Citizenship Conference, 20 West 40th Street, New York, N.Y. 10018, was founded in 1954 as a coordinating and informational agency. It was the successor to an earlier group.

INDIVIDUALISM

Definitions: the act or philosophy of asserting the individual as the most important element of society; that which is self-centered rather than group-centered; egoism; independent individual action or thought; the personal element; first person singular; me first; capital I.

Quotations:

It is in vain to talk of the interest of the community, without understanding what is the interest of the individual. *Jeremy Bentham,* **An Introduction to the Principles of Morals and Legislation,** *1789.*

Nature never rhymes her children, nor makes two men alike. *Ralph Waldo Emerson,* **Essays, Second Series:** *Character, 1844.*

God helps them that help themselves. *Benjamin Franklin,* **Poor Richard's Almanac,** *1733 (drawn from maxim going back to ancient Greece).*

When the war closed . . . we were challenged with a peacetime choice between the American system of rugged individualism and a European philosophy of diametrically opposed doctrines — doctrines of paternalism and state socialism. *Herbert Hoover, Presidential campaign speech in New York, October 22, 1928.*

The strongest man in the world is he who stands alone. *Henrik Ibsen,* **An Enemy of the People,** *1882.*

Down to Gehenna or up to the throne,/He travels the fastest who travels alone. *Rudyard Kipling, "The Winners," 1888.*

Let me emphasize that serious as have been the errors of unrestrained individualism, I do not believe in abandoning the system of individual enterprise. *President Franklin D. Roosevelt, radio address, August 24, 1935.*

If a man does not keep pace with his companions, perhaps it is because he hears a different drummer. Let him step to the music which he hears, however measured or far away. *Henry D. Thoreau,* **Walden,** *Conclusion, 1854.*

. . . the frontier is productive of individualism. *Frederick Jackson Turner, "The Significance of the Frontier in American History," 1893.*

Anonymous aphorisms:

It takes all sorts to make a world.

One of a kind isn't much of a poker hand, but it's a pretty good description of a real leader.

It's fine to stand out from the crowd, but not when they're shooting at you.

Everyone to his own taste.

One man's meat is another man's poison.

He stands the tallest who stands alone.

Anecdotage:

"I don't want to suggest that he is an egotist," said an opponent of a notoriously independent candidate, "but after he was made *he* threw away the mold."

Because people insist on doing things their own way doesn't mean they will do things individually. Consider what happens when the kids at school are told they can dress as each one pleases. They all come in looking exactly the same.

Facts:

Conformism is a social pressure, common to most societies. The person who looks or acts different is somehow set apart. That which is individual is regarded as eccentric, at best, if not downright heretical. Yet the history of the world has been made very largely by people who were highly individualistic, and did not behave according to the standard for their class, or their people, or their time. This, of course, has been the story of many of the world's great scientists, philosophers and political leaders, who started with the courage of their convictions and ended up by leading the world into new frontiers of knowledge or accomplishment. In the United States, the first written guarantee of individual rights was written into the Constitution, derived in part from the tradition of mother England; but every attempt to guarantee individualism in the world today traces back to the U.S. seminal document, the Declaration of Independence, and its lineal descendant, the Constitution. Perhaps the most dedicated advocate of individualism was Henry David Thoreau, particularly in such writings as "Civil Disobedience" and *Walden*.

INSPIRATION

Definitions: an infusion of light or spirit that provides a solution for a challenge; a flash of revelation for the solution of a problem; a subconscious message that impels a course of conduct; a moment of genius; a revelation of wisdom; accomplishment that doesn't come with perspiration.

Quotations:

Genius is one percent inspiration and 99 percent perspiration. *Thomas A. Edison, 1890s.*

Any new formula which suddenly emerges in our consciousness has its roots in long trains of thought; it is virtually old when it first makes its appearance among the recognized growths of our intellect. *Oliver Wendell Holmes,* **The Autocrat of the Breakfast-Table,** *1858.*

An idea, to be suggestive, must come to the individual with the force of a revelation. *William James,* **The Varieties of Religious Experience,** *1902.*

No man ever became great by imitation. *Samuel Johnson,* **The Rambler,** *September 7, 1751.*

A god dwells within our breast; when he awakens us, we are inspired with a holy rapture that grows from the seed of divine thought planted in man. *Ovid,* **Fasti,** *about 5 A.D.*

Anonymous aphorisms:

Inspiration is sometimes another name for desperation.

Inspiration starts with aspiration.

It's only an inspiration when somebody makes it work.

Inspiration is sometimes used to explain what cannot be explained.

Inspiration and imagination go hand in hand.

Anecdotage:

A maker of pornographic movies was asked how he came to his line of work and said it was pure inspiration. "Yes," said a critic, "he was inspired by a hunger for money."

Ambitious young Joe Smith never missed a day of submitting a new idea to his boss, and his boss never missed a day rejecting Joe's idea. One day Joe submitted a suggestion and his boss said, "That's sheer inspiration!" "No," said Joe, "99% aspiration, 1% inspiration."

Why do most people seem to get their inspirations overnight? Because inspiration comes from dreams.

INVENTION

Definitions: a device, mechanism or procedure that did not previously exist; a new way of doing something; the secret of progress; the act of devising new machines or processes; what necessity is the mother of; *"The Mother of Necessity" (Thorstein Veblen).*

Quotations:

. . . God hath made man upright: but they have sought out many inventions. **Ecclesiastes,** *VII:29.*

'Tis frivolous to fix pedantically the date of particular inventions. They have all been invented over and over fifty times. *Ralph Waldo Emerson,* **The Conduct of Life:** *Fate, 1860.*

Invention breeds invention. *Ralph Waldo Emerson,* **Society and Solitude:** *Works and Days, 1870.*

What good is a new-born baby? *Benjamin Franklin, August 27, 1783, when somebody asked what good was served by the first balloon ascension in Paris.*

What hath God wrought! *Samuel F. B. Morse, first message on opening of first telegraph line, between Washington and Baltimore, May 24, 1844.*

Anonymous aphorisms:

Did you ever think how much labor went into inventing a labor-saving device?

One civilization after another has reinvented the wheel.

It takes one invention to replace another.

Necessity is the mother of invention.

Invention is the son of need and the father of prosperity.

These days invention requires subvention, defies convention and often calls for divine intervention.

The inventor's motto is: If you don't see what you want, make it.

Anecdotage:

An American and an Englishman were arguing the virtues of their countries. "In England," said the American, "when we said we had a new way to process cotton, you said 'impossible.' When we came up with the airplane, you said it was simply an interesting invention. When we produced the computer, you said it was promising. Apart from the steam engine and some looms, what have you invented?" "Your language," said the Englishman.

An inventor and an explorer compared their callings. "I go out looking for new things," said the explorer. "I stay home making new things," said the inventor.

"Surely you don't classify any inventor as more important to the world than Christopher Columbus." "How about the guy who invented the boat?" asked the inventor.

Facts:

Invention constantly changes the nature of human life. From the wheel to the computer, invention has made it possible for man to be more productive, to expand his horizons, to make life easier and more fruitful. The Constitution of the United States took pains to protect the rights of inventors by providing in Article I, Section 8 (8) that Congress shall have the power "To promote the Progress of Science and useful Arts, by securing for limited Times to Authors and Inventors the exclusive Right to their respective Writings and Discoveries." The U.S. issues patents for inventions at the rate of more than 75,000 a year. Not every invention, of course, is an earth-shaking one; but one need only recall those in the field of transportation and energy to realize how much of modern life is the product of inventive genius. An annual report is published by the U.S. Commissioner of Patents. *The New York Times* began publishing a Saturday news column about patents many years ago.

JOBS

(See also Labor, Opportunity)

Definitions: work; occupations; gainful employment; tasks for which one is paid; assigned functions; what people do for a living; bread and butter.

Quotations:

Work is not the curse, but drudgery is. *Reverend Henry Ward Beecher*, **Proverbs from Plymouth Pulpit,** *1887.*

Blessed is he who has found his work; let him ask no other blessedness. *Thomas Carlyle*, **Past and Present,** *1843.*

He that hath a trade hath an estate; he that hath a calling hath an office of profit and honor. *Benjamin Franklin*, **The Way to Wealth,** *1757.*

Too many young men and women face long and bitter months of job hunting or marginal work after leaving school. Our society has not yet established satisfactory ways to bridge the gap between school and work. *President Lyndon B. Johnson, message to Congress, May 1, 1967.*

People who are hungry and out of a job are the stuff of which dictatorships are made. *President Franklin D. Roosevelt, message to Congress, January 11, 1944.*

Far and away the best prize that life offers is the chance to work hard at work worth doing. *President Theodore Roosevelt, September 7, 1903.*

In order that people may be happy in their work, these three things are needed: They must be fit for it: They must not do too much of it: And they must have a sense of success in it. *John Ruskin,* **Pre-Raphaelitism,** *1850.*

. . . work saves us from three great evils: boredom, vice and need. *Voltaire,* **Candide,** *1759.*

. . . there is as much dignity in tilling a field as in writing a poem. *Booker T. Washington,* **Up from Slavery,** *1901.*

Anonymous aphorisms:

First get the job, then get the job done.

Don't send a boy to do a man's job these days; send a woman.

A job is regular work you get paid for before you find a position.

Finding a job is sometimes harder work than doing a job.

All work and no play makes Jack a dull boy.

All work and no play makes jack.

Make the best of a bad job.

Anecdotage:

"If you can't find employment," said Mr. Jones to his son, "at least go down and collect your unemployment insurance." "No," said the son, "it's too much of a job."

When Willie was caught robbing the poorbox at the church, he pleaded for mercy, "I've been looking day and night for a job," he said. "This is a funny place to look," said the sexton.

"Young man," said Mr. Brown, "I have selected you for this job over scores of other applicants. You should regard that as a clear vote of confidence in your ability and your training. Work hard and this could be the start of a fine career." The young man fidgeted for a moment and then answered, "Thanks, Dad."

Facts:

Jobs are one of the measures of the success of any society. When there is not enough work for everybody who wants to work, there are problems; and there are also problems when there is work enough but not reward enough. In earlier generations — as in Japan today — jobs were for a lifetime. Today, both because of the mortality rate in business enterprises and because of the desire for upward mobility on the part of jobholders, one person is apt to hold many, or at least several, jobs in a lifetime. The technological revolution is outmoding some jobs and creating new ones. Alvin Toffler in *Future Shock* noted a *Fortune* magazine survey that found one out of three young executives with major U.S. corporations was in a job that had not previously existed. For the past several decades, the labor turnover in manufacturing industries in the U.S., from one cause or another, has been about 16 employees out of every hundred per month. The U.S. Department of Labor checks periodically on the average length of time that workers keep their jobs and in recent surveys has found that the tenure was roughly between four and five years. (This doesn't mean leaving a company after that amount of time; it takes into account promotions as well as new employment.) But the problems of changing jobs are infinitely less crucial than those of joblessness.

For the latest figures on unemployment, consult the Bureau of Labor Statistics, whose monthly reports on Employment and Earnings are widely covered in the press. The Bureau is a unit of the U.S. Department of Labor, at 200 Constitution Avenue NW, Washington, D.C. 20210.

JOURNALISM
(See also Radio, Television)

Definitions: writing, editing and publishing material on contemporary news and trends; reporting current events; "literature in a hurry" (*Matthew Arnold*); the news.

Quotations:

In a democracy, the public has a right to know not only what the government decides, but why and by what process. *President Gerald Ford, September 13, 1976.*

How beautiful upon the mountains are the feet of him that bringeth good tidings . . . **Isaiah,** *52:7.*

. . . were it left to me to decide whether we should have a government without newspapers or newspapers without a government, I should not hesitate a moment to prefer the latter. *Thomas Jefferson, letter to Colonel Edward Carrington, January 16, 1787.*

In a world of daily—nay, almost hourly—journalism every clever man, every man who thinks himself clever, or whom anybody else thinks clever, is called upon to deliver his judgment point-blank and at the word of command on every conceivable subject of human thought. *James Russell Lowell, "Democracy," 1884.*

All the news that's fit to print. *Adolph S. Ochs first printed this slogan on the editorial page of* **The New York Times** *October 25, 1896.*

. . . in recent years, both print and broadcast journalism have been the subject of a growing if irrational suspicion—sometimes expressed in high places—that the press is somehow to blame for unhappy events and trends, merely because it performs its duty of reporting them. *CBS Chairman William S. Paley, December 7, 1976.*

We live under a government of men and morning newspapers. *Wendell Phillips, January 28, 1852.*

As cold waters to a thirsty soul, so is good news from a far country. **Proverbs, 25:25.**

The men with the muckrakes are often indispensable to the well-being of society; but only if they know when to stop raking the muck . . . *President Theodore Roosevelt, April 14, 1906.*

Nobody likes the bearer of bad news. *Sophocles,* **Antigone,** *about 440 B.C.*

It is a newspaper's duty to print the news, and raise hell. *Wilbur F. Storey, editor of the* **Chicago Times,** *statement of editorial purpose, 1861.*

When we hear news we should always wait for the sacrament of confirmation. *Voltaire, letter to Le Comte d'Argental, August 28, 1760.*

Anonymous aphorisms:

Freedom of the press is a right; freedom from the press is an illusion.

News is where you find it.

Bad news travels fast.

No news is good news.

Journalism consists of producing headlines against deadlines.

It isn't news until it's reported.

News is instant history.

Anecdotage:

"Where is your story on the big game today?" the editor asked the new reporter. "I did not write it," said the reporter, "because the game was called off when the stadium collapsed." "Then where is the story on the stadium collapse?" "That wasn't my assignment."

To illustrate the fact that each day's news is reported in the perspective of the day, journalism professors like to tell the story of successive days' headlines in a Parisian gazette on Napoleon's escape from Elba. The day the news came the headline spoke of the Corsican Monster. Two days later he was the Pretender. Then he was Bonaparte and finally the headline said "His Imperial Majesty Will Be in Paris Tomorrow."

"My father," said the boy proudly, "has been in the newspaper business for 30 years." "What does he do?" the boy was asked. "Oh, he sells them at his stand on the corner."

Facts:

Journalism is considered a relatively modern innovation, which flowered at the time of the American Revolution. Freedom of the press was largely an American product, and journalism has been more varied and more free in this country than anyplace else on earth. Although the number of daily newspapers has been reduced in the age of broadcasting, there are still more daily newspapers in this country than in any other. With some 1700 daily papers, 8,000 weekly newspapers and 8,000 broadcasting stations, the multiplicity of journalistic voices in the U.S. far surpasses the rest of the world. The newspapers of largest circulation in the world, however, are not in the U.S. They are nationally circulated newspapers in such other countries as the U.S.S.R., Japan and the United Kingdom. Journalism used to be a profession that one learned only from experience, but today there are hundreds of schools and departments of journalism in colleges and universities; a number of them award advanced degrees.

The annual *Editor & Publisher Yearbook* offers interesting statistics on the newspaper as an American institution.

JUSTICE

(See also Courts, Law)

Definitions: the administration of law; that which is just and right; "the crowning glory of the virtues" (*Cicero*); "the great standing policy of civil society" (*Edmund Burke*); "truth in action" (*Joseph Joubert*).

Quotations:

Peace and justice are two sides of the same coin. *President Dwight D. Eisenhower, February 6, 1957.*

One man's justice is another's injustice. *Ralph Waldo Emerson,* **Essays, First Series:** *Circles, 1841.*

Eye for eye, tooth for tooth, hand for hand, foot for foot. **Exodus,** *21:24.*

. . . moderation in the pursuit of justice is no virtue. *Arizona Senator Barry M. Goldwater, speech accepting Republican Presidential nomination in San Francisco, July 16, 1964.*

Justice delayed is democracy denied. *Robert F. Kennedy, "To Secure These Rights," 1964.*

The love of justice in most men is only the fear of suffering injustice. *François, Duc de La Rochefoucauld,* **Maxims,** *17th century.*

Why should there not be a patient confidence in the ultimate justice of the people? Is there any better or equal hope in the world? *President Abraham Lincoln, first Inaugural Address, March 4, 1861.*

Yet shall I temper so/Justice with mercy. *John Milton,* **Paradise Lost,** *1667.*

. . . this even-handed justice. . . *William Shakespeare,* **Macbeth,** *1606*

Expedience and justice frequently are not even on speaking terms. *Michigan Senator Arthur H. Vandenberg, March 8, 1945.*

Justice, sir, is the great interest of man on earth. It is the ligament which holds civilized beings and civilized nations together. *Daniel Webster, September 12, 1845.*

Judging from the main portions of the history of the world, so far, justice is always in jeopardy. *Walt Whitman,* **Democratic Vistas,** *1870.*

Justice has nothing do with expediency. *President Woodrow Wilson, February 26, 1916.*

Anonymous aphorisms:

Justice wears different faces for different people.

Justice is blind.

Justice is done as often as anybody is done.

He couldn't get justice so he went to court.

Everyone sees his own cause as just.

Justice often satisfies neither side.

Justice can always be found in court, even if sometimes it is only the title of the official on the bench.

Justice always needs a friend at court.

Anecdotage:

We all define justice the same way in the abstract, said the scholarly judge, but we are bound to differ in the concrete. For example, ask the two parties in the case I just decided what they thought of the verdict, and I think you'll find that they have different concepts. So the two parties were asked about the verdict. "That's justice," said one. And the other asked, "that's justice?"

"Justice," says a lawyer of our acquaintance, "is like meat. Everybody comes into court to see justice done, but some want it rare, some medium and some well done."

"Excuse," said the jury foreman to the judge, "but we have a question of law. What is justice?" "That's not a question of law," said the judge, "it's a question of judgment."

Facts:

Justice is one of the first functions of any society, whether it is dispensed on the basis of free and fair trial or by dictatorial fiat, and whether it is in fact just or not. The administration of justice cealls for a vast machinery: in the U.S. there are well over 300,000 lawyers and thousands of courts, as well as correctional institutions and law enforcement agencies. It involves guarantees not only of basic rights, fairness of evidence and the machinery for appeals to higher jurisdictions, but also a system of checks and balances in the selection of judges, a requirement for jury trials in various kinds of cases and, above all, constant reaffirmation of the basic principles of justice embodied in the Constitution.

There are numerous organizations dedicated to insuring justice through adequate legal representation (the Legal Aid Society, for example), through seeking protection of the interests of particular groups (as for example the American Association of Retired Persons or the National Association for the Advancement of Colored People) and through the normal voicings of conscience by religious groups.

KNOWLEDGE

Definitions: direct perception; understanding or cognition; a body of information; that which has been learned and remembered; "the only elegance" (*Ralph Waldo Emerson*); "the great sun in the firmament" (*Daniel Webster*); "the amassed thought and experience of innumerable minds" (*Ralph Waldo Emerson*); "a species of money" *Jean Jacques Rousseau*).

Quotations:

Knowledge is power. *Sir Francis Bacon,* **Religious Meditations,** *Of Heresies, 1597.*

Knowledge is the only good, and ignorance the only evil. *Diogenes Laertes,* **Lives of the Philosophers:** *Socrates, probably around 200 A.D.*

To be conscious that you are ignorant is a great step to knowledge. *Benjamin Disraeli,* **Sybil,** *1845.*

We are wiser than we know. *Ralph Waldo Emerson,* **Essays, First Series:** *The Over-Soul, 1841.*

Knowledge is the antidote to fear . . . *Ralph Waldo Emerson,* **Society and Solitude:** *Courage, 1870.*

To be proud of knowledge is to be blind with light. *Benjamin Franklin,* **Poor Richard's Almanac,** *1756.*

Knowledge and timber shouldn't be much used till they are seasoned. *Oliver Wendell Holmes,* **The Autocrat of the Breakfast-Table,** *1858.*

It is the province of knowledge to speak and it is the privilege of wisdom to listen. *Oliver Wendell Holmes,* **The Poet at the Breakfast-Table,** *1872.*

I think by far the most important bill in our whole code, is that for the diffusion of knowledge among the people. No other sure foundation can be devised, for the preservation of freedom and happiness. *Thomas Jefferson, letter to George Wythe, August 13, 1786.*

The gathering of knowledge is the supreme achievement of man. *President Lyndon B. Johnson, January 22, 1964.*

Promote then as an object of primary importance, institutions for the general diffusion of knowledge. In proportion as the structure of a government gives force to public opinion, it is essential that public opinion be enlightened. *President George Washington, Farewell Address, September 1796.*

Anonymous aphorisms:

What you don't know can hurt you.

He that knows little soon repeats it.

The most important thing to know is what you don't know.

If you don't know, ask.

We know so many things that aren't so.

The more you know, the more you want to know more.

The person who thinks he knows everything has a lot to learn.

Anecdotage:

At a dinner for U.S. winners of the Nobel Prize in 1962, President John F. Kennedy remarked: "I think this is the most extraordinary collection of talent, of human knowledge, that has ever been gathered together at the White House—with the possible exception of when Thomas Jefferson dined alone."

Every time somebody asked Mr. Jones a question he couldn't answer he would say something like, "I think you'll have to find that out for yourself" or "look it up yourself" or "ask somebody with more time to explain it to you." His problem, of course, was that he didn't know how to say he didn't know.

Facts:

The world's store of knowledge is growing at an ever-increasing rate of speed, partly because more people are working to find out more things than ever before, partly because they have better means of learning than ever before, such as the computer. In chemistry, for example, we have discovered new elements that nobody ever knew existed. In astronomy and planetary science we have had machines dig up samples of the soil on planets that previous generations could never reach. We can store more in a room of microfilm than the entire array of knowledge in the great library of Alexandria, and scan it quicker. It has been estimated that in the space of a single generation, the world will have four times as much knowledge as it has today and more than 90 percent of what will be known 50 years from now is unknown today. There is a simple way to illustrate the march of knowledge. Take an old edition of your favorite encyclopaedia and compare it to a new one. Pick a sample volume from each and see how many more entries there are in the newer one. And think of what additional knowledge we will have when fiber optics, transistors, and cellular structure are better utilized.

LABOR

(See also Jobs)

Definitions: work; collective word for those who are organized employees; those who are salaried; unions; the working class; horny-handed sons of toil (*Denis Kearney*).

Quotations:

There can be no distress, there can be no hard times, when labor is well paid. The man who raises his hand against the progress of the workingman raises his hand against prosperity. *W. Bourke Cockran, speech in New York, August 18, 1896.*

There is no right to strike against the public safety by anybody, anywhere, any time. *Governor Calvin Coolidge, telegram on strike by Boston police, September 14, 1919.*

Honest labour bears a lovely face. *Thomas Dekker,* **Patient Grissell**, *1603.*

The right to work, I had assumed, was the most precious liberty that man possesses. *Associate Justice William O. Douglas of Supreme Court, dissent in* **Barsky v. Regents,** *April 26, 1954.*

Take not from the mouth of labor the bread it has earned. *President Thomas Jefferson, Inaugural Address, March 4, 1801.*

I like work: it fascinates me. I can sit and look at it for hours. *Jerome K. Jerome,* **Three Men in a Boat**, *1889.*

American labor, whenever it gathers, does so with love for its flag and country and loyalty to its government. *New York Mayor Fiorello H. LaGuardia, speech at Chicago World's Fair, Labor Day, September 3, 1934.*

No man is born into the world whose work/Is not born with him...*James Russell Lowell, "A Glance Behind the Curtain," 1843.*

Far and away the best prize that life offers is the chance to work hard at work worth doing. *President Theodore Roosevelt, September 7, 1903.*

. . . work saves us from three great evils: boredom, vice and need. *Voltaire,* **Candide,** *1759.*

Anonymous aphorisms:

Labor is a working combination.

One man's labor is another man's capital.

The real secret power of labor is that it works.

Labor is a striking phenomenon.

In unions there is a strength.

Organized labor is a big business.

Labor is the ultimate power of the people.

Anecdotage:

Why are members of unions supposed to refer to their fellow members as brothers and sisters? Because they're all waiting for the same cry of "uncle."

Years ago a middle aged man in working clothes used to come religiously to every free evening lecture at Cooper Union in New York, no matter what the subject. No matter who the lecturer was, this same man would always rise to ask the same question, and it always elicited an answer. The question always was: "Now, all this that you've been telling us, is it good or bad for the working man?"

Labor and capital have opposite views of collective bargaining. Labor puts the accent on the first part of the phrase: collect. Capital is more interested in the second part, the word whose first two syllables say bar gain.

Facts:

Between 1940 and 1968, union membership in the U.S. more than doubled. Thereafter, there was a period of plateau. The growth was due in large measure to success in organizing the previously unorganized, and in gaining contracts in fields such as public education where there had not previously been union agreements. The growth of labor unionism in this country has been promoted by a variety of factors, ranging in some instances from management's insensibility to the demands of workers to favorable laws enacted by political bodies responsive to their labor constituencies. In addition to the growth of labor unions, labor has won a steadily greater degree of government protection as far as minimum wages, basic working conditions and fair employment practices are concerned. At times, however, organized labor has found itself part of the establishment, confronted with demands from working people. This has been true in the case of the efforts of minorities to obtain union membership and employment in industries where a closed union shop controls the jobs. Labor has also, as the custodian of various pension and welfare plans, found itself somewhat a part of capital management and the investment group. Not all labor unions are "horny handed sons of toil." The so-called talent unions—actors, musicians, dramatists, for example—have salary scales far beyond those of some of their brethren in the labor movement.

For a helpful list of unions, see the material provided by the U.S. Bureau of Labor Statistics or the AFL-CIO in the leading annual almanacs.

LANGUAGE

Definitions: oral or printed combinations of words to convey messages from one being to another; the vehicle of communication between people; tongue; the way human beings express thoughts to each other; a distinctive vocabulary understood by a definable group of people; "the archives of history" (*Ralph Waldo Emerson*).

Quotations:

All words are pegs to hang ideas on. *Reverend Henry Ward Beecher*, **Proverbs from Plymouth Pulpit**, *1887.*

It is with language as with manners: they are both established by the usage of people of fashion...*Lord Chesterfield*, **Letters to His Son**, *April 5, 1754.*

Language gradually varies, and with it fade away the writings of authors who have flourished their allotted time . . . *Washington Irving*, **The Sketch Book:** *The Mutability of Literature, 1820.*

I am sorry when any language is lost, because languages are the pedigree of nations. *Samuel Johnson, September 18, 1773 (quoted by James Boswell in* **Journal of a Tour to the Hebrides with Samuel Johnson, LL.D.***)*

Man does not live by words alone, despite the fact that sometimes he has to eat them. *Democratic Presidential nominee Adlai E. Stevenson, speech in Denver, September 5, 1952.*

It is the man who determines what is said, not the words. *Henry D. Thoreau,* **Journal,** *July 11, 1840.*

Language, as well as the faculty of speech, was the immediate gift of God. *Noah Webster, preface to* **American Dictionary of the English Language**, *1828.*

Wondrous the English language, language of live men...*Walt Whitman, "As I Sat Alone," 1856.*

Anonymous aphorisms:

The test of your command of language is whether you can describe a spiral staircase or a bathing beauty without using your hands.

More people have been hurt by words than by guns.

Language sometimes interferes with communication.

Talk is cheap and silence is golden.

Watch your language.

Harsh words are hard to heal.

Choose your words or your words will keep you from being chosen.

Anecdotage:

Three cows were grazing in a pasture. The first one said "Moo!" The second one said "Moooo!." The third one barked. "See," said the proud farmer, "she speaks another language."

An American college student was assigned a dormitory room with a young Englishman. The American's father asked how he liked rooming with the Englishman. "Except for the one standing argument," said the student, "it's fine." "What's the argument?" "Each of us accuses the other of having an accent."

Two men were having a very heated discussion. Both were very voluble and neither was having much success with convincing the other. Finally one clenched his fist and hit the other on the jaw, knocking him down. The fallen gentleman looked up and said, "Why didn't you say that in the first place?"

Facts:

Language is a fluid and changing art. Most modern languages are derived from earlier versions which we would find hard to understand today; and it is hard enough to understand other people's accents and dialects in our own mother tongue. All told, the world today has more than 150 languages characterized as major, and we can't even agree on the alphabets we use to record them. The top five are Chinese, English, Russian, Spanish and Hindi, in terms of the number of people who speak them, followed by Bengali, Arabic, Japanese and German. Surprisingly, Portugese is the mother tongue of more people than French, although French is one of the major languages of international communication. One of the marks of a vigorous language is that it adds new words and new shades of meaning. That is why, for example, different generations sometimes have trouble understanding each other even when they think they are both speaking the same language. The slang of one group of people can be virtually unintelligible to their language compatriots. In your local library or book store, you will find specialized dictionaries of ethnic English, hobby group English (such as Citizen's Band language) and the like. For a list of the current languages of the world, see the principal annual almanacs, such as the World Almanac.

LAW

(See also Courts, Justice, Law and Order)

Definitions: rule of conduct established and enforced by government; the body of such rules; the process and practice of administering such rules; the professional practice of the law; "the last result of human wisdom acting upon human experience for the benefit of the public" (*Samuel Johnson*).

Quotations:

. . . you cannot live without the lawyers, and certainly you cannot die without them. *Joseph H. Choate, speech in New York, May 13, 1879.*

Laws must be justified by something more than the will of the majority. They must rest on the eternal foundation of righteousness. *Calvin Coolidge, January 7, 1914.*

Anyone who takes it on himself, on his own authority, to break a bad law, thereby authorizes everybody else to break the good ones. *Denis Diderot,* **Supplement to the Voyage of Bougainville,** *1796.*

Law is not self-executing. Unfortunately, at times its execution rests in the hands of those who are faithless to it. And even when its enforcement is committed to those who revere it, law merely deters some human beings from offending, and punishes other human beings for offending. This does not make men good. This task can be performed only by ethics or religion or morality. *North Carolina Senator Sam J. Ervin, Jr., statement as Chairman of Senate Watergate Committee with its final report, July 12, 1974.*

Laws too gentle are seldom obeyed; too severe, seldom executed. *Benjamin Franklin,* **Poor Richard's Almanac,** *1756.*

There are not enough jails, not enough policeman, not enough courts to enforce a law not supported by the people. *Vice President Hubert H. Humphrey, May 1, 1965.*

. . . a strict observance of the written laws is doubtless *one* of the high duties of a good citizen, but it is not the *highest*. The laws of necessity, of self-preservation, of saving our country when in danger, are of higher obligation. *Thomas Jefferson, letter to John B. Colvin, September 20, 1810.*

Our nation is founded on the principal that observance of the law is the eternal safeguard of liberty and defiance of the law is the surest road to tyranny. *President John F. Kennedy, September 20, 1962.*

Ye shall have one manner of law, as well for the stranger, as for one of your own country. **Leviticus** *24:22*.

Wherever Law ends, Tyranny begins. *John Locke,* **Two Treatises of Government,** *1690.*

Ignorance of the law excuses no man; not that all men know the law, but because 'tis an excuse every man will plead, and no man can tell how to confute him. *John Selden,* **Table Talk***: Equity, 1689 (published in that year, although he had died 35 years before).*

To make laws that man cannot, and will not obey, serves to bring all law into contempt. *Elizabeth Cady Stanton, testimony before New York State Senate Judiciary Committee, 1861.*

Anonymous aphorisms:

A lawyer's briefs aren't.

A government of law is a government of lawyers.

Necessity hath no law.

A lawsuit helps keep the lawyers clothed.

The more laws the more offenders.

Law is a bottomless pit.

God save us from a lawyer's etceteras.

Anecdotage:

Two angels in heaven had a furious argument and decided to go to higher authority to get it settled; they asked St. Peter where they could get lawyers to plead their case. "You'll have to ask for a change of venue," said St. Peter, "we don't get the lawyers up here."

A doctor and a lawyer were discussing the merits of their respective professions. "In my profession," said the doctor, "we cure people." "And in mine," said the lawyer, "we probate your failures."

In a backward kingdom the King issued a law that ordered the sun to stand still. The sun, of course, continued to rise and set in its accustomed way. The King was furious, but when his counsellors tried to explain to him that it was his law, not the sun, that was at fault, he refused to accept this fact. "Ignorance of the law," he said, "is no excuse."

Facts:

It is said that even in a primitive society there is medicine, but law comes with civilization. In that case, the United States is becoming more civilized all the time, not only because we have more laws but because we are steadily acquiring more lawyers. At the turn of the century, the proportion of the American population in the legal profession was less than .09 percent, less than one lawyer per 1,000 people. Today, it is about one lawyer for every 500 people. The same trend has been evident in most of the principal Occidental nations. Some of this is due to the fact that the government keeps adding more laws to the books, providing more reasons for litigation. Part of the reason is that the opportunities to go to law school have been broadened, particularly for minorities and women. And part of the reason is that the profession of the law has become, more than ever before, a good means of entry into both government and business management.

Your local bar association library can provide pertinent statistics on the growth of the profession both in your area and throughout the nation. The American Bar Association is located at 1155 East 60th Street, Chicago, Illinois 60637.

LAW AND ORDER

(See also Crime, Justice, Law, Violence)

Definitions: the absence of crime in an orderly society; the protection of the rights of law-abiding citizens and of their safety; safe streets and safe homes.

Quotations:

Law is order, and good law is good order. *Aristotle,* **Politics,** *c. 330 B.C.*

Of all the tasks of government, the most basic is to protect its citizens against violence. *Secretary of State John Foster Dulles, April 22, 1957.*

History shows us, demonstrates that nothing, nothing prepares the way for tyranny more than the failure of public officials to keep the streets safe from bullies and marauders. *Senator Barry M. Goldwater of Arizona, accepting Republican Presidential nomination in San Francisco, July 16, 1964.*

Law enforcement cannot succeed without the sustained—and informed— interest of all citizens. It is not enough to reflect our concern over the rise in crime by seeking out single answers or simple answers. The people will get observance of the law and enforcement of the law if they want it, insist on it, and participate in it. *President Lyndon B. Johnson, message to Congress, March 8, 1965.*

There is no greater wrong in our democracy than violent, willful disregard of law. *President Lyndon B. Johnson, August 15, 1965.*

There is no grievance that is a fit object of redress by mob law. *Abraham Lincoln, speech in Springfield, Illinois, January 27, 1838.*

The age of the social conscience, social justice and concern seems to have coincided with the age of crime, pornography, mugging and international terrorism. What started out as a liberalization of restrictive social conventions seems to have developed into a dictatorship of license. *Prince Philip of Great Britain, October 17, 1977.*

Anonymous aphorisms:

Law and order are not necessarily partners.

The best protection for people on a street is a lot of other people on the street.

Many of those who call for law and order mean the old order.

Law and order are far surer when they reflect the popular will than when imposed upon a dissident public.

The value of law and order depends on whose law it is, and who gives the order.

When you read the riot act, be prepared to enforce it.

A vigilante is the product of not keeping a sharp enough vigil and having to raise the ante.

Anecdotage:

The leader of a mob attacking the town jail to get hold of a hated prisoner told the sheriff, "We're taking the law into our own hands." "If it's in your own hands," said the sheriff, "it isn't the law. Nobody owns the law." "Oh, yeah," said the mob leader, "you seem to think you own it." "No," said the sheriff, quietly, "the law owns me."

"How can you have law and order and still have a democracy?" a foreign dictator asked an American visitor. "It depends," said the American, "on who orders the law."

Facts:

Throughout American history there have been challenges to law and order, ranging from Shays' Rebellion to the excesses of the Barbary Coast in San Francisco to the era of lynchings to the student rebellions and anti-war demonstrations of only a few years ago. It becomes clear that our society has succeeded more in defusing the violence and intimidation of mob action than in solving the problems of criminal attacks on the individual citizen. The great dilemma in safeguarding law and order is to maintain decent order without offending the law. We are still fighting the battle of keeping people from taking the law into their own hands. To that end, governments have steadily expanded the ways the individual citizen can have recourse to public help in protecting his rights and safety.

The problem is that in expanding individual freedom we have had, of necessity, to limit the freedom of government. In an earlier era, it was commonplace to say that law and order was enforced by the policeman's nightstick; but today the use of the nightstick has been circumscribed to protect individual citizens' rights. At different positions in the law and order spectrum can be found such organizations as the American Civil Libertites Union, 22 East 40 Street, New York, N.Y. 10016, and the National Council on Crime and Delinquency, 411 Hackensack Avenue, Hackensack, New Jersey 07601.

LEADERSHIP

Definitions: the ability, duties or act of leading; the art of directing and guiding others; the ship that leads the way.

Quotations:

There are men, who, by their sympathetic attractions, carry nations with them, and lead the activity of the human race. *Ralph Waldo Emerson,* **The Conduct of Life***: Power, 1860.*

The American people want leadership which believes in them, not leadership which berates them. *President Lyndon B. Johnson, October 14, 1964.*

In time of peril, like the needle to the lodestone, obedience, irrespective of rank, generally flies to him who is best fitted to command. *Herman Melville,* **White Jacket***, 1850.*

No man is fit to command another that cannot command himself. *William Penn,* **No Cross, No Crown***, 1669.*

People ask the difference between a leader and a boss...The leader works in the open, and the boss in covert. The leader leads, and the boss drives. *Theodore Roosevelt, October 24, 1910.*

Reason and judgement are the qualities of a leader. *Tacitus,* **Histories,** *c. 116 A.D.*

Anonymous aphorisms:

You can always tell a leader, but you can't tell him much.

Before a leader can come first, he has to come forth.

Judge a leader by the followers.

Take me to your leader.

In any group of people, a small fraction will be leaders, a larger fraction will be followers and a substantial proportion just won't want to get involved.

Leadership is the only ship that doesn't pull into a safe port in a storm.

Leadership casts a long shadow.

Anecdotage:

President John F. Kennedy told the story of "the leader in the French Revolution who said, 'There go my people. I must find out where they are going so I can lead them.' "

Harry Truman, lecturing at Columbia University, provided a down-to-earth definition of political leadership. He said, "When a leader is in the Democratic Party he's a boss; when he's in the Republican Party he's a leader." Mr. Truman, of course, had his tongue in his cheek. He also once commented on the tactics of Republican leadership as being, "If you can't convince them, confuse them."

LEISURE
(See also Hobbies and various sports)

Definitions: time free from work; activities pursued for entertainment or relaxation: spare time; rest and relaxation.

Quotations:

There can be no high civilization where there is not ample leisure. *Reverend Henry Ward Beecher,* **Proverbs from Plymouth Pulpit,** *1887.*

Increased means and increased leasure are the two civilizers of man. *Benjamin Disraeli, April 3, 1872.*

A life of leisure and a life of laziness are two things. *Benjamin Franklin,* **Poor Richard's Almanac,** *1746.*

No man is so methodical as a complete idler, and none so scrupulous in measuring out his time as he whose time is worth nothing. *Washington Irving,* **Wolfert's Roost,** *"My French Neighbor," 1855.*

All intellectual improvement arises from leisure...*Samuel Johnson, April 13, 1773 (per James Boswell).*

Idle folks have the least leisure. *John Ray,* **English Proverbs,** *1670.*

He enjoys true leisure who has time to improve his soul's estate. *Henry D. Thoreau,* **Journal,** *February 11, 1840.*

In itself and in its consequences the life of leisure is beautiful and ennobling in all civilized men's eyes. *Thorstein Veblen,* **The Theory of the Leisure Class,** *1899.*

Anonymous aphorisms:

Half a loaf is better than not loafing at all.

Some people merely spend their leisure time; others enjoy it.

The busiest people have the most leisure—or get the most out of it.

The best way to appreciate leisure is to work hard for it.

Time to spare spares the soul.

All work and no play isn't much better than all play and no work.

Anecdotage:

"Would you care to define your leisure activities?" "Nothing doing."

Once there was a man whose job entailed carpentry day after day. A friend called on him at home one day and found him busy in his workshop, doing more carpentry. "What kind of leisure activity is that?" the friend asked, "it's the same thing you do to earn a living." "Yes," said the carpenter, "but here I am able to hang around my own joints."

Facts:

There are two principal reasons for the proliferation of leisure activities. The first and most important is that the average American has more time for leisure. In production, labor saving devices have cut the working hours; in industry in the U.S. the average weekly hours worked was 39.8 in 1950, and 35.7 in 1975. Improvements in transportation—more ownership of cars, better roads, speedier air travel—have increased the availability of leisure time activities too. Finally, the wisdom of medicine is spreading the gospel that relaxation, the pursuit of a hobby, can be good for your health.

LIBERTY

Definitions: freedom; "the right to do what the laws allow" (*Charles de Secondat Montesquieu*); absence from restraint; the original free-for-all.

Quotations:

The greatest dangers to liberty lurk in insidious encroachment by men of zeal, well-meaning but without understanding. *Associate Justice Louis D. Brandeis of the Supreme Court, dissent in* **Olmstead v. U.S.**, *June 4, 1928.*

Now, we Americans understand freedom. We have earned it; we have lived for it, and we have died for it. This nation and its people are freedom's models in a searching world. We can be freedom's missionaries in a doubting world. *Arizona Senator Barry M. Goldwater, accpeting Republican Presidential nomination in San Francisco, July 16, 1964.*

Give me liberty or give me death! *Patrick Henry, speech to the Virginia Assembly, March 23, 1775.*

The very aim and end of our institutions is just this: that we may think what we like and say what we think. *Oliver Wendell Holmes,* **The Professor at the Breakfast-Table,** *1860.*

The most stringent protection of free speech would not protect a man in falsely shouting fire in a theatre and causing a panic. *Associate Justice Oliver Wendell Holmes, Jr., of the Supreme Court, decision in* **Schenck v. U.S.,** *March 3, 1919.*

If there is any principle of the Constitution that more imperatively calls for attachment than any other it is the principle of free thought—not free thought for those who agree with us but freedom for the thought we hate . . . *Associate Justice Oliver Wendell Holmes, Jr., of the Supreme Court, dissent in* **U.S. v. Schwimmer,** *May 27, 1929.*

It behooves every man who values liberty of conscience for himself, to resist invasions of it in the case of others . . . *President Thomas Jefferson, letter to Dr. Benjamin Rush, April 21, 1803.*

Where the press is free and every man able to read, all is safe. *Thomas Jefferson, letter to Charles Yancey, 1816.*

It has been observed that they who most loudly clamour for liberty do not most liberally grant it. *Samuel Johnson,* **Lives of the English Poets,** *Milton, 1779.*

Our reliance is in the love of liberty which God has planted in us. Our defense is in the spirit which prized liberty as the heritage of all men, in all lands everywhere. Destroy this spirit and you have planted the seeds of despotism at your own doors. *Abraham Lincoln, speech in Edwardsville, Illinois, September 11, 1858.*

Four score and seven years ago our fathers brought forth on this continent a new nation, conceived in liberty and dedicated to the proposition that all men are created equal. *President Abraham Lincoln, address at Gettysburg, Pennsylvania, November 19, 1863.*

. . . that this nation, under God, shall have a new birth of freedom...*ibid.*

Since the general civilization of mankind, I believe that there are more instances of the abridgment of the freedom of the people by gradual and silent encroachments of those in power than by violent and sudden usurpations. *James Madison, speech to the Virginia Convention, June 16, 1788.*

. . . the freedom of the press is one of the great bulwarks of liberty, and can never be restrained but by despotic governments. *George Mason, Virginia Bill of Rights, adopted June 12, 1776.*

We look forward to a world founded upon four essential human freedoms. The first is freedom of speech and expression—everywhere in the world. The second is freedom of every person to worship God in his own way—everywhere in the world. The third is freedom from want . . . everywhere in the world. The fourth is freedom from fear . . . everywhere in the world. *President Franklin D. Roosevelt, message to Congress, January 6, 1941.*

My country, 'tis of thee,/Sweet land of liberty,/Of thee I sing:/Land where my father died,/Land of the pilgrims' pride,/From every mountain-side/Let freedom ring. *Reverend Dr. Samuel F. Smith, "America," 1831.*

A free press stands as one of the great interpreters between the government and the people. To allow it to be fettered is to fetter ourselves. *Associate Justice George Sutherland of the Supreme Court, decision in* **Grosjean v. American Press Co.,** *February 10, 1936.*

God grants liberty only to those who love it, and are always ready to guard and defend it. *Massachusetts Senator Daniel Webster, June 3, 1834.*

The history of liberty is a history of limitation of government power, not the increase of it. *New Jersey Governor Woodrow Wilson, 1912 (credited to several different dates and places).*

Anonymous aphorisims:

Nothing is more precious than freedom.

Better to be a free bird than a lion in chains.

Too often, liberty is not appreciated until it is taken away.

To protect your liberty, respect the liberty of others.

Liberty is the freedom of people you agree with; license is for those of other views.

Liberty is not free; it is paid for with good citizenship.

Anecdotage:

Why do they describe an actor who isn't working as being at liberty? Because his time is free.

At a town meeting, a couple of obstreperous citizens kept monopolizing the floor. Finally, one outraged townsman demanded to know whether they were on the town tax rolls. He was asked why and replied, "Because I don't think people should get liberty free."

Why is liberty symbolized by a statue of a lady with a torch? Because it is a thing of beauty that can only be seen when its light shines.

Facts:

Liberty is a perishable commodity. In the first half of the 1970s, freedom gained in such nations as Spain and Portugal, and declined in such countries as the Philippines. Freedom House, 20 West 40th Street, New York, N.Y., does an annual survey of the state of freedom in the world, and such organizations as the Reporters Committee for Freedom of the Press, in

Washington, and the national and state and city units of the American Civil Liberties Union also maintain current dossiers on the subject.

LIFE

(See also Nature)

Definitions: the condition or experience of existing as a human being; the way a person lives; the original one-way street; the first thing we get and the last we give up.

Quotations:

Life is an incurable disease. *Abraham Cowley, "To Dr. Scarborough," 1656.*

. . . for a living dog is better than a dead lion. **Ecclesiastes,** *9:4.*

Life is a series of surprises. *Ralph Waldo Emerson,* **Essays, First Series:** *Circles, 1841.*

Life is too short to waste/In critic peep or cynic bark,/Quarrel or reprimand;/ 'Twill soon be dark;/Up! mind thine own aim, and/God save the mark! *Ralph Waldo Emerson,* **Poems,** *To J.W., 1847.*

Tell me not in mournful numbers,/Life is but an empty dream!/For the soul is dead that slumbers,/And things are not what they seem./Life is real! Life is earnest!/And the grave is not its goal;/Dust thou art, to dust returnest,/Was not spoken of the soul. *Henry Wadsworth Longfellow, "A Psalm of Life," 1839.*

We breathe today the same air that Julius Caesar breathed. Thanks, however, to the recycling labors of chlorophyl-bearing plants on land and plankton in the sea, we can safely inhale the air that has already served a thousand emperors. *Chairman Russell W. Peterson of U.S. Council on Environmental Quality, September 29, 1976.*

As for man, his days are as grass: as a flower of the field, so he flourisheth. For the wind passeth over it, and it is gone; and the place thereof shall know it no more. **Psalms,** *103:15-16.*

Life's but a walking shadow, a poor player/That struts and frets his hour upon the stage/And then is heard no more: it is a tale/Told by an idiot, full of sound and fury,/Signifying nothing. *William Shakespeare,* **Macbeth,** *1606.*

Let us endeavor so to live that when we come to die even the undertaker will be sorry. *Mark Twain,* **The Tragedy of Pudd'nhead Wilson,** *1894.*

Why is it that we rejoice at a birth and grieve at a funeral? It is because we are not the person involved. *Ibid.*

...this world is a comedy to those who think, a tragedy to those who feel...*Horace Walpole, December 31, 1769.*

Anonymous aphorisms:

Life is what you make it.

Nobody gets out of life alive.

While there's life there's hope—and while there's hope there's life.

To everyone, life in the first person is a mystery.

Life is the same old story, but every individual reaches his own ending.

Life is the only thing worth living.

Life doesn't seem so bad when you consider the alternative.

Anecdotage:

George Washington Carver, the scientist who found so many worthwhile uses for the peanut, was credited with the story that when he was waxing philosophical he asked the Lord to explain the mystery of the universe and the secret of life, and the Lord told him such knowledge was not within the scope of human existence. "Well, then," said Mr. Carver, "what about the mystery of the peanut?" "That," said the Lord, "is closer to your size."

A young student enbarking on a career as a philosopher went into the mountains of the far Himalayas to speak to an elderly seer. He asked the sage, "Master, what is life?" The sage closed his eyes in thought for a few moments, then replied, "Life is the smell of a fresh new rose." "But, master," said the young student, "in the Andes an elderly Inca told me that life was a sharp stone." "That's *his* life," said the Himalayan sage.

LINCOLN

Definitions: Abraham Lincoln; 16th U.S. President; "The Great Emancipator"; "Honest Abe."

Quotations:

In him was vindicated the greatness of real goodness and the goodness of real greatness. *Reverend Phillips Brooks, sermon at Independence Hall, Philadelphia, April 1865.*

His heart was as great as the world, but there was no room in it to hold the memory of a wrong. *Ralph Waldo Emerson,* **Letters and Social Aims***: Greatness, 1876.*

There is a singular quality about Abraham Lincoln which sets him apart from all our other Presidents . . . a dimension of brooding compassion, of love for humanity; a love which was, if anything, strengthened and deepened by the agony that drove lesser men to the protective shelter of callous indifference. *President Lyndon B. Johnson, February 12, 1967.*

That nation has not lived in vain which has given the world Washington and Lincoln, the best great men and the greatest good men whom history can show. *Massachusetts Senator Henry Cabot Lodge, February 12, 1909.*

Here was a man to hold against the world,/A man to match the mountains and the sea. *Edwin Markham, "Lincoln, the Man of the People," 1901.*

. . . the well assured and most enduring memorial to Lincoln is invisibly there, today, tomorrow and for a long time yet to come in the hearts of lovers of liberty, men and women who understand that wherever there is freedom there have been those who fought, toiled and sacrificed for it. *Carl Sandburg, speech to joint session of Congress on Lincoln's 150th birthday, February 12, 1959.*

Now he belongs to the ages. *Secretary of War Edwin M. Stanton on the day Lincoln died, April 15, 1865.*

Oh Captain! My Captain! *Walt Whitman, "Oh Captain! My Captain!" 1865.*

Anonymous aphorisms:

Lincoln was a rail splitter; he was followed by hair splitters.

Only a man with the common touch would get his picture on the penny.

If Lincoln were alive today, he'd ride around in a Ford.

They called him Father Abraham because he kept the American family together.

Anecdotage:

Although the anecdotes told by and about Abraham Lincoln are endless, these two capture particularly his attitude toward life:

Adlai Stevenson recalled Lincoln's remark after losing an election. Lincoln said he felt like a youngster who had stubbed his toe, and was too old to cry, but it hurt too much to laugh.

Lincoln himself, when asked in the White House how it felt to be the President of the United States, told the story of the man who was tarred and feathered and ridden out of town on a rail. The man was asked how he felt about being treated that way and replied, "If it wasn't for the honor of the thing, I'd just as soon walk."

Facts:

Abraham Lincoln was the first martyred President, the last of the frontier Presidents (his successor, Andrew Johnson, was the only Chief Executive since Lincoln to be virtually entirely self-educated) and indubitably the most eloquent. If lay sainthood can be bestowed upon a leader, it has come closest to Lincoln. He is undoubtedly the President most depicted in drama, most often cited as an advocate of reconciliation and tolerance. In this context, the personal tragedies of his life—the family losses and difficulties which, along with the Civil War, etched those great lines on his familiar face—have become part of the drama which keeps Lincoln so familiar a figure to the people of America and the world. One place and several dates have always been particularly associated with him. The place, of course, is the magnificent Lincoln Memorial in Washington, D.C., dedicated in 1922. One date is February 12, Lincoln's birthday, which is celebrated more widely each year. He was born in Kentucky on that date in 1809. The other date which is closely tied to the remembrance of Lincoln is November 19, the anniversary of his dedication in 1863 of the National Cemetery at Gettysburg, when he delivered the immortal Gettysburg Address. Lincoln was shot by John Wilkes Booth at Ford's Theatre in Washington at a performance of "Our American Cousin" on the evening of April 14, 1865. He died shortly after seven the following morning.

LITERATURE

(See also Books)

Definitions: written compositions in prose or verse; the field of endeavor concerned with the writing, publication, preservation and study of such work; prose or verse collectively; the magic of words; "an investment of genius which pays dividends to all subsequent times" (*John Burroughs*).

Quotations:

Life comes before literature, as the material always comes before the work. The hills are full of marble before the world blooms with statues. *Reverend Phillips Brooks, "Literature and Life," late 19th century.*

All literature is yet to be written. *Ralph Waldo Emerson, "Literary Ethics," 1838.*

An old author is constantly rediscovering himself in the more or less fossilized productions of his earlier years. *Oliver Wendell Holmes,* **Over the Teacups**, *1891.*

The literary world is made up of little confederacies, each looking upon its own members as the lights of the universe; and considering all others as mere transient meteors, doomed soon to fall and be forgotten, while its own luminaries are to shine steadily on to immortality. *Washington Irving,* **Tales of a Traveller**: *Literary Life, 1824.*

It takes a great deal of history to produce a little literature. *Henry James,* **Hawthorne**, *1879.*

The chief glory of every people arises from its authors . . . *Samuel Johnson, Preface to* **A Dictionary of the English Language**, *1755.*

Our American professors like their literature clear and cold and pure and very dead. *Sinclair Lewis, speech accepting Nobel Prize for Literature in Stockholm, December 12, 1930.*

. . . poetry . . . says more, and in fewer words, than prose. *Voltaire,* **Philosophical Dictionary,** *1764.*

Anonymous aphorisms:

Literature is the art of words and the wordiest of the arts.

Write makes might.

Great books are the voices of their times; the greatest literature is timeless.

Literature bridges the centuries.

One man's letter is another man's literature.

Literature to be popular usually combines the shock of recognition and the recognition of shock.

Anecdotage:

A college student asked his adviser whether he could obtain permission to skip the compulsory course in English literature. "After all," he said, "it's nothing but dead books." "No," said the professor, "they aren't dead. Books are the living thoughts that dead people leave behind." "Well," said the student, "if books aren't dead, they are still too old—at least the ones in the literature course." "No," said his adviser, "they're not old. They're vintage."

The first person to write down a particular composition of words is an originator; then somebody else polishes his words, as an editor; then three or four more people do their own variations, switching names of characters, or settings; and finally somebody writes a learned treatise about all this. When you put all this work together, it is what we call literature.

What's the difference between today's best sellers and great literature? One or more generations.

Facts:

As the world grows more populous and more literate, and the frontiers of human experience and imagination expand, literature grows. Literature does not wither with time; some items may be outdated and become archaic, but great literature—of which the Bible is perhaps the greatest example—has lasting values. The opportunities and reward for literary effort in all its forms, playwriting, documentation, the novel, are greater than ever; but so is the competition. A best seller today sells more copies, at a higher price, than ever before in the history of literature. But the study of the history of literature, and of the literature of the past, is not high on the list of priorities for today's students. What has happened is that the formal study has become less attractive than the kind of self-study reflected in the tremendous surge in the purchase of reading materials. Literature began as a transcript of tales and comments heard around a primitive campfire. Literature today is once again relating to the continuity of experience from one generation to the next. The riches of literature past and present are more readily available today than ever before, in the age of the paperback reprint, the library and the used book exchange.

LONGEVITY

(See also Age)

Definitions: long duration of life; the condition of living a long time; the extent of the length of one's life; life expectancy; biology's holy grail.

Quotations:

'Tis very certain the desire of life/Prolongs it. *George Gordon Lord Byron,* **Don Juan,** *1819.*

I have been asked, "How do you grow old so easily?" I reply, "Very easily. I give all my time to it." *Representative Emanuel Celler of New York, comment as Dean of the House of Representatives on his 83rd birthday, May 6, 1971.*

Few envy the consideration enjoyed by the oldest inhabitant. *Ralph Waldo Emerson,* **Society and Solitude***: Old Age, 1870.*

Wish not so much to live long as to live well. *Benjamin Franklin,* **Poor Richard's Almanac,** *1738.*

All would live long, but none would be old. *Benjamin Franklin,* **Poor Richard's Almanac,** *1749. (See Swift quote below.)*

The longer thread of life we spin,/The more occasion still to sin. *Robert Herrick,* **Noble Numbers,** *1647.*

. . . whoever lives long must outlive those whom he loves and honours. Such is the condition of our present existence, that life must one time lose its associations, and every inhabitant of the earth must walk downward to the grave alone and unregarded, without any partner of his joy or grief, without any interested witness of his misfortunes or success. *Samuel Johnson,* **The Idler,** *January 27, 1759.*

. . . Age is opportunity no less/Than Youth itself, though in another dress. *Henry Wadsworth Longfellow, "Morituri Salutamus," 1874.*

Nobody loves life like an old man. *Sophocles,* **Acrisius,** *5th century B.C.*

Every man desires to live long; but no man would be old. *Jonathan Swift,* **Thoughts on Various Subjects,** *1711. (See Franklin quote above.)*

Anonymous aphorisms:

Life is habit forming.

Life has a certain ending and uncertain timing.

Long life is a gift that nobody gets to keep.

The people who live long are those who long to live.

The years in your life are less important than the life in your years.

Life should be measured by its breadth, not its length.

Anecdotage:

Old man Jones worried his children because he smoked regularly, partied enthusiastically and gambled frenziedly. "You're killing yourself," they warned him. "Then it must be a slow death," he replied, "because I've been doing it already for so many years."

"How come the ancient fathers in the Bible and even the dinosaurs lived so much longer than we do?" the professor was asked. "Because they didn't know they weren't supposed to," he replied.

The average elephant lives longer than the average human being, which proves that there may be something to working for peanuts; but some people think that it proves the secret of long life is a thick skin.

Facts:

The highest life expectancy rate in the history of the United States up to that time was recorded in 1975, when the average male baby could look forward to living 68.5 years and the newborn girl 76.4 years. These rates were 15 years higher for men and 22 years greater for women than in 1920. The longer life expectancy for females is worldwide, except in some parts of Asia where life expectancy generally is quite low. The explanation used to be that the males faced more pressures to their health from trying to support their families; but in the age of working women, when presumably the pressures of earning a living are greater upon them, the difference in life expectancy has grown. Nevertheless, statistics at best are generalizations. Longevity is somewhat a matter of heredity, somewhat a matter of circumstance—and somewhat a matter of fate.

The Statistical Yearbook of the United Nations, the Statistical Abstract of the U.S. and state and local health department reports can provide further details.

LOVE

(See also Marriage, Sex)

Definitions: strong affection; an emotional bond of mutual attraction; emotional attachment involving sexual desire; intimate concern for some person or thing; "the river of life in this world" (*Henry Ward Beecher*); what we keep by giving.

Quotations:

Whoso loves /Believes the impossible. *Elizabeth Barrett Browning*, **Aurora Leigh**, *1856*.

All mankind love a lover. *Ralph Waldo Emerson*, **Essays, First Series**; *Love*, *1841*.

Life's greatest happiness is to be convinced we are loved. *Victor Hugo*, **Les Miserables**, *1862*.

There is no fear in love; but perfect love casteth out fear . . . **I John** *4:18*.

There's nothing in this world so sweet as love,/And next to love the sweetest thing is hate. *Henry Wadsworth Longfellow*, **The Spanish Student**, *1842*.

The course of true love never did run smooth. *William Shakespeare*, **A Midsummer Night's Dream**, *1595*.

'Tis better to have loved and lost/Than never to have loved at all. *Alfred Tennyson*, **In Memoriam**, *1850*.

There is no remedy for love but to love more. *Henry D. Thoreau*, **Journal**, *July 25, 1839*.

Love conquers all. *Virgil*, **Eclogues**, *10, 37 B.C.*

. . . love has never known a law/Beyond its own sweet will. *John Greenleaf Whittier*, "*Amy Wentworth*," *1862*.

Men always want to be a woman's first love—women like to be a man's last romance. *Oscar Wilde*, **A Woman of No Importance**, *1893*.

Anonymous aphorisms:

All's fair in love and war.

Love makes the world go square.

The love that lasts is the love that's last.

Love will find a way.

Love and a cough cannot be hid.

The difference between love and lust is what makes the world go round in circles.

Love is blind.

Anecdotage:

A young man staggered into a small bakery just as it was opening at the crack of dawn on a miserable, stormy day. "Thank goodness you're open," he said, "I've been walking all over town looking for a place where I can get her the fresh blueberry buns she wants. I must have walked miles. And at last I find them—right here. She'll love them. Give me three." The clerk wrapped them and said, "Are these for your mother?" "Come on," said the young man, "would my mother send me out on a night like this? And would I go?"

"Love," said the devotee of romance, "is the last word." "Only in a telegram," said the cynic.

After their son came home and announced he had fallen in love at first sight with a girl he had just met, his mother said to his father, "What do you think of that?" "Well," said the father, "it's a great time-saver."

LOYALTY

Definitions: fidelity; faithfulness, consistent adherence to and support of a cause, principle or person; something that arouses oaths; the original high fidelity system.

Quotations:

Trust men and they will be true to you; treat them greatly, and they will show themselves great. *Ralph Waldo Emerson,* **Essays, First Series**: *Prudence, 1841.*

Enlightened loyalty requires that each citizen take the trouble to learn about, to discuss, to think through, the crucial issues of our time. *President Lyndon B. Johnson, Loyalty Day Proclamation, April 6, 1967.*

Since this country was founded, each generation of Americans has been summoned to give testimony to its national loyalty. *President John F. Kennedy, Inaugural Address, January 20, 1961.*

Statesman, yet friend to truth! of soul sincere,/In action faithful, and in honor clear;/Who broke no promise, serv'd no private end,/Who gain'd no title, and who lost no friend. *Alexander Pope,* **Moral Essays**, *VII, To Mr. Addison, 1720.*

. . . be thou faithful unto death, and I will give thee a crown of life. **The Revelation of St. John the Divine,** *2:10.*

. . . go on, and I will follow thee,/To the last gasp, with truth and loyalty. *William Shakespeare,* **As You Like It***, 1600.*

My kind of loyalty was loyalty to one's country, not to its institutions or its office-holders. *Mark Twain,* **A Connecticut Yankee in King Arthur's Court***, 1889.*

Loyalty to petrified opinion never yet broke a chain or freed a human soul. *Mark Twain, inscription in the Hall of Fame.*

I do solemnly swear (or affirm) that I will support and defend the Constitution of the United States against all enemies, foreign and domestic; that I will bear true faith and allegiance to the same; that I take this obligation freely, without any mental reservation or purpose of evasion, and that I will well and truthfully discharge the duties of the office on which I am about to enter. So help me God. *U.S. Oath of Office, adopted July 11, 1868.*

Anonymous aphorisms:

Loyalty is an animal instinct; we can take lessons in it from dogs.

Loyalty oaths are words, not deeds.

Loyalty can be blind but it can't be lame.

The best way to get loyalty is to give it.

Any loyalty that is bought can be bought away.

Anecdotage:

During one of those sedition scares an investigator came to the home of Mr. and Mrs. Smith. Mrs. Smith answered the door. "I'm here to find out what party Mr. Smith belongs to," the investigator said. "I'm the party he belongs to," said Mrs. Smith, and she slammed the door.

Mr. Brown always described himself as a loyal supporter of the local college football team, but a friend ran into him on the street when the team was playing a game. "I thought you were a loyal rooter," said the friend. "Oh," said Mr. Brown, "I root for them all the time, but I only go to see them when they're likely to win." "My loyalty," said Mr. Jones, "is a matter of principle. I can change it, of course, when the interest is raised."

Facts:

Few societies are immune to the idea that loyalty can be brought about by coercion. The Russians see "counter-revolutionaries" in their midst more often than we insist on loyalty oaths, but the Western democracies in the age of security-consciousness worry periodically about how to determine and insure the loyalty of their own key people. This is not a human characteristic of modern vintage. It existed among the ancient Greeks and in every other civilization. Different philosophies, of course, have different ideas of loyalty. In a dictatorship, loyalty is non-deviationism, no straying from the absolute party line. In a democracy, loyalty involves less absolute criteria. The U.S. Oath of Office, which is in essence a loyalty oath, was adopted after the Civil War. The Constitution to which it refers has freedom of conscience guaranteed in it; hence loyalty in this country has become a catchword referring more to reliability than to beliefs. In an age of complicated defense secrets involving thousands of people, the question of loyalty is a euphemism for the basic question of trustworthiness.

LUCK

Definitions: chance; fortune; the way the cookie crumbles; the roll of the dice; a failure's explanation for someone else's success; being at home when opportunity knocks.

Quotations:

Better be born lucky than rich. *John Clarke*, **Paroemiologia Anglo-Latina**, *1639*.

Shallow men believe in luck. *Ralph Waldo Emerson*, **The Conduct of Life: Worship**, *1860*.

Diligence is the mother of good luck. *Benjamin Franklin*, **Poor Richard's Almanac**, *1735*.

Luck is a mighty queer thing. All you know about it for certain is that it's bound to change. *Bret Harte, "The Outcasts of Poker Flat," 1869*.

True luck consists not in holding the best of the cards at the table:/Luckiest he who knows just when to rise and go home. *John Hay*, **Distichs**, *latter 19th century*.

Fortune never seems blinder than to those she doesn't favor. *Francois Duc de La Rochefoucauld*, **Maxims**, *1665*.

Fortune gives too much to many, but enough to none. *Martial*, **Epigrams**, *1st century*.

Luck never made a man wise. *Seneca*, **Moral Letters to Lucilius**, *65 A.D.*

Times go by turns, and chances change by course, From foul to fair, from better hap to worse. *Robert Southwell, "Times Go By Turns," about 1595*.

Anonymous aphorisms:

Luck is how the other guy made it.

He who puts his trust in luck is apt to end up putting himself in hock.

If you can't change your luck, change your game.

Not all luck is good, and not all good is luck.

Lucky at cards, unlucky at love.

~~The people who believe most in luck are those who lack it.~~

Luck often masquerades as wisdom.

Anecdotage:

No matter what happened to Tommy Brown, he always described it as pure luck. He decided to prospect for gold and went into the mountains through a bitter winter, nearly freezing to death as he kept looking for a golden vein in the rugged ground. Finally, as the ground thawed in the Spring and he was down to his last meagre ration of food and his mule was gasping its last, he broke into the earth in a likely looking spot and dug and dug until at last he hit a box. With no food left and his strength fast ebbing, a million miles from nowhere, he managed to lift the box out and open it. Inside was a carton of Army C rations. "Boy am I lucky," he said, "it could have been gold."

When Jane Jones, a beautiful, hard-working girl, married an ugly, shift-less man, her mother had a simple explanation. "Jane's bad luck was his good luck."

Facts:

Luck is one of humanity's names for the unexplainable. Other names are fate, chance, destiny. Throughout history we have sought to explain the unex-plainable things that happen to people. Religion, superstition, dream interpre-tation, mathematical odds formulas all are used to try to explain and to insure the smile of Lady Luck. We pray and we do things which we hope will "make things turn out better" for us. We base businesses on mankind's indomitable belief in luck—not merely gambling businesses and gaming tables and lot-teries, but also ventures which we go into "taking a chance" with venture capital. The selling of good luck charms and tokens is itself a steady business, and perhaps the best commentary is that the rabbit's foot which some people carry to bring them luck didn't do too well for the rabbit.

MAIL

Definitions: the postal system; letters and other material sent and delivered through the postal system; correspondence.

Quotations:

A Committee on the Post office, too, have found, a thousand difficulties. The Post is now very regular, from the North and South, altho it comes but once a Week. It is not easy to get faithfull Riders, to go oftener. The Expence is very high, and the Profits (so dear is every Thing, and so little Correspondence is carried on, except in franked Letters), will not Support the office. *John Adams, letter to Thomas Jefferson, May 26, 1977.*

The United States may give up the postoffice when it sees fit, but while it carries it on, the use of the mails is almost as much a part of free speech as the right to use our tongues. *Associate Justice Oliver Wendell Holmes, Jr., dissent in Supreme Court case of* **Milwaukee Social Democratic Publishing Company v. Burleson**, *1921.*

A short letter to a distant friend is, in my opinion, an insult like that of a slight bow or cursory salutation—a proof of unwillingness to do much, even where there is a necessity of doing something. *Samuel Johnson, letter to Joseph Baretti, June 10, 1761.*

The mailman is the agent of impolite surprises. *Friedrich Wilhelm Nietzsche,* **Human, All Too Human**, *1878.*

The postal service touches the lives of all Americans. Many of our citizens feel that today's service does not meet today's needs, much less the needs of tomorrow. I share this view. *President Richard M. Nixon, message to Congress, February 25, 1969.*

There is no Democratic or Republican way of delivering the mail. There is only the right way. *President Richard M. Nixon, message to Congress, May 27, 1969.*

Correspondences are like small-clothes before the invention of suspenders; it is impossible to keep them up. *Sydney Smith, letter to Mrs. Crowe, January 31, 1841.*

I never received more than one or two letters in my life—I wrote this some years ago—that were worth the postage. *Henry D. Thoreau,* **Walden:** *Where I lived and What I Lived For, 1854.*

Neither snow, nor rain, nor heat, nor gloom of night stays these couriers from the swift completion of their apponted rounds. *Inscription on Manhattan Post Office, adapted from "The Histories" of Herodotus.*

Anonymous aphorisms:

The way it comes through, they ought to call it partial post.

Some mail goes out under a frank and some ends up in a john.

The postal system has two sexes—mail and miss.

The mails must go through.

As welcome as a letter from home.

Anecdotage:

A goodwill ambassador for the Postmaster General was addressing a school class about the U.S. mail system. "What's the fastest thing in the Postal Service?" he asked. A boy in the back raised his hand and replied, "The fastest thing in the Postal Service is the way the rates go up."

A student of language wondered why the words for postal service and for a masculine human being sound so similar. His professor told him it was because both kinds of mail (male) have a lot of room for improvement.

A foreigner asked why the Post Office called its address system the Zip Code. The answer was because without the numbers you're apt to get zip.

What's the difference between a postage stamp and the postal system? You can lick the stamp but you can't lick the system.

Facts:

Back in 1966, President Lyndon B. Johnson reported that America was "generating mail at the rate of 76 billion pieces a year. That is more than all of the rest of the mail generated in the entire world combined." Since then, the Postal Service has been changed from a Cabinet department to an independent establishment of the executive branch. The Postmaster General is elected by the Board of Governors of the U.S. Postal Service. The Service still has the obligations and privileges which go with its governmental relationship. The privileges are principally related to the fact that the Postal Service is a chosen instrument. It monopolizes access to mail boxes; it is the instrument of international postal operations. The obligations are those, which come from being a chosen instrument—including the necessity of maintaining full postal service to communities where such business incurs a substantial loss. Under repeated Congressional mandates, the Postal Service has sought to become self-supporting, but without success. When it raises rates, which requires the approval of the Postal Rate Commission, it also raises public wrath. When it cuts its own services, or seeks to protect portions of them from the competition of private deliveries, it is also subjected to criticism.

MANNERS

Definitions: deportment; social conduct; the style and custom of social intercourse; civility with polish.

Quotations:

If a man be gracious, and courteous to strangers, it shows he is a citizen of the world . . . *Sir Francis Bacon,* **Essays:** *Of Goodness, 1597 or later.*

In the days of old/Men made the manners; manners now make men. *George Gordon Lord Byron,* **Don Juan,** *1824.*

Good manners are, to particular societies, what good morals are to society in general: their cement and their security. *Lord Chesterfield, letter to his son, November 3, 1749.*

Fine manners need the support of fine manners in others. *Ralph Waldo Emerson,* **The Conduct of Life:** *Behavior, 1860.*

Civility costs nothing, and buys everything. *Lady Mary Wortley Montagu, Letter to Countess of Bute, May 30, 1756.*

We cannot learn from one another until we stop shouting at one another—until we speak quietly enough so that our words can be heard as well as our voices. *President Richard M. Nixon, Inaugural Address, January 20, 1969.*

We meet at meals three times a day, and give each other a new taste of that old musty cheese that we are. We have had to agree on a certain set of rules, called etiquette and politeness, to make this frequent meeting tolerable and that we need not come to open war. *Henry D. Thoreau,* **Walden:** *Solitude, 1854.*

There are few things that so touch us with instinctive revulsion as a breach of decorum. *Thorstein Veblen,* **The Theory of the Leisure Class,** *1899.*

Anonymous aphorisms:

Other times, other manners.

You can learn good manners from the bad manners of others.

It takes good manners to put up with bad ones.

Knowing good manners depends on practicing them.

Man is judged by his manners more than by his looks.

Anecdotage:

The little boy at family dinner was asked whether he'd like some french fries, and he said, "yes." His mother said, "yes, what?" "Yes, before the meat," he answered.

An old grouch, about to enter a building, found that the door was being held open for him, with considerable effort, by a little boy. "Never mind that," said the old grouch, "I don't need your help." The little boy smiled up at him and said, "You're welcome."

MARRIAGE

(See also Love, Sex)

Definitions: the state of wedlock; the condition of having a husband or wife; the legal union of a man and woman; "the state or condition of a community consisting of a master, a mistress and two selves, making in all, two" (*Ambrose Bierce*); altar ego.

Quotations:

Can two walk together, except they be agreed? **Amos,** *3:3.*

. . . to have and to hold from this day forward, for better, for worse, for richer, for poorer, in sickness and in health, to love and to cherish, till death do us part. **Book of Common Prayer,** *Solemnization of Matrimony.*

One was never married, and that's his hell; another is, and that's his plague. *Robert Burton,* **The Anatomy of Melancholy,** *1621.*

Marriage is a feast where the grace is sometimes better than the dinner. *Charles Caleb Colton,* **Lacon,** *1820s.*

Every woman should marry—and no man. *Benjamin Disraeli,* **Lothair,** *1870.*

Is not marriage an open question, when it is alleged, from the beginning of the world, that such as are in the institution wish to get out, and such as are out wish to get in? *Ralph Waldo Emerson,* **Representative Men:** *Montaigne, 1850. (See also Montaigne quote below.)*

Where there's marriage without love, there will be love without marriage. *Benjamin Franklin,* **Poor Richard's Almanac,** *1734.*

Keep your eyes wide open before marriage, half shut afterwards. *Benjamin Franklin,* **Poor Richard's Almanac,** *1738.*

More belongs to marriage than four legs in a bed. *Thomas Fuller,* **Gnomologia,** *1732.*

I believe it will be found that those who marry late are best pleased with their children, and those who marry early with their partners. *Samuel Johnson,* **Rasselas,** *1759.*

What therefore God hath joined together, let not man put asunder. **Mark,** *10:9.*

Marriage may be compared to a cage: the birds outside frantic to get in and those inside frantic to get out. *Michel Eyquem de Montaigne,* **Essays, III,** *1588. (See Emerson quote above.)*

Marriage is popular because it combines the maximum of temptation with the maximum of opportunity. *George Bernard Shaw,* **Man and Superman,** *1903.*

Remember, it's as easy to marry a rich woman as a poor woman. *William M. Thackeray,* **Pendennis,** *1850.*

Anonymous aphorisms:

In the ideal marriage one partner is blind and the other deaf.

If a wife always laughs at her husband's jokes, is he funny or she smart?

Some people say marriage is an outmoded institution; the question is whether they want to rebuild it or tear it down.

Marriage is a mutual assistance pact.

Marriage may be made in heaven, but sometimes it can be hell on earth.

Marriage is an institution run by the inmates.

Marriage runs the risk of going from bed to worse.

Marriage is a union with a limited membership.

Marry in haste, repent at leisure.

Anecdotage:

Mr. and Mrs. Jones on their 75th wedding anniversary were asked what they felt their marriage had taught them. "Patience," said Mr. Jones; "Fortitude," said Mrs. Jones.

You never can tell about a marriage from the outside, said the old philosopher. Some couples hold hands because they're afraid that if they let go they'd kill each other.

When Dr. Samuel Johnson heard that a man who had survived one unhappy marriage had married for a second time, the good Doctor remarked that the remarriage was "the triumph of hope over experience."

Lady Nancy Astor, listening to Winston Churchill and growing more and more angry over the views he was expressing, said to him, "If you were my husband I'd put poison in your coffee." Churchill replied, "If I were your husband, I'd drink it."

Facts:

In the age when more and more young men and women are living together without the possession of a marriage certificate, divorces have been going up while marriage has been at a declining rate. In 1975, there were over a million divorces in the U.S. and the marriage rate was the lowest in the past four years. There were slightly more than two marriages for every divorce. Marriage in recent years has, if anything, become somewhat more difficult in the U.S. and divorce has become easier. Further, with the growth of community property laws and the acceptance of open non-married partnerships, as well as unmarried parenthood, the institution of marriage has become less attractive to some men and women. In the mid-1970s California had the highest ratio of divorces to marriages, and Nevada, once the divorce capital, had the lowest.

The World Almanac and Statistical Abstract of the United States contain comparative figures for the states, and historical figures as well.

MEDICINE
(See also Drugs, Health)

Definitions: the science, art or materials used in the treatment of prevention of illness and disease; the profession of providing medical treatment; the healers.

Quotations:

There are no such things as incurables, there are only things for which man has not found a cure. *Bernard Baruch, April 1954.*

. . . the only profession that labors incessantly to destroy the reason for its own existence. *James Bryce, March 23, 1914.*

God heals, and the doctor takes the fees. *Benjamin Franklin,* **Poor Richard's Almanac,** *1736.*

Into whatever houses I may enter I will go for the benefit of the sick and will abstain from every voluntary act of mischief and corruption, and further from the seduction of females or males, bond or free. Whatever in connection with my professional practice or not in connection with it I may see or hear I will not divulge, for I hold that all such things should be kept secret. *Hippocrates, substantial portion of the Hippocratic oath for doctors, supposedly written about 400 B.C.*

. . . if the whole materia medica, as now used, could be sunk to the bottom of the sea, it would be all the better for mankind—and all the worse for the physicians. *Dr. Oliver Wendell Holmes, address to the Massachusetts Medical Society, Boston, May 30, 1860.*

The patient, treated on the fashionable theory, sometimes gets well in spite of the medicine. *President Thomas Jefferson, letter to Dr. Casper Wistar, June 21, 1807.*

Diseases desperate grown /By desperate appliances are relieved . . . *William Shakespeare,* **Hamlet,** *1600.*

The miserable have no other medicine/But only hope. *William Shakespeare,* **Measure for Measure,** *1604.*

Anonymous aphorisms:

In medicine, the more practice a doctor has, the less practice he needs.

Anyone who sees a psychiatrist should have his head examined.

Only a fool will make his doctor his heir.

Why do the best doctors have the sickest patients?

Under medicare even the bills are doctored.

The family physician is disappearing faster than a healthy man's symptoms.

The doctors cure all kinds of ills, except the shock of doctors' bills.

Call the doctor early and you won't have to call the doctor late.

Good doctors are usually bad patients.

Nobody cares about the doctors till we need them.

Anecdotage:

The doctor tried in vain to impress on his patient the seriousness of his illness. He said, "There's no point in hiding from you the fact that you are very,

very, very sick. Do you have any last requests?" "Yes," said the patient, "get me another doctor."

A man telephoned his doctor and said, "I have this shooting pain in my throat when I swallow and I'm very hoarse. What should I do?" The doctor replied, "Until you can see me at the office tomorrow, just keep your neck swathed in hot compresses." "My maid told me to use cold compresses," protested the man. "Nonsense," said the doctor. "My maid says hot compresses."

"Doctor," the patient complained, "every morning when I get up I'm nauseous for an hour." "What you should do," said the doctor, "is to get up an hour later."

Facts:

Medicine is an ancient science, but professional medical education is relatively modern in the United States. When one reflects that only in the 19th century was modern anesthesia developed, and that surgeons routinely perform countless operations today that would have been impossible in our grandparents' time, the incredible speed with which the professional practice of medicine has developed can be better appreciated. In the U.S. some 75 years ago, 5,700 new doctors were graduated each year from medical school. In 1930, there were only some 4,500 new medical graduates and there were less medical schools than a generation before. To make up the difference between our home-grown supply of new doctors and the mounting needs of the population, more and more graduates of foreign medical schools came to practice in the U.S. In the early 1970s, even though the American medical schools were vastly increasing the number of doctors they educated, it was estimated that as many as 20 percent of the physicians practicing in the U.S. were the products of foreign medical schools—including Americans who went to Mexico, Canada and Europe because they couldn't get into U.S. medical schools. In 1977, *The New York Times* said that about half of all medical residencies in New York State hospitals were held by doctors with foreign educations, and in New Jersey, 75 percent. At the same time, more than 13,000 new doctors annually were being graduated by U.S. medical schools and the number was going up every year. The story of medical costs was similar—more care available, at more cost than ever. Your state, city or county medical association and hospital association has the latest statistics.

MEMORY

Definitions: the process or faculty of remembering; that which is recalled or remembered; "the diary we all carry about with us" (*Oscar Wilde*).

Quotation:

Memory is the mother of all wisdom. *Aeschylus*, **Prometheus Bound**, *5th Century B.C.*

. . . let us remember that the times which future generations delight to recall are not those of ease and prosperity, but those of adversity bravely borne. *Harvard President Charles W. Eliot, December 22, 1877.*

That which is bitter to endure may be sweet to remember. *Thomas Fuller,* **Gnomologia,** *1732.*

'Tis sweet to thinke on what was hard t'endure. *Robert Herrick, "Satisfaction for Suffering," 17th century.*

Memory is a net; one finds it full of fish when he takes it from the brook; but a dozen miles of water have run through it without sticking. *Oliver Wendell Holmes,* **The Autocrat of the Breakfast-Table,** *1858.*

The tumult and the shouting dies;/The capitans and the kings depart:/Still stands Thine ancient sacrifice,/An humble and a contrite heart./Lord God of Hosts, be with us yet,/Les we forget—lest we forget! *Rudyard Kipling, "Recessional," 1897.*

Everyone complains of his lack of memory, but nobody of his want of judgement. *Francois Duc de La Rochefoucauld,* **Maxims,** *17th centyry.*

If I do not remember thee, let my tongue cleave to the roof of my mouth . . . **Psalms,** *137:6.*

Better by far that you should forget and smile/Than that you should remember and be sad. *Christina Rossetti, "Remember," 1862.*

When to the sessions of sweet silent thought/I summon up remembrance of things past,/I sigh the lack of many a thing I sought,/And with old woes new wail my dear time's waste. *William Shakespeare,* **Sonnets,** *30, 1609.*

It is not so easy to forget. *Richard Brinsley Sheridan,* **The Rivals,** *1775.*

Anonymous aphorisms:

Things that live in memory have no visible means of support.

I'll never forget what's-his-name.

Some of our most vivid memories are of things that never happened, for we remember the images and the imagination of our childhood dreams.

We are apt to remember most vividly what we are most anxious to forget.

Memory plays strange tricks.

Anecdotage:

"I am trying desperately to remember why I came here." "Forget it." "That's it! That's what I came here for—to forget."

"People attach much too much importance to memory," said the absent-minded professor. "I disagree," said his colleague. "Disagree with what?" asked the professor.

The classic story of memory is about the man who had gone to the circus as a small boy and returned years later. He was sitting in a cheap seat when an elephant came along, reached up into the stand, wrapped his trunk gontly about the man and carried him over to deposit him gently in the best seat in the circus tent. The man turned to his neighbor and said, "The elephant remembered that the last time I was here, years ago, I fed him peanuts." Just then the elephant came back, lifted his trunk, pointed it straight at the man and blew a stream of water in his face. "I forgot I gave them to him in the bag," said the man.

Facts:

Memory is a mental faculty which occurs naturally, but which can also be developed. There is a constant stream of books and courses in how to develop a better memory. As the world has developed, humans have had to remember more with each passing generation, but students of physiology insist that the capacity of the human brain to retain information is far greater than what we currently use. Remembering is easier when what we are trying to memorize or store away in our minds is related to something we already know; hence many memory methods urge that we try to associate something new with something we know very well. Memory is not always a conscious process. We all have memories that come to mind seemingly by themselves, sometime even unwelcome ones.

MEN

Definitions: human adult males; humans of the gender God made first, before he worked out improvements; former boys.

Quotations:

Remember, all men would be tyrants if they could. *Abigail Adams, letter to her husband, John Adams, March 31, 1776.*

The best works, and of greatest merit for the public have proceeded from the unmarried or childless men. *Sir Francis Bacon,* **Essays:** *Of Marriage and Single Life, 1600s.*

Men are but children of a larger growth. *John Dryden,* **All for Love,** *1678.*

Men are what their mothers made them. *Ralph Waldo Emerson,* **The Conduct of Life:** *Fate, 1860.*

Our self-made men are the glory of our institutions. *Wendell Phillips, December 21, 1860.*

I wonder men dare trust themselves with men. *William Shakespeare,* **Timon of Athens,** *1605-9.*

We do not ask man to represent us; it is hard enough in times like these for man to carry backbone enough to represent himself. *Elizabeth Cady Stanton, March 19, 1860.*

There is no escape—man drags man down, or man lifts man up. *Booker T. Washington, address to Howard University alumni, 1896.*

Men become old, but they never become good. *Oscar Wilde,* **Lady Windermere's Fan**, *1892.*

At thirty man suspects himself a fool;/Knows it at forty, and reforms his plan;/At fifty chides his infamous delay,/Pushes his prudent purpose to resolve:/In all the magnanimity of thought/Resolves; and re-resolves; then dies the same. *Edward Young,* **Night Thoughts**, *1740s.*

Anonymous aphorisms:

A good man isn't only hard to find—he's hard to keep good.

A real man's man is no man's man.

Man's chief pursuit is neither fame nor fortune; man's chief pursuit is woman.

Men like to make the wheels go round, which is why so many men go around in circles.

A man is like a plank of wood—soft until seasoned.

A self-made man is judged by his product.

Anecdotage:

The angry father kept objecting to his son's light-hearted approach to adult life. "When I was a boy your age," he said, "I was a man."

Why did the Lord make man first and woman thereafter? Because after He saw Adam, He realized man needed some help.

What is the message of civilized man? If you don't wear a beard life is one close shave after another.

MIDWEST

Definitions: the central section of the United States between the East and the Continental Divide, above the South and Southwest; the corn belt; the hinterland; America's heartland; the breadbasket of the nation.

Quotations:

Ohio is the farthest west of the east and the farthest north of the South. *Louis Bromfield,* **Pleasant Valley**, *1945.*

These are the gardens of the Desert; these/The unshorn fields, boundless and beautiful,/For which the speech of England has no name—/The Prairies. *William Cullen Bryant, "The Prairies," 1832.*

Minnesotans are used to their people running for President. We usually have two or three in there. *Minnesota Senator Walter F. Mondale, 1972.*

. . . covered partly with majestic trees, partly with flowery prairies, immeasurable to the eye, and intersected with large rivers and broad lakes—a land where everybody could do what he thought best, and nobody need be poor, because everybody was free. *Carl Schurz, 1850s.*

I come from a state that raises corn and cotton and cockleburs and Democrats, and frothy eloquence neither convinces nor satisfies me. I'm from Missouri. You have got to show me. *Missouri Congressman Willard D. Vandiver, 1899.*

When anything is going to happen in this country, it happes first in Kansas. *William Allen White, quoted by John Gunther.*

Anonymous aphorisms:

Iowa, where the tall corn grows.

A Missouri mule isn't stubborn. He's just hard to convince.

The Midwest isn't one region; it's several that you can't really tell apart.

Great Lakes make great states.

Illinois calls itself the land of Lincoln, but Lincoln is a city in Nebraska.

The Midwest is what you have to cross to get to there from here.

Anecdotage:

Perhaps the oldest intercity rivalry is that of those called the Twin Cities. It can be illustrated by the story that a bookstore in Minneapolis refused to stock a popular book whose title was *In the Steps of Saint Paul.*

Midwesterners are accused of pronunciation that makes merry, marry and Mary sound exactly the same; Midwesterners say the rest of the country thinks everything is the same throughout the Midwest.

Then there's the man from Kansas who objects to New York City because it isn't centrally located.

Where are the old people in Iowa? In California.

Facts:

Although there is a tendency to think of the Midwest as a single entity, it is much more aptly described as an inland empire, with terrain ranging from forests to prairies, climate that ranges from very cold to quite hot and a combination of vast farm acreage and great cities. Its Eastern states have five times the population per square mile of land of its Western states. Much of its metropolitan growth has been a direct result of its raising of food—wheat and corn processing, stockyards and meat processing, and transportation of foodstuffs.

MINORITIES

(See also Blacks, Ethnicity, Immigration, Prejudice, Race)

Definitions: those groups of the population not of the same race, ethnic stock or religion as the majority; also applied in some senses to classes of people such as the aged, and at times along sexual lines as well; those with less votes.

Quotations:

The history of most countries has been that of majorities—mounted majorities, clad in iron, armed with death, treading down the tenfold more numerous minorities. *Oliver Wendell Holmes, May 30, 1860.*

Though the will of the majority is in all cases to prevail, that will, to be rightful, must be reasonable; the minority possess their equal right, which equal laws must protect, and to violate would be oppression. *President Thomas Jefferson, Inaugural Address, March 4, 1801.*

If by the mere force of numbers a majority should deprive a minority of any clearly written constitutional right, it might in a moral point of view justify revolution—certainly would if such a right were a vital one. *President Abraham Lincoln, Inaugural Address, March 4, 1861.*

Governments exist to protect the rights of minorities. The loved and the rich need no protection—they have many friends and few enemies. *Wendell Phillips, December 21, 1860.*

One, with God, is always a majority, but many a martyr has been burned at the stake while the votes were being counted. *Maine Representative Thomas B. Reed, 1885.*

No democracy can long survive which does not accept as fundamental to its very existence the recognition of the rights of minorities. *President Franklin D. Roosevelt, letter to National Association for Advancement of Colored People, June 25, 1938.*

Anonymous Aphorisms:

If you put together enough minorities, you have a majority.

Uncle Sam isn't married to antecedents.

This country was settled by people who found themselves to be minorities, for one reason or another, in the lands they came from.

There are two kinds of minorities—those that the majority sets apart, and those that set themselves apart.

In every minority there are two groups—those who take pride in being different and those who differ with that pride.

A nation that doesn't have minorities manufactures them.

Anecdotage:

Two members of distinguished First Families were discussing the way members of minorities had poured into their city. "Do you know the worst thing about them?" one asked the other. "It isn't their clothes, or their looks. It is their obvious determination to outnumber us."

"If you look at the history of the United States," said the professor, "you will see very clearly what the greatest weapon of the minorities has been." "Bombs? Riots? Arson? Welfare?" asked the student. "No," said the professor, "the conscience of the majority."

Facts:

Minorities are the inevitable consequences of two primitive human instincts—tribal and territorial. The first possessors of a piece of land become a tribe, with a feeling of kinship. They find themselves fearing, fighting or perhaps merely resenting other neighboring tribes, and when different tribes are part of the same geographic or political unit, some find themselves to be minorities. The history of Western democracy has shown a growing attempt to expand the idea of the greatest good for the greatest number, to bring more minorities into the mainstream. At times, however, this well-intentioned effort ignores the fact that there are some respects in which minorities may not want to be brought into the mainstream. They may value some of the things which set them apart. The great difficulty is to guarantee both equality and respect for differentness. The laws of the United States bar discrimination in employment and, to a large extent, in housing. But the line between desegregation and homogenization is one over which many words have been and will continue to be spilled, and the extent to which a majority culture destroys minority cultures is not purely a matter of law.

Local, state and federal human rights agencies and organizations generally have annual reports available to the public which give some idea of current problems and accomplishments.

MOTION PICTURES

(See also Censorship)

Definitions: a series of photos projected on a screen which give the effect of continuous motion, accompanied by sound; filmed theatrical presentations reproduced by projection in theatres; the flicker; the flicks; pix; also known by nicknames for specialized categories such as horse operas, musicals etc.

Quotations:

If we paid serious attention to one tenth of one percent of what looks like legitimate protest, it would be utterly impossible for us to make any pictures at all, or have any kind of villain unless he were a native born, white American citizen, without a job and without any political, social, religious or fraternal affiliations of any kind. *Joseph I. Breen, Production Code Administrator, 1938.*

It cannot be doubted that motion pictures are a significiant medium for the communication of ideas. They may affect public attitudes and behavior in a variety of ways, ranging from direct espousal of a political or social doctrine to the shaping of thought which characterizes all artistic expression. The importance of motion pictures as an organ of public opinion is not lessened by the fact that they are designed to entertain as well as to inform...*Associate Justice Tom Clark of the Supreme Court, decision in* **Burstyn v. Wilson,** *1952.*

A wide screen just makes a bad film twice as bad. *Samuel Goldwyn, 1956.*

Everybody has two businesses—his own and the movies. *Will Hays, about the time he took over as "czar" of the U.S. motion picture industry, 1923.*

Most arts appeal to the mature. This art appeals at once to every class, mature, immature, developed, undeveloped, law abiding, criminal....*Production Code of the Motion Picture Association of America, early 1960s.*

Anonymous aphorisms:

Read the book, see the picture.

Basically there are three kinds of movies—skin flicks, sin flicks and kin flicks.

The movies are larger than life, and any resemblance is sometimes entirely coincidental.

These days in the movie theatres the porn is green and the plot sickens.

The big question in the movie rating system is this: when a movie is rated PG, indicating parental guidance required, who is supposed to guide the parents?

Anecdotage:

A long time ago, the movie industry in the U.S. decided to conduct a mammoth promotional campaign to bring people back to the movie theatre. They adopted as a motto "Movies Are Your Best Entertainment" and prepared to go to town. Then somebody noticed that the initials of their slogan spelled MAYBE.

A. H. Weiler of *The New York Times* was one of the film reviewers who, in the early days of color movies, found himself inundated with adjectival descriptions of the chromatic values of upcoming films—to the point where he announced happily in one review that he had just seen a picture "in glorious black and white."

The late Sam Goldwyn is credited with devising the all-purpose answer when someone closely connected with a new film comes up to you after the preview to ask what you thought of it. Say "What a picture!" and leave fast.

Facts.

The motion picture was the first mass sight and sound medium to bring drama and entertainment to millions of people around the world at the same time. Until the advent of television, it was unchallenged for the attention of the world's largest audiences. Because it served so universal a public, it was also the first of the mass entertainment media to adopt a code of standards, which for many years it enforced with varying degrees of rigidity. As television cut down the volume of attendance at motion picture theatres, particularly in the United States, pressure to loosen the standards of the Motion Picture Production Code steadily increased, and ultimately a classification system was adopted. Pictures rated X, or for adults only, became box office attractions. Supreme Court decisions greatly restricted the scope of any possible censorship. The movies found new fortunes in doing what television could not—some of it spectacular, suitable for general audiences, some of it for children, and a great deal in the area of what became known as "exploitation pictures"— pornography, ethnic violence themes, sensationalism of every kind. The motion picture industry prospered, even though the costs of picture making rose, by selling films for television showing, by also making television series, and by high ticket prices and sensational themes for theatrical films.

MUSIC

Definitions: the art or profession of creating combinations of tones and rhythms to produce vocal or instrumental melody or emotional effects; "the universal language of mankind (*Henry Wadsworth Longfellow*); "the food of love" (*William Shakespeare*); "the only cheap and unpunished rapture on earth" (*Sydney Smith*).

Quotations:

Music is well said to be the speech of angels; in fact, nothing among the utterances allowed to man is felt to be so divine. It brings us near to the Infinite. *Thomas Carlyle*, **On Heroes, Hero-Worship and the Heroic in History**, *1841*.

Music has charms to soothe a savage breast...*William Congreve*, **The Mourning Bride**, *1697*.

Take a music-bath once or twice a week for a few seasons, and you will find that it is to the soul what the water-bath is to the body. *Oliver Wendell Holmes*, **Over the Teacups**, *1891*.

Music is invaluable where a person has an ear. Where they have not, it should not be attempted. *Thomas Jefferson, letter to Nathaniel Burwell, March 14, 1818.*

And the night shall be filled with music,/And the cares that infest the day,/ Shall fold their tents, like the Arabs,/And as silently steal away. *Henry Wadsworth Longfellow, "The Day Is Done," 1845.*

Hell is full of musical amateurs. Music is the brandy of the damned. *George Bernard Shaw,* **Man and Superman**, *1903.*

Let music swell the breeze,/And ring from all the trees/Sweet Freedom's song...*Reverend Samuel F. Smith, "America," 1832.*

Of all the arts I think Music has the most mighty, universal, and immediate effect. *Sir Arthur Sullivan, May 2, 1891.*

...music is perpetual, and only hearing is intermittent. *Henry D. Thoreau,* **Journal**, *February 8, 1857.*

I hear America singing, the varied carols I hear...*Walt Whitman, "I Hear America Singing," 1855.*

Anonymous aphorisms:

I care not who writes the nation's laws, if I can write its songs.

Music is the international language because everybody responds to its notes.

The song is ended but the melody lingers on.

Face the music.

Some of the strongest people in the world can't carry a tune.

Anecdotage:

An ardent music lover came to New York especially to attend a concert by a great European pianist never before heard live in this country. The music lover got lost walking to the concert, so he stopped at a doorway where an old man was playing the violin and said, "Excuse me, but this is something you would know. How do I get to Carnegie Hall?" "Practice," said the old man, "practice."

The orchestra played Tschaikowsky's *Romeo and Juliet* overture, and the long-haired elderly man in the audience wept and wept. "You must be an incurable romantic," said the lady next to him. "No," he said, "I'm a musician."

Facts:

In the explosion of the arts that has occurred in the United States in recent years, music has not been neglected. Sales of phonograph records and tapes have soared; the American Symphony Orchestra League, headquartered in Vienna, Virginia, reported 40 per cent more symphony orchestras operated in 1974 than in 1955, and the Statistical Abstract of the United States showed comparable growth for opera companies. The number of musical instrument stores grew similarly. In the field of creativity, one cannot point to statistics as easily. Although the American Society of Composers, Authors and Publishers (ASCAP) and other musical societies have also grown, one cannot measure the impact of music simply in the number of compositions or composers. But music is more present than ever in our everyday world. Your ears will tell you.

NATURE
(See also Life)

Definitions: the physical world; that which exists in the world independent of mankind; the forces of life, vegetable, animal, mineral and kinetic; "but a name for an effect/Whose cause is God" (*William Cowper*); "the art of God" (*Sir Thomas Browne*); the iron law of life; the environment; the earth, land, water and air in which we live.

Quotations:

To him who in the love of Nature Holds/Communion with her visible forms, she speaks/A various language . . . *William Cullen Bryant, "Thanatopsis," 1817.*

We must realize that we can no longer throw our wastes away because there is no "away". *New Jersey Governor William T. Cahill, 1971.*

Nature works on a method of all for each and each for all. *Ralph Waldo Emerson,* **Society and Solitude:** *Farming, 1870.*

We have met the enemy and he is us. *Walt Kelly, "Pogo" comic strip, 1970.*

It were happy if we studied nature more in natural things, and acted according to nature, whose rules are few, plain and most reasonable. *William Penn,* **Fruits of Solitude,** *1693.*

Men and Nature must work hand in hand. The throwing out of balance of the resources of Nature throws out of balance also the lives of men. *President Franklin D. Roosevelt, message to Congress, January 24, 1935.*

The conservation of our natural resources and their proper use constitute the fundamental problem which underlies almost every other problem of our national life. *President Theodore Roosevelt, message to Congress, December 3, 1907.*

Everything is good when it leaves the hands of the Creator; everything degenerates in the hands of man. *Jean Jacques Rousseau,* **Emile,** *1762.*

...the laws of nature are the same everywhere. Whoever violates them anywhere must always pay the penalty. *Carl Schurz, 1889.*

One touch of nature makes the whole world kin. *William Shakespeare*, **Troilus and Cressida**, *1602*.

Nature never did betray the heart that loved her. *William Wordsworth, "Lines Composed A Few Miles Above Tintern Abbey," 1798.*

Anonymous aphorisms:

Nature does nothing without a purpose.

Nature is the greatest show on earth.

Mother Nature and Father Time have only one sun between them.

Nature is a revolving door: what goes out in one form comes back in another.

Nature's laws are the real wisdom of the ages.

Nobody fools nature over the long run.

Nature always wins in the end.

Anecdotage:

A real estate developer bought a large plot of land including a beautiful mountain. He flattened the top of the mountain to build a lodge there, removed all the trees on one side of the hill to put in a terraced swimming pool, and built a sculpture garden on the other side. Then he advertised in the travel journals under the slogan, "Ain't nature grand!"

"The first law of nature," said the professor, "is survival." "No," said a second scholar, "the first law is that nothing lasts forever." "Prove it," said the professor. "That's easy," said the scholar. "If the first law of nature were survival, how come no plant, animal or human being lives forever?"

"Nature isn't perfect," said the old philospher, "which is why cosmetics were invented." "Long before cosmetics," said his wife, "nature came up with another invention—the darkness of night."

Facts:

The world and laws of nature are constant, but man's knowledge of them keeps expanding. And the more knowledge we have, the more miraculous nature seems, with its constant balancing of forces, its mathematical preciseness and its inexorable workings. Man's use of the resources of nature constantly grows, although in our time we have come to learn that some of these resources, such as oil, are not inexhaustible. But increased interest in natural resources and nature's wonders is not all based on utilitarian reasons. More and more Americans, for example, have been relaxing by rediscovering nature. Since 1950, the number of visitors to U.S. national parks has quadrupled, according to the National Park Service. In about the same period, according to the U.S. Fish and Wildlife Service, the number of hunting and fishing licenses issued annually has more than doubled.

NEIGHBORS

Definitions: people living adjacent to each other, with a common boundary or meeting place; residents of the same or adjacent areas; those who share a common spirit or interest in a given geographical area; one's human environment; the folks next door.

Quotations:

No man is an island, entire of itself; every man is a piece of the continent, a part of the main; . . . any man's death diminishes me, because I am involved in mankind; and therefore never send to know for whom the bell tolls; it tolls for thee. *John Donne,* **Devotions,** *XVII, 1624.*

Nor knowest thou what argument/Thy life to thy neighbor's creed has lent./All are needed by each one/Nothing is fair or good alone. *Ralph Waldo Emerson, "Each and All," 1839.*

Good fences make good neighbors. *Robert Frost, "Mending Wall," 1914.*

Your own safety is at stake when your neighbor's house is burning. *Horace,* **Epistles,** *1, about 10 B.C.*

The impersonal hand of government can never replace the helping hand of a neighbor. *Vice President Hubert H. Humphrey, February 10, 1965.*

Thou shalt love thy neighbor as thyself. **Leviticus,** *19:18.*

. . . better is a neighbor that is near than a brother far off. **Proverbs,** *21:10.*

In the field of world policy, I would dedicate this nation to the policy of the good neighbor. *President Franklin D. Roosevelt, First Inaugural Address, March 4, 1933.*

As we have recaptured and rekindled our pioneering spirit, we have insisted that it shall always be a spirit of justice, a spirit of teamwork, a spirit of sacrifice, and, above all, a spirit of neighborliness. *President Franklin D. Roosevelt, October 4, 1933.*

. . . I am as desirous of being a good neighbor as I am of being a bad subject . . . *Henry D. Thoreau,* **Civil Disobedience,** *1849.*

Anonymous aphorisms:

We can live without our friends, but not without our neighbors.

When you have a plot of land, the best thing to cultivate is your neighbors.

Two's company, three's a neighborhood.

Check the neighbors before you buy the house.

A good neighbor is the next best thing.

The best next-door neighbor is the one who overlooks things.

The greatest luxury in life is to be able to pick your neighbors.

Anecdotage:

Two Indians watched the Pilgrims landing at Plymouth Rock, and one said to the other, "There goes the neighborhood!"

Then there's the man who puts a sign on his front door when he goes off on vacation, reading: Attention thieves; do not bother to enter here; everything of value has already been borrowed by my neighbors.

A young couple planning to buy a new home were interested in a particular suburban development, so they rang a few doorbells to see what kind of neighbors they would have if they moved in. They decided not to buy because every neighbor tried to sell them his house, saying he was getting too old to worry about the neighborhood.

Facts:

The concept of neighborhood is at the root of much of contemporary life in the United States and elsewhere. For example, the question of how much neighborhood control of schools there should be, how many neighborhoods should be in a single school district, has been a burning issue not only in disputes involving school desegregation but also with regard to questions of funding and taxation. Many metropolitan and suburban areas are still trying to determine where the neighborhood community prerogative in government lies and where it must be overridden. The right to regulate residential construction and the size of building lots is bitterly fought for by communities determined to maintain the existing character of their neighborhood and just as bitterly fought against by those who think that such neighborhoods are un-neighborly.

NEW ENGLAND

Definitions: the northeast section of the United States; "Down East"; baked bean country; Yankee country.

Quotations:

And this is good old Boston,/The home of the bean and the cod,/Where the Lowells talk only to Cabots/And the Cabots talk only to God. *John C. Bossidy, "On the Aristocracy of Harvard," 1910.*

The courage of New England was the "courage of conscience." *Rufus Choate, speech at bicentennial of Ipswich, Mass., 1834.*

. . . a sup of New England's air is better than a whole draft of old England's ale. *Reverend Francis Higginson,* **New England's Plantation,** *1630.*

O, Eleazar Wheelock was a very pious man;/He went into the wilderness to teach the Indian,/With a Gradus ad Parnassum, a Bible, and a drum,/And five hundred gallons of New England rum . . . *Richard Hovey, "Eleazar Wheelock," song of Dartmouth College, late 19th century.*

New England has a harsh climate, a barren soil, a rough and stormy coast, and yet we love it, even with a love passing that of dwellers in more favored regions. *Henry Cabot Lodge, Forefathers' Day speech in New York City, December 22, 1884.*

The New Englanders are a people of God, settled in those which were once the Devil's territories. *Reverend Cotton Mather,* **Wonders of the Invisible World,** *1693.*

. . . New England, where the clergy long held a monopoly of what passed for learning. *Francis Parkman, article in* **The Nation,** *1869.*

There is a sumptuous variety about the New England weather that compels the stranger's admiration—and regret . . . In the spring I have counted one hundred and thirty-six different kinds of weather inside four-and-twenty hours. *Mark Twain, speech in New York City, December 22, 1876.*

Anonymous aphorisms:

New England is neither new nor England; it is its own tradition.

New England, where ever since Myles Standish people have spoken for themselves.

Living through a New England winter develops Yankee ingenuity.

You can always tell a Yankee but you can't tell him much.

If New England did not exist it would never have been invented.

Anecdotage:

New Englanders' lack of loquaciousness is legendary, as perhaps is this story of a New England President named Calvin Coolidge, who was asked what had been the subject of the pastor's sermon in church that Sunday and said, "Sin." "What did the preacher say?" "He's agin it," said Mr. Coolidge.

"The trouble with New Englanders," said Mr. Jones, "is that they refuse to argue. No matter how stupid you accuse them of being, they refuse to argue." "You don't say," said his New England friend.

Facts:

New England is geographically the smallest of the great regions of the United States, but it wasn't always. Back in the days of the Founding Fathers, the U.S. was largely confined to the Eastern seaboard states, and New England was one of the larger sections. Today, the influence of New England remains larger than its area. The names of cities as far west as Oregon (Portland, Salem) bear witness to the extent of the New England heritage, and among the great colleges of America, Harvard, Yale, Dartmouth, Brown, Williams, Amherst and others retain Down East's claim to historic intellectual leadership. There are great colleges all over the country today, but the chances are that more of them have grown from seeds sown in New England than from any other region. In the mid-1970s, the six New England states—Maine, New Hampshire, Vermont, Massachusetts, Rhode Island, Connecticut—contained slightly less than 6 percent of the total U.S. population. In 1920 they had 7 percent. According to the 1970 census, New England had the highest percentage of foreign-born or foreign parentage population of any region of the country; the highest group, in terms of country of origin, were Canadian.

NUCLEAR ENERGY

Definitions: energy resulting from nuclear fission or nuclear fusion; atomic energy; power derived from atomic processes; A-power; atom splitting.

Quotations:

We are here to make a choice between the quick and the dead. *Bernard M. Baruch, speech at United Nations Atomic Energy Commission, June 14, 1946.*

We are now facing a problem more of ethics than physics. *ibid.*

We have grasped the mystery of the atom and rejected the Sermon on the Mount. *General Omar N. Bradley, Armistice Day speech, 1948.*

. . . the element uranium may be turned into a new and important source of energy in the immediate future. Certain aspects of the situation which has arisen seem to call for watchfulness and, if necessary, quick action on the part of the Administration *Albert Einstein, letter to President Franklin D. Roosevelt, August 2, 1939.*

It is not enough just to take this weapon out of the hands of the soldiers. It must be put into the hands of those who will know how to strip its military casing and adapt it to the arts of peace. *President Dwight D. Eisenhower, speech to United Nations General Assembly, December 8, 1953.*

Today at last we really have good reason for believing that the atom can be made the servant and not the scourge of mankind. *President Lyndon B. Johnson, message to International Conference on Peaceful Uses of Atomic Energy, August 30, 1964.*

This energy is to propel the machines of progress; to light our cities and our towns; to fire our factories; to provide new sources of fresh water; and to really help us solve the mysteries of outer space as it brightens our life on this planet. We have moved far to tame for peaceful uses the mighty forces unloosed when the atom was split. And we have only just begun. *President Lyndon B. Johnson, August 26, 1966.*

There is no evil in the atom; only in men's souls. *Adlai E. Stevenson, September 18, 1952.*

Never in history has society been confronted with a power so full of promise for the future of man and for the peace of the world. *President Harry S. Truman, message to Congress, October 3, 1945.*

Anonymous aphorisms:

The world has atomic ache.

The question of nuclear energy has created more heat than nuclear energy itself has produced.

Nuclear energy provides endless fuel for discussion.

The idea of self-sustaining nuclear energy is that there is no fuel like an old fuel.

The problem of nuclear energy is a fission expedition.

Anecdotage:

Johnny Brown wanted a career in atomic energy but he found it was too dangerous. It was not because of radiation; it was because everybody wanted to argue with him.

"I don't belive in nuclear energy," said Mr. Jones. "I think we would be better off trying to get energy from sunlight." "What exactly do you think the source of sunlight is?" asked Mr. Smith.

Facts:

Few contemporary issues have generated as much heat as the question of nuclear energy. In the wake of the atom bomb, the peaceful use of atomic energy was envisioned as the hope of mankind, and exciting progress has been made in the development of this source of power. But at the same time there has been a sustained effort to block the development of nuclear energy plants on the basis of allegations of potential danger from leakage and problems of waste disposal. There has been no proof of the alleged extent of the danger; but the question of whether the risk is worth taking has produced sufficient uncertainty to delay the age of nuclear power by at least a generation. In the mid-1970s, not even the manipulation of oil prices and supplies, and the resultant cost spirals and shortages, persuaded the United States to embark on the degree of nuclear power capacity that atomic energy champions advocated.

OPPORTUNITY

(See also Jobs)

Definitions: a chance to advance oneself or profit; the occasion of being in the right place at the right time with the right qualifications; the knock that's a boost; that which comes disguised as hard work.

Quotations:

A wise man will make more opportunities than he finds. *Sir Francis Bacon,* **Essays,** *Of Ceremonies and Respect, 1625.*

God helps them that help themselves. *Benjamin Franklin,* **The Way to Wealth,** *1757.*

Our country has become the land of opportunity to those born without inheritance . . . *Republican Presidential candidate Herbert Hoover, October 22, 1928.*

We have set out in this country to improve the quality of American life. We are concerned with each man's opportunity to develop his talents. *President Lyndon B. Johnson, July 12, 1966.*

All of us do not have equal, talent, but all of us should have an equal opportunity to develop our talents. *President John F. Kennedy, June 6, 1963.*

. . . Age is opportunity no less/Than Youth itself, though in another dress. *Henry Wadsworth Longfellow, "Morituri Salutamus," 1874.*

I seen my opportunity and I took it. *George Washington Plunkitt, quoted by William L. Riordon in* **Plunkitt of Tammany Hall,** *1905.*

When the iron is hot, strike. *John Heywood,* **Proverbs,** *1546.*

There is a tide in the affairs of men,/which, taken at the flood, leads on to fortune;/Omitted, all the voyage of their life/Is bound in shallows and in miseries. *William Shakespeare,* **Julius Caesar,** *1599.*

Since the days when the great fleet of Columbus sailed into the waters of the New World, America has been another name for opportunity . . . *Frederick Jackson Turner, "The Significance of the Frontier in American History," 1893.*

Anonymous aphorisms:

Some people get the breaks; some people make their own.

Opportunity makes the man.

Today's opportunity is yesterday's dream and tomorrow's memory.

Opportunity doesn't necessarily knock on the door; it may be leaning against the wall waiting to be noticed.

Opportunity comes to those who go looking for it.

Not every opportunity is a good one; some are invitations to disaster.

Opportunity makes the thief.

Anecdotage:

The salesman at the door was very persistent. When Mr. Jones slammed the door in his face, he yelled through it about what a wonderful opportunity he was offering, a once in a lifetime opportunity at a special sale price. "I've heard of opportunity knocking," said Mr. Jones, "but when it starts pounding on the door there's got to be a catch to it."

How would you define the situation when a group of 100 people were locked in with you in an abandoned theatre? "A potential lawsuit," said the attorney. "An emergency for the fire department or the police," said the building inspector. "A great opportunity," said the comedian.

PARENTS

(See also Adolescence, Babies, Children, Family, Marriage)

Defintions: those who beget offspring; mothers and fathers; heir conditioners; immediate progenitors; line of descent.

Quotations:

We never know the love of our parents for us till we have become parents. *Reverend Henry Ward Beecher,* **Proverbs from Plymouth Pulpit**, *1887.*

Honor thy father and thy mother . . . **Exodus,** *20:12*

The longer we live, and the more we think, the higher value we learn to put on the friendship and tenderness of parents and of friends. Parents we can have but once; and he promises himself too much, who enters life with the expectation of finding many friends. *Samuel Johnson, 1766 quotation in James Boswell's* **The Life of Samuel Johnson**, *1791.*

Men are generally more careful of the breed of their horses and dogs than of their children. *William Penn,* **Some Fruits of Solitude**, *1693.*

It is a wise father that knows his own child. *William Shakespeare,* **The Merchant of Venice**, *1597.*

All women become like their mothers. That is their tragedy. No man does. That's his. *Oscar Wilde,* **The Importance of Being Earnest**, *1895.*

Anonymous aphorisms:

Parenthood is the sin—or the virtue—of repetition.

There are two stages for parents—when your children ask all the questions and when they think they know all the answers.

In loco parentis—Latin for "Children can drive their parents crazy."

"Why" is the question children ask their parents and parents sometimes ask each other.

Life is richer when one gives it to another.

A parent's training starts when that future parent is still a child.

Parents should be their children's parents first, their children's friends later.

Anecdotage:

The classic story of the generation gap is of the man who murdered both his parents and then called for the court's mercy as an orphan.

The ambitions of parents of Old World stock have been the subject of many jokes, as for example, the one about Mrs. Smith, who was asked about her two children in elementary school and answered, "The Doctor is in the third grade and the lawyer is in the first!"

How many times, as the kids were growing up, has a harried mother or father said to them, "I hope you have a child just like you, so you'll go through what I'm going through now!"

Facts:

The status of parenthood in our modern era has changed considerably from that in past generations. Families are smaller, parents are younger, and more of them aren't married. From 1950 to 1965 the average family size went up; from 1965 to the mid-1970s it went down. The U.S. Bureau of the Census estimated that, in 1975, 46 percent of all U.S. families had no children under 18, 19.7 percent had one child under 18, and 18 percent had two children under 18 years of age. The development of contraceptive methods has resulted in more families without children or with only one or two.

PEACE

(See also Armed Forces, War)

Definitions: condition of amity or concord among parties who might otherwise be engaged in strife or combat; the opposite of war; the time between wars; "in international affairs, a period of cheating between two periods of fighting" (*Ambrose Bierce*); something mankind persists in fighting over.

Quotations:

Peace upon any other basis than national independence, peace purchased at the cost of any part of our national integrity, is fit only for slaves, and even when purchased at such a price it is a delusion, for it cannot last. *Idaho Senator William E. Borah, speech in the Senate, November 19, 1919.*

There never was a good war or a bad peace. *Benjamin Franklin, letter to Josiah Quincy, September 11, 1783.*

They shall beat their swords into plowshares, and their spears into pruning-hooks; nation shall not lift up sword against nation, neither shall they learn war any more. **Isaiah,** *2:4.*

In this age when there can be no losers in peace and no victors in war, we must recognize the obligation to match national strength with national restraint. *President Lyndon B. Johnson, speech to joint session of Congress, November 27, 1963.*

The mere absence of war is not peace. *President John F. Kennedy, State of the Union message to Congress, Janurary 14, 1963.*

Blessed are the peacemakers: for they shall be called the children of God. **Matthew,** *5:9.*

Peace hath her victories/No less renown'd than war. *John Milton, "To the Lord General Cromwell," 1652.*

Peace, like charity, begins at home. *President Franklin D. Roosevelt, August 14, 1936.*

We desire the peace which comes as of right to the just man armed; not the peace granted on terms of ignominy to the craven and the weakling. *President Theodore Roosevelt, December 3, 1901.*

No nation ever yet enjoyed a protracted and triumphant peace without receiving in its own bosom ineradicable seeds of future decline. *John Ruskin,* **Modern Painters,** *Vol. IV, 1856.*

When the bells of peace ring there will be no hands to beat the drums of war. Even if they existed, they would be stilled. *Egypt's President Anwar el-Sadat, address to Parliament of Israel, November 20, 1977.*

Where they make a desert, they call it peace. *Tacitus,* **Life of Agricola**, *about 100.*

Peace hath higher tests of manhood/Than battle ever knew. *John Greenleaf Whittier, "The Hero," 1853.*

Only a peace between equals can last . . . *President Woodrow Wilson, speech to the Senate, January 22, 1917.*

Anonymous aphorisms:

Peace makes plenty.

Better to keep peace than to have to make peace.

If peace is to last it must come first.

War breaks out, peace settles in.

It isn't real peace if it includes a piece of somebody else's property.

Better an uneasy peace than an easy war.

Peace is for the strong, subjugation for the weak.

Anecdotage:

It is a measure of the normal state of things that some years ago the *New York Daily News*, noting that there was no war going on in the world, headlined its story: "Peace Breaks Out."

Two pacifists were arguing about who was more idealistic. "I love peace so much," said one, "that I am willing to fight for it." "And I love peace so much," said the other, "that I am willing not to fight for it."

POLITICAL PARTIES

(See also Candidates, Elections, Government, Voting)

Definitions: organizations dedicated to a particular political philosophy and/or espousing the candidacy of groups of candidates under a common banner; organizations of voters seeking to elect their group's choices to public office; the ins and the outs; the government and the opposition.

Quotations:

Any man who can carry a Republican primary is a Republican. *Idaho Senator William E. Borah, 1923.*

I think probably politicians are about half ego and half humility. *Jimmy Carter, April 11, 1975.*

Turn the rascals out. *Attributed to Charles A. Dana, and used as 1872 slogan of Liberal Republican Party.*

The Democratic party is like a mule. It has neither pride of ancestry nor hope of posterity. *Ignatius Donnelly, speech in the Minnesota legislature, September 13, 1860. Also attributed to at least three other people.*

Of the two great parties, which at this hour almost share the nation between them, I should say that one has the best cause, and the other contains the best men. *Ralph Waldo Emerson,* **Essays, Second Series***: Politics, 1844.*

...the conservative is an old democrat. *Ralph Waldo Emerson,* **Representative Men***: Napoleon, 1850.*

...I have never yet seen a political organization that was an eleemosynary institution. *North Carolina Senator Sam J. Ervin, Jr., August 1, 1973.*

You cannot adopt politics as a profession and remain honest. *Louis McHenry Howe, January 17, 1933.*

They see nothing wrong in the rule that to the victor belong the spoils of the enemy. *New York Senator William L. Marcy, speech in the Senate, January 21, 1832.*

Any party which takes credit for the rain must not be surprised if its opponents blame it for the drought. *Dwight W. Morrow, October 10, 1930.*

The fact is that a reformer can't last in politics. He can make a show for a while, but he always comes down like a rocket. Politics is as much a regular business as the grocery or the drygoods or the drug business. *George Washington Plunkitt, quoted by William L. Riordon in* **Plunkitt of Tammany Hall***, 1905.*

The best system is to have one party govern and the other party watch. *Maine Representative Thomas B. Reed, speech in House of Representatives, April 22, 1880.*

I am not a member of any organized political party. I am a Democrat. *Attributed to Will Rogers in the 1920s.*

When a leader is in the Democratic Party he's a boss; when he's in the Republican Party he's a leader. *Harry S. Truman, speech at Columbia University, April 28, 1959.*

Anonymous aphorisms:

Promise them anything but get out the vote.

Politicians don't like to talk turkey because they hate to eat crow.

A mugwump is a political animal with his mug on one side of the fence and his wump on the other.

Conservative means small change and radical means large bills.

A political club is better than a policeman's club.

A political party always tries to take the cake.

Politics is the art of the passable.

Anecdotage:

The story is told that Theodore Roosevelt was once heckled by a man who kept interrupting to proclaim, "I'm a Democrat. My father was a Democrat. My grandfather was a Democrat," Roosevelt finally turned to him and said, "If your father had been a jackass, and your grandfather a jackass, what would you be?" The heckler replied, "A Republican."

A candidate had spent the evening at the home of a local opinion leader, trying to woo her and her family to his candidacy. The evening went very pleasantly and when he was leaving the lady said to him, "You have made a great impression here. We are delighted that you're running, and there's only one person in the whole world that I would rather vote for." "That's very complimentary," the candidate said, "but I'd like to know who that one person is." The lady smiled sweetly and said, "Your opponent."

Facts:

Political parties follow different patterns in different countries. In the United States and England, there have generally been two major parties contending, although not always the same two. (Labor replaced the Liberals as the British opponents of the Conservatives, and the Republicans in the U.S. came on the scene after the Whigs faded.) On the Continent the democratic nations are apt to have more parties competing more equally in the political arena, and more coalition governments as a result.

POPULATION

(See also Children, Family)

Definitions: the people or total number of people of a given area or governmental entity; humanity.

Quotations:

If government knew how, I should like to see it check, not multiply the population. *Ralph Waldo Emerson*, **The Conduct of Life:** *Considerations by the Way, 1860.*

I was ever of the opinion that the honest man who married and brought up a large family, did more service than he who continued single and only talked of population. *Oliver Goldsmith*, **The Vicar of Wakefield**, *1766.*

A reliable estimate shows that, at present rates of growth, the world population could double by the end of the century. The growing gap—between food to eat and mouths to feed—poses one of mankind's greatest challenges. It threatens the dignity of the individual and the sanctity of the family. *President Lyndon B. Johnson, message to Congress, February 2, 1966.*

Population, when unchecked, increases in a geometrical ratio. Subsistence only increases in an arithmetical ratio. *Thomas R. Malthus,* **An Essay on the Principle of Population,** *1798.*

The people are a many-headed beast. *Alexander Pope,* **First Epistle of First Book of Horace,** *1735.*

Men, like all other animals, naturally multiply in proportion to the means of their subsistence. *Adam Smith,* **The Wealth of Nations,** *1776.*

We have been God-like in our planned breeding of our domesticated plants and animals, but we have been rabbit-like in our unplanned breeding of ourselves. *Arnold Toynbee, June 1963.*

Anonymous aphorisms:

People are people's number one problem.

The world is full of people getting closer all the time.

People try to get away from it all, but it all comes along with them.

The rich get richer and the poor get children.

People speak of the problem of growing population, but even when population is standing still it is growing—growing older.

It isn't the heat, it's the humanity.

Anecdotage:

A young woman asked to express her views of the population problem said "It is better to be gotten than to beget; it is better to beget than to be gone."

A young student was asked to summarize the state of the population of the world. "The population of the world," he answered, "shows that you don't have to go to school to learn how to multiply."

Then there's the character who thinks that Zero Population Growth means we're breeding more people who amount to nothing.

Facts:

Growth of population has helped to spark both the advance of civilization and the crisis of modern times. It has been one of the forces that made possible the development of new worlds in the Americas and the growth of old tensions elsewhere. It has created a vast appetite for the world's natural resources and outstripped those natural resources. Between 1970 and 1975, the fastest growing area of the world, in terms of population, was Latin America, with an annual rate of 2.8 percent, and the lowest was Europe, at .7 percent. The U.S. rate of population growth in 1975 was .8 percent. These various rates reflect not only the birth and longevity statistics of the various parts of the world but also the movement of people. A country's population growth, as in the case of the United States, comes in part from a higher ratio of births to deaths and in part from immigration. The Population Reference Bureau, Inc., 1754 N. Street, N.W. Washington, D.C. 20036, was credited in 1976 with estimating that between 1976 and the year 2000 world population would go up from approximately 4 billion to 6.2 billion. It was estimated that at the 1976 world population growth rate of 1.9 percent, the number of people on earth will double in less than 40 years. History tends to show that the more people there are, the faster they increase. If the general estimate is correct that world population reached a billion in 1850, after thousands of years of man on earth, then it took only 75 years to double, 50 years thereafter to double again. In the past, starvation and diseases such as cholera limited population growth; but man's ingenuity has grown with man's numbers. The biggest part of the population challenge is that, in general, those segments of population least able to take care of themselves are the segments that most prolifically reproduce.

POVERTY

Definitions: the condition of being poor; lack of possessions or resources; "life near the bone" (*Henry D. Thoreau*).

Quotations:

Over the hill to the poor-house I'm trudgin' my weary way . . . *Will Carleton, "Over the Hill to the Poor-House," 1871. (Sometimes rendered as "Over the Hills . . . ")*

Thousands upon thousands are yearly brought into a state of real poverty by their great anxiety not to be thought poor. *William Cobbett,* **Advice to Young Men***, 1829.*

Poverty is the open-mouthed, relentless hell which yawns beneath civilized society, *Henry George,* **Progress and Poverty***, 1878.*

Poverty has many roots, but the tap root is ignorance. *President Lyndon B. Johnson, message to Congress, January 12, 1865.*

A decent provision for the poor is the true test of civilization. *Samuel Johnson, quoted in James Boswell's* **The Life of Samuel Johnson***, 1770.*

If a free society cannot help the many who are poor, it cannot save the few who are rich. *President John F. Kennedy, Inaugural Address, January 20, 1961.*

No men living are more worthy to be trusted than those who toil up from poverty . . . *President Abraham Lincoln, message to Congress, December 3, 1861.*

For ye have the poor always with you . . . **Matthew,** *26:11.*

How the Other Half Lives. *Jacob A. Riis, title of book, 1890.*

I see one-third of a nation ill-housed, ill-clad, ill-nourished. *President Franklin D. Roosevelt, Second Inaugural Address, January 20, 1937.*

There is only one class in the community that thinks more about money than the rich, and that is the poor. The poor can think of nothing else. That is the misery of being poor. *Oscar Wilde,* **The Soul of Man Under Socialism,** *1891.*

Anonymous aphorisms:

Poverty is rich in all the wrong things.

Being poor provides plenty of room for improvement.

Poverty is no disgrace, but it's hardly a mark of distinction.

There is none so poor as he who knows not the joy of what he has.

Poverty seems worst when there is wealth alongside it.

The rich get richer and the poor get children.

It is possible to be poor in purse but rich in blessings.

Anecdotage:

Sam Levenson often describes the funny and warm incidents of growing up in a family that was hard pressed for a decent income, and he explains it by saying. "We didn't know we were poor."

The impoverished son of an impoverished family was asked how he could have managed to live so pennilessly for so long. "You must remember," he said, "I had a head start."

Facts:

Two simple statistics point up the problem of poverty in the United States. A 1977 report by the Congressional Budget Office said that the number of poor people in the nation had increased in 1975 by 10.7 percent or 2,500,000 people over 1974, a record increase, but that if you count the benefits of Medicare, Medicaid, food stamps and other government assistance, in terms of dollar value, the incidence of poverty among families was down about 60 percent since 1965. The Congressional Budget Office and the U.S. Census Bureau disagree on how many poor people there are here, but they do not disagree that poverty remains a problem. According to the Census Bureau's 1976 report, the percentage of Americans below the poverty level was more than 20 percent in 1960 and declined until 1969. The Census figures show a slight increase since then, particularly in periods of mass unemployment. Between 1960 and 1975, expenditures for every form of welfare service more than doubled. The Congressional Budget Office noted that one of the slight effects of our tax system has been to transfer some income—if you count benefits as income—from the rich to the poor.

PREJUDICE

(See also Blacks, Minorities, Race)

Definitions: a preformed bias; an attitude or opinion based on prejudgment; "a vagrant opinion without visible means of support" (*Ambrose Bierce*); "an opinion without judgment" (*Voltaire*); a closed mind, often combined with an open mouth.

Quotations:

He prided himself on being a man without prejudices; and this itself is a very great prejudice. *Anatole France,* **The Crime of Sylvestre Bonnard**, *1881.*

For, when you assemble a number of men to have the advantage of their joint wisdom, you inevitably assemble with those men all their prejudices, their passions, their errors of opinion, their local interests, and their selfish views. *Benjamin Franklin at the Constitutional Convention, Philadelphia, September 17, 1787.*

Prejudice is the child of ignorance. *William Hazlitt,* **Sketches and Essays**, *"On Prejudice," 1839.*

Our nation's long neglect of minorities whose skin is dark is perhaps only a little worse than our neglect of another minority whose hair is white. *President Lyndon B. Johnson, September 5, 1966.*

Irrational barriers and ancient prejudices fall quickly when the question of survival itself is at stake. *Massachusetts Senator John F. Kennedy, April 12, 1959.*

There is nothing stronger than human prejudice. *Wendell Phillips, January 28, 1852.*

Ignorance is stubborn and prejudice dies hard. *U.S. Ambassador to the U.N. Adlai E. Stevenson, October 1, 1963.*

It is never too late to give up our prejudices. *Henry D. Thoreau,* **Walden**, *Economy, 1854.*

Anonymous aphorisms:

Prejudice isn't just a closed mind; it's an open wound.

Prejudice is the iron curtain of the mind.

Hate does as much harm to the one who hates as to the target.

Prejudice is blanket judgment without looking under the blanket.

To be tolerant of prejudice is to be part of it.

Prejudgment is no judgment.

Prejudice has an insatiable appetite for believing the worst.

Anecdotage:

A notorious bigot was attempting to show how broadminded he was by talking about his daily habits. "Every day," he told a Black woman, "I walk through your neighborhood and pass your house." "Thanks for not stopping," she said.

"There isn't a single Jew or non-white or Catholic in my little village." "Maybe that's why it's still a village."

Facts:

Prejudice has more forms than a cat has lives. That is why, in this country, there are so many organizations fighting it. Local, state and federal equal or civil rights offices of the government can provide information about particular aspects of prejudice and the names of organizations active in those areas.

PRIVACY

Definitions: the condition of or right to be secure from other people's presence or knowledge of one's affairs; the right to be left alone; that which is nobody else's business.

Quotations:

. . . the right to be let alone—the most comprehensive of rights, and the right most valued by civilized men. *Associate Justice Louis D. Brandeis, of Supreme Court, dissenting opinion in Olmstead v. U.S., June 4, 1928.*

The right of every person "to be let alone" must be placed in the scales with the right of others to communicate. *Chief Justice Warren E. Burger, May 4, 1970.*

There has been too much Government secrecy and not enough respect for the personal privacy of American citizens. *Democratic Presidential nominee Jimmy Carter, debate with President Ford, September 23, 1976.*

. . . a man's house is his castle . . . *Sir Edward Coke,* **Third Institute**, *1644.*

A man must ride alternately on the horses of his private and his public nature. *Ralph Waldo Emerson,* **The Conduct of Life:** *Fate, 1860.*

I want to be alone. *Attributed to Greta Garbo in the 1930s.*

Some persons who were intended by nature to adorn an inviolable privacy are thrust upon us by paragraphers and interviewers whose existence is a dubious blessing . . . *Sir Henry Irving, February 14, 1898.*

Every man should know that his conversations, his correspondence, and his personal life are private. *President Lyndon B. Johnson, March 10, 1967.*

A man has a right to pass through this world, if he wills, without having his picture published, his business enterprises discussed, his successful experiments written for the benefit of others, or his eccentricities commented upon, whether in handbills, circulars, catalogues, newspapers or periodicals. *Chief Judge Alton B. Parker of New York State Court of Appeals, decision in* **Roberson v. Rochester Folding Box Co.,** *1901.*

I feel the necessity of deepening the stream of life; I must cultivate privacy. It is very dissipating to be with people too much. *Henry D. Thoreau,* **Journal,** *August 2, 1854.*

Anonymous aphorisms:

In the computer age it is disturbing to realize that a machine has your number.

There are always casualties in the invasion of privacy.

People who live in glass houses are still entitled to window shades.

The government has no more right than anybody else to be a Peeping Tom.

Not everybody wants to be on Candid Camera.

Goldfish, not men, are supposed to live in transparent bowls.

Nobody's life is expected to be a totally open book.

Anecdotage:

"My daughter," said Mrs. Brown, "is only 13 and already she has her own apartment." "Where?" asked Mrs. Smith. "In ours," said Mrs. Brown.

A certain college professor likes to stress that privacy is defined differently, depending on your perspective. "The Government," he says, "isn't usually interested in finding out who lost money gambling; but they are forever trying to identify the winners."

Beverly Hills is known as a community with a passion for privacy, even to the fact that there are practically no sidewalks. As comedians point out, in what is by now a piece of faulty folklore, it's such a private community that even the police have an unlisted phone number.

Facts:

The Federal government, in response to concerns voiced by so many citizens and groups, set up a commission to see what could be done without protecting privacy; but it is a very difficult job, when we are required to file details of our income annually with the Internal Revenue Service, when our credit history is stored in business companies' files, our reading habits are recorded in magazine subscription lists and private and government computers follow us virtually from birth to death. The courts and the legislatures have attempted to codify and define the limits of such governmental invasions of privacy as wire-tapping and interception or reading of mail. Efforts are being made to strengthen provisions against self-incrimination, and protect the confidentiality of various types of messages and notes, such as those between patient and doctor, or a newsman's unpublished notes or tapes. Part of the difficulty in some cases arises from the fact that the federal government very legitimately acquires more information about more people all the time—through the workings of the Social Security System, for example.

PSYCHOLOGY

Definitions: the science of mental processes and behavior; mind matter; heady stuff; head shrinking, civilized style.

Quotations:

Happiness, or misery, is in the mind. It is the mind that lives. *William Cobbett,* **Grammar of the English Language,** *1819.*

Neurosis seems to be a human privilege. *Sigmund Freud,* **Moses and Monotheism,** *1938.*

Castles in the air—they are so easy to take refuge in. And so easy to build as well. *Henrik Ibsen,* **The Master Builder,** *1892.*

Depend upon it, Sir, when a man knows he is to be hanged in a fortnight, it concentrates his mind wonderfully. *Samuel Johnson, quoted in James Boswell's* **Life of Samuel Johnson** *as a 1777 remark.*

Every man values himself more than all other men, but he always values others' opinion of him more than his own. *Marcus Aurelius,* **Meditations,** *2nd century.*

The mind is its own place, and in itself,/Can make a Heaven of Hell, a Hell of Heaven. *John Milton,* **Paradise Lost,** *Book I, 1667.*

Suspicion always haunts the guilty mind . . . *William Shakespeare,* **King Henry VI,** *Part III, 1592.*

Among all the diseases of the mind there is not one more epidemical or more pernicious than the love of flattery. *Richard Steele,* **The Spectator,** *December 3, 1711.*

Anonymous aphorisms:

Psychology sometimes determines what's in your head by getting under your skin.

Anyone who goes to a psychologist should have his head examined.

Psychologists say a lot of people lie on the couch, but some tell the truth.

Was the world happier before psychology, or was that a delusion?

Psychology is only a state of mind.

Pyschology is the science of predicting how people behave—and explaining why they don't.

Anecdotage:

Probably the most familiar of all psychologist stories is that of the two who met at an elevator. The first one smiled at the second and said, "Hello. How are you?" And the second one said to himself, "Now why did he say that?"

A psychologist was administering a test to an applicant for a police job, and asked the applicant to say the first word that popped into his head after every word the psychologist gave him. "Food," said the pscyhologist. "Dirty," said the applicant. "Vacation," said the psychologist. "Dirty," said the applicant. "Love," said the psychologist. "Dirty," said the applicant. "Excuse me," said the psychologist, "but no matter what I say, you keep replying 'dirty'. Why are you doing that?" "Because," said the applicant, "you keep using dirty words." "Well, then," said the psychologist, "suppose you give me a few words that aren't dirty." "What," said the applicant, "and let you dirty them?"

Facts:

Psychology is a comparatively modern science. In 1960 in the U.S. there were 772 doctorates in psychology conferred; in 1974 there were more than 2,500. The employment of psychological profiles and psychological criteria keeps growing as this field of knowledge keeps expanding. But the science of human behavior is far from exact and few fields are still as wide open to further discovery.

PUBLIC OPINION

Definitions: attitude or opinion held generally or collectively by the public; popular consensus; the voice of the people; the views of two cab drivers and a bartender as transmuted in the telling.

Quotations:

Public opinion is no more than this./What people think that other people think. *Alfred Austin,* **Prince Lucifer,** *1887.*

When the people have no other tyrant, their own public opinion becomes one. *E. G. Bulwer-Lytton,* **Ernest Maltravers,** *1837.*

The constant appeals to public opinion in a democracy, though excellent as a corrective of public vices, induce private hypocrisy, causing men to conceal their own convictions when opposed to those of the mass, the latter being seldom wholly right, or wholly wrong. *J. Fenimore Cooper,* **The American Democrat,** *1838.*

. . . what we call public opinion is generally public sentiment. *Benjamin Disraeli, August 3, 1880.*

With public sentiment, nothing can fail; without it, nothing can succeed. *Abraham Lincoln, August 21, 1858.*

There is no group in America that can withstand the force of an aroused public opinion. *President Franklin D. Roosevelt, June 16, 1933.*

Public opinion is a weak tyrant compared with our own private opinion. *Henry D. Thoreau,* **Walden:** *Economy, 1854.*

Public opinion is stronger than the legislature, and nearly as strong as the ten commandments. *Charles Dudley Warner,* **My Summer in a Garden,** *1870.*

In proportion as the structure of a government gives force to public opinion, it is essential that public opinion should be enlightened. *President George Washington, Farewell Address, September 1796.*

Anonymous aphorisms:

Everybody knows better than anybody.

A great leader molds public opinion; a wise leader listens to it.

What the public thinks depends on what the public hears.

Public opinion is itself a matter of opinion.

The voice of the people sometimes depends on which people you hear.

Public opinion and the weather are equally hard to predict, and equally changeable.

Public opinion is sometimes shown by public silence.

Anecdotage:

A Congressman was asked how he determined public opinion on pending issues in his district. "On most questions," he said, "the first thing I have to try to find out is whether there *is* a public opinion."

A journalist who travels all over the world has gotten used to being asked about public opinion in this country or that on this or that issue, and he has found what he describes as the absolutely safe and accurate answer, no matter what the subject. When asked to describe public opinion on anything, anyplace, he always says, "It's divided."

Facts:

Public opinion—or, more exactly, the reporting of it—has become a big business first in the United States and increasingly around the world. It is a tool of market research, through readership and viewing surveys to determine what the public watches and likes. It is used by every major candidate in planning his campaign, to find out which issues and which points of view interest his or her constituency. The biggest problem is that while surveys can be quite accurate, the time lag between the field interviews and the compilation of the report is such that people may change their minds.

PUBLIC RELATIONS

Definitions: the business or profession of representing a person or enterprise to the public; "the engineering of consent" (*Edward L. Bernays*); "the hidden persuaders" (*Vance Packard*); putting your best foot forward; the strategy of dealing with the press and the representatives of the public.

Quotations:

All propaganda has to be popular and has to accommodate itself to the comprehension of the least intelligent of those whom it seeks to reach. *Adolf Hitler*, **Mein Kampf**, *1925*

Be it true or false, what is said about men often has as much influence upon their lives, and especially upon their destinies, as what they do. *Victor Hugo*, **Les Miserables**, *1862*.

Perhaps the most direct way to attain fame is to insist, confidently and consistently, that we already have it. *Count Giacomo Leopardi, 19th century*.

What rage for fame attends both great and small!/Better be damn'd than mentioned not at all. *John Wolcot (Peter Pindar), "To the Royal Academicians," later 18th century*.

Anonymous aphorisms:

The idea of public relations is that if you lead a horse to water, even if you can't make him drink, maybe you can make him swim.

A bistro is a saloon with a public relations man.

Public relations is the art of best foot forward.

Public relations is sometimes like the practice of medicine: sometimes you can improve a condition but often your major success is to keep a bad condition from getting worse.

The difference between press agentry and public relations is that a press agent gets your name in the paper and a public relations counsel knows when you should not get your name in the paper.

Some public relations people are suppress agents.

Getting the press to mention you is press agentry; getting them to mention you kindly is public relations.

Anecdotage:

Public relations is like the farmer with his stubborn old mule. The farmer hit the mule over the head with a bat. Why? For the same reason that so many causes need public relations. The first thing you have to do is to make sure you have your target's attention.

A publicist in New York insists that his is one of the professions mentioned in the Bible, and Aaron was the first public relations counsel. If you look in the *Book of Exodus*, Chapter IV, Verse 16, it becomes clear; for the Bible tells us that the Lord said to Moses, of Aaron, that "he shall be thy spokesman unto the people."

PUBLIC SPEAKING

Definitions: addressing gatherings of people; the art or process of oration or declamation; platform appearance; oratory; forensics.

Quotations:

Discretion of speech is more than eloquence. *Sir Francis Bacon,* **Of Discourse,** *1625.*

That which we are capable of feeling, we are capable of saying. *Miguel de Cervantes Saavedra,* **Novelas Ejemplares,** *El Amante Liberal, 1613.*

Let your speech be always with grace, seasoned with salt, that ye may know how ye ought to answer every man. **Colossians,** *4:6.*

All the great speakers were bad speakers at first. *Ralph Waldo Emerson,* **The Conduct of Life:** *Power, 1860.*

Every man is eloquent once in his life. *Ralph Waldo Emerson,* **Society and Solitude:** *Eloquence, 1870.*

A soft tongue may strike hard. Benajamin Franklin, **Poor Richard's Almanac,** *1744.*

Amplification is the vice of modern oratory. . . .Speeches measured by the hour die by the hour. *Thomas Jefferson, letter to David Harding, April 20, 1824.*

True eloquence does not consist in speech. Words and phrases may be marshalled in every way, but they cannot compass it. It must consist in the man, in the subject, and in the occasion. *Massachusetts Representative Daniel Webster, August 2, 1826.*

Anonymous aphorisms:

Public speaking is an audience participation event; if it weren't, it would be private speaking.

A good speech is like a pencil; it has to have a point.

Great public speakers listen to the audience with their eyes.

Exhaust neither the topic nor the audience.

No good speech ever came to a bad end.

Do not open mouth until brain is in gear.

When a speaker is on too long, his audience may get short with him.

Anecdotage:

The story is told of the way Secretary of State William M. Evarts began a Thanksgiving dinner speech. He said, "You have been giving your attention to a turkey stuffed with sage; you are now about to consider a sage stuffed with turkey."

"Why is it," a famous lecturer was asked, "that the speeches always come after the dinner?" "Because," said the lecturer, "it's hard for the speaker to talk when empty stomachs are growling."

The story is told of a public speaker whose problem was that he couldn't cope with hecklers. This was discovered one evening in a college town, when his prepared remarks were interrupted, rather mildly, and he said, "Why is it every time I open my mouth, some jackass speaks?"

RACE

(See also Blacks, Ethnicity, Prejudice)

Definitions: a distinctive group within a biological species, in the case of mankind involving physical characteristics such as color of skin; broadly categorized among humans as white, yellow, black, brown and red; differences that are sometimes more apparent than real; tribal differentiation.

Quotations:

The difference of race is one of the reasons why I fear war may always exist; because race implies difference, difference implies superiority, and superiority leads to predominance. *Benjamin Disraeli, February 1, 1849.*

Every man has pride of race, and under appropriate circumstances when the rights of others, his equals before the law, are not to be affected, it is his privilege to express such pride and to take such action based upon it as to him seems proper. . . . Our Constitution is color-blind, and neither knows nor tolerates classes among citizens. *Associate Justice John Marshall Harlan of Supreme Court, dissenting opinion in* **Plessy v. Ferguson,** *May 18, 1896.*

Men are not superior by reason of the accidents of race or color. They are superior who have the best heart—the best brain. *Robert G. Ingersoll, lecture on "Liberty," late 19th century.*

Men of different ancestries, men of different tongues, men of different colors, men of different environments, men of different geographies do not see everything alike. Even in our own country we do not see everything alike. *President Lyndon B. Johnson, February 11, 1964.*

We must learn to live together as brothers or perish together as fools. *Reverend Dr. Martin Luther King, Jr., March 23, 1964.*

After all, there is but one race—humanity. *George Moore,* **The Bending of the Bough,** *1900.*

Morality knows nothing of geographical boundaries or distinctions of race. *Herbert Spencer.* **Social Statics,** *1850.*

I believe in the brotherhood of man, not merely the brotherhood of white men but the brotherhood of all men before the law. *Missouri Senator Harry S. Truman, June 15, 1940.*

We conclude that in the field of public education the doctrine of "separate but equal" has no place. Separate educational facilities are inherently unequal. *Chief Justice Earl Warren, Supreme Court decision in* **Brown v. Board of Education of Topeka,** *May 17, 1954.*

Our nation is moving toward two societies, one black, one white—separate and unequal. *Report of National Advisory Commission on Civil Disorders, February, 29, 1968.*

Anonymous aphorisms:

Things might be simpler if we were all born polka-dotted.

The stock they come from is some people's stock in trade.

When some people see black, they see red.

The real colors of the United States are red, white, black, yellow and brown.

The surest way to go broke is to put all your money on a single race.

Mankind consists of five races and an infinite number of heats.

We are all brothers and sisters under the skin, but some people only look at the color of the skin.

Anecdotage:

A black man who had tried for years, in vain, to become a member of an exclusive club, died and went to heaven, where he had no trouble, because of his upright life, in getting in. He said to St. Peter, "Isn't it strange that I can get into heaven, but I couldn't get into the club I wanted, because they would not accept Blacks or Jews as members?" "We knew that before you came," said St. Peter; "the Boss's son ran into the same thing."

This is a variation of a World War II story that makes a universal point. An American Indian, very proud of his heritage, was drafted and sent to a remote Polynesian island where there were only a handful of people, all of Polynesian stock. The Indian's first letter home complained that there was nobody of his own kind on the island; but in later letters this point gradually disappeared and one day he wrote to his mother that the longer he stayed there the more red-skinned the girls all looked.

A Korean millionaire went to the optometrist for a pair of glasses and was shown a thick tortoise shell frame. He tried it on, looked doubtful, and said to the optometrist, "You don't think it makes me look too Japanese?"

Facts:

Race is a fact of life; its impact through the years has been a problem. In the U.S. the doctrine of "separate but equal" facilities was used to separate blacks from whites, and also to segregate Indians, Orientals and others in facilities that were certainly separate but hardly equal to those of the white majority. The first reaction of those who believed in equality among the races was to try to bar any official governmental recognition of race; for a time, in some areas, the maintaining of records indicating race or religion of individuals was considered an evil practice. That view changed most dramatically with the passage of the Civil Rights Act and the Equal Employment Opportunity regulations. In order to prove compliance with anti-discrimination statutes now, businesses and institutions are required to keep records of the race, sex, color, ethnic surname and other pararacial connotations of the individuals they hire, or enroll.

RADIO

(See also Journalism, Television)

Definitions: the transmission, through the air, of electric signals that carry sound from a transmitting antenna to receivers tuned to the proper frequency; wireless; the sound box; the disembodied voice; where talk is cheap; the chatterbox.

Quotations:

There have been few developments in industrial history to equal the speed and efficiency with which genius and capital have joined to meet radio needs. *Secretary of Commerce Herbert Hoover, about 1925.*

The radio is doing a great job in our country in extending the real spirit of democracy. . . . The radio has changed and elevated the technique of political campaigns. And what is more important, it has done a great deal to debunk, and to compel political parties to state the facts and stick to the issues. *New York Mayor Fiorello H. LaGuardia, November 6, 1936.*

Broadcasting gets broader all the time. *William S. Paley, May 25, 1954.*

. . . we had to learn what our new broadcasting medium was for. Some people thought broadcasting would be for education. Some thought merely that it would replace the phonograph. Some thought it would remake the world, which it hasn't. Some thought it would revolutionize politics, which it has. . . . But, of course, broadcasting did not limit itself to any one of these. Instead it became almost all the things that were imagined for it. *William S. Paley, May 25, 1954.*

The broadcasting industry has, indeed, a very great opportunity to serve the public, but along with this opportunity goes an important responsibility to see that this means of communication is made to serve the high purposes of a democracy. *President Franklin D. Roosevelt, message to National Association of Broadcasters, February 1938.*

Anonymous aphorisms:

Radio is the talk of the town.

The miracle of radio is that you can always tune in on another voice.

So many people are fanatics for CB radio they should call it citizens' bund.

Radio made the whole world an echo chamber.

Radio reaches everywhere; it's the world you take with you.

From the crystal set to the transistor, radio has had the last word.

Anecdotage:

Being afraid of a microphone is rare today because it's such a familiar gadget, but mike fright has afflicted some prominent people. Several generations ago Elihu Root, the eminent Republican statesman, found someone putting a microphone in front of him. Mr. Root said, "Take that away. I can talk to a Democrat but I cannot speak into a dead thing." Perhaps that was how they came to refer to a turned-on microphone as being "live."

Radio preceded television, of course, but a child of the TV age, asked to describe radio, said it was "television without pictures."

Facts:

The prominence of television in the nation's attention has a tendency to overshadow public awareness of the dimensions of radio broadcasting. The fact is that there are more coast-to-coast radio networks than TV ones, and about nine times as many radio as TV stations in the U.S. There are four times as many radio stations as there are daily newspapers in the U.S. There are so many thriving radio stations that they can specialize to a degree unheard of in television—all-news stations, all-classical music, all-ethnic and so forth. In some services, such as up-to-the-minute rush hour traffic and road condition reports, radio has developed unique capabilities unmatched. Radio has the smallest, most portable receivers, the longest reach in terms of mileage and the most instantaneous immediacy of any communications medium today.

RELIGION

Definitions: belief in a system of faith, a divinity or supernatural force; an organized ritual and/or hierarchy of worship and faith; a set of beliefs and tenets; "a daughter of Hope and Fear, explaining to Ignorance the nature of the Unknowable" (*Ambrose Bierce*); "the opium of the people" (*Karl Marx*); the explanation of the unexplainable; the Church.

Quotations:

The First Amendment has erected a wall between Church and State which must be kept high and impregnable. *Associate Justice Hugo L. Black, Supreme Court decision in* **McCollum v. Board of Education of Champaign County District 71,** *March 8, 1948.*

In God We Trust. *Authorized by Secretary of the Treasury Salmon P. Chase to be imprinted on U.S. currency in 1864.*

All religions united with government are more or less inimical to liberty. All separated from government are compatible with liberty. *Speaker Henry Clay, speech in House of Representatives, March 24, 1818.*

. . . the most acceptable service of God is the doing of good to man . . . *Benjamin Franklin,* **Autobiography,** *1784.*

Mine eyes have seen the glory of the coming of the Lord;/He is trampling out the vintage where the grapes of wrath are stored;/He hath loosed the fateful lightning of his terrible, swift sword;/His truth is marching on. *Julia Ward Howe, "Battle Hymn of the Republic," February 1862.*

An honest God is the noblest work of man. *Robert G. Ingersoll,* **The Gods,** *1872.*

. . . religion is a matter which lies solely between man and his God, that he owes account to none other for his faith or his worship . . . *President Thomas Jefferson, letter to Danbury Baptist Association of Connecticut, January 1, 1802.*

To be of no church is dangerous. Religion, of which the rewards are distant and which is animated only by Faith and Hope, will glide by degrees out of the mind unless it be invigorated and reimpressed by external ordinances, by stated calls to worship, and the salutary influence of example. *Samuel Johnson,* **Life of Milton,** *1799.*

I believe in an America where the separation of church and state is absolute . . . . where religious intolerance will someday end—where all men and all churches are treated as equal—where every man has the same right to attend or not attend the church of his choice . . . . I do not speak for my church on public matters—and the church does not speak for me. *Massachusetts Senator John F. Kennedy, speaking as Democratic Presidential candidate in Houston, September 12, 1960.*

Every religion is good that teaches man to be good. *Thomas Paine,* **The Rights of Man,** *1792.*

Going to church doesn't make a man a Christian any more than going to a garage makes him an automobile. *Billy Sunday, about the 1920s.*

We have just religion enough to make us hate, but not enough to make us love one another. *Jonathan Swift,* **Miscellanies,** *1711.*

No people can be bound to acknowledge and adore the invisible hand, which conducts the affairs of men, more than the People of the United States. *President George Washington, First Inaugural Address, April 30, 1789.*

God requireth not any uniformity of religion to be enacted and enforced in any civil state; which enforced unanimity (sooner or later) is the greatest occasion of civil war, ravishment of conscience, persecution of Jesus Christ in his servants, and of the hypocrisy and destruction of millions of souls. *Reverend Roger Williams,* **The Bloudy Tenent of Persecution for the Cause of Conscience,** *1644.*

. . . we are bounde by the law of God and men to doe goode unto all men and evil to noe one. *The Flushing Remonstrance, addressed by citizens of Flushing, N.Y. to Governor Peter Stuyvesant of New Amsterdam, December 27, 1657.*

Congress shall make no law respecting an establishment of religion, or prohibiting the free exercise thereof . . . *Constitution of the United States, First Amendment, adopted December 15, 1791.*

Anonymous aphorisms:

A man's faith, more than his house, is his castle.

I'd rather deal with a God-loving person than with a God-fearing one.

Religion's greatest miracle is the survival of faith.

Religion is a combination of the hereafter and the heretofore.

Belief in God is part of religion; acting like God's children is the rest.

There are no atheists in foxholes.

Faith is stronger than steel.

Anecdotage:

President John F. Kennedy remarked that he had asked the Chief Justice whether a proposed new education bill was constitutional, and the Chief Justice had told him, with no further amplification, that "It's clearly constitutional—it hasn't got a prayer."

Then there's the story of the devoted worker in the congregation who couldn't believe she was in heaven because they didn't have a Las Vegas Night.

A group of congregants were asked by their pastor whether they prayed regularly to God, and if so, what they always prayed for. One said for health, another for happiness, another for salvation in the world to come. But one congregant kept shaking his head, and when it came his turn, he said, "It's very simple. I believe in God and what I pray for is that He believe in me."

Facts:

In the mid-1970s the U.S. had more than 330,000 churches, with a membership of over 130 million, plus innumerable smaller religious groups with uncounted members; but the appearance of the statistics was misleading; virtually every church was having problems of lapsed or inactive members. At the same time, almost a billion dollars a year was being spent in church-related construction.

The annual Yearbook of American Churches contains much information about the numerical position and trends in the religions of America. The World Almanac lists the leading denominations and their headquarters.

SCHOOL

(See also College, Education)

Definitions: an educational institution, particularly below college level; a place where subjects are taught to students; class warfare; the learning experience; the world of the classroom.

Quotations:

I believe that the school is primarily a social institution. Education being a social process, the school is simply that form of community life in which all those agencies are concentrated that will be most effective in bringing the child to share in the inherited resources of the race, and to use his own powers for social ends. *John Dewey, article in* **School Journal,** *January 16, 1897.*

The public school is in most respects the cradle of our democracy. *Associate Justice William O. Douglas, dissent in Supreme Court case of* **Adler v. Board of Education,** *1952.*

You send your child to the schoolmaster, but 'tis the schoolboys who educate him. *Ralph Waldo Emerson,* **The Conduct of Life:** *Culture, 1860.*

No greater nor more affectionate honor can be conferred on an American than to have a public school named after him. *Herbert Hoover, June 5, 1956.*

Tomorrow's school will be the center of community life, for the grownups as well as the children: "a shopping center of human services." . . . It will employ its buildings round the clock and its teachers round the year. We just cannot afford to have an $85 billion plant in this country open, less than 30 percent of the time. *President Lyndon B. Johnson, February 16, 1966.*

. . . the common school, improved and energized as it can easily be, may become the most effective and benignant of all the forces of civilization. *Horace Mann, 1848.*

A teacher works in a sensitive area in a schoolroom. There he shapes the attitude of young minds towards the society in which they live. In this, the state has a vital concern. It must preserve the integrity of the schools. *Associate Justice Sherman Minton, Supreme Court decision in* **Adler v. Board of Education,** *1952.*

In the first place God made idiots. This was for practice. Then he made school boards. *Mark Twain,* **Following the Equator,** *1897.*

Anonymous aphorisms:

The first victory for women's lib was the idea of sending kids to school.

For too many of today's school population, there aren't three Rs, there are six—remedial 'ritin', remedial readin' and remedial 'rithmetic.

You can't expect schools for children to solve the problems of adults.

Too many people stop caring about the schools when their own kids are grown.

The first thing to learn in school is how to learn.

Too many schoolteachers these days seem to be setting a striking example.

Some kids learn more about life going to and from school than in the school-room.

Anecdotage:

At Open School Day the teacher told Johnny's parents that he didn't take part in classroom discussion, so when they got home they instructed Johnny to mend his ways. The next day when he came back from school his mother asked him, "Johnny, did you raise your hand today?" "Yes," said Johnny. "And what did you talk about?" his mother asked. "Nothing," said Johnny; "By the time I got back to the room it was time for recess."

Children in school are not exactly putty in the hands of their teachers. Sometimes they can teach precision to their elders. For example, a teacher once instructed her students to write a composition on the subject of "My Ideal Room." One youngster turned in an one sentence paper and received a zero. His father promptly came to school to find out why, and when the teacher showed him the composition he pointed out that instead of a zero it deserved 100 percent, because it was a fair response to the teacher's topic. The student had carefully entitled his composition "My Ideal Room," and then had written, "I like my room just as it is."

They call the custodian of this particular school Daniel, because he's always reading the writing on the walls.

Facts:

A number of recent trends in our school system deserve to be noted. Busing to maintain racial integration is widespread, even though attacks on the concept continue. (This, of course, is applicable only to the public school system; while segregated private schools face growing governmental and public pressure, busing is not proposed as a viable answer for the non-public schools.) Another developing trend is the action in various states to overturn or diminish the concept of local funding of schools in favor of a method whereby richer communities help support poorer communities' public school systems. In most communities, members of the local school board hold periodic public meetings, at which the particular problems of that community are discussed.

The National Education Association, sometimes described as the largest professional association in the world, is headquartered at 1201 16th Street NW, Washington, D.C. 20036.

SCIENCE

Definitions: study or knowledge of laws and products of nature; particularly and collectively, physics, chemistry, biology, astronomy, geology and related subjects; subjects based on the workings of natural laws of action, reaction, persistence of matter etc.; "organized knowledge" (*Herbert Spencer*); "nothing but developed perception, interpreted intent, common sense rounded out and minutely articulated" (*George Santayana*); "the knowledge of consequences and dependence of one fact upon another" (*Thomas Hobbes*); "the slaying of a beautiful hypothesis by an ugly fact" (*Thomas H. Huxley*).

Quotations:

Science has not yet mastered prophecy. We predict too much for the next year and yet far too little for the next ten. *Astronaut Neil A. Armstrong, address to joint session of Congress, September 16, 1969.*

Nine-tenths of modern science is in this respect the same: it is the produce of men whom their contemporaries thought dreamers—who were laughed at for caring for what did not concern them—who, as the proverb went, "walked into a well from looking at the stars"—who were believed to be useless, if anyone could be such. *Walter Bagehot*, **The English Constitution,** *1867.*

Men love to wonder, and that is the seed of our science. *Ralph Waldo Emerson*, **Society and Solitude:** *Works and Days, 1870.*

Today, our enormous investment in science and research is our evidence of our faith that science can not only make man richer—but science can make man better. *President Lyndon B. Johnson, February 6, 1967.*

Let both sides seek to invoke the wonders of science instead of its terrors. Together let us explore the stars, conquer the deserts, eradicate disease, tap the ocean depths . . .*President John F. Kennedy, Inaugural Address, January, 20, 1961.*

. . . man is still the most extraordinary computer of all. *President John .F. Kennedy, May 21, 1963.*

The language of science is universal, and perhaps scientists have been the most international of all professions in their outlook. *President John F. Kennedy, October 22, 1963.*

The simplest schoolboy is now aware of truths for which Archimedes would have given his life. *Ernest Renan*, **Souvenirs d'Enfance et de Jeunesse,** *1883.*

Our science and industry owe their strength to the spirit of free inquiry and the spirit of free enterprise that characterize our country. *President Harry S. Truman, letter to Senator Brien McMahon, February 1, 1946.*

The Congress shall have Power . . . to promote the Progress of Science and useful Arts, by securing for limited Times to Authors and Inventors the exclusive Right to their respective Writings and Discoveries . . . . *Constitution of the United States, Article I, Section 8, adopted by the Constitutional Convention of 1787, ratified June 21, 1788, effective March 4, 1789.*

Anonymous aphorisms:

Science is the ascertainment of facts and the refusal to regard facts as permanent.

To err is human; to try to prevent recurrence of error is science.

Every science thinks it is *the* science.

Yesterday's dreams are today's science.

Great science is an art.

Science is forever rewriting itself.

The banker asks, "how much?" The scientist asks, "how come?"

Anecdotage:

A science professor attended a party with a group of university colleagues from the drama department. During an impromptu entertainment one comic dropped his pants; everybody laughed uproariously except the science professor. "Why weren't you laughing?" he was asked. "Because," he said, "it reminded me that my next lecture was on the law of gravity."

"One of the great quests of science," the teacher said to his class, "has been to design a perpetual motion machine. What do you think has been the biggest problem?" "Easy," said one student; "getting it to stop."

Three scientists were in a travel group that visited the Grand Canyon. The geologist said, "I wonder how old it is." The mathematician said, "I wonder how many inches it erodes each year." The meteorologist said, "How hot is it down there?"

"For every action," said the science teacher to the class, "there is a reaction. For example, what happens when you step into a bathtub?" "The telephone rings," said a student.

Facts:

Science, which in the broadest sense is the accumulation of knowledge, has been growing at an ever increasing rate. That is because every increase in scientific knowledge or in the sophistication of scientific techniques opens up new areas for study. The U.S. Bureau of Labor Statistics estimated that total employment of natural scientists and engineers virtually tripled in the U.S. from 1950 to 1970. The annual report on *Research and Development in Industry* by the U.S. National Science Foundation estimated that in 1974 more than 356,000 man-years of research and development were chalked up; and the Foundation said that, although the percentage of Federal funds went down, the total expenditure in the nation for research and development in 1975 was almost six times that of 1955. In between those years, of course, we saw the "science explosion" produced by man's success in space exploration and the step-up in the search for new sources of energy.

SEASONS

Definitions: the four divisions of the year, based on the changing positions of regions of the earth in relation to the sun; particular periods of the year distinguished by special characteristics, as the graduation season; summer, autumn, winter and spring.

Quotations:

The melancholy days are come, the saddest of the year/Of wailing winds, and naked wood, and meadows brown and sere. *William Cullen Bryant, "The Death of the Flowers," 1825.*

To every thing there is a season, and a time to every purpose under the heaven . . . **Ecclesiastes,** *3.1.*

Hot midsummer's petted crone,/Sweet to me thy drowsy tone/Tells of countless sunny hours,/Long days, and solid banks of flowers . . . *Ralph Waldo Emerson, "The Humblebee," 1839.*

Oh, the long and dreary Winter!/Oh, the cold and cruel Winter! *Henry Wadsworth Longfellow,* **The Song of Hiawatha,** *1855.*

Came the Spring with all its splendor,/All its birds and all its blossoms,/All its flowers and leaves and grasses. *Ibid.*

What is so rare as a day in June? *James Russell Lowell,* **The Vision of Sir Launfal,** *1848.*

No price is set on the lavish summer;/June may be had by the poorest comer. *ibid.*

When the frost is on the punkin. . . . *James Whitcomb Riley, "When the Frost Is on the Punkin," 1883.*

In the Spring a young man's fancy lightly turns to thoughts of love. *Alfred Tennyson, "Locksley Hall," 1842.*

We remember autumn to best advantage in the spring; the finest aroma of it reaches us then. *Henry D. Thoreau,* **Journal,** *May 10, 1852.*

Anonymous aphorisms:

Summer heals winter's scars and winter cools summer's passions.

The fashions make the season.

Spring is what separates the snow from the heat waves.

Spring hopes eternal.

Every summer is headed for a fall.

If there were no natural seasons, people would invent them.

In some parts of the world, there are two seasons—rainy and rainier, in others, dry and drier.

Nature saves her biggest shocks for solstice and for equinox.

There are five seasons—winter, spring, summer, fall and slack.

Anecdotage:

A South American was explaining to a New Yorker that when it is summer in New York it is winter in Brazil. "I prefer," said the New Yorker, "to think that one of us has cold summers and warm winters, so that it's the same season at the same time with just a few changes." "Fine," said the South American. "Have a good winter this July."

Facts:

Man is a creature of the seasons—in his leisure habits, in his clothing, his shelter, his occupations. The farmer's year is governed by the season, because the products of nature are governed by the seasons. Even in an age where we build domed, heated, air conditioned structures to defy normal seasonal climate, there is a seasonal cycle. We follow it with the school year, or the crop cycle. But if nature has created the climate and the natural conditions that identify each season, man has provided artificial characteristics. Christmas in the Northern hemisphere is a winter holiday, Easter a spring one. Thanksgiving is an autumn highlight in the U.S. January is the time of department store white sales, September or thereabouts the time for the new model cars—and so forth. For every single thing, there is a season.

SEX

(See also Love, Marriage

Definitions: the physical qualities which differentiate between male and female; the act of coition by male and female; gender; the method of reproduction of species; where surrender is often victory.

Quotations:

The Greeks Had a Word for It *Title of play by Zoe Akins, 1929.*

Sex and obscenity are not synonymous. *Associate Justice William J. Brennan, Jr., decision in Supreme Court case of Roth v. U.S., June 24, 1957.*

Sex, a great and mysterious motive force in human life, has indisputably been a subject of absorbing interest to mankind through the ages. *ibid.*

. . . men and women do not always love in accordance with the prayer. . . *Sinclair Lewis, accepting Nobel Prize for Literature, Stockholm, December 10, 1930.*

. . . . is there any greater or keener pleasure than physical love? No, nor any which is more unreasonable. *Plato,* **The Republic,** *6th century B.C.*

Give me chastity and continence, but not just now. *Saint Augustine,* **Confessions,** *5th century.*

Is it not strange that desire should so many years outlive performance? *William Shakespeare,* **Henry IV, Part II,** *1598.*

Whatever may befall me, I trust that I may never lose my respect for purity in others.. . . Can I walk with one who by his jests and by his habitual tone reduces the life of men and women to a level with that of cats and dogs? *Henry D. Thoreau,* **Journal,** *April 12, 1852.*

Is Sex Necessary? *Title of book by James Thurber and E. B. White, 1929.*

Anonymous aphorisms:

The battle of the sexes has more surrenders than casualties, and a great many hand-to-hand encounters.

Remember way back when we had only two sexes?

The difference between men and women doesn't come between them; it's what brings them together.

A sexpot is sometimes self-heating.

It isn't important that we be able to tell the boys from the girls. It's important that they be able to tell.

Only in the so-called civilized world is sex an over-the-counter—or under-the-counter—commodity.

Anecdotage:

The dignified doctor was caught in lovers' lane with his pretty nurse and tried to explain it away to the police by telling them he was conducting an exploratory operation.

The little boy looked very upset as he came in to talk to his parents. "What's the matter?" they asked him. "Tommy Jones just told me how I got here, and I can't believe it. It sounds terrible." "Oh no," said his mother. "It isn't terrible at all. I guess I should tell you about it." "I don't want to hear any more about it," said the little boy. "Everybody else came here in a car; why did I come in a baby carriage?"

Why isn't there more sex in nudist camps? Because a near miss is apt to have no mystery.

Myron Cohen's most famous story is probably about the suspicious husband who came home sure that his wife was entertaining a lover, threw open the closet door and found a little man cowering there. What the little man said is as good an explanation of sexual dalliance as any. "Everybody," said the little man, "got to be someplace."

Facts:

Probably every generation since the dawn of time has contemplated the sexual mores of its offspring and decided that the world was going to pot. Attitudes toward the relations between the sexes, and toward what used to be regarded as obscenities and perversions, have changed; but unless all the lessons of history are to go for naught, there will be an inevitable cycle. There always has been, from permissiveness to Puritanism to prurience and back. In some areas of subject matter, however, the march of events has not been cyclical. Sex education, once regarded as the work of the devil, is now accepted as an idea, even though the degree of explicitness and the age at which such education should be begun are still subjects of considerable argument, as is the role of the school compared with that of the home. In dress the age of the hoop skirt or the neck-to-ankle woman's bathing suit seems unlikely to return. Psychology, a science which came to maturity on the basis of recognizing the primal role of sexual instincts in the now-debated work of Sigmund Freud, has combined with other fields of medical expertise to produce a whole new area of treatment and advice for the troubled. Planned families, methods of birth control—some not involving religious problems—and even marital blood tests all reflect a modern expansion of the permissible and socially acceptable contemporary approaches to the subject of sex. At the same time, attitudes toward sex are among the great controversies in various religions and between differing sects.

SOCIETY

(See also Civilization)

Definitions: the community as a whole; the upper caste or exclusive portion of the population; everybody else; the club to which everybody belongs; the 400.

Quotations:

There never has yet existed a wealthy and civilized society in which one portion of the community did not, in point of fact, live on the labor of the other. *South Carolina Senator John C. Calhoun, speech in Senate defending slavery, 1837.*

All men plume themselves on the improvement of society, and no man improves. Society never advances. It recedes as fast on one side as it gains on the other. It undergoes continued changes; it is barbarous, it is civilized, it is christianized, it is rich, it is scientific; but this change is not amelioration. For every thing that is given something is taken. Society acquires new arts and loses old instincts. *Ralph Waldo Emerson*, **Essays, First Series:** *Self-Reliance, 1841.*

It is not from top to bottom that societies die; it is from bottom to top. *Henry George*, **Progress and Poverty,** *1879.*

The original of all great and lasting societies consisted not in the mutual good will men had towards each other, but in the mutual fear they had of each other. *Thomas Hobbes*, **Philosophical Rudiments Concerning Government and Society,** *1650.*

[The great society] is a place where men are more concerned with the quality of their goals than the quantity of their goods. *President Lyndon B. Johnson, May 22, 1964.*

In civilized society we all depend upon each other, and our happiness is very much owing to the good opinion of mankind. *Samuel Johnson, July 20, 1763, as quoted in James Boswell's* **Life of Samuel Johnson.**

Man is a social animal. *Seneca,* **On Benefits,** *about 55 A.D.*

To get into the best society nowadays, one has either to feed people, amuse people, or shock people. *Oscar Wilde,* **A Woman of No Importance,** *1893.*

The society of excess profits for some and small returns for others, the society in which a few prey upon the many, the society in which a few took great advantage and many took great disadvantage, must pass. *Republican Presidential candidate Wendell L. Willkie, October 18, 1940.*

High society is for those who have stopped working and no longer have anything important to do. *President Woodrow Wilson, February 24, 1915.*

Anonymous aphorisms:

High society sometimes favors low dives.

The great society found it still needed dues-paying members.

When people talk about what society needs, they are apt to be talking about what they need; but when they talk about what society should do, they are talking about other people.

Society always seems to thrive by keeping somebody out.

Society is based on the fact that misery loves company.

Society is what some people yearn to break into and others yearn to get away from.

Society is composed of the classes, the masses, the full cups and the demi-tasses.

Anecdotage:

Mr. Brown was very impressed with his new neighbors when he heard from Mrs. Jones that Mr. Jones moved in society circles—till he found out that Mr. Jones was a moving man.

The college graduating class was being addressed by a commencement speaker whose theme was their debt to society. Finally, one father of a graduate could stand it no longer; he muttered to the new graduate's mother, "Maybe these others have a debt to society, but I paid for his tuition in cash."

A lawyer was pleading for his slumborn client, who was on trial for a mugging. "You should not blame him" said the attorney, "because he is, after all, simply a product of his society." When the prosecutor's turn came to address the jury, he said, "My worthy opponent has described the defendant as the product of society. It might have been more accurate to describe him as the waste product."

Facts:

One of the notable characteristics of the American society is not that it is classless, though it often likes to think of itself as such, but that it is open to upward class mobility. Unlike some older European societies, particularly where the heritage of an established nobility and a landed aristocracy persists, America has lived the Horatio Alger rags-to-riches story time and again, men of the humblest origins have become society's stars and family position conversely has been no guarantee of success.

SOUTH

Definition: that portion of the United states below the Mason-Dixon line; the states which formed the Confederacy in the Civil War; the grits, chitlins and cotton country; Carter country; the solid South; "way down upon the Swanee River" (*Stephen Foster*); Dixie.

Quotations:

"Carry Me Back to Old Virginny," Title of song by James A. Bland, 1875.

The North excels in business, but the South leads in romance. *Irvin S. Cobb, speech in New York, January 6, 1917.*

The North has put her heroes on a pension, but the South has put hers on a pedestal. *ibid.*

Then I wish I was in Dixie! Hooray! Hooray!/In Dixie's land we'll take our stand,/To live and die in Dixie!/Away, away, away down South in Dixie. *Daniel Decatur Emmett, "Dixie," 1859.*

"My Old Kentucky Home." Title of song by Stephen C. Foster, 1853.

There is a New South, not through protest against the old, but because of new conditions, new adjustments and, if you please, new ideas and aspirations. *Henry W. Grady, December 22, 1886.*

Anonymous aphorisms:

Very few people speak of Northern charm, or Northern hospitality—or Northern fried chicken.

The girls in the South are pretty because the weather gives them more time to bloom.

From corn pone to Cape Kennedy in one generation.

The South shall rise again.

Go North for your living; go South for your health.

The people in the South are warmer.

Anecdotage:

When Jimmy Carter of Georgia was elected President, a common comment in the South was that he was the first President in more than a hundred years who "spoke English without an accent."

The story is told of a student in the South who was asked to describe the Atlantic Ocean and said it was a large body of water extending from Virginia to Florida.

In Officer Candidate School, a candidate from Florida in a group of aspiring Army officers during World War II announced, "One Southerner can lick ten Yankees." One of the others grinned and replied, "Hold out your tongue."

Facts:

The new South that Henry W. Grady talked about in 1886 has grown a lot newer since then. Today it is a section where agriculture and manufacturing share with tourism the credit for a great economic step forward. Tobacco and cotton, while still great staples, are no longer the only bellwether crops; President Carter made his money with peanuts, and the orange and grapefruit groves of Florida, as well as the vegetable farms and cattle, are part of the Southern agricultural landscape. Textiles and other manufactures which can use the relatively plentiful hydroelectric power and timber and mineral resources make the South view the future with enthusiasm.

SPACE

(See also Exploration)

Definitions: the universe beyond earth; out of this world; physical infinity; where there is always room for improvement.

Quotations:

The Universe is but one vast Symbol of God. *Thomas Carlyle,* **Sartor Resartus,** *1834.*

Think of our world as it looks from that rocket that's heading toward Mars. It is like a child's globe, hanging in space, the continents stuck to its side like colored maps. We are all fellow passengers on a dot of earth. *President Lyndon B. Johnson, Inaugural Address, January 20, 1965.*

Space is the stature of God. *Joseph Joubert,* **Pensées, 1842.**

(The universe) is an infinite sphere whose center is everywhere and boundary nowhere. *Blaise Pascal,* **Pensées,** *1670.*

From a wild weird clime that lieth, sublime,/Out of Space—out of Time. *Edgar Allan Poe, "Dreamland," 1845.*

The poet's eye, in a fine frenzy rolling,/Doth glance from heaven to earth, from earth to heaven;/And as imagination bodies forth/The forms of things unknown, the poet's pen/Turns them to shapes, and gives to airy nothing/A local habitation and a name. *William Shakespeare,* **A Midsummer Night's Dream,** *1596.*

It is easier to suppose that the universe has existed from all eternity than to conceive a Being beyond its limits capable of creating it. *Percy Bysshe Shelley,* **Queen Mab,** *notes, 1813.*

Anonymous aphorisms:

Space exploration is a weighty problem without any gravity.

We're back where Alexander the Great was thousands of years ago, looking for new worlds to conquer.

The further out in space we go, the more space we find to go in.

They don't sing about racing for the moon any more, because that boat has landed.

The bigger our discoveries about space, the smaller we become.

There may be other creatures in space, but we see no air apparent.

Anecdotage:

Did you hear about the crooked astronaut? He ran a rocket racket.

Apollo 8 astronauts Anders, Borman and Lovell, televising the earth from outer space, provided a commentary that truly seemed amazing. They simply read the words of the Book of Genesis, and they were incredibly accurate as captions for pictures: . . . and the earth was without form, and void; and darkness was upon the face of the deep. . . . And God said, Let there be light: and there was light. . . .

Facts:

In the 1960s, mankind explored a greater expanse of the unknown than in the entire history of the world to that time. No other decade contributed more to our knowledge of other planets. But it was also a decade when difficulties and dissent on earth caused us ultimately to look more toward our own planet, even as we continued to try to reach other worlds. In the 1970s, our instruments reached Mars, and for a time we seemed to pause for breath.

The Office of Public Affairs of the National Aeronautics and Space Administration, 400 Maryland Avenue SW, Washington, D.C. 20546, is a central governmental source for current information.

TAXES

Definitions: fees or levies imposed by government on property or income or transactions; duties, tariffs or assessments; "what we pay for civilized society" (*Justice Oliver Wendell Holmes, Jr.*); the eternal revenue service.

Quotations:

I am in favor of an income tax. When I find a man who is not willing to bear his share of the burdens of the government which protects him, I find a man who is unworthy to enjoy the blessings of a government like ours. *William Jennings Bryan, July 8, 1896.*

The present tax structure is a disagrace to this country. It's just a welfare program for the rich. *Democratic Presidential candidate Jimmy Carter, first debate with President Gerald R. Ford, September 23, 1976,*

. . . in this world nothing is certain but death and taxes. *Benjamin Franklin, letter to Jean-Baptiste Leroy, November 13, 1789. (It is not known whether he was deliberately paraphrasing Daniel Defoe's reference to "as certain as death and taxes" in* **Political History of the Devil,** *1726.)*

The wisdom of man never yet contrived a system of taxation that would operate with perfect equality. *President Andrew Jackson, Proclamation to the People of South Carolina, warning against secession over states' rights, December 10, 1832.*

Taxation is, in fact, the most difficult function of government—and that against which their citizens are most apt to be refractory. *Thomas Jefferson, letter to bookdealer Joseph Milligan, April 6, 1816.*

The power to tax is the power to live, at least as far as local government is concerned. *New York Mayor John V. Lindsay, April 26, 1971.*

. . . the power to tax involves the power to destroy . . . *Chief Justice John Marshall, Supreme Court decision in* **McCulloch v. Maryland,** *March 6, 1819.*

Nothing brings home to a man the feeling that he personally has an interest in seeing that Government revenues are not squandered, but intelligently expended, as the fact that he contributes individually a direct tax, no matter how small, to his Government. *Secretary of the Treasury Andrew Mellon, Annual Report, 1925.*

In constitutional states liberty is compensation for heavy taxes; in dictatorships the substitute for liberty is light taxes. *Charles de Montesquieu,* **The Spirit of the Laws,** *1748.*

We shall never make taxation popular, but we can make taxation fair. *President Richard M. Nixon, message to Congress, April 21, 1969.*

Taxation without representation is tyranny. *Attributed years later to James Otis, argument before the Superior Court of Massachusetts, February 1761.*

Taxes, after all, are the dues that we pay for the privilege of membership in an organized society. *President Franklin D. Roosevelt, October 21, 1936. (See Justice Holmes' definition, above.)*

Anonymous aphorisms:

Government is an endless pursuit of new ways to tax.

Things are so bad now the Internal Revenue Service even taxes your patience.

Carpet tacks—the only tax that doesn't keep going up.

Taxes are the price we pay for a government that guarantees us the freedom to earn enough money to pay our taxes.

It's tough enough to pay taxes, but making out the income tax forms seems to make it worse.

I don't know why they couple death and taxes. Death only comes once.

They used to say that the only thing the government didn't tax was taxes. Then they invented the surtax.

Anecdotage;

Oscar Wilde is said to have protested about the taxes on his house. When told that it was taxed because, by living there, he used the protection and services of the government, which operated even while he slept, Wilde is supposed to have answered, "But I sleep so badly."

"What bracket are you in?" Mrs. Gotrocks asked Mr. Loaded. "I'm not in a bracket," he replied, "I'm in a pincer."

The history teacher asked the class, "What caused the American Revolution?" Immediately a little girl raised her hand and said, "Taxation." A little boy raised his hand at that and the teacher said, "Tommy, do you have anything to add?" "Yes," said Tommy, "why do they teach that we won?"

Facts:

We all know that government has grown more expensive, not only because the cost of goods and services has risen, but also because government is doing so many more things than it used to, from space exploration to relief and welfare. The U.S. Bureau of the Census reported that between 1950 and 1974 the total taxes per capita in the U.S.—the total collected in taxes by federal, state and local governments, divided by the number of people in the country—more than quadrupled. In 1972, there were over 66,000 local governments with some kind of taxing power, plus the 50 states and the federal government. In that same year, the average per capita tax was $738 federal and $522 state and local, a total of $1,260 for each man, woman and child in the nation. (This, of course, includes taxes paid by corporations and other businesses. Individual income tax per capita figures were $455 federal and $73 state and local.)

TEENAGERS

(See also Adolescence, Youth)

Definitions: people in their teens, that is age 13 through 19; the one age when you feel complimented to be told you look older.

Quotations:

. . . your budding Miss is very charming,/But shy and awkward at first coming out,/So much alarmed, that she is quite alarming,/All Giggle, Blush; half Pertness and half Pout. *George Gordon Lord Byron,* **Beppo,** *1818.*

The imagination of a boy is healthy, and the mature imagination of a man is healthy; but there is a space of life between, in which the soul is in a ferment, the character undecided, the way of life uncertain, the ambition thick-sighted: thence proceeds mawkishness. *John Keats,* **Endymion,** *preface, 1818.*

When the brisk minor pants for twenty-one. *Alexander Pope*, **Imitations of Horace,** *Epistles, Book 1, about 1733.*

Just at the age 'twixt boy and youth,/When thought is speech, and speech is truth. *Sir Walter Scott*, **Marmion,** *1808.*

Eighty odd years of sorrow have I seen,/And each hour's joy wreck'd with a week of teen. *William Shakespeare*, **Richard III,** *1593.*

He has quit the awkward stage; he is out of his teens. *Terence*, **Andria,** *166 B.C.*

Anonymous aphorisms:

Teenage is a moment that seems like an eternity.

Teenage means perpetual emotion.

Teenage is cured by time, which brought it on in the first place.

Teenage is life viewed through a magnifying glass.

Teens are folks in jeans, full of beans and low in means.

Teenage is a rest and relaxation stop in the march of time.

Anecdotage:

Comedienne Jean Carroll used to like to describe her teenage daughter's life style this way: She has her own apartment, in mine.

Psychologists define teenage as the time when an individual exchanges the silver cord for the telephone cord.

Mr. Jones was asked to describe his son's desperate attempt to look older than his actual teen age. "He's growing a beard on the installment plan," said Mr. Jones. "You know, just a little down, and more when he can manage it."

Facts:

Few elements of our population have had as great a change in their status in recent years as teenagers. Where they used to be minors, they are now eligible to vote at 18. Where they used to be more or less at the mercy of parents, they are now recognized as having individual rights. And they are also targeted by the business community as probably the most impressionable and lucrative market for many different types of goods and services. But the idea that teenagers conform to a single pattern is one of the great myths of our time. They may tend to dress alike; so, in the aggregate, do their parents. They are the age group with generally the most difficult employment problems. Because of their liability record, their automobile insurance rates, particularly for males, are the highest in many areas. But if these and other problems lump them together as a class of our population, they are also separated into many different types and categories. They differ in race, in educational interests and attainments, regional attitudes. What they have in common is that they are eager, as were their parents before them, to become the "command generation." They don't watch the clock; but they watch the calendar.

TELEVISION

(See also Journalism, Radio)

Definitions: transmission and reception over long distances of both sight and sound; the home screen; the tube; the magic box: TV.

Quotations:

The most powerful social force in the world's most powerful nation—this is what broadcasting, and television broadcasting in particular, has been called with increasing frequency during the past two decades. *DuPont-Columbia Survey and Awards Jurors, 1969.*

Like most basic national institutions, television operates at the center of American life. As a result, it is always under pressure from the left and the right. *NBC President Julian Goodman, June 23, 1970.*

When television is good, nothing—not the theater, not the magazines or newspapers—nothing is better. But when television is bad, nothing is worse. . . . a vast wasteland. *Federal Communications Commission Chairman Newton H. Minow, May 9, 1961.*

This instrument can teach, it can illuminate, it can even inspire, but only if human beings are willing to use it to those ends. Otherwise it is only wires and lights in a box. *Edward R. Murrow of CBS, January 1, 1952.*

The revenues from advertising support the free, competitive American system of telecasting, and make available to the eyes and ears of the American people the finest programs of information, education, culture and entertainment. *National Association of Broadcasters, Preamble to the Television Code, first adopted in 1952.*

. . . broadcasting has consistently demonstrated a remarkable and ever-expanding capacity to serve the needs of both commerce and society. *CBS Chairman William S. Paley, April 18, 1973.*

Anonymous aphorisms:

Everybody is an authority on television.

Veni, video, vici, I came, I appeared on television, I conquered.

In the age of television, they still describe secret proceedings as being in camera, when what they really mean is that they aren't *on* camera.

Television is everybody's window on the world.

~~Television bears watching.~~

TV or not TV, that is the question.

Television is the great democratizer; it gives everybody the same front row seat.

Facts:

It was estimated in 1976 that 97 percent of all U.S. households had television sets, which probably means that there are more households with television than with telephones. Television has long since established itself as the nation's leading medium of information, entertainment and advertising. Merely recalling such events as the impeachment hearings, Kennedy-Nixon and Carter-Ford debates, Kennedy assassination aftermath, Vietnam, Murrow-McCarthy or "Roots" testifies to the impact of the most total communications medium yet devised.

TENNIS

Definitions: a game played across a net by two or four players, using rackets and a felt-covered, rubber, air-filled ball; netiquette; the bouncing ball set.

Quotations:

When we have match'd our rackets to these balls,/We will, in France, by God's grace play a set/Shall strike his father's crown into the hazard. *William Shakespeare*, **King Henry V,** *1598.*

They must either . . . leave those remnants/Of fool and feather that they got in France . . ./. . . renouncing clean/The faith they have in tennis. . . . *William Shakespeare*, **King Henry VIII,** *1612.*

My advice to young players is to see as much good tennis as possible and then attempt to copy the outstanding strokes of the former stars. *William T. Tilden, July 1926.*

Anonymous aphorisms:

In tennis even a grudge game can be a love match.

His tennis game is a net loss.

Some people play tennis as if they are relying on a higher court.

In mixed doubles the mix is very important.

Tennis is like a lawsuit; you can always be surprised by what happens on the other side of the court.

There are would-be bullies on a tennis court whose net game can be described as gross.

Tennis is a sport in which an unseeded player can still flower.

Anecdotage:

Supreme Court Justice Hugo Black was one of the more famous elderly tennis players. He liked to joke about being advised by his doctor that a man in his forties shouldn't play tennis. Justice Black said he couldn't wait to reach 50 so he could play the game again.

Tennis used to be known for the strictness with which its very strict etiquette was observed not only by the players but by the galleries. Contemplating the uninhibited behavior of players and audiences alike in the 1970s, one veteran observer said that "they've substituted flannel mouths for flannel pants."

Facts:

In the 1970s, tennis was perhaps the fastest growing sport both for participants and for spectators, in the U.S. Its growth was greatly stimulated by allowing professionals and amateurs to play in the same tournaments—and indeed by recognizing that it was a profession for professional players. It led the way in providing amphitheatre and television program attractions in which both men and women could take part. The development of winterized bubble roofs brought an explosion of indoor tennis court facilities to the point where what had been basically a summer pastime became an all-year sport.

The U.S. Tennis Association (which used to be the U.S. Lawn Tennis Association until other surfaces replaced the previously dominant lawn courts) is located at 51 East 42 Street, New York, N.Y. 10017. In 1975, it was estimated, some 35 million U.S. tennis players spent over half a billion dollars on clothes and equipment for the game and more than $400 million was expended on construction of new facilities.

THEATER

(See also Drama)

Definitions: presentation of drama or other entertainment on a stage before on audience; performances before the public; the stage; the legitimate theater; performances in the setting of an auditorium designed for this purpose.

Quotations:

A play ought to be a just and lively image of human nature, representing its passions and humors, and the changes of fortune to which it is subject, for the delight and instruction of mankind. *John Dryden*, **An Essay of Dramatic Poesy,** *1668.*

On the stage he was natural, simple, affecting;/'Twas only that when he was off he was acting. *Oliver Goldsmith,* **Retaliation,** *1774.*

The Fabulous Invalid. *Title of play about the theater by George S. Kaufman and Moss Hart, 1938.*

To wake the soul by tender strokes of art,/To raise the genius, and to mend the heart;/To make mankind, in conscious virtue bold,/Live o'er each scene, and be what they behold:/For this the Tragic Muse first trod the stage. *Alexander Pope, "Prologue to Mr. Addison's Cato," 1713.*

Judge not the play before the play is done:/Her plot hath many changes. . . . *Francis Quarles, "Epigram, Respice Finem," early 1600s.*

All the world's a stage,/And all the men and women merely players:/They have their exits and their entrances;/And one man in his time plays many parts. . . . *William Shakespeare,* **As You Like It,** *about 1599.*

It is an extremely difficult thing to put on the stage anything which runs contrary to the opinions of a large body of people. *George Bernard Shaw, July 30, 1909 (testimony before a committee).*

Whoever condemns the theater is an enemy of his country. *Voltaire, June 20, 1733.*

Anonymous aphorisms:

There's a broken heart for every light on Broadway.

Real life is not necessarily good theater.

The show must go on.

Comedy on the stage is very serious business.

The stars may be on stage, but the audience is king.

Theater is whatever people will buy tickets to see.

Theater is like baseball; it depends on hits and runs.

Anecdotage:

Then there's the actor who describes himself as "the off Broadway type." He doesn't mean he specializes in little theater. He means he can't get a job *on* Broadway.

A showman was asked to define theater. "When a man falls down in the street and a crowd gathers round him," he said, "that's an event. But when a crowd pays money at a box office to go into a building to see a man fall down, that's theater."

It was Oscar Wilde who commented after the opening of a play of which he had a high opinion that "the play was a great success but the audience was a failure."

Facts:

The theater has been called the fabulous invalid because for at least half a century it has been described as dying. Broadway, the legendary "great white way" of the stage, was labeled as doomed when talking pictures came upon the scene, and every movie theater could present the sight and sound of stage triumphs. Then, when television developed into the nation's most popular theatrical form, the prophets of doom for the legitimate theater renewed their prophecies. But, although the number of successes on Broadway went down, the vitality of living theater went up. Off Broadway and Off Off Broadway bloomed. Regional theater became a thriving reality. Theater studies at such universities as Yale, Carnegie-Mellon and Northwestern prospered. Foundation and government support for resident companies was a new development of the 1960s and 1970s. In any community of size, the theater today is still among those facilities present. Contact your local newspaper for information about theatrical activities in your community.

TIME

Definitions: the period during which a condition exists, a process occurs or an action continues; the duration of a condition, process or action; a fixed moment during a period; "that which man is always trying to kill, but which ends up killing him" (*Herbert Spencer*); the one thing that never stands still; "a very shadow that passeth away" (*Solomon*).

Quotations:

Backward, turn backward, O Time, in your flight,/Make me a child again, just for tonight. *Elizabeth Chase Akers, "Rock Me to Sleep, Mother," 1860.*

Take care of the minutes, for the hours will take care of themselves. *Lord Chesterfield, letter to his son, October 4, 1746.*

This time, like all times, is a very good one, if we but know what to do with it. *Ralph Waldo Emerson, "The American Scholar," 1837.*

. . . time is money. *Benjamin Franklin,* **Advice to a Young Tradesman,** *1748.*

If Time be of all Things the most precious, wasting Time must be, as Poor Richard says, the greatest Prodigality; since, as he elsewhere tells us, Lost Time is never found again. *Benjamin Franklin,* **The Way to Wealth,** *1757.*

Art is long, and Time is fleeting. . . . *Henry Wadsworth Longfellow, "A Psalm of Life," 1839.*

Lives of great men all remind us/We can make our lives sublime,/And, departing, leave behind us/Footprints on the sands of time. *ibid.*

Time makes more converts than reason. *Thomas Paine, "Common Sense," 1776.*

For a thousand years in thy sight are but as yesterday when it is past, and as a watch in the night. **Psalms,** *90.4.*

Never before have we had so little time in which to do so much. *President Franklin D. Roosevelt, February 23, 1942.*

Time is but the stream I go a-fishing in. *Henry D. Thoreau,* **Walden,** *1854.*

Anonymous aphorisms:

One today is worth two tomorrows.

Time is a great legitimizer.

Time heals all wounds, and wounds all heels.

When you're out of time, you're out.

You can save time but you can't bank it.

It is always later than you think.

When it's high time there's no time to spare.

Time and tide wait for no man.

Anecdotage:

"Time," said the sage," is a great healer." "But," asked his pupil, "what if you're feeling fine in the first place?"

"How do you explain the relativity of time?" the professor was asked. "Well," he said, "if I am rushing to catch a plane, and the check-in clerk is so slow that I miss it, the extra two minutes don't mean much to him but they sure make a difference to me. That's relativity."

The explorers, a man and wife, had returned from spending several years on a lonely expedition. "Did you get tired of just being with each other," they were asked. "Well," said the woman explorer, "he was away for one night." "Then you were together virtually all the time?" "No," she replied, "you see we were in the Arctic; the night was six months long."

VIOLENCE

(See also Crime, Law and Order)

Definitions: use of physical force to destroy or coerce; conflict; brawn over brain; disorder.

Quotations:

It is organized violence on top which creates individual violence at the bottom. *Emma Goldman, June 15, 1917.*

When a fact can be demonstrated, force is unnecessary; when it cannot be demonstrated, force is infamous. *Robert G. Ingersoll,* **Prose-Poems and Selections,** *1884.*

. . . violence is the sign of temporary weakness. *Jean Jaures,* **Studies in Socialism,** *1902.*

It is easier today to buy a destructive weapon, a gun, in a hardware store, than it is to vote. *President Lyndon B. Johnson, December 20, 1963.*

Democracy will never solve its problems at the end of a billy club. *President Lyndon B. Johnson, July 28, 1964.*

. . . for all they that take the sword shall perish with the sword. **Matthew,** *26.52.*

Perseverance is more prevailing than violence; and many things which cannot be overcome when they are together, yield themselves up when taken little by little. *Plutarch,* **Parallel Lives,** *about 100 A.D. (Sertorius)*

These violent delights have violent ends. *William Shakespeare,* **Romeo and Juliet.** *1596.*

Anonymous aphorisms:

Violence is self-destructive.

Violence is as American as apple pie.

Don't start a fight if you're not prepared to finish it.

Violence on behalf of the right side can make it the wrong side.

People who live in glass houses shouldn't throw stones.

When there is an epidemic of violence, nobody can consider himself immune.

Some people think the only way to shut 'em up is to shoot 'em up.

Anecdotage:

The leader of an urban youth gang visited a Quaker community where he saw everyone settle his differences by quietly talking to those of differing view. "Don't you think this is better than fighting?" the youth gang leader was asked. "No," he replied, "it takes all the fun out of life."

Every time that a controversial issue came up at the town meeting, the town dissenter said "We'll stage a demonstration." Finally one of the elders lost his temper. "You don't accomplish anything by your demonstrations," he said. "They always end up in a riot, and what good is that?" "Well," said the dissenter, "it gets a lot more attention than when I talk in the town meeting."

There was a violence-prone young man who got into a fight by smashing a merchant's window, starting a fire, and battling with the firemen. When the police came, he went after them with a knife and, in defending themselves, they beat him to a pulp. As he lay moaning on the sidewalk, he raised his head and snarled at them, "Have you had enough?"

Facts:

Violence has always been a fact of human existence, in every civilization. Today there is great concern over depictions of violence. The concern is a reaction not exclusively to what is reported or depicted in the communications media, but also the result of recent events. It was fact, not fiction, that terrorists murdered Israeli athletes at the 1972 Olympic games. It was in real life, not fiction, that airport terminals were bombed, planes hijacked, hostages taken. The assassinations of President John F. Kennedy, Robert Kennedy and Martin Luther King, Jr. were not the work of fiction writers, nor was the violence that erupted in city after city thereafter. In March, 1968, the report of the National Advisory Commission on Civil Disorders was published. That was the Commission known popularly as the U.S. Riot Commission. It dealt with violence stemming from racial unrest, which is only one cause, but its observations and recommendations deal with a far broader canvas: opening up opportunities for jobs, education and housing; giving the disadvantaged more control of their own lives and stimulating better intergroup communication. These are all internal remedies for internal national problems. Like the problem of international violence, however, they depend on one fact: violence continues to exist as long as the practice of violence goes unpunished and the causes go unsolved. It should be remembered too that not all the increase in real-life violence comes in crime and war. Contact sports have become more violent. Basketball today, for example, permits a degree of contact which would have been illegal 20 years ago. The development of high-speed automobiles has led to an increase in violent accidents. Violence is a fact of life; its control is a problem of life.

VOTING

(See also Candidates, Elections, Political Parties)

Definitions: the expression of choices and preferences among candidates and issues by casting ballots; suffrage; the exercise of the franchise; the voice of the people; the poll that counts.

Quotations:

At the bottom of all the tributes paid to democracy is the little man, walking into the little booth, with a little pencil, making a little cross on a little bit of paper—no amount of rhetoric or voluminous discussion can possibly diminish the overwhelming importance of the point. *Prime Minister Winston Churchill of Great Britain, speech in Commons, October 31, 1944.*

Your every voter, as surely as your chief magistrate, under the same high sanction, though in a different sphere, exercises a public trust. *President Grover Cleveland, Inaugural Address, March 4, 1885.*

A straw vote only shows which way the hot air blows. *O. Henry,* **Rolling Stones,** *"A Ruler of Men," 1913.*

Voting is the first duty of democracy. *President Lyndon B. Johnson, August 11, 1964.*

The ignorance of one voter in a democracy impairs the security of all. *President John F. Kennedy, May 18, 1963.*

The ballot is stronger than the bullet. *Abraham Lincoln, about 1856.*

Inside the polling booth every American man and woman stands as the equal of every other American man and woman. There they have no superiors. There they have no masters save their own minds and consciences. *President Franklin D. Roosevelt, October 21, 1936.*

Nobody will ever deprive the American people of the right to vote except the American people themselves. *President Franklin D. Roosevelt, October 5, 1944.*

Even *voting* for the right is *doing* nothing for it. *Henry D. Thoreau, "Civil Disobedience," 1849.*

By their votes ye shall know them. *President Harry S. Truman, September 23, 1948.*

Act as if the whole election depended on your single vote . . . *John Wesley, "A Word to a Freeholder," 1748.*

Anonymous aphorisms:

If you walk past the polling place without casting your vote, you are voting with your feet.

The most important single exercise for the adult American is the exercise of the franchise.

A write-in vote is often designed to keep some candidates right out.

The votes that count are the votes you *can* count.

Anecdotage:

Harry Truman is supposed to have asked a man in the crowd, during his whistle-stop campaign for the Presidency in 1948, how the man planned to vote. The man said, "I wouldn't vote for you if you were the only man on the ballot." "Put that man down as doubtful," said President Truman to one of his aides.

A defeated candidate came back to the little community of ten voters he had visited during the campaign. "I'm disappointed in you," he said. "When I was here before the election all ten of you said you would vote for me, and when the votes were counted not one of you had. Now if only one of you had been smart enough to vote for me, I wouldn't know which one of you had told the truth. Instead, I know you all lied."

Then there's the man who describes voting the straight ticket as putting all his "exes" in one basket.

Facts:

The most important single fact about voting in the United States is that, although we are the oldest major democratic, popularly elected representative government in the world, we have proportionately less people participating in our elections than in the rest of the self-governing world. In the 1976 Presidential election, less than 55 percent of the eligible voters cast ballots, compared to better than 70 percent virtually everywhere else. The U.S., of course, has greatly expanded the number of citizens eligible to vote by abolishing poll taxes, enfranchising 18-year-olds and enforcing voting rights legislation. The Statistical Abstract of the United States contains comparative information through the years on the number of eligible voters and the extent of their participating in elections.

WAR

(See also Peace)

Definitions: a state or period of armed conflict between states or peoples; the clash in battle of opposing military, naval and air forces; "a by-product of the arts of peace" (*Ambrose Bierce*); that which determines not who is right, but who is left.

Quotations:

In peace the sons bury their fathers and in war the fathers bury their sons. *Sir Francis Bacon,* **Apothegms,** *1624.*

It takes twenty years or more of peace to make a man; it takes only twenty seconds of war to destroy him. *King Baudouin I of Belgium, address to joint session of Congress of U.S., May 12, 1959.*

There is no greater pacifist than the regular officer. Any man who is forced to turn his attention to the horrors of the battlefield, to the grotesque shapes that are left there for the burying squads—he doesn't want war! *General of the Army Dwight D. Eisenhower, June 19, 1945.*

By the rude bridge that arched the flood,/Their flag to April's breeze unfurled,/Here once the embattled farmers stood,/And fired the shot heard round the world. *Ralph Waldo Emerson, "Concord Hymn," April 19, 1837.*

Older men declare war. But it is youth that must fight and die. *Herbert Hoover, June 27, 1944.*

It is well that war is so terrible—we would grow too fond of it. *Confederate General Robert E. Lee, December 13, 1862.*

I know war as few other men now living know it, and nothing to me is more revolting. I have long advocated its complete abolition, as its very destructiveness on both friend and foe has rendered it useless as a means of settling international disputes. . . . In war there is no substitute for victory. *General of the Army Douglas MacArthur, speech to joint session of Congress, April 19, 1951.*

It is always easy to begin a war, but very difficult to stop one, since its beginning and end are not under the control of the same man. *Sallust,* **Bellum Jugurthinum,** *1st century B.C.*

There is many a boy here today who looks on war as all glory, but boys, it is all hell. *General William T. Sherman, August 11, 1880.*

For it is all too obvious that if we do not abolish war on this earth, then surely, one day, war will abolish us from the earth. *Harry S. Truman, January 25, 1966.*

Anonymous aphorisms:

War is blind.

People used to go off to war, but modern science can now bring it to your doorstep.

Those who yearn for war have already started it in their hearts.

In the next war there will be no rear echelon.

War brings more evils than it cures, and yet war against evil cannot always be avoided.

Many a victorious war turned to ashes in peace.

The only good war is a war to make a good peace.

Man seems to know how to make war better than how to make peace.

Anecdotage:

An elderly cannibal sage and a missionary were comparing their philosophies. The cannibal reminisced about the tribal wars he had fought, and how he had eaten his foes. The missionary said, "We fight wars for higher reasons—for truth, for defense of democracy, for freedom." "You must eat many, many people," said the cannibal. "Oh, no," said the missionary, "we don't eat human beings." "Then," said the cannibal sage, "you have no reason to kill each other."

'We will bomb your cities, set fire to your crops, defoliate your forests, kill your people by the millions," the belligerent dictator roared across the conference table at the ambassador from overseas. "We will reduce your country to nothing. We will fight—and we will win the war." "Given your description," said the ambassador, "just what do you expect to win?"

Facts:

War is mankind's oldest weakness. No civilization yet created has been able to abolish it. In this century alone, the United States has been involved in four major wars—World Wars I and II, Korea and Vietnam—plus various minor military confrontations. In that same period, the world has tried to abolish war through non-aggression compacts, United Nations sessions, disarmament and arms limitation agreements, peaceful sanctions against aggressors etc. But military preparedness continues to be reflected around the world in mounting armament sales and the increasing sophistication of equipment. The war against war is being waged at great cost.

WASHINGTON, D.C.

Definitions: the capital city of the United States; "a city of southern efficiency and northern charm" (*John F. Kennedy.*)

Quotations:

Washington is no place for a civilized man to spend the summer. *President James Buchanan (attributed), 1857-1861.*

There are a number of things wrong with Washington. One of them is that everyone has been too long away from home. *President Dwight D. Eisenhower, May 11, 1955.*

Washington is not a place to live in. The rents are high, the food is bad, the dust is disgusting and the morals are deplorable. *Horace Greeley, July 13, 1865.*

Washington is full of famous men and the women they married when they were young. *Mrs. Oliver Wendell Holmes, Jr., January 8, 1903.*

The condition of our capital city is a sign of the condition of our nation—and is certainly taken as such by visitors, from all the states of the Union, and from around the globe. *President Richard M. Nixon, message to Congress, April 28, 1969.*

Every man who takes office in Washington either grows or swells, and when I give a man an office, I watch him carefully to see whether he is swelling or growing. *President Woodrow Wilson, May 15, 1916.*

Anonymous aphorisms:

When Congress is in session, the city is so crowded that the D.C. stands for Don't Come.

When you work in Washington a few years you are apt to stay.

Washington, where the buck starts.

Washington, D.C. was named for the only President who didn't have to live there.

The only reason Washington is the nation's capital is that Boston was too far North, Philadelphia didn't want New York, New York didn't want Philadelphia and nobody yet had heard of Las Vegas.

Washington, where the lame ducks are on the pond.

Anecdotage:

Why do they call it D.C.? Because you wouldn't expect it to be A.C. like the rest of the country.

A visitor to Washington in the Spring said "The cherry blossoms are absolutely lovely, but is it always this windy?" "Madam," said the guide, "you must remember this is the nation's capital. Where the government meets it's always windy."

During a Washington rainstorm, the lawn sprinklers in front of the White House suddenly turned on and began operating full force. A passerby turned to his companion and said, "Why do you suppose those sprinklers went on now?" "It's an old rule in Washington," said the other. "Whatever nature does, Washington thinks it can do better."

Facts:

Washington, D.C. has been an anomaly. It is represented in Congress, but, for years has been without a vote. It is where the President lives, but the people who live in Washington could not vote in the Presidential election until 1964. It is a city with a population more heavily Black than any other major American metropolis, and one with more people paid by the same employer—the Federal government—than any other of comparable size. But it is also a city where almost everybody has some roots elsewhere. Because it is the place where the nation's elected representatives meet, it has something of every state of the Union.

WASHINGTON, GEORGE

Definitions: the first President of the United States under the Constitution; "the Father of his Country."

Quotations:

Surely Washington was the greatest man that ever lived in this world uninspired by divine wisdom and unsustained by supernatural virtue. *Henry P. Brougham (Lord Brougham and Vaux),* **Historical Sketches of Statesmen Who Flourished in the Time of George III,** *1839-1843.*

. . . I know that it is impossible for me to bestow anything like adequate praise on a character which gave us, more than any other human being, the example of a perfect man; yet, good, great, and unexampled as General Washington was, I can remember the time when he was not better spoken of in this House than Bonaparte is now. *Charles James Fox, speech in House of Commons, February 3, 1800.*

To contemplate his unselfish devotion to duty, his courage, his patience, his genius, his statesmanship and his accomplishments for his country and the world, refreshes the spirit, the wisdom and the patriotism of our people. *President Herbert Hoover, proclamation for Washington's 200th birthday, issued February 2, 1932.*

. . . never did nature and fortune combine more perfectly to make a man great . . . *Thomas Jefferson, January 2, 1814.*

. . . first in war, first in peace, first in the hearts of his countrymen. *Henry ("Light Horse Harry") Lee, text of resolution introduced in Congress on his behalf by John Marshall December 19, 1799.*

Washington is the mightiest name on earth—long since mightiest in the cause of civil liberty; still mightiest in moral reformation. *Abraham Lincoln, February 22, 1842.*

That nation has not lived in vain which has given the world Washington and Lincoln, the best great men and the greatest good men whom history can show. *Massachusetts Senator Henry Cabot Lodge, February 12, 1909.*

Anonymous aphorisms:

When George Washington beat the forces of George III, many of his fellow Americans wanted to make him King George I; but he didn't like the idea, which two centuries later saved us from having King Richard I.

George Washington couldn't tell a lie because it would have had a harmful effect on American mythology.

If George Washington slept every place they say he did, he must have won the war in his sleep.

Washington was a man of great accomplishments, but there was one thing he couldn't do; he couldn't tell a lie.

Anecdotage:

"Why was Washington a great man?" the young student was asked. "Because he was born on a national holiday."

Why was Washington, D.C. named after George Washington? Because he was born first.

WEALTH

Definitions: abundant supply of property or resources; riches; affluence; prosperity; "a conventional basis of reputability" (*Thorstein Veblen*); "the holiest of our gods" (*Juvenal*).

Quotations:

The men who have earned five million dollars have been so busy earning it that they have not had time to collect it; and the men who have collected five million dollars have been so busy collecting it that they have not had time to earn it. *William Jennings Bryan, "The Price of A Soul," early 20th century.*

The problem of our age is the proper administration of wealth, so that the ties of brotherhood may still bind together the rich and poor in harmonious relationship. *Andrew Carnegie, "Wealth," 1889.*

It requires a great deal of boldness and a great deal of caution to make a great fortune, and when you have got it, it requires ten times as much wit to keep it. *Ralph Waldo Emerson,* **The Conduct of Life:** *Power, 1860.*

The Affluent Society. *Title of book by John K. Galbraith, 1958.*

Ill fares the land, to hastening ills a prey,/Where wealth accumulates and men decay. *Oliver Goldsmith,* **The Deserted Village, 1770.**

Put not your trust in money, but put your money in trust. *Oliver Wendell Holmes,* **The Autocrat of the Breakfast-Table, 1858.**

Few rich men own their own property. The property owns them. *Robert G. Ingersoll, October 29, 1896.*

It is easier for a camel to go through the eye of a needle, than for a rich man to enter into the kingdom of God. **Mark,** *10:25.*

The loved and the rich need no protection—they have many friends and few enemies. *Wendell Phillips, December 21, 1860.*

. . . a man is rich in proportion to the number of things he can afford to let alone. *Henry D. Thoreau,* **Walden,** *1854.*

Anonymous aphorisms:

The rich get richer and the poor get children.

One man's wealth is another man's pocket money.

He is a poor man if he has to watch his wealth.

A fat purse never lacks friends.

Money can't buy happiness, but it certainly doesn't discourage it.

The share-the-wealth movement appeals the most to those with the least to share.

A little among neighbors is better than riches in a wilderness.

Anecdotage;

The story is told of a multimillionaire who insisted on doing business in a genteel but very shabby office. His lawyer said to him, "A man of your position and resources should really have a better furnished office." "Why?" asked the multimillionaire. "Everybody will charge me more for what I buy."

A feeble old rich man, confined to his bed with the infirmities of age, pointed out the window at a husky teenager who was having a laughing conversation with a pretty girl. "I wish I was as rich as he," said the old man. "But he has no job, his family has ten mouths to feed and he doesn't even know whether he'll be able to go to college," the rich man's nurse said. "Yes," said the rich man, "but he has health and youth and hope—he's rich in all the things that money can't buy."

Humphrey, who loved to spout statistics, was an ardent share-the-wealther until somebody gave him a little pocket calculator. Then he announced that he had changed his political philosophy. When asked why, he said, "Well, I did a little figuring and discovered that if they shared the wealth I wouldn't be getting any, I'd have to give some up."

Facts:

Wealth, in the last analysis, is not an absolute thing, but a comparative one. The wealthy family is usually given that distinction because it has more than other families rather than because it has everything. This is illustrated by a few simple statistics. In the United States in the latter half of the 1970s, a family that had an income of just below $30,000 a year was in the top 10 percent of family income. Being in the top 10 percent is regarded as being wealthy—but obviously that is true only on a comparative basis. The top 5 percent of income in the United States in the mid-1970s required a family to be bringing in

$40,000 a year. Perhaps a better indication of the true dimensions of U.S. wealth came in 1976 in figures credited variously to the World Bank and the Swiss Banking Society. They show that the 1975 per capita gross national product of various nations, in U.S. dollars, put the United States below such nations as Kuwait, Switzerland, Sweden, Norway and Denmark. On the other hand, in terms of available creature comforts, the rankings might be different.

The U.S. Internal Revenue Service publishes annual Statistics of Income which can also provide helpful information.

WEST

Definitions: that portion of the United States adjacent to or west of the Continental Divide; generally speaking, the states of Montana, Wyoming, Colorado, New Mexico, Arizona, Utah, Idaho, Oregon, Washington and California; where men are men; the wide open spaces.

Quotations:

Westward the course of empire takes its way . . . *Bishop George Berkeley, "On the Prospect of Planting Arts and Learning in America," 1752.*

Out where the handclasp's a little stronger,/Out where the smile dwells a little longer,/That's where the West begins. *Arthur Chapman, "Out Where the West Begins," 1917.*

. . . westward, look, the land is bright. *Arthur H. Clough, "Say Not the Struggle Naught Availeth," 1862.*

Go West, young man, go West and grow up with the country. *Credited to Horace Greeley, who indeed said it, but attributed the initial thought to John L. Soule, 1850s.*

East is East and West is San Francisco, according to Californians. Californians are a race of people; they are not merely inhabitants of a State. They are the Southerners of the West. *O. Henry, "A Municipal Report," 1910.*

Westward, Ho! *Title of novel by Charles Kingsley, 1855.*

I come . . . from the West where we have always seen the backs of our enemies. *Major General John Pope, July 14, 1862.*

We go eastward to realize history and study the works of art and literature, retracing the steps of the race; we go westward as into the future, with a spirit of enterprise and adventure. *Henry D. Thoreau, "Walking," 1862 (published posthumously.)*

Anonymous aphorisms:

The West is yet to come.

Every Western state seems to regard itself as all that's left of the old West.

There is no more enthusiastic Westerner than a transplanted Easterner.

They used to say when someone died, that he "went West." When they say someone went West these days, it usually means he got a new lease on life.

The greatest mineral riches of the West are found in the gold mine known as Las Vegas.

California is a state, but southern California is a state of mind.

The sun rises in the East and smiles on the West.

Anecdotage:

I suppose you've heard about the prospector who was looking for gold and hit it rich. He struck water.

One of the effects of the West on new settlers throughout its history is that they have become its biggest boosters. So when Mr. Jones in his cowboy clothes monopolized the conversation at the Nevada bar by talking about how weak and helpless he felt when he first saw the West, an Eastern visitor said, "What part of the East did you come from, Mr. Jones?" "I didn't come from the East," said Mr. Jones, "I was weak and helpless because I was so young. I was born here."

A Westerner died and found himself in the next world full of comfort and sunshine and delightful ways to pass the time. "How do you like it here?" he was asked. "Well," he said, "for Hell it isn't too bad." "What do you mean Hell?" said his companion. "This isn't Hell. It's Heaven." "You must be from the East," said the Westerner. "Anything you come to after living in the East seems like Heaven. But I'm from the West, and believe me, anything else seems like Hell to me."

Facts:

The American West is by far the largest of the traditional regions of our land, and potentially the richest. It already contains the most populous state in the nation, California, and its other states are growing steadily. Its mineral resources are still being explored; its climate is generally salubrious, particularly with the growth of air conditioning and solar energy. Its coastline is picturesque, its mountains the largest America has except for Alaska (which in spirit is an extension of the West) and its pioneering tradition is the youngest of American traditions. With the development of the Pacific world, the American West has become as important for its ports and international atmosphere as for its inland empires.

WOMEN

(See also Feminism)

Definitions: adult female humans; the distaff side; formerly the weaker sex; the ladies; the first improvement on man; the female of the species; "the last thing civilized by man" (*George Meredith*); the eternal feminine.

Quotations:

. . . can't live with them, or without them. *Aristophanes*, **Lysistrata**, *411 B.C.*

A sufficient measure of civilization is the influence of good women. *Ralph Waldo Emerson*, **Society and Solitude:** *Civilization, 1870.*

Man has his will—but woman has her way. *Oliver Wendell Holmes*, **The Autocrat of the Breakfast-Table**, *1858.*

There is in every true woman's heart a spark of heavenly fire, which lies dormant in the broad daylight of prosperity, but which kindles up and beams and blazes in the dark hour of adversity. *Washington Irving*, **The Sketch Book**, *"The Wife," 1820.*

It is a good time to be a woman because your country, now more than at any time in its history, is utilizing your abilities and intelligence. *Claudia Taylor (Mrs. Lyndon B.) Johnson. March 31, 1964.*

. . . the colonel's lady an' Judy O'Grady/Are sisters under their skins. *Rudyard Kipling, "The Ladies," 1895.*

The female of the species is more deadly than the male. *Rudyard Kipling, "The Female of the Species," 1911.*

Women are not entirely wrong when they reject the rules of life prescribed for the world, for these were established by men only, without their consent. *Michel Eyquem de Montaigne*, **Essays, Book III**, *1588.*

Too often the great decisions are originated and given form in bodies made up wholly of men, or so completely dominated by them that whatever of special value women have to offer is shunted aside without expression. *Mrs. Eleanor Roosevelt, speech at U.N., December 1952.*

Anonymous aphorisms:

Woman's work is never done—by a man.

Woman's intuition is man's tuition.

It is an incontrovertible fact that women bear watching and men watch their bearing.

When a woman has no answer, the sea has no salt.

It is easier for a woman to be famous for her genius than to be forgiven for it.

Working women used to be a male tactic.

God took one look at Adam and brought out a new design called Eve.

Anecdotage:

A captain of industry who had been dealing with the representatives of a women's rights committee was warned that they were outspoken. "By whom?" he asked.

A pretty woman got on the crowded bus; there were no seats available, but as she began to pass him an elderly man arose and offered her his seat. Instead of accepting and sitting down, she smiled at him and said, "Sir, it's nice that you are so old-fashioned but this is a new era and men don't have to get up to offer seats to women any more." "They do if they want to get off at the next stop," said the old gentleman, as he moved to the exit.

It has now become less revolutionary to hear someone advised to "have faith in God. She will protect you." But that didn't prevent Mr. Jones from being surprised when he heard the first book of the Bible referred to as "Jennie's Sis."

Why is it always Mother Nature and Father Time? because Mother always knows best and Time is bound to tell.

Facts:

The changing status of women can be noted in many ways. They are working more often outside the home, they are increasingly independent of men and they have more recourse to the protection of the law in their search for equality of opportunity and status. But in the mid 1970s it was still a fact, noted officially by the U.S. Department of Labor, that men were still getting the better jobs and the better pay. The *Wall Street Journal* ran a terse headline summarizing this: "Less Rank and More File." In 1975, according to the Department of Labor, the median income of working women was little more than half—57 percent—that of men. And one other spin-off of the fact that more women were working was that more men seemed to be exercising the option of letting their wives be the principal breadwinners in the family. Nevertheless, there were encouraging signs of progress—great increases in the number of women in law school, more women executives in business, more women going to college. It was generally felt that the opportunities for the new generation of women would be better than for their predecessors.

WORRY

Definitions: anxiety; nervous concern; sleepless nights; fear of what is to come; that which is almost always premature.

Quotations:

A crust eaten in peace is better than a banquet attended by anxiety. *Aesop, "The Town Mouse and the Country Mouse," 6th century B.C.*

There are two days in the week about which and upon which I never worry . . . .One . . . is Yesterday. . . .And the other day I do not worry about is Tomorrow. *Robert J. Burdette, "The Golden Day," late 19th century.*

As a rule, men worry more about what they can't see than about what they can. *Julius Caesar,* **Gallic War,** *1st century B.C.*

When you're laying awake with a dismal headache, and repose is tabooed by anxiety,/ I conceive you may use any language you choose to indulge in, without impropriety. *W. S. Gilbert, lyric in* **Iolanthe,** *1882.*

How much pain have cost us the evils which have never happened. *Thomas Jefferson, letter to Thomas Jefferson Smith, February 21, 1825.*

. . . the misfortunes hardest to bear are those which never come. *James Russell Lowell,* **Democracy and Other Addresses,** *1887.*

Deep into that darkness peering, long I stood there wondering, fearing,/ Doubting, dreaming dreams no mortal ever dared to dream before. *Edgar Allan Poe, "The Raven," 1845.*

Anonymous aphorisms:

Worry makes the world go round and round and round.

He who never worries never cares.

You can always find something to worry about.

Worry comes before wisdom.

It takes a lot of imagination to worry.

Worry never paid a bill.

Worry tries to cross the bridge before you come to it.

Anecdotage:

"Most of the things you worry about," the psychiatrist told Mr. Brown, "never happen." "I know that," said Mr. Brown, "but then I find myself worrying about *why* they didn't happen."

A passenger on the airplane was obviously a member of the white knuckle brigade. The plane hadn't even begun its take-off, and he was clutching his seat with evident anxiety. His seat mate, trying to relieve the tension, "said, "You're jumping the gun; we're not even in the air yet." "That's your worry," said the anxious passenger. "Mine is that I missed the flight I should have been on an hour ago, and I'm going to miss my connecting flight." It's easy to see when someone is worried, but not so easy to know what he's worrying about.

Two men were going to fly to the moon together. One was calm and the other anxious. The calm one said, "He should be calm." The worried one said, "He should be worried."

YOUTH

(See also Adolescence, Teenagers)

Definitions: the period between childhood and full maturity; young adulthood; "a stuff will not endure" (*William Shakespeare*); that which is old to children and young to their parents; "perpetual intoxication . . . a fever of the mind" (*La Rochefoucauld*).

Quotations:

The young are in a state like intoxication; for youth is sweet and they are growing. *Aristotle*, **Nicomachean Ethics**, *4th century B.C.*

Young men think old men are fools, but old men know young men are fools. *George Chapman*, **All Fools**, *1605.*

America is a country of young men. *Ralph Waldo Emerson*, **Society and Solitude:** *Old Age, 1870.*

. . . the young must fight in the ranks. *Homer*, **Iliad**, *about 800 B.C.*

Every old man complains of the growing depravity of the world, of the petulence and insolence of the rising generation. He recounts the decency and regularity of former times, and celebrates the discipline and sobriety of the age in which his youth was passed; a happy age that is now no more to be expected, since confusion has broken in upon the world, and thrown down all the boundaries of civility and reverence. *Samuel Johnson*, **The Rambler**, *September 8, 1750.*

The mental disease of the present generation, is impatience of study, contempt of the great masters of ancient wisdom, and a disposition to rely wholly upon unassisted genius and natural sagacity. The wits of these happy days have discovered a way to fame, which the dull caution of our laborious ancestors durst never attempt; they cut the knots of sophistry which it was formerly the business of years to untie, solve difficulties by sudden irradiations of intelligence, and comprehend long processes of argument by immediate intuition. *Samuel Johnson,* **The Rambler,** *September 7, 1851.*

How beautiful is youth! How bright it gleams/With its illusions, aspirations, dreams! *Henry Wadsworth Longfellow, "Morituri Salutamus," 1875.*

If youth be a defect, it is one that we outgrow only too soon. *James Russell Lowell, November 8, 1886.*

Certainly the time when the young are to be seen and not heard is gone in America—and gone for good. *President Richard M. Nixon, December 1, 1971.*

We cannot always build the future for our youth, but we can build our youth for the future. *President Franklin D. Roosevelt, September 20, 1940.*

My salad days,/When I was green in judgment. *William Shakespeare,* **Anthony and Cleopatra,** *1606.*

The youth of America is their oldest tradition. It has been going on now for three hundred years. *Oscar Wilde,* **A Woman of No Importance,** *1893.*

Anonymous aphorisms:

The younger generation is always displaced by a younger generation.

Instead of chips off the old block some people think we now have saps out of the old trees.

We are so concerned with making a good world for our heirs that it can be said we are heir conditioned.

You're only young once. How long that once lasts is the question.

Youth will have its fling, even if it means flinging away its youth.

Youth is much too precious to be wasted on the young.

Young people live in their own world—which used to be ours.

Anecdotage:

"What would you give to be young again?" a man was asked at his 40th birthday party. "That's easy," he replied. "I'd give twenty years off my life."

"What is the line between youth and age?" "It is that point in your life when you stop yearning to look older and begin to hope that you look younger than your years. In other words, youth gives way to a new wrinkle."

"Why," a psychiatrist was asked, "do young people always seem to feel they can get away with things?" "It's because they know they have more time to improve."

At the college commencement, the senior alumni whispered to each other about how young the faculty looked, the faculty said the same thing about the graduating class and the graduating class said the same thing about the freshmen. Youth is a relatively old story.

Facts:

In recent years, America has had a split personality about its young people. On the one hand, it has lowered the age for voting eligibility and broadened the charters of student rights; on the other hand, it has had discriminatory rates for car insurance for young men below 25 (based on actuarial considerations), considerable prejudice against the views expressed by people in that age bracket and resentment of their attempts to make themselves separate from the bosom of the family. Part of this is what has existed throughout time, but it has been heightened by the pace and scope of modern life. Part has been due to the fact that recent youth, the product of the post-World War II baby boom, were so much more numerous than their predecessors. One notable result of all this has been a distinct decrease in the age of our political leadership, reflected, among other ways, in the abolition of the iron rule of entrenched senior chairmen of Congressional committees. Between 1957 and 1975, the number of Representatives under 40 rose and the number over 60 went down, although in the Senate the trend was less pronounced.

Volume 2

Apt
Comparisons

How to Use This Volume

A list of the words for which comparisons and symbols are given in this volume appears on the next several pages. Thereafter, each listed word has its own section, which includes comparisons, symbols, cross references and opposites.

If you can't find the particular word you want, look in the word list for a word of similar meaning. For example, you won't find the word "afraid," but you will find the word "frightened."

Some of the symbols have varying shades of meaning, and in such cases they may be used to signify different things. Midas, for example, is a symbol for being both acquisitive and miserly. Words and the names that symbolize them are often flexible; they can conjure up different pictures in different contexts. This volume provides a variety of the pictures provided by apt comparisons.

Words Listed

A

abandoned
abbreviated
abiding
abrupt
absolute
absorbent
absorbing
abstinent
absurd
abundant
abused
abusive
accidental
accommodating
accomplished
accountable
accurate
acquisitive
active
acute
adaptable
adjustable
admirable
admired
adventurous
affected
affectionate
affirmative
afflicted
affluent
aged
aggravated
aggressive
agile
agitated
agreeable
aimless
airy
alien
alike
allergic
alone
aloof
amateurish
amazing
ambitious
amiable

ample
ancient
anemic
angelic
angry
anguished
annoying
anonymous
antagonistic
anxious
apathetic
apologetic
apparent
appealing
appreciated
approachable
appropriate
arbitrary
arguable
argumentative
arid
aromatic
arresting
arrogant
artful
artistic
assertive
assorted
athletic
atrocious
attentive
attractive
austere
authentic
authoritative
automatic
available
average
awful
awkward

B

backhanded
backward
bad
baffling
balanced
bald

balky
bankrupt
barbarous
bare
barefaced
barren
basic
beastly
beautiful
becoming
believable
beloved
bent
bewildered
big
bigoted
binding
biting
bitter
black
blank
bleak
blemished
blended
blessed
blind
bloody
blue
boisterous
bold
booming
bored
boring
botched
bothered
bottomless
bountiful
brave
breathless
breezy
brief
bright
brilliant
bristling
brittle
broad
broke
brutal
bulging

bulky
bumpy
bungled
burdensome
buried
busy

C

calculating
callous
calm
camouflaged
carefree
careful
careless
carnal
casual
catching
cautious
ceaseless
celebrated
censored
certain
changeable
changed
changeless
chaotic
charitable
charming
chaste
cheap
cheated
cheerful
cherished
childish
choked
chronic
civilized
classic
classified
clean
clear
clever
close
closed
cloudy
coarse
cold
colorful
colorless
colossal
comfortable
comforting
comical
commanding

commendable
commercial
committed
common
commonplace
compelling
competitive
complete
complex
complicated
complimentary
compressed
compulsory
concealed
concentrated
concerned
concise
condensed
condescending
conditional
confident
confidential
confined
conformist
confused
congenial
congested
conscientious
considerate
consistent
constant
contagious
continuous
contrived
convenient
convincing
cool
cooperative
corny
correct
corrupt
cosmetic
cosmopolitan
courageous
courteous
cowardly
cracked
crafty
cranky
crass
craven
crazy
creative
criminal
critical
crooked

crowded
crucial
crude
cruel
crumby
cultured
curious
cutting
cynical

D

dainty
damaged
damaging
damned
dangerous
daring
dark
dashing
dated
dead
deadly
deaf
deafening
dear (affectionate)
dear (costly)
debatable
decadent
decayed
deceitful
deceptive
decisive
dedicated
deep
defensive
defiant
definite
delayed
deliberate
delicate
demonic
dense
dependable
deprived
deserted
deserving
desirable
desolate
desperate
despondent
destructive
detached
detestable
devious
devoted

dictatorial
different
difficult
dignified
diplomatic
direct
dirty
disagreeable
disastrous
discounted
discouraged
discreet
disguised
dishonest
dismal
disorganized
disposable
dissipated
distant
distinguished
distorted
distracting
divided
dizzy
docile
doctored
dogged
dogmatic
dopey
doubtful
downhearted
dreadful
dreary
drowsy
drunk
dry
dubious
dull
dumb
duplicit
durable
dutiful

E

eager
early
earthy
easy
economical
edgy
educated
eerie
effective
efficient
egotistical

elastic
electrifying
elegant
elementary
elevated
eligible
eloquent
elusive
embarrassed
eminent
emphatic
empty
enchanting
encouraging
endangered
endless
enduring
energetic
engaging
enigmatic
envious
erratic
erroneous
essential
established
estimable
euphoric
evasive
evil
exaggerated
exalted
excessive
exciting
exclusive
excusable
exemplary
exhausted
expensive
experienced
experimental
explicit
explosive
expressive
extended
extinct
extravagant
extreme

F

faceless
faded
faint
faithful
false

familiar
famous
fancy
far
fascinating
fast
fat
fatal
faulty
favorable
feeble
fertile
festive
feverish
fierce
filthy
final
fine
finished
firm
fishy
fit
flabby
flashy
flat
flattering
flawless
fleeting
flexible
flowery
foggy
foolish
forgetful
forgivable
forgotten
formal
forsaken
fortunate
fragrant
frail
frank
frantic
fraudulent
free
frequent
fresh
friendly
frightened
frightful
frugal
fruitful
fruitless
furious
fussy
futile
fuzzy

G

gallant
gaseous
gaudy
generous
genial
gentle
genuine
ghastly
gifted
glaring
gloomy
glorified
glorious
glossy
good
graceful
gracious
gradual
grand
grasping
grateful
greedy
gripping
gross
grouchy
grudging
guilty

H

habitual
hairy
handicapped
handsome
happy
hard
hard-core
hardy
harmful
harmless
harmonious
harsh
hasty
hateful
haughty
haunted
healing
healthy
hearty
heated
heavenly
heavy
heavy handed
hellish

helpful
helpless
heretical
hesitant
hidden
high
holy
honest
hopeful
hopeless
horrible
hospitable
hot
huge
humble
hungry
hurried
hybrid
hypocritical

I

icy
ideal
idealistic
idle
idolatrous
ignorant
ill advised
illegible
ill mannered
illogical
ill tempered
imaginary
imitative
immaculate
immature
immediate
imminent
immodest
immoral
impartial
impatient
impersonal
important
impressive
improper
impudent
impulsive
impure
inaccessible
inaccurate
inadequate
incalculable
incompetent
incongruous

indelible
independent
indifferent
indiscreet
indulgent
ineffective
inefficient
ineligible
inept
inert
inevitable
inexcusable
infinite
inflamed
inflammable
inflated
informal
innocent
innovative
inquisitive
insincere
insistent
inspired
instantaneous
instinctive
instructive
insulting
intangible
intimate
intolerant
intoxicating
intricate
intrusive
intuitive
inventive
inviting
involved
irrational
irregular
irrelevant
isolated

J

jaded
jammed
jarring
jealous
Jewish
juicy

K

keen
kind
knotty
knowledgeable

L

laborious
large
lasting
late
lavish
lawless
lazy
leakproof
leaky
learned
left handed
leftist
left out
legal
legendary
lethal
liberal
light
limited
limp
lingering
little
lonely
lonesome
long
loose
loud
lovable
lovely
low
loyal
lucky
lying

M

mad
magnificent
magnified
majestic
matchless
mature
meager
mean
meddlesome
meek
memorable
menacing
messy
mighty
militant
minimal
miraculous
misplaced

mistaken
misunderstood
mixed
mixed up
modern
modest
momentary
monotonous
monumental
moody
moving
muddled

N

naive
naked
narrow
nasty
natural
near
neat
necessary
needless
needy
negative
neglected
negligent
neighborly
nervous
neurotic
neutral
new
nice
nimble
noble
noisy
normal
nostalgic
noticeable
notorious
nourishing
numerous
nutty

O

obedient
objectionable
oblivious
obscure
obsolete
obvious
odorous
offensive
officious
old

old fashioned
ominous
open
opinionated
optimistic
original
overlooked
overwhelmed
overwhelming
overworked

P

packed
padded
painful
pale
panic-stricken
paradoxical
parched
parochial
particular
partisan
passionate
patient
patronizing
peaceful
perfect
permanent
permissive
perpetual
personal
persuasive
pessimistic
pestilential
picky
piratical
pitiful
pitiless
placid
plain
planned
plausible
playful
pleasant
pleased
pliable
pointed
poisonous
polished
polite
political
polluted
pompous
poor
popular
porous

portable
positive
possessive
powerful
precious
precise
predictable
prejudiced
premature
pretty
prevalent
privileged
productive
profitable
promising
prophetic
prosperous
provocative
prudent
public
pugnacious
punctual
pure
puzzled

Q

quaint
qualified
quarrelsome
queasy
queer
questionable
quick
quiet
quoted

R

rabid
radiant
radical
random
rapid
rare
rash
raw
reactionary
real
reasonable
rebellious
reckless
red
refined
regular
regulated
rejected
relaxed

relentless
reliable
repentant
repetitious
replaceable
representative
repressed
resented
resolute
respectable
restless
revolutionary
rich
ridiculous
righteous
rigid
ripe
rotten
rough
rude
run-down
rushed
rusty

S

sacred
sacrificial
sad
safe
satisfied
savage
scandalous
scanty
scarce
scared
scattered
scornful
secret
seldom
selective
selfish
sensitive
sentimental
serious
sexy
shady
shallow
sharp
short
shrewd
shrill
shy
sick
silent
simple
skinny
slim

slippery
slow
sly
small
smelly
smooth
smug
sneaky
sober
soft
solemn
solid
soothing
sore
sought after
soulful
sound
sour
sparse
special
spectacular
speculative
spoiled
spontaneous
spotless
square
steadfast
sticky
stingy
straight
strange
strong
stubborn
subtle
subversive
superficial
sure
surprised
suspicious
sweet
sympathetic
systematic

T

tactless
talkative
tame
tangled
tarnished
tasteful
tasteless
taxing
temporary
tense
tentative
thick
thin
threatening

tight
timeless
timely
tolerant
tough
transient
transparent
treacherous
tricky
true
trustworthy

U

ugly
uncertain
unclean
uncomfortable
uncompromising
underdeveloped
understandable
unfinished
unlucky

unnecessary
unpopular
unprepared
untruthful
urgent
useful
useless

V

vague
vain
varied
vast
versatile
violent
virtuous
visionary
volatile
vulgar

W

warm
watered

wayward
weak
wealthy
weary
welcome
wicked
wily
windy
winning
wise
worried
wrong

Y

yellow
young
youthful

Z

zealous

A

Abandoned: as a ghost town; as Salome's veils; as a used Kleenex; as an X-rated orgy.
symbols: Jezebel; wreck of the Hesperus; the Mary Celeste; Dorian Gray.
see also: deserted; empty; forgotten; decadent; immoral; dissipated.
opposite: crowded; noble; virtuous; jammed.

Abbreviated: as a grouch's smile; as a frost in August; as a classified ad.
symbols: Tom Thumb; pocket edition; cablese.
see also: condensed; short; small; brief.
opposite: windy; large; big; vast; long; excessive.

Abiding: as the Constitution; as mother love; as a family feud; as a permanent house guest.
symbols: Rock of Ages; the Phoenix.
see also: enduring; endless; lasting; permanent.
opposite: temporary; momentary.

Abrupt: as a station break; as a telephone call at 2 AM; as a sudden dip in cold water; as a head-on crash.
symbols: bolt from the blue; thunderbolt.
see also: rude; hasty; hurried.
opposite: gradual; smooth; leisurely.

Absolute: as the law of nature; as the state of virginity; as a miser's greed.
symbols: Tsar; monarch of all he surveys.
see also: arbitrary; rigid.
opposite: flexible; limited.

Absorbent: as a child's mind; as cereal soaking up cream; as the bread you use to sop up the gravy.
symbols: sponge; blotting paper.
see also: imitative; pliable; porous.
opposite: closed; leakproof.

Absorbing: as a good book by a cozy fire; as a fairy tale to a two-year-old; as a love affair.

symbols: Diogenes' tub.

see also: exciting; fascinating; inviting.

opposite: dull; forgotten; overlooked.

Abstinent: as a pious monk; as a reformed sinner; as a penitent on a bed of nails.

symbols: Alcoholics Anonymous; Nazarite; the wagon.

see also: sober; dry; chaste.

opposite: drunk; dissipated.

Absurd: as a clown's make-up; as a monkey in a dinner jacket; as heavy underwear in Hell.

symbols: Alice in Wonderland.

see also: queer; strange; ridiculous; foolish.

opposite: wise; reasonable.

Abundant: as the salt in the sea; as the corn in Kansas; as popcorn in the peanut gallery; as excuses in traffic court.

symbols: Cornucopia; horn of plenty.

see also: numerous; fruitful.

opposite: scarce; sparse; rare.

Abused: as a betrayed confidence; as a battered child; as the privileges of rank.

symbols: Job; Oliver Twist.

see also: damaged; deprived; excessive.

opposite: privileged; blessed; cherished.

Abusive: as a heckler with a foul mouth; as a baseball fan disagreeing with the umpire; as an anonymous letter.

symbols: billingsgate; fishwife.

see also: nasty; insulting; impudent.

opposite: courteous; kind; polite.

Accidental: as a slip on a banana peel; as an automobile crash; as being hit by lightning, as the whims of the gods.

symbols: Joe Btflspk.

see also: casual; lucky; unlucky.

opposite: planned; deliberate.

Accommodating: as Conrad Hilton; as a salesman with something he's anxious to sell; as a head waiter whose palm has been greased; as a doting mother.

symbols: Little Dorrit; Mother Hubbard.
see also: hospitable; helpful; welcome; neighborly.
opposite: disagreeable; cold; offensive.

Accomplished: as the roster of *Who's Who in America*; as an old master; as a finished performance; as a stroke of genius.

symbols: The Renaissance Man; Leonardo da Vinci.
see also: gifted; finished; complete.
opposite: unfinished; incompetent; inept.

Accountable: as a defendant in court; as a businessman's books; as an income tax return; as the manager of the mint.

symbols: where the buck stops.
see also: guilty; reliable; responsible.
opposite: innocent; evasive; fraudulent; negligent; slippery.

Accurate: as a pinpoint bullseye; as a dictionary definition; as a hole in one; as perfect pitch.

symbols: Kentucky rifleman.
see also: correct; perfect.
opposite: inaccurate; faulty; erroneous.

Acquisitive: as a go-getter with "the gimmes"; as an empire builder; as the guy with his eye on the pie in the sky.

symbols: gold digger; Midas.
see also: greedy; grasping; wealthy; rich.
opposite: generous; poor; kind.

Active: as an angry volcano; as a tumbler on a trampoline; as a restless child; as a bucko with a bumblebee in his britches.

symbols: whirling dervish.
see also: busy; restless; involved.
opposite: inert; lazy; quiet.

Acute: as a rupturing appendix; as a wise one's vision; as the pangs of hunger; as a glutton's indigestion.

symbols: the razor's edge.
see also: sharp; keen; quick.
opposite: dull; dumb; slow.

Adaptable: as putty; as a two-way stretch; as an ambidextrous athlete; as an all-purpose wheel.
symbols: chameleon.
see also: adjustable; flexible; pliable; changeable.
opposite: rigid; changeless; reactionary; arbitrary.

Adjustable: as a pair of suspenders; as a tripod; as an insurance claim; as a bargainer's prices.
symbols: Proteus.
see also: adaptable; flexible; changeable.
opposite: rigid; final; changeless.

Admirable: as a good example; as other people's courage in the face of adversity; as a young man's respect for an old man's years.
symbols: The Admirable Crichton.
see also: exemplary; respectable; good; attractive.
opposite: hateful; detestable.

Admired: as a teenage idol; as a sex symbol; as an old master; as the other guy's good luck.
symbols: folk hero; household god.
see also: cherished; lovable.
opposite: detestable; hateful.

Adventurous: as Columbus on an unknown sea; as a fledgling fleeing the nest; as a soldier of fortune.
symbols: Lochinvar; Daniel Boone; Davy Crockett.
see also: brave; aggressive; daring.
opposite: hesitant; frightened; scared; shy.

Affected: as a fashion model; as a sophomore trying to look like a senior; as a ham actor; as an egotist acting humble.
symbols: Gongora; Gongorism; Restoration comedy.
see also: superficial; shallow.
opposite: plain; simple; humble; natural.

Affectionate: as a pet puppy; as newly weds on their honeymoon; as a miser toward his money.
symbols: lovebirds; Tristan and Isolde; Romeo and Juliet; turtledoves.
see also: dear; warm; devoted.
opposite: distant; disagreeable; cold; threatening.

Affirmative: as a standing ovation; as a double negative; as a unanimous vote.

symbols: yes man.

see also: positive; confident; agreeable.

opposite: neutral; negative.

Afflicted: as an itcher who can't scratch; as the lame, the halt and the blind; as the first born sons of ancient Egypt; as a miser whose money turns out to be counterfeit.

symbols: Job.

see also: painful; pitiful; run-down.

opposite: blessed; healthy; happy.

Affluent: as a land of milk and honey; as the age of plenty; as a spendthrift who never runs out of money; as a collector with the key to the mint.

symbols: Croesus; the Rockefellers.

see also: rich; wealthy.

opposite: poor; deprived.

Aged: as the old family heirlooms; as choice Scotch whiskey; as ancient history; as the Petrified Forest.

symbols: Methuselah; senior citizen.

see also: old; ancient.

opposite: young; youthful.

Aggravated: as atrocious assault; as a gambler on a losing streak; as a wound rubbed with salt.

symbols: The Terrible Tempered Mr. Bang.

see also: angry; anguished; bothered; furious.

opposite: soothing; relaxed; calm.

Aggressive: as a fighting cock; as a shopper at a bargain counter; as a hungry tiger.

symbols: Mars; Aries.

see also: adventurous; menacing; threatening; assertive.

opposite: relaxed; friendly; peaceful.

Agile: as a circus acrobat; as a mountain goat; as a tap dancer on a bed of glowing coals; as a climbing cat.

symbols: Hermes, Mercury.

see also: nimble; fast; graceful.

opposite: awkward; confused; left handed.

Agitated: as a fly in a mixmaster; as a fat man's middle in a
                  vibrator belt; as troubled waters.
symbols: Jeremiah; nervous Nellie; the Terrible Tempered
                  Mr. Bang.
see also: nervous; chaotic; frantic; anxious.
opposite: relaxed; calm; placid.

Agreeable: as a lovers' tryst; as ecstasy in excelsis; as a cool
                  breeze on a hot night.
symbols: Elysium; Elysian fields.
see also: amiable; pleasant; happy; kind.
opposite: disagreeable; annoying; bristling.

Aimless: as a blind man's arrow; as a shot in the dark; as a
                  stroll in the park.
symbols: drifter; beatnik; hippie; Kerouac character.
see also: vague: bored; limp.
opposite: ambitious; decisive; dedicated; deliberate.

Airy: as an eagle's lair; as the holes in Swiss cheese; as
                  riding in a balloon.
symbols: Olympus.
see also: carefree; light; windy; breezy.
opposite: heavy; worried; tense.

Alien: as corn in a field of rice; as man on the moon; as a
                  fish out of water; as a basketball player in a
                  pygmy village.
symbols: a man from Mars; visitors from outer space; a
                  greenhorn.
see also: different; strange.
opposite: familiar; conformist; natural.

Alike: as two peas in a pod; as grains of sand; as the hairs
                  on your head.
symbols: Mike and Ike; Tweedledum and Tweedledee;
                  Bobbsey Twins.
see also: conformist.
opposite: different; matchless.

Allergic: as a hay fever victim in a field of pollen; as a case of
                  hives.
symbols: Allergy Ike; sneezy.
see also: sensitive; inflamed.
opposite: fit; fortunate; healthy.

Alone: as a hermit on a desert island; as garlic amid the scent of roses; as a man without a friend.
symbols: Robinson Crusoe; Adam.
see also: abandoned; desolate; isolated; lonely; lonesome; aloof.
opposite: dense; crowded; jammed.

Aloof: as a man avoiding a process server; as a cat that doesn't want to be bothered; as a lady that doesn't want to be wooed.
symbols: Mrs. Van Astorbilt; Howard Hughes; the invisible man.
see also: alone; cool; distant; icy; indifferent; haughty.
opposite: friendly; amiable; charming; warm; approachable

Amateurish: as a Sunday painter; as a first music lesson.
symbols: duffer; candidate for The Gong Show; dabbler; amateur night.
see also: inept; awkward.
opposite: experienced.

Amazing: as landing on the moon; as the recurrent miracle of sunrise; as a child's imagination.
symbols: The Twilight Zone; Believe It or Not.
see also: surprised; miraculous.
opposite: predictable.

Ambitious: as a stage mother; as a Horatio Alger hero; as a go-getter going out to get; as a politician with his eye on the White House.
symbols: Sammy Glick; young man in a hurry; the new woman.
see also: aggressive; hopeful.
opposite: aimless; vague; relaxed.

Amiable: as a well-tipped waiter; as a happy drunk; as a class reunion; as a candidate catching up with a crowd.
symbols: Happiness Boys; Sunshine Sammy; life of the party; Smiling Jack.
see also: agreeable; friendly; pleasant.
opposite: disagreeable; nasty.

Ample: as a fat man's waistline; as a rich person's purse; as a mother's love.
symbols: the groaning board; cornucopia; horn of plenty.
see also: abundant; fat; numerous; large.
opposite: scarce; limited.

Ancient: as the Pyramids; as the age of the dinosaurs; as the
                    waters of the sea; as the Joe Miller joke book.
symbols: Father Time; Father Abraham; Methuselah.
see also: aged; old; dated; old-fashioned.
opposite: modern; new.

Anemic: as a pauper's bankroll; as the soup in the poorhouse;
                    as an overdrawn bank account.
symbols: tired blood.
see also: weak; sick.
opposite: healthy; rich; strong.

Angelic: as an innocent babe; as the heavenly choir; as the
                    backers of a Broadway show; as the cherubim.
symbols: Gabriel; Ezriel; St. Peter
see also: heavenly; pure; kind; good.
opposite: disagreeable; bad; evil.

Angry: as a lynch mob on the loose; as a shopper who got
                    there too late for the bargains; as an open wound;
                    as a spoiled child.
symbols: The Terrible Tempered Mr. Bang; a seething vol-
                    cano.
see also: mad; ill-tempered; sore; inflamed.
opposite: calm; peaceful.

Anguished: as a rejected parent; as a day of mourning; as a
                    deserted lover.
symbols: Elektra.
see also: sad; painful; afflicted; worried; anxious.
opposite: happy; breezy; calm.

Annoying: as an itch where you can't scratch; as rain on your
                    best clothes.
symbols: Dennis the Menace; pain in the neck; the nasties.
see also: disagreeable; hateful.
opposite: agreeable; pleasant.

Anonymous: as an obscene phone call; as a graffiti writer; as a
                    nickel in the church collection box.
symbols: John Doe; Jane Doe; Richard Roe.
see also: secret; hidden.
opposite: barefaced; open.

Antagonistic: as oil and water; as fighters in the ring; as sin and redemption.
symbols: The Hatfields and the McCoys.
see also: argumentative; defiant; ill-tempered; pugnacious.
opposite: friendly; agreeable; affectionate; pleasant; apathetic.

Anxious: as an expectant father in the hospital waiting room; as a taxpayer about to be audited by the Internal Revenue Service.
symbols: Nervous Nellie.
see also: agitated; bothered; worried; concerned.
opposite: calm; placid.

Apathetic: as an off-year election; as the audience at a dull funeral; as the reaction to a chronic last-place team.
symbols: zombie.
see also: dull; placid.
opposite: anxious; eager.

Apologetic: as a defendant trying to appease the judge; as a guest who comes too early; as an errant spouse who's caught erring.
symbols: Caspar Milquetoast; repentant sinner.
see also: embarrassed; hesitant; humble.
opposite: nasty; cutting; ill mannered.

Apparent: as the blush on the bride; as the newness of a honeymoon couple; as the guilt of a man holding a smoking gun.
symbols: first blush.
see also: obvious; clear; certain; sure; noticeable.
opposite: debatable; uncertain; arguable; dubious; questionable.

Appealing: as an uncrowded beach; as a free sample; as a child's tears; as a friendly puppy.
symbols: Kewpie Doll; cutie pie; matinee idol; heart-throb.
see also: attractive; sympathetic; charming; nice.
opposite: ugly; hateful; nasty; rotten.

Appreciated: as a kind word in a tense moment; as an unexpected compliment; as a pair of free tickets to a hit show.

symbols: best seller; people's choice; hot property.
see also: popular; welcome; desirable.
opposite: unpopular; objectionable.

Approachable: as a prostitute plying her trade; as a candidate looking for another hand to shake; as a puppy that wants to be petted.

symbols: open door; outstretched hand.
see also: amiable; friendly; pleasant; agreeable; affectionate.
opposite: aloof; haughty; antagonistic.

Appropriate: as a coat in a cold wave; as a bottle in a barroom; as a bowl in a china shop.

symbols: according to Hoyle.
see also: ideal; correct.
opposite: wrong; unnecessary.

Arbitrary: as a papal bull; as a dictator's dictum; as the count for a knockdown in a prizefight; as the points of the compass.

symbols: Dutch uncle; little tin god.
see also: rigid; uncompromising; dictatorial.
opposite: adjustable; flexible; pliable.

Arguable: as an umpire's call; as what came first, the chicken or the egg; as a lawyer's brief; as a case in court.

symbols: the great debate; the question before the house.
see also: questionable; uncertain; debatable; dubious; doubtful.
opposite: certain; sure; clear; obvious.

Argumentative: as a session of the United Nations; as a spoiled child; as rival candidates in a hot election.

symbols: Philadelphia lawyer; barracks lawyer; jailhouse lawyer.
see also: quarrelsome; antagonistic; defensive; opinionated.
opposite: peaceful; agreeable; reasonable.

Arid: as a sand box in the Sahara; as a dry spell in the dust bowl.

symbols: Gobi Desert; Death Valley; dry bones.
see also: dry; parched; dull; empty.
opposite: watered; fruitful; deep; memorable.

Aromatic: as attar of garlic; as a perfume counter; as a salami.
symbols: smellovision; the nose knows
see also: smelly; fragrant; odorous.
opposite: blank.

Arresting: as an overworked cop; as a banner headline; as a growl from a police dog.
symbols: John Law; a clock-stopper.
see also: impressive; noticeable; spectacular.
opposite: dull; blank; boring.

Arrogant: as a civil servant with seniority; as a haughty head waiter; as the Caesars.
symbols: gauleiter; commissar; Dutch uncle.
see also: haughty; rude; offensive; officious.
opposite: humble; kind; courteous.

Artful: as contrived simplicity; as a pitchman's presentation; as a master craftsman; as an old master.
symbols: The Artful Dodger; Michelangelo.
see also: wily; sly; tricky; calculating; artistic; devious.
opposite: simple; plain.

Artistic: as the Metropolitan Museum; as a fight by Muhammad Ali in his prime; as a sonata by Beethoven.
symbols: Picasso; Mozart; Leonardo da Vinci; the Muses.
see also: beautiful; tasteful; gifted.
opposite: coarse; vulgar; tasteless.

Assertive: as a stage mother; as a ham actor fighting for the spotlight; as a hungry puppy.
symbols: Stentor; town crier.
see also: loud; positive; argumentative.
opposite: apathetic; neutral; hesitant; quiet.

Assorted: as a laundry list; as a fancy antipasto; as the items at a rummage sale; as the contents of the melting pot.
symbols: hash; a mixed bag.
see also: varied; mixed; blended; different.
opposite: alike.

Athletic: as a decathlon champion; as two hours on the tennis court; as a physical fitness fanatic.
symbols: the Olympics; Mercury; the bionic man.
see also: healthy; active; strong; fit.
opposite: inert; flabby.

Atrocious: as an axe murder; as the crime of the century; as
                    the scrapbook of Attila the Hun.
symbols: Ivan the Terrible; Genghis Kan.
see also: awful; cruel; horrible; frightful; hellish; evil.
opposite: kind; warm; gentle; good; angelic.

Attentive: as someone hoping to be remembered in your will;
                    as a spellbound audience; as a taxpayer at an
                    I.R.S. audit.
symbols: "His Master's Voice"; Argus.
see also: devoted; obedient; considerate; warm.
opposite: indifferent; distant; cool.

Attractive: as beauty to the beast; as a cool drink on a hot day;
                    as young love; as sunlight after a storm.
symbols: Helen of Troy; the Sirens; the Lorelei.
see also: appealing; charming; fascinating; beautiful.
opposite: ugly; crumby; beastly.

Austere: as the halls of Westminster Abbey; as an audience
                    with the Pope; as a hearing in the Supreme
                    Court.
symbols: Spartan; Draco.
see also: harsh; hard; frugal; minimal.
opposite: extravagant; lavish; soft; rich.

Authentic: as a fingerprint; as an Act of Congress; as a cer-
                    tified check.
symbols: the real McCoy.
see also: real; true; genuine.
opposite: false; lying; untruthful.

Authoritative: as the Ten Commandments; as a decision of the
                    Supreme Court; as holy writ; as divine inspira-
                    tion.
symbols: the horse's mouth; the Delphic Oracle; the Al-
                    manach de Gotha.
see also: reliable; compelling; true; trustworthy; positive.
opposite: untruthful; false; evasive; uncertain.

Automatic: as the twelve o'clock whistle; as the stroke of mid-
                    night; as a recorded message; as the blink of an
                    eye.
symbols: Robby the Robot; the computer age.
see also: certain; predictable; constant; habitual; planned;
                    sure.
opposite: spontaneous; uncertain; chaotic; disorganized.

Available: as a jobless politician; as an actor at liberty; as a vacant billboard.
symbols: Available Jones; Mr. Barkis.
see also: open; abundant; numerous.
opposite: scarce; sparse.

Average: as the middle of the road; as the Dow Jones index; as the man on the street.
symbols: John Q. Public.
see also: normal; regular.
opposite: special; different; extreme.

Awful: as sin; as the face of death; as a shriek in the night; as the truth when it hurts.
symbols: the fires of Hell; the Days of Awe; the wrath of the gods.
see also: bad; atrocious; horrible; disastrous; impressive; mighty.
opposite: modest; small; cheerful; good; exemplary; pleasant.

Awkward: as an adolescent; as a toddlers' dancing class; as a flimsy alibi.
symbols: the awkward age; a penguin.
see also: inept; heavy-handed; left-handed.
opposite: graceful; gracious; agile; nimble.

B

Backhanded: as damning with faint praise; as a tennis shot at Wimbledon; as praising with faint damns.
symbols: the sly fox.
see also: devious; duplicit; sly; awkward; hypocritical.
opposite: direct; barefaced; graceful; gracious.

Backward: as a horse and buggy on a superhighway; as the glances of a gangster on the lam; as a ten-year-old in kindergarten; as a trip in reverse.
symbols: Simple Simon; dinosaur; village idiot; Mickey Mouse.
see also: slow; delayed; ignorant.
opposite: bright; wise; quick.

Bad: as rotten apples; as the wicked witch of the west; as a mob's manners; an an illiterate's spelling; as burning books.

symbols: the big bad wolf; the Devil; Satan; Lucifer.
see also: evil; rude; mean; sick.
opposite: good; pleasant; amiable.

Baffling: as the mystery of life; as the cure for aging; as the dimensions of outer space.

symbols: the Sphinx.
see also: confused; complex; complicated; difficult.
opposite: understandable; clear; easy.

Balanced: as a man on a tightrope; as a banker's checkbook; as the scales of justice; as a report by Price, Waterhouse.

symbols: wirewalker; Mexican standoff; tightrope walker.
see also: alike; harmonious; honest.
opposite: extravagant; extreme; distorted.

Bald: as the proverbial billiard ball; as the American eagle; as the classic coot; as a barefaced lie.

symbols: Mexican Hairless; skinhead.
see also: bare; smooth; naked; obvious.
opposite: hairy; hidden; devious.

Balky: as a donkey's disposition; as a baby with a bad case of colic; as a spoiled child; as a bickerer driving a bargain.

symbols: Missouri mule; bad actor.
see also: stubborn; rigid; cranky.
opposite: pliable; agreeable; cooperative.

Bankrupt: as a treasury without a trace of treasure; as a broken cookie jar; as a wiped-out gambler.

symbols: gone to the cleaners; taking a bath; ten cents on the dollar.
see also: broke; poor; deprived; run down.
opposite: rich; wealthy; affluent; prosperous.

Barbarous: as a human sacrifice; as a caveman clobbering his next-door neighbor; as the law of the jungle.

symbols: Attila the Hun; saber-toothed tiger; nature in the raw.
see also: savage; brutal; cruel.
opposite: civilized; kind; cultured.

Bare: as the naked truth; as a rose bush in February; as a new-born babe.
symbols: kewpie doll; September morn.
see also: bald; naked; simple; barren; open.
opposite: concealed; camouflaged; closed.

Barefaced: as a bully's bluster; as a man who's just shaved off his beard; as a super-salesman's enthusiasm; as a mother's pride.
symbols: Mr. Brass.
see also: impudent; bold; naked.
opposite: hidden; cowardly; polite; courteous.

Barren: as the surface of the moon; as a blank page; as an empty landscape; as a pauper's prospects.
symbols: desert; Death Valley.
see also: arid; fruitless; parched; bare.
opposite: fruitful; productive.

Basic: as Run Dick Run; as the Constitution; as the law of supply and demand; as the Ten Commandments.
symbols: First Principles; base one.
see also: essential; elementary; necessary.
opposite: unnecessary; excessive; fancy.

Beastly: as the animals of the Ark; as a heat wave in Hell; as the occupants of the zoo.
symbols: the law of the jungle; tooth and claw.
see also: cruel; fierce.
opposite: civilized; kind; polite.

Beautiful: as a happy memory; as a bride; as the sunset that ends a perfect day; as the face of true love.
symbols: Venus; Helen of Troy.
see also: lovely; attractive; appealing; handsome; pretty.
opposite: ugly; awful; coarse; dirty; frightful.

Becoming: as a garland for a hero; as ham to eggs; as a bouquet to a bride; as a waltz at a wedding.
symbols: the crowning glory; the final touch.
see also: appropriate; fit; appealing; complimentary.
opposite: ugly; improper.

Believable: as seeing for yourself; as being there; as a certified check; as a deathbed confession.

symbols: Mr. Integrity; the real McCoy.

see also: trustworthy; convincing.

opposite: transparent; treacherous; lying.

Beloved: as a nursery rhyme; as an uncle with money; as Siegfried was to Brunhilde.

symbols: Daphnis and Chloe; Romeo and Juliet; Tristan and Isolde.

see also: affectionate; dear; lovable; precious.

opposite: detestable; hateful; nasty.

Bent: as a pipe going around a corner; as a kneeling knee; as a tuba; as a pretzel.

symbols: the crooked man who walked a crooked mile; a clover-leaf turn.

see also: crooked; distorted.

opposite: direct; straight.

Bewildered: as a drunk with a dizzy spell; as a baby first seeing itself in a mirror; as a lost child; as one suddenly awakened.

symbols: the lost soul; Hazy Daisy; orphan of the storm.

see also: confused; puzzled; mixed up.

opposite: confident; commanding; calm; correct.

Big: as a billionaire's bankroll; as a swollen elephant; as a braggart's mouth.

symbols: Behemoth; Leviathan; Gargantua.

see also: huge; large; colossal.

opposite: small; minimal.

Bigoted: as the voice of hate; as a color bar; as a skin test for scapegoats; as the Inquisition.

symbols: Salem witch trial; the burning of the books.

see also: narrow; prejudiced; ignorant; intolerant; exclusive.

opposite: tolerant; liberal; friendly; neighborly.

Binding: as a ball and chain; as a contract signed and sealed; as a ball of twine; as the bonds of blood.

symbols: Ten Commandments; Bushido; Loyalty Oath.

see also: compulsory; effective.

opposite: ineffective; tentative.

Biting: as a berserk shark with hunger pangs; as gallows humor; as the flavor of a hot pepper; as a watch-dog's welcome; as a bumblebee.
symbols: Mr. Vitriol; Dr. Knock.
see also: sharp; bitter; nasty; cutting.
opposite: kind; sweet; soft.

Bitter: as a sour lemon; as a Boston winter; as spoiled wine.
symbols: Eumenides; the Furies; Xanthippe.
see also: cold; sour; sharp; harsh; bleak.
opposite: happy; soft; sweet; kind.

Black: as a coal mine before the light goes on; as midnight without a moon; as a storm cloud; as the other side of the moon.
symbols: River Styx; Soul.
see also: dark.
opposite: pale; light.

Blank: as a wall before the graffiti artists find it; as a baf-fled student's expression; as a bankrupt's check-book.
symbols: clean slate.
see also: empty; clean; clear; desolate; bare; barren.
opposite: crowded; messy; congested.

Bleak: as a sandstorm in the Sahara; as a fall guy's future; as the surface of the moon; as a bad weather forecast.
symbols: Slough of Despond; Wuthering Heights.
see also: dismal; bitter; colorless; alone.
opposite: colorful; warm; hospitable; encouraging.

Blemished: as a roue's reputation; as a broken mirror; as a fac-tory second.
symbols: damaged goods; Adam after Eden.
see also: impure; tarnished; damaged; faulty.
opposite: pure; flawless; perfect.

Blended: as hash in a mixmaster; as the colors of the rainbow; as most Scotch whiskey; as a Bloody Mary.
symbols: mulligan; melting pot; stew.
see also: mixed; varied.
opposite: divided.

Blessed: as the Good Book; as the meek who shall inherit the earth; as it is to give, rather than to receive; as the Sabbath day; as the pure in heart.
symbols: Fortunate Isles; God's favorites.
see also: exalted; happy; sacred; holy; lucky; fortunate.
opposite: damned; unlucky.

Blind: as one who will not see; as a bat in a bright light; as the three mice who ran after the farmer's wife.
symbols: Justice; Braille.
see also: oblivious; handicapped.
opposite: sensitive; visionary

Bloody: as an operating room; as a battlefield; as an axe murder; as shaving with a dull razor.
symbols: slaughterhouse; Aceldama.
see also: red; brutal; savage.
opposite: kind; happy; safe; peaceful.

Blue: as the skies above; as a pornographic movie; as a disappointed lover; as the waters of the sea.
symbols: rated X; blue Monday.
see also: colorful; anguished; worried; dirty; sexy.
opposite: colorless; happy; cheerful; clean.

Boisterous: as sailors on liberty fresh from the sea; as the winning team's locker room; as Saturday night in the corner saloon; as high school kids when school is let out.
symbols: Hotspur; Gadarene swine; the roar of the crowd.
see also: loud; noisy; rough.
opposite: quiet; refined; silent.

Bold: as polished brass; as an avenging angel; as a lion on the loose.
symbols: Hector; Achilles; Sir Galahad; Sir Lancelot.
see also: daring; brave; courageous.
opposite: cowardly; quiet.

Booming: as business in a bank on payday; as a 21-gun salute.
symbols: Big Bertha; Stentor; Midas touch.
see also: loud; noisy; busy; rushed; prosperous.
opposite: quiet; slow; poor.

Bored: as a two-year-old at a talk on metaphysics; as the audience when an after-dinner speech becomes a forever-after speech; as an illiterate in a bookstore.

symbols: Sleeping Beauty; Job's comforter.
see also: jaded; apathetic
opposite: active; involved.

Boring: as somebody else's snapshots; as an oft told tale told once too often; as a doctor's waiting room with no magazines to read.

symbols: Sleeping Beauty.
see also: dull; empty.
opposite: fascinating; gripping; compelling; exciting; charming.

Botched: as hard boiled oatmeal; as burnt bacon; as a lumpy carpet.

symbols: Watergate; Waterloo.
see also: bungled; spoiled, mixed up.
opposite: perfect; right.

Bothered: as a bubble in a windstorm; as a face with a fist stuck into it; as a baby with a balky bootie; as three women wearing the same dress at the party.

symbols: Old Fortunatus (*Thomas Dekker*); the Terrible Tempered Mr. Bang.
see also: aggravated; worried; anxious; downhearted; bewildered; concerned.
opposite: calm; cool; relaxed; placid

Bottomless: as a nudist camp; as the depths of despair; as the basement of Hades.

symbols: quicksand; Tartarus; the lower depths.
see also: endless; deep; unfinished.
opposite: high; narrow.

Bountiful: as a bumper crop; as an unexpected bonus; as being remembered in your rich uncle's will; as the winning lottery ticket.

symbols: last of the big-time spenders; the horn of plenty; Lady Bountiful.
see also: fruitful; rich; fertile.
opposite: poor; meager; sparse; arid.

Brave: as Daniel in the lion's den; as a voyage into the unknown; as the roster of the Congressional Medal of Honor.

symbols: lion; Achilles; Galahad; David.
see also: courageous; bold; daring.
opposite: afraid; frightened; cowardly; scared.

Breathless: as a middle-aged marathon runner; as an excited teenager; as a sports crowd watching a sudden-death overtime.

symbols: Mr. Excitement.
see also: exhausted; excited.
opposite: calm.

Breezy: as Chicago in March; as a song and dance man; as the birds of spring.

symbols: Zephyr; Pollyanna; cave of Aeolus.
see also: windy; airy.
opposite: calm; quiet.

Brief: as a grouch's smile; as lightning in collied night (*Shakespeare*); as the life span of a raindrop.

symbols: abridged edition; nutshell; Tacitean.
see also: abbreviated; abrupt; quick; fast.
opposite: extended; long.

Bright: as sunshine; as the lights on Broadway; as the sparkle of a pure white diamond.

symbols: the Milky Way; the Great White Way.
see also: light; flashy; glaring; brilliant.
opposite: dull; dark; slow.

Brilliant: as a flash of lightning; as the invention of the wheel; as a no-hit game.

symbols: Einstein; da Vinci; summer sunshine; ball of fire.
see also: glaring; bright; electrifying; inspired.
opposite: dull; dark; slow; blank.

Bristling: as a porcupine with quills at the ready; as an unfriendly witness; as a fighting gamecock.

symbols: Xanthippe; wild boar.
see also: angry; aggressive; nasty; rough.
opposite: amiable; friendly; peaceful; calm.

Brittle: as an entertainer's reputation; as an eggshell; as a
miniature made of matchsticks.

symbols: eggshell, glass windowpane.

see also: frail; weak.

opposite: strong; firm; solid.

Broad: as the passage to Hell; as an elephant's bottom; as
the day is long.

symbols: Dan to Beersheba; the Milky Way; the Big Dipper.

see also: ample; large; big.

opposite: narrow; small.

Broke: as a pauper whose credit cards have been stolen; as
the man who cornered the market in Confeder-
ate money.

symbols: poorhouse; poverty row.

see also: bankrupt; poor.

opposite: rich; affluent.

Brutal: as beating a baby; as the law of the jungle; as cutting a throat.

symbols: Yahoo; Roman holiday.

see also: cruel; savage; barbarous; fierce; harsh.

opposite: civilized; cultured; kind.

Bulging: as a millionaire's wallet; as a bankrupt's credit file;
as a beer guzzler's waistline.

symbols: overstuffed chair; Falstaff.

see also: fat; excessive; bulky.

opposite: thin; anemic; skinny.

Bulky: as a fat man in a full length fur; as the postman's
Christmas mailbag.

symbols: Goliath; Falstaff; Gargantua.

see also: large; big; fat.

opposite: small; thin.

Bumpy: as an unpaved road; as a ride down the rapids; as a
ride on a roller-coaster with square wheels.

symbols: air pocket; rocky road to Dublin.

see also: rough; uncomfortable.

opposite: smooth; calm; comfortable.

Bungled: as Watergate; as the war on crime; as the unsettled state of the weary world.

symbols: butterfingers; wreck of the Hesperus.
see also: botched; spoiled; mixed up.
opposite: perfect; accomplished; brilliant.

Burdensome: as a fur coat in July; as a bag of rocks; as the trials of Job.

symbols: labors of Hercules; Sisyphus.
see also: heavy; uncomfortable.
opposite: light; carefree; comfortable; comforting.

Buried: as Captain Kidd's treasure; as the late George Apley; as illegal profits.

symbols: R.I.P.; Lethe.
see also: concealed; secret; hidden; repressed.
opposite: open; apparent; noticeable; obvious.

Busy: as a bee on a business trip; as a one-armed paperhanger in a windstorm.

symbols: beehive.
see also: ceaseless; crowded; feverish; overworked; rushed.
opposite: idle; carefree; quiet.

C

Calculating: as a fortune hunter; as a taxpayer in search of a refund; as an adding machine running amok.

symbols: Delilah; Caesar's Cassius; Iago.
see also: wily; sly; artful; tricky.
opposite: simple; plain; honest.

Callous: as the heel of the barefoot boy; as a hardened criminal; as a dictator's conscience; as a clerk in the complaint department.

symbols: Mr. Hard Heart; heart of stone; cold shoulder.
see also: hard; indifferent; cruel.
opposite: soft; considerate; sympathetic; kind.

Calm: as still waters; as the quiet after the storm; as sleeping dogs.

symbols: Sunday vespers; deserted village; ghost town; Nirvana.
see also: placid; quiet; relaxed.
opposite: agitated; frantic; chaotic; worried; anxious; edgy.

Camouflaged: as a wolf in sheep's clothing; as laundered money.
symbols: chameleon; Trojan horse.
see also: concealed; hidden; secret.
opposite: apparent; obvious; noticeable.

Carefree: as a kid on vacation; as a prepaid holiday; as a happy
ending.
symbols: the lotus eaters.
see also: happy; relaxed; airy.
opposite: anxious; worried.

Careful: as a barefoot boy in a field of broken glass; as a cat
on a tightrope.
symbols: by the numbers; by the book.
see also: cautious; conscientious.
opposite: negligent; careless.

Careless: as lighting a match to find a gas leak; as a drunken
driver; as a spendthrift with borrowed money.
symbols: unguided missile.
see also: negligent; hasty.
opposite: conscientious; careful.

Carnal: as a satyr's stare; as sex in the barnyard; as an
X-rated movie.
symbols: Circean cup; Messalina; Casanova.
see also: earthy; sexy.
opposite: innocent; pure.

Casual: as a passing shower; as an adolescent's attitude; as
a beachcomber's costume.
symbols: pot luck; que sera sera.
see also: carefree; relaxed; informal.
opposite: formal; regular; frantic.

Catching: as a cold; as the enthusiasm of a crowd; as a sprinter
chasing a crawler; as a fisherman's net.
symbols: hit parade; epidemic.
see also: contagious; attractive.
opposite: elusive; isolated; ugly.

Cautious: as a new keeper with an old gorilla; as a doctor
without malpractice insurance; as a buffalo in a
rug factory; as a statement from the State Department.
symbols: Fabian.
see also: careful; discreet.
opposite: careless; negligent.

Ceaseless: as the battle of the sexes; as the search for sun-
                    shine; as the cycle of life.
symbols: perpetual motion.
see also: endless; constant; perpetual; permanent.
opposite: temporary; momentary.

Celebrated: as the Saviour's birth; as the wages of sin; as chil-
                    dren's birthdays; as Heaven and Hell and all that
                    lies between.
symbols: the hero of the hour; the talk of the town.
see also: famous; important.
opposite: quiet; obscure.

Censored: as a prisoner's mail; as a mouth washed out with
                    soap; as a Soviet encyclopedia.
symbols: Mrs. Grundy; Bowdler; book burning.
see also: classified; repressed; concealed; hidden; secret.
opposite: public; permissive; open.

Certain: as death and taxes (*Benjamin Franklin*); as water
                    flowing downhill; as the probability of change; as
                    fate.
symbols: sure thing; money in the bank.
see also: sure; constant; definite.
opposite: uncertain; arguable; changeable.

Changeable: as a fickle lover; as a baby's diaper; as the mood of a
                    mob; as the latest fashions; as the weather.
symbols: Proteus; chameleon.
see also: moody; volatile; elastic.
opposite: constant; steadfast; definite.

Changed: as a patient after a sex operation; as the value of a
                    dollar; as yesterday's innocence; as a convert's
                    faith.
symbols: new look.
see also: different; varied; dated.
opposite: alike; conformist.

Changeless: as the expression of the Sphinx; as the sun in the
                    sky; as human nature.
symbols: rock of ages.
see also: steadfast; true; constant.
opposite: changeable; uncertain; different.

Chaotic: as the bargain basement when the big sale is on; as World War III; as rush hour downtown; as the first day at kindergarten.

symbols: bedlam; Tower of Babel.

see also: agitated; busy; frantic; panic-stricken; disorganized.

opposite: calm; quiet; peaceful; relaxed.

Charitable: as giving of yourself; as a helping hand; as forgiving a sinner; as giving people faith and hope.

symbols: the good Samaritan; Lady Bountiful.

see also: generous; kind; helpful; considerate.

opposite: cruel; harsh; mean.

Charming: as a person persuading a snake to do tricks; as a performer making a pitch for a part; as innocent young love; as a candidate at a fund-raising party.

symbols: Price Charming; the three Graces.

see also: appealing; attractive; beautiful; enchanting.

opposite: hateful; objectionable; ugly.

Chaste: as a vestal virgin; as ice (*Shakespeare*); as a suitor who's still chasing; as the mind of a new-born babe.

symbols: an innocent; Artemis; Galahad.

see also: pure; clean; innocent.

opposite: blemished; tarnished; impure.

Cheap: as dirt; as a miser's mite; as unsolicited advice; as a rummage sale.

symbols: Scrooge; Jack Benny; Mickey Mouse.

see also: stingy; crumby.

opposite: dear; generous.

Cheated: as a customer who buys the Brooklyn Bridge; as the person who plans to con the con man; as the victim of a stacked deck.

symbols: sucker; bag holder.

see also: damaged; forsaken; left out; overlooked; unlucky.

opposite: prosperous; rich; wealthy; winning.

Cheerful: as the bearer of good news; as an infectious laugh; as a good meal in pleasant company; as an incurable optimist.

symbols: Pollyanna; Thalia; the Cheshire cat.
see also: pleasant; agreeable; amiable; happy.
opposite: sad; moody; downhearted; dreary; gloomy.

Cherished: as the family heirlooms; as a fond memory; as a good reputation.

symbols: Queen of Hearts; America's sweetheart.
see also: beloved; dear; precious; appreciated.
opposite: forsaken; rejected; forgotten.

Childish: as chewing a pacifier; as a security blanket; as a rubber duck in the bathtub.

symbols: the children's hour; kindergarten.
see also: young; youthful; immature; foolish.
opposite: old; mature; wise.

Choked: as a bunter's baseball bat; as an engine coming up for air; as a clogged chimney.

symbols: garrotte.
see also: jammed; brief; dead; short.
opposite: clear; strong; long; loose.

Chronic: as complaints from critics; as crabgrass; as hay fever; as wondering about the weather.

symbols: four-time loser.
see also: regular; constant; lasting; continuous; permanent.
opposite: temporary; uncertain; acute.

Civilized: as paper plates; as drinking through a plastic straw; as a drawing room comedy; as a hearing in the Supreme Court.

symbols: Attic (Attica).
see also: educated; cultured; refined.
opposite: coarse; vulgar; rude.

Classic: as the Bible; as the beauty of Venus de Milo; as the Pyramids; as The Odyssey and The Iliad.

symbols: Attic; Augustan.
see also: lasting; enduring.
opposite: transient; momentary.

Classified: as a secret in the Pentagon; as the ranks of the
                      Army and Navy; as the genuses of Nature; as a
                      card catalogue.
symbols: official secrets; Iron Curtain; caste system.
see also: assorted; censored; varied.
opposite: open; public; disorganized.

Clean: as a pastor's parable; as the bones picked by a vul-
                      ture; as a hound's tooth; as a whistle.
symbols: new broom; Simon pure.
see also: pure; flawless; spotless; immaculate.
opposite: dirty; blemished; tarnished; impure; unclean.

Clear: as a cloudless sky; as an open road; as an ultimatum;
                      as a fist in the face; as crystal.
symbols: plain English; open book.
see also: obvious; certain; apparent; understandable.
opposite: foggy; fuzzy; cloudy.

Clever: as a cautious cat; as clockwork; as a campus politi-
                      cian.
symbols: old fox; Attic salt.
see also: calculating; intuitive; sly; wise.
opposite: simple; innocent; dumb.

Close: as the air in a smoke-filled room; as the fingers of
                      your hand; as a disputed call at home plate; as
                      next year is to New Year's Eve.
symbols: a hair's breadth; Damon and Pythias; Black Hole of
                      Calcutta.
see also: near; stingy; arguable; debatable; questionable;
                      dear.
opposite: distant; certain; sure; obvious; far; antagonistic.

Closed: as a bigot's mind; as a deal where the seller has
                      already cashed the check; as kindergarten at
                      midnight; as a restricted community; as death.
symbols: Berlin wall; Iron Curtain.
see also: bigoted; narrow; repressed; isolated; censored.
opposite: open; available; liberal; expressive.

Cloudy: as a defective crystal ball; as milk of magnesia; as a scene viewed through a gauze curtain; as uncertain weather.

symbols: nimbus; cumulus.
see also: foggy; fuzzy; dark; dense; uncertain.
opposite: bright; clear; apparent; obvious; certain.

Coarse: as cotton canvas; as convicts' conversation; as the inscriptions on rest room walls; as adolescent humor.

symbols: Caliban; Goth; philistine.
see also: vulgar; rude; rough.
opposite: gentle; smooth; refined.

Cold: as a hermit's hospitality; as a polar bear's living room; as midnight on the moon; as Kansas in February.

symbols: North Pole; Arctic; Jack Frost; iceberg.
see also: bitter; windy; icy; antagonistic.
opposite: warm; friendly; hospitable.

Colorful: as a peacock's plumes; as a painter's palette; as the flowers that bloom in the spring.

symbols: rainbow; Joseph's coat.
see also: flashy; bright; brilliant; gaudy.
opposite: colorless; bleak; barren; bare; desolate.

Colorless: as the air we breathe; as a deprived chameleon; as a bashful mouse.

symbols: Plain Jane.
see also: bleak; dull; boring; barren.
opposite: colorful; flashy; gaudy; brilliant; spectacular.

Colossal: as Caesar's gall; as the expanding universe; as the birth rate of bacteria; as a ham actor's ego.

symbols: Colossus of Rhodes; Gargantua.
see also: huge; vast; ample; big.
opposite: small; little; meager.

Comfortable: as a cow in a corncrib; as your own bed; as a friendly conversation.

symbols: Land of Cockaigne; bosom of the family.
see also: easy; relaxed; convenient.
opposite: restless; uncomfortable.

Comforting: as a vote of confidence; as victory snatched from the jaws of defeat; as love reciprocated; as a hot cup on a cold morning.

symbols: Nirvana.
see also: encouraging; soothing; sympathetic; warm.
opposite: callous; cool; indifferent; cruel.

Comical: as a circus clown; as an ape acting human; as somebody else slipping on a banana peel; as the Sunday funnies.

symbols: slapstick; Gilbertian; French farce; Hellzapoppin'.
see also: absurd; nutty; playful.
opposite: serious; dull; boring; sad.

Commanding: as the tablets from Mount Sinai; as an imperial monarch; as a spoiled child; as the tug of fate; as a date with destiny.

symbols: Zeus; the brass.
see also: dictatorial; compelling; decisive.
opposite: weak; shy; uncertain.

Commendable: as keeping the faith; as virtue in a sea of trouble; as kindness in a selfish world, as valor on the field of battle.

symbols: seal of approval: Congressional Medal of Honor; applause.
see also: good; desirable; admirable.
opposite: bad; inexcusable; objectionable.

Commercial: as a sponsor's message; as a shopping center; as an auction; as a pitchman's spiel; as a sales demonstration in a store.

symbols: the street; over the counter.
see also: profitable; speculative; competitive.
opposite: amateurish; bankrupt; broke.

Committed: as a convict with a life sentence; as a miser is to money; as the folks that signed the contract.

symbols: dues payer; working member.
see also: dedicated; loyal; involved.
opposite: indifferent; evasive; cool; casual; left out.

Common: as clay; as a crowd; as the lowest denominator; as
~~the ground we share; as horse sense.~~

symbols: run of the mill.
see also: earthy; average.
opposite: rare; special.

Commonplace: as the union of consenting adults; as the standard
set of sins; as growing old.
symbols: Tom, Dick and Harry.
see also: average; square; frequent.
opposite: rare; affected; special.

Compelling: as a court order; as a gun at your head; as the law of
nature; as a successful drama; as the Sermon on
the Mount.
symbols: Hobson's choice; Fate; the Fates.
see also: binding; persuasive; effective; commanding; convincing; gripping.
opposite: weak; inadequate; debatable; dull.

Competitive: as cut-throat capitalism; as two prospectors staking
out the same claim; as a grudge match; as three
horse traders in a one-horse town.
symbols: dog eat dog; price war; survival of the fittest.
see also: commercial; antagonistic.
opposite: apathetic; indifferent; cooperative.

Complete: as a family with 27 children; as Adam's exile from
the Garden of Eden; as a total eclipse; as the
unabridged dictionary.
symbols: the works; the whole cosmos.
see also: absolute; final; finished.
opposite: partial; underdeveloped; unfinished.

Complex: as the instructions on an income tax form; as
French irregular verbs; as the question of nu-
clear energy; as explanations of the new math.
symbols: Gordian knot.
see also: baffling; complicated; difficult.
opposite: understandable; clear; easy; simple.

Complicated: as the directions for an assemble-it-yourself toy; as
a maze with moving walls; as a bureaucrat's ex-
planation of the rules; as a French farce.
symbols: labyrinth.
see also: difficult; complex; baffling.
opposite: clear; simple; understandable; easy.

Complimentary: as a vote of confidence; as a standing ovation; as a testimonial dinner.
symbols: blue ribbon; four stars.
see also: gracious; flattering.
opposite: insulting; rude.

Compressed: as a three-page summary of the Bible; as the gas in a high pressure tank; as the Lord's Prayer on the head of a pin; as a whale in a sardine can.
symbols: microfilm; cablese.
see also: condensed; concentrated; concise; brief; tight.
opposite: loose; excessive; long.

Compulsory: as wearing clothes in public; as going to school; as paying taxes; as plowing is for a farmer.
symbols: a must; the law of the land.
see also: arbitrary; dogmatic; rigid; dictatorial.
opposite: adjustable; pliant; free.

Concealed: as a secret sex life; as a worm inside an apple; as a hero's fears; as the beauties of poverty; as the identity of an anonymous obscene phone caller.
symbols: hide and seek; closed doors.
see also: secret; hidden; buried; camouflaged; censored.
opposite: open; obvious; apparent; noticeable.

Concentrated: as a hypnotist's stare; as the pain of a hangover; as frozen orange juice.
symbols: Johnny one-note.
see also: compressed; concise; condensed; attentive.
opposite: indifferent; weak; apathetic; loose.

Concerned: as an investor watching his stock hit zero; as the bookies when a 100 to 1 shot wins the race; as a catcher whose pitcher is wild; as a taxpayer who's been invited in by Internal Revenue.
symbols: Nervous Nellie; worry wart.
see also: anxious; worried; agitated; bothered; tense.
opposite: relaxed; calm; placid; apathetic.

Concise: as a headline; as a nice girl's no; as the "I do" in a wedding ceremony.
symbols: Tacitean; nutshell; Spartan brevity.
see also: brief; compressed; concentrated; tight.
opposite: loose; windy; excessive; long.

Condensed: as dehydrated soup; as a college cram course; as the milk of human kindness.

symbols: pocket edition; thumbnail; digest.

see also: concise; compressed; concentrated; short; abbreviated; brief.

opposite: long; windy; excessive.

Condescending: as a sophomore to a freshman; as a music critic trying to make a reputation; as a self-professed connoisseur telling you why you know nothing; as a cat putting up with being petted.

symbols: Lord of the manor; cock of the walk; lord of creation.

see also: haughty; arrogant; officious; patronizing.

opposite: polite; courteous; free; friendly.

Conditional: as a politician's ultimatum; as what a bargainer says is a "last offer"; as a postponed foreclosure; as a doctor's prognosis.

symbols: the big if; the yes but syndrome.

see also: tentative; uncertain.

opposite: absolute; certain.

Confident: as a champion fighting a chump; as a rooster in a henhouse; as the only candidate on the ballot; as a man with lots of money in his pocket.

symbols: Mr. Micawber; Pollyanna.

see also: sure; bold; certain; positive; resolute.

opposite: hopeless; anxious; worried; concerned.

Confidential: as a state secret; as a midnight tryst; as an accountant's audit; as a church confessional.

symbols: sealed lips; closed doors; "Deep Throat."

see also: classified; secret; censored.

opposite: open; public.

Confined: as a goldfish in a teacup; as a dog on a short leash; as a kid in a crib; as a cow in a corset.

symbols: caged bird; Devil's Island; Black Hole of Calcutta; house arrest.

see also: limited; close.

opposite: free.

Conformist: as a corps of cadets passing in review; as the dancers in a chorus line; as a flock of sheep.

    symbols: by the book; the establishment; when in Rome.

    see also: alike.

    opposite: different.

Confused: as a mouse in a maze; as a sea horse whose father has turned into its mother; as a compass in a magnet factory.

    symbols: Tower of Babel; Mrs. Malaprop; lost soul.

    see also: bewildered; chaotic; disorganized.

    opposite: certain; sure; knowledgeable.

Congenial: as corned beef and cabbage; as peace and quiet; as a happy drunk.

    symbols: peaches and cream; sweetness and light; Arcadia.

    see also: friendly; harmonious; happy; hospitable.

    opposite: angry; annoying; bitter; disagreeable.

Congested: as the throughway at rush hour; as a chest cold; as a boom town in a gold rush; as steerage; as Times Square on New Year's Eve; as the aisles in the bargain basement.

    symbols: S. R. O. (standing room only); mob scene; Black Hole of Calcutta.

    see also: crowded; busy; rushed.

    opposite: clear; airy; empty.

Conscientious: as a religious objector; as a worried watchdog; as a scared patient following the doctor's orders.

    symbols: Trojan; Trojan service; on the ball.

    see also: careful; cautious; honest; devoted.

    opposite: indifferent; careless; duplicit; dishonest.

Considerate: as a groom to his new bride; as a good host; as an act of courtesy; as an offer of a second chance.

    symbols: Sir Walter Raleigh; Good Samaritan; Mr. Nice Guy.

    see also: kind; generous; attentive; charitable.

    opposite: callous; indifferent; distant; cruel; cool; harsh.

Consistent: as salmon swimming upstream; as the course of a ferryboat; as a cock's crowing.

    symbols: steady Eddie.

    see also: changeless; uncompromising; certain.

    opposite: changeable; varied.

Constant: as the northern star (*Shakespeare*); as the laws of nature; as the leopard's spots; as the cycle of night and day; as a miser's penny pinching.

symbols: Penelope; Rock of Gibraltar.
see also: ceaseless; endless; steadfast; faithful; permanent; changeless,
opposite: changeable; uncertain; temporary; false.

Contagious: as the common cold; as laughter; as a popular tune; as a mob's panic.

symbols: the hit parade; epidemic.
see also: catching; attractive.
opposite: elusive; exclusive.

Continuous: as the stars that shine (*Wordsworth*); as an endless circle; as a self-winding watch; as the earth revolving around the sun.

symbols: the task of Sisyphus.
see also: ceaseless; constant; endless; perpetual; chronic; permanent.
opposite: temporary; final; fleeting.

Contrived: as a corny commercial; as a bad plot; as a complicated alibi.

symbols: a Rube Goldberg; bag of tricks; deus ex machina.
see also: false; lying; untruthful; complicated.
opposite: simple; true; honest; sincere.

Convenient: as a timely interruption; as having your own gold mine around the corner.

symbols: deus ex machina.
see also: helpful; near; appropriate; useful.
opposite: useless; awkward; jarring.

Convincing: as a sign from God; as seeing it for yourself; as being hit on the head.

symbols: an Academy Award performance; certified check.
see also: reasonable; reliable; trustworthy.
opposite: uncertain; untruthful; transparent.

Cool: as the proverbial cucumber; as last night's ardor in the light of day; as the morning dew; as a meeting between neighbors who aren't talking.

symbols: Jack Frost; iceberg.
see also: aloof; indifferent; cold; relaxed; icy.
opposite: warm; hot; bothered; worried; anxious; bewildered; tense.

Cooperative: as bill and coo; as coition; as a matched team of horses; as give and take; as a football center and the quarterback.

symbols: helping hand; team play.
see also: helpful; friendly.
opposite: stubborn; balky; quarrelsome.

Corny: as a can of succotash; as the crops in Kansas; as the Joe Miller joke book; as pone in Paducah; as the kernels on the cob.

symbols: an old vaudeville act; an old familiar story.
see also: dated; old-fashioned; familiar.
opposite: new; original; modern.

Correct: as a courtier's conduct; as a curtsey to a queen; as 100% on an exam.

symbols: Emily Post.
see also: polite; courteous; perfect; accurate.
opposite: rude; ill-mannered; impolite; wrong; erroneous.

Corrupt: as a slush fund; as a black market in counterfeit currency; as a stuffed ballot box; as a professional turncoat.

symbols: another Watergate; Teapot Dome.
see also: dishonest; crooked; deceitful; evil; bad; treacherous; dirty.
opposite: clean; honest; innocent; good.

Cosmetic: as a bobbed nose; as a new coat of paint; as lipstick and powder; as a toupe on a bald man.

symbols: paint job; plastic surgery.
see also: beautiful; attractive; lovely; deceitful.
opposite: ugly; raw; harsh.

Cosmopolitan: as blintzes in Little Italy; as the United Nations; as the crossroads of the world; as a carnival in Cannes.

symbols: the Melting Pot; international house; the jet set.
see also: mixed; tolerant;
opposite: parochial; narrow.

Courageous: as the lone defender of a lost cause; as eating a full course dinner in a dirty restaurant; as doing something you're scared to death to do.

symbols: Captains Courageous; Hairbreadth Harry; Dick Daring.
see also: brave; bold; daring; gallant.
opposite: cowardly; scared; frightened.

Courteous: as a courtier to a queen; as a bus queue in London; ~~as a waiter working for a big tip; as the salesman~~ who wants your business.
symbols: Sir Walter Raleigh; Alfonse and Gaston.
see also: considerate; polite; correct.
opposite: ill-mannered; rude; impolite.

Cowardly: as a hyena with a food phobia; as a coyote that's afraid of the dark; as a stab in the back; as an anonymous phone call.
symbols: the Cowardly Lion in *The Wizard of Oz*; Bob Acres.
see also: scared; frightened; yellow.
opposite: bold; brave; daring; gallant.

Cracked: as a broken mirror; as the ice in a frozen daiquiri; as the cookies in the asylum.
symbols: a nut; a coot.
see also: crazy; faulty; damaged.
opposite: sane; reasonable; wise; healthy.

Crafty: as a conspirator in a cloakroom; as a crow in a cornfield; as a con man on the make; as a kid conning his grandma.
symbols: Cassius of the lean and hungry look (*Shakespeare*);
see also: the sly fox.
opposite: innocent; pure; frank; honest.

Cranky: as a colicky kid or the parent awakened at 2 AM; as a 1910 tin lizzie; as a cat in a contretemps.
symbols: the terrible tempered Mr. Bang; fussbudget.
see also: balky; disagreeable; bristling.
opposite: aggreable; amiable; pleasant; nice.

Crass: as profiteering in penicillin; as ignorance calling itself erudition; as a dollop of dolts.
symbols: Elmer Gantry.
see also: gross; vulgar; ignorant; selfish.
opposite: fine; straight; generous; estimable; nice.

Craven: as a coward's whimper; as life on one's knees; as voluntary slavery.
symbols: white feather; yellow streak.
see also: cowardly; afraid; scared; frightened.
opposite: bold; daring; brave; courageous.

Crazy: as a berserk bedbug; as a cuckoo coot; as a loco loon; as a skeleton man trying to lose weight.
symbols: Mad Hatter; Bedlam.
see also: cracked; mad; irrational.
opposite: responsible; reasonable; normal.

Creative: as the gift of life; as a seed sprouting in the earth; as a painting by Picasso.
symbols: Michelangelo; da Vinci; William Shakespeare.
see also: artistic; original; inventive; innovative; inspired.
opposite: dull; amateurish; useless; imitative.

Criminal: as a killer caught in the act; as everything listed in the penal code; as a mugger in the park.
symbols: Public Enemy No. 1; now starring on a wanted poster; Jesse James.
see also: evil; lawless; immoral; corrupt; wicked; bad; crooked; hard-core.
opposite: legal; correct; pure.

Critical: as a reviewer telling you how bad a play is; as the moment of nuclear fission; as a confrontation between two killers.
symbols: Devil's advocate; seat on the aisle.
see also: scornful; crucial; serious; attentive.
opposite: safe; secure; friendly; relaxed.

Crooked: as a corkscrew; as an inviting finger; as a politician on the take; as a coiled spring.
symbols: Tweed ring; loaded dice; stacked dack.
see also: bent; distorted; dishonest; criminal; corrupt.
opposite: straight; honest.

Crowded: as a bank on payday; as a safe port in a storm; as the theater with the hit show.
symbols: S.R.O. (standing room only); mob scene; rush hour.
see also: congested; busy; rushed; packed; thick; jammed.
opposite: blank; quiet; empty.

Crucial: as the last game of the world series; as life and death; as a finger on the trigger.
symbols: moment of truth; the last straw; Judgment Day; the payoff.
see also: important; serious; decisive; urgent.
opposite: useless; needless; unnecessary.

Crude: as raw petroleum; as country cactus; as rubber
                    dripping from the tree.
symbols: Yahoo; sons of Belial; Goth.
see also: raw; rough; harsh.
opposite: smooth; polished.

Cruel: as death by inches; as a creeping cancer; as a cold
                    shoulder in a hot spot; as a kick in the pants.
symbols: Attila the Hun; Marquis de Sade; Genghis Khan.
see also: awful; atrocious; hellish; horrible; mean.
opposite: kind; amiable; gentle; friendly.

Crumby: as the bottom of the breadbox; as cracked biscuits;
                    as the lower crust of life; as a baker's leaving.
symbols: Grub Street; Poverty Row.
see also: messy; crass; nasty.
opposite: clean; neat; nice.

Cultured: as the Harvard bookshelf; as a college professor; as
                    buttermilk; as a pearl in a captive oyster.
symbols: highbrow; intellectual.
see also: knowledgeable; educated.
opposite: ignorant; crass; dopey.

Curious: as an inquiring photographer; as a nosy neighbor; as
                    a snowstorm in July; as a cat.
symbols: The Old Curiosity Shop; Mr. Snoop; Nosy Nellie.
see also: meddlesome; strange; inquisitive.
opposite: indifferent; apathetic; normal; regular.

Cutting: as a surgeon's scalpel; as a kitchen knife; as a razor's
                    edge; as a cold shoulder.
symbols: surgery; the axe.
see also: biting; sharp; keen.
opposite: dull; friendly.

Cynical: as a sinner scorning salvation; as a psalm by a
                    sadist; as the state of mind of a solid skeptic.
symbols: Diogenes; doubting Thomas.
see also: biting; bitter; pessimistic; doubtful; dubious.
opposite: optimistic; eager; innocent.

D

Dainty: as a dewdrop on a daisy; as a dish to set before the queen; as a dancing doll; as a daffodil.
symbols: lifted pinkie; Dresden doll;
see also: delicate; graceful.
opposite: heavy-handed; coarse; gross.

Damaged: as a broken wing; as the serpent's reputation after the Garden of Eden; as a car that lost an argument with a trailer truck.
symbols: the wreck of the Hesperus; the ruins of Pompeii.
see also: spoiled; faulty; tarnished; blemished; run-down.
opposite: flawless; perfect; pure; fresh.

Damaging: as a Nixon tape; as a bite from a black widow spider; as a fire in an oil refinery; as being caught with a smoking gun at the scene of a shooting.
symbols: bull in a china shop; accident going someplace to happen; one-man wrecking crew; Vandals.
see also: destructive; harmful; guilty.
opposite: harmless; innocent; helpful.

Damned: as a deal with the Devil; as a forlorn Faust; as an unrepentant sinner; as from here to eternity.
symbols: Cain; the mark of Cain; the Devil's disciple; lost soul.
see also: haunted; dreadful; evil; unlucky; wicked.
opposite: good; exalted; blessed; holy; sacred.

Dangerous: as a pothole on a speedway; as a ticking bomb; as a psychopathic killer; as a dive in the dark.
symbols: sword of Damocles; dynamite; the razor's edge.
see also: threatening; ominous; menacing; critical; harmful.
opposite: safe; secure; harmless; trustworthy; reliable.

Daring: as the young man on the flying trapeze; as a dance in a den of lions; as a duel to the death; as tickling a tiger.
symbols: Nimrod; Lochinvar; Columbus.
see also: adventurous; defiant; bold; brave; reckless; courageous.
opposite: scared; cowardly; careful; cautious.

Dark: as the other side of the moon; as the bottom of the deep blue sea; as the doom of the damned; as a moonless night at midnight.

symbols: Erebus; blackout.
see also: black; cloudy; gloomy; sad.
opposite: bright; light; brilliant; cheerful; happy.

Dashing: as a cavalier courting a queen; as a sprinter racing to the tape; as a dude with new duds.

symbols: Lochinvar; Don Juan.
see also: bold; attractive; adventurous; sexy.
opposite: slow; dreary; dull.

Dated: as the Nina, the Pinta, and the Santa Maria; as a dowager; as the dipsy doodle; as the divine right of kings.

symbols: Model T; an antique; a throwback; a dodo.
see also: obsolete; old; ancient; old fashioned; corny; quaint.
opposite: new; original; fresh; modern.

Dead: as driftwood; as a doorknob; as an abandoned dream; as the air in a sealed tomb; as yesterday's headlines.

symbols: a corpse; gone West; six feet under; dodo.
see also: finished; dull; quiet; buried; flat; inert.
opposite: fresh; new; hot; innovative; original; young.

Deadly: as the seven sins; as a tiger shark; as the black plague; as the bite of a cobra; as Cleopatra's asp.

symbols: kiss of death; appointment in Samarkand.
see also: lethal; fatal; destructive.
opposite: harmless; safe.

Deaf: as one who will not hear; as justice is blind; as a doorpost; as a spoiled child with selective hearing.

symbols: tuned out; wearing earmuffs.
see also: indifferent; oblivious; selective.
opposite: involved; concerned.

Deafening: as the amplifer for adolescent music; as a blast in the ear; as the drums of war.

symbols: thunder; Big Bertha.
see also: noisy; loud.
opposite: quiet; silent.

Dear (affectionate):   as remembered kisses after death (*Alfred Tennyson*); as days of delight; as the scenes of a happy childhood; as the dawn of love.

symbols: apple of one's eye.

see also: cherished; precious; beloved; lovable.

opposite: rejected; forgotten; forsaken; hateful.

Dear (costly):   as a dollop of radium; as a flawless diamond; as ordinary fish roe masquerading as caviar; as the price of coffee in a rising market.

symbols: a king's ransom; highway robbery.

see also: high; inflated.

opposite: free; cheap.

Debatable: as who won the argument; as a question of judgment; as a campaign issue; as the definition of happiness.

symbols: the jury is out; a hung jury; you pays your money and you takes your choice.

see also: questionable; arguable; uncertain; dubious; doubtful.

opposite: established; obvious; certain; sure.

Decadent: as the younger generation has seemed to the elder since the dawn of time; as Rome during its decline and fall; as the French court right before the French Revolution.

symbols: Marquis de Sade; Sodom and Gomorrah.

see also: decayed; rotten; evil; immoral.

opposite: virtuous; good.

Decayed: as garbage gone to seed; as an apple core in the open air; as a cadaver in a haunted house; as a mouthful of cavities.

symbols: Cheap John; the wreck of the Hesperus.

see also: rotten; spoiled; damaged.

opposite: fresh; new; good.

Deceitful: as a dodo declaring he can fly; as a fixed deck of cards; as loaded dice; as a doublecrosser covering his tracks; as a turncoat with a reversible vest.

symbols: Ananias; a double agent.

see also: lying; tricky; treacherous; dishonest; insincere; false; duplicit.

opposite: honest; true; sincere; trustworthy; faithful.

Deceptive: as a pair of falsies; as a promise from a pitchman; as a deliberate decoy; as wishful thinking.

symbols: mirage; fool's gold.
see also: false; duplicit; lying; deceitful.
opposite: honest; trustworthy; true.

Decisive: as death; as the Day of Judgment; as a knockout; as the Battle of Waterloo.

symbols: crossing the Rubicon; the die is cast.
see also: crucial; final; definite; certain; emphatic.
opposite: uncertain; changeable; debatable; uncompromising; compelling.

Dedicated: as a martyred missionary; as the Founding Fathers; as a national monument.

symbols: a saint; crusader.
see also: devoted; attentive; holy.
opposite: indifferent; aloof; lazy; insincere.

Deep: as the bottom of the sea; as the Devil's domicile; as first love (*Alfred Tennyson*); as Death Valley.

symbols: the lower depths; bottomless pit; Hades.
see also: bottomless; endless.
opposite: shallow; superficial.

Defensive: as a middle line backer; as an early warning system; as a moat.

symbols: Alibi Ike; foxhole.
see also: bristling; cautious; defiant; frightened.
opposite: unprepared; hesitant; helpless.

Defiant: as a rebellious teenager; as Horatio at the bridge; as an untamed tiger.

symbols: William Tell; Sons of Liberty; Boston Tea Party; the Lost Battalion.
see also: bold; rebellious; fierce; uncompromising.
opposite: yellow; reasonable; cowardly; docile.

Definite: as a fingerprint; as money in the bank; as a signed contract; as an oath signed in blood.

symbols: in black and white; exhibit A.
see also: certain; sure; clear; positive; decisive; emphatic.
opposite: uncertain; questionable; changeable; vague.

Delayed: as a double take; as a limelight lover's entrance; as a derailed train.

symbols: Quintus Fabius Maximus Cunctator; Fabian; slow burn.

see also: slow; late; hesitant.

opposite: fast; dashing; instantaneous.

Deliberate: as a five-year plan; as an Act of Congress; as a court order; as aiming a gun.

symbols: game plan; blueprint; slow motion.

see also: thoughtful; planned; slow; precise.

opposite: spontaneous; accidental; quick; uncertain.

Delicate: as gossamer lace; as fine crystal; as a spider's web; as a surgeon's touch.

symbols: touching a nerve; sensitive area; walking on eggs.

see also: frail; sensitive; dainty; airy; light; intricate.

opposite: coarse; gross; heavy; crude.

Demonic: as the cabinet of Dr. Caligari; as a trip through Hell; as the adventures of Ulysses; as the eternal underworld.

symbols: Beelzebub; Satan; Lucifer; the Devil; Pluto.

see also: hellish; bad; evil; mean; disagreeable; hateful.

opposite: angelic; heavenly; good; noble; virtuous.

Dense: as the heart of the jungle; as a peasoup fog; as a dummy's brain.

symbols: a thicket; a forest; a logjam.

see also: foggy; thick; cloudy; crowded; stupid.

opposite: clear; thin; bright; brilliant.

Dependable: as clockwork; as the cycle of the tides; as sunrise.

symbols: Old Reliable.

see also: steadfast; reliable; trustworthy; faithful.

opposite: changeable; uncertain; dishonest; lying; false.

Deprived: as a baseball team without a bat; as a bull left by himself; as a miser without money.

symbols: the 100 neediest cases; the disadvantaged; the slums.

see also: poor; broke; needy; neglected; hungry.

opposite: rich; wealthy; prosperous; affluent; privileged.

Deserted: as an empty island; as a golf course at midnight; as a
                         sunken ship.

symbols: ghost town; haunted house; wide open spaces.
see also: empty; blank; desolate.
opposite: crowded; congested; busy.

Deserving: as a doer of good deeds; as a good Samaritan; as a
                         helpful friend; as one good turn.

symbols: the good guys; the Golden Rule gang.
see also: admirable; good; needy.
opposite: objectionable; wayward; wicked.

Desirable: as power to a politician; as dinner to a dieter; as
                         detente to the diplomats; as a date with destiny.

symbols: sine qua non; primary objective; holy grail.
see also: sought after; welcome; popular.
opposite: unpopular; objectionable.

Desolate: as the sea of despair; as a lonely wasteland; as a
                         garbage dump; as rejected love.

symbols: Death Valley; the sands of the desert; a haunted
                         house.
see also: alone; isolated; barren; bare; abandoned; empty;
                         dismal.
opposite: crowded; abundant; fertile; hospitable.

Desperate: as a last stand; as a cornered rat; as a gamble with
                         death.

symbols: forlorn hope; Frantic Frank.
see also: frantic; mad; extreme; worried.
opposite: calm; hopeful; confident.

Despondent: as a dying duck; as a sea of sadness; as a bookie
                         paying off a 1000-to-1 shot; as a spurned suitor.

symbols: Slough of Despond; sad acres.
see also: sad; gloomy; downhearted; pessimistic; discour-
                         aged.
opposite: happy; glad; cheerful; optimistic.

Destructive: as moths in a woolens closet; as crows in a cornfield;
                         as a temper tantrum; as an earthquake with a ten
                         rating on the Richter scale.

symbols: the sacking of Rome; the Vandals.
see also: damaging; harmful; disastrous; lethal.
opposite: harmless; safe; helpful.

Detached: as an innocent bystander; as a neutral observer; as a colonel a continent away from his command; as a caboose without a locomotive.

symbols: in dreamland; separate tables.

see also: aloof; apathetic; distant.

opposite: anxious; eager; involved.

Detestable: as a head full of hate; as a hymn to Hitler; as a dastardly deed.

symbols: the man you love to hate; public enemy number 1.

see also: hateful.

opposite: lovable.

Devious: as a disguised detour; as a double-dyed deceiver; as a counter counter spy; as a secret agent.

symbols: Fifth Column; Uriah Heep; the sly fox; Iago.

see also: sneaky; backhanded; sly; hypocritical.

opposite: direct; honest; clear; barefaced.

Devoted: as a patriot to a fatherland; as a Midas to his money; as a mother to her child; as a prophet to a faith.

symbols: Penelope; Damon and Pythias; Tristan and Isolde.

see also: attentive; dedicated; dear; loyal; committed.

opposite: indifferent; cool; callous; negligent; false.

Dictatorial: as a gun at your head; as a master over a slave; as a domineering parent; as the guy who owns the ballpark.

symbols: Der Fuehrer; Il Duce; Hitler; the Generalissimo; the Godfather.

see also: commanding; arbitrary; rigid; threatening.

opposite: flexible; changeable; free; open.

Different: as night and day; as the elephant and the eel; as apples and oranges; as democracy and dictatorship; as male and female.

symbols: the other side of the street; one man's meat.

see also: varied; assorted; hybrid.

opposite: alike.

Difficult: as the labors of Hercules; as governing the ungovernable; as making dreams come true; as defying Destiny.

symbols: the $64 question; the hat trick; Gordian knot.

see also: complicated; baffling; hard.

opposite: easy; understandable; simple.

Dignified: as a deacon; as a sermon at the summit; as a session of the Supreme Court; as a college commencement; as a state funeral.

symbols: the striped pants set; a formal tea party.
see also: solemn; grand; formal; quiet.
opposite: boisterous; noisy; ill-mannered; loud.

Diplomatic: as a white lie; as a caution phrased as a compliment; as looking the other way; as an artful ambassador.

symbols: striped pants; protocol.
see also: gracious; dignified; artful; tasteful; wily.
opposite: tactless; ill-mannered; rude.

Direct: as a bullet; as a straight line between two points; as a dentist's drill.

symbols: straight arrow; blunt instrument.
see also: straight; honest; clear.
opposite: devious; sneaky; sly; crooked.

Dirty: as the linen in the laundry; as dishonest dollars; as uncollected garbage; as a doublecross.

symbols: ring around the collar; a pigsty; Augean stable.
see also: unclean; dishonest; tarnished; rusty.
opposite: spotless; clean; honest; straight.

Disagreeable: as a haughty head waiter; as the neighborhood grouch; as a dirty name; as stormy weather.

symbols: pain in the neck; pretty kettle of fish; Pandora's box.
see also: annoying; nasty; rotten; bad.
opposite: agreeable; amiable; kind; friendly; good.

Disastrous: as lighting a match to look at a gas line; as the devil's triumph; as the day of doom; as someone snuffing out the sun.

symbols: Armageddon; Waterloo.
see also: damaging; destructive; harmful; horrible.
opposite: harmless; safe.

Discounted: as an unsuccessful rumor; as a cut-rate drugstore; as the clearance prices in a bargain basement.

symbols: markdown; cynics' corner.
see also: cheap; dubious; doubtful.
opposite: dear; believable.

Discouraged: as a drunk in a dry county; as a poet who can't get published; as a three-time loser; as a baseball player who can't get to first base.

symbols: Listening to Cassandra; in the dumps.

see also: sad; despondent; downhearted; blue; gloomy; pessimistic

opposite: confident; happy; glad; cheerful; optimistic.

Discreet: as a plain brown wrapper on a tactless book; as a diplomat; as a cautious whisper.

symbols: soul of discretion; tiptoe; one step at a time.

see also: cautious; prudent; wise; careful.

opposite: rash; careless; indiscreet.

Disguised: as a wolf in sheep's clothing; as a painted clown; as a man in a mask.

symbols: chameleon; protective coloration; the invisible man; man of many faces.

see also: camouflaged; concealed; hidden; doctored.

opposite: obvious; apparent; open; clear; frank.

Dishonest: as a forged signature; as a meow by a mouse; as a false set of books; as cheating your mother.

symbols: Ananias; Baron Munchausen; confidence man; Jesse James; Cagliostro.

see also: crooked; corrupt; evil; lying; false.

opposite: honest; true; genuine; real; frank.

Dismal: as a decaying swamp; as bad news on a nasty day; as a dull speech before dinner.

symbols: Wuthering Heights; nightmare alley; poverty row.

see also: gloomy; bad; dark; desolate; bleak.

opposite: happy; cheerful; bright.

Disorganized: as a do-it-yourself instruction sheet; as a day in a dreamworld; as a riot; as a really spontaneous demonstration; as recess in high school.

symbols: mob scene; bedlam; tower of Babel.

see also: confused; chaotic.

opposite: planned; calculating; neat.

Disposable: as a paper diaper; as common trash; as extra income; as biodegradable waste.

symbols: a throwaway; orphan of the storm.

see also: obsolete; replaceable.

opposite: permanent.

Dissipated: as a roving roue; as a wastrel's wealth; as a departed dollar; as the pleasure of the chase when it is past.

symbols: Dorian Gray; Bacchanalia.
see also: wayward; loose; immoral; wicked.
opposite: moral; straight; good.

Distant: as from here to eternity; as a dowager's disapproval; as the Day of Judgment; as outer space.

symbols: the ends of the earth; a trillion light years; different wave lengths.
see also: far; cool; indifferent; cold; aloof; haughty.
opposite: near; sympathetic; comforting.

Distinguished: as a Nobel Prize; as divine inspiration; as winning your letter in the college of hard knocks.

symbols: top drawer; pillar of the community; head of the class.
see also: eminent; famous; exemplary.
opposite: obscure; overlooked; shady.

Distorted: as a paranoiac's perspective; as looking at the world through the wrong end of the telescope; as a much traveled rumor; as a double jointed skeleton.

symbols: a horse designed by a committee; a pretzel gone amok.
see also: crooked; bent; changed; false.
opposite: straight; clear; genuine; true.

Distracting: as squeaky shoes in a quiet library; as a coughing fit at a concert; as hot pants in a poolroom; as an interruption during a soliloquy.

symbols: sideshow; second feature; interruption in the broadcast.
see also: arresting; irrelevant; questionable.
opposite: pointed; absorbing; accurate.

Divided: as the Grand Canyon; as the wheat and the chaff; as a loaf of bread after it has been sliced.

symbols: choosing sides; a house divided; separate tables.
see also: different; mixed; partisan; quarrelsome.
opposite: alike; cooperative; harmonious.

Dizzy: as a drunk on a dromedary; as a loon that's lapped up loco water; as a rider on a roller-coaster; as a lover of LSD.

symbols: a fruitcake; falling off the wire; wound up.
see also: confused; crazy; foolish.
opposite: straight; solid; wise.

Docile: as a little lamb; as a devoted dog; as smart kids the night before Christmas.

symbols: a dishrag; Mr. Meek; Caspar Milquetoast.
see also: obedient; meek; gentle.
opposite: stubborn; nasty; rough.

Doctored: as loaded dice; as a stacked deck; as the second version of an unsuccessful recipe; as a kid with a cold.

symbols: Mickey Finn; a mickey.
see also: changed; distorted; polluted; mixed.
opposite: true; genuine; clean; original.

Dogged: as the devil's determination; as a preacher's patience; as a ploughman plodding home his weary way.

symbols: sticktoitiveness; a bulldog; Spartan.
see also: stubborn; committed; insistent.
opposite: flexible; easy; lazy.

Dogmatic: as a catechism; as a professor's pet theory; as the Communist Manifesto.

symbols: Holy Writ; gospel; written in stone; ipse dixit.
see also: opinionated; positive; rigid; changeless.
opposite: flexible; pliant; changeable; loose.

Dopey: as a dose of opium; as a pill popper; as the Disney dwarf; as a dimwitted donkey.

symbols: hophead; Simple Simon; the village idiot; Boeotian.
see also: foolish; ignorant; dumb; doctored; drunk.
opposite: wise; knowledgeable; clever; sober; inspired.

Doubtful: as a five-day weather forecast; as a mule's fertility; as full payment of the wages of sin.

symbols: Doubting Thomas; dark horse.
see also: questionable; uncertain; debatable; dubious.
opposite: certain; sure; affirmative; positive.

Downhearted: as a ghost without a house to haunt; as a devil caught doing a good deed; as a dieter who hasn't lost an ounce.

symbols: Slough of Despond; sea of despair; blue funk.
see also: discouraged; despondent; gloomy; sad.
opposite: happy; cheerful; optimistic.

Dreadful: as a reign of terror; as a day of infamy; as the plagues in ancient Egypt; as fooling around with Mother Nature.

symbols: Roman holiday; blood bath; the Devil and his dam.
see also: awful; evil; frightful; atrocious; bad; hellish.
opposite: good; pleasant; heavenly; angelic; nice.

Dreary: as a dark, damp day; as a garbage dump on a dull, drab dawn; as the dregs of despair; as a deserted house.

symbols: Wuthering Heights; dullsville; blue Monday.
see also: gloomy; dismal; sad; dark.
opposite: cheerful; bright; happy; pleasant.

Drowsy: as a lazy dog by a friendly fire; as the audience for a heavy speech after an even heavier dinner; as a ten o'clock town at 2 AM.

symbols: Sleeping Beauty; arms of Morpheus; Rip van Winkle.
see also: weary; relaxed; bored.
opposite: restless; active; excited.

Drunk: as he who prostrate lies, without the power to drink or rise (*Thomas Love Peacock*); as a one-martini man on a six-martini streak; as a barfly with a barrel of bourbon.

symbols: Bacchus; John Barleycorn; the old soak; Dutch courage.
see also: dizzy; wet.
opposite: sober; dry.

Dry: as the sands of the desert; as dehydrated dust; as a drought in Death Valley.

symbols: Pythagorean brotherhood; on the wagon; Encratites; total abstention.
see also: parched; arid.
opposite: watered.

Dubious: as the justice given in a kangaroo court; as a forced confession; as the testimony of a proven per-jurer; as a bargainer's bargain.

symbols: on the fence; doubting Thomas.

see also: uncertain; questionable; doubtful.

opposite: certain; sure; positive; affirmative.

Dull: as a boring story that you've heard before; as a knife that can't cut; as a pause between yawns.

symbols: Boeotian; dullsville; Nirvana.

see also: boring; colorless; dead; dumb.

opposite: exciting; fascinating; keen; sharp; bright.

Dumb: as a beast of the field; as a dolt in a duncecap; as the luck of the favored few.

symbols: Boeotian; lockjaw; Chelm; galloping ignorance.

see also: dopey; ignorant; silent.

opposite: wise; clever; talkative.

Duplicit: as a worthless guaranty; as a double doublecross.

symbols: double dyed deceiver; fifth column; stacked deck.

see also: hypocritical; sneaky; tricky; doctored; fraudulent.

opposite: true; honest; genuine.

Durable: as the sands of time; as eternal love; as the war between men and women.

symbols: Rock of Gibraltar; rock of ages.

see also: constant; strong; perpetual; permanent; lasting.

opposite: faded; changeable; temporary; weak.

Dutiful: as a child's thank you letter; as a compliment to a harried hostess; as a call home on Mother's Day; as a devoted daughter.

symbols: Galahad; a Trojan; Gal or Man Friday.

see also: obedient; devoted; attentive; considerate; courte-ous; polite.

opposite: indifferent; negligent; careless; antagonistic; nasty.

E

Eager: as an eagle eying his prey; as two lovers heading for
a hideaway; as an early bird after a worm; as a
hungry free loader.

symbols: old up 'n' at 'em; full of beans; eager beaver; Boy
Scout.

see also: hot; zealous; bold; hungry.

opposite: indifferent; slow; cool.

Early: as Adam and Eve; as the light of dawn; as the Book
of Genesis; as Cro-Magnon Man.

symbols: Aurora; dawn patrol; early bird.

see also: fast; quick; young.

opposite: late; delayed; old.

Earthy: as gutter English; as a farmer's figures of speech; as
life in a sod hut; as the farmer's daughter.

symbols: Mother Nature; barnyard philosophy.

see also: carnal; crude; vulgar; coarse; natural.

opposite: refined; cultured; delicate; flowery.

Easy: as rolling off a log; as drawing breath in the open
air; as relaxing in a rocking chair; as the proverbial pie.

symbols: the Lotus Eater; easy street; piece of cake; cake-
walk.

see also: comfortable; understandable; simple.

opposite: complicated; difficult; hard.

Economical: as energy from the wind; as walking to work; as
hash at home; as living off the land.

symbols: Mr. Pennysaver; pinch purse; close to the vest.

see also: stingy; frugal; close; tight; cheap.

opposite: expensive; generous; dear.

Edgy: as a bartender on the brink of a brawl; as a boiler at
the breaking point; as a perturbed porcupine; as
a prophet of doom.

symbols: Damocles; Terrible Tempered Mr. Bang; short fuse;
tenterhook time.

see also: nervous; agitated.

opposite: calm; relaxed; placid.

Educated: to the nth degree; as a post-doctoral pundit; as a master's touch.
symbols: a Ph.D.; the cap and gown set; the brain trust.
see also: learned; cultured; civilized.
opposite: ignorant; barbarous; savage; crude.

Eerie: as the aura of the unknown; as the pit and the pendulum; as a voice from the dead; as the silence of a haunted house.
symbols: Queer Street; nightmare alley.
see also: frightful; dismal; bleak; gloomy; threatening.
opposite: warm; colorful; hospitable; friendly; encouraging.

Effective: as balm in Gilead; as fuel in a fire; as eyes for an eagle; as food in the fight against famine.
symbols: ball of fire; dynamite.
see also: useful; appropriate; accomplished; convincing.
opposite: useless; inefficient; idle; empty.

Efficient: as the heat in Hades; as a sharp knife on a Gordian knot; as a ball bearing; as a bulldozer on a demolition job.
symbols: new broom; a machine.
see also: accomplished; systematic; productive.
opposite: inefficient; incompetent; inadequate.

Egotistical: as kissing the image in the mirror; as awarding yourself a medal; as a braggart's boasts.
symbols: The Great I Am; first person singular; Mr. Bumble.
see also: immodest; vain; selfish.
opposite: humble; meek; modest.

Elastic: as a criminal's conscience; as a campaign promise; as a garter belt.
symbols: two-way stretch; rubber band.
see also: flexible; changeable; uncertain.
opposite: constant; changeless; certain; tight.

Electrifying: as a bolt of lightning; as new-found hope; as a high voltage line.
symbols: live wire; dynamo; a charged battery; thunderbolt.
see also: exciting; brilliant; inventive.
opposite: boring; dull; hopeless.

Elegant: as a master's touch; as a royal coronation; as a
                      peacock's preen; as an ermine robe.

symbols: Fancy Dan; Beau Brummel; fashion plate.
see also: fancy; handsome; beautiful; refined; tasteful.
opposite: coarse; cheap; noisy; dull; gross; frightful.

Elementary: as the primary colors; as the air we breathe; as 2
                      plus 2; as fire and water.

symbols: bread and butter; the nitty gritty; the basics.
see also: basic; simple.
opposite: complicated; complex; intricate; difficult.

Elevated: as a snob's eyebrows; as an egotist's opinion of him-
                      self; as heaven above; as a king on a throne.

symbols: Olympus; highbrow.
see also: high; exalted; special.
opposite: low; common; average; commonplace.

Eligible: as a handsome millionare bachelor; as a petunia
                      waiting to be picked; as a hot dog is for eating.

symbols: Available Jones; favorite son.
see also: qualified; fit; deserving.
opposite: ineligible; unprepared.

Eloquent: as the Sermon on the Mount; as action clear and
                      prompt; as naked truth; as the Gettysburg Ad-
                      dress.

symbols: Demosthenes; Daniel Webster.
see also: expressive; authoritative.
opposite: dull; corny.

Elusive: as the source of a rumor; as a pesky gnat; as the
                      charm of a nagging spouse; as a snake swiveling
                      in the grass.

symbols: Scarlet Pimpernel; will-o'-the-wisp.
see also: evasive; slippery; tricky; uncertain.
opposite: catching; definite; certain; straight.

Embarrassed: as a memory expert who forgets his name; as the
                      cook who burns the beef; as a saint caught sin-
                      ning; as a Welcome Wagon lady who is asked to
                      leave; as a nudist caught with clothes on.

symbols: blushing violet; in the soup.
see also: uncomfortable; confused.
opposite: relaxed; calm.

Eminent: as the wisdom of the Founding Fathers; as the sun in the sky; as the eagle among birds and the lion among beasts.

symbols: Olympian; Jovian.

see also: distinguished; celebrated; noticeable; admired; important

opposite: obscure; hidden; overlooked.

Emphatic: as a punch on the proboscis; as reading the riot act; as an ultimatum; as a kick in the pants.

symbols: table-pounding; Stentor.

see also: loud; positive; dogmatic.

opposite: hesitant; indifferent; soft; apathetic; tentative.

Empty: as a pauper's pocket; as a bottomless pit; as the desert wastes; as a nitwit's noodle; as the barrel that rattles loudest.

symbols: the hole in the doughnut; wide open spaces; no man's land.

see also: bare; barren; blank; deserted.

opposite: crowded; congested; jammed.

Enchanting: as a fairy godmother; as a magic kingdom; as a dream of glory; as young love.

symbols: Titania; Queen Mab; Cupid's arrow.

see also: charming; attractive; beautiful; lovable.

opposite: awful; hateful; frightful; wicked; ugly.

Encouraging: as a round of applause; as sweet success; as fuel is to a fire.

symbols: Pollyanna; cheerleader.

see also: comforting; sympathetic; helpful; hopeful.

opposite: cool; indifferent; hopeless.

Endangered: as a lamb lying down with a lion; as a pickle at a picnic; as a sinner's soul; as a vanishing species.

symbols: Damocles; Hairbreadth Harry.

see also: abused; afflicted; damaged.

opposite: safe; enduring.

Endless: as the march of time; as all eternity; as the vastness of space; as the line around a circle.

symbols: continuous performance; world without end.

see also: constant; continuous; perpetual; permanent; infinite; ceaseless.

opposite: complete; limited; final; definite; temporary.

Enduring: as the sands of the desert and the waters of the sea; ~~as eternal truth; as Holy Writ.~~

symbols: Rock of Ages; a fixture; the establishment.
see also: endless; permanent; perpetual; lasting.
opposite: fleeting; temporary.

Energetic: as a daily decathlon; as internal combustion; as perpetual motion; as a mountain climber.

symbols: eager beaver; dynamo; Trojan.
see also: active; busy; restless; feverish.
opposite: relaxed; inert; idle; lazy.

Engaging: as a siren's smile; as the promise of profit; as the scent of sex; as the prospect of a good deal.

symbols: Amoret; Don Juan; Lochinvar.
see also: appealing; fascinating; attractive; charming.
opposite: nasty; detestable; hateful; crumby.

Enigmatic: as the mystery of life; as a riddle without an answer; as which came first—the chicken or the egg.

symbols: Sphinx; Mona Lisa.
see also: uncertain; obscure; hidden.
opposite: clear; certain; understandable.

Envious: as a rich relation thinks a poor relation is; as a social climber; as a psychopathic sibling.

symbols: green-eyed monster; keeping up with the Joneses.
see also: jealous; greedy.
opposite: indifferent; apathetic; generous; kind; charitable.

Erratic: as a compass gone amuck; as a bird flying with one wing; as an egg rolling down a hill; as a drunk's footsteps.

symbols: an unguided missile; an accident going someplace to happen.
see also: queer; strange; absurd.
opposite: sure; steadfast; reasonable.

Erroneous: as a case of mistaken identity; as mistaking a tiger for a tabby; as a typo in a banner headline; as reasoning with a gorilla.

symbols: the blunderworld; wrong way Corrigan; a Brodie.
see also: wrong; false; mistaken; inaccurate.
opposite: correct; true; accurate.

Essential:	as food and water; as the breath of life; as the salt in the sea; as a heartbeat.
symbols:	meat and potatoes; a must; sine qua non.
see also:	necessary; basic.
opposite:	unnecessary; needless.
Established:	as the seats of the mighty; as the myths of our time; as the law of supply and demand; as the Constitution.
symbols:	Rock of Gibraltar; the way the cookie crumbles.
see also:	firm; old; constant; certain; permanent.
opposite:	uncertain; temporary.
Estimable:	as a doctor who works without fees; as a guardian angel; as a good Samaritan in a bad time; as a star who doesn't fall for his own publicity; as a good deed in a selfish world.
symbols:	man in the white hat; the good guys.
see also:	appreciated; respectable; popular.
opposite:	objectionable; disagreeable; unpopular.
Euphoric:	as a lottery winner; as an immigrant in heaven; as a pair of newlyweds; as a proud new parent.
symbols:	seventh heaven; Eden; Paradise; Arcadia.
see also:	happy; exalted; glad; optimistic.
opposite:	sad; unhappy; gloomy; downhearted; pessimistic.
Evasive:	as an unfriendly witness; as a debtor dodging process servers; as a halfback heading for the goal-line.
symbols:	Reynard the Fox; will o' the wisp; slippery eel.
see also:	elusive; wily; tricky; sneaky; untruthful.
opposite:	honest; true; real; approachable.
Evil:	as the devil in the depths; as a bad seed; as the serpent in the Garden of Eden.
symbols:	Satan; Lucifer; Beelzebub; snake in the grass.
see also:	bad; corrupt; mean; immoral; wicked.
opposite:	good; kind; innocent; pure; trustworthy.
Exaggerated:	as the report of Mark Twain's death; as calling a pond an ocean; as making a mountain out of a molehill; as a rumor growing from mouth to mouth; as a braggart's adjectives.
symbols:	gilding the lily; laying it on with a trowel; Baron Munchausen.
see also:	magnified; extravagant; overwhelming.
opposite:	modest; small; little; compressed; concise.

Exalted: as a king on a throne; as the stars in the sky; as the wisdom of the All High; as a sinner being born again.

symbols: monarch of all he surveys; king of kings; lord of the manor; the high and the mighty.

see also: high; glorified; elevated; blessed; holy; glorious.

opposite: low; damned; crumby; heretical.

Excessive: as a fanatic's zeal; as the lust for power; as too much of a good thing.

symbols: Nero; Saturnalia; laid on with a trowel; a bit much.

see also: extreme; needless; unnecessary; tasteless.

opposite: essential; necessary; basic; modest.

Exciting: as passion reciprocated; as the smell of blood to a raging beast; as the prospect of a golden opportunity.

symbols: the thrill of a lifetime; electric moment.

see also: electrifying; heated; moving.

opposite: dull; boring; placid; quiet.

Exclusive: as a locked door; as a restricted community; as a journalistic scoop.

symbols: Nob Hill; snob hill; closed corporation; private club.

see also: selective; closed; narrow; privileged.

opposite: broad; open; hospitable.

Excusable: as a childish error; as a dirty diaper; as a slip of the lip.

symbols: white lie; Alibi Ike.

see also: forgivable; understandable; reasonable.

opposite: inexcusable.

Exemplary: as a model citizen; as a preacher's parable; as the courage of a Medal of Honor winner.

symbols: perfect specimen; Sir Galahad; the Admirable Crichton.

see also: admirable; classic; good; clear.

opposite: bad; poor; wrong; spoiled.

Exhausted: as a finished oil field; as a pauper's bank account; as the patience of a short-tempered man after a long wait; as a tot at the end of a hectic day.

symbols: wreck of the Hesperus; end of the line; totalled.

see also: finished; empty; weary.

opposite: strong; full; energetic.

Expensive: as the wages of sin; as the price of progress; as a bad investment; as a seller's market.

symbols: highway robbery.
see also: dear; high; inflated.
opposite: cheap; low; economical.

Experienced: as one who's been there oft before; as a graduate of the school of hard knocks; as a man of the world.

symbols: Nestor; sachem; old pro; old hand.
see also: qualified; educated; wise.
opposite: amateurish; incompetent; unprepared.

Experimental: as a child learning to walk; as a laboratory exercise; as a stab in the dark.

symbols: breadboard model; trial and error; run it up the flagpole.
see also: tentative; uncertain.
opposite: certain; sure; absolute; experienced.

Explicit: as X marks the spot; as a court injunction; as a gun at your head.

symbols: in black and white.
see also: clear; certain; obvious; definite; precise.
opposite: uncertain; fuzzy; cloudy; inaccurate.

Explosive: as the bomb at Hiroshima; as a bolt of lightning; as dry gunpowder; as a riot waiting to happen.

symbols: dynamite; TNT.
see also: volatile; inflamed.
opposite: calm; mild.

Expressive: as a blush; as a bended knee; as falling asleep in the middle of a speech; as a baby's lower lip.

symbols: telltale smile; the cat that swallowed the canary.
see also: eloquent; clear.
opposite: flat; faceless; vague.

Extended: as the hand of friendship; as a bankrupt's credit; as a booking that's held over.

symbols: stretchout; long stretch.
see also: long; delayed.
opposite: brief; short.

Extinct: as a dead volcano; as the mastodon and the sabre-toothed tiger; as the lost continent of Atlantis.

symbols: the dodo; the dinosaur.
see also: dead; finished.
opposite: new; modern; timely.

Extravagant: as a politician's promises; as a wastrel's wildness; as a high pressure salesman's pitch; as a spend-thrift's standards.

symbols: gilding the lily; the last of the big time spenders; good-time Charlie.

see also: exaggerated; flattering; lavish; generous.

opposite: cheap; tight; small; economical.

Extreme: as the end of the spectrum; as the lengths to which desperation drives people; as your opponent's position.

symbols: the nth degree; all the way.

see also: final; desperate; narrow.

opposite: cautious; moderate; tolerant.

F

Faceless: as a disembodied voice; as a headless horseman; as a scream in the night; as a masked bandit.

symbols: masked ball; the man in the iron mask.

see also: anonymous.

opposite: familiar; obvious.

Faded: as high fashion denim; as the leaves that fall from the trees; as the light at the end of the day.

symbols: twilight; the invisible man.

see also: colorless; cloudy.

opposite: colorful; brilliant; gaudy; durable.

Faint: as the heart that ne'er won fair lady; as the praise that damns; as a distant star; as a glimmer in the black of night.

symbols: fadeaway; weak in the knees; small signal from outer space.

see also: weak; feeble; frail.

opposite: strong; brillant; loud; bold.

Faithful: as old dog Tray; as a good friend; as the word of an honest man.

symbols: fidus Achates; Old Faithful; Penelope.

see also: constant; trustworthy; loyal; true; steadfast.

opposite: false; changeable; lying; uncertain.

False: as the tears of the crocodile; as a fool's illusions; as heathen gods; as a phony witness.

symbols: Apples of Sodom; Achitophel; Cressid (Cressida).

see also: dishonest; lying; treacherous; untruthful.

opposite: true; loyal; trustworthy; steadfast; honest; accurate.

Familiar: as an old mistake (*Edwin Arlington Robinson*); as a fond memory; as the old faces; as your father's favorite story; as the face in the mirror.

symbols: Everyman; déja vu; return engagement; rebroadcast; rerun.

see also: normal; natural; common; average.

opposite: rare; strange; different; alien; special.

Famous: as the names of the Apostles; as the Ten Commandments; as the best sellers, the football stars and the home run kings; as the plays of Shakespeare.

symbols: a household word; Hall of Fame; headliner.

see also: celebrated; eminent; distinguished.

opposite: obscure; forgotten.

Fancy: as a fiddler's fingering; as a peacock's plumage; as the clothes at a costume ball; as the flights of imagination; as a fighter's fast footwork.

symbols: Marivaudage.

see also: gaudy; colorful; intricate; elegant; imaginary.

opposite: dull; quiet; incompetent.

Far: as angels ken (*John Milton*); as from here to eternity; as the furthest star; as a faded memory.

symbols: the ends of earth; light years.

see also: distant; infinite; endless.

opposite: close; near; imminent.

Fascinating: as first love; as a fan dancer's fandango; as a rendezvous with destiny; as a foretaste of Paradise.

symbols: Siren; Aphrodite's girdle; Venus; Apollo; Adonis.

see also: engaging; attractive; exciting; charming; appealing.

opposite: dull; boring.

Fast: as a flash in the pan; as the flight of a rumor; as the speed of light; as the shades of nightfall.

symbols: Atalanta; greased lightning.

see also: quick; rapid; brief; early.

opposite: slow; delayed; hesitant.

Fat:	as a well-to-do whale; as a rich man's wallet; as a porker ready for the pot; as a contented cow.
symbols:	Big Bertha; Wouter van Twiller; Two-Ton Tessie; Falstaff; tub of lard.
see also:	flabby; broad; padded; big; large.
opposite:	skinny; thin; slim; small.
Fatal:	as the gift of beauty (*Lord Byron*); as the passage of time; as two feet in the grave.
symbols:	Grim Reaper; angel of death; appointment in Samarra; Thanatos.
see also:	lethal; deadly; destructive.
opposite:	safe; harmless; secure.
Faulty:	as a leaking faucet; as a plane with one wing; as a TV set without a picture tube; as a phoney alibi.
symbols:	a lemon; a basket case; a dodo.
see also:	cracked; messy; damaged; disastrous.
opposite:	flawless; perfect.
Favorable:	as a vote of confidence; as a friendly breeze; as flattery; as a fond mother's view of her family.
symbols:	the smile of the gods; four stars; thumbs up; good omen.
see also:	good; friendly; hopeful; optimistic.
opposite:	bad; antagonistic; hopeless; pessimistic.
Feeble:	as a punctured alibi; as a con man's conscience; as the mind of a moron; as a coward's courage.
symbols:	milksop; tired blood.
see also:	weak; anemic; frail.
opposite:	strong; powerful; hearty; firm; fierce.
Fertile:	as the lower forty; as the cornfields of Kansas; as a flowering field.
symbols:	Ashtoreth; Ceres; Mother Earth; Cybele; Aphrodite; Demeter.
see also:	fruitful; bountiful; rich.
opposite:	barren; fruitless; poor; meager.
Festive:	as a golden wedding; as a Labor Day picnic where the beer flows like water; as the Fourth of July; as the fanciest feast.
symbols:	Saturnalia; Roman holiday; red letter day.
see also:	happy; flowery.
opposite:	bleak; gloomy; despondent.

Feverish: as an attack of malaria; as a hothouse in a heat wave; as panic in the streets; as the activity in an agitated ant hill.

symbols: boiling point; bonfire; beehive.

see also: busy; energetic; active; hot.

opposite: cool, calm, relaxed; inert; quiet; placid.

Fierce: as nature in the raw; as the claws of a jungle cat; as the call of the wild; as a bully facing a smaller opponent.

symbols: Mars; Bellona; Hotspur.

see also: bold; powerful; strong; firm; antagonistic.

opposite: feeble; weak; shy.

Filthy: as man-made muck; as a fetid garbage dump; as the pitch of a pornographer; as dishonest dollars.

symbols: Augean stables; flea bag; pigsty.

see also: dirty; messy; unclean; impure.

opposite: clean; spotless; pure.

Final: as the grave; as going under for the third time; as three strikes; as the third day of hash in the boarding house; as the Last Supper.

symbols: Götterdämmerung; Judgment Day; Twilight of the Gods; a wrap; the grand climax.

see also: finished; complete; definite.

opposite: continuous; unfinished; endless; partial.

Fine: as rare silk; as the point of a pin; as the perfection of paradise; as filigree.

symbols: gossamer; Augustan.

see also: dainty; delicate; precise; perfect.

opposite: gross; coarse; crude; heavy.

Finished: as the Middle Ages; as the fadeout to the closing titles; as a fine performance; as a polished parquet floor.

symbols: closed chapter; end of the line; masterpiece.

see also: complete; perfect; accomplished; final.

opposite: unfinished; partial; coarse; crude; underdeveloped.

Firm: as the faith of the fathers; as the mountains stand against the sky; as a strong foundation; as the devil with the damned.

symbols: The Rock of Gibraltar; Stonewall Jackson.

see also: arbitrary; rigid; strong; commanding; established.

opposite: weak; feeble; brittle; delicate; shy.

Fishy: as a school of flounder; as good red herring; as the one that got away; as a phony pedigree.

symbols: old wives' tale; whale of a story; mare's nest.
see also: suspicious; questionable; dubious; false.
opposite: true; correct; established; sure; certain.

Fit: as a finely-tuned fiddle; as a crown for a king; as a champion in top form.

symbols: Charles Atlas; Mr. Universe; Mr. America; right time; right place.
see also: appropriate; becoming; strong; qualified; healthy.
opposite: inadequate; weak; sick; hopeless.

Flabby: as the moral fiber in a fleshpot; as a fat man's middle; as a weak handshake; as a limp lump of lard.

symbols: Falstaff; soft stuff.
see also: fat; ample.
opposite: slim; strong; fit.

Flashy: as the lights on the Great White Way; as the slot machines in Las Vegas; as a shooting star in the night; as a diamond glinting in the night.

symbols: Roman candle; Corinthian; rhinestone cowboy.
see also: bright; brilliant; colorful; gaudy; loud.
opposite: colorless; dark; quiet.

Flat: as an empty wallet; as the endless prairie; as the ground under a steamroller; as the world before Columbus.

symbols: pancake; collapsible top hat; stale beer.
see also: thin; skinny; endless; colorless; dreary.
opposite: thick; fat; colorful; gaudy.

Flattering: as a testimonial dinner; as soft light for a lovely woman; as an unexpected compliment.

symbols: Blarney stone; gilding the lily.
see also: complimentary; gracious.
opposite: insulting; rude; nasty.

Flawless: as a perfect diamond; as love's young dream; as a plaster saint.

symbols: Augustan; Attic; Utopia.
see also: perfect; correct.
opposite: blemished; faulty; tarnished; impure.

Fleeting: as a momentary memory; as the blink of an eye; as the estate of man (*Marcus Aurelius*); as an instant in eternity.
symbols: April shower; mayfly; passing fancy.
see also: momentary; brief; fast; temporary; quick.
opposite: enduring; lasting; permanent.

Flexible: as a bending knee; as a bargainer's last offer; as picture wire; as a murderer's morals.
symbols: two-way stretch; India rubber man.
see also: adjustable; pliable; adaptable; elastic.
opposite: rigid; firm; solid; uncompromising.

Flowery: as a spring bouquet; as a gangster's funeral; as a garden in bloom; as a fulsome introduction.
symbols: Gongorism; Euphuism.
see also: flattering; complimentary; eloquent; expressive; fancy.
opposite: dreary; dull; modest.

Foggy: as steamed-up eyeglasses; as a Turkish bath; as a mountain in the clouds.
symbols: pea soup; London special.
see also: dense; cloudy; gloomy; dark.
opposite: bright; clear; brilliant.

Foolish: as the man who thinks he knows it all; as rushing in where angels fear to tread; as getting your courage from a bottle; as young and old each think the other is.
symbols: Pickwickian; Boeotian; Chelm.
see also: stupid; dopey; dumb; absurd; indiscreet; rash.
opposite: wise; clever; prudent; careful; cautious.

Forgetful: as an advanced case of senility; as he who chooses not to remember; as a student who didn't stop to study; as a victim of total amnesia.
symbols: Lethe; waters of Lethe; absent-minded professor.
see also: oblivious; negligent; careless.
opposite: attentive; conscientious; careful.

Forgivable: as honest human error; as a wrong step in a righteous cause; as an excess of enthusiasm; as pre-election promises.
symbols: little white lie; on the side of the angels.
see also: excusable; understandable; reasonable.
opposite: inexcusable; wrong.

Forgotten: as a dead man out of mind (*Bible: Psalms*); as fanaticism that goes out of fashion; as old ways in new times; as the dreams of yesteryear; as last year's styles.
symbols: the forgotten man; watered by Lethe.
see also: forsaken; deserted; abandoned; neglected.
opposite: memorable; timely.

Formal: as the look of a penguin; as a state dinner; as white tie and tails; as the proceedings of the Supreme Court; as an audience with the Pope.
symbols: black tie; soup and fish; by the numbers.
see also: solemn; dignified; grand.
opposite: boisterous; noisy; ill-mannered; rude.

Forsaken: as a wanderer in the desert; as the primrose path to a practicing puritan; as the way of the wicked; as a lonely grave.
symbols: ghost town; orphan of the storm; lost world.
see also: neglected; desolate; forgotten; deserted.
opposite: cherished; sought-after.

Fortunate: as a favorite of fickle Fate; as one loved for himself alone; as a farmer with a fertile field; as a sweepstakes winner.
symbols: Midas touch; darling of the gods.
see also: lucky; blessed.
opposite: unlucky; damned.

Fragrant: as the flowers that bloom in the spring; as the sweet smell of success; as French perfume with the stopper open.
symbols: garden of roses; incense; balsam; balm.
see also: aromatic; flowery; odorous; smelly.
opposite: arid; dead.

Frail: as a blade of grass bending in the breeze; as tissue paper; as fleeting fame; as a fading friendship.
symbols: house of cards; eggshell; 90-pound weakling.
see also: brittle; weak; anemic; feeble; delicate.
opposite: strong; powerful; firm; solid; heavy.

Frank: as an unrehearsed insult; as a family argument; as a puppy's emotions; as a nudist's costume.
symbols: true confession; brass tacks; talking turkey.
see also: open; honest.
opposite: insincere; dishonest; affected.

Frantic: as a commuter running for the last train of the morning; as a frog in a frying pan; as a fox in a furrier's shop; as a photographer without film.

symbols: Bedlam; hoopla; three-ring circus.

see also: agitated; bothered; chaotic; desperate.

opposite: calm; relaxed; quiet; peaceful; casual.

Fraudulent: as counterfeit money; as a doctored dissertation; as false piety; as a phony affidavit.

symbols: Cagliostro; confidence game; snake oil salesman; medicine show.

see also: false; dishonest; lying; untruthful; deceitful; devious; duplicit.

opposite: genuine; honest; true; correct.

Free: as the open road; as the breeze in the trees; as the air we breathe; as unsolicited advice.

symbols: Statue of Liberty; Liberty Bell; on the house.

see also: independent; liberal; generous; permissive.

opposite: limited; confined; rigid.

Frequent: as a baby's diaper changes; as a frog's jumps; as the cackles in a henhouse.

symbols: epidemic; morning, noon and night.

see also: numerous; repetitious.

opposite: rare; scarce; seldom.

Fresh: as a new coat of paint; as a daisy with the dew on; as an unrepentant sinner sneering at salvation; as a teenager tangling with a parent.

symbols: mint condition; sons of Belial; hot off the press.

see also: new; rude; insolent; bold; modern.

opposite: ancient; old; rotten; decayed; old fashioned.

Friendly: as a helping hand; as a kind word at a bad moment; as a vote of confidence; as a salesman trying to make a sale.

symbols: Damon and Pythias; fidus Achates; Three Musketeers; Welcome Wagon.

see also: amiable; pleasant; agreeable; approachable; warm; affectionate.

opposite: aloof; haughty; nasty; antagonistic.

Frightened: as Miss Muffet spotting the spider; as a mouse confronted by a cat; as a startled fawn; as a gunman when somebody else has the gun.

symbols: seeing a Gorgon; Bob Acres; gooseflesh.

see also: scared; cowardly.

opposite: brave; daring; bold; courageous.

Frightful:	as man's inhumanity to man; as the Devil's dwelling place; as a mob in motion; as the depths of despair; as a holocaust remembered.
symbols:	Godzilla; Caliban; Armageddon; Attila the Hun.
see also:	atrocious; awful; cruel; horrible; hellish; dreadful.
opposite:	good; kind; pleasant; warm; angelic; blessed.
Frugal:	as a hermit's housewarming; as a bride on a budget; as a miser with his money; as a thrifty Scot.
symbols:	Spartan; Diogenes.
see also:	economical; stingy; close; cheap.
opposite:	lavish; generous; extravagant.
Fruitful:	as the seed that multiplies; as the land of milk and honey; as the lessons of experience; as the parents of a large family.
symbols:	Demeter; Pomona; Freya.
see also:	bountiful; fertile; rich; productive.
opposite:	fruitless; barren; poor; meager; arid.
Fruitless:	as a forlorn hope; as an overage apple tree; as the search for the Holy Grail; as synthetic breakfast drinks.
symbols:	wild goose chase; labor of Sisyphus; Penelope's web.
see also:	barren; poor; arid; bare.
opposite:	productive; fruitful; bountiful; fertile.
Furious:	as the courage of a cornered rat; as the frenzy of the damned; as a barroom brawl; as a fight to the death.
symbols:	Eumenides; the Terrible Tempered Mr. Bang.
see also:	angry; mad; ill-tempered.
opposite:	placid; calm; peaceful; relaxed.
Fussy:	as a prissy pussycat; as a thoroughbred at the starting gate; as a dude with dandruff; as a hypochondriac with heartburn.
symbols:	fussbudget; Mr. Prim.
see also:	nervous; careful; cautious.
opposite:	careless; negligent; reckless; breezy.
Futile:	as a rain dance in Death Valley; as a spear in a nuclear war; as a conversation with a stone; as a forlorn hope.
symbols:	Don Quixote; Sisyphus.
see also:	useless; vain; hopeless; helpless; inadequate.
opposite:	effective; helpful; useful; hopeful.

Fuzzy: as a bad connection; as a faulty memory; as doubleknit gone to seed.
symbols: out of focus; smog city; fogbound.
see also: unclear; uncertain; foggy.
opposite: clear; certain.

G

Gallant: as the good fight; as a fighting flag flying in the breeze; as a dashing cavalier; as a knight in shining armor.
symbols: Sir Galahad; Robin Hood; Sir Walter Raleigh.
see also: dashing; brave; courageous; bold; courteous.
opposite: scared; frightened; cowardly; rude; nasty.

Gaseous: as a leaking stove; as the bubble in a glass of soda pop; as a windbag; as a blimp.
symbols: gas bag; hot air balloon; lighter than air.
see also: light; volatile; windy; talkative.
opposite: heavy; dense; silent.

Gaudy: as all that glitters; as the baubles of the night; as an overloaded Christmas tree; as the Great White Way.
symbols: circus poster; rainbow; Christmas tree.
see also: flashy; colorful; brilliant; festive; lavish.
opposite: colorless; dark; dismal; desolate.

Generous: as a doting grandparent; as a forgiving heart; as an act of mercy; as an unsolicited gift; as a helping hand.
symbols: Santa Claus; Kris Kringle; Lady Bountiful; Good Samaritan; Fairy Godmother.
see also: kind; charitable; considerate; free; helpful.
opposite: grudging; tight; cheap; close.

Genial: as a gentle jest; as a gracious host; as the mood of spring; as the look of love.
symbols: gladhander; life of the party.
see also: amiable; friendly; cheerful; agreeable; happy; gracious; congenial.
opposite: quarrelsome; gloomy; disagreeable; biting; gloomy.

Gentle: as a little lamb; as Jesus meek and mild (*Charles Wesley*); as a healing angel; as a mother's touch.
symbols: timid soul; Caspar Milquetoast.
see also: kind; meek; docile.
opposite: biting; nasty; sharp; strong.

Genuine: as the dark of night; as the light of day; as envy undisguised; as a baby's burp.
symbols: the real McCoy; Simon Pure; 14 carat.
see also: authentic; real; true; original.
opposite: false; imitative; untruthful.

Ghastly: as the fate of Hamlet's father; as a ghoul in a graveyard; as the haunts of Hell; as a night in a haunted house.
symbols: the Flying Dutchman; the mystery of the Mary Celeste.
see also: dismal; bleak; desolate; gloomy.
opposite: bright; happy; cheerful.

Gifted: as a favorite of fickle fate; as a spoiled child at Christmas-time; as the darling of the gods; as a golden voice.
symbols: Talent Incorporated; Renaissance man.
see also: blessed; fortunate.
opposite: handicapped; deprived.

Glaring: as an error in open view; as the brightness of the summer sun; as the glance of a grumpy grouch; as the center of the spotlight.
symbols: front and center; eye stopper; eye opener.
see also: bright; obvious; brilliant; noticeable; apparent; angry.
opposite: overlooked; obscure; hidden.

Gloomy: as the grave; as a friendless funeral; as the lonely night; as a pessimist's predictions; as the trackless wastes of the dark unknown.
symbols: Hamlet; Slough of Despond; cave of Trophonius; Erebus.
see also: black; dark; sad; pessimistic; dismal; dreary; downhearted; discouraged; eerie.
opposite: happy; cheerful; warm; glad; optimistic.

Glorified: as a braggart's boast; as hero worship; as dreams of grandeur; as the golden age of Greece; as the grandeur that was Rome.

symbols: star billing; matinee idol; household name.

see also: exalted; elevated; magnified.

opposite: low; common; average.

Glorious: as the sunlight after the storm; as the coming of the Lord; as the ascent of man; as the gift of laughter; as the triumph of good over evil; as the flag of truth flying triumphant.

symbols: Paradise; heaven; Eden.

see also: exalted; spectacular; beautiful; harmonious.

opposite: mean; ugly; low.

Glossy: as a dandy's lacquered hair; as a cover girl; as a picture postcard; as a fancy sales brochure.

symbols: tinsel; plastic.

see also: smooth; colorful; polished.

opposite: dull; colorless; unappealing.

Good: as gold; as glad tidings; as a nice deed in a naughty world; as the fish that are left in the sea; as the man you can't keep down.

symbols: Mithra; Themis; Galahad.

see also: commendable; admirable; exemplary; pleasant; desirable.

opposite: bad; hellish; horrible; atrocious; mean; awful.

Graceful: as a gazelle; as a ballerina; as the eagle in its flight; as the willow waving in the wind; as the man on the flying trapeze.

symbols: Hebe.

see also: agile; nimble; dainty; delicate.

opposite: awkward; heavy-handed; heavy.

Gracious: as a good loser; as a thoughtful host; as the kingdom of Heaven; as good manners under pressure.

symbols: Attic; Sir Walter Raleigh; Emily Post.

see also: courteous; amiable; polite; kind; pleasant; hospitable.

opposite: ill-mannered; gross; rude; impolite.

Gradual: as the passage of time; as the road to hell; as the water torture; as the pace of a tortoise; as the progress of a snail.

symbols: Fabian.
see also: slow; delayed; hesitant; deliberate.
opposite: fast; instantaneous; dashing.

Grand: as the canyon of the Colorado; as the great design of life; as the manner of the mighty; as the ultimate illusion.

symbols: Olympian; Jovian.
see also: exalted; solemn; formal; high; dignified.
opposite: low; mean; meek; humble; rotten; relaxed.

Grasping: as a miser for more money; as a politician's push for power; as an adolescent lover feeling his way; as a stage mother.

symbols: Scrooge; Midas; Harpagon; Silas Marner.
see also: selfish; vain; cheap; tight; crass.
opposite: idealistic; generous; kind.

Grateful: as one who wants another gift; as a puppy for a pat on the head; as those who recognize their debts; as the giver of thanks.

symbols: Thanksgiving; grace.
see also: pleased; appreciated.
opposite: indifferent; arrogant.

Greedy: as the lust for lucre; as a hungry dog is for a bone; as one who is searching for sin; as a money grubber in the mint.

symbols: Midas; gold-digger; green-eyed monster; Scrooge.
see also: envious; jealous; cheap; grudging.
opposite: generous; charitable; kind.

Gripping: as a bulldog's bite; as a baby's hold on your finger; as the pulse of passion; as a ghost story told by candlelight; as a mysterious noise in the night.

symbols: cliffhanger; crowd-stopper.
see also: fascinating; compelling; exciting; strong.
opposite: dull; boring; weak.

Gross: as a belch at a banquet; as picking your nose in public; as orgy time in Sodom and Gomorrah; as a grudge in the Garden of Eden.

symbols: Goth; Caliban.
see also: crass; rude; coarse; vulgar; insulting.
opposite: elegant; educated; refined; cultured.

Grouchy: as an overworked complaint clerk; as a bothered bus driver; as a sore loser; as a tired child; as a demon with dyspepsia; as a hermit facing a horde of visitors.

symbols: crab; Tartar.
see also: ill-tempered; angry; mad; nasty; grudging.
opposite: agreeable; genial; friendly; pleasant; amiable.

Grudging: as a curmudgeon's compliments; as a tip from a tightwad; as a smile from a sourpuss; as praise from a political opponent.

symbols: Scrooge; left-handed.
see also: grouchy; stingy; tight.
opposite: generous; genial; kind; considerate; overwhelming.

Guilty: as a killer caught in the act; as a thief with his hand in the collection box; as the serpent in Paradise.

symbols: cop a plea; mea culpa.
see also: criminal; wrong.
opposite: innocent; excusable.

H

Habitual: as breathing; as brushing your teeth; as hoping for the best.

symbols: daily dozen; custom of the house.
see also: automatic; regular; constant; changeless.
opposite: irregular; rare; changeable.

Hairy: as an ape; as an unkempt camel; as a tale of horror; as the floor of a busy barbershop.

symbols: wooly bear; barber bait.
see also: menacing; ominous; fuzzy.
opposite: smooth; bare; clear.

Handicapped: as a homing pigeon without a home; as a cook without a kitchen; as a one-armed octopus; as a filibusterer who's lost his voice; as a one-armed paperhanger.

symbols: behind the eight-ball; the lame, the halt and the blind.

see also: limited; underdeveloped.

opposite: privileged; gifted.

Handsome: as a Greek god; as a matinee idol; as the bull that kidnapped Europa (*Cicero*); as a heavy bankroll.

symbols: Adonis; Apollo; Ganymede.

see also: attractive; beautiful; fascinating.

opposite: ugly; beastly.

Happy: as a lark on the loose; as a fool in love; as the man that hath his quiver full (*Bible: Psalms*); as the hope of heaven; as being in the right place at the right time; as a carefree kitten; as those with blessings they can count.

symbols: Arcadia; Elysium; Elysian fields; Paradise.

see also: euphoric; carefree; cheerful; exalted.

opposite: sad; moody; gloomy; dismal.

Hard: as nails of stubborn steel; as teaching an old dog new tricks; as the way of transgressors (*Bible: Proverbs*); as the heart of the vilest villain.

symbols: task of Sisyphus; labors of Hercules; Rock of Gibraltar.

see also: tough; difficult; austere; baffling.

opposite: easy; soft; simple.

Hard-core: as a teen-age two-time loser; as a drop-out with a drug habit.

symbols: child of the streets; the unrepentant; misfit.

see also: abandoned; forsaken; criminal; immoral; lawless.

opposite: correct; pure; cherished.

Hardy: as a healthy hound dog; as a prizefighter in the pink; as the weed that won't let go of your lawn.

symbols: Hercules; Amazon; Hygeia.

see also: strong; tough; firm; solid; enduring.

opposite: weak; frail; feeble.

Harmful: as a cyanide cocktail; as a taste of toadstool; as a bull in a china shop; as an atom bomb.

symbols: Pandora's box.

see also: damaging; destructive; lethal; fatal; deadly; disastrous.

opposite: safe; harmless; helpful; good.

Harmless: as a eunuch in a harem; as a moth in a closetful of dacron; as a barking dog without teeth.

symbols: placebo; the good guys.

see also: safe; helpful.

opposite: damaging; harmful; destructive; fatal; lethal; deadly; disastrous.

Harmonious: as the music of the spheres; as a pair of lovebirds; as a heavenly choir; as two minds with but a single thought.

symbols: Orpheus; Entente Cordiale.

see also: alike; agreeable; peaceful; friendly; amiable.

opposite: different; antagonistic; difficult; disagreeable.

Harsh: as a drill sergeant's dressing down; as the school of hard knocks; as nature in the raw; as naked hate.

symbols: Draco; Eumenides (The Furies).

see also: austere; sharp; rough; biting; rude; bitter.

opposite: soft; gentle; smooth; kind; gracious.

Hasty: as leaving through a window; as a retreat that turns into a rout; as a marriage on the spur of the moment; as a last-minute substitution.

symbols: quickstep; French leave; greased lightning.

see also: fast; quick; hurried; rushed.

opposite: hesitant; slow; delayed; cautious.

Hateful: as the gates of Hell (*Homer*); as the other person's bad habits; as treason in a time of trial; as malice pure and simple.

symbols: Devil incarnate; Eumenides; harpies; men in the black hats.

see also: detestable; offensive; nasty; annoying.

opposite: admirable; beloved; dear; lovable.

Haughty: as the pride that goes before a fall; as a dowager looking down her nose; as a snob among the hoi polloi; as a commoner playing king.

symbols: Mrs. Van Astorbilt; high horse.
see also: arrogant; rude; distant; cool.
opposite: humble; meek; approachable; warm; friendly.

Haunted: as holy ground (*Lord Byron*); as a ghost's gazebo; as one whose mind is full of memories; as an old graveyard; as a house of horrors.

symbols: The Flying Dutchman; Rosemary's Baby; Friar Rush.
see also: ghastly; damned.
opposite: blessed.

Healing: as an angel's touch; as nature's nostrums; as the passage of time.

symbols: Aesculapius; Imhotep; Hippocrates; Apollo.
see also: helpful; healthy.
opposite: harmful; damaging; fatal; deadly; lethal.

Healthy: as a sound mind in a sound body (*Juvenal*); as a happy horse; as the prime of life; as heaven on earth.

symbols: Hygeia; Salus.
see also: sound; strong.
opposite: sick.

Hearty: as a heavenly hosannah; as an overwhelming welcome; as the handshake of friendship; as spontaneous applause.

symbols: Falstaff; the works.
see also: strong; powerful; sincere; warm; zealous.
opposite: feeble; weak; frail; false; insincere.

Heated: as the temperature in a Turkish bath; as the peak of passion; as a hundred degrees in the shade; as the halls of Hell.

symbols: volcano; fireworks.
see also: hot; fierce; angry; inflamed; explosive.
opposite: calm; icy; cold; peaceful; amiable.

Heavenly: as the abode of angels; as all eternity; as the celestial skies; as the soul's salvation.

symbols: Nirvana; Valhalla; Elysium; pearly gates.
see also: angelic; good; pure; high.
opposite: evil; demonic; bad; low; hellish.

Heavy: as the hand of fate; as the weight of the world; as a heart of stone; as the burden of guilt.

symbols: Two Ton Tessie; Big Bertha; labor of Sisyphus; millstone; backbreaker.

see also: burdensome; laborious; big.

opposite: light; dainty; delicate; airy; easy.

Heavy handed: as painting with a club; as a gorilla grasping a straw; as a surgeon using a meat-axe; as crocheting with boxing gloves.

symbols: Draconian; Prussian; overkill.

see also: crude; coarse; harsh; severe; cruel.

opposite: fine; delicate; dainty; graceful; agile; soft; smooth.

Hellish: as a housewarming in Hades; as the Devil's disposition; as the fury of a woman scorned; as a Puritan's private conscience; as unholy wedlock.

symbols: Satanic; Tartarus; inferno; Gehenna.

see also: awful; horrible; frightful; dreadful.

opposite: heavenly; angelic; good; pleasant.

Helpful: as a guardian angel; as a fairy godmother; as the gift of hope; as a hand up when you're down; as a place to hide.

symbols: Good Samaritan; friend in need; good right arm.

see also: convenient; encouraging; generous; kind.

opposite: cool; indifferent; distant; callous.

Helpless: as a newborn babe; as an unarmed man in a gun battle; as an innocent in a kangaroo court; as a leaf in a hurricane; as a fledgling in the nest.

symbols: babe in arms; tied to the tracks; Achilles heel.

see also: inadequate; futile.

opposite: strong; effective.

Heretical: as every orthodoxy when it was first suggested; as the other person's concept of truth; as the first suggestion that the earth was round.

symbols: fallen angel; stray lamb; off the reservation.

see also: different; radical; revolutionary; rebellious.

opposite: sacred; blessed; holy; regular.

Hesitant: as a bashful bride; as a timid toe in the water; as a man caught between two women; as an unconvinced customer.

symbols: shrinking violet; cold feet; hot and cold.

see also: slow; lingering; delayed; tentative.

opposite: instantaneous; immediate; emphatic; fast; dashing; impulsive; bold.

Hidden: as buried treasure; as a secret psyche; as an ulterior
                    motive; as a hermit's hideaway.
symbols: Trojan horse; star chamber; chameleon.
see also: buried; concealed; secret; camouflaged; censored;
                    disguised; obscure.
opposite: obvious; open; apparent; noticeable.

High: as a kite on the climb; as the heavens; as the top of
                    the mountain; as the price of progress; as a bird
                    on the wing.
symbols: Olympus; Everest; the Alps; outer space.
see also: elevated; exalted; expensive; heavenly; dear.
opposite: low; cheap; economical; mean.

Holy: as the ground where the Law was given; as the
                    words of the prophets; as the Ten Command-
                    ments; as the Lord of Creation.
symbols: scripture; Gospel; the anointed.
see also: blessed; exalted; sacred.
opposite: damned; heretical.

Honest: as the day is long; as the man Diogenes couldn't
                    find; as a baby's smile.
symbols: Fabricius; a man for Diogenes; true blue.
see also: frank; open.
opposite: lying; dishonest.

Hopeful: as a gambler with money to put on the table; as a
                    persistent suitor; as a stagestruck performer; as
                    a new salesman.
symbols: Pollyanna; Mr. Micawber.
see also: confident; promising; optimistic.
opposite: hopeless; desperate; uncertain; pessimistic.

Hopeless: as a lost cause; as getting blood from a stone; as
                    happiness in Hell; as a deal with the Devil; as the
                    dream of eternal youth.
symbols: Slough of Despond; Cave of Despair; Cassandra.
see also: desperate; pessimistic.
opposite: hopeful; confident; optimistic.

Horrible: as hate on the march; as man's inhumanity to man;
                    as the triumph of terror; as the remembrance of
                    evil; as the depths of Hell.
symbols: Gorgon; Medusa; Pandora's box; the plagues of
                    Egypt.
see also: atrocious; awful; hellish; mean; evil; disastrous.
opposite: good; exemplary; angelic; noble; pleasant.

Hospitable: as an outstretched hand beckoning to a well-stocked table; as a warm welcome on a cold night; as an open door and a friendly fireplace; as a place of shelter in a weary world.

symbols: open house; mine host; kill the fatted calf; Boniface.
see also: friendly; gracious; pleasant; warm; welcome.
opposite: antagonistic; aloof; haughty; mean.

Hot: as Hades in a heat wave; as a bed of burning coals; as a tin roof in the summer sun; as a full head of steam.

symbols: Turkish bath; sauna; sweatbox; bonfire.
see also: heated; inflamed; explosive; volatile.
opposite: cold; icy; calm; gentle; mild.

Huge: as an egotist's ego; as the mileage to Mars; as the heavens are high.

symbols: Leviathan; Colossus of Rhodes; Brobdingnagian.
see also: colossal; big; large.
opposite: small; minimal.

Humble: as a contrite heart; as ignorance at the feet of wisdom; as he who finds his pride is false; as a petitioner before a prince.

symbols: Caspar Milquetoast; shrinking violet; eating crow.
see also: modest; docile; meek; gentle.
opposite: exalted; mighty; haughty; affected; glorified.

Hungry: as a starving hyena; as a vulture on a vegetable diet; as an adolescent between meals; as a bear on the prowl.

symbols: torment of Tantalus; tightened belt.
see also: empty; bottomless.
opposite: satisfied.

Hurried: as a hasty exit; as a candidate's campaign schedule; as a quick count.

symbols: Hermes; Mercury.
see also: hasty; rushed; fast; quick.
opposite: slow; hesitant; delayed; lingering.

Hybrid: as a cross between a worm and a giraffe; as a mule with feathers; as a cat that barks.

symbols: Pan; half man, half beast.
see also: mixed; varied; assorted; different.
opposite: pure.

Hypocritical: as a humble dictator; as a pious pervert; as sin calling itself salvation; as hate masquerading as
love.
symbols: Pecksniff; Uriah Heep.
see also: duplicit; false; devious; insincere.
opposite: honest; barefaced; believable; trustworthy.

I

Icy: as the northern wastes; as the hand of death; as a
cold shoulder; as the inside of a refrigerator.
symbols: Jack Frost; Siberia; Arctic.
see also: cold; bitter; aloof; distant.
opposite: warm; friendly; heated; hot; approachable.

Ideal: as Paradise before the fall; as life in an ivory tower;
as Heaven come to earth; as a perfect specimen.
symbols: Utopia; New Jerusalem; millennium; Erehwon;
Shangri-La.
see also: perfect; heavenly; happy.
opposite: wrong; sad; faulty.

Idealistic: as the dreams of sophomores; as the hope of Heaven
on earth; as the view that all men are good; as
the perceptions of young love.
symbols: Don Quixote; castles in the air.
see also: noble; exalted; optimistic; visionary.
opposite: crass; cynical; pessimistic; bitter.

Idle: as a painted ship upon a painted ocean (*Samuel T.
Coleridge*); as an unused mind; as empty words;
as lost time.
symbols: lotus-eater; sloth.
see also: lazy; inert; quiet.
opposite: active; busy; feverish.

Idolatrous: as the worship of the Golden Calf; as serving false
gods; as worship of the wind; as praying to the
pyramids.
symbols: Baal; the Golden Calf; Lares and Penates.
see also: heretical.
opposite: sacred; holy.

Ignorant:　　as those who will not learn; as babes in arms; as an idle mind; as one who doesn't know he doesn't know.

symbols:　　Philistine; Yahoo; Boeotian; Jukes.

see also:　　oblivious; blind; dumb; foolish.

opposite:　　clever; wise; knowledgeable.

Ill advised:　　as teasing a tiger; as atheism in a seminary; as punching a policeman; as putting your head in the lion's mouth.

symbols:　　counsel of Iago.

see also:　　foolish; tactless; dumb; tasteless; wrong.

opposite:　　wise; appropriate; correct; clever; sound.

Illegible:　　as a doctor's handwriting; as a fourth carbon; as a department store receipt.

symbols:　　hen scratching; Greek.

see also:　　fuzzy; uncertain; cloudy.

opposite:　　clear; understandable; obvious.

Ill mannered:　　as a slob at a soirée; as a weasel in a henhouse; as a bolshevik in a boardroom; as a poltergeist.

symbols:　　bull in a China shop; Goth; Jukes.

see also:　　rude; nasty.

opposite:　　polite; refined; courteous.

Illogical:　　as a throwing the baby out with the bathwater; as biting your nose to spite your face; as wearing a tie with a turtleneck; as blaming the weatherman for the weather; as chopping off a finger to cure a hangnail.

symbols:　　pipe dream; Pickwickian.

see also:　　irrational; incongruous; absurd; strange; mistaken.

opposite:　　wise; sound; natural.

Ill tempered:　　as a prickly porcupine; as a tired taxpayer; as a starving baby at 4 AM; as a tot in a tantrum.

symbols:　　Xanthippe; Terrible Tempered Mr. Bang; spitfire.

see also:　　mad; angry; antagonistic; grouchy; rude; pugnacious; quarrelsome.

opposite:　　agreeable; charming; calm; peaceful; amiable; pleasant.

Imaginary: as a hypochondriac's complaints; as the castles of the mind; as a child's view of life; as what we think we know.

symbols: castle in the air; pipe dream; Arabian Nights; Chimera.

see also: legendary; false; visionary.

opposite: real; true; accurate.

Imitative: as monkey see, monkey do; as the tastes of adolescents; as a child of its parents; as the sincerest form of flattery.

symbols: spittin' image; when in Rome (do as the Romans do); carbon copy.

see also: repetitious.

opposite: original; creative; inventive; innovative; genuine.

Immaculate: as a floor you can eat off; as a saint's reputation; as a new page in the book of life.

symbols: Simon pure; Galahad; Astraea.

see also: clean; pure; spotless.

opposite: dirty; blemished; tarnished; unclean; impure.

Immature: as a sapling in the sun; as a babe in arms; as an acorn waiting to be an oak.

symbols: green apple; tadpole; wet behind the ears.

see also: young; youthful; childish; foolish.

opposite: wise; ripe; old; knowledgeable.

Immediate: as love at first sight; as the next breath; as right now.

symbols: Johnny on the spot; before you can say Jack Robinson.

see also: instantaneous; automatic; spontaneous.

opposite: delayed; late; hesitant; slow; tentative.

Imminent: as day is to dawn; as the next tick of the clock; as a blink of the eye.

symbols: waiting in the wings; just around the corner.

see also: threatening; close; near.

opposite: uncertain; distant; far.

Immodest: as the man who rates himself a genius; as a boaster's braggadocio; as a salvo of self-praise.

symbols: Falstaff; strutting peacock; Pistol.

see also: egotistical; vain; exaggerated; selfish.

opposite: modest; humble; meek; docile.

Immoral: as tearing up the Ten Commandments; as sin on the loose; as selling your soul.

symbols: Jezebel; Paphian; Sodom and Gomorrah; Messalina; Nero; Heliogabalus.

see also: evil; corrupt; bad; wrong.

opposite: angelic; good; exemplary.

Impartial: as an honest judge; as the law of nature; as a man who doesn't care; as an outsider should be in a family spat.

symbols: Ateraea; Themis; Rhadamanthus.

see also: neutral; detached.

opposite: prejudiced; opinionated; bigoted; sympathetic; involved; partisan.

Impatient: as an anxious lover; as a thoroughbred at the starting gate; as a hurricane waiting to happen; as a child whose presents are still gift wrapped; as a glutton looking at the food on the table.

symbols: Hotspur; Mr. Short Fuse; the Terrible Tempered Mr. Bang.

see also: hasty; rushed; hurried; tense.

opposite: calm; relaxed; placid.

Impersonal: as junk mail; as an income tax form; as a conversation with a computer.

symbols: any Tom, Dick and Harry; form letter.

see also: anonymous; aloof; cool; detached.

opposite: personal; warm; approachable; involved.

Important: as the breath of life; as food to the famished; as prayer for the pious; as the sun in the sky.

symbols: Olympian; VIP; Mr. Big; top of the list; high priority.

see also: crucial; famous; decisive; serious; celebrated; urgent; necessary.

opposite: unnecessary; useless; needless; obscure.

Impressive: as the Seven Wonders of the World; as a miracle on your doorstep; as a lion's roar; as lightning and thunder in the night.

symbols: Olympian; four stars.

see also: arresting; convincing; spectacular; compelling; fascinating.

opposite: dull; boring; colorless; empty.

Improper:	as thumbing one's nose at the Pope; as counterfeit in the collection box; as dirty thoughts during transcendental meditation; as a peeping tom.
symbols:	Machiavellian; Old Adam; under the table.
see also:	indiscreet; wrong; inexcusable; corrupt.
opposite:	correct; discreet; wise; prudent.
Impudent:	as a disrespectful child; as a know-it-all who knows nothing; as the pot calling the kettle black.
symbols:	sons of Belial; Leo the Lip.
see also:	rude; insulting; arrogant; bold; tactless.
opposite:	quiet; courteous; discreet.
Impulsive:	as hate at first sight; as an unplanned purchase; as sin on the spur of the moment.
symbols:	Hotspur.
see also:	daring; bold; reckless; spontaneous.
opposite:	hesitant; lingering; delayed; slow.
Impure:	as a doctored drink; as a half-truth; as spoiled food; as a masochist's imagination.
symbols:	Sodom; Augean.
see also:	blemished; tarnished; doctored; dirty.
opposite:	pure; chaste; perfect; flawless; innocent.
Inaccessible:	as an eagle's nest; as an igloo on an iceberg; as a deadbeat ducking the bill collectors.
symbols:	Ultima Thule; Shangri-La.
see also:	far; distant; elusive; isolated.
opposite:	near; close.
Inaccurate:	as calling a spade a club; as a shot in the dark; as a wrong number.
symbols:	Mrs. Malaprop; Wrong Way Corrigan; Pickwickian.
see also:	wrong; erroneous; faulty.
opposite:	correct; true; accurate.
Inadequate:	as a putter on a driving range; as bailing out a boat with a sieve; as a rhesus monkey trying to be King Kong; as hammering nails with a fly swatter.
symbols:	Sisyphean labor; 4 F.
see also:	futile; useless; limited; vain; incompetent.
opposite:	helpful; ample; effective.

Incalculable: as the average hospitable bill; as the rewards of whiplash; as an advance estimate of the cost of car repairs.

symbols: pi to the nth degree; counting the stars.

see also: uncertain; vague; infinite.

opposite: certain; sure; clear; definite; limited

Incompetent: as a glove maker who's all thumbs; as an exterminator who encourages ants; as a cashier who can't count.

symbols: Mr. Bungle; Colonel Blimp; Sad Sack.

see also: inefficient; inept; inadequate; amateurish.

opposite: accomplished; qualified; fit; useful.

Incongruous: as a houseboat on the high seas; as steak sauce on ice cream; as a snowstorm in a steaming jungle.

symbols: fish out of water; strange bedfellows; apples and oranges.

see also: strange; ridiculous; absurd; illogical.

opposite: normal; natural; appropriate; correct; conformist.

Indelible: as a tattoo; as the bleaching of bones; as a bad impression; as an inherited trait.

symbols: the leopard's spots; Mnemosyne; mark of Cain.

see also: permanent; lasting; enduring; perpetual; changeless.

opposite: uncertain; changeable; temporary.

Independent: as the U.S. of A.; as a candidate without a party; as a runaway teenager.

symbols: Statue of Liberty; Liberty Bell; Spirit of '76.

see also: free.

opposite: confined; limited; committed.

Indifferent: as a snooty sales clerk; as an auto salesmen when cars are selling; as a eunuch confronted with a bathing beauty.

symbols: Laodicean; cold shoulder; deaf ear.

see also: aloof; cool; distant; callous; negligent.

opposite: sympathetic; comforting; devoted; attentive; involved.

Indiscreet: as a a bedroom without a window shade; as salting the hostess' prize dish before tasting it.

symbols: bull in a china shop; blabbermouth.

see also: ill-advised; careless; tactless; rude; foolish; hasty.

opposite: prudent; discreet; careful; cautious.

Indulgent: as a doting grandparent; as an audience of friends
                  and relatives; as the parents who spare the rod.

symbols: sugar daddy; Lady Bountiful; guardian angel.
see also: permissive; tolerant; considerate; kind; amiable.
opposite: callous; cool; cruel; rigid.

Ineffective: as an umbrella in a hurricane; as eating soup with a
                  fork; as a rowboat with a hole in the hull.

symbols: paper tiger; labor of Sisyphus; love's labor lost.
see also: useless; fruitless; futile; inadequate; helpless; hope-
                  less; weak.

opposite: effective; fruitful; useful; strong; helpful; convinc-
                  ing.

Inefficient: as smoke signals in a high wind; as a postage stamp
                  that won't stick; as serving soup with a sieve.

symbols: The Poor Soul; Sad Sack; basket case.
see also: incompetent; inadequate; futile.
opposite: effective; smooth; accomplished.

Ineligible: as a duffer for the Masters Tournament; as a
                  bigamist at the bridal altar; as a teenager trying
                  to get a pension.

symbols: beyond the pale.
see also: left out; picky; inadequate.
opposite: eligible; qualified; deserving.

Inept: as a finger painter who's all thumbs; as a juggler
                  with the shakes; as a cook who can't remember a
                  recipe; as a dancer with two left feet.

symbols: Mr. Thumbs; Sad Sack.
see also: incompetent; awkward; amateurish; inefficient.
opposite: accomplished; efficient; effective.

Inert: as a cornerstone; as a statue in the park; as the
                  water in a stagnant pool; as a limp wet rag.

symbols: Sleeping Beauty; Rock of Gilbraltar; Mount Ever-
                  est.

see also: lazy; relaxed; limp; dead.
opposite: active; busy; agitated; energetic.

Inevitable: as the Day of Judgment; as morning, noon and
                  night; as the march of time.

symbols: The Fates; Kismet.
see also: certain; sure; clear; definite.
opposite: questionable; uncertain; debatable.

Inexcusable: as a streaker in a seminary; as graffiti in the Sistine Chapel; as lighting a match to look for a gas leak.

symbols: beyond the pale; over the line.

see also: ill-advised; wrong.

opposite: excusable; exemplary; commendable; admirable.

Infinite: as a braggart's boasts; as the expanding universe; as the duration of eternity; as the power of nature.

symbols: world without end.

see also: endless; perpetual.

opposite: limited; definite; confined.

Inflamed: as an angry boil; as a mob in white heat; as a strep throat; as an adolescent's first pass at passion.

symbols: The Furies; active volcano.

see also: heated; passionate; angry; sick; painful.

opposite: calm; placid; gentle; peaceful; healthy.

Inflammable: as high octane gasoline; as a dry forest; as a demagogue's call to arms.

symbols: tinder box; powder keg.

see also: explosive; dangerous; threatening; ominous.

opposite: safe; harmless.

Inflated: as a pneumatic tire; as a braggart's ego; as a pumped-up air mattress; as a hot air balloon.

symbols: lighter than air; blowfish.

see also: exaggerated; magnified; huge; booming; high.

opposite: small; minimal; low.

Informal: as a leisure dress in a nudist colony; as a picnic in the park; as dirty overalls; as a pajama party.

symbols: pot luck; homespun.

see also: casual; relaxed.

opposite: formal; rigid.

Innocent: as a newborn babe; as a lamb led to slaughter; as a new-laid egg (*W. S. Gilbert*); as a passing bystander.

symbols: Arcadian; babes and sucklings; Astraea; babe in the woods.

see also: pure; clean; chaste; harmless.

opposite: blemished; tarnished; crafty; wily corrupt; deceitful; guilty.

Innovative: as an automobile in mule country; as the invention of the wheel; as the first fashion designer.

symbols: new broom; New Look; New Deal.
see also: original; creative; inventive; inspired.
opposite: old fashioned; obsolete; overworked; normal.

Inquisitive: as a curious cat; as a grand jury on the scent of sin; as the neighborhood snoop.

symbols: Nosy Parker; Polly Pry; Paul Pry; peeping Tom.
see also: curious; meddlesome.
opposite: indifferent; apathetic; aloof.

Insincere: as a flatterer's flowery phrases; as canned laughter; as the polished prose of diplomats; as a candidate's compliments.

symbols: Judas kiss; Punic faith; Machiavellian.
see also: false; contrived; lying; duplicit; dishonest; hypocritical.
opposite: honest; trustworthy; true.

Insistent: as a nagging backache; as a life insurance salesman; as a collection agency; as a drug habit; as a migraine.

symbols: Hobson's choice; Siren song.
see also: dogged; stubborn; committed.
opposite: hesitant; relaxed; apathetic.

Inspired: as a work of genius; as Tschaikovsky's Fourth or a fifth of Jack Daniels; as a spontaneous demonstration in the Kremlin; as a Beethoven sonata.

symbols: brainstorm; Moses; the vision of the prophets.
see also: electrifying; innovative; brilliant; eager.
opposite: bored; dull; apathetic; normal.

Instantaneous: as the shock of recognition; as turning on a light; as a bolt of lightning; as the blink of an eye.

symbols: split second; spur of the moment; Johnny on the spot.
see also: immediate; automatic.
opposite: slow; delayed.

Instinctive: as ducking for cover; as a tigress protecting her cubs; as the relationship between cat and mouse; as the act of breathing.

symbols: nature of the beast; Pavlovian; in the blood.
see also: natural; automatic; predictable; intuitive.
opposite: uncertain; contrived.

Instructive: as six lessons from Madame La Zonga; as learning from a master; as the school of hard knocks; as seeing for yourself.
symbols: Nestor; Mentor.
see also: explicit; plain; clear.
opposite: dumb; obscure.

Insulting: as a slap in the face; as an audience that talks through the performance; as a snooty sales clerk; as a snub at a soirée.
symbols: sons of Belial; billingsgate.
see also: rude; tactless; impudent.
opposite: complimentary; polite; diplomatic.

Intangible: as human ethics; as the spirit of '76; as memories in the mists of time; as the holes in Swiss cheese.
symbols: a creature of the mind.
see also: vague; uncertain.
opposite: definite; clear.

Intimate: as a secret tryst; as bedmates in a boudoir; as an underwear ad.
symbols: bedroom diplomacy; Venus Genetrix; tête-à-tête.
see also: personal; familiar; close; near; secret.
opposite: public; distant; far; impersonal.

Intolerant: as Carry Nation contemplating a saloon; as a Puritan who thinks he sees a sinner; as young success is of old failure; as the sinner is of the saint.
symbols: Spanish Inquisition; iron hand.
see also: bigoted; dogmatic; narrow; prejudiced; closed; parochial.
opposite: tolerant; liberal; understanding.

Intoxicating: as 100 proof whiskey in a ten ounce glass; as the sweet sensual scent of sex; as sheer beauty beckoning; as the sense of power.
symbols: John Barleycorn; Bacchanalian.
see also: drink; dizzy; euphoric; overwhelming; strong.
opposite: sober; calm; placid; gloomy.

Intricate: as a family tree; as the complications of the income tax; as the language of the bureaucrat.
symbols: Daedalian; Gordian knot; jigsaw puzzle.
see also: complex; complicated; difficult; baffling.
opposite: simple; clear; elementary; basic.

Intrusive: as the neighborhood gossip; as an unexpected com-
                 mercial; as a foot in the door; as a peeping Tom.

symbols: the uninvited guest; buttinsky.

see also: meddlesome; insistent; ill-mannered; personal.

opposite: aloof; apathetic.

Intuitive: as a woman's hunches; as a good poker player; as a
                 baby's grasping fingers; as a mother's love.

symbols: feel it in your bones; hunch player; a little bird's
                 whisper.

see also: instinctive; automatic.

opposite: uncertain; bewildered.

Inventive: as a gifted liar; as the man who made the wheel; as
                 the design of the universe.

symbols: Thomas A. Edison; Daedalian.

see also: imaginative; fertile; creative.

opposite: dull; boring; futile.

Inviting: as a lifetime supply of all your favorite foods; as the
                 applause of your peers; as the promise of power;
                 as the immediate availability of a magnificent
                 companion of the opposite sex.

symbols: siren song; golden apples.

see also: attractive; provocative; promising; fascinating; ap-
                 pealing.

opposite: disagreeable; gross; hellish; horrible; insulting;
                 ugly.

Involved: as the meat balls are with the spaghetti; as the
                 electric circuits in a pinball machine; as a net-
                 work of Swiss bank accounts.

symbols: partners in crime; Daedalian; Gordian knot.

see also: committed; dedicated; complex; complicated; intri-
                 cate; baffling.

opposite: clear; simple; aloof; cool; casual; left out; indifferent.

Irrational: as a hysteric at the height of a fit; as the blindness
                 of hate incarnate; as fear of the unknown; as suc-
                 cess in the rock music field.

symbols: Mad Hatter; Alice in Wonderland; Through the
                 Looking Glass.

see also: illogical; angry; mad.

opposite: normal; reasonable.

Irregular: as French verbs; as a shirt with three sleeves; as a dyspeptic's digestion; as a rigged election.

symbols: cutting corners; not according to Hoyle.

see also: erratic; wrong; uncertain; changeable.

opposite: normal; regular; average; constant.

Irrelevant: as matzoh balls are to clam chowder; as a lawn mower in a field of artificial grass; as water wings in the desert.

symbols: another ballgame; a different kettle of fish; a horse of another color.

see also: alien; foreign; needless.

opposite: appropriate; essential; necessary.

Isolated: as an atom on an asteroid in outer space; as a good example in a bad situation; as a poached egg on toast; as a lonely crouton in a sea of soup.

symbols: Stylites (pillar saints); Robinson Crusoe; sent to Coventry.

see also: alone; exclusive; inaccessible; forsaken; left out; lonely; lonesome; abandoned.

opposite: near; close; crowded; jammed; involved.

J

Jaded: as a polygamist on his 27th honeymoon; as the oldest elephant in the circus; as a sinner in Sodom; as a tea taster in his cups.

symbols: Dorian Gray; the disenchanted; battle fatigue.

see also: bored; weary; apathetic; indifferent; dull; casual.

opposite: eager; zealous; anxious.

Jammed: as a commuter bus in rush hour; as the road to the beach on a sunny Sunday in July; as a two-passenger car with a ten-passenger load.

symbols: S.R.O. (standing room only); Black Hole of Calcutta; sardine can.

see also: crowded; congested; packed; thick.

opposite: isolated; alone; abandoned; empty.

Jarring: as the stop when somebody pulls the emergency cord; as a siren in the still of night; as a no vote in a chorus of ayes; as a cat-call at a convocation.

symbols: apple of discord; upset the applecart.

see also: harsh; rude; loud; noisy.

opposite: quiet; calm; peaceful; polite.

Jealous: as a discarded lover; as a petty official guarding his privileges; as a suspicious spouse; as a sibling rivalry.

symbols: the green-eyed monster; keeping up with the Joneses.

see also: envious; greedy.

opposite: indifferent; generous; charitable; kind.

Jewish: as Abraham, Isaac and Sholem Aleichem; as chicken soup with matzoh balls; as the three B's— bagels, blintzes and borscht; as Tel Aviv; as John the Baptist.

symbols: the chosen people; the people of the Book.

see also: timeless; legendary.

opposite: transient.

Juicy: as a ripe orange; as grapes ready for the pressing; as a chaw of chewing tobacco; as scandalous scuttlebutt.

symbols: Rabelaisian; mouth watering.

see also: fruitful; fascinating.

opposite: fruitless; dry; dull.

K

Keen: as a brand new razor blade; as a cutting edge; as the pain of a stab in the back; as the mind of an Einstein.

symbols: Damascus steel; Toledo blade.

see also: cutting; sharp; brilliant; biting.

opposite: dull; slow.

Kind: as kings upon their coronation day (*John Dryden*); as an act of love; as a helping hand in an hour of need; as a kiss.

symbols: Good Samaritan; knight errant; guardian angel; Lady Bountiful; fairy godmother.

see also: generous; charitable; considerate; genial.

opposite: cruel; brutal; harsh; savage; threatening.

Knotty: as a pockmarked pine; as tangled twine; as a fouled fishing line.

symbols: Gordian; Chinese puzzle; between Scylla and Charybdis.

see also: complex; difficult; complicated; mixed up.

opposite: simple; clear; easy.

Knowledgeable: as a nosey neighbor; as the man who wrote the book; as Father Time.
symbols: Einstein; walking encyclopedia.
see also: learned; cultured; educated; wise.
opposite: ignorant; immature; dopey; dumb.

L

Laborious: as the labors of Hercules; as a tyro's technique; as teaching a new dog old tricks; as a hike up Mount Everest.
symbols: Sisyphus; Hercules; the curse of Adam.
see also: hard; difficult; tough.
opposite: easy; simple; clear.

Large: as life and twice as natural (*Lewis Carroll*); as the tail that wags the dog; as an elephant seems to a gnat; as the world is round.
symbols: Gargantua; Colossus of Rhodes.
see also: colossal; big; huge; vast; broad.
opposite: small; minimal; little.

Lasting: as a stain on the family escutcheon; as a happy memory; as a diamond.
symbols: Rock of Ages; laws of the Medes and the Persians; Rock of Gibraltar.
see also: enduring; chronic; endless; perpetual; permanent.
opposite: fleeting; temporary; limited; momentary.

Late: as lunch at midnight; as a Christmas card on the Fourth of July; as the horse that finished last; as the dear departed.
symbols: last minute; tail-ender; eleventh hour.
see also: delayed; slow; dead.
opposite: early; new; immediate; punctual.

Lavish: as a Roman orgy; as the treasure of the Tsars; as the flattery of a man with an axe to grind; as a Hollywood party in the good old days.
symbols: Lucullus; groaning board.
see also: extravagant; grand; exaggerated; generous.
opposite: stingy; frugal; economical; close; cheap; modest; simple.

Lawless: as the James brothers; as the robber barons; as anarchy on the loose; as the top ten public enemies; as mob rule.

symbols: Judge Lynch; street justice; reign of terror.
see also: corrupt; crooked; wicked; evil; dishonest; immoral.
opposite: legal; innocent; trustworthy; good; correct.

Lazy: as Ludlam's dog that leaned his head against a wall to bark (*John Ray*); as a languid river in the noonday sun; as a hound dog dozing in the heat; as lolling in a hammock.

symbols: Castle of Indolence; Lotus-eaters.
see also: idle; relaxed; limp; inert.
opposite: energetic; active; busy; athletic; feverish.

Leakproof: as an empty glass; as a plumber's prize pipejoint; as a space capsule.

symbols: Fort Knox; hermetically sealed.
see also: solid; tight; strong.
opposite: loose; leaky.

Leaky: as an unfixed faucet; as a rickety roof in a rainstorm; as a tent with mothholes; as an old tub.

symbols: sieve; blabbermouth.
see also: porous; loose.
opposite: leakproof; tight.

Learned: as a Ph.D. with a photographic memory; as a senior sage; as the one who wrote the book.

symbols: Socrates; Aristotle; Maimonides.
see also: educated; cultured; knowledgeable; wise.
opposite: ignorant; immature; blank.

Left handed: as an invitation from a hermit; as damning with faint praise; as British traffic.

symbols: portsider; Wrong Way Corrigan.
see also: backhanded; awkward; tactless; heavy-handed.
opposite: artful; gracious; diplomatic.

Leftist: as the dogma in the Kremlin; as a manifesto from Marx; as the radicals who are convinced they're right.

symbols: Red; Marxist; Maoist.
see also: radical; revolutionary; liberal; heretical; rebellious.
opposite: conformist; reactionary; prudent.

Left out:	as a pup in the doghouse; as a wallflower at a junior prom; as the player neither team wants.
symbols:	beyond the pale; sent to Coventry.
see also:	forsaken; abandoned; overlooked; isolated; deserted; neglected.
opposite:	sought after; involved; popular.
Legal:	as the Bill of Rights; as a decision by the Supreme Court; as the law of the land.
symbols:	Astraea; Themis; the Bar.
see also:	correct; authoritative.
opposite:	lawless; corrupt.
Legendary:	as the knights of the Round Table; as the prowess of Paul Bunyan and his blue ox Babe; as the cremation of Sam McGee; as the Loch Ness monster; as the abominable snowman.
symbols:	chimera; household names; folk heroes.
see also:	imaginary; uncertain; doubtful; questionable; popular.
opposite:	true; accurate; real; boring.
Lethal:	as a dose of arsenic; as a leap off the Eiffel Tower; as a dumdum bullet between the eyes; as the black plague.
symbols:	Thanatos; Aceldama; Grim Reaper.
see also:	deadly; fatal; destructive.
opposite:	harmless; safe; encouraging.
Liberal:	as a cheerful giver; as a politician with public money; as an indulgent parent; as the New Deal.
symbols:	Good Samaritan; left of center; "bleeding heart."
see also:	generous; leftist.
opposite:	stingy; tight; reactionary; conformist.
Light:	as a lamp in the darkness; as a load of helium; as the heart of a happy human; as the noonday sun in a cloudless sky; as the air above.
symbols:	Apollo; Mithra.
see also:	airy; carefree; brilliant; delicate; gaseous; dainty.
opposite:	heavy; dark; burdensome.
Limited:	as liberty in a dictatorship; as a pinch-penny's pocket money.
symbols:	Iron Curtain; closed company; short tether.
see also:	confined; close; inadequate; selective; stingy; endangered.
opposite:	free; generous; infinite; overwhelming.

Limp: as a wet rag; as a string of licorice; as a serving of
~~well-done spaghetti; as a milksop's handshake.~~

symbols: dish rag; marshmallow; Caspar Milquetoast.
see also: inert; relaxed.
opposite: rigid; active; busy; agitated; energetic; steadfast.

Lingering: as a four-week head cold; as a long liquid lunch; as
the scent of perfume in a boudoir; as a favorite
memory.

symbols: slow death; staying power.
see also: endless; continuous; constant; perpetual; ceaseless.
opposite: fleeting; momentary; final.

Little: as the law allows; as a single drop of water in the
deep blue sea; as a midget in Lilliput; as a grain
of sand.

symbols: Tom Thumb; Munchkin; pocket edition; Lilliput.
see also: minimal; meager; small; abbreviated.
opposite: big; large; huge; colossal; vast.

Lonely: as life at the top; as solitary senility; as the road to
nowhere; as the craters of the moon.

symbols: pillar saint; Timon of Athens; Diogenes in his tub;
Coventry.

see also: isolated; alone; forsaken; lonesome; abandoned; left
out.

opposite: crowded; involved.

Lonesome: as a haunted house; as the last of the Mohicans; as a
wallflower; as a sailor on an endless sea.

symbols: The Man Without a Country; Robinson Crusoe;
Ishmael.

see also: alone; lonely; forsaken; abandoned; left out.
opposite: sought after; involved.

Long: as the Lincoln Highway; as a speech by Fidel Castro; as the limits of outer space; as life has lived
on earth.

symbols: from here to eternity; slow boat to China; beat
around the bush.

see also: endless; infinite; slow; broad; extended.
opposite: short; abbreviated; brief; quick; fast.

Loose:	as a fallen woman; as the wind (*George Herbert*); as a worn-out girdle; as goose grease; as a liar is with the truth; as the tongue of the town gossip.
symbols:	rope of sand; long leash; on the town; Nirvana.
see also:	relaxed; immoral; slippery; dishonest; lying; false.
opposite:	tight; rigid; confined; honest; accurate.
Loud:	as the howl of a hurricane; as the beat of a big bass drum; as a clap of thunder; as the caw of the crow in the cornfield.
symbols:	Stentor.
see also:	noisy; harsh; boisterous.
opposite:	soft; quiet.
Lovable:	as Elaine the fair, the lily maid of Astelot (*Alfred Tennyson*); as a little puppy; as a cuddle bunny.
symbols:	Eros; Cupid; Aphrodite.
see also:	beloved; friendly; winning; charming; cherished; enchanting.
opposite:	hateful; nasty; disagreeable; objectionable; rotten; awful.
Lovely:	as love remembered; as the light of day; as the gift of laughter; as a rose in full bloom.
symbols:	The Graces; Helen of Troy; Miss Universe; Hebe; Venus.
see also:	beautiful; appealing; charming; enchanting; lovable.
opposite:	frightful; ugly; awful; disagreeable; rotten.
Low:	as a gnat's knee; as the depths of Hell; as a coward hangs his head; as a basso's bottom note; as the bottom of the barrel.
symbols:	below sea level; bottomed out; down in the dumps.
see also:	deep; bottomless; downhearted; mean; nasty.
opposite:	high; elevated; cheerful.
Loyal:	as a faithful dog; as mother love; as an old friend.
symbols:	fidus Achates; The Three Musketeers; Bushido.
see also:	constant; faithful; true; steadfast; trustworthy; changeless.
opposite:	false; uncertain; treacherous; tricky; changeable.

Lucky: as stumbling on a pot of gold; as hitting the bullseye
                    in the dark; as the man who broke the bank of
                    Monte Carlo; as the man who owns a golden
                    goose.
symbols: Fortuna; Midas touch; Tyche.
see also: fortunate; blessed; happy.
opposite: unlucky; damned.

Lying: as a false witness; as a teller of tall tales; as an
                    affidavit by Judas Iscariot.
symbols: Ananias; Baron Munchausen.
see also: dishonest; false; tricky.
opposite: honest; frank; true; trustworthy.

M

Mad: as a March hare (*John Heywood*); as a dog that's
                    foaming at the mouth; as a fool in a full moon.
symbols: Bedlam; Alice in Wonderland; Terrible Tempered
                    Mr. Bang.
see also: crazy; angry; irrational; agitated; feverish; ill-
                    tempered.
opposite: calm; reasonable; peaceful; relaxed; placid.

Magnificent: as the Taj Mahal; as the music of the spheres; as the
                    gift of genius; as the heavens in their glory.
symbols: Seven Wonders of the World; Olympian.
see also: glorious; beautiful; impressive; majestic.
opposite: ugly; dreadful; frightful; awful; horrible.

Magnified: as a molecule viewed through a microscope; as a
                    coward's fears; as a molehill masquerading as a
                    mountain; as a ham actor's ego.
symbols: Baron Munchausen; piling Pelion on Ossa; cock-
                    alorum.
see also: exaggerated; overwhelming; extravagant.
opposite: small; little; minimal; modest.

Majestic: as a royal coronation; as the music of Bach; as the
                    mountain tops; as the basilica of St. Peter in the
                    Eternal City.
symbols: Olympus; Triton among the minnows.
see also: magnificent; glorious; impressive; monumental.
opposite: modest; minimal; small.

Matchless: as a smoker without a light; as a man without a mate; as Mount Everest; as the morning sun.

symbols: Kohinoor; Taj Mahal; the greatest; one in a million.

see also: alone; different.

opposite: alike; conformist.

Mature: as Methuselah approaching his millennium; as ripe cheese; as a giant redwood; as grapes ready to be wine.

symbols: aged in the wood; prime of life; vintage wine.

see also: ripe; experienced; aged.

opposite: naive; raw; immature; childish; young; youthful.

Meager: as a know-nothing's knowledge; as a pauper's purse; as a mess of pottage.

symbols: Spartan; Spartan fare; bread and water; slim pickings.

see also: poor; little; minimal; scanty; scarce.

opposite: affluent; rich; wealthy.

Mean: as a miser with a migraine; as a bad-tempered bully on a binge; as a man who kicks puppies.

symbols: Scrooge; dog in the manger; rogue elephant.

see also: cruel; demonic; detestable; objectionable; awful; hellish.

opposite: agreeable; pleasant; charming; angelic; generous; kind.

Meddlesome: as too many cooks in the kitchen; as a prying neighbor; as a squirrel eating the birdseed; as a grandstand quarterback.

symbols: Nosy Parker; buttinsky; Paul or Polly Pry.

see also: intrusive; curious; inquisitive.

opposite: aloof; indifferent; apathetic; cold.

Meek: as a modest mouse; as a little lamb; as a milksop.

symbols: Caspar Milquetoast; timid soul; Job; a pussycat.

see also: docile; gentle; quiet; humble; tame; repressed.

opposite: assertive; aggressive; argumentative; pugnacious; menacing; loud.

Memorable: as Moses on the mountain top; as the discovery of the New World; as man's first steps on the moon.

symbols: Mnemosyne; big moment; one for the book.

see also: famous; indelible; enduring; monumental.

opposite: forgotten; colorless; dull; fuzzy.

Menacing: as Dracula looking for a drink at midnight; as Frankenstein's monster; as a glare from Godzilla; as a strain of madness; as a mysterious disease; as a ransom note.

symbols: sword of Damocles; saber rattling; brinkmanship.
see also: threatening; ominous; dangerous; pungnacious.
opposite: meek; docile; safe; harmless; trustworthy; kind; gentle.

Messy: as a madman's logic; as the town dump; as a beach after a beer bust; as an unmade bed.

symbols: mare's nest; Bedlam; Babel; Augean stable.
see also: dirty; disorganized; confused; unclean; muddled; mixed up.
opposite: clean; neat; planned; efficient.

Mighty: as a tidal wave; as an atom bomb; as the truth on the march.

symbols: Titan; Hercules; Gargantua; Samson.
see also: strong; powerful; overwhelming; monumental; colossal.
opposite: weak; feeble; meager; humble; small; little; underdeveloped.

Militant: as an activist with an itch; as a riot looking for a place to happen; as a hungry lioness protecting her cubs; as a mob on the march.

symbols: Bellona; Mars; Samurai; soldier of fortune.
see also: aggressive; pugnacious; positive.
opposite: quiet; peaceful; meek; docile; quiet.

Minimal: as a nudist's negligee; as a hermit's hospitality; as a miser's gifts to charity.

symbols: Lilliput; drop in the bucket; sub-compact.
see also: small; little.
opposite: big; huge; large.

Miraculous: as the spark of life; as blood from a stone; as a walk on the water; as our ability to find explanations for the unexplainable.

symbols: act of God; heaven-sent; parting of the waters.
see also: baffling; amazing.
opposite: logical; understandable.

Misplaced: as a bull in a china shop; as cash with a con man; as a saddle on a sea lion; as a saloon in a seminary.

symbols: fish out of water; square peg in a round hole.

see also: irrelevant; confused; mixed up; wrong; mistaken.

opposite: representative; right.

Mistaken: as a miser who collects counterfeit money; as a mouse at a cats' convention; as applause at a funeral; as seeds in concrete.

symbols: a Brodie; a blooper.

see also: erroneous; wrong.

opposite: right; correct.

Misunderstood: as English in Omsk; as another man's pride; as a wink at the wrong time in the wrong direction.

symbols: false impression; wrong end of the stick.

see also: muddled; mixed up; confused; puzzled; uncertain.

opposite: clear; understandable; certain.

Mixed: as a malted; as the merchandise in a flea market; as a melting pot; as cement waiting to be poured; as boarding house hash.

symbols: Tower of Babel; Noah's Ark; crazy quilt.

see also: varied; assorted; blended; hybrid.

opposite: alone; divided; lonely; lonesome.

Mixed up: as a scrambled egg; as alphabet soup; as the contents of a cocktail shaker; as a combination of two days' hash; as a lost child; as a homing pigeon without a home.

symbols: Tower of Babel; Bedlam.

see also: confused; bewildered; puzzled; mistaken.

opposite: clear; right; accurate.

Modern: as the day after tomorrow; as the exploration of outer space; as the latest nostalgia fad.

symbols: the now generation; the new improved model; the rage.

see also: new.

opposite: old; ancient.

Modest: as a maiden's blush; as a poor man's purse; as a mere moment in the vast expanse of eternity; as an inferiority complex.

symbols: shrinking violet; Encratite; vestal virgin; Artemis.
see also: humble; frugal; chaste; meek; docile; economical.
opposite: immodest; egotistical; loose; lavish; haughty; affected.

Momentary: as the beginning of a blink; as a passing twinge; as a single click of the clock of time.

symbols: nine days wonder; flash in the pan.
see also: fleeting; transient; temporary.
opposite: lasting; constant; permanent; enduring; continuous.

Monotonous: as the roar of the surf; as breathing; as turnpike driving in heavy traffic; as a thrice-told tale.

symbols: task of Sisyphus; same old story; broken record.
see also: boring; dull; repetitious.
opposite: exciting; fascinating; gripping.

Monumental: as the great Sphinx; as a hundred-story building in a one-horse town; as Mount Everest.

symbols: Eiffel Tower; Colossus of Rhodes; Titan; Herculean.
see also: majestic; impressive; memorable; mighty; colossal; overwhelming.
opposite: modest; dull; little; small; forgotten.

Moody: as a brooding beatnik; as a paranoid's psyche; as the mists of time; as fickle fortune.

symbols: Hamlet; the cave of Trophonius; Slough of Despond.
see also: volatile; changeable; gloomy; nervous; neurotic.
opposite: cheerful; steadfast; changeless; happy; constant.

Moving: as a mother's love; as a miracle before your eyes; as a letter from a cherished past; as a shove from a tractor.

symbols: Siren song; tear jerker; hearts and flowers.
see also: warm; appealing.
opposite: cold; cool; ineffective.

Muddled: as a mess in a Mixmaster; as a message written in molasses.

symbols: mare's nest; Gongorism.
see also: mixed up; confused; puzzled; messy; unclean.
opposite: clear; clean; neat; logical.

N

Naive:	as a rookie falling for the same old routine; as un-tried youth trying to seem mature; as most of the people who think they are city slickers; as the yearnings of young love.
symbols:	Arcadian; Simple Simon; wet behind the ears.
see also:	idealistic; simple.
opposite:	mature; experienced.
Naked:	as a newborn babe in its birthday suit; as a jaybird bathing; as a bald man's scalp; as the unvarnished truth.
symbols:	streaker; flasher; topless; bottomless; the altogether.
see also:	bare; bold; obvious.
opposite:	concealed; camouflaged; hidden.
Narrow:	as a bigot's mind; as the straight path of life; as a bureaucrat's vision; as a patrician nose for looking down on people.
symbols:	Mrs. Grundy; bluenose; know-nothing.
see also:	bigoted; prejudiced; intolerant.
opposite:	tolerant; broad; liberal; open.
Nasty:	as a nagging spouse; as a nervous hyena; as a batch of paper cuts; as a deliberate doublecross.
symbols:	The Furies; goon squad; Xanthippe; snake in the grass.
see also:	hateful; detestable; disagreeable; cruel; mean; harsh.
opposite:	friendly; agreeable; pleasant; warm; kind.
Natural:	as Mother Nature herself; as the breath of life; as the sunshine and the rain; as human mortality.
symbols:	Simon Pure; the real McCoy; Arcadian; the art of God.
see also:	true; real; instinctive; spontaneous; innocent.
opposite:	false; affected; insincere; fraudulent.
Near:	as your next-door neighbor; as the end of your nose; as a close shave; as a voice in your ear.
symbols:	around the corner; close quarters; hair's breadth.
see also:	close; convenient.
opposite:	far; distant.

Neat:	as the proverbial pin; as a straight drink of whiskey; as a trick by Houdini.
symbols:	apple-pie order; ship-shape.
see also:	clean; precise; spotless; immaculate.
opposite:	disorganized; messy; tangled; confused; unclean.

Necessary:	as eggs in an omelet; as print in a newspaper; as oxygen in the air we breathe.
symbols:	a must; an absolute; will of the gods.
see also:	essential; basic; useful.
opposite:	needless; unnecessary; useless.

Needless:	as pits in cream cheese; as bones in ice cream; as extra warts; as a hole in the head.
symbols:	coals to Newcastle; gilding the lily.
see also:	unnecessary; useless.
opposite:	necessary; useful; essential; basic.

Needy:	as an orphan of the storm; as a waif on welfare; as a deserted family.
symbols:	Poverty Row; over the hill to the poorhouse; wolf at the door.
see also:	poor; deprived.
opposite:	rich; affluent; wealthy; privileged.

Negative:	as a door slammed in your face; as a Presidential veto; as a rejection slip.
symbols:	downbeat; nihilism; black ball.
see also:	pessimistic; downhearted; uncertain; dubious.
opposite:	positive; affirmative; optimistic; sure; certain.

Neglected:	as a ghost town gone to seed; as an unwanted child; as a loafer's chores.
symbols:	on the shelf; limbo; out to pasture.
see also:	abandoned; deserted; forgotten; forsaken; overlooked; run-down.
opposite:	cherished; appreciated; welcome; beloved.

Negligent:	as a drunken driver; as a sleeping watchman; as a teacher who plays hookey.
symbols:	Sad Sack; goof-off; grasshopper (compared to the ant).
see also:	careless; indifferent; improper; lazy.
opposite:	attentive; conscientious; devoted; careful; considerate; cautious.

Neighborly:	as a nearby friend; as a helping hand; as a shared lawnmower.
symbols:	block party; fence friendship.
see also:	helpful; friendly; pleasant; approachable; amiable; hospitable.
opposite:	aloof; haughty; nasty; antagonistic; indifferent; cold.
Nervous:	as a cat on the prowl; as a newlywed; as a crap-shooter waiting for the roll of the dice; as a caged lion.
symbols:	sword of Damocles; razor's edge; anxious seat.
see also:	edgy; agitated; restless; neurotic; worried; tense; anxious.
opposite:	calm; relaxed; placid.
Neurotic:	as a psychiatrist's most constant client; as a cat with a complex; as a kid whose id has slid; as a lost libido.
symbols:	Freudian; walking wounded; Momus.
see also:	nervous; worried; tense; anxious.
opposite:	calm; relaxed; healthy; placid.
Neutral:	as the friend of both sides; as the one who doesn't want to be involved; as weakness caught between two strengths; as tasteless grain spirits before the whiskey flavor's added.
symbols:	golden mean; straight down the middle.
see also:	impartial; detached; independent; indifferent.
opposite:	involved; active; partisan.
New:	as money straight from the mint; as today at sunrise; as the latest bulletin; as the wine that's just been pressed; as a pickle not yet dilled; as the baby fresh from the womb.
symbols:	Genesis; world premiere; hot off the press.
see also:	modern; fresh; immediate; young.
opposite:	old; obsolete; dated; ancient; aged.
Nice:	as new clothes; as the guys who finish last (derived from Leo Durocher); as sugar and spice.
symbols:	Attic; Arcadian; peaches and cream.
see also:	appealing; attractive; charming; becoming; friendly; pleasant.
opposite:	mean; detestable; nasty; disagreeable.

Nimble: as the feet of a Fred Astaire; as the mind of a man who lives by his wits; as a monkey maneuvering from tree to tree; as Jack jumping over the candlestick.

symbols: Hermes; Mercury; twinkletoes.

see also: agile; fast; active; quick.

opposite: awkard; slow; inept.

Noble: as the greatest works of man; as the noblest Roman of them all; as the stature of a saint; as good deeds in a lost cause.

symbols: Galahad; Bayard; Olympus; Sir Lancelot.

see also: elevated; exalted; high; pure; sacrificial; good; kind; generous.

opposite: nasty; mean; low; selfish; cruel.

Noisy: as teatime in the Tower of Babel; as the sound of angry surf; as barking dogs at midnight; as the cocks crowing at dawn.

symbols: Stentor; the cave of the winds.

see also: loud; boisterous; jarring.

opposite: soft; calm; quiet.

Normal: as 98.6 degrees; as red tape in a bureaucracy; as April showers and May flowers.

symbols: S.O.P. (standard operating procedure); according to Hoyle.

see also: average; familiar; common; representative.

opposite: rare; special; different; high; low.

Nostalgic: as a class reunion; as the songs our mothers taught us; as a letter from a long-lost friend; as the old family album.

symbols: memory book; the good old days.

see also: old-fashioned; sentimental; memorable.

opposite: forgotten; indifferent; cold.

Noticeable: as a wart on the end of your nose; as a banner headline; as a star in a spotlight; as a badly fitting toupe.

symbols: exhibit A; front and center.

see also: obvious; glaring; eminent.

opposite: obscure; overlooked; hidden.

Notorious: as the nightlife of the gods; as the sins of Sodom and the grossness of Gomorrah; as the habits of a happy hooker.

symbols: talk of the town; hot copy; household word.

see also: celebrated; famous; scandalous.

opposite: hidden; secret.

Nourishing: as three square meals a day; as food for thought; as milk and meat.

symbols: Hygeia; Ceres; Demeter.

see also: healthy; hearty.

opposite: poor; poisonous; rotten.

Numerous: as the fish in the sea; as a plague of locusts; as the children of God; as the grains of sand; as the sins of the Devil.

symbols: Briareus; legion.

see also: abundant; fruitful.

opposite: scarce; sparse; scanty.

Nutty: as a pecan pie; as a package of pistachios; as a nougat; as a field of filberts.

symbols: full moon; Tom o' Bedlam; fruitcake.

see also: crazy; mixed up; cracked; mad; irrational.

opposite: reasonable; responsible; normal.

O

Obedient: as a trained seal; as a yes-man in a no-win situation; as a faithful dog; as a dutiful child; as a good soldier.

symbols: Myrmidon; Pavlov's dog.

see also: dutiful; faithful; trustworthy; available; agreeable.

opposite: antagonistic; negligent; uncertain; rebellious.

Objectionable: as stealing from the poorbox; as foul language in a nursery; as child abuse; as setting fire to your neighbor's house.

symbols: gall and wormwood; public nuisance.

see also: disagreeable; nasty; criminal; evil; hateful; wicked; mean.

opposite: attractive; appealing; lovable; good; beautiful.

Oblivious: as a blind man in a blaze of color; as a drunk on a bender; as a sleeping baby in the midst of bedlam.

symbols: Lethe; limbo.
see also: forgetful; apathetic; blind; ignorant; deaf; forgetful.
opposite: attentive; anxious; concerned; worried; careful; tense.

Obscure: as the language of diplomacy; as a black crow in a dark field on a moonless midnight; as the mood of the Mona Lisa; as the paths of destiny that lie ahead.

symbols: Cimmerian darkness; Erebus; Gongorism.
see also: concealed; enigmatic; uncertain; dark; secret; hidden.
opposite: obvious; clear; open; certain; understandable.

Obsolete: as a horse and buggy on a high speed turnpike; as last year's fashions; as the Wright brothers' first airplane; as the Spanish Inquisition.
symbols: dodo; dinosaur; Colonel Blimp.
see also: ancient; old fashioned; dated.
opposite: new; modern; fresh.

Obvious: as a nudist in a store window; as a diamond tiara; as a wolf whistle; as a Rolls Royce in a poor neighborhood.
symbols: landmark; written on one's face.
see also: noticeable; clear; apparent; open.
opposite: obscure; hidden; concealed; camouflaged; overlooked.

Odorous: as the wind from a pigpen; as the smell of decay; as a flower garden in full bloom; as limburger cheese.
symbols: nose music; smellevision; what the nose knows.
see also: smelly; fragrant; aromatic.
opposite: blank; faded.

Offensive: as an ugly drunk; as an open insult; as a slap in the face.
symbols: Belial; gall and wormwood; public nuisance.
see also: annoying; insulting; ill-mannered; antagonistic; rude; menacing; threatening.
opposite: polite; complimentary; friendly; amiable.

Officious: as an uncivil servant; as government prose; as a head waiter with the help; as a bureaucrat hiding his lack of power.

symbols: Mr. Bumble; bureaucrat; fussbudget; apparatchik.

see also: haughty; arrogant; rude; pompous; condescending.

opposite: courteous, correct, polite, amiable.

Old: as the hills and the heavens; as the battle of the sexes; as the Ten Commandments; as an overage century plant.

symbols: Methuselah; Nestor; Father Abraham.

see also: aged; ancient; dated; obsolete.

opposite: new; modern; young; youthful; fresh.

Old fashioned: as hoop skirts and buggy whips; as the wedding march; as a nickel candy bar; as 2¢ plain that still costs two cents.

symbols: Mid-Victorian; Model T; stone age; square.

see also: ancient; dated; nostalgic; corny; quaint; square.

opposite: new; modern; fresh; original.

Ominous: as a dark cloud coming fast; as a burst of gunfire; as a message from the mafia.

symbols: handwriting on the wall; storm cloud; Cassandra.

see also: threatening; menacing; dangerous; pessimistic.

opposite: favorable; encouraging; cheerful; hopeful; optimistic; safe.

Open: as a chatterbox's mouth; as a road with nobody on it; as the trackless seas; as a wastrel's wallet; as the wide spaces of the west.

symbols: broad daylight; cards on the table; above board.

see also: clear; obvious; talkative; generous.

opposite: closed; grudging; concealed; hidden; tight.

Opinionated: as a pompous pundit with a permanent pulpit; as one who claims a monopoly on truth; as one who prides himself on defying public opinion.

symbols: Sir Oracle; know-it-all; the Great I Am.

see also: dogmatic; positive; aribtrary; stubborn; partisan; uncompromising.

opposite: flexible; pliable; changeable; neutral; impartial.

Optimistic: as describing a half empty bottle as half full; as
                    asking a miser for a hand-out; as an unrepentant
                    sinner's plan to get to heaven; as a high-pressure
                    door-to-door salesman.

symbols: Dr. Pangloss; Pollyanna.
see also: hopeful; cheerful.
opposite: pessimistic; gloomy; hopeless.

Original: as the first sunrise; as Adam and Eve; as the Crea-
                    tion of the earth; as a sketch by da Vinci.
symbols: new departure; prototype; Genesis.
see also: creative; inspired; innovative; inventive.
opposite: imitative; repetitious.

Overlooked: as a hidden valley; as a forgotten mistake; as a favo-
                    rite child's failings; as what we do not wish to
                    see.
symbols: a sleeper; pigeon-hole; dust-gatherer.
see also: forgotten; neglected; forsaken; left out.
opposite: sought after; glaring; obvious; noticeable; clean.

Overwhelmed: as a mouse facing a mastodon; as the Punxatawney
                    team playing the Pittsburgh Steelers; as light is
                    by darkness and later the darkness by the light;
                    as a calm sea by a tidal wave; as man in the face
                    of the wrath of nature.
symbols: Waterloo; bite the dust.
see also: finished; repressed.
opposite: overwhelming; strong.

Overwhelming: as the odds for a 100 to 1 shot; as high pressure
                    hospitality; as the temptations of envy and the
                    taste of greed; as the unbridled excesses of ambi-
                    tion; as a take-charge hostess.
symbols: Superman; the Six Million Dollar Man; Bionic Wo-
                    man; Wonder Woman; Olympian.
see also: extravagant; mighty; monumental; exaggerated;
                    magnified; strong.
opposite: underdeveloped; weak; feeble; indifferent; little;
                    small.

Overworked: as a relief pitcher on a bad baseball team; as the doorbell on trick or treat night; as an excuse people know the judge will accept; as a glutton's epiglottis; as the circus sweepers when the elephants have digestive problems; as a fatty's two-way stretch.

symbols: nose to the grindstone; galley slave.

see also: exhausted; weary; tired; busy.

opposite: idle; lazy; relaxed.

P

Packed: as rush hour on the Tokyo subway; as a souvenir hunter's suitcase; as a crooked election.

symbols: S.R.O. (standing room only); can of sardines; Black Hole of Calcutta.

see also: crowded; congested; jammed; dishonest; crooked; tight; close.

opposite: empty; lonely; lonesome; honest; loose; isolated.

Padded: as a psycho's cell; as a false expense account; as a politician's pork barrel; as a fat one's figure.

symbols: Parkinson's law; falsies.

see also: fat; ample; false; contrived; lying; untruthful.

opposite: flat; thin; skinny; slim; true; honest.

Painful: as paying the piper; as the pangs of conscience; as the school of hard knocks; as a soul in torment; as a rude surprise.

symbols: the rack; Job's comforter; trial by ordeal.

see also: afflicted; anguished; inflamed; raw; uncomfortable; cruel; sore.

opposite: soothing; comforting; easy; comfortable.

Pale: as a ghost with pernicious anemia; as the fading light of winter sunset; as a starveling who has never seen the sun.

symbols: Death warmed over; the color of chalk.

see also: ghastly; colorless; anemic.

opposite: colorful; bright; healthy; dark.

Panic-stricken: as a herd of cattle in full stampede; as a crowd of cowards contemplating a catastrophe; as speculators in a sinking market; as a village in the path of a new volcano.

symbols: Deimos; Phobos; gutless wonder; bowl of Jello; trembling aspen.

see also: frantic; scared; chaotic.

opposite: calm; relaxed.

Paradoxical: as feasting in the face of famine; as waging war to produce peace; as the thin line between love and hate; as the wonders and the wastes produced by the same sun in the same sky.

symbols: Pickwickian; cross purposes; reductio ad absurdum.

see also: illogical; strange.

opposite: reasonable; simple.

Parched: as a sand dune in the desert; as a dipsomaniac in a dry county; as dirt in the dust bowl; as ancient parchment.

symbols: Sahara; Death Valley; torment to Tantalus.

see also: dry; arid.

opposite: watered; juicy.

Parochial: as a parish the Pope forgot; as the local gossip; as a secret society; as a forgotten backwater.

symbols: Lares and Penates; home territory; charmed circle.

see also: narrow; secret; close; familiar.

opposite: broad; cosmopolitan; open.

Particular: as an itemized bill; as a picky eater; as a dude with his duds; as a secret snob; as a personal birthmark.

symbols: Mr. Finicky; tough shopper; Craig's Wife.

see also: special; selective; exclusive; explicit; intolerant; precise; picky.

opposite: tolerant; open; random; relaxed.

Partisan: as a plea by a defense attorney; as a campaign platform; as a cheer leader; as a proud parent.

symbols: fidus Achates; man Friday; cheering section.

see also: sympathetic; political; prejudiced; opinionated; involved.

opposite: impartial; neutral; detached.

Passionate: as a pair of lovers; as the power of lust; as a pleader trying to convince himself he's right; as those who really care.

symbols: Aphrodite; Eros; fire in the belly; heavy breathing; Savonarola.

see also: inflamed; inspired; rabid; opinionated; fierce; hot.

opposite: cold; cool; icy; indifferent; relaxed.

Patient: as those who suffer in silence; as a spider spinning its web; as a cat watching a canary; as the wise man who gives an opponent enough rope to hang himself.

symbols: Job; Fabian; trust in Providence.

see also: tolerant; indulgent; meek; enduring; calm.

opposite: impatient; intolerant; ill-tempered.

Patronizing: as a snob in a slum; as a public servant dispensing the public's money; as a know-it-all trying to show you how much he knows; as a salesclerk who confers attention on customers like a Papal blessing; as youth can be to age—and age to youth.

symbols: Snob Hill; lord of the manor; cock of the walk.

see also: haughty; condescending; smug; rude.

opposite: gracious; accommodating; polite; courteous.

Peaceful: as the house of the Lord; as the sleep of the just; as the lilies of the field; as the dreams of lovers; as the pleasures of home and hearth.

symbols: Arcadia; green pastures; Ferdinand the Bull; Irene.

see also: calm; quiet; relaxed; easy.

opposite: aggressive; militant; agitated; chaotic.

Perfect: as Paradise before Adam ate the apple; as the peace that passeth understanding; as a hole in one; as the place where angels dwell.

symbols: Sir Galahad; paragon; Superman; Minerva; Apollo; Wonder Woman.

see also: flawless; ideal; chaste; pure.

opposite: blemished; tarnished; faulty; impure.

Permanent: as the persistence of matter; as the pyramids; as the inevitability of change; as the pursuit of power; as a grouch's grumbling.

symbols: Rock of Gibraltar; law of the Medes and the Persians; Rock of Ages.

see also: perpetual; endless; enduring; lasting; indelible; timeless; constant.

opposite: momentary; temporary; brief; replaceable.

Permissive: as free enterprise in an open society; as a Roman orgy; as the parents that spare the rod and spoil the child; as an asylum run by the inmates.

symbols: laissez-faire; blank check.

see also: indulgent; tolerant.

opposite: intolerant; censored.

Perpetual: as the revolution of the earth around the sun; as human emotion; as the pairing of the sexes; as the search for something new.

symbols: Rock of Ages; evergreen; hardy perennial.

see also: permanent; continuous; constant; endless; enduring; timeless; indelible; lasting.

opposite: fleeting; momentary; limited; changeable; replaceable; temporary.

Personal: as the inner soul; as a loin cloth; as the pangs of conscience; as a love letter.

symbols: first person singular; nobody's business.

see also: intimate; secret.

opposite: public; open.

Persuasive: as a super-salesman; as the lure of something for nothing; as a good example; as the power of public opinion; as the promise of power.

symbols: Demosthenes; Grey Eminence.

see also: convincing; winning; compelling; eloquent; powerful.

opposite: dull; inadequate; weak; futile.

Pessimistic: as a compulsive crepehanger; as a speculator who sells short; as a candidate who asks for a recount before the vote is in; as a manufacturer of air raid shelters.

symbols: Cassandra; Calamity Jane.

see also: gloomy; downhearted; hopeless.

opposite: optimistic; hopeful; cheerful.

Pestilential: as a plague of locusts; as jungle rot; as tsetse flies.
symbols: the plagues of Egypt.
see also: contagious; deadly; fatal; lethal; horrible.
opposite: clean; safe; healing; healthy.

Picky: as a dentist checking your teeth for cavities; as a horserace bettor; as a critic with an ulcer; as a selective shopper.
symbols: Mr. Finicky; bargain hunter; fruit squeezer.
see also: particular; selective; precise; explicit.
opposite: open; reasonable; adaptable; agreeable.

Piratical: as the buccaneers who sailed the Spanish Main; as the bandits of the Barbary Coast; as those who live by the skull and crossbones.
symbols: Bluebeard; Captain Kidd; the Jolly Roger; the black flag.
see also: lawless; criminal; dishonest; wicked; bad; evil.
opposite: honest; generous; correct; trustworthy.

Pitiful: as a pauper's pittance; as a beggar's plea; as the plight of a homeless orphan; as the pride that goeth before a fall.
symbols: Sad Sack; feeble imitation.
see also: sad; incompetent; poor; needy; anguished; hopeless.
opposite: happy; accomplished; rich; wealthy; cheerful; hopeful.

Pitiless: as a hanging judge; as the law of the jungle; as persistent poverty; as the savagery of nature in the raw.
symbols: Attila the Hun; Eumenides (The Furies).
see also: cruel; savage; barbarous; callous; indifferent; harsh; hard.
opposite: kind; considerate; gentle; charitable; soft.

Placid: as the aftermath of rapture; as a miser sitting on a mound of money; as a summer day when not even the flies are stirring; as a town that time forgot; as the waters of a soft, still pool.
symbols: Arcadia; Utopia; sea of tranquility.
see also: calm; relaxed; quiet; cool.
opposite: agitated; feverish; restless; chaotic; frantic; anxious; busy.

Plain:	as the nose that lies naked upon your face; as a hermit's search for solitude; as the simple pleasures of a little child; as the blunt speech of an honest soul.
symbols:	Plain Jane; open book; point-blank; written on one's face.
see also:	simple; average; bald; open; commonplace; average.
opposite:	involved; affected; complicated; complex; special; rare.
Planned:	as an architect's blueprint; as the plot of the perfect detective story; as D-Day; as a spontaneous demonstration in a dictatorship.
symbols:	Machiavellian; by the numbers; laid out; according to Hoyle; foregone conclusion.
see also:	deliberate; calculating.
opposite:	spontaneous; unprepared; random; disorganized; aimless.
Plausible:	as a perfect alibi; as seeing it for yourself; as the testimony of ten eyewitnesses.
symbols:	honest face; a likely story; a leg to stand on.
see also:	logical; reasonable; believable.
opposite:	illogical; absurd; ridiculous.
Playful:	as a pack of porpoises; as a puppy with a friend; as a kitten with a ball of string.
symbols:	life of the party; kitten on the keys.
see also:	comical; nutty; absurd; abandoned.
opposite:	dull; serious; sad; gloomy.
Pleasant:	as the days of wine and roses; as a land of milk and honey; as having money and knowing how to spend it; as good company in happy surroundings; as the far off fields of home.
symbols:	Saturnian; Arcadia; Garden of Eden.
see also:	congenial; cheerful; genial; gracious; charming; nice; friendly; amiable.
opposite:	disagreeable; nasty; mean; rude; cold.
Pliable:	as picture wire; as soft plastic; as a lover anxious to please; as a candidate who follows the crowd.
symbols:	putty; India rubber man.
see also:	flexible; adjustable; elastic; adaptable.
opposite:	rigid; arbitrary; firm; uncompromising; opinionated.

Pointed: as the tip of the needle; as a huntsman's arrow; as a
kick on the shin under the table; as a gun aimed
at a bullseye.

symbols: on target; on the button.

see also: accurate; sharp; keen; biting; acute.

opposite: dull, inaccurate; vague.

Poisonous: as a gossip's tongue; as the sting of an adder; as one
man's meat is to another man; as mustard gas; as
the doctrines of the devil.

symbols: a glass of wine with the Borgias; the tongue of the
viper.

see also: lethal; fatal; dangerous; treacherous; harmful.

opposite: healthy; kind; friendly; harmless.

Polished: as the language of diplomacy; as the handle of the
big front door (*W. S. Gilbert*); as a lady's finger-
nails; as a prize performance.

symbols: Chesterfieldian; Mayfair; kid gloves; beau monde;
savoir faire.

see also: smooth; glossy; subtle; accomplished; fine; courteous.

opposite: dull; rough; rude; impolite; awkward.

Polite: as as a waiter working for a good tip; as a salesclerk
to a good customer; as a person of breeding; as a
discreet diplomat.

symbols: Emily Post; Amy Vanderbilt; Alphonse and Gaston;
minding one's P's and Q's.

see also: courteous; refined; considerate; attentive; kind; cultured.

opposite: rude; ill mannered; savage; officious; callous.

Political: as a nominating convention; as a campaign speech;
as a candidate kissing babies; as a party caucus;
as a pork-barrel bill.

symbols: cloakroom government; party time; vote-chasing; a
play to the gallery.

see also: partisan; selfish; opinionated; prejudiced.

opposite: impartial; idealistic.

Polluted: as the sewage that flows to the sea; as a festering
swamp; as a smog-ridden sunset; as spoiled wa-
ter.

symbols: Augean stable; poisoned well.

see also: poisonous; dirty; unclean; impure.

opposite: pure; clean; healthy; immaculate.

Pompous: as a braying jackass in love with the sound of his voice; as a strutting peacock parading for the peahens; as a windbag uttering what he thinks are words of wisdom; as a posturing ham actor sunning himself in the spotlight.

symbols: Mr. Bumble; stuffed shirt; bag of wind.
see also: officious; egotistical; rude.
opposite: meek; quiet; shy; modest; courteous.

Poor: as a churchmouse in a rundown parish; as the beggar at the gate; as one with nothing left to sell; as one who cannot afford to dream; as a rich man's opinion of poverty.

symbols: Poverty Row; Queer Street; wolf at the door.
see also: deprived; needy.
opposite: rich; prosperous; wealthy; affluent; privileged.

Popular: as cotton candy at the circus; as hot dogs in a ball park; as peanuts with elephants; as going over to the enemy in the war between the sexes; as a prom queen.

symbols: charisma; everybody's sweetheart; bandwagon; matinee idol.
see also: appreciated; sought after; estimable; welcome; prevalent; famous.
opposite: unpopular; objectionable; tarnished.

Porous: as a coffee filter; as blotting paper; as a poor excuse; as a gauze bandage.
symbols: sieve; sponge.
see also: open; leaky.
opposite: solid, leakproof.

Portable: as a penknife; as a folding umbrella; as a paperback book; as a package of peppermints.
symbols: pocket edition.
see also: light; small.
opposite: heavy; burdensome; big.

Positive: as a fingerprint identification; as a bigot's prejudices; as a test for pregnancy; as the fact that the paths of glory lead but to the grave.
symbols: Sir Oracle; know-it-all.
see also: dogmatic; affirmative; assertive; emphatic; authoritative; certain; sure.
opposite: negative; uncertain; neutral; dubious; doubtful; tentative.

Possessive: as a miser with his money; as a child with a new toy; as a dog with a bone; as the owner of a security blanket.

symbols: Scrooge; silver cord.

see also: affectionate; acquisitive; selfish; jealous.

opposite: generous, open, kind.

Powerful: as the iron laws of nature; as the idea whose time has come; as the force of nuclear fission; as the mightiness of right.

symbols: Hercules; Samson; Aaron's serpent.

see also: strong; mighty; overwhelming.

opposite: weak; feeble; frail; delicate; underdeveloped.

Precious: as the rarest gem in a jeweled crown; as a good name; as time which once past can never be regained; as the gift of life.

symbols: a king's ransom; pearl without price; worth its weight in gold.

see also: dear; beloved; cherished.

opposite: cheap; rejected; little.

Precise: as a dictionary definition; as the work of a master watchmaker; as a perfect fit; as a punctilious professor.

symbols: like clockwork; on the buttom; to a tee.

see also: accurate; explicit; certain; fine; flawless; perfect; appropriate.

opposite: crude; coarse; gross; vague; uncertain.

Predictable: as the Ides of March; as baked beans in Boston; as the timing of the tides; as a total eclipse of the sun; as church bells.

symbols: Pavlov's dog; Big Ben; in the cards; foregone conclusion.

see also: certain; sure; inevitable.

opposite: uncertain; dubious; vague; doubtful; questionable.

Prejudiced: as a kangaroo court; as a bigot with his back to the wall; as one looking for excuses for his own failures; as a bought jury.

symbols: knee-jerk reaction; foregone conclusion.

see also: partisan; bigoted; narrow; corrupt; partial; intolerant; opinionated.

opposite: impartial; neutral; tolerant; sympathetic; straight.

Premature: as a review printed before the show opens; as a birth after four months of human pregnancy; as the claims of victory for Dewey in the 1948 election; as talking about a no-hit game in the seventh inning.

symbols: jumping the gun; too much too soon.
see also: unprepared; hasty; early; young.
opposite: mature; ripe; late; old.

Pretty: as the flowers that bloom in the spring; as a picture of happiness; as the songs of the birds; as a happy daydream.

symbols: The Graces; Miss Universe; Miss America; sight for sore eyes.
see also: attractive; lovely; beautiful; pleasant; handsome.
opposite: ugly; frightful; beastly; awful.

Prevalent: as the persistence of poverty; as the hope that springs eternal; as fleas in a dog pound; as sunburn on the beach.

symbols: the rage; the reigning influence; the in thing.
see also: popular; common; commonplace.
opposite: unpopular; rare; scarce.

Privileged: as a child of wealth; as a member of the ruling class; as a princess in a golden kingdom; as a spoiled brat.

symbols: born with a silver spoon; the upper crust; the haves.
see also: rich; wealthy; exclusive; prosperous; selective.
opposite: deprived; needy; neglected; forsaken; poor; broke.

Productive: as a fertile piece of farmland; as a maternity ward; as sowing seeds in fruitful soil; as an assembly line.

symbols: the horn of plenty; fertile soil; fruitful acres.
see also: fruitful; fertile; bountiful; profitable; prosperous.
opposite: barren; fruitless; bare; arid; dry.

Profitable: as striking oil; as finding gold; as betting on winners; as printing money.
symbols: money in the bank; black ink side of the ledger.
see also: productive; commercial; winning; rich; fruitful; prosperous.
opposite: bankrupt; unlucky; broke; futile.

Promising: as a child prodigy; as a number one draft choice; as a day that starts with a glorious sunrise; as a supersalesman's spiel.

   symbols: bright prospect; a comer; a likely; rising star.

   see also: hopeful; encouraging; optimistic; engaging.

   opposite: hopeless; pessimistic; dubious; doubtful.

Prophetic: as a preview; as the lessons of the past; as the handwriting on the wall; as a premonition.

   symbols: Cassandra; Elijah; Nostradamus.

   see also: predictable; inevitable.

   opposite: uncertain; cloudy.

Prosperous: as an Arab with an oil well; as the man who broke the bank at Monte Carlo; as he who has a lot of what the public wants to buy; as a man with money to rent.

   symbols: Golconda; El Dorado; Rockefeller; Croesus.

   see also: rich; wealthy; affluent; privileged.

   opposite: poor; bankrupt; broke needy.

Provocative: as profanity in church; as an invitation to lust; as a knothole in the fence around a nudist colony; as a preview of pleasure.

   symbols: temptation of Eve; Siren song; girdle of Venus.

   see also: inviting; appealing; fascinating; compelling; attractive.

   opposite: boring; dull; burdensome; aimless.

Prudent: as steering with both hands; as spotting the exits the moment you enter; as looking before you leap; as a squirrel saving nuts for the winter; as worrying more about the hereafter than the heretofore.

   symbols: Fabian; weather eye to windward; eye to the future; ear to the ground.

   see also: wise; discreet; cautious; careful.

   opposite: careless; rash; indiscreet; foolish.

Public: as putting it in Macy's window; as a lighted billboard in the heart of town; as a Presidential proclamation; as an announcement by the town crier.

   symbols: general knowledge; everybody's business; posted on the wall.

   see also: open; obvious; free; apparent; available.

   opposite: personal; secret; intimate; censored.

Pugnacious: as an ugly drunk; as one whose brains are in his fists; as a street bully spoiling for a fight; as a dictator trying to divert his people from their problems; as a cornered rat.

symbols: Ares; Eris; Mars.

see also: militant; threatening; antagonistic; ill tempered; quarrelsome.

opposite: peaceful; congenial; plesant; genial; calm; meek; docile; shy.

Punctual: as the Naval Observatory; as children for a meal they love; as Big Ben; as the seasons; as the equinox and solstice; as the tides; as the sunrise.

symbols: Johnny on the spot; on the button.

see also: timely; accurate; precise; correct.

opposite: late; inaccurate; faulty.

Pure: as the driven snow; as the heart of a new-born babe; as Paradise; as water from a crystal spring; as a miser's greed.

symbols: Sir Galahad; Arcadia; vestal virgin; Artemis.

see also: chaste; immaculate; angelic; flawless; clean; innocent.

opposite: blemished; polluted; tarnished; spoiled; poisonous; doctored; impure.

Puzzled: as a mouse in a maze; as a kid trying to figure how they got that great big tuna in that little bitty can; as the audience watching a master magician; as a man trying to understand woman's intuition.

symbols: Gordian knot; up a tree; horns of a dilemma.

see also: bewildered; baffling; confused; muddled; uncertain.

opposite: clear; understandable; knowledgeable.

Q

Quaint: as a teashop in the tenderloin; as hoopskirts and hansom cabs; as an assembly-line antique factory; as the contents of the old trunk in the attic.

symbols: Gilbert and Sullivan world; pure P. G. Wodehouse.

see also: corny; dated; old-fashioned; queer.

opposite: new; efficient; modern.

Qualified: as a politician's promise; as Methuselah would be for social security; as a canary is to sing.

symbols: up to the mark; know-how.

see also: eligible; fit; appropriate; experienced; accomplished; limited.

opposite: amateurish; inadequate; unprepared; absolute.

Quarrelsome: as a camel with a nasty disposition; as the two partners in a bad bargain; as Punch and Judy.

symbols: Montague and Capulet; Kilkenny cats; the Hatfields and the McCoys.

see also: argumentative; pugnacious; ill-tempered; disagreeable.

opposite: cooperative; peaceful; genial; congenial; pleasant; calm.

Queasy: as a dyspeptic on a loop-the-loop; as a gourmet with a greasy spoon; as a seasick sailor on a stormy sea; as a drunk with dysentery.

symbols: bromo bait; the turistas; up tight; Montezuma's revenge.

see also: ill; sick; uncomfortable.

opposite: comfortable; healthy.

Queer: as a three-dollar bill; as gravy on ice cream; as a camel's shape; as the people other people marry.

symbols: Alice in Wonderland; bohemian.

see also: absurd; strange; erratic; irrational; illogical.

opposite: reasonable; normal; average; logical.

Questionable: as a hermit's hospitality; as the wisdom of the state; as a deposition by Ananias; as a plea for mercy by a man who kills both his parents and then seeks clemency as an orphan; as an anonymous letter; as a confidence man's conscience.

symbols: anybody's guess; fast shuffle; the jury's out; Shady Lane.

see also: arguable; dubious; doubtful; fishy; suspicious; debatable; uncertain.

opposite: clean; honest; clear; certain; sure;

Quick: as the wink of any eye; as the brown fox that jumped over the lazy dog; as a cat's reaction; as cream turns sour.

symbols: Mercury; greased lightning.

see also: fast; brief; nimble; agile; rapid.

opposite: slow; hesitant; left-handed; awkward.

Quiet: as the still of the grave; as a stone; as the sleep of
                the just; as a tiger stalking its prey; as silent
                prayer.
symbols: Amyclean silence; still of the night.
see also: calm; placid; relaxed; idle; peaceful.
opposite: loud; deafening; feverish; noisy; boisterous; busy.

Quoted: as a favorable review; as the good Book; as a popu-
                lar joke; as the prices on the New York Stock
                Exchange; as Bartlett's Familiar Quotations.
symbols: Echo; author credit
see also: repetitious; corny; familiar.
opposite: original.

R

Rabid: as a hound with hydrophobia; as a lynch mob look-
                ing for a victim; as a dog that's foaming at the
                mouth; as a fan who cheers by throwing a temper
                tantrum.
symbols: mad dog; Corybants; The Furies.
see also: passionate; fierce; inflamed; opinionated; sick.
opposite: aloof; cool; placid; meek; shy; docile; healthy; rea-
                sonable.

Radiant: as the summer sun; as the light of heaven; as a
                rainbow after a storm; as a bright new star.
symbols: Milky Way; Great White Way; Roman candle;
                Hyperion.
see also: brilliant; bright; electrifying.
opposite: dull; dark; gloomy.

Radical: as armed revolution; as the red flag; as the bands
                that throw the bombs; as turning the world on its
                ear.
symbols: Marxism; nihilism; bolshevism; populism; Left;
                Red.
see also: revolutionary; extreme; heretical; subversive; in-
                novative.
opposite: cautious; reactionary; docile; peaceful; old fashion-
                ed.

Random: as a scattergun; as a lottery; as an arrow shot in air, that falls to earth we know not where (*Henry Wadsworth Longfellow*); as the rain.

symbols: potluck; luck of the draw.
see also: casual; aimless; accidental; uncertain.
opposite: planned; deliberate; definite; certain.

Rapid: as a speeding bullet; as an SST; as the spread of a rumor; as the speed of light.

symbols: Hermes; Mercury; high-tail; wildfire.
see also: fast; quick.
opposite: slow; delayed.

Rare: as a day in June (*James Russell Lowell*); as steak tartare; as discretion in a town gossip; as a close-up of the Loch Ness monster.

symbols: one in a million; rara avis.
see also: scarce; sparse; scanty.
opposite: common; familiar; frequent; normal; numerous; abundant.

Rash: as teasing a tiger; as Russian roulette; as playing tag with a juggernaut; as salting your food without tasting it first.

symbols: Hotspur; Don Quixote; fire eater.
see also: reckless; bold; daring; adventurous.
opposite: cautious; careful; repressed.

Raw: as an open wound; as uncooked kidney beans; as the weather at the North Pole; as a dirty deal; as nature on the half shell.

symbols: nature's nasty side; uncut stone; red meat and green apples.
see also: crude; coarse; immature; painful; rough; harsh.
opposite: smooth; polished; ripe; pleasant.

Reactionary: as a return to the seventh century; as calling for the resumption of slavery; as turning the clock back.

symbols: Col. Blimp; the radical right; dinosaur.
see also: backward; changeless; stubborn.
opposite: liberal; modern; flexible.

Real: as a rotten apple; as the rocks along the road; as a punch on the nose; as the red of the rose; as the Rock of Gilbraltar.
symbols: the McCoy; fact of life.
see also: authentic; true; genuine; honest.
opposite: false; lying; dishonest.

Reasonable: as a plausible alibi; as a friendly discussion; as the prices in the bargain basement.
symbols: Athena; Minerva; golden mean; a likely story.
see also: convincing; understandable; cheap.
opposite: illogical; irrational; mad; angry; dear.

Rebellious: as an angry adolescent; as a revolutionary; as a thankless child; as the Founding Fathers.
symbols: Ate; Loki; young Turk.
see also: radical; revolutionary; defiant; subversive.
opposite: agreeable; docile; meek; placid; reasonable.

Reckless: as a jaywalker on a throughway; as a drunken driver; as highdiving into a bathtub; as tasting toadstools.
symbols: daredevil; brinkmanship; desperado.
see also: rash; bold; daring; adventurous; careless.
opposite: cautious; careful; scared; repressed.

Red: as a radiant rose; as a boiled lobster; as third-degree sunburn; as a Russian schoolroom.
symbols: rosy dawn; carrot-top; bricktop; hammer and sickle.
see also: colorful; bloody; radical.
opposite: colorless; cautious.

Refined: as quality sugar; as the Queen's conversation; as motor oil; as the conversation in a seminary.
symbols: Attic; The Graces.
see also: gentle; elegant; polite; courteous; cultured; quiet.
opposite: loud; coarse; vulgar; rude; boisterous; ill-mannered; tough.

Regular: as the ticking of a clock; as a career sergeant in the Army; as a daily routine.
symbols: clockwork; daily dozen.
see also: chronic; steadfast; constant; repetitious; changeless.
opposite: irregular; changeable; uncertain.

Regulated: as the heat in a room with a thermostat; as traffic lights.
symbols: public utility; under control; computer-run.
see also: systematic; adjustable.
opposite: disorganized; mixed up.

Rejected: as a bad manuscript; as a slug in the slot machine; as a bad credit risk; as an unsuccessful suitor.
symbols: Ishmael; blackball; sent to Coventry.
see also: forsaken; neglected; deserted.
opposite: sought-after; popular; cherished.

Relaxed: as a sleeping baby; as a limp washrag; as a spent spring; as a used-up rubber band; as a worn-out girdle.
symbols: laissez faire; breathing spell.
see also: calm; casual; inert; peaceful; cool; placid; comfortable.
opposite: tense; agitated; edgy; feverish; nervous; active; bothered; worried.

Relentless: as the pressure of poverty; as the hounds of hell; as a nagging tongue.
symbols: Javert; avenging angel; bloodhound.
see also: steadfast; pitiless.
opposite: pliable; changeable; kind.

Reliable: as money in the bank; as the rotation of the earth; as the Federal Reserve Bank; as the wisdom of holy writ.
symbols: real McCoy; steady Eddie; from the horse's mouth.
see also: trustworthy; responsible; steadfast; faithful; authoritative; loyal.
opposite: treacherous; untruthful; false; uncertain; changeable.

Repentant: as a crook who cops a plea; as a diner who mistook the hot mustard for mayonnaise; as a sinner caught in the act; as many who marry in haste.
symbols: St. Mary Magdalene; sackcloth and ashes.
see also: sad; apologetic.
opposite: cheerful; callous; indifferent.

Repetitious: as a recorded message; as the route of a merrygo-
                    ~~round; as an old man's story-telling; as a stuck~~
                    needle.
symbols: Little Sir Echo; Echo; a parrot.
see also: dull; boring; familiar.
opposite: new; original; final.

Replaceable: as rubber tires; as light bulbs; as a substitute
                    teacher; as golf tees; as an office temporary.
symbols: revolving door; throwaway model.
see also: temporary; transient; changeable.
opposite: permanent; lasting; perpetual; constant; change-
                    less.

Representative: as a town meeting; as a random survey; as a secret
                    ballot; as the letters to the editor; as a show of
                    hands.
symbols: John Q. Public; the man in the street; Gallup Poll;
                    straw vote.
see also: normal; average; regular; accurate.
opposite: special; different.

Repressed: as a thwarted sneeze; as a puritan's libido; as dis-
                    sent in a dictatorship.
symbols: Iron Curtain; Bamboo Curtain; reign of terror;
                    1984.
see also: censored; hidden; concealed; secret; docile.
opposite: open; free; aggressive; reckless; rash; noticeable.

Resented: as a new broom in an old mess; as a reformer in a
                    political clubhouse; as the teacher's pet; as a snub
                    at a soiree.
symbols: Dr. Fell; bête noire.
see also: hateful; offensive; annoying; disagreeable.
opposite: beloved; dear; lovable; precious; genial; congenial.

Resolute: as Columbus sailing into the unknown; as St.
                    George in search of the dragon; as the hunt for
                    the Holy Grail; as a curmudgeon refusing to
                    smile.
symbols: Joan of Arc; never say die.
see also: confident; bold; stubborn; sure; positive; certain.
opposite: hesitant; uncertain; cautious; anxious.

Respectable: as an Archbishop; as high tea at Buckingham Palace; as a pious pilgrim in a church pew; as a pillar of wisdom.

symbols: good name; pillar of the community.

see also: estimable; virtuous; dependable; trustworthy.

opposite: criminal; objectionable; corrupt; rebellious.

Restless: as a willow waving in the breeze; as a rolling stone; as an insomniac with hives; as Midas smelling money; as a nervous racehorse at the starting gate; as an adolescent waiting for the phone to ring.

symbols: Ulysses; Wandering Jew; Flying Dutchman; The Disinherited.

see also: nervous; edgy; agitated; anxious; feverish; uncertain.

opposite: calm; placid; relaxed; quiet; docile.

Revolutionary: as the invention of the wheel; as the dogma of Marx; as a victory of the downtrodden; as mob law.

symbols: civil war; rabble in arms; Red flag; tables turned.

see also: radical; rebellious; Red; heretical; subversive; new.

opposite: reactionary; peaceful; old fashioned; cautious.

Rich: as a double dip banana split; as the coffers of Fort Knox; as an Arab potentate with a penchant for petroleum; as a sugar diet.

symbols: Croesus; Rockefeller; El Dorado; Midas.

see also: wealthy; affluent.

opposite: poor; deprived; needy.

Ridiculous: as putting mustard on honey; as a line backer dancing the Specter of the Rose; as snowshoes on a swan; as asking a hermit to the Mardi Gras.

symbols: Alice in Wonderland; Momus; crazy quilt; theater of the absurd.

see also: absurd; illogical; incongruous; foolish; comical; strange.

opposite: serious; wise; reasonable; correct.

Righteous: as those in the armor of a just cause; as the judgments of the Lord; as the nation which keepeth the truth (*Isaiah*); as those who walk the straight and narrow path.

symbols: salt of the earth; pillar of the community.

see also: holy; honest; exemplary; correct.

opposite: bad; evil; dishonest; wrong.

Rigid: as a steel girder; as the morals of a bluenose; as a cadet's posture; as a contract without an escape clause.

symbols: Procrustean; Draco; Spartan.
see also: aribtrary; uncompromising; stubborn.
opposite: flexible; pliable; accommodating; adjustable.

Ripe: as a rich red raspberry; as corn that's ready to pop; as the cheese that shows its age; as red apples; as the wine grapes waiting to be pressed.

symbols: harvest time; heavy on the vine.
see also: mature; perfect; finished.
opposite: raw; crude; underdeveloped; immature.

Rotten: as mackerel that shines and stinks by moonlight (*John Randolph*); as limburger cheese that's past its prime; as a skunk's reputation; as a grouch's disposition.

symbols: Augean stable; gangrene; Sodom and Gomorrah.
see also: decayed; smelly; decadent; objectionable.
opposite: pleasant; agreeable; amiable; good.

Rough: as an uncut diamond; as a barroom brawl; as coarse sandpaper; as a rhino's hide; as a walk on a wild waterfront.

symbols: Donnybrook Fair; Vandal; the wild bunch.
see also: boisterous; coarse; violent.
opposite: smooth; quiet; polite; finished; docile.

Rude: as the manger where the babe was born; as an insult to Emily Post; as an uncivil servant; as an obscene gesture; as a slap in the face.

symbols: billingsgate; fishwife.
see also: insulting; coarse; vulgar; tactless; gross; nasty; impudent; insolent.
opposite: polite; kind; gentle; courteous; complimentary.

Run-down: as a neglected neighborhood; as a ruined reputation; as a broken watch; as an abandoned building.

symbols: Poverty Row; a shanty in old shantytown.
see also: abandoned; neglected; forsaken; poor; bankrupt.
opposite: profitable; prosperous; neat.

Rushed: as a short order cook with a long line of customers; as an emergency operation; as the most popular student on campus; as the umbrella counter in a sudden rainstorm.

symbols: juggling act; three-ring circus.

see also: booming; busy; hurried; popular; fast.

opposite: slow; delayed; relaxed; unpopular.

Rusty: as neglected armor; as an old nail; as an athlete gone to pot; as a buried beer can; as a scrap iron dump.

symbols: overage destroyer; mothball fleet.

see also: tarnished; blemished; old; dirty.

opposite: new; clean; polished; flawless; perfect.

S

Sacred: as a cow in Calcutta; as the Gospel; as life, liberty and the pursuit of happiness; as the honor of brave and honest folk.

symbols: Holy Writ; holy of holies; the word of God.

see also: holy; blessed; dedicated.

opposite: damned; heretical; idolatrous.

Sacrificial: as a burnt offering; as selfless love; as a bunt by a home run hitter; as dying so that others may live.

symbols: Alcestis; scapegoat.

see also: noble; dedicated; devoted; loyal; committed.

opposite: insincere; negligent; callous; selfish.

Sad: as a centipede with foot trouble; as sackcloth and ashes; as the loss of hope; as sudden sorrow.

symbols: Slough of Despond; Acheron; Angerona.

see also: anguished; blue; gloomy; despondent; downhearted; hopeless; discouraged.

opposite: happy; cheerful; amiable; hopeful.

Safe: as the vaults at Fort Knox; as a soul in Heaven; as the Federal Reserve; as money in the bank.

symbols: snug harbor; sanctuary.

see also: secure; reliable; trustworthy; dependable; enduring.

opposite: endangered; dangerous; deadly; lethal; disastrous; harmful; fatal.

Satisfied: as a lover loved; as a parent who can answer all the children's questions; as a gourmet after a deluxe dinner; as hunger at the festive board.

symbols: contented cow; cat that ate the canary.

see also: pleased; happy; grateful.

opposite: angry; hungry; anxious; worried; concerned.

Savage: as the law of the jungle; as man's inhumanity to man; as a cornered rat; as a Roman circus; as the uncharted wilderness.

symbols: Attila the Hun; jungle beast; beast of prey.

see also: barbarous; cruel; pitiless; beastly; brutal; harsh.

opposite: kind; civilized; cultured; polite; gentle.

Scandalous: as the morals of the Marquis de Sade; as gutter gossip; as sin on a silver platter; as a scarlet past.

symbols: talk of the town; whispering campaign; overnight sensation.

see also: notorious; evil; wicked; corrupt; heretical; bad; immoral.

opposite: pure; good; innocent; admirable; clean; nice; chaste; exemplary.

Scanty: as a nudist's wardrobe; as a baby's vocabulary; as the dialogue in a pantomime; as a poor man's purse.

symbols: starvation diet; slim pickings.

see also: meager; minimal; scarce; little; poor.

opposite: large; numerous; big; overwhelming; huge; abundant; monumental.

Scarce: as bones in ice cream; as water in a wasteland; as five-cent cups of coffee; as the hair on a bald man's head.

symbols: black market; one for the ration board.

see also: meager; minimal; sparse.

opposite: numerous; abundant; overwhelming.

Scared: as a frightened fawn; as the food taster for the Borgias; as a rabbit on the run; as a new student on the first day of school.

symbols: panicsville; white knuckle flight.

see also: frightened; cowardly.

opposite: brave; bold; courageous; daring.

Scattered: as the stars in the heavens; as the driftwood on the shore; as dust upon the wind; as the applause for a bad act.

symbols: buckshot; blunderbuss.

see also: dissipated; thin; sparse; meager.

opposite: thick; crowded; packed, jammed; abundant.

Scornful: as one who wishes he had thought of it himself; as a snob sizing up the hoi polloi; as a skeptic confronted by honest emotion.

symbols: cold shoulder; curled lip.

see also: critical; disagreeable; smug.

opposite: friendly; amiable; agreeable; cooperative; helpful; kind.

Secret: as the silence of the grave; as hidden vanity; as the thoughts that cannot be shared; as the history that's told in whispers; as scandal in high places.

symbols: arcanum arcanorum; C.I.A.; "the company".

see also: anonymous; buried; hidden; concealed; intimate; personal; camouflaged; disguised.

opposite: obvious; apparent; clear; certain; open; noticeable.

Seldom: as a borrower remains a friend; as great and good occur in the same person; as the blooming of a century plant.

symbols: once in a blue moon; a sometime thing.

see also: rare; scarce.

opposite: regular; frequent; repetitious.

Selective: as a spoiled child's hearing; as a snooty club; as the law of the survival of the fittest.

symbols: choice not chance; Rhadamanthes.

see also: closed; narrow; particular.

opposite: open; broad; hospitable.

Selfish: as the practice of me first; as stealing from a baby; as a one-seater automobile.

symbols: looking out for number one.

see also: grasping; egotistical.

opposite: idealistic; generous.

Sensitive: as a hair trigger; as a top secret weapon; as a ~~psychopath with a thin skin; as an allergic reac-~~ tion.

symbols: litmus paper; pressure point.
see also: allergic; delicate; inflamed; painful.
opposite: secure; safe; crude; gross; indifferent; aloof; cold.

Sentimental: as a golden wedding; as Auld Lang Syne; as love's old sweet song; as mother love.

symbols: hearts and flowers; tear jerker.
see also: nostalgic; affectionate; precious; soulful; cherished.
opposite: indifferent; cold; callous; hard; tough.

Serious: as a comic's ambition to do tragedy; as the task of being funny; as a doctoral dissertation; as the last rites.

symbols: Old Sobersides; down to cases.
see also: important; urgent; crucial; sober.
opposite: foolish; comical; absurd; nutty; ridiculous.

Sexy: as the pros of procreation; as a lesson in love; as the back seat at an X-rated drive-in movie; as the opposites that attract each other; as a matched pair of passion flowers.

symbols: Eros; Casanova; Aphrodite; oomph; Astarte; Venus; the Lorelei; Sirens.
see also: carnal; earthy.
opposite: pure; innocent; chaste.

Shady: as an arbor in full bloom; as a con man under the old oak tree; as a dark night in a pine grove; as a deal with the devil; as a disgraceful past.

symbols: Stygian; Plutonian; Erebus; under a rock.
see also: questionable; immoral; dark; lying; dishonest.
opposite: honest; open; bright; good.

Shallow: as a wading pool; as the Los Angeles River in the dry season; as a bird bath; as the conversation in a cocktail lounge; as a hasty judgment.

symbols: Philistine; Babbitt.
see also: superficial; narrow; low.
opposite: deep; cultured; wise.

Sharp: as a two-edged sword (*Proverbs*); as the tooth of the tiger; as the eye of the eagle; as the point of a tack; as the tongue of a nag.

symbols: the razor's edge; the needle.

see also: pointed; cutting; keen; biting; harsh.

opposite: soft; dull; kind; friendly; dull.

Short: as the simple annals of the poor (*Thomas Gray*); as the breath of age (*William Shakespeare*); as an embezzling bank teller; as a sudden stop; as a midget's measurements.

symbols: Tom Thumb; abridged edition; flash in the pan.

see also: abbreviated; brief; condensed; dishonest; simple.

opposite: long; large; excessive; honest; windy.

Shrewd: as a rat with a high IQ; as Sherlock Holmes; as the business agent for the business agents' union.

symbols: Machiavelli; David Harum.

see also: wily; calculating; tricky, wise; crafty.

opposite: simple; dull; open.

Shrill: as the shriek of an air raid siren; as a whistling teapot with a full head of steam; as a soprano with a head cold; as a scared woman's scream.

symbols: screech owl; glass shatterer; steam whistle.

see also: noisy; loud; deafening.

opposite: quiet; soft; low; silent.

Shy: as a modest maiden; as a sheik without an oil well; as a bankrupt's bank account; as a cautious two-year-old.

symbols: John Alden; shrinking violet.

see also: quiet; meek; docile; repressed; humble; frightened.

opposite: assertive; aggressive; bold; pugnacious; loud; argumentative.

Sick: as a dog with dyspepsia; as a soul in torment; as smallpox; as a patient in intensive care.

symbols: Camille; under the weather.

see also: weak; pestilential; inflamed; anemic; feeble.

opposite: healthy; strong.

Silent: as the stillness of the grave; as the language of pan-
~~tomime; as he who has no answer;~~ as the empti-
ness of space.

symbols: Amyclae; Sphinx; Harpocrates.
see also: quiet; soft; low.
opposite: noisy; loud; shrill; deafening.

Simple: as the songs of children; as the plain pleasures of
the people; as the basic virtues; as adding one
and one; as an honest smile.

symbols: Simple Simon; Tommie Traddles.
see also: plain; commonplace; average; easy; understandable.
opposite: baffling; complicated; difficult; affected.

Skinny: as a skeleton on a diet; as bones with binding; as an
empty wallet.

symbols: skin and bones; walking skeleton.
see also: slim; thin.
opposite: fat; flabby; padded; ample.

Slim: as a streamlined whippet; as a fashion model; as a
pauper's pickings.

symbols: toothpick; wasp-waist.
see also: skinny; thin; flat.
opposite: fat; flabby; padded; broad; ample.

Slippery: as an elusive eel; as a banana peel on a newly
polished floor; as a master of disguise.

symbols: greased pig; Machiavellian.
see also: sly; elusive; tricky; wily; evasive; loose
opposite: catching; open; honest; simple.

Slow: as a tortoise taking its time; as funeral march; as
the mills of the gods that grind so small (*Henry
Wadsworth Longfellow*).

symbols: molasses in January; snail.
see also: delayed; hesitant.
opposite: quick; fast; nimble; instantaneous.

Sly: as a superspy; as a sneaky double entendre; as a
sneakthief; as a fox in the forest.

symbols: Machiavelli; Reynard the Fox; Volpone; the Artful
Dodger.
see also: wily; shrewd; artful; calculating; subtle; tricky;
slippery.
opposite: straight; simple; plain; honest.

Small: as the hopes of a pessimist; as a gnat's knee; as a single candle in a galaxy of light; as a grain of sand; as home for a humming bird.

symbols: pocket edition; Tiny Tim; Tom Thumb; Lilliput; the little people.

see also: little; minimal; meager.

opposite: big; large; huge; vast; colossal; ample.

Smelly: as a pigpen in a high wind; as a fish too long out of water; as a garbage dump.

symbols: B.O.; halitosis; stinkweed; skunk.

see also: aromatic; odorous; fragrant.

opposite: blank; airy.

Smooth: as silk and just as gentle; as the soft cheek of a maiden fair; as monumental alabaster (*William Shakespeare*); as a baby's brow.

symbols: velvet touch; kid gloves; clear sailing; sweetness and light.

see also: glossy; polished; fine.

opposite: rough; coarse; harsh.

Smug: as a sophomore sneering at the freshmen; as the cynic who told you so; as a man who makes his own medals; as a self-made man who admires his product; as the driver who gets 50 miles to the gallon; as a reformed smoker; as the cat that swallowed the canary.

symbols: fat cat; Babbitt; the establishment.

see also: patronizing; condescending; arrogant; officious; immodest; vain.

opposite: modesty; humble.

Sneaky: as a sidewinder; as a snake in the grass; as a peeping tom; as walking on tiptoe.

symbols: Uriah Heep; Pearl Harbor.

see also: deceitful; crafty; wily; tricky; duplicit; devious; evasive.

opposite: honest; direct; trustworthy; reliable.

Sober: as an undertaker's outerwear; as a reformed drunk; as the sound of sorrow; as a judge in the halls of justice.

symbols: water wagon; temperance man.

see also: dignified; solemn; sad; quiet.

opposite: intoxicating; ill-mannered; boisterous; loud.

Soft: as a baby's bottom; as the answer that turneth away wrath (*Proverbs*); as the sound of sweet music; as the words that are spoken in love.

symbols: life of Riley; Easy Street; velvet touch; kid gloves; feather bed.

see also: smooth; gentle; kind; gracious.

opposite: hard; pitiless; harsh; austere.

Solemn: as a sinner suing for salvation; as a state ceremony; as the Day of Judgment; as the stillness of the unknown.

symbols: Old Sobersides; striped pants.

see also: dignified; formal; holy; sober.

opposite: boisterous; ill-mannered; rude; noisy; loud.

Solid: as the Rock of Gibraltar; as a citizen of substance; as stale cheesecake; as a knockout punch.

symbols: money in the bank; 14 carat; old reliable.

see also: firm; strong; hardy; tough.

opposite: frail; weak; feeble; porous; volatile.

Soothing: as the charms of music for a savage breast; as a soft word at a tough time; as a mother's touch; as the balm they should have had in Gilead.

symbols: Nirvana; the pause that refreshes.

see also: comforting; soft; calm; relaxed.

opposite: frantic; agitated; anxious; bothered; worried; nervous.

Sore: as an aching joint; as a bad loser after a tough decision; as a Sunday driver in a weekday traffic jam.

symbols: Terrible Tempered Mr. Bang; salt in the wound.

see also: painful; mad; angry; anguished; uncomfortable.

opposite: comfortable; calm; peaceful; healthy.

Sought after: as public enemy number one; as a Presidential nomination; as the keys to the kingdom; as the winning ticket in the lottery.

symbols: charisma; matinee idol; oomph.

see also: popular; famous; scarce; rare.

opposite: unpopular.

Soulful: as the birth of the blues; as the sweet spirit of sisterhood; as the sighs of love.

symbols: charisma; the inner id.

see also: sentimental; euphoric; cherished; exalted.

opposite: indifferent; callous; downhearted.

Sound: as the old dollar; as a healthy horse; as the sleep of the just; as the soul of a saint.
symbols: Salus; Simon Pure; Rock of Gibraltar.
see also: healthy; reasonable; solid; wise.
opposite: sick; ill-advised; dumb.

Sour: as spoiled grapes; as the bitterness of a broken friendship; as an off-key symphony; as stale wine; as the grapes of wrath.
symbols: Adullamites; vinegar.
see also: bitter.
opposite: sweet; happy.

Sparse: as waterholes in the wasteland; as compliments in the complaint department; as credit at a collection agency; as a pauper's pennies; as halos in Hell.
symbols: slim pickings; desert.
see also: meager; scarce; scattered; dissipated.
opposite: numerous; abundant; crowded; jammed; packed.

Special: as a diamond jubilee; as a pipeline to Santa Claus; as the return of a prodigal; as the gift of grace.
symbols: four-star; red-letter.
see also: rare; original.
opposite: average; common; regular; natural.

Spectacular: as the view from outer space; as a home run in the last of the ninth with the bases full; as a rocket rising into the soaring sky; as Niagara Falls in full flow.
symbols: Seven Wonders of the World; Roman holiday; Roman candle; Aurora.
see also: impressive; magnificent; monumental; glorious; beautiful.
opposite: dull; bleak; ugly; colorless; weary.

Speculative: as trying to predict which way a fly will jump; as strip poker; as borrowing money to get into a bingo game; as a plunge on the horses.
symbols: toss of the dice; luck of the draw; Fortuna; Lady Luck.
see also: uncertain; changeable; rash.
opposite: certain; sure; definite.

Spoiled: as a child that never hears a no; as a burnt offering at a banquet; as rancid butter; as the vines the little foxes find.

symbols: sour wine; rotten apples; snafu.

see also: damaged; decayed; faulty; tarnished; rotten.

opposite: flawless; pure; perfect.

Spontaneous: as a burst of laughter; as combustion in a pile of oily rags; as a sudden sneeze; as the tears of a toddler.

symbols: spur of the moment; self-starter.

see also: instantaneous; instinctive; unprepared.

opposite: planned; automatic; constant.

Spotless: as a blank sheet; as an angel's reputation; as a broadcast without commercials; as a black leopard.

symbols: Galahad; Vestal virgin.

see also: immaculate; pure; flawless; perfect.

opposite: blemished; tarnished; unclean; dirty; polluted.

Square: as a box; as the deal you get from an honest man; as old-fashioned virtue.

symbols: old school; old fogy; Fides.

see also: old fashioned; corny; honest; frank; straight.

opposite: new; dishonest; lying.

Steadfast: as the spirit of never say die; as a guiding star; as true love through thick and thin; as faithful friendship.

symbols: patience of Job; fidus Achates.

see also: true; constant; changeless; reliable; dependable; trustworthy; loyal.

opposite: changeable; uncertain; volatile; fickle; treacherous.

Sticky: as rubber cement; as spilled syrup; as soothing an angry porcupine.

symbols: Old Man of the Sea; flypaper.

see also: difficult; tough; uncomfortable.

opposite: neat; easy; comfortable.

Stingy: as a miser with his money; as a hostess serving a five-portion pie to a table of ten; as a curmudgeon with his compliments.

symbols: Scrooge; pinchpenny.

see also: cheap; tight; frugal; economical; grudging; close.

opposite: generous; open; charitable; kind; helpful.

Straight: as the path the crooked cannot walk; as the shortest distance between two points; as the line before the punchline; as an arrow that knows just where it's going.

symbols: the McCoy; dead level; 14 carat.

see also: direct; honest; neat; pointed.

opposite: crooked; dishonest; subtle.

Strange: as the bedfellows of politics; as somebody else's ideas; as the attitudes of adolescence; as tomorrow's fashions looked yesterday.

symbols: one for the books; creature from outer space.

see also: absurd; queer; erratic; different; alien; illogical; incongruous.

opposite: familiar; natural; normal; average; alike.

Strong: as a bull moose full of beans; as iron bands (*Henry Wadsworth Longfellow*); as the scent of gorgonzola; as the staying power of garlic; as Paul Bunyan and his blue ox.

symbols: Atlas; Hercules; Amazon; Samson; John Henry.

see also: powerful; mighty; compelling; overwhelming.

opposite: weak; frail; feeble; overwhelmed.

Stubborn: as a Missouri mule with its mind made up; as the fancies of a fool; as a spot that won't come out; as the kid who keeps coming back for more; as a goal-line stand.

symbols: a mule; block of granite.

see also: rigid; balky; obstinate; arbitrary; dogmatic; opinionated; uncompromising.

opposite: flexible; pliable; adjustable; weak.

Subtle: as the serpent's slither; as the messages of silence; as the loss of youth; as a pickpocket's touch; as the surgeon's skill.

symbols: Machiavellian; Philadelphia lawyer; Artful Dodger.

see also: artful; calculating; polished; shrewd.

opposite: straight; direct; open.

Subversive: as corned beef with lettuce; as working for a rerun of the American Revolution; as a spy in the Oval Office.

symbols: fifth column; Quisling; the underground.

see also: radical; heretical; revolutionary.

opposite: loyal; cooperative.

Superficial: as a thin coat of paint; as a surface scratch; as a social lion's small talk; as the forced smile of a harried hostess.
symbols: Philistine; tempest in a teapot; tip of the iceberg.
see also: shallow; thin; contrived; affected.
opposite: deep; wise; authentic.

Sure: as the certainty of death; as daylight after the darkness; as the master's touch.
symbols: Sir Oracle; open and shut case; lead-pipe cinch.
see also: clear; certain; definite; inevitable.
opposite: questionable; tentative; speculative; doubtful; surprised; dubious; uncertain.

Surprised: as a criminal caught in the act; as a mother-in-law by her son-in-law's success; as a drinker who didn't know he was loaded.
symbols: bolt from the blue; bombshell.
see also: miraculous; amazing; baffling.
opposite: predictable; certain; sure.

Suspicious: as a smoking gun; as a man who's been offered something for nothing; as one who knows his own guilt; as a copper looking for a clue.
symbols: Doubting Thomas; Sherlock Holmes; Ellery Queen.
see also: fishy; questionable; uncertain; dubious; doubtful.
opposite: aloof; clean; clear.

Sweet: as the smell of success; as the satisfaction of revenge; as money to a miser; as sugar and molasses in a honey haze; as solitude is to a hermit.
symbols: attar of roses; balm of Gilead; music of the spheres; honey.
see also: appealing; attractive; fragrant; tasteful.
opposite: sour; bitter.

Sympathetic: as a mother's hug; as a helping hand; as a friend who's looking for a favor.
symbols: milk of human kindness; friendly ear; echoing chord; shoulder to lean on.
see also: comforting; soothing; encouraging; partisan.
opposite: indifferent; cool; callous; impartial; antagonistic.

Systematic: as the order of nature; as a computer run; as building blocks; as a tax audit.

symbols: by the numbers; by the book; blueprint; assembly-line.

see also: efficient; regulated.

opposite: disorganized; mixed up; messy.

T

Tactless: as interrupting the Pope; as a tap dance in a tomb; as tipping a tycoon; as clapping a Queen on the back; as being drunk at a temperance meeting.

symbols: bull in a china shop; foot in the mouth; Philistine.

see also: ill-advised; indiscreet; tasteless; foolish; left-handed; rude.

opposite: exemplary; courteous; tasteful; wise.

Talkative: as a teenager on the telephone; as the town gossip; as a parrot who likes the spotlight.

symbols: diarrhea of the mouth; chin music; cave of the winds; magpie; chatterbox.

see also: windy; gaseous; loud.

opposite: silent; quiet.

Tame: as a dull party; as a tabby; as a timid toddler; as a tiny titter.

symbols: trained seal; performing dog; pussycat.

see also: docile; meek; gentle; obedient.

opposite: fierce; savage; pugnacious; aggressive.

Tangled: as a fishline full of knots; as the web we weave when first we practice to deceive (*Sir Walter Scott*); as a goat's hair; as an octopus in a fishnet.

symbols: Gordian knot; jumble; snafu.

see also: messy; sticky; mixed; confused.

opposite: smooth; neat; clear.

Tarnished: as the town tramp's reputation; as neglected silver; as a rusty nail; as a tainted title.

symbols: damaged goods; blot on the escutcheon; mark of Cain; faded halo.

see also: blemished; spoiled; rusty; dirty; damaged; impure.

opposite: perfect; flawless; polished; pure; clean.

Tasteful: as forbidden fruit; ~~as a wine of rarest vintage~~ elegantly served; as a well-turned phrase; as the tact of a true diplomat.

symbols: Attic; savoir-faire; to the Queen's taste.

see also: appropriate; elegant; refined; cultured; graceful; correct.

opposite: tactless; heavy-handed; foolish; awkward; wrong; tasteless.

Tasteless: as well chewed gum; as praying with crossed fingers; as chewing gum in church; as winking at the Pope.

symbols: Philistine; Roman holiday; X-rated.

see also: tactless; ill-advised; indiscreet; rude; heavy-handed.

opposite: tasteful; refined; cultured; elegant.

Taxing: as the Internal Revenue Service; as Congress at money-raising time; as Social Security; as tiptoeing on a bed of coals; as a tour on the run.

symbols: labors of Hercules; Sisyphian task; hard row to hoe.

see also: burdensome; heavy; laborious; difficult.

opposite: easy; light; simple.

Temporary: as a passing shower; as tomorrow when it comes; as the rooster who rules the roost today; as a permanent wave.

symbols: passing show; One-Shot Willie; ships that pass in the night.

see also: momentary; transient; fleeting.

opposite: permanent; enduring; perpetual; continuous; timeless; constant; lasting; chronic.

Tense: as a snake getting set to strike; as a sprinter at the starting block; as a hermit expecting company; as a miser waiting for the tax collector; as an expectant father who's been told to expect triplets.

symbols: the jitters; the willies; touch and go; coiled spring.

see also: impatient; rushed; nervous; neurotic.

opposite: relaxed; casual; carefree; happy.

Tentative: as a toe in the water; as the first sip of the soup; as a buyer's first bid; as a poor man's prosperity.

symbols: trial run; dry run; trial balloon.

see also: experimental; questionable; hesitant; conditional; uncertain.

opposite: positive; affirmative; emphatic; sure; certain.

Thick: as autumnal leaves (*John Milton*); as three in a bed (*Sir Walter Scott*); as hasty pudding; as thieves in the state pen; as a heavy accent; as piano legs.

symbols: laid on with a trowel; Boeotian; pea soup.

see also: heavy; crowded; congested; packed; jammed; numerous; tough.

opposite: thin; sparse; scanty; light; meager; scattered.

Thin: as a poor excuse; as the way they try to slice salami; as a touchy person's skin; as a dime in a time of inflation; as the line between self confidence and sheer conceit.

symbols: walking skeleton; bag of bones; watered soup.

see also: skinny; slim.

opposite: thick; fat; flabby.

Threatening: as an angry murmur rising from an unruly mob; as a lawyer's letter that begins with the word "unless"; as an unfriendly fist an inch from your nose; as a black cloud.

symbols: sword of Damocles; handwriting on the wall; storm cloud.

see also: ominous; menacing; imminent; offensive; antagonistic; dangerous.

opposite: friendly; hospitable; safe; kind; helpful.

Tight: as a well-tuned drum; as a miser with his money; as a hermit with his invitations; as a two-day drunk; as a closed circle.

symbols: slow on the draw; penny pincher; close shave; Scrooge.

see also: stingy; grudging; cheap; close; leakproof; drunk.

opposite: generous; charitable; loose; open; sober.

Timeless: as the sound of the surf at the edge of the sea; as the Ten Commandments; as the laws of nature.

symbols: Rock of Ages; eternity; infinity.

see also: infinite; endless; perpetual; durable; permanent; lasting.

opposite: limited; fleeting; momentary; brief; temporary.

Timely: as tomorrow's news; as a birthday party; as a tax refund; as a reminder that today is your wedding anniversary.

symbols: psychological moment; Johnny on the spot; on the button.

see also: appropriate; punctual; helpful.

opposite: ill-advised; late; wrong.

Tolerant: as a doting sugar daddy; as a psychoanalyst who gets paid for listening; as a patient parent.

symbols: laissez-faire; carte blanche; open society; patience of Job.

see also: understanding; indulgent; permissive; patient.

opposite: callous; intolerant; allergic.

Tough: as a hippo's hide; as teakwood; as a Tartar; as a tiger with a titanic appetite; as overcooked steak.

symbols: Amazon; Hercules; bulldog; uphill going; Spartan; Procrustean; Draconian.

see also: strong; hard; hardy; difficult.

opposite: weak; soft; easy.

Transient: as a wandering breeze; as a leaf tossed by the wind; as a passing shower; as an idea in an empty head.

symbols: bird of passage; shooting star; flash in the pan.

see also: temporary; fleeting; momentary; replaceable.

opposite: lasting; enduring; permanent; abiding; chronic.

Transparent: as window glass; as a miser's greed; as the water in a goldfish bowl; as false modesty; as a peacock's pride.

symbols: an open book; wrapped in cellophane.

see also: obvious; clear.

opposite: hidden; concealed; obscure.

Treacherous: as the undertow along the beach; as Lady Luck; as a false friend; as a knife in the back.

symbols: Borgia; Quisling; Vicar of Bray; fifth column.

see also: deceitful; poisonous; false; lying; untruthful.

opposite: friendly; honest; loyal; trustworthy; true.

Tricky: as a master magician; as Dicky; as a crooked card game; as a shell game; as outfoxing a cool cat; as a wolf in sheep's clothing.

symbols: Artful Dodger; Till Eulenspiegel; Cagliostro.

see also: artful; wily; contrived; duplicit; elusive; evasive; sly.

opposite: simple; honest; innocent; trustworthy.

True: as many a word spoken in jest; as the words of the wise; as the green of the grass, the blue of the sky and the red of the sunset; as the fact that fish live in the sea.

symbols: the real McCoy; the way it is; straight goods.

see also: authentic; honest; genuine; real; faithful; steadfast; loyal.

opposite: false; lying; contrived; dishonest; untruthful.

Trustworthy: as a faithful friend; as the truth that time has tested; as the love of a loyal dog; as the power of the profit motive.

symbols: square shooter; true blue; fidus Achates.

see also: faithful; reliable; dependable; loyal.

opposite: sneaky; lying; uncertain; fickle; piratical.

U

Ugly: as the underside of the rock when you turn it over; as the face of hate; as a grouch's disposition; as the sense of sin.

symbols: Gorgon; Medusa; gargoyle.

see also: ill-tempered; disagreeable; beastly.

opposite: appealing; beautiful; handsome; lovely; attractive.

Uncertain: as the glory of an April day (*William Shakespeare*); as a weather prediction; as the way the cookie crumbles; as man's destiny.

symbols: Buridan's ass; horns of a dilemma; blow hot and cold; thin ice.

see also: questionable; debatable; doubtful; dubious; arguable; incalculable.

opposite: certain; sure; clear; positive; definite.

Unclean: as a clogged sewer; as a foul mouth; as a grabbag of garbage; as an X-rated movie.

symbols: Augean stable; town dump; pigsty.

see also: dirty; messy; blemished; impure; tarnished.

opposite: clean; pure; spotless; neat.

Uncomfortable: as a moose at a taxidermists' convention (*Bill Leonard*); as the sixth year of the seven year itch; as a hair shirt under a hot sun; as a collision with a cactus.
symbols: Gehenna; gall and wormwood.
see also: burdensome; painful; sticky; tense.
opposite: comfortable; easy; relaxed.

Uncompromising: as put up or shut up; as a challenge to a duel; as the man who won't take yes for an answer.
symbols: Procrustean; bulldog; pig iron; stiff-necked.
see also: arbitrary; rigid; stubborn; dogmatic; changeless.
opposite: adjustable; pliable; flexible; changeable.

Underdeveloped: as a badly processed photograph; as a country that kept its innocence; as a hermit's hospitality; as an oilfield waiting to be worked.
symbols: stone age; have-not; MTC (more to come).
see also: raw; crude; immature.
opposite: ripe; mature; old.

Understandable: as an outstretched hand; as a fist in the face; as a wolf whistle; as a come-hither wink.
symbols: plain English; words of one syllable.
see also: logical; easy; simple; clear.
opposite: baffling; difficult; complicated; dark.

Unfinished: as that symphony by Schubert; as the average self-made man; as the world on the fifth day.
symbols: work of Penelope; task of Sisyphus; rough cut; breadboard model.
see also: endless; underdeveloped; raw.
opposite: finished; final; complete.

Unlucky: as a florist with rose fever; as the rabbit who lost the foot you carry for luck; as crossing a black cat's path under a ladder on Friday the 13th and breaking a mirror on the way; as a miser with a hole in his strongbox.
symbols: jinx; Jonah; hex; Joe Btflspk.
see also: haunted; damned.
opposite: fortunate; blessed.

Unnecessary: as an extra tonsil; as shipping sand to the desert; as sugar in your honey; as icing on the icing.

symbols: coals to Newcastle; boondoggle.

see also: needless; excessive; irrelevant.

opposite: essential; necessary; crucial.

Unpopular: as a polecat in the parlor; as heresy before it becomes orthodoxy; as long hair in the Marines; as a barber among the beatniks; as a weasel in the henhouse.

symbols: bête noire; rogue elephant; sent to Coventry.

see also: hateful; detestable.

opposite: sought-after; popular.

Unprepared: as the student who didn't do the homework; as a sudden gasp; as raw potatoes.

symbols: caught short; wet behind the ears; half-cocked.

see also: premature; raw; spontaneous.

opposite: ripe; mature; planned.

Untruthful: as a con man's come-on; as the winning entry in the contest at the Liars' Club; as the acclaim of a hired claque.

symbols: Ananias; Baron Munchausen.

see also: lying; false; dishonest.

opposite: true; honest; accurate; correct.

Urgent: as an emergency operation; as an SOS from a ship at sea; as a five-alarm fire call; as rescue for a drowning man.

symbols: top priority; a must; matter of life and death.

see also: crucial; serious; essential.

opposite: needless; unnecessary; irrelevant.

Useful: as an extra hand; as teeth for a tiger; as tools for a mechanic.

symbols: means to an end; working model; a leg up.

see also: effective; helpful.

opposite: futile; ineffective; useless.

Useless: as a pocket with a hole in it; as an extra adenoid; as last year's calendar; as a rain dance in the Sahara.

symbols: exercise in futility; spiked gun; wild goose chase; tilting at windmills.

see also: futile; helpless; inadequate; ineffective; vain.

opposite: useful; necessary; essential; basic; effective.

V

Vague: as the shifting sands; as a faint memory; as the outline of a distant shore; as a politican's promises; as an unwilling witness's memory.

symbols: anybody's guess; needle in a haystack.
see also: uncertain; intangible; confused.
opposite: definite; certain; sure; clear.

Vain: as a peacock on parade; as a pussycat pretending to be a tiger; as the delights of the flesh; as valor in a lost cause.

symbols: Narcissus; Don Quixote; labor of Sisyphus; wild goose chase.
see also: smug; immodest; arrogant; egotistical; useless; futile.
opposite: modest; simple; humble; useful; productive.

Varied: as the vistas in the valley of Kashmir; as the languages in the Tower of Babel; as the faces of the races of the world; as a mixed box of nuts.

symbols: Noah's Ark; U.N.; melting pot; salmagundi.
see also: mixed; blended; hybrid.
opposite: pure; straight.

Vast: as the endless world of space; as the emptiness of the ocean seas; as the Russian steppes.

symbols: Atlantean; Atlas; Texas; all over the map.
see also: huge; big; large; colossal.
opposite: small; little; limited; minimal.

Versatile: as a one-man band; as a fish that flies; as a triple-threat man in football; as a decathlon champion.

symbols: jack of all trades; Renaissance man; man of parts; Proteus; many strings to the bow.
see also: accomplished; adaptable.
opposite: rigid; ignorant.

Violent: as the passions of the poor; as the fury of war; as a battle to the death; as the ability of man to self-destruct.

symbols: The Furies; battle of the Titans; volcano; Juggernaut; Aceldama.
see also: brutal; lethal; destructive; explosive; extreme.
opposite: quiet; peaceful; gentle.

Virtuous: as a mortal trying to become a saint; as a Horatio Alger hero; as a blushing bride; as the sweet sisters of charity.

symbols: Xenocrates; Diana; Artemis; Galahad.
see also: good; chaste; pure; innocent.
opposite: bad; decadent; corrupt; wicked.

Visionary: as a dream of glory; as a picture of paradise; as most people's hopes for the hereafter;

symbols: catles in the air; Joan of Arc; Utopia; Promised Land.
see also: idealistic; electrifying; ideal.
opposite: cynical; pessimistic; blind.

Volatile: as high pressure gas; as liquid oxygen; as a live volcano.

symbols: Mercury; mercurial; boiling point; vanishing act; full head of steam.
see also: explosive; changeable; moody; hot; gaseous.
opposite: quiet; steadfast; changeless; solid; mild.

Vulgar: as the common crowd; as the lowest bunch in town; as the vices of the many; as gutter language in the living room.

symbols: Trimalchio; the great unwashed; nouveau riche; street stuff.
see also: coarse; gross; crass; rude.
opposite: refined; cultured; gentle; polite.

W

Warm: as a hero's welcome; as a round of applause; as a sunny day in August; as the glow of friendship; as the heart behind a helping hand.

symbols: torrid zone; the tropics; bubbling over; open arms.
see also: affectionate; comforting; friendly; amiable; hospitable; pleasant.
opposite: cool; aloof; indifferent; callous.

Watered: as a well-kept lawn; as a diluted drink; as the sand that meets the surf; as weak soup.

symbols: less than meets the eye; thin stuff.
see also: doctored; thin.
opposite: solid; condensed.

Wayward: as the twists of fate; as the primrose path; as the life
                that moves too fast.
symbols: off the beam; problem child.
see also: loose; dissipated; immoral; bad.
opposite: good; moral; straight; righteous.

Weak: as watered tea; as the average person's resistance
                to flattery; as the fallen sinner; as a man's will
                compared to a woman's wont.
symbols: jellyfish; creampuff; tired blood.
see also: feeble; anemic; faint; exhausted.
opposite: strong; healthy; stubborn.

Wealthy: as Howard Hughes in his heyday; as a covey of
                Vanderbilts; as the man who broke the bank at
                Monte Carlo.
symbols: Croesus; Midas touch; El Dorado.
see also: rich; affluent.
opposite: poor; needy; deprived.

Weary: as the way of the transgressor; as an oldster's ach-
                ing bones; as a tortoise in a track meet.
symbols: Hercules after his labors; Sisyphus between trips.
see also: exhausted; overworked; jaded; bored.
opposite: eager; dashing; active; busy.

Welcome: as a letter from home; as the flowers that bloom in
                May (*Charles Macklin*); as Santa Claus at
                Christmas; as water in the desert.
symbols: open arms; outstretched hand; waiting at the sta-
                tion.
see also: appreciated; popular; desirable.
opposite: unpopular; objectionable.

Wicked: as the Devil's disciples; as a dozen dens of iniquity;
                as the worst of the witches; as evil incarnate.
symbols: Belial; Satan; the serpent in the Garden of Eden.
see also: evil; bad; immoral; hellish; lawless; loose.
opposite: good; righteous; moral; admirable; exemplary.

Wily: as a fox in a farmyard; as a weasel at work; as a
                master spy; as the witch of Endor.
symbols: the Artful Dodger; cutie-pie; Reynard the Fox.
see also: sly; tricky; calculating; crafty.
opposite: simple; plain.

Windy: as the weather at the top of the world; as a corner
                    on the Chicago lakefront; as an orator who gets
                    paid by the word; as a blow by blow description;
                    as a filibuster.

symbols: Aeolus; the cave of the winds.

see also: airy; talkative; gaseous; breezy.

opposite: calm; quiet; silent.

Winning: as the Superbowl champions; as the prize ticket in
                    the lottery; as a grand slam; as a royal flush; as
                    an angel's smile.

symbols: blue ribbon; championship belt; the laurel wreath.

see also: profitable; lucky; attractive; sought after.

opposite: unlucky; left out; ineffective; futile.

Wise: as the sages of the ages; as time; as a wary wildcat;
                    as the word of God; as one who knows when to
                    watch his words; as he who says nothing rather
                    than say something wrong.

symbols: Solomon; the Magi; Athena; Mentor; the Founding
                    Fathers.

see also: prudent; knowledgeable; discreet; learned; cau-
                    tious; bright; brilliant.

opposite: stupid; dumb; dull; rash; immature.

Worried: as a mouse in cat country; as the captain of a leaky
                    boat a hundred miles at sea; as the man who can't
                    pay back the loan shark; as a hypochondriac
                    without symptoms; as an elephant who forgets.

symbols: weight of the world; cliffhanger; nail biter.

see also: anxious; anguished; concerned; nervous;

opposite: calm; relaxed; euphoric; oblivious; indifferent; aloof.

Wrong: as the road to Hell; as waterwings on the desert; as
                    a love letter addressed "to whom it may con-
                    cern"; as the divine right of kings.

symbols: booby prize; dunce cap; Devil's disciple.

see also: erroneous; inaccurate; immoral; dishonest.

opposite: correct; accurate; true; moral; honest.

Y

Yellow: as the dying leaves of autumn; as buttercups in bloom; as a canary with jaundice; as cowardice in living color.

symbols: white feather; streak down the back; lily livered.
see also: cowardly; scared.
opposite: brave; daring; courageous.

Young: as first love; as a woman thinks she looks and a man thinks he acts; as everybody's kid sister; as one whose fancy lightly turns to thoughts of love (*Alfred Tennyson*).

symbols: the now generation; the tomorrow generation; small fry.
see also: childish; youthful; immature.
opposite: aged; old; ancient; mature.

Youthful: as trying to decide what you want to be when you grow up; as growing a beard to look older; as the frisbie crowd; as the eternal juvenile; as braces on your teeth.

symbols: Aeson's bath; Endymion; Juventas.
see also: childish; immature; young.
opposite: aged; dated; ancient; old; mature.

Z

Zealous: as a bill collector on commission; as Zorro leaving his mark; as a missionary on the scent of souls to save; as the neighborhood gossip keeping tab on the neighbors.

symbols: mover and shaker; bulldog; bitter-ender; mono-mania; wearing blinders.
see also: eager; dedicated; anxious; devoted.
opposite: aimless; aloof; apathetic; bored; jaded; indifferent.

Volume 3

The
Day
and
Date
Book

Introduction

For every single day of the year, there are several possible timely pegs on which to hang a speech.

In this volume of Speaker's Lifetime Library, angles and speech themes for every day of the year are listed, in chronological order from January 1 to December 31.

In addition to these specific entries, you should bear in mind the events that have occurred within the past year or five years. Very often, in local terms, for example, a news event of a year or two ago provides the same kind of peg that the national and international occurrences offer in the listings on the following pages. The other point is that our entries are finite. They go up to the date of publication of this book, but every day new things are happening—and every day, therefore, brings new anniversaries, new memories, new pegs for the speaker.

There are over a thousand speech angles in this volume. Every one of them can be related to the most contemporary or the most eternal of values. Some offer jumping-off points for a variety of themes and treatments.

If you use this volume, you should never find yourself stopped by the question, "What should I speak about?" The pegs are here.

A final hint: The day on which a speech is to be delivered is not the only day from which to draw your lead. Today is the eve of tomorrow; you can always draw an angle from the day after your speaking date, and speak of tomorrow's timely peg. The same can be done with a speech angle that applies to yesterday: "Only yesterday, it was 100 years since . . ."

Indeed, one can even apply this sort of chronological association to the week or the month. A speech pegged to the coming of Spring is timely for the whole week of March 21. A speech on the subject of Thanksgiving is timely for much of November.

So, as you consult this volume, look up not merely the particular day but also the days surrounding it. And keep in mind as well that every single year is a significant one. In 1989, for example, the U.S. observes the 200th anniversary of the adoption of the Constitution. Any time that year is appropriate for speeches celebrating the glory of our law.

It is wise, therefore, to remember that every year, as well as every day of every year, is something special.

JANUARY 1

President Lincoln issued Emancipation Proclamation in 1863.

Brooklyn merged with New York in a single city in 1898.

26 nations signed United Nations Declaration in World War II in Washington, D.C. in 1942.

First issue of *The Liberator*, William Lloyd Garrison's anti-slavery periodical, 1831.

Birthday of Paul Revere (1735), Betsy Ross (1752), General Anthony Wayne, (1745).

Introductions:

This is the day when, traditionally, our good resolutions are put to the test. Historically, it is a day full of good intentions, and, happily, of the beginning of the triumph of good.

It was on this day in 1831 that William Lloyd Garrison's first issue of his anti-slavery publication, *The Liberator*, produced a pretty good statement for all of us who have occasion to make our voices heard. He said: "I am in earnest. I will not equivocate; I will not excuse; I will not retreat a single inch; and I will be heard." That sets a pretty high mark for all of us.

On New Year's Day, no matter what the past, we look forward with hope. President Lincoln's Emancipation Proclamation in 1863 made that New Year's Day—and every New Year's Day since then—particularly meaningful. That proclamation was issued exactly 128 years after one of the most famous messengers of freedom, Paul Revere, was born. This day of the year is also the birthday of two other famous names of the American Revolution, Betsy Ross and General "Mad Anthony" Wayne. The New Year in America begins with many reminders of a heritage of dedication to liberty.

A New Year is always a time of hope. No matter what the problems of the past, we renew our dedication. In 1942, in the midst of a time of reverses in World War II, 26 nations signed the United Nations Declaration in Washington. In 1898, the citizens of Brooklyn and that smaller island in the harbor chose January 1 to merge their two cities into what became known as Greater New York.

As with the bowl games that are a feature of this day, not everybody comes out a winner. But we address ourselves to the matters at hand with confidence, with all-out effort and most assuredly with hope. It is in that spirit that I speak to you now.

JANUARY 2

New York Jets signed Joe Namath from the University of Alabama to play professional football in 1965 for a reported $400,000.

The first successful heart transplant operation was performed in South Africa in 1968.

Queen Victoria announced in 1900, "We are not amused."

Introductions:

Many a person, by the second day of the year, is already spiritually in tune with the attitude voiced by Queen Victoria on this date at the turn of the century, when she said regally, "We are not amused." As we look back at the era to which the Victorian Queen gave her name, it certainly seems more solid, less exciting and infinitely simpler than our own times; but we would probably change only a bit of her comment, to describe our attitude today. "We are not amazed."

It has been said that we live in an era of rising expectations. Perhaps that era is past, but we certainly live in an era of rising accomplishments. Everything is going up. And one phase of that upward trend was begun on this very day in 1965, when Joe Namath was signed to play professional football for the New York Jets for what was then regarded as an astronomical figure of $400,000. If there was a single dramatic monument to the age of onward and upward, it was that financial breakthrough—the echoes of which we certainly find around us today. We are truly in the era of "the sky's the limit."

Our modern era is not, as we sometimes think, one characterized mainly by higher and higher prices. It is also characterized by higher and higher accomplishment. A whole era of such accomplishment opened up on this date in 1968 when Dr. Christiaan Barnard performed the first successful heart transplant operation. He captured the imagination of the world and dramatized a whole new frontier for science. New frontiers, indeed, are all around us, some much closer than we think. I should like to discuss some of them with you here today.

JANUARY 3

Congress convenes on or about this date, usually.

Alaska was admitted as a state, 1959.

Cicero was born, 106 B.C.

Oscar Wilde told U.S. Customs, "I have nothing to declare but my genius," 1882.

Introductions:

Today is a fairly auspicious day for the platform speaker. It is the birthday of one of the greatest orators of all time, the Roman Cicero. He was the artist of the spoken word, and all of us are, at best, his students. His orations in the Roman Senate were masterpieces. Please do not expect the same from me here and now.

It may be simple coincidence that Cicero's birthday is also the time, approximately, when the Congress convenes in Washington. Today's Senate or House of Representatives may not be oversupplied with voices as golden as that of Cicero, but it is safe to say that we have more voices, more issues, and probably more people listening. It behooves us, therefore, to follow some anonymous sage advice about the public speaker, which I shall observe as follows: "Get up, get going, get down to cases, get off."

When Alaska was admitted as a state of the U.S. on this day in 1959, it was the first time the U.S. admitted to membership a territory not contiguous to the other states. There is no telling now where, with that tradition broken, other traditions will stand fast. But in exploring such prospects with you here today, I will try to avoid the state of mind exemplified by Oscar Wilde's comment, on this very day in 1882, when he said, "I have nothing to declare but my genius." I speak to you with no feeling of genius whatsoever, but with a sense of deep conviction.

JANUARY 4

First successful appendectomy performed, in Iowa, 1885.

Shorthand inventor Sir Isaac Pitman born, 1813.

"General Tom Thumb" born 1838.

Introductions:

This is a day whose anniversaries remind us of the virtues of doing without excess baggage and being willing to recognize limitations; these are virtues particularly important for a speaker to bear in mind and I will do so today.

When Dr. William West Grant in Davenport, Iowa, performed the first successful appendectomy on this day in 1885, he proved that man can live without an appendix. The same is true of a speech; it can get along fine without an appended flow of extra conversation.

It is helpful in reminding me not to trespass too heavily on your time today to know that we are meeting on the birthday of two men who, in different ways, exemplified the virtues of brevity, terseness and compactness. One was Sir Isaac Pitman, who invented the system of shorthand that bears his name.

The other was General Tom Thumb, billed in his time as the smallest man in the world. Following, so to speak, in their footsteps, I shall endeavor to make my remarks short and sweet, bearing in mind the ancient maxim that good things come in small packages.

JANUARY 5

Twelfth Night.

George Washington Carver Day (he died on this day in 1943).

Henry Ford announced minimum wage of $5 for eight-hour day, 1914.

Voltaire said, "Opinion has caused more trouble on this little earth than plagues or earthquakes," 1759.

Introductions:

Today brings us Twelfth Night, the end of the Christmas season. Some of us may feel that in this commercial era Twelfth Night comes not a day too soon. But today brings inspiration of its own.

January 5 is George Washington Carver Day, commemorating the death of a onetime slave in 1943, a man who proved that the American dream isn't— or maybe is—peanuts. Long before Jimmy Carter made peanuts a symbol of American indigenous success, George Washington Carver had given us all visions of greatness in the humble goober. There are many roads to greatness, for an individual as well as a nation.

Another man of humble beginnings, Henry Ford, helped to make his company and his nation great on this day in 1914 when he announced that he would institute an eight-hour working day and a minimum wage of $5 a day—both concepts fairly revolutionary for their time. As with many new ideas, a lot of people found it crazy, heretical, subversive or what-have-you. That is probably because, as Voltaire said—on this very day in 1759—"Opinion has caused more trouble on this little earth than plagues or earthquakes."

I am here today to express opinions, without the least desire to cause trouble, but with a firm conviction that even a nut has a right to come out of the shell.

JANUARY 6

Three Kings Day; Greek Cross Day.

President Franklin D. Roosevelt's Four Freedoms speech to Congress, 1941.

Joan of Arc was born, 1412.

Introductions:

The Feast of Epiphany is observed today in Latin America as Three Kings Day, a gift-giving holiday. So there are two ways of looking at my speech. Either I am giving you the gift of my brilliant thoughts eloquently expressed, or I am giving you, much more likely, the gift of not taking too much of your time.

One of today's interesting traditions is that it is Greek Cross Day, when devout men jump into the waters of such oddly assorted places as Tarpon Springs, Florida, and New York Harbor to retrieve Orthodox crosses in an ancient and always exciting combination of devotion and athletics. Much of life—and of that portion of life known as public speaking—is like the diving for the Greek Cross. You can get into deep water, and the water can be cold. And you have a choice of diving in quickly or sliding in gradually. I believe I have dwelt on this point sufficiently so that I have managed to get gradually into my prepared remarks.

Every serious speech made today might well spring from the remarks of Franklin D. Roosevelt when he addressed Congress on this day in 1941. He spoke then of "a world founded upon four essential freedoms . . . freedom of speech and expression . . . freedom of every person to worship God in his own way . . . freedom from want . . . [and] freedom from fear." There is no field of human endeavor where these four freedoms are not—or should not be—the basic, jumping-off point.

Life is not merely the state of things as they are, but the vision of what they might be. Different people, different times produce different visions. Today, more than most days, reminds us, because it is the birthday of the simple peasant maid, Joan of Arc, that visions are a real force in the world. Today's vision, often enough, is tomorrow's reality. And what do we envision today?

JANUARY 7

Baltimore & Ohio Railroad Company began rail service, using horse-drawn carriage, 1830.

Surveyor VII landed on the moon, 1968.

Introductions:

Rising to speak today, today in particular, I am reminded of how much easier it is for the modern speaker than for Demosthenes or Cicero. For them, apart from their eloquence, the ability to be heard was a rare attribute; there was no public address system, no acoustical tile, no means of amplification.

When that great American orator, Daniel Webster, was a rising statesman, communication was in its infancy. On this very day in 1830, a newfangled idea called a railroad began operating out of Baltimore. That first U.S. train, believe it or not, was horse-drawn, which illustrates that nothing can keep a good idea down, even when you have to have a substitute source of energy.

One hundred and thirty eight years to the day after a horse pulled the first Baltimore and Ohio train—on this very day in 1968—Surveyor VII landed on the moon. Communication has come a long, long way indeed. We span the universe as once we dared to hope we could span the continent. But for all the increase in the speed and breadth of communication, we still have no substitute for the oldest process of communication, simply speaking to each other. And so, without rocketry or radar or a computer hook-up, I am here today to talk to you.

JANUARY 8

Battle of New Orleans, 1815.

President Lyndon B. Johnson "declares unconditional war on poverty in America," 1964.

Introductions:

We do not widely celebrate today as Andrew Jackson Day, which marks his victory over the British at the Battle of New Orleans in 1815. Our relative calmness about that anniversary may be because, in the annals of history, that battle was largely meaningless; the War of 1812 was already over. The battle was fought because neither side got the news in time. That, of course, is true of many battles in life. They are fought needlessly, because the issue has already been decided, or has disappeared. That is why speakers sometimes address themselves to non-issues—the sanctity of motherhood, the importance of kindness and so forth. But, even in the Battle of New Orleans, there was a point to be made about the character of the American defense. And today, without seeking to start a war, I nevertheless feel there are some points of importance to be made.

Perhaps it is in the nature of humankind to have to envision life as a battleground. It need not be a combat zone. In 1964 President Lyndon B. Johnson on this day spoke of what he conceived as a crucial struggle, but he was not talking of armies and Vietnam. It was on this day that President Johnson said his Administration "here and now declares unconditional war on poverty in America." Some aspects of that still undeclared and most assuredly unfinished war—the battle for better life—are my topic today.

JANUARY 9

William Pitt, the elder, addressing the House of Lords: "Where law ends, tyranny beings . . . Unlimited power is apt to corrupt the minds of those who possess it." 1770.

Richard M. Nixon born, 1913.

United Nations headquarters opened in New York City in 1951.

Introductions:

It is surprising, sometimes, the way time can jump a century or two and words or events of the past gain new impact many years later. Today is such a day. It is the anniversary of the opening of the United Nations headquarters in New York City in 1951, and of the birth of one of the most controversial figures of our time, Richard M. Nixon, in 1913. And it is the day of the year when, in 1770, generations before the clamorousness of the UN and the agony of Richard Nixon, the wise William Pitt, the elder, told the British House of Lords, "Where law ends, tyranny begins" and "Unlimited power is apt to corrupt the minds of those who possess it." We are in a time when the question of where law ends is very real, and the challenge of the power that corrupts is ever-present. It is against that framework and in that perspective that I welcome this opportunity to speak with you today.

JANUARY 10

Texas oil boom started with discovery of oil in Beaumont, 1901.

Ethan Allen born, 1738.

Introductions:

Today is the birthday of Ethan Allen, the Revolutionary War commander who, when he demanded the surrender of Fort Ticonderoga, said he did so "In the name of the great Jehovah and the Continental Congress." Ethan Allen knew what to put first. He regarded himself as an instrument of a supreme Being or will, next to which the Continental Congress took second billing. We must all take second billing to nature. We must match our thoughts and our efforts with the larger and supreme laws of existence. My purpose here today is to state some particular thoughts against the broader framework of the world we live in.

We progress; we invest; we make changes. But in the last analysis we are still subject to the vagaries of life. On this day in 1901, oil was discovered in

Beaumont, Texas. It started an era of American prosperity and revolutionized the energy of the world. Our world today is still very largely dependent on where the next source of energy is found, and on who controls it. But let us think of energy in its broadest terms, not merely as a deposit in the ground. Let us address ourselves today to the broad question of how our energy, our efforts, can make things better.

JANUARY 11

Caesar crossed the Rubicon, 49 B.C.

Amelia Earhart Putnam became the first woman to fly solo across the Pacific, from Honolulu to Oakland, California, 1935. (Completed flight January 12.)

Alexander Hamilton born, 1755.

Introductions:

The great decision in a person's life is sometimes described as "crossing the Rubicon." The phrase comes from Julius Caesar's crossing of the river Rubicon on this day in 49 B.C. By crossing the river, Caesar committed himself irrevocably to war against Pompey and the Roman Senate. "The die is cast," Caesar said. For most of us, there is a personal Rubicon that, sooner or later, we have to cross. For whole nations as well—and this is such a time.

Human destiny is at least in part what we ourselves make it. The beasts behave on instinct, but humans choose their own paths. In 1935, on this day, Amelia Earhart Putnam set out to do what no woman had ever done before—to fly herself across the Pacific. She flew from Honolulu to California, proving again the motto that is the watchword of human progress, it can be done. It can be done!

On January 11, 1755, a man named Alexander Hamilton was born in the British West Indies. His name is one of the great ones in American history; his face one of the most familiar, since it appears on the ten dollar bill; his fate also familiar, since he was probably America's most famous victim of a duel, killed in just such an "affair of honor" by Aaron Burr. I mention Hamilton's story at the outset of these remarks as a reminder that none of us, however brilliant, can really know what lies ahead. We must do what we can—as much as we can—as soon as we can. Tomorrow, after all, is what we make today.

JANUARY 12

(See Amelia Earhart Putnam entry for January 11)

First museum in U.S. established in Charleston, S.C., 1773.

Mrs. Hattie Caraway became first elected U.S. woman Senator, 1932.

Introductions:

Although there is probably no country where women have consistently been given their due, the United States can point with pride to some notable distaff pioneers. One such was Amelia Earhart, who on this day in 1935 singlehandedly conquered the Pacific by flying from Honolulu to Oakland, California. Another, in a different arena, was Mrs. Hattie Caraway, who in 1932 became the first woman to be elected to the United States Senate. Women have come a long way since then—some nations have had women heads of government—but it is good for Americans to remember that to a large extent the pioneering by women in public life was done right here. Every period of history has its own frontiers, and ours is no exception. Today you need only look around to find shining examples of women in every area of human endeavor here, in what is still the greatest land of opportunity in the world. Consider, if you will, the opportunities which we enjoy.

America, it has been said, is a nation of volunteers. We have more people giving of their time and talent for more causes than do other countries. This is an old American tradition, particularly worth noting here because today is the anniversary of the establishment of the first public museum in this country. It was the Charleston Museum in Charleston, South Carolina, founded in 1773. That is a landmark in a tradition of public service, education and preservation of knowledge that continues still to build. I offer my remarks, then, against the backdrop of that great tradition.

JANUARY 13

Stephen Foster Memorial Day.

Zola's "J'accuse" published in Paris, 1898.

Introductions:

The most powerful thing in the world is not a bomb or a chemical reaction. The most powerful thing in the world, as a couple of anniversaries today remind us, is an idea, the planting of a seed in the human brain. Today, on this very day in 1898, a man named Emile Zola published in Paris an article entitled "J'accuse" (I accuse). It was a defense of a French soldier named Alfred Dreyfus, who was being railroaded on treason charges. The Zola article aroused France and the world. Before the case was over, not only was Captain Dreyfus vindicated, but the government of France and the French military establishment were rocked to their heels and drastically changed. This was the power of an idea.

On this same day in 1864 a gentle man died in Bellevue Hospital in New York—a man who rocked no governments, roused no great pangs of conscience; but a man who wrote songs that have conjured up ever since, for millions upon millions of people, a mind's eye image of America. This is Stephen Foster Memorial Day, in memory of the author of gentle songs that have contributed so much to our picture of ourselves, of the Swanee River, of the old folks at home, of Jeannie with the light brown hair. Times change, and some of Stephen Foster's lyrics are no longer sung because their connotations do not fit the times, but the essential spirit that he caught—the celebration of the gentle bucolic America that was—remains as part of the American heritage. It is in the shadow of that heritage that I speak to you today.

JANUARY 14

Fundamental Orders of Connecticut, pioneer written constitution in America, adopted in 1639.

Benedict Arnold born, 1741.

Albert Schweitzer born, 1875.

Introductions:

Man's greatest enemy, it has been said, is man himself. Two of today's anniversaries remind us of that fact, and a third confutes it. Today is the birthday of one whose very name has come to symbolize treachery—Benedict Arnold, a brave and doughty fighter in the American Revolution until he decided to cast his lot with the enemy and became a turncoat. But today is also the birthday of a man who came to symbolize what was good in human nature—service to his fellow man, love of the arts, dedication and sacrifice. On this day in 1875, Dr. Albert Schweitzer was born—medical missionary, musician, philosopher, opposite in so many ways to Benedict Arnold, and a reminder that human beings are cast in no single mold. We like to arrange our society so that we can seek out, promote and reward that which is good, and prevent that which is bad. And on this same day, back in 1639, America developed a means of doing just that. It was a document called the Fundamental Orders of Connecticut, the pioneer written Constitution. That was the concept of what we like to think of as government by laws rather than by men. Men can be Benedict Arnolds or Albert Schweitzers or something in between; but a written Constitution is a specific set of fundamental doctrines which, to a large extent, saves us from ourselves. As we look at the world today, we look at it against this great American backdrop of Constitutional doctrine and basic principle. And this is what we see.

JANUARY 15

Martin Luther King, Jr., born in 1929. His birthday is observed as Human Relations Day.

Kellog-Briand Pact for peaceful settlement of international disputes ratified by U.S. Senate, 1929.

"The Man with the Hoe" published, 1899.

Introductions:

Today is Human Relations Day, the name chosen to mark the birthday of the Reverend Doctor Martin Luther King, Jr., born in Atlanta in 1929. Dr. King, the man who had that glorious dream of brotherhood and equality, did not live to see the greatest progress up that road; but certainly, on his day, we now can look back and see how far we have come toward the light. On his day, indeed, we have a moral obligation to examine the human condition and ask how we can make it better.

Man is a creature of hope. Back in 1929, on this date, on the very day of the birth of Martin Luther King, Jr., the U.S. Senate ratified a treaty whose very title expressed its hope—the Kellogg-Briand agreement for the peaceful settlement of international disputes. We know how well that worked! Ten years later the world was at war. But the anniversary reminds us that we keep on trying, over the years, and we are trying still.

We, all of us to some degree, remain like "The Man with the Hoe" whom poet Edwin Markham described in a great poem published on this day in 1899:

> "Bowed by the weight of centuries he leans
> Upon his hoe and gazes on the ground,
> The emptiness of ages in his face,
> And on his back the burden of the world."

The burden is there. What are we doing about it?

JANUARY 16

Eighteenth Amendment to the Constitution (Prohibition) went into effect, 1920.

U.S. Civil Service established as merit system by Pendleton Act, 1883.

Introductions:

From the time we are able to walk, we are encouraged to be brave enough to try. Experimentation, we are told, is the road to progress. Today we mark the anniversary of what was called "the noble experiment." It didn't work, but we like to think that it taught us something. The experiment was Prohibition; the Eighteenth Amendment, which established it, went into effect this day in 1920. In 1933 it was abandoned. In the meantime we learned, among other things, that law depends on the people for its effectiveness in a democracy. Perhaps that lesson was worth the experiment. At least it has led us, since then, to try harder and harder to find out what the people want, and, conversely, to create a state of mind before we impose a new law. And so it behooves us today to address ourselves to the question of what exactly do we want.

On this day in 1883 we thought we had solved the problem of governmental corruption. We thought we had solved it by enactment of the Pendleton Act, which established the U.S. Civil Service as a merit system of employment. We had no idea then of the infinite complications and ingenious devices which would grow up in public employment, and in private attitudes toward the operations of government. Life has grown more complicated—or is it merely government that has grown more complicated? That is the question we must ask ourselves today.

JANUARY 17

Benjamin Franklin born, 1706.

St. Anthony the Abbot, patron saint of animals, died 346 A.D.

Cable car patented, 1871.

Introductions:

The first great American user of words and master of expression was Benjamin Franklin, born on this day in 1706. Benjamin Franklin is remembered more as a writer—an inventor and patriot leader and diplomat—than as a speaker, but many a speaker has built his oratory on the wisdom of the author of *Poor Richard's Almanac.* He wrote, for example, that "A word to the wise is enough and many words won't fill a bushel." In that spirit, I shall not try to pile up a bushel's worth of words, but shall speak in full confidence that what I am about to say, as far as this audience is concerned, is most assuredly a word to the wise.

Today is devoted, in the calendar of saints' days, to St. Anthony the Abbot, regarded as the patron saint of animals. On this day, in many parts of the world, the animals are formally blessed in observance of the occasion. It is a fitting commentary on our present standards and way of life, therefore, to look at ourselves today in the light of the way we treat animals. How do we care for our pets? How do we hunt and respect the wild beasts? What do we do for our animal friends? I think the answers to these questions can provide an allegory for the quality of human life today.

Life has been described as the struggle of man against man, the struggle of man against the beasts, the partnership of man and nature, and sometimes, in a vein of simple optimism, as the progress of humankind. One story that began on this day in 1871 summarizes part of the tug and pull of human existence. It is the story of the cable car, patented on this day in 1871, put into operation two and a half-years later on the hills of San Francisco and still in operation there. Through the years, other more efficient forms of transportation have been developed, and San Francisco has started to use them; but every time it is suggested that the cable cars be discontinued, the human beings of San Francisco rediscover their past and insist on keeping it—while hundreds of thousands of visitors to that spectacular city enthusiastically applaud. Life for all of us is a constant challenge to decide what of the past we should retain and what we should replace. So today let us look at our own beloved cable cars, and consider which of them are worth keeping.

JANUARY 18

Week of Prayer for Christian Unity, January 18-25.

Captain Robert Scott reached South Pole, 1912; but Amundsen had gotten there first.

Daniel Webster born, 1782.

Introductions:

This is either a very well-omened or a very challenging day for a public speaker. It is the birthday of the most awesome and eloquent public speaker the United States has yet known, a man named Daniel Webster, born 1782. It was Daniel Webster, you may recall, whom Stephen Vincent Benet chose as the man to argue a case against the Devil in that epic chronicle, "The Devil and Daniel Webster." I am no Daniel Webster, but I hope his spirit will at least loosen my tongue as I rise to address you today.

Being second best somehow has never meant quite what it should. When we say someone is second-ranked in the world tennis rankings, that is very impressive; but when we say he is second-best—even the second-best player in the world, it doesn't sound quite as good. This comes to mind today because in 1912, on this date, a great explorer came in second and, subsequently was largely forgotten. The explorer was Captain Robert Scott, who reached the South Pole on this day in 1912. It was an epic feat of heroism, made further memorable by the fact that Captain Scott and his party died on the way back. But the glory was greatly dimmed by the fact that Roald Amundsen had reached and discovered the Pole a month earlier—and Amundsen survived. There is no disgrace in coming in second; but there is insufficient glory. Particularly in America, we have a tendency to revel in that which we have done first, perhaps at the expense of that which we do best. And so today I would like to talk about a number of things which America did not invent or discover, but which America does very well indeed.

Christian unity, which can and should be regarded as a prelude to total human unity, is not a goal unique to America. But in America we have set aside a particular week in which to strive for it; and that Week begins today. What more fitting theme for comment in America, where so many different strains have come together, than this theme of unity.

JANUARY 19

Robert E. Lee born, 1807.

Tin canning process for food patented, 1825.

James Watt born, 1736.

Introductions:

Most of us at some point in our lives are faced with an important decision. Few of us ever can have the kind of choice that was offered to a man born on this date in 1807. The man was Robert E. Lee, and the choice came when he was offered the command of the Union Army in what was to be the great Civil War. He chose, as we all know, to turn down that offer and instead to become the Commander of the Confederate Army. And despite his ultimate defeat in that war he became one of the great men of America. What he so amply demonstrated was that in lost causes men can find themselves; that nobility of spirit can somehow survive and triumph over defeat. These are certainly things worth remembering as, on the anniversary of his birth, we share here today some thoughts about our own times.

There are a number of people and events that stand as milestones in the history of human progress. One such person is James Watt, the man who put the machine to work. James Watt was born on this day in 1736. It was he who saw how steam could be harnessed; he who brought to actuality the idea of a steam engine. Since his time many other forms of engine have been produced; but James Watt in large measure began the modern age of civilization. On his birthday, it is timely to ask ourselves what we have done with the greater horizons the machine age made possible.

Today I would like to recall to you the names of Ezra and Thomas Kinsett. They are not household words; but their monument is in every household. In 1825, on this day, Ezra and Thomas Kinsett of New York City patented a process for the tin canning of food. If others ushered in the machine age, they can be said to have pioneered the age of convenience. Not every revolutionizer of the way we live enjoys immortal fame—as witness the Kinsetts. And so it behooves us to remember that what each of us does can have more of an impact than we know. Today I call your attention to some little noted examples of the effect of lighting one small candle in the darkness, like Ezra and Thomas Kinsett.

JANUARY 20

Presidential Inauguration Day.

First basketball game, 1892.

Introductions:

Anyone who rises to speak on this day, the twentieth day of January, speaks in the shadow or the glory of some of the most noble phrases ever uttered, phrases spoken by men as they were inaugurated President of the United States. Since 1937, January 20 has been Presidential Inauguration Day, when Franklin D. Roosevelt saw "one third of a nation ill-housed, ill-clad, ill-nourished"—when John F. Kennedy urged his fellow Americans to "ask not what your country can do for you; ask what you can do for your country"— when Harry Truman observed that "The supreme need of our time is for men to learn to live together in peace and harmony"—and when Dwight D. Eisenhower said that "whatever America hopes to bring to pass in the world must first come to pass in the heart of America." What better introduction than these great words to my humble remarks today?

In a hall in Springfield, Massachusetts, on this day in 1892, a great tool of international communication was born. It wasn't intended that way. It was simply a game designed by a YMCA worker named James Naismith and called basketball. Basketball did not merely catch on. It took the world by storm. It is played everywhere; it is a great vehicle of international team competition. It has brought glory to depressed peoples, excitement and inspiration to those in need. As a sport, it has the frailties of every sport—the exaggerated competitiveness, the tensions, the unbridled rewards and anxieties. But what it tells us all, in essence, is that there are ways that people who speak different languages and come from different cultures can still find a common ground. That is indeed a worthy theme to explore at this time and in this place.

JANUARY 21

Stonewall Jackson born, 1824.

First atomic-powered submarine launched, 1954.

Alger Hiss convicted of perjury, 1950.

Introductions:

Adversity is a hard school; but its alumni are apt to shine. Today marks the birth, in 1824, of a man who has come, even more since his death, to symbolize the integrity of stubborn courage. His name was Thomas Jackson, but we all know him better as "Stonewall" Jackson—not merely one of the great tacticians and military leaders of the Confederate Army in the U.S. Civil War, but the personification of strength and steadfastness. At a time when we are called upon once again to stand fast for fundamental beliefs, it is only fitting to recall the man who, in Robert E. Lee's famous phrase, stood like a stone wall. Who and where are our stone walls today?

Occasionally an event leaves a by-product that dwarfs the original occurrence itself. Such was the case with a court trial that ended in a conviction on this day in 1950. It was the trial of Alger Hiss for perjury in a case which brought to the attention of the nation and the world a young Congressman from California, a man named Richard M. Nixon. The case itself was a cause celebre from the moment the verdict was brought in; but perhaps in the annals of history it will be most remembered as a sort of launching pad for the amazing career thereafter of Richard Nixon. At any rate, it makes a point worth emphasizing at the start of these remarks. We speak and act, at any given moment, without really knowing what the lasting effect, if any, will be—and so we must be ever-mindful that we are on trial, awaiting a future verdict in the courtroom of history. What will history say of us?

The first atomic-powered submarine, the Nautilus, was launched on this day in 1954. Atomic power—and we along with it—seems to have been getting into deep water ever since. This is the modern dilemma: How much can and should we venture to make life easier; how much failure to venture forth makes life harder than it should be? Where is the line to be drawn and who is to draw it? That is the broad question which dominates all others in the world today.

JANUARY 22

Queen Victoria died, 1901.

"Red Sunday" in St. Petersburg bloodily foreshadowed the Russian Revolution, 1905.

Introductions:

Not too many people give their name to a whole era, but one who did was Queen Victoria of Great Britain. In a literal sense, the Victorian era ended on this day in 1901, when, after a reign of 60 years, Queen Victoria died. We live today in far more complicated times. No nation and no individual symbolize them as did Victoria and her empire. But Victoria symbolized more than her time. She symbolized a whole set of rules in the relationships between individuals. They were rules which we now regard—in further tribute to her impact—as "mid-Victorian." And so, on the anniversary of her death, one may well ask what we now have to take the place of Victoria's rules, the Victorian concept of responsibility and dignity and human obligation.

In the long view of history we can look back and find turning points which we did not really recognize at the time. One such was "Red Sunday," on this date in 1905, when the Czar's soldiers fired on marching Russian workers who were demonstrating peacefully for better conditions. Not only were many killed; thousands were arrested and sent to prison, many to camps in Siberia. We know now that had "Bloody Sunday" been less bloody, and the Czar's forces less repressive, there might have been no Bolshevik revolution. The whole history of the world might have been different. Yet, as we look around, we also know of more recent "Bloody Sundays" and we have a right to wonder what can be done to prevent extremism from dominating the destiny of the world.

JANUARY 23

Dr. Elizabeth Blackwell received the first M.D. awarded to a woman in the U.S., 1849.

Communist leaders confessed to anti-Stalin conspiracy in U.S.S.R., 1937.

Poll tax barred in Federal elections in U.S., 1964.

Introductions:

Today is not one of the days normally devoted to saluting the female portion of our population, like Mother's Day or Equal Rights Day. But today is a very significant day for women, and for all the rest of us who would be nothing without women. It is the anniversary of the awarding of a medical degree to Dr. Elizabeth Blackwell in 1849, the first U.S. woman doctor. This is and should be a milestone in the annals of the relationship of men and women, a topic in which there are still sufficient complications not just for one speech today but for much more to come.

The way people think, their relationships with each other, have complicated life since the days of Adam and Eve. But only in recent times have we come to discover such an insidious tool as what is euphemistically called "brain washing." Today is a day on which to remember the battle for control of people's minds. On this day, in 1937, a group of Communist leaders confessed in court to an anti-Stalin conspiracy in Russia. Why and how they came to confess brought new attention to the whole subject of psychological warfare, breaking down of will and the dubious art of thought manipulation. The anniversary is a good time to raise the question of how free can and should the human mind be kept, and what we can do to preserve that freedom.

The history of the human race in some respects is a history of attempting to persuade people to raise their voices and cast their votes. But it is also a history of attempts to prevent people from making their voices heard through the ballot. In 1964 on this date, the Twenty-fourth Amendment to the Constitution barred the poll tax in Federal elections. You no longer had to pay for the privilege of casting your vote. Voting was recognized as a right, not simply a privilege. That, it seems to me, provides an excellent text for the day. Citizenship is not merely a privilege; it is a collection of rights. How well are we doing with protecting and advancing those rights?

JANUARY 24

John W. Marshall discovered gold at Sutter's Mill, California, 1848.

"The man who makes no mistakes does not usually make anything else."—
Edward John Phelps, 1899.

Introductions:

Among the great forces which drive men, none through history has been
more potent than the lure of gold. It brought the Spanish to explore the New
World, and it opened up the vast spaces of the American continent to settlement. Today marks the day when a good bit of this began, the anniversary of
the discovery of gold by John W. Marshall at Sutter's Mill in California in 1848.
This was the event which started the gold rush that sent thousands of '49ers
west to seek their fortunes, opened the hills and the trackless wastes to prospectors and set the groundwork for the coming of what we laughingly call
civilization. It was not accidental that when oil was later being hunted for in
the same frantic way, it became known as black gold. Yes, the search for gold
has vastly broadened the world's horizons. We have reason to wonder now
where that search will take us next, and what the "black gold" of tomorrow will
turn out to be.

In 1899 on this day a lawyer-diplomat named Edward John Phelps made a
speech in which he said, "The man who makes no mistakes does not usually
make anything." That is my text for today—the need to dare, the need to do
things, the need not to be terrified by fear of being wrong.

JANUARY 25

Nellie Bly's trip around the world was completed, 1890.

Transcontinental U.S. telephone service began, 1915.

Pope John XXIII called an ecumenical council to promote unity, 1959.

Introductions:

This day of the year was a red-letter day in 1890 for Elizabeth Cochrane,
who wrote for *The New York World* as Nellie Bly. On this day, she completed
her fantastic trip around the world in the amazing time of 72 days, 6 hours, 11
minutes. On this same day in 1915, Alexander Graham Bell completed the first
transcontinental phone call, from New York to San Francisco, inaugurating a
new era in speedy communication. Obviously, today is a time when, through
the years, we have been thinking of how to be closer to each other. It is a
subject on which further thought is certainly to the point.

A simple priest, who became Pope John XXIII, on this date in 1959 took a giant step toward bringing the world closer together without depending on the miracles of science. He called for an ecumenical council to explore ways of promoting unity among humankind. I think it is fair to say that the echoes of that call and that spirit deserve to be with us today, and to be heard again.

JANUARY 26

Australia Day, commemorating settlement in 1778.

Daniel Webster's reply to Senator Hayne, 1830.

Introductions:

Today is Australia Day, commemorating the settlement and raising of the British flag in the harbor of Sydney, Australia in 1778. Ordinarily, this would seem to be principally of interest in Australia, but it has very real meaning for all of us. If the American Revolutionary War had not been raging in that period, the settlers who were landed in Australia would have been sent to America—and we probably would have had a tremendous outcry, because those first settlers were convicts. There were too many to keep in England, and so they were sent to a new land. It is a comment on both the hardiness and the resilience of disadvantaged people that from these convict settlers Australia developed into one of the great civilized lands in the South Pacific. When tested, the goodness of people emerged—and more good people were attracted. Thus Australia Day gives us today a timely reminder that faith in people can be well rewarded.

On this day in 1830, the Senate of the United States was the scene of an impartial debate on the issue that, a generation later, was to lead to Civil War—the issue of states' rights and nullification. And on this day the eloquent Daniel Webster summarized, as well as it has ever been done, the cornerstone doctrines of our nation. Replying to Senator Hayne, he saluted, in his words, "Liberty and Union, now and for ever, one and inseparable." They remain our watchwords—Liberty and Union. Let us consider what they mean today.

JANUARY 27

Electric light bulb patented, 1880.

Mozart born, 1756.

Three U.S. astronauts killed in fire aboard spaceship, 1967.

Introductions:

I doubt that my remarks today will be able to shed as much light as was made possible on this date in 1880. That was when Thomas A. Edison received a patent for his incandescent electric light bulb. Ever since, it has been easier to shed light in dark places. And also, ever since, there have been people seeking to turn off the lights. Sometimes the purpose has been innocent or amatory. Sometimes the purpose has been to hide something. I rise here today to suggest that a more old-fashioned method of shedding light in dark places is still in order. I rise in behalf of that ancient custom of asking questions. Here are some areas where I believe questions are in order.

Wolfgang Amadeus Mozart lived a short life and a productive one. He was born on this date in Austria in 1756. He wrote 626 musical compositions including magnificent operas and symphonies and he died at the age of 35. If he had been asked to come before such a group as this, he would probably have produced a masterpiece. For those of us, however, to whom masterpieces do not come easily, whether in music or in words, there are still opportunities to be heard, and I thank you for providing me with such an opportunity tonight.

I wonder how much—if anything—these names mean to you: Virgil Grissom, Edward White, Roger Chaffee. Some of you may recognize them as the three astronauts who were killed by fire in their Apollo spaceship at Cape Kennedy, Florida. That happened on this day in 1967. I mention it to remind you that while we have our eyes on the heights, the trouble may be right at our feet. Astronauts Grissom, White and Chaffee died not in outer space but on the ground. Even though we look abroad and afar for the causes of the problems which perplex us, let us be sure we are safe right here on the ground at home.

JANUARY 28

Louis D. Brandeis became first Justice of Jewish faith nominated for U.S. Supreme Court, 1916.

"There is nothing stronger than human prejudice." Wendell Phillips, 1852.

Introductions:

If we care to measure the progress of our nation, one anniversary marked today provides a convenient yardstick. On this date in 1916, Louis D. Brandeis became the first American of Jewish faith to be nominated to the Supreme Court. Today there seems to be nothing particularly remarkable about that appointment. The name of Brandeis lives not only in his historic opinions and dissents but in the title of a great American university. But in 1916 his nomination aroused a tremendous furor. His religion and his liberal views made him repugnant to many Americans. Ladies and gentlemen, we have come a long way since then. We have not defeated prejudice, political, religious or racial; but we have learned that great men surmount labels and cataloguing, and healthy nations have room for minority beliefs and need of their champions. The times have changed since the days of Louis D. Brandeis; but let us look to see whether we are as far along the path of mutual respect and open opportunity as we like to think we are.

On this date in 1852, Wendell Phillips, the New England orator and abolitionist leader, said, "There is nothing stronger than human prejudice." How far have we come? Can we rest on our laurels, or is human prejudice still the strongest power in the world—and if so, where is it taking us?

JANUARY 29

Congress established Commission to decide the Hayes-Tilden election, 1877.

William McKinley born in 1843.

Introductions:

When I began to prepare my remarks for this occasion, I consulted the history books, and I found something interesting—and heartening. On this date in 1877, there was such a tangle of charges and confusion over the 1876 Presidential election that Congress established a special Electoral Commission to decide whether Samuel Tilden or Rutherford B. Hayes had been elected. We have had our Watergates since then, but we might as well face the fact that we have come a goodly distance in representative government since Messrs. Hayes and Tilden. So I speak to you today not as a cynic, but rather as one convinced that, however slowly, we do move onward and upward.

Not too long ago, one of our political leaders described a concept of public policy with which he disagreed as "creeping McKinleyism." That was probably the only modern reference to the man who was born on this date in 1843, was the President at the turn of the century and became the symbol for a totally passé style of laissez-faire conservatism. William McKinley is best remembered these days as the President whose assassination made Teddy Roosevelt President. Politically, modern times in the U.S. began with Teddy Roosevelt, and the Stone Age, by popular belief, ended with William McKinley. We have a great tendency to think in eras, to compartmentalize this age or that. Tonight I propose to challenge that tendency—to talk about the problems of our times not in terms of *when* they are—or how modern they may be—but rather in terms of how long we have somehow failed to solve them.

JANUARY 30

Adolf Hitler became Chancellor of Germany, 1933.

Mahatma Gandhi assassinated, 1948.

Franklin D. Roosevelt born, 1882.

Introductions:

Some of the television news broadcasters like to start off their reports by asking, "What kind of a day has it been?" I thought I might do the same, so I checked to see what kind of a day this has been. I wonder whether I should have bothered. On this date in 1835, a demented painter named Richard Lawrence tried to assassinate President Jackson. In 1889 the tragedy of Mayerling ended with the suicide of Crown Prince Rudolf of Austria and Baroness Marie Vetsera. In 1925 Floyd Collins was trapped in a cave in Kentucky in which he later died. But dire as the events of this date were, I have saved what I must call the black letter day for last. On this date in 1933, Adolf Hitler became the Chancellor of Germany, launching that nation on a suicidal path of hate and war. Looking back on all these anniversaries, I have come to the conclusion that it's a good day to be here talking to you. Certainly it is good by comparison with the past.

One of the ironies of this date is that probably the greatest apostle of non-violence of modern times, Mahatma Gandhi of India, the father of modern non-violent civil disobedience, was assassinated in 1948 in New Delhi. Life is not all what we make it; it is what other people make it for us. With that in mind, let us look at the world that other people are making—and what we are doing about it.

When the history of the twentieth century is written, there will be much attention devoted to the giants of their times—and one of them will have to be the man who was born in Hyde Park, New York, on this date in 1882. His name, of course, was Franklin D. Roosevelt, whose greatest triumph was probably not as President but as one who overcame a great physical handicap after he was stricken with infantile paralysis. I hope that, in reminding you of his story today, I may proceed to explore with you how and where his kind of courage is needed in the world today.

JANUARY 31

Alexander Selkirk, "Robinson Crusoe," rescued after four years on an island in the Pacific, 1709.

Jackie Robinson born, 1919.

Introductions:

Truth, they say, is stranger than fiction. Whether that is itself true or fictitious, truth is not the point. The fact is that, on this date, a true story—which nobody really remembers—provided the basis for a piece of fiction that everybody knows. The true story was that of Alexander Selkirk, a British sailor who was rescued on this date in 1709 after four years alone on an island in the Pacific. Not many people recognize the name of Alexander Selkirk. But they all recognize the story his real-life adventure inspired, the story of Robinson Crusoe. Somehow, we seem to prefer to deal with facts in fictional, storytelling terms. That may be why commentaries about current conditions—social, cultural or political—all seem more effective when they "tell a story." Today I would like to tell you about the facts on which some current story themes are based.

Occasionally it falls to the lot of one person to become the living embodiment of an idea, the symbol of something in which a lot of people believe. When that happens, although there is apt to be a strong rooting section, the person who is the symbol usually has to do most of the hard work alone. That's the way it was with a great athlete who was born on this date in 1919—a man named Jackie Robinson. It fell to Jackie Robinson to integrate major league baseball and thereby to open the door in all organized sport to Blacks who had previously been barred. Jackie Robinson endured much for the sake of a cause where, as an individual, he would have fought back. It took much greater courage to endure—and in the end to win. That symbol of courage and wisdom, of dedication to a cause more important than a single individual's suffering, is in my mind today because we are in a time when the same challenge falls on many of us—not because of the color of our skins but because of the repressive weight of orthodoxy. The old expression was "quicker than you can say Jack Robinson." Today I rephrase it: As courageous as you remember Jackie Robinson. We need that kind of courage now.

FEBRUARY 1

U.S. Supreme Court convened for the first time, in New York in 1790.

The birth of "the 400," 1892.

American Heart Month starts.

American History Month and Black History Month start.

Introductions:

We observe many anniversaries in the United States. One that we somehow overlook occurs today. On this date, in 1790, the U.S. Supreme Court convened for the first time. The Supreme Court may well be America's unique contribution to the science of government, because it is the living symbol of what has been called a government of laws rather than a government of men. The separation of powers, the system of checks and balances designed by the Founding Fathers, is part of the glory of this country, and today was—and is—a red letter day. So it is in a spirit of pride in our heritage that I speak to you.

In 1892, Mrs. William B. Astor gave a society ball on this day in New York City. A man named Ward McAllister drew up the guest list, and it was referred to in terms of the number of people considered eligible to be invited. They were called "the 400." Ever since then, "400" has been synonymous with high society. This prompts me to say that anything more or less than 400 is probably a far more interesting and challenging audience. I have not counted the house here today, but I am reasonably sure of the quality of the audience. And I appreciate the opportunity to speak to you as I am about to do.

Today marks the start of American Heart Month, when the nation musters up its resources once again to support the fight against ailments of the heart and circulatory system. It is an interesting commentary that the main reason for the enthusiasm with which America supports American Heart Month is that we are so often inclined to put our money where our heart is. The impulses of the heart are generous and—I know no other way to put it—heartfelt. We tend to approach our problems from the heart, and today as I talk to you I want you to know that I am speaking from the heart. If the head happens to agree, that is so much the better.

George Santayana said that those who cannot remember the past are condemned to repeat it. Since today is the start of the observance of American History Month, you will be hearing enough about the past from others. I prefer to address myself today to the future.

FEBRUARY 2

Groundhog Day.

The "Cardiff Giant" was exposed as a hoax in 1870.

Introductions:

Today, as you may have heard from a television weather forecaster, is Groundhog Day. Legend says that if the groundhog comes out today and happens to see his shadow, it means six more weeks of winter. I presume that if it is too cold or stormy for him to come out, the Lord alone knows how much longer winter will be. I must report to you that there is no similar test for speakers. It is very difficult for you to tell, from the way I come out, how long my speech is going to be. Some speakers themselves can't tell, until they see how friendly the audience is. But I want to assure you that I will not speak one minute longer than it will take me to finish what I have to say.

Back in 1869, a seemingly petrified giant human figure was discovered on a farm in Cardiff, New York. It created a sensation, for a while; but on this day, in 1870, the Cardiff Giant was exposed as a hoax. It was neither the first nor the last time people have been asked to put their faith in something that turned out to be a fake. That, indeed, may be the greatest challenge of life—to figure out what is real, what is true, and what is fake. I am not here to overwhelm you with carefully tailored statistics or to play upon natural fears. I am here to report some relatively simple facts that I think you ought to know—and that, indeed, you can test for yourselves.

FEBRUARY 3

Four Chaplains Day marks four chaplains' heroic death in World War II, 1943.

Lincoln at Civil War peace conference, 1865.

Introductions:

I daresay that not too many of you are aware that today is not merely the third day of February. Today has a name—a very special name. It is Four Chaplains Day. It marks the heroic death of four men of the cloth—a Catholic priest, a Jewish rabbi and two Protestant ministers—who gave their life jackets to others and went down together in the sinking of the troop transport Dorchester in the North Atlantic during World War II, in 1943. The priest was named Washington; the rabbi was named Goode; and the ministers were named Fox and Poling. Theirs are names to be remembered; and their sacrifice is worth remembering. Their brotherhood should be an example for us all. It should transcend differences of opinion, and enable us to talk together and to work together in that sense of common purpose which those men had in such abundance.

Working together is not always easy. On this date, in 1865, President Lincoln and the Vice President of the Confederacy, Alexander H. Stephens, met aboard a ship in the harbor of Hampton Roads, Virginia, to try to settle the Civil War. The meeting failed because the Confederacy insisted on independence. A bare two months later, after more killing and more suffering, that independence was lost anyway. Talk, it has been said, is cheap; and actions speak louder than words. But sometimes words are wiser. And always it is wiser to talk to each other than to remain silent. Except, of course, in the case of a public speaker, who naturally expects the audience to remain silent while the words fall from his lips. You do, of course, retain the option of applauding if the spirit moves you.

FEBRUARY 4

Confederate States of America organized in Montgomery, Alabama, 1861.

Patty Hearst kidnapped, 1974.

Introductions:

As Americans, we seem to have a particular fondness for lost causes—and very much so for causes which went down fighting hard and gallantly. One such, which has been a state of mind for more than a hundred years, was the Confederate States of America, born on this date in 1861. It took a long time to bind up the wounds of the bloody Civil War which was fought with the Confederacy. But out of that war and its aftermath came some great men and some great events. A cause was lost, but the greater cause of unity was ultimately won. Every one of us has a cause that is yet to be won. My remarks today may be judged by the impact they have on your own particular cause or dream. In the end, somehow, though it takes a long time to come, decent causes, honest dreams and devoted advocates find a way to work things out. Perhaps the best dividend of the Civil War was that we haven't had another Civil War since then. Or, to put it another way, how much better for us to be talking together instead of shooting!

Kidnapping is an old and nasty crime, and not the kind of subject one would ordinarily use to introduce a speech. But today happens to be the anniversary of a rather unusual kidnapping. On this date, in 1974, Patty Hearst was kidnapped by the Symbionese Liberation Army, the beginning of a strange story of mind warfare and attacks upon the psyche. Though rarely as violent as in the case of Patty Hearst, there seems to be a stepped-up effort on the part of all too many people to hold the minds of others for ransom. To demand conformism in thinking. To impose orthodoxies, new or old, and to seek to manipulate that sleeping giant called public opinion. We find ourselves asking not so much "What did he say?" as "Why did he say it?" The remarks I am about to make are being spoken to you with no ulterior motive, but simply because I think they deserve saying. And, of course, to go with that, there is the satisfaction of being able to exercise freedom of the mouth. It is a great privilege and I thank you for extending it to me.

FEBRUARY 5

Roger Williams arrived in America, 1631.

Adlai E. Stevenson was born in 1900.

Introductions:

More than 300 years ago, on this date, a young Englishman arrived in the colonies, to serve as a minister. He became our first great dissenter. His name was Roger Williams, and he was the founder of religious tolerance in America. He established religious freedom as the law in Rhode Island. The roots of freedom, it seems, go back to very early days in this land. And what moved Roger Williams motivates us still today—to speak out, to speak our minds. If he had not acted out of conscience as he did, who knows how free we would be to exchange our ideas here today?

The gift of words is a great gift indeed. When one is called upon to speak in public, one walks in the shadow of the great orators, the men of golden tongues and shining phrases. Today is the birthday of one such man. There were controversies aplenty about his qualifications for our highest office, but none about his eloquence. His name was Adlai Stevenson. Among the many memorable things he said was this: "Government [in a democracy] cannot be stronger or more tough-minded than its people. It cannot be more inflexibly committed to the task than they. It cannot be wiser than the people." That, my friends, is a pretty good text for today. Adlai Stevenson said it in 1952.

FEBRUARY 6

College of William and Mary chartered in Williamsburg, Va., 1693.

Twentieth Amendment (Lame Duck Amendment) went into effect in 1933 for future years.

Babe Ruth born, 1895.

Introductions:

If there is a single most notable aspect of the growth of our nation, it is probably wrapped up in one word—education. The point is timely today because, on this date in 1693, the first charter for a college in this country was granted, at Williamsburg, Virginia. The college which opened later thanks to that charter is the College of William and Mary. Years later, it became the founding home of the national collegiate honor fraternity, Phi Beta Kappa. So, in a sense, today can be regarded as the anniversary of America's determination to make itself the best educated nation on earth. Of course, that is a goal which can never be completely gained. There is always more to be learned, more to be seen, more to be explored. Even here today, in our own small way, we carry on that never-ending process.

Probably the most picturesquely named portion of the supreme law of the land is the Twentieth Amendment to the Constitution. It became part of the law on this day in 1933 and it is popularly known as the Lame Duck Amendment. You all know what a lame duck is—a politician who has been defeated for reelection but is still in office. Before the Lame Duck Amendment, a President and a Congress were elected in November and not sworn in until the following March, four months later. In the interim, the lame ducks continued to run the government. That was the schedule that had been adopted in the eighteenth century, when communication was slow and changes took time. Communication today is so fast that even the two months or so between Election Day and the dates when the newly elected take office leave time for a limited amount of lame duckery, but the increased speed and immediacy of broadcast and press coverage makes for greater responsiveness to and by the public. And of course that is particularly true when you deal with a live audience. There is no canned laughter machine in this room and no mechanically augmented sound track. I am working from a script but you are not. I trust you will not make me a lame duck.

Today is the birthday of one of America's greatest heros. He was cheered longer and louder than virtually anybody of his time—and he never ran for office or made feminine hearts flutter or discovered a cure for a disease. His name was George Herman Ruth, possibly the outstanding baseball player of all time but something more—the epitome of irreverent, roistering, hail-fellow-well-met masculine America. On his birthday, it is worth remembering that America has a particular fondness for rough diamonds, for people who do whatever it is they do better than anybody has ever done it before. Babe Ruth's records have been broken. No record lasts forever, and a lot of young Americans today still harbor the dream of being the Babe Ruth of tomorrow. That is what I would like to talk to you about today—the constant and usually correct belief of the younger generation that they can do better than the heroes of their parents' generation. I have a few suggestions as to where they might concentrate their efforts.

FEBRUARY 7

John L. Sullivan won the last bare-knuckle heavyweight boxing championship, 1882.

Charles Dickens born 1812.

Sinclair Lewis born, 1885.

Introductions:

Back in 1882, in Mississippi City, Mississippi, on this date, the gentleman known as the Boston Strong Boy, John L. Sullivan, won the bare-knuckle heavyweight championship of the world by knocking out one Paddy Ryan in the ninth round. In later years the boys fought with their gloves on. Today I propose to make what I will call a bare-knuckle speech. I am taking the gloves off to speak to you bluntly and frankly on issues which deserve that kind of attention.

Today is the birthday of an Englishman and an American who were both writers, both adept at creating characters who personified attitudes of their times, both among the most honored writers of their time. One was Charles Dickens, who turned his spotlight on social conditions in nineteenth century England; the other was Sinclair Lewis, who did the same for the America of the 1920s and 1930s. They created characters who live forever—Fagan, Babbit, Pickwick, Elmer Gantry and many others. They had one particular quality in common; when they saw injustice, they tried to do something about it. It is in that spirit that I rise to speak to you now.

FEBRUARY 8

Birth of a Nation world premiere, 1915.

Jules Verne born, 1828.

Introductions:

Today is an anniversary for motion pictures—and I think it has a message for all of us. In Los Angeles on February 8, 1915, a motion picture that was to gain world fame as *The Birth of a Nation* had its world premiere. It was like no picture ever made before. It was a lot longer than most. Its director, D.W. Griffith, used camera and editing techniques that revolutionized the whole business of picture making. It dealt with a subject, the rise of the Ku Klux Klan in the South, that was controversial in an industry which had been spending its time trying to please everybody. It was priced higher than most motion pictures. And it surmounted all these obstacles—because it was made and marketed by people willing to take a chance on the power of their own imaginations. They did what a lot of people told them couldn't bé done. And it is that spirit that I want to talk about today. I think we should take a good look at some of the things that couldn't be done, but that we are doing anyway.

We like to say that fact is stranger than fiction. Maybe it would be more accurate to say that fact has a way of catching up with fiction. Jules Verne, who was born in 1828 on this day, was the king of science fiction in his time. He practically invented the form. He wrote about ships that traveled in the depths of the sea, voyages to the moon and to the center of the earth and other fantasies. Of course, they turned out not to be quite so fantastic after all. Today, it is very difficult to know what is fantasy and what is fact. I hope that tonight we can separate the fantasy from the fact, not in matters of science, but in regard to the way we live.

FEBRUARY 9

National Weather Service established, 1870.

William Henry Harrison born, 1773.

Introductions:

Today is the birthday of the National Weather Service, which was established as a unit of the U.S. Army in 1870. In honor of the occasion I am authorized to give a weather forecast for this room for the next half hour. The forecast is: Windy.

It probably is appropriate for a speaker on this date to take note that today is the birthday of William Henry Harrison, born in 1773 and the undisputed holder of the record for the shortest time in office of any U.S. President. He was inaugurated on March 4, caught cold and died exactly one month later. The moral for a speaker is clear: say what you have to say while you still have breath. So I will take a deep breath and begin.

FEBRUARY 10

Normandie capsized at pier in New York, 1942.

First singing telegram, 1933.

Free hand for the Gestapo in Germany, 1936.

Introductions:

It was on this day, the tenth of February, in 1942, that a former luxury liner from France named the *Normandie*, being converted into a troopship for World War II in New York, met its doom. It had caught fire the day before, and the firefighters poured tons of water on the flames. On February 10 it was so full of water that it overturned and capsized, like a beached whale on the New York waterfront. I suppose the moral is that if you water down something too much, it will end up totally destroyed. I have therefore tried to keep my remarks today—if not dry as dust—from becoming so heavy that they end up waterlogged.

It came as a great surprise to me to discover first that today was the birthday of the singing telegram, which began in 1933, and second to find that there are adults, perhaps some even in this audience, who never even heard of the singing telegram. For their benefit, let me hastily explain that a singing telegram was simply an arrangement whereby you had your message delivered in the form of a song—such as "Happy Birthday"—sung to your addressee instead of being delivered in an envelope. It was a cute idea, and it was popular for a generation or so; but now you can sing to anyone you want simply by placing a phone call. We are in an era of "speak for yourself." So I apologize. Instead of having John Denver or Barbra Streisand or your favorite performer sing my message to you, I stand here to speak it for myself.

There are many police states, where the gendarmerie or the secret police observe no law but their own. In 1936, on this date, that kind of power was given to the secret police organization whose name has been synonymous ever since with evil and repression, the German Geheimstaatspolizei, or Gestapo. It is worth remembering that this kind of gathering—and my remarks to it— probably could not have taken place under the rule of the Gestapo, because at least some of us would have been otherwise engaged. I say this not to add solemnity to my remarks or to your reception of them, but merely to start on the happy note that in this year of our Lord this very day is a lot better than it used to be.

FEBRUARY 11

Thomas A. Edison born, 1847. (Observed for some years as National Science Youth Day.)

Birth of the gerrymander, 1812.

Introductions:

Since today is the birthday of Thomas A. Edison, born in 1847 in Milan, Ohio, I suppose a speaker has a special obligation to be inventive. For some years, the occasion has been observed as National Science Youth Day, which sounds like a rather interesting invention itself. Youth is not a science and science is not a youth, but I am perfectly willing to go along with the celebration and wish a happy birthday to any science youth I happen to encounter. It seems to me, however, that essentially Thomas A. Edison was not so much a scientist as a man who was forever asking the question "why don't they . . . ?", except that the way he looked at things he was more likely to be asking "how can we . . . ?" I ask you all to consider adopting the same attitude. Today I propose to talk to you not about why we should do certain things but rather how.

Back on this date in 1812, the Governor of Massachusetts, a man named Elbridge Gerry, signed a bill setting district lines in his state. A cartoonist looked at the new district borders and drew a caricature that made the redistricting look like a salamander, since the borders were so strange. Combining the name of the Governor with the shape of the specially designed district, he came up with a new word. It was gerrymandering. It means distorting a natural contour to suit your own ends. And you can, so to speak, gerrymander a speech as well as an area. You can take a situation and pick and choose the borders that you propose to discuss. That is particularly easy when you have a complicated subject. But I prefer to address myself to what I believe is the central issue, the core question.

FEBRUARY 12

Lincoln's birthday, 1809.

Georgia Day.

Kosciusko Day.

General Omar N. Bradley born, 1893.

Introductions:

This is a very special day to many Americans. It is Lincoln's birthday. Honest Abe was born in 1809 in Kentucky. And if you come further south you may be observing Georgia Day today, the anniversary of the landing of James Oglethorpe in what is now Savannah, Georgia. If you are of Polish descent, you probably know that it is Kosciusko Day, marking the birth, in 1746, of a Polish patriot who fought in the American Revolutionary War. Many older miners remember today as the birthday, in 1880, of the man who built the United Mineworkers union, John L. Lewis. It is obviously a day for an upbeat speech about America, and I propose to proceed along just that line.

For many Americans, there is a special warmth about this day because it is the birthday of a man named Omar N. Bradley, General Omar N. Bradley, who was known as the G.I.'s general in World War II. Born in Missouri in 1893, he turned out to be one of the nation's most loved as well as longest lived top generals, and a plain and gentle man. If we are looking for the model of a dedicated public servant, we don't have to look beyond Omar Bradley. I would like to quote something he said in an Armistice Day speech in 1948: ". . . humanity is in danger of being trapped in this world by its moral adolescents." That is a pretty good springboard for my remarks today.

FEBRUARY 13

Boston Latin School founded, 1635.

First state university opened in North Carolina, 1795.

Introductions:

This is an important day for enlightenment in America. On this date, back in 1635, the oldest American public school, the Boston Latin School, began. This nation has been dedicated to free public education ever since. We have always wanted Americans to be educated people. We haven't always succeeded. But we started trying to educate young Americans a long time ago. I think we have a lot of room for improvement, after more than three hundred years of trying. For example, there are some elements of primary education on which I believe we could put a greater emphasis.

There have been many more changes in American higher education, I suspect, than in the elementary grades. When the first state university in the United States opened on this date in 1795—the University of North Carolina at Chapel Hill—not too large a number of our young men, and none of our young women, were able to go to college. There wasn't room, and most of them had jobs they had to do. We know that the college situation has changed. But I think we are not always up to date on what the college situation is, as of right now. It is high time we looked at the relationship between government and education. That is my subject today.

FEBRUARY 14

Valentine's Day

Malthus born, 1766.

Introductions:

I greet you on Valentine's Day, the celebration dedicated to lovers, greeting card companies and the people who sell those heart-shaped candy boxes.

Not accidentally, it comes smack in the middle of American Heart Month. I speak to you on the proposition that the heart is right just about as often as the head. My proposition is that when America acts for heartfelt reasons, the action is usually for the best.

It is interesting that Valentine's Day should be the birthday of the man who propounded one of the gloomier theses about life. Thomas Malthus, born in England in 1766, argued that population increases in a geometrical ratio, unless checked, while subsistence only increases in an arithmetical ratio. He argued that what he called "moral restraint," postponing the age of marriage, was the best way to prevent the supply of people from outrunning the supply of food. So on February 14, you have your choice of Valentine's Day romance or the "wait a while" counsel of that man born on this day so many years ago, Thomas Malthus. Who is right?

FEBRUARY 15

Battleship *Maine* blown up in Havana harbor, Cuba, 1898.

Galileo born, 1564.

Introductions:

I wonder how many people here remember the slogan, "Remember the *Maine!*" And of those who recognize the reference to the blowing up of the battleship *Maine* in the harbor of Havana, Cuba on this day in 1898, I wonder how many are convinced that it was done by the country with which we went to war thereafter, the Kingdom of Spain. We seem to have a need for a "last straw," an incident which finally brings on a war, even when there are other, better reasons for it. That, of course, is true of many vital decisions other than war. One startling murder can trigger better funding for a police force that has been needing money for years; one publicized good deed can win public trust for a figure whose private good deeds have been deserving of that trust for most of a lifetime. It took a whole parade of such "last straws," including boycotts and price rises and extreme shortages, to begin even to crack the wall of public indifference to the fuel problem. I would like to ask you today about a number of similar public problems that seem to be waiting for that "last straw."

On this date in 1564, Galileo Galilei was born in Italy. His story is as pertinent today as it was 400 years ago. When he developed the telescope to the point where he was able to observe the heavens, he was loaded down with honors. When he supported the theory that the earth revolved around the sun, he ran into trouble with the Inquisition, because the Church was still committed to the idea that the earth, not the sun, was the center of the known universe. The establishment is not always friendly to ideas which challenge presumed truth. We like to think today that we are much more tolerant than our forefathers. But are we?

FEBRUARY 16

Grant's demand for unconditional surrender, 1862.

Edgar Bergen born, 1903.

Introductions:

Some words, like some names, are far more dramatic and meaningful than others. When General U.S. Grant, on this date in 1862, laid down his terms to the besieged Confederate forces at Fort Donelson, Tennessee, the phrase became his nickname—and a yardstick by which the totality of victory has been measured ever since. After that day, U.S. Grant was known as Unconditional Surrender Grant. And nowhere is there a greater fondness for the idea of unconditional surrender than in the safe confines of the speaker's platform. Calls to fight until the unconditional surrender of the opposing forces on this issue or that are sometimes couched as calls for all-out campaigns, unconditional vigilance and so forth. Today I will ignore the search for unconditional surrender and talk in terms of perhaps more reasonable solutions. We face many issues where even a partial victory represents tremendous progress. Let me address myself to that goal now.

Edgar Bergen, who became a star entertainer, was born on this day in 1903. But that isn't why I stand here telling you about his birthday. Edgar Bergen did something not too many entertainers do. He contributed to the English language. When we refer to a Charlie McCarthy or a Mortimer Snerd, we are using names Bergen devised for his ventriloquist's act. The ventriloquist dummies he named were very different in personality, and their names have become synonymous with kinds of human behavior and human relationships. They remind me that the first obligation of a public speaker is simply not to be a Charlie McCarthy or a Mortimer Snerd when he gets up to speak. With that goal in mind, I clear my throat and get going.

FEBRUARY 17

Miles Standish made military captain of the Pilgrim colony, 1621.

Thomas Jefferson elected President on the 36th ballot, 1801.

Introductions:

Back in 1621, news was made this day by a gentleman named Miles Standish. Now you all know who Miles Standish was—or do you?—and so I will wager that most of you assume this was the day he sent John Alden to propose to Priscilla Mullen on his behalf. If Miles Standish is known at all today, it is because Henry Wadsworth Longfellow wrote a poem called "The Courtship of Miles Standish." But that isn't what happened on this day in 1621. As a matter of fact, it never happened at all. The poem was pure fiction; but Miles Standish was a very real character, and on this day in 1621 he was made the military captain of the Pilgrim colony in Massachusetts. Incidentally, he was married not once but twice. It is appropriate to mention this today, because it demonstrates how people can be remembered for the wrong things, and how, once set loose, a misconception can be more powerful and widespread than the truth. Today I am here to set a few facts straight.

There is no confusion in the public mind, I dare say, about who Thomas Jefferson was or about his greatness. It may come as something of a shock to many Americans, therefore, to recall that, on this day in 1801, when Jefferson was elected the third President of the United States by the House of Representatives, that election came on the 36th ballot. Things which we take for granted as having come very easily were sometimes very hard-won indeed. So as we sit here in comfort and luxury, I think we should take a good hard look at the sacrifice and the effort behind our current situation.

FEBRUARY 18

First cow to fly, 1930.

"All we ask is to be let alone"—Jefferson Davis, 1861.

Introductions:

There are any number of earth-shaking events which we file away in our memories. Today marks the anniversary of an event that I think may very possibly have escaped the attention of every single person here. On this date in 1930, for the first time, it is recorded that a cow flew—or more exactly, a cow was taken for an airplane ride, and milked en route, in the middle west. The reasons for this high-flying dairy exercise are shrouded in the mists of time, but it just goes to show that people will stop at nothing to make a point. Let me assure you that my remarks today will be a little more down to earth.

When Jefferson Davis was inaugurated as the President of the Confederate States of America on this date in 1861, he said something which is as understandable and worthy of sympathy today as it was then. "All we ask," said the Confederate President, "is to be let alone." How many of us have felt that same way. Unfortunately, we live in times when it is increasingly difficult to be let alone. There seem to be less and less private compartments on this spaceship Earth. And so my subject today is simply this: In times like ours, what is there that we can call our own and nobody else's?

FEBRUARY 19

Copernicus born, 1473.

David Garrick born, 1717.

Introductions:

Did you ever stop to think about what the world today would look like to a man who lived 500 years ago? Well, I know of a man, born on this date in 1473, who might be surprised by this city but would not be at all surprised by the modern universe. His name was Copernicus, and it was he who founded the modern science of astronomy, the idea of the planets revolving around the sun. If it hadn't been for the concept that Copernicus propounded—and Galileo helped to prove—we might still be earthbound creatures today, there would have been no human footsteps on the moon and all the science fiction would be about events on earth. Life is a succession of building blocks, of one idea leading to another, and another, and another. That is why it is so important to encourage impractical thinkers as well as practical ones. For Copernicus's ideas, the sky was the limit. We need to encourage more of the impractical thinkers of today. Let me give you a couple of examples.

Acting is, of course, an ancient profession, only comparatively recently an honorable one. One reason for its being well regarded today is that David Garrick was born—in 1717, on this date. Garrick was not only the greatest actor of his time on the London stage; he made the theater a center of culture. He was an intimate of Dr. Samuel Johnson, and he is buried in Westminster Abbey. His career reminds us that it isn't what you do, but how well you do it, that makes the difference. I would like to speak out here today for a new emphasis on quality in what we do. My theme is: what can we do to promote pride in what we do?

FEBRUARY 20

John Glenn Day.

Anthony Eden resigned as Foreign Secretary of Great Britain, 1938.

Council of Economic Advisers established by U.S., 1946.

Introductions:

There are not too many people living in this country who can say there is a national day named after them, but today is such a day. It is John Glenn Day, proclaimed after John Glenn became the first U.S. astronaut to orbit the earth on this date in 1962. That trip took him a good deal less time than was subsequently required for him to get elected later to the U.S. Senate from Ohio. And John Glenn Day is a good time to remember that going into orbit is fine for a while, but you finally have to come down to earth. We have been in orbit for quite a while on some pressing national issues; now let's come back to earth.

Politics has been described as the art of the practical. It is not supposed to be a pursuit with much room for idealism; but on this day in 1938 a politician put idealism first. His name was Anthony Eden, and he resigned as Foreign Secretary of Great Britain in protest against Prime Minister Chamberlain's policy of appeasement toward Nazi Germany. It was a gallant gesture. There does not appear to have been any profound effect on international affairs, but a public display of conscience may have helped the esprit de corps of Great Britain in the hard days that were to come. One man's conscience is only symbolic. What counts is its effect on mass conscience. And there are many questions to be asked about the presence—or absence—of mass conscience in our troubled world today.

A note in passing. The Council of Economic Advisers to the President of the United States was established in 1946 on this date. Obviously that is why we have not had any economic problems since then. When considering the proliferation of government agencies, just remember that a camel is a horse designed by a committee. And now let us look at a few of our current camels.

FEBRUARY 21

First woman dentist, 1866.

U.S. Army versus Senator Joe McCarthy, 1954.

President Nixon visited Communist China, 1972.

Introductions:

I am speaking on a historic day. In 1866, on February 21, a lady named Lucy Hobbs graduated from the Ohio College of Dental Surgery in Cincinnati as the first American woman dentist. This made possible that most unusual of all events—a woman asking a man to open his mouth. In honor of that occasion, I am opening my mouth here today.

Today is the anniversary of one of the Army's most historic declarations of war. Declarations of war are not usually handled by the Army; they fight the wars that Congress declares. But in this case it was a war of ideas, not bullets. On this date, in 1954, the Army accused Senator Joseph R. McCarthy of browbeating Army personnel in his pursuit of his hunt for Communists. It was the Army accusation that led to the Senate hearings which in turn led to censure of the Senator and brought him low. It has become unfashionable to think of the U.S. Army as a defender of the rights of individuals. Like so many unfashionable ideas, perhaps it should be given some renewed consideration.

It isn't always what is done; it's who does it. That point was made clear to Americans on this date in 1972 when a man whose whole political career had been built on fighting communism journeyed in friendship to Communist China as the representative of the United States. The man, of course, was President Nixon, and it was generally agreed that only as ardent an anti-communist as he could have persuaded American anti-communists to sit still for this change of U.S. policy. It was a Southern or Southwestern President who got the Civil Rights program enacted by Congress. Perhaps we should ask ourselves when, if ever, issues will be decided on the issues themselves, rather than by force of personality or because of trust in a particular leader. Certainly we are confronted today by issues which should not depend on who is carrying the flag.

FEBRUARY 22

Washington's Birthday.

Popcorn anniversary, 1630.

Introductions:

Today is Washington's birthday. It may not be observed as a holiday on this date every year because we like to have our national holidays on Mondays so as to have long weekends. But that doesn't matter because George Washington was not really born on February 22, 1732, anyway. When he was born, the country was still on the old calendar. He was actually born on February 11; but then we adopted the Gregorian calendar, which added 11 days. After many years of celebrating his birthday on February 11, Washington himself finally changed it to February 22. I mention this so that you will understand that the old timers had some options we no longer enjoy today. Having your choice of birthdates was a minor option. You also had a lot of empty land to build a farm on, if you wished. You could go to sea. You couldn't take a plane, or a truck, or a railroad train. But it seemed to be a time of much more hope for free men. Perhaps we should ask ourselves why.

America is a collection of folkways and family recipes that, put together, make up a way of life. One of the ingredients was given to us by the Indians on this date in 1630. That was when the redmen introduced the Pilgrims to popcorn. Things have been popping ever since.

FEBRUARY 23

Siege of the Alamo began, 1836.

Electrolytic process for manufacture of aluminum invented, 1886.

Birthday of Rotary Club, 1905.

Iwo Jima flag-raising, 1945.

Introductions:

This is, so to speak, a flag-waving day for Americans. As a matter of fact, it is literally a flag-waving day in American history, for on this date, in 1945, the famous picture was taken of the Marines raising the American flag at Iwo Jima. The picture, taken by Associated Press photographer Joe Rosenthal at the height of the fighting on that embattled Pacific island, was the inspiration for the Iwo Jima monument in Washington, outside the Arlington National Cemetery. And it represents a spirit of valor which continues as an inspiration to all of us today.

Valor is a tradition not at all unique to America; nor is it a unique American custom to hand down from one generation to another the key words which recall a particularly epic incident of courage. Today is the anniversary of the beginning of a siege in the city of San Antonio in 1836, a siege which millions of Americans continue to be reminded to remember. Inside was a small band of determined men. Outside was a Mexican Army. The place was the Alamo. The gallantry of the defenders of the Alamo is well remembered. And we Americans have many Alamos to remember.

Sometimes a thing is so commonplace and ordinary today that we pay very little attention to its birthday. That is certainly the case on February 23, which happens to be the birthday of Charles M. Hall's invention of the electrolytic process which made possible the manufacture of aluminum. If you stop to think of it, that invention probably played a very real part in making possible the aviation industry—because aluminum was so light a metal—as well as creating a whole new generation of pots and pans. Charles Hall went on to make a fortune from his invention, but he is one of a vast army of relatively unsung Americans—though infinitely better rewarded than most of them—who have made this world better for their presence. Making the world better, of course, is everybody's business, and it is done in many ways.

One way that people try to arrive at a common cause is through regularly meeting together to discuss common problems or voice common concerns. On this date in 1905 a small group of businessmen in Chicago organized a club that now is worldwide and that has become a recognizable community institution. It is called the Rotary Club. I don't know how many Rotary Clubs around the world have met how many times and heard how many speakers since it all started on this day in 1905; but for public speakers what happened on that date has certainly helped provide a great many more platforms.

FEBRUARY 24

Supreme Court in *Marbury v. Madison* ruled an Act of Congress unconstitutional, 1803.

Honus Wagner born, 1874.

Introductions:

One of the glories of our American heritage is that we have a Constitution which is so unquestionably the supreme law of the land. Over the course of generations, we seem to have come to believe that it was ever thus. But the fact is that we owe a great deal of the supremacy of that law—and the resultant stability of our governmental system—to a court decision which was handed down on this date in 1803. The case was *Marbury v. Madison,* known to legal scholars everywhere and studied at school but largely forgotten by the rest of us. In that case, for the first time, the Supreme Court voided an Act of Congress because the law that Congress had passed was in violation of the Constitution. This case not only established beyond doubt that the Constitution was supreme but also crystalized the power of the Supreme Court to rule finally on what was or was not Constitutional. So today's anniversary is a landmark worth remembering and a fitting introduction indeed to a consideration of where we are today.

In the early days of professional baseball, when it was laying claim to the title of America's national pastime, there were some very accomplished and colorful players who became popular heroes. Not too many of them carried over into later years. Some remained simply as legends, but there was one who, long after his playing days were over, was a familiar figure in the great ballparks. His name was Honus Wagner; he started playing professionally in 1895, was the only infielder of the five immortals first named to the Baseball Hall of Fame, and was active in baseball as a coach until the World War II era. Honus Wagner, who spanned baseball from its stone age to modern times, was born on this date in 1874. His career reminds us that we may not be as far away from our beginnings as we sometimes think. We would have a hard time today finding the equal of his record as a fielder or a hitter or an all-around player. Maybe we should examine what in America gave rise to the Honus Wagners and how we can do it again.

FEBRUARY 25

Income Tax Amendment to Constitution went into effect, 1913.

Enrico Caruso born, 1873.

George ("Beatles") Harrison born, 1943.

Introductions:

Today is an anniversary which prompts no great celebration, but is very much worth noting. On this date, in 1913, the Sixteenth Amendment to the U.S. Constitution went into effect. The Sixteenth Amendment authorized the income tax. It reminds us that the helping hand of government has been known on occasion to help itself. None of us works alone. We all have Uncle Sam as a partner. I doubt that the authors of the income tax ever had any idea of the size of the bite that such taxes would ultimately take. We know about the bite; but how is it being digested?

Seventy years apart, two men were born on this date whose careers invite an interesting comparison. One was Enrico Caruso, born in Italy in 1873, perhaps the most famous opera singer of all time. The other was George Harrison of "The Beatles," born in England in 1943, one of the four members of a singing group that did more to change popular music than any performers in history. "The Beatles" and Caruso moved in far different musical worlds, but they had in common a strong integrity about doing their jobs their own way. They sang with gusto; they believed in what they were doing. Both Caruso and Harrison—the latter much earlier in his career—became cult heroes, so to speak. The moral seems to be that it is fine to sing for your supper but it is best to sing in your own way—and ultimately, whether in an opera company or a pop quartet, the individual is bound to emerge. We put a tremendous emphasis on teamwork, but as we look at the world around us we depend to a great extent on individual stars. That is as true today as ever before.

FEBRUARY 26

Napoleon escaped from Elba, 1815.

Buffalo Bill born, 1846.

Introductions:

On this very day in 1815, Napoleon Bonaparte, who had been exiled to the island of Elba after his reign as self-made Emperor of France, escaped to begin the war that climaxed at the Battle of Waterloo. In one hundred days, countless lives were lost, and when it was over, Napoleon was back in exile, permanently, on another island, St. Helena. It seems to be the destiny of humankind to be very hard to convince. Ambition and the lust for power die very hard. That can be seen around us today as surely as when Napoleon's legions were reforming for their last futile battle.

Today is Buffalo Bill Day. Buffalo Bill Day "ain't what it used to be." In his time, Buffalo Bill, or Colonel William F. Cody, to give him his full name, was a symbol of the old west, the wild west show, the thrills of the frontier. It didn't matter that a lot of what he presented was purely show business—it was the original cowboys and Indians show, and it gave not only Americans but the whole world a thrill and a circusy idea of what America was like. Buffalo Bill Cody was born on this day in 1846. With some help from an ingenious press agent named Ned Buntline, who dubbed him Buffalo Bill, he made the American west glamorous and adventurous and postponed for three or four generations most public review of the ethics or the wisdom of our relationships with the Indians. Among other things, Buffalo Bill claimed to have killed some 4,280 buffaloes, which would also not endear him to us now. So, if we want to consider where we are today, we might look at a hero of the day before yesterday named Buffalo Bill and make some comparisons. Maybe we have made more progress than we think.

FEBRUARY 27

Reichstag fire, 1933.

Henry Wadsworth Longfellow born 1807.

John Steinbeck born, 1902.

Introductions:

The world, Shakespeare wrote, is a stage; sometimes events are staged in that world on a scale and with consequences that boggle the mind. One such event occured on this day in 1933 in a Germany that had seen Adolf Hitler ushered in as Chancellor of a politically divided nation where his Nazi party did not as yet command a convincing majority. On this day, the Reichstag building, symbol of Germany's fragile democracy, was burned; the Nazis promptly denounced the fire as a Communist plot, went in for a show trial of Communist leaders and sought to inflame the people with the imminence of a Red threat as an excuse for giving dictatorial powers to Hitler. The verdict of history is that the fire was much more likely set by the Nazis themselves, through a dimwitted dupe or two. Life is a theatrical exercise; we must always try to look below the surface of events and examine possible motives. So I shall speak to you today not only about what seems to be happening, but about why.

When we look at America today, what we see is not only what is before our eyes but also the images that have been bequeathed to us. Few have given us more such images than a poet who was born on this day in 1807 in Portland, Maine. Henry Wadsworth Longfellow gave us *Hiawatha*, "The Wreck of the Hesperus," *Evangeline*, "The Courtship of Miles Standish" and "Paul Revere's Ride," among the many word pictures he painted. Longfellow wrote of a different world and a different America than we have today; but his concepts still affect our thinking. On his birthday, I can't help wondering how he would view his country today.

John Steinbeck was born on Henry Wadsworth Longfellow's birthday, but 95 years later. Times had changed. Longfellow wrote of the distant past and contributed to American mythology. Steinbeck wrote of the present. His masterpiece, *The Grapes of Wrath*, told the story of the dispossessed Okies of the Depression and dust bowl era. It has been compared in impact to *Uncle Tom's Cabin*. It not only became a part of history; it helped to make history. Not too many of us can capture and record our own times as Steinbeck did in that book; but on his birthday we can certainly follow his model and take a long, hard, searching and—I hope—compassionate look at our world.

FEBRUARY 28

Bachelors Day in non-leap years.

Geraldine Farrar born, 1882.

Introductions:

Today, traditionally, is Bachelors Day three years out of four. In leap years, the bachelors' day is the 29th. I mention Bachelors Day only for histori-cal reasons, of course; in the old sense, the idea of the observance is as old-fashioned as the bustle. Bachelors Day was drawn from the idea that only once every four years—later made once a year—was it proper for a lady to take the initiative and propose to a man. In those bygone days, it was also understood that what was proposed was marriage. Period. As I said, times have changed; and with a sigh for the uncomplicated world of Bachelors Day, I proceed to ask you to join me in looking at the world as it is, regardless of what it used to be.

American patriots seem never to make much of the birthday of Geraldine Farrar, born on this date in 1882. But I think the occasion deserves to be noted, because Miss Farrar became so glamorous an American opera star. Even in America, there was an ingrained prejudice against American opera singers. Even after Miss Farrar, some American singers felt it necessary to change their names to sound Italian in order to be accepted on the operatic stage. Geraldine Farrar paved the way for the end of a senseless prejudice. That is a pretty good reason to remember her. And on her birthday, it carries a lesson for all of us.

FEBRUARY 29

Leap Year Day (Bachelors Day).

President's National Advisory Commission on Civil Disorders warned of ra-cism, 1968.

Introductions:

This is a most unusual day. We get a February 29th only once every four years, so we had better make the most of it. Years ago, it was commended to single females as the day they could make the most of by proposing to the bachelors instead of waiting for the men to make the move. You can see how times have changed!

In 1968, this was the day when the President's National Advisory Com-mission on Civil Disorders, established to find out why such disorders were plaguing the nation and what could be done about the problem, issued a report. I would like to read a brief quotation from that report. It said: "Our nation is moving toward two societies, one black and one white—separate and unequal." What would a similar commission say today?

MARCH 1

First U.S. census authorized, 1790.

Baby Charles A. Lindbergh, Jr. was kidnapped, 1932.

U.S. Peace Corps established, 1961.

Introductions:

Did you ever stop to think how much of what we do depends on counting? Today is a good day for that thought, because it is the anniversary of the authorization of the first U.S. census in 1790. We have been counting heads ever since, to determine Congressional districts, to allocate government money, to figure out unemployment rates and so forth. But counting is a part of every phase of life, from baseball—three strikes you're out, four balls you walk and so forth—to commercial payment terms like 2 percent off for payment in ten days. So much of life is arithmetical that, particularly in the computer age, the time seems to have come to ask whether the number is not taking over from the person.

Americans like to think that vicious, senseless kidnapping is more characteristic of overseas societies than of our own. Today reminds us otherwise. On this date in 1932, a baby named Charles A. Lindbergh, Jr., the son of one of our great aviation heroes, was kidnapped, only to be found dead a short while later. The trial of the man accused of that crime became somewhat of a Roman holiday, and was conducted in an atmosphere of revulsion at what many people then thought had been the crime of the century. Unfortunately, we learn over and over again that horror can always top—or bottom—itself. We live in a world where we have not yet solved the question of how to defend mankind from itself. Are we any further along than we were when the nation prayed that little Baby Lindbergh would be found alive?

John F. Kennedy was a man of charm and wit, martyred tragically before he had completed a term as President. Probably his most notable monument for many years was not a collection of papers or a noble building but rather an idea which survived him and was known throughout the world. It was the Peace Corps, born on this date in 1961. Years later, when Jimmy Carter went to the White House, one of the things which commended him to voters was that his mother, when in her sixties, had been a Peace Corps volunteer in India. The Peace Corps, unlike other American help abroad, was not a flow of supplies from a rich nation to poorer ones; it was, literally, a helping hand—it was people who went abroad to share their know-how; to work side-by-side with native farmers and teachers. It is good for us to remember this day as the anniversary of a notable characteristic of Americans—giving of themselves.

MARCH 2

Hayes-Tilden election decided by special Commission, 1877.

Vietnam peace treaty signed in Paris, 1973.

Texas Independence Day, 1836.

Introductions:

I wonder what present-day editorial writers would say if the people had voted in an election back in November, and nobody had been able to decide by now who had been elected, and a special commission finally decided which votes to count and which ones to throw out. That is a somewhat oversimplified account of exactly what happened up to and including this date in 1877, when a special Electoral Commission declared Rutherford B. Hayes elected as President over Samuel J. Tilden. That was only a dozen years after the Civil War; it could hardly have been described as a long era of peace and tranquility. It was an era, however, when people seem to have been more patient. There may be a lesson for all of us in the way the nation of 1877 dealt with what could have been one of the most divisive events in our history.

How did you feel on this day in 1973? You may wonder why I ask that particular question, until I tell you that on this date in 1973 the United States, the Viet Cong, the North Vietnamese and the South Vietnamese signed a peace treaty in Paris that ended so many bloody years of a far-off bloody war—a war that divided America, prompted riots, affected elections and, to a frightening extent, disaffected a substantial fraction of a generation. Before we judge the efforts of current diplomats in the uncertain international arena, we might look back to March 2, 1973 and ask ourselves what we thought should have been done then, and whether we now, in the perspective of history, think we should have done something else. As we ponder the future, let us remember the past.

I have never been certain of what degree of coincidence was involved that on the very day when Sam Houston celebrated his 43rd birthday, Texas declared its independence. The Lone Star Republic ultimately became the Lone Star State of the United States. Sam Houston served as President of the Republic of Texas and then 14 years as the senator from Texas, only to go into retirement when his opposition to the secessionist movement led to his political downfall. That he influenced the original independence movement is beyond doubt; but important as he was in bringing that about, he was not able to stem another political tide a quarter of a century later. There is a lesson in this for every working politician. The public does not forever vote for old heroes. New generations of issues bring new generations of statesmen; and the wisest leaders know not only when to stand firm, but also when to move with the times. Take our own times, for example.

MARCH 3

"Star Spangled Banner" became national anthem, 1931.

Alexander Graham Bell born, 1847.

Introductions:

"The Star Spangled Banner" was written in 1814. On this date in 1931, 117 years later, it officially became our national anthem. Acts of legislative bodies sometimes lag considerably behind public sentiment and public practice. I imagine everyone here today could recite a list of laws or actions that Congress long since should have gotten around to, and cite the delay as the reason for this or that problem still being with us. But I ask you to remember that we were using "The Star Spangled Banner" as our national anthem long before it became official. There is no law that says we have to wait for Congress to move before we tackle a problem through other means. We pride ourselves on being a nation of doers, on being able to work together voluntarily. Okay. We have plenty of opportunities to dig right in.

Today is the birthday of the man responsible for more conversation than anybody else who ever lived. He was born in Edinburgh, Scotland, in 1847 and he came to Boston as a young man to teach what he called "visible speech"—a sort of sign language—to the deaf. In the course of his work, he began to experiment with a device to transmit sound electrically. He finally made it work. Just seven days after his 29th birthday, his voice, saying "Mr. Watson, come here. I want you," was heard by his assistant, Mr. Watson, through a wire into another part of the house. The instrument was the telephone and the man was Alexander Graham Bell. Somebody once wondered whether if the inventor of the telephone had been named Alexander Graham Boom, the signal for an incoming call would have been a clap of thunder rather than a ringing bell. Joking aside, the telephone opened a new era for America—and for the world. It helped knit sprawling cities and the whole American continent together. It spawned new businesses. It created a new necessity for the American home. And it certainly changed life for teenagers. Today I ask you to join me in an affectionate but critical look at the age of communication that Alexander Graham Bell's invention ushered in.

MARCH 4

Presidential Inauguration Day, until 1937, when the date was shifted to January 20.

U.S. Constitution went into effect, 1789.

Knute Rockne born, 1888.

Introductions:

This is one of those days when a person who gets up to speak can deliver an entire speech of quotations from other, better speeches made in past years on this same date. Up until Franklin D. Roosevelt's second term, this was the date for the inauguration of the President of the United States. This was the date when FDR told the nation, "The only thing we have to fear is fear itself." That was in 1933, with banks closing and the great Depression grinding us down. This was the date in 1861, on the eve of the Civil War, when the new President, Abraham Lincoln, said: "This country, with its institutions, belongs to the people who inhabit it. Whenever they shall grow weary of the existing government, they can exercise their constitutional right of amending it, or their revolutionary right to dismember or overthrow it." Yes, that is precisely what Lincoln said. If there is one paramount thread in the inaugural addresses, it is that the people ultimately decide their own destiny. That is a pretty good text for our own times.

The instrument the founding Fathers designed to make this government of ours work is called the Constitution of the United States. It went into effect on this date, March 4, in 1789. It has been challenged; it has been amended, but it has remained, ever since, as the supreme law of the land. Yet, time after time, when various clauses or amendments of the Constitution are the subject of public opinion polls in which the people are not told that the concept is in the Constitution, the public vote them down. This does not mean that the Constitution is at odds with the people. It does mean that the Constitution is not a weathervane nor a sometime thing. It stands as much as a bulwark against the passions of the moment as a protection against governmental encroachment. It was artfully written; sometimes both sides in a dispute cite the Constitution as proving they are right. Today I would like to talk about some of the lesser-known aspects of this remarkable document, such as its recognition of scientists and writers.

It isn't quite as fashionable today as it was 50 years ago to regard the United States as a melting pot, forging a unity and sense of common purpose among immigrants from all corners of the world. But today is the birthday of an immigrant who has come to epitomize America—maybe to some, middle America. The immigrant I have in mind was born in Voss, Norway, on this date in 1888. He came to this country with his family when he was five years old. He went to college and became a chemistry instructor, as well as assistant coach of the football team. His name was Knute Rockne. If anyone can be said to have revolutionized American football and put it on the map, it was this man, Knute Rockne of Notre Dame. What Knute Rockne did for America in his time, I am sure, is being done now, or will be done soon, by newer immigrants. We have only to look around us to see that the melting pot is still cooking.

MARCH 5

Boston Massacre, 1770.

Winston Churchill's "Iron Curtain" speech, 1946.

Introductions:

This is the date when, in 1770, British troops fired into a crowd of unruly Bostonians in what became known as the Boston Massacre. The event is widely regarded as having been a prelude to the American Revolutionary War which broke out five years later. In light of later developments in the world, it is interesting to know that five men died in the Boston Massacre. At the battle of Lexington, where the Revolution started, eight men were killed and ten were wounded. In Belsen and Auschwitz, thousands were killed; even when the gangsters perpetrated the St. Valentine's Day massacre in Chicago in 1929, the death toll was higher than in 1770 in Boston. But massacre, like so many other words in our language, is a relative term. It can refer to the coldbloodedness as well as the volume of slaughter. It is a reminder that mere numbers are not the measure of good or evil. It is also a reminder that in some ways we hold human life much cheaper today than our forefathers did.

When we look back at the past, we have captions for significant events that summarize a whole array of concepts in a simple phrase. Probably no phrase has been a more eloquent summary of an attitude and an era than the expression used by Winston Churchill in a speech in Fulton, Missouri, on this date in 1946. "From Stettin in the Baltic to Trieste in the Adriatic, an iron curtain has descended across the Continent," Churchill said. For a generation, at least, the Iron Curtain separated two hostile camps in an uneasy world. It didn't start with Winston Churchill's speech; but that speech helped crystallize the realization that we were confronted with a breach among the allies of World War II. When and how the age of the Iron Curtain comes to an end has been a concern of most of the world ever since.

MARCH 6

Alamo Day.

Michelangelo born, 1475.

Introductions:

Today is Alamo Day. Down in Texas they don't have to be reminded to remember the Alamo. For the rest of us, a reminder may be in order. On this day in 1836, the Battle of the Alamo ended with the entire garrison wiped out by the victorious Mexicans. In the end, it was a pyrrhic victory for Mexico, because Texas won its war for independence, and in the process made a battlecry that lives in history. The Alamo brought greater glory to its defenders, in the long view of history, than might have been theirs, perhaps, if they had won their battle. What inspires human beings is not simply victory; it is the conviction that what they have done, whether successful or not, has been done nobly in a righteous cause. It matters not that the other side may be just as firmly convinced of the righteousness of its cause and the nobility of its performance. This is something we have a tendency to forget or to overlook. I suggest that as we contemplate some of our current challenges, we try putting ourselves in the other fellow's shoes. Occasionally, it is helpful to remember the other guy's Alamo.

Some people leave their mark on the world in the shape of ideas; some in the form of deeds; some seem to leave no mark at all. But few have left behind as great a mark of genius as a man who was born on this date in 1475. His name was Michelangelo. What he left behind includes the dome of the great Church of St. Peter's in the Vatican, the immortal statue of David in Florence, the glorious figure of Moses, the glorious altar wall and ceiling of the Sistine Chapel. Michelangelo thought of himself basically as a sculptor; but he was a man with the courage of his ideals who brought new realism, in heroic proportions, to the world of the arts. If very few of us can hold a candle to Michelangelo, we can at least remember—and emulate—his dedication to the truths in which he so strongly believed.

MARCH 7

Burbank Day.

Capture of Remagen Bridge, 1945.

Introductions:

Today is Burbank Day. To youngsters, it may seem that we are honoring a city in California, which is a measure of the briefness of fame. Burbank Day is the birthday of Luther Burbank, the horticulturist who developed over 200 varieties of fruits and vegetables, as well as any number of hybrid flowers. He was one of the forerunners of the so-called "green revolution" of our times. Strangely, people who work to get better crops from the land never seem to enjoy the lasting fame of those who lead fighting men into battle or win elections. Perhaps it would be refreshing for us here today to look at the gentle art of growing things as it exists in the world today.

Every step in world history, it has been said, is another building block on the eternal road. Sooner or later, every road at one time or another becomes a bridge, enabling us to continue moving forward. Today, in a very real sense, we remember a bridge—the bridge at Remagen, Germany. On this date in 1945, the U.S. Ninth Armored Division captured the bridge across the Rhine

at Remagen. It was not only a dramatic feat of valor; it helped speed the
victory over a stubborn foe in World War II. And the men who captured the
bridge had one rare privilege. They knew quite well how important an
achievement it was. All too often, there is no way at the time of knowing the
real importance of what we have done—or for that matter, the real unimpor-
tance, depending on the circumstance. We have only to look at some recent
events to realize the way our sense of history can sometimes be off-target.

MARCH 8

Oliver Wendell Holmes, Jr. born, 1841.

Arnold Schuster killed in Brooklyn, 1952.

Introductions:

When the man who was to become Supreme Court Justice Oliver Wendell
Holmes was born on this date in 1841, his name was already famous—because
he was Oliver Wendell Holmes, Jr., son of the doctor and author who was one
of the great literary figures of New England's golden age. Oliver Junior chose,
like so many sons of famous fathers, to walk a different path. His world was the
law. On the Supreme Court, during his long tenure, he became as famous for
the brilliance of his dissents as for the power of his judgments. Like his noted
father, he was a brilliant writer. Like his father, he was long-lived. He served
on the Supreme Court for some 30 years. He resigned from the Court when he
was past 90. I begin today's remarks by quoting something which should be a
watchword for every speaker, something he wrote in 1919. ". . . the best test
of truth," said Justice Holmes, "is the power of the thought to get itself accepted in the competition of the market." That is the competition I propose to
enter here and now.

Not too many people today recognize the name of Arnold Schuster. He
was the law abiding citizen who recognized a legendary bank robber named
Willie Sutton, told the police, and was later shot and killed in Brooklyn, in
1952, on this date. His murder was never solved, and I dare say it discouraged
many other law abiding citizens from turning criminals in to the police. One of
the unsolved problems of our time is how adequately to protect, let alone
compensate, those who at the risk of their own welfare give public aid to law
enforcement agencies. Time and again we read of cases where a good Samaritan ends up in the hospital or on welfare while the suspected criminal he helped
apprehend is happily out on bail. The question is not whether to abridge the
rights of the accused, but rather how to aid those who find themselves victims.

MARCH 9

Amerigo Vespucci Day.

Benjamin Franklin's creed, 1790.

Introductions:

Today is Amerigo Vespucci Day, marking the anniversary of the birth, in 1451 in Florence, Italy, of the man after whom America is named. I don't pretend to understand why America is named after the first name of Signor Vespucci whereas Columbus, Ohio, for example, is named after the last name of Christopher Columbus. But it is hard to imagine the United States of Vespucci. So we start off this day with a feeling which I hope will be strengthened by my remarks, namely that no matter how things are, they could have been worse.

On March 9, 1790, toward the last days of a long and incredibly productive life, Benjamin Franklin took pen in hand and wrote a letter to the Reverend Ezra Stiles, who had asked about Dr. Franklin's religious beliefs. I am grateful to the Reverend Stiles for asking, because Franklin's answer is so appropriate today. "I believe in one God," wrote Ben Franklin, "Creator of the Universe. That he governs it by his Providence. That he ought to be worshipped. That the most acceptable Service we render to him is doing good to his other children."

MARCH 10

First words spoken over a telephone, 1876.

Defenestration of Jan Masaryk, 1948.

Introductions:

Some words gain immortality because of their eloquence, but there was nothing very eloquent about the few words a young Scottish teacher of the deaf spoke on this day in Boston in 1876. Yet they live on, and when I repeat them, you will probably know why. The young Scotsman said, "Mr. Watson, come here. I want you." Do you recognize them? Of course you do. They were the immortal words that were first spoken over a telephone. And the young man who spoke them, to his assistant at the other end of a wire connection, was Alexander Graham Bell. I must in all honesty admit that, while I will have more than Alexander Graham Bell to say tonight, it will not be anywhere nearly as earth-shaking.

There is a question mark that hangs over this day of the year. It goes back to 1948, when the late Jan Masaryk, son of the founder of the Republic of Czechoslovakia and a champion of democratic self-government, was the anti-communist Foreign Minister of his country. He died when he fell from a window in Prague. Many believe, but have not conclusively proved, that he was pushed. Certainly his sudden and tragic death made it easier for the Reds to consolidate their control of the nation. History is full of mysteries that in themselves seem minor but that can, when and if solved, throw considerable light on larger matters. We, in our own present time, face some of these mysteries—why certain people behave as they do in certain situations, why this leader or that chooses to make a mountain of some particular molehill. Even asking the questions reveals the extent of the puzzle.

MARCH 11

Blizzard of 1888.

Lend-Lease Law signed, 1941.

Introductions:

It is said of the weather that everybody talks about it, but nobody does anything about it. If you ask the average person what subject makes news more often than any other, chances are that you'll get some such answer as sports or crime; but the fact is that the subject that is news day after day is the weather. That was particularly true when the snow began to fall in the northeastern United States back in 1888. It snowed from March 11 to March 14 that year, piling up the white stuff in record proportions. The people who lived through it talked about it for the rest of their lives. And I suppose we do the same thing about the great events through which we have lived. Each generation up to now has felt that its great war topped, or bottomed, the wars of the past; each has thought its challenges were the most severe. We are no different in that respect from those who came before us. We look at the same world from different perspectives—not necessarily violently different, but certainly not the same. Let us try then to look at the world with some perspective other than our own.

On this day, in 1941, President Franklin D. Roosevelt signed the Lend-Lease Law, which was a device for giving aid to England and other nations fighting Nazi Germany in World War II without going to war ourselves. We might remember this the next time we equate neutrality and impartiality. Very often we describe ourselves as neutral when what we really mean is non-belligerent. There is a considerable difference between these two attitudes, and we should ask ourselves, as we face the world, on which issues we are really neutral, on which simply non-belligerent, and on which we are indeed mentally in a state of war.

MARCH 12

President Roosevelt's first radio fireside chat, 1933.

Nazis occupied Austria, 1938.

Introductions:

When our country was very young, the President was seen by the people only in the few places he had occasion to visit personally. As the nation grew, the Chief Executive was seen and heard personally by a relative handful of the electorate, but his picture and his words were carried in the nation's press. Then came Franklin D. Roosevelt. In 1933, on this date, he tried something new—a fireside chat, by radio, heard throughout the nation. Thanks not only to the pervasiveness of broadcasting but also to the charisma of FDR, the fireside chat began a whole new era for the Presidency. Ever since—and more so in the age of television—the President has been brought directly to the people. Perhaps today will not go down in history books as a key anniversary in the evolution of the democratic process, but maybe it should.

History is a chain of events; as we look back at it we find ourselves wondering what would have happened if this or that particular link in the chain had been broken. On this date in 1938, history might have been changed. That was the day when Adolf Hitler's Nazi Germany invaded Austria and set about what they called Anschluss, the incorporation of Austria into Germany. It shocked the world—but the world did nothing about it, and Hitler, emboldened, went on to further aggressions that climaxed in World War II. We will never know whether the chain of events could have been broken on March 12, 1938; whether the democracies could have dissuaded Hitler with something stronger than mere words of protest. And so we must ask ourselves, I suppose, at every hour of decision, have we stood up as strongly as we might for what we believe is right.

MARCH 13

World standard time established, 1884.

First Uncle Sam cartoon, 1852.

Introductions:

As I stand here before you, the clocks all over the world are synchronized. It isn't the same time everywhere, of course, but we can look at our clocks here and know exactly what time it is in Singapore or Moscow or Timbuktu. We've only been able to do that since 1884, when an international conference on this date in Washington, D.C. established a world system of standard time, based on Greenwich Mean Time. I wonder what would happen if such a conference, for such a purpose, were called today. Would there be a third world coalition demanding that the base time be moved from Greenwich, England to some spot in a have-not nation? Would the whole idea be denounced as a plot of this or that coalition of powers? Would a vast bureaucracy be created—or at least sought—to administer a complicated set of agreements and regulations? And how long would it take to settle matters? After all, where time is concerned, time is no object.

Uncle Sam is our favorite relative, and a figure of admiration or hate for most of the world. Uncle Sam, as you may know, has been around a long time—but not as long as some people think. The lanky Yankee in the star spangled outfit was born in the issue of a New York weekly called *The Lantern* on this date in 1852. With variations to suit the times, Uncle Sam has been around ever since, but before he came on the scene the symbol for cartoon references to the nation was someone known as Brother Jonathan. We seem to be the only country whose national popular symbol is everybody's relative. I think that says something—and something rather good—about Uncle Sam, his nephews and his nieces. We are, in a very real sense, everybody's relatives.

MARCH 14

Albert Einstein born, 1879.

Eli Whitney received patent for the cotton gin, 1794.

Introductions:

Today is the birthday of Albert Einstein, who came into this world in 1879 in Ulm, Germany. Einstein's story points up quite a few morals. For one thing, the man who became one of the great thinkers of all time was not a particularly good student. He was not really a late bloomer, just an individualist who went at his own pace in his own way. He won the Nobel Prize in 1921 for Physics, a field in which he had created a tremendous revolution by propounding the theory of relativity. Einstein was a Jew, so when Hitler began the Nazi anti-Semitic era in Germany, Albert Einstein came to the United States, where he spent the rest of his life. And it was Einstein who wrote to President Roosevelt to persuade the President to start research on what became the atomic bomb. If there is any truth in our belief that right makes might, the story of Albert Einstein seems to bear it out. He was a man of peace, who helped unlock the key to the most terrible weapon of war the world has yet seen. He was a German whose own country turned him out, and he became one of the great assets of his adopted country. There won't be many Einsteins in our lifetime; but his story is one that we would all do well to remember.

This is the anniversary of the granting of a patent to Eli Whitney, who is remembered in history as the inventor of the cotton gin. The patent for the cotton gin, however, turned out to be one of the least rewarding items in Whitney's career, even though his machine, by greatly reducing the need for hand labor, had a tremendous impact on the development of the South. So many other people marketed cotton gins in defiance of his patent, that the bloom was off when he finally had his priority recognized years later. But, in the meanwhile, Eli Whitney had become the father of the idea of mass production, using the first primitive sort of assembly line and a system of interchangeable parts to manufacture muskets. Very few Americans have contributed as much to American economic development as the little known Eli Whitney. Next time you go to your mechanic to have the car fixed, you might stop and think of what would happen if Eli Whitney hadn't come up with the idea of interchangeable parts.

MARCII 15

The Ides of March.

Julius Caesar assassinated, 44 B.C.

Buzzard Day in Hinckley, Ohio.

Introductions:

The Ides of March are upon us. It was William Shakespeare who reminded us, "Beware the Ides of March." We used to think the advice was prophetic, because March 15, the Ides of March, used to be the date for filing and paying your Federal income tax. We now have an extra month for that delightful exercise. But there is enough in history to keep reminding us of the Ides of March.

Julius Caesar was the man who was told to beware the Ides of March, and it was an accurate warning. He was stabbed to death on that very day in 44 B.C. by a group including his friend Brutus. Being killed is bad enough, but having it done by a friend is even worse. I am not suggesting you had better check up on your friends, because, as Caesar said, the die is cast. Just remember the sage advice of Satchel Paige, a baseball player rather than a dramatist, who counseled, "Don't look back; someone might be gaining on you."

Nature has a clock more regular than the finest timepiece manufactured by man. And on nature's clock certain events happen every year at the same time. Today one such event is commemorated in the town of Hinckley, Ohio. It is worth mentioning because it shows the degree of tolerance which human beings have for familiar things—even things not usually regarded as attractive. In this instance, what we are talking about is Buzzard Day, when the buzzards are supposed to return to Hinckley. The town sets aside the first Sunday after this date as Buzzard Sunday. So let us remember, with an eye to the buzzards, that there is a time and place for everything.

MARCH 16

Law establishing U.S. Military Academy signed, 1802.

First liquid-fuel rocket flight, 1926.

Introductions:

On this date, in 1802, President Thomas Jefferson signed a law that established a great educational institution. It was—and is—the United States Military Academy at West Point, New York. Through its history, it has been far more than a military institute. We sometimes forget that, at a time when higher education was beyond the reach of all but a handful of Americans, West Point offered it on the basis of selection for merit. The long gray line of cadets produced great generals; it also produced men who performed distinguished public service as civilians. Presidents, college presidents, captains of industry—West Point nurtured them all. Its motto has on occasion been derided, but I commend it to your attention here and now—duty, honor, country.

It was in 1926, on this date, that the first liquid-fueled rocket was flown. It happened at Auburn, Massachusetts, and the man responsible was Robert H. Goddard, the pioneer of rocket flight. Ironically, not too much attention was paid in this country to Goddard's work—although many years later the Goddard Space Flight Center was named after him. But if the United States in the 1920s and 1930s was not interested in rocketry, another country was. When World War II was raging, Germany—with a young man named Wernher von Braun pushing the development of Goddard's idea—used buzz bombs and other rocket missiles as weapons of war. After the war, von Braun came to the U.S. and helped guide our historic space program; so Dr. Goddard's idea finally blossomed into full flower in his homeland after all. But the story of what happened after this historic day in 1926 reminds us that we have not always been as ready to accept change, as ready to work on new ideas, as we like to think.

MARCH 17

St. Patrick's Day.

National Gallery of Art opened, Washington, D.C., 1941.

Introductions:

It will come as less than headline news that today is St. Patrick's Day. Few celebrations are as enthusiastic as those on behalf of the man who drove the snakes from Ireland. In Boston, a city rich in Irish-American tradition, the date, by happy coincidence, also is Evacuation Day, marking the British evacuation of that city in 1776 in the American Revolutionary War. It is a day worth noting because the bands march and pipes play not in memory of war but in fond celebration of a goodly heritage. We salute the wearers of the green and the greening of the wearers.

The National Gallery of Art opened on this date in 1941. It is a great treasure trove of art for the public to see and enjoy. But it raises a point. Like the Smithsonian Institution, its senior organization, it is a public museum originally made possible by private funds. In a nation which can find public money to set up all kinds of ventures, we have been singularly unable or unwilling to provide a publicly funded start for buildings and collections of art treasures. Art has never ranked high on our list of priorities. Maybe we should redo our list.

MARCH 18

North Atlantic Treaty Organization formed, 1949.

Grover Cleveland born, 1837.

Introductions:

It was four years after the end of World War II when the basic Western Allies of that conflict, the United States, Great Britain and France among them, formed the North Atlantic Treaty Organization on this date in 1949. NATO was a noble experiment—an attempt to share a common defense responsibility among the armed forces of a group of nations. To the amazement of many, and despite defections and dissensions, NATO lasted. It became a reality of international relations in its time, and the term North Atlantic was stretched considerably as a geographical definition. It certainly encourages us today to believe that if people want to get along and make common cause, they can, despite differences of language, geography and culture. Perhaps we ought to try to work out a domestic NATO here at home.

Grover Cleveland holds a unique place among our Presidents. He was the only man to be elected President for two non-consecutive terms. He was both the twenty-second and the twenty-fourth President of the United States. He was also the target of perhaps the most vicious campaign in American history, in the election of 1884. He was called the candidate of "Rum, Romanism and Rebellion," in a speech by a supporter of James G. Blaine that repulsed the electorate. As if that were not enough, Cleveland was accused of fathering an illegitimate child. He defused that campaign issue by admitting the charge. If you think that politics plays rough today, bear in mind the story of Grover Cleveland, born on this date in 1837 in Caldwell, New Jersey.

MARCH 19

The swallows return to Capistrano, California.

Earl Warren born, 1891.

U.S. Senate rejected League of Nations, 1920.

Introductions:

One swallow does not a summer make, but today the swallows bring a pretty certain sign of spring, in an area where spring is not that easy to differentiate from winter. This is the day when the swallows come back to the mission of San Juan Capistrano in California, according to the tradition. It is a tradition celebrated in legend and song by people who have never been within a thousand miles of Capistrano, but it helps remind them and us that spring is about to come. We are at the season when we begin to wonder what will be budding.

When Earl Warren was born on this date in Los Angeles in 1891, California was barely past its frontier days and the U.S. was, so to speak, still in short pants. Before he died, Chief Justice Earl Warren presided over two contrasting chapters in American history, that helped this nation to grow up. One was the case of Brown v. Topeka Board of Education, in 1954, in which the Supreme Court rendered the historic decision that banned racial segregation as public policy, and reversed the previously accepted idea of separate but equal facilities for blacks and whites. Justice Warren's other historic role was as Chairman of the Commission which investigated the assassination of John F. Kennedy and decided that Lee Harvey Oswald was an assassin who had acted alone. It was largely because of the tremendous prestige and integrity of Earl Warren that this decision remained so little questioned for so many years. Earl Warren was an example of one of America's most consistent products— integrity. His birthday is a welcome reminder that we have always had public servants who came from that mold—and we could always have used more.

In 1920, the United States Senate, on this nineteenth day of March, rejected the Treaty of Versailles and kept the U.S. out of the League of Nations. Some historians have contended that if the U.S. had joined the League there might have been sufficient international agreement there to prevent the second World War. That, of course, is moot. But today we mark the anniversary of the last time the United States saw fit to return to the policy of "no entangling alliances." Soon thereafter, perhaps inevitably, it became impossible for the U.S. to maintain a posture of isolation. Today, though, as in 1920, we are still debating where and how far the policy of the U.S. should be involved with international organizations.

MARCH 20

King George III succeeded to throne of England, 1751.

"Uncle Tom's Cabin" published in book form, 1852.

Introductions:

We are somewhat past the era in history when the disposition of a king helped determine history. The last king whose disposition affected us here in America was George III of England. He succeeded to the throne on this day in 1751. George III thought he could push the colonists around, and he found Prime Ministers who agreed with him. If he had not, we might all be British today. Like the late Mayor LaGuardia of New York, it may be said of George III that when he made a mistake it was a beaut. In pondering what nice things have happened to us since George's day, let us pause for a moment to remember—and to hope that stubbornness such as his will not do for our country what his did for England.

Jimmie Walker once said that he had never heard of a girl who was ruined by a book—a remark much quoted by enemies of all censorship. Today I call to your attention the anniversary of a book which helped write the ruination of a way of life. The way of life was slavery—which of course deserved to be gotten rid of—and the book was *Uncle Tom's Cabin.* Harriet Beecher Stowe had published it in serial form as a magazine series, but on this day in 1852 it appeared as a bound book. It played a major role in arousing sentiment against slavery. When we speak of a Simon Legree, we are still reflecting the influence of *Uncle Tom's Cabin.* So today is not without its very special meaning.

MARCH 21

First day of Spring.

Martin Luthor King, Jr., led civil rights march from Selma, Alabama, 1965.

Introductions:

It can be snowing or freezing but the calendar is very clear about it; today, give or take a few hours for a vagrant vernal equinox, is the coming of Spring. It colors our outlook, makes us generally a bit more optimistic, has us looking for the first buds. Maybe the calendar is smarter than we are. Maybe the idea of Spring in our hearts is simply good medicine after a long hard winter—or a short dull winter, for that matter. What kind of Spring can we look forward to?

On this day in 1965, the Reverend Dr. Martin Luther King, Jr., led a civil rights march out of Selma, Alabama, headed for Montgomery. It was neither the first, nor the last, nor the most unusual instance of the leadership of this remarkable man. But on the first day of Spring, there is a special note of hope in recalling that out of bad situations America has always seemed to find inspirational leaders like Martin Luther King. What he had as his dream is still a goal for us today—the brotherhood of man and the age of peace.

MARCH 22

Edwards Law outlawed polygamy in U.S., 1882.

First American non-aggression treaty, 1621.

Arab League formed, 1945.

Introductions:

In 1882, on this date, the guardians of public morality breathed a sigh of relief with the adoption of the Edwards Act which outlawed polygamy. It was aimed at dissident Mormons who were clinging to that sect's earlier belief in the idea of multiple wives. If you think back to 1882, it was a time when nice people did not talk about sex, women didn't have very many rights and the opponents of polygamy were convinced that they were striking a mighty blow for morality. The solution adopted in our own times has been a different version of multiple wives—or husbands. To phrase it in electrical terms, it is now done in series instead of in parallel. A human is apt to have more than one mate, but not two at the same time. Whether that is an improvement in morality I leave to your own judgment—the judgment, however, of the community rather than of the individual. Morality changes with the times, but there is a constant dispute between those who think they are with it and those who think they are beyond it. We are in that kind of dispute today.

If I mention the words non-aggression treaty you probably imagine I am going to talk about some piece of modern diplomacy. No. I am talking about the first such agreement in America, which was made on this date, in 1621, between Governor John Carver of Plymouth and Chief Massasoit of the Indians. As such agreements go, it was a pretty good one. It lasted half a century. If we can do as well today, we should be happy.

The Arabs are a great force in the world and they go back a long way in history. It may come as a surprise, therefore, to know that it was only in 1945, on this day, that the Moslem countries of the Middle East organized the Arab League. Unity among the Arab states, as we are reminded every now and then when it seems to come apart at the seams, is a comparatively recent development—not quite what the world had in mind when Israel came into being. We have a tendency to confuse recent developments with age-old traditions, so it is well to remind ourselves that some of those traditions are not quite as old as the ages.

MARCH 23

World Meteorological Day.

Patrick Henry's greatest speech, 1775.

Introductions:

When the Reverend Dr. Martin Luther King, Jr., said, on this day in 1964, that "We must learn to live together as brothers or perish together as fools," he was voicing what we must regard as the spirit which lies behind the observance today of World Meteorological Day by the members of the United Nations. Meteorologists and weather experts know that, regardless of lines on maps or walls that separate the nations, we are all sharing the same cycles of weather. The storm that starts in one country ends up in another; one land's heat wave is another land's drought—and so forth. Nobody yet has found a way of fencing in the air we breathe. Let us keep that in mind on World Meteorological Day—and all year long.

On this day in 1775, at the Virginia convention, a fire-breathing lawyer named Patrick Henry rose and spoke the words that generation after generation of Americans would remember as the heart of our national heritage: "Is life so dear," asked Patrick Henry, "or peace so sweet as to be purchased at the price of chains and slavery? Forbid it, Almighty God ! I know not what course others may take, but as for me, give me liberty or give me death!" Spoken on this day in 1775. Do we say less today?

MARCH 24

Robert Koch announced discovery of the tubercle bacillus, 1882.

Thomas E. Dewey born, 1902.

Introductions:

If it were just because this was the day Robert Koch announced the discovery of the bacillus that caused tuberculosis, in 1882, March 24 would be a significant day of the year. Dr. Koch's discovery, one of many this great German doctor made, paved the way for saving many lives. But above all, it showed the need for using the skills of science to isolate the microorganisms that bring so many other diseases. If the anniversary of Dr. Koch's discovery can give us the message to encourage those scientists who are exploring the microscopic unknown, it will be a day well worth remembering. We have a tendency to ask that scientists work on that which is immediately practical; but today's impracticality is the hope of tomorrow.

Thomas E. Dewey was born on this day in 1902 in Owosso, Michigan. He was renowned as a prosecutor of crime, as Governor of New York State and as twice a candidate for the Presidency of the United States; but he will probably be best remembered in history for Election Night, 1948, when at least one great newspaper, *The Chicago Tribune*, was so sure of the outcome that they printed an edition declaring Dewey the victor over Truman. So Mr. Dewey's birthday comes as a reminder not to be too sure—any time—of what you think is a sure thing.

MARCH 25

Triangle Shirt Waist fire, 1911.

Gutzon Borglum born, 1871.

Introductions:

It is a sad fact of life that some things that need doing are not done until a shocking event awakens the conscience of the public. That comes to mind particularly now because today is the anniversary of the great Triangle Shirt Waist Company fire in 1911. The Triangle fire in a crowded New York factory resulted in the death of 147 people, who had been working in disgraceful sweatshop conditions. The labor laws and factory building codes were revised thereafter, following a great public outcry. But it took a disaster to bring the reform. Are we doing better now?

It is one of the ironies of history that sometimes the work of men is well known while the men who did the work are forgotten. Probably every American has heard of or would recognize a picture of the Mount Rushmore National Memorial, the huge faces of Washington, Lincoln, Jefferson and Theodore Roosevelt carved from a natural rock mountain in South Dakota. But how many of us know, or indeed care, that this was the inspiration of Gutzon Borglum, one of the greatest and certainly the most monumental of American sculptors? Gutzon Borglum was born in Bear Lake, Idaho, on this date in 1871. As we ponder the glories of America let us not forget the people who made those glories real.

MARCH 26

Prince Kuhio Day.

Commercial motion picture film first manufactured by George Eastman, 1885.

Dr. Salk announced a polio vaccine, 1953.

Introductions:

What Prince served in Congress? That's a question that might stump some of the experts, unless they know something about today, which happens to be Prince Kuhio Day. Prince Kuhio Day is Hawaii's commemoration of the birthday of Prince Jonah Kuhio Kalanianaole, who represented the early Territory of Hawaii as a Delegate in the United States House of Representatives. Hawaii, it is worth noting, is the only State that once had its own royal family. Prince Kuhio Day is a reminder that American roots go back to many strains and many levels, in many different parts of the world.

Among the things we take for granted these days, few seem simpler than a roll of film. But on this day back in 1885, a man named George Eastman created a communications miracle by manufacturing the first commercial motion picture film. We all know what happened thereafter—how the ability to photograph motion pictures of great dramas and of breaking news events helped create a communications revolution. That's what can happen with a simple idea. Indeed, most of the progress in the world has come not from complicated concepts that were difficult to comprehend but from simple ideas. And so today I want to talk in simple, basic terms.

It was on this day, in 1953, that Dr. Jonas Salk announced the development of a vaccine against polio. The Salk vaccine had a stringent test ahead of it, but this was the day when a long-sought victory against dread infantile paralysis at last appeared likely. If nothing else had happened on this day throughout history, that one event would still make it a day to remember. And it reminds us, very strongly, that for every problem there is ultimately a good solution.

MARCH 27

Marconi sent radio signals across the English Channel, 1899.

Washington signed act to build a U.S. Navy, 1794.

Wilhelm Roentgen born, 1845.

Introductions:

We live in the age of communication. In the past century or so, we have made it possible to communicate quickly with masses of people all over the world. On this day, in 1899, that sort of communication took a giant step forward when Guglielmo Marconi sent signals through the air on radio waves across the English Channel. This was one of the milestones in the march to the worldwide radio and television transmissions available today. As I talk to you today, ham radio operators and even citizen's band walkie talkies make a commonplace of Marconi's miracle. And in the age of communication, no speaker is really talking just to the group he or she faces; in the press, in films, in sound recordings or even video, the whole world can listen in . . . if the world wishes. But where there is no press or radio or television coverage, we also live in the sunshine age, where the best motto for any speaker is, if you have to go off the record, if you think you can keep what you say secret, your best bet is to keep your mouth shut. You may therefore be assured that since I am continuing to talk from this platform, what I have to say is not confidential, not off the record.

We live in an intrusive age. X-rays are used not merely in medicine, but also to examine luggage at airports. That may be a commentary on our times. It is appropriate today because today is the birthday of Wilhelm Roentgen, the man who discovered what was originally called the Roentgen Ray. In the long view of history, Wilhelm Roentgen, born on this date in Lennep, Germany in 1845, opened a door through which modern physics has enlarged its view and understanding of the previously unknown. If we have a better idea of what is going on, Wilhelm Roentgen is partly responsible.

The United States was born as a seafaring nation, and its naval victories began with the American Revolution. But after the Revolution, we had no Navy to speak of. On this day in 1794, President George Washington, an old Army man himself, signed the Act of Congress designed to get a Navy built. I am happy to cite that fine spirit of cooperation as the prelude to my remarks today.

MARCH 28

First washing machine patent issued, 1797.

Constantinople became Istanbul, 1930.

Introductions:

We like to think of our times as the great age of convenience—pre-cooked foods, convenient labor-saving devices. But it has been a long time coming. For example, it was way back in 1797, on this date, that the U.S. granted a patent to one Nathaniel Briggs of New Hampshire for a washing machine. It took more than a hundred years after that before electricity and human ingenuity produced the ancestor of the present-day machines. So my message today is one of patience. It takes time to go from the first primitive expression of a new idea to the final, perfected product.

Throughout history, cities and towns have disappeared with a stroke of the pen. They aren't destroyed. The buildings don't come down into a mess of rubble. They just change their names. You won't find St. Petersburg, Russia, on the map any more; but Leningrad is where St.Petersburg used to be. You may have misplaced Mauch Chunk, Pennsylvania—not an easy place name to misplace, to be sure, until it changed its name, in honor of a famous Indian athlete, and became Jim Thorpe, Pennsylvania. I mention this because, probably the most ancient city to go through a modern name change, changed its name on this date, in 1930. The city was Constantinople; it is now Istanbul. It just goes to show that the name is less important than what is underneath it.

MARCH 29

Last U.S. prisoners of war and armed forces left Vietnam, 1973.

Washington, D.C. residents won right to vote in Presidential elections, 1961.

John Tyler born, 1790.

Introductions:

This day is an anniversary worth remembering. It is the day, in 1973, when the last prisoners of war and armed forces from the U.S. left Vietnam. Today, before we crystallize our opinions about the policies now being followed by the U.S., we might get a better perspective if we try to recall how we felt before and after the exit from Vietnam. No time exists in a vacuum; we can judge the present only by the past.

Until 1961, there was a whole class of citizens of the United States, law abiding, literate and tax paying, who were denied the right to vote in Presidential elections—not because of their color, not because of racial or religious prejudice, but simply because they happened to live in the District of Columbia, rather than in a state. On this date in 1961, the Twenty-third Amendment to the Constitution finally let the people who live in the President's town help decide who should be President. Democracy sometimes takes a long time to pay attention to its own front yard.

Today is the birthday of John Tyler. If you don't immediately recognize why we should take note of that fact, perhaps it would help if I recall the phrase, "Tippecanoe and Tyler too." That's our John Tyler, born in 1790 in Greenway, Virginia. And the reason I want to take note of his birthday is that he was the first vice president to wake up one day and find himself the President of the United States. "Tippecanoe" was William Henry Harrison, who died one month after being inaugurated as President; John Tyler thereupon moved into the White House, but not with much enthusiasm manifest in the Congress. We have had all too much experience since then with sudden accessions to the Presidency, and so we should be grateful that the first time it became necessary, in 1840, a man born on this day some years before was there to make it work. And we should always remember that this country has always been able to get the job done.

MARCH 30

Seward's Day.

Beau Brummell died in poverty, 1840.

Lead pencil with eraser patented, 1858.

Introductions:

I am encouraged to start my remarks by noting that one of the wisest decisions—or luckiest ones—ever made was made on this day—or, more exactly, sealed on this day. Today is Seward's Day, marking the date in 1867 when Secretary of State William H. Seward completed the negotiations for the U.S. purchase of Alaska. The price was $7,200,000 and critics called it Seward's Folly. I hope you will join me in prayer that we may commit similar follies in our time.

And now a word to people who have trouble looking neat or keeping up with the fashions. On this day in 1840, the man whose name became synonymous with the last word in elegance, Beau Brummell, died in France—in poverty. There is hope, ladies and gentlemen, that sartorial splendor and good fortune do not necessarily go hand in hand.

What was the greatest invention? Some will say the wheel; some will nominate electricity. My own favorite is the invention which a man named H.

L. Lipman of Philadelphia patented on this date in 1858. It was so simple an idea that one is amazed it hadn't been developed sooner. Mr. Lipman patented the idea of a lead pencil with an eraser on the other end, attached. Any man who gives the world a chance to erase a mistake has got to be a public benefactor. I must tell you that I used his invention many times in composing my remarks for you today.

MARCH 31

Ten-hour government work day, 1840.

Treaty of Kanagawa opened Japan to U.S. trade, 1854.

Introductions:

Anniversaries are a convenient way of pointing up how times have changed. On this date in 1840, for example, President Van Buren established a ten-hour working day for government employees. You may choose your own comment on this landmark in the progress of the civil servant. I merely mention it as a backdrop for my remarks on the conditions of life today.

This is the anniversary of the Treaty of Kanagawa of 1854. You may not recognize the name, but most of you will recognize the event. It was the agreement that opened the ports of Japan to U.S. ships, the beginning of bringing Japan into closer touch with the Western world. One cannot help wondering what the history of the world might have been if the Treaty had never been signed, if Commodore Perry had stayed in the North Atlantic and if the transistor didn't work. The game of "what if . . ." is, of course, an endless one; but the story of the Treaty of Kanagawa tells us once again that when we open a door, we never know what is going to be coming through that door or when.

APRIL 1

April Fool's Day.

The House of Representatives finally achieved a quorum and went to work, 1789.

First wartime U.S. conscription law, 1863.

Introductions:

Today is a difficult day on which to be taken seriously. It is the day when a lot of calls come to the aquarium for Mr. Fish, and the practical jokesters go to town. It is hard to be serious on April Fool's Day. But I shall make the effort, secure in the knowledge that even on All Fool's Day life is not all foolishness.

I believe that the April Fool's Day tradition was very much alive in 1789, but it is an interesting point because on this date in that year, for the first time, the newly established House of Representatives of the United States was finally able to assemble a quorum and get down to business. It had taken them almost a month to get that far. I shall try to get down to business here today just a trifle more speedily.

The United States was not fooling around on April 1, 1863, during the Civil War, when our first wartime conscription law went into effect. By then we had fought at least three wars—if you count the Mexican War as a major one—on a volunteer basis. Conscription is, so to speak, a latter-day phenomenon in the United States. The foundations of our nation were built by volunteers. That is a spirit worth remembering in our own times.

APRIL 2

International Children's Book Day.

Ponce de Leon landed in Florida, 1513.

Congress authorized U.S. Mint, 1792.

Introductions:

Today is International Children's Book Day, which is observed on the birthday of Hans Christian Andersen, the great story teller who was born in Odense, Denmark, in 1805. Did you ever stop to think—and International Children's Book Day is a good time to think about it—that the most international of all forms of story is the children's fairy tale? The works of the Grimm brothers, Andersen, and Charles Perrault, who created the immortal world of children's literature, are as familiar to the English speaking world as they are in their native lands. What appeals to children, what is understandable to children, deals with basic emotions and simple confrontations. We have a tendency to talk down to children. But there is a difference between talking clear, talking plain and talking down. Today, in the spirit of clarity, I propose to talk plain.

On this date, in 1513, a Spanish explorer landed in what is now Florida, near the present-day city of St. Augustine. He was looking for the Fountain of Youth; it is an odd quirk that the land where so many older people go to retire should have been first explored in a search for the secret of youth. Today, more than 450 years later, we are still looking for the fountain of youth, even as our median age gets older and older. We are caught between two conflicting facts—one, that people still want to work, as they get older or enjoy the income they can only get by working; two, that apparently the only way to provide enough work for all our young people is to persuade older people to turn the work over to them. That, I dare say, is not what Ponce de Leon bargained for; but it is a situation which confronts us today.

Somebody once said that the thing that marks the difference between a government and a mob is that a government makes its own hard money. I guess from that point of view, today is a notable anniversary for us; for on this date in 1792, Congress authorized the establishment of the U.S. Mint. Ever since then, we seem to have been engaged in a dispute between those who thought we were running out of money and those who thought we could always mint more. As I address this problem before you today, I am afraid I cannot report any greater unanimity than heretofore.

APRIL 3

Marshall Plan enacted by Congress, 1948.

Washington Irving born, 1783.

Jesse James killed, 1882.

Bruno Richard Hauptmann executed, 1936.

Introductions:

I am speaking to you today on the anniversary of Congress's enactment of the Marshall Plan in 1948. The Marshall Plan, which provided billions of dollars for a European Recovery Program after World War II, was probably the greatest instance of enlightened national generosity in history. As we contemplate the goodness or badness of the American public in these times, it is well to be reminded of a record of international neighborliness which, I believe, has been matched by no other nation in the long history of mankind. Let us view our present situation against that heartening backdrop.

Today is the birthday of Washington Irving, that first great American author who invented Father Knickerbocker and the Headless Horseman and Rip Van Winkle, who told the story of Granada's glorious Alhambra to the world and who taught America to laugh at itself. He was born in New York City in 1783. As long as we can look at ourselves and at the world with the combination of good humor, imagination and wisdom which characterized the work of Washington Irving, we will be all right. And as I speak to you today, I shall try to avoid turning any of you into Rip Van Winkles.

There is an interesting contrast brought to mind by this day. It happens to be the anniversary of the killing of Jesse James in 1882 in St. Joseph, Missouri and the execution of Bruno Richard Hauptmann in New Jersey in 1936 for the kidnap-murder of baby Charles A. Lindbergh, Jr. By all accounts, Jesse James was a professional thief who did not hesitate to kill, yet he has become—and was, even in his own time—somewhat of a folk hero. Bruno Hauptmann was convicted amid a wave of revulsion for the crime, in a trial that was the Roman holiday of its time. If we are fascinated with the seamy side today, so were our parents and grandparents. The only difference is that today the seamy side is a much bigger business.

APRIL 4

Our briefest Presidency, 1841.

Rhodes scholarships established, 1902.

NATO became official, 1949.

Introductions:

This is the day when the shortest term of any President of the United States came to an end. William Henry Harrison died in 1841 after serving only 31 days as President. He was the first Chief Executive to die in office, and Vice President John Tyler was the first Veep to move suddenly to the White House. We have had all too many such changes since then. Tyler, indeed, was not only the first but one of the least blessed. He couldn't do a thing with Congress. Later Vice Presidents, like Teddy Roosevelt, Harry Truman and Lyndon Johnson, were a great deal more in command of the situation. Our system is somewhat different from that of other parliamentary democracies. We try always to have someone waiting in the wings. The only time that wasn't the case was when Richard M. Nixon's Vice President, Spiro Agnew, resigned; then Gerald Ford was named to succeed him. There was no thought then that this would lead him also to the White House. I have made these long comments about short Presidential terms, on the anniversary of the shortest, to emphasize that we always need a little something, or someone, as a spare.

On this day, in 1901, $10 million from the will of Cecil Rhodes, the British empire builder in Africa, was set aside to make possible that most coveted of awards to American college graduates, the Rhodes scholarship. Rhodes Scholars since then have come from every part of the country and every walk of life, and their studies in the great English universities have helped both nations to understand each other a little better. It has been suggested that we might explore the possibility of domestic Rhodes scholarships to help the disparate portions of our own nation understand each other better too. Today I ask you to consider with me how we can promote that kind of mutual understanding in our land, which needs it so badly.

The North Atlantic Treaty Organization, born a month earlier, became official on this date in 1949, when the Treaty was signed by the various nations in Washington, D.C. It was another of those ringing affirmations of human optimism that keep the peace for at least a little while; and it deserves to be remembered today in a world rather different from the simple days of 1949.

APRIL 5

First Presidential veto, 1792.

Booker T. Washington born, 1856.

Introductions:

For almost three years, the President of the United States had not taken a stand; but on this day, in 1792, President George Washington, for the first time, used his power to veto a bill passed by Congress. He rejected a measure dealing with apportioning the districts for representation in the government. It was a precedent for a President, and Washington's successors have been far less reluctant than he to use their veto power. Our system of checks and balances in government was designed to give each of the three branches some kind of governance over the other two. Whether this would have continued if the first President had not chosen to use the veto is something we will never know. On the anniversary of that first veto, our Congress and our people are not always willing to take no for an answer.

Today is the birthday of Booker T. Washington, born in 1856 as a slave in Franklin County, Virginia. Booker T. Washington pioneered in the education of Black Americans and was the first head of the famous Tuskegee Institute. He worked within the racially segregated structure of his time, and has been criticized by later generations for his willingness to accept segregation of the races as a way of life. Yet, in his own lifetime, he was an inspirational and progressive force for improving the lot and the abilities of American Blacks. His story is a graphic reminder that every generation sets its own standards not only for its own time but also in judgment for the past. Each of us is the creature of our own times. I dare say that what I am here to say to you today is not the same as what I might have said or you would have wanted to come to hear in Booker T. Washington's time; but that time was several days before yesterday, and we must look forward to tomorrow.

APRIL 6

First Church of Latter Day Saints (Mormons) organized, 1830.

Discovery of the North Pole, 1909.

U.S. entered World War I, 1917.

Introductions:

In the history of the United States, religious intolerance and persecution wrote a new and unhappy chapter as a result of the organization of a new church on this date, in 1830, in Seneca County, New York. It was called the Church of Jesus Christ of the Latter Day Saints, founded by Joseph Smith and known more generally as the Mormons. Driven from more than one community, the Mormons ultimately made a heroic trek across the continent to Utah, where they built a flourishing community. Today, Mormons are prominent in government and business, and they have maintained a religious community probably heightened by the remembrance of a now distant era of persecution. Out of adversity, we are reminded, comes strength—a good point to remember as we face our own problems today.

On this date, in 1909, Robert E. Peary and Matthew Henson reached, or discovered, if you prefer that word, the North Pole. They didn't really discover it because they knew it was there all the time. The whole world knew it was there. But for some time there was a good deal of doubt over who had reached it first. Dr. Frederick A. Cook claimed to have reached the Pole a year earlier, and it was a long time before Cook's claim was dismissed. Ever since, Peary's reaching the North Pole first has been a great story of successful American adventure. There is only one aspect of it that has been rather generally overlooked—recognized rather tardily even by our own government. That is the feat of Matthew Henson. If he was not the first American to reach the Pole—and he may well have been, if only a pace ahead of Peary—he was certainly the first Black American. Peary was in command of the expedition, but Matthew Henson was right there with him when they and their Eskimo associates reached the North Pole. As we contemplate what history we remember, we should spare a thought for the history that somehow gets overlooked.

History and April 6 have come together many times, none more meaningful than this date in 1917, when, for the first time, the United States entered a World War. World War I has faded somewhat alongside the more recent horrors of World War II, Korea and Vietnam, but it was our first war outside our own hemisphere (except for the Philippine phase of the Spanish American War). It was our first expedition into armed conflict on the soil of Europe—not a foray against the Barbary pirates, but a full scale overseas land and sea war. Whatever we accomplished was not enough. Looking back today on the anniversary, it would be nice to feel that it can never happen again, so that we can turn our thoughts to more peaceful pursuits.

APRIL 7

World Health Day.

Walter Winchell born, 1897.

John McGraw born, 1873.

Introductions:

This is World Health Day. It was established because the member states of the United Nations wanted to mark the anniversary of the founding of the World Health Organization in 1948. The World Health Organization is uniquely privileged; it is concerned with a subject which transcends national borders and the ordinary prejudices. Medical science does not usually consider its processes state secrets, does not wage economic warfare and does not hold human life to be merely a cheap and replaceable commodity. World Health Day is therefore a happy time on which to take a good look at the human condition.

The impact some people make is often misunderstood in their own time. That was probably true of a man named Walter Winchell, born on this date in 1897. In his time, which was really the 1930s and 1940s, Walter Winchell was probably the most influential columnist—in newspapers and on the air—in the whole world. But as a lasting influence, he made a contribution more as a maker of words than as a peddler of rumors. When we hear words like scram, or infanticipating, or people being "that way," or a couple having phfft or melted, or hear Broadway referred to as the Hardened Artery, or alcohol called giggle water, or dozens of other colloquial usages, we are reflecting a language that Winchell not only popularized but in large part invented. Some of his word usages, of course, have faded, but they will undoubtedly be resurrected. We may never again refer to divorce as Reno-vation, because you don't have to go to Reno, as you did in Winchell's heyday, to get an easy divorce. But referring to a wife as a squaw—while far more offensive now than in the Winchell era—is still quite clear. In the long view of history, what Winchell said was not as significant as the words he used to say it. I am not sure I would want my remarks here today to leave that same kind of mark. I hope my meaning will outlast my words.

When John J. McGraw was born on this date in 1873, baseball was a fairly new game of some popularity. John McGraw helped more than probably any other single man to make it not only the national pastime but to spread its fame and charm around the world. He was a fine player, but his greatness came as a manager. He not only developed championship teams and trained disciples who also became outstanding managers; he led the New York Giants on several international tours—in 1914, for example; he wrote books about the game and he created a whole standard of conduct for the playing field, combative, arguing with umpires, running his ball club with the iron hand that earned him the nickname of "Little Napoleon." We were probably fortunate that his passion was baseball, not politics. Is there room today in life for the John McGraws. Or are we playing by a new set of rules.

APRIL 8

Oleomargarine anniversary.

Consecration of first synagogue in New York, 1730.

Introductions:

We live in the era of synthetic foods. Today may be its birthday. On this date, in 1873, a patent was issued to a man described as the first successful manufacturer of oleomargarine. Within a year, laws to protect dairymen against the competition of the substitute for butter were being put on the books, but oleo persisted. If there is a market for a product—or for an idea— you need more than a set of laws to stamp it out. With that preliminary observation, let us proceed to talk about some of our problems which are not synthetic, but very very real.

Even people who are tolerant of differing ideas sometimes find it attractive to be a little intolerant as well. In New York City there was a Jewish congregation in the 1650s, but they were not permitted to build a place of worship. Only in 1730, on this day, were they able to consecrate their synagogue, the temple of Congregation Shearith Israel, better known today as the Spanish and Portugese Synagogue. Freedom of worship took a while, in colonial America, to make it all the way. Even after the enactment of the Bill of Rights, later on, it was, for a time, an uphill fight. Maybe that is what makes this basic freedom one that people are still so willing to fight for.

APRIL 9

Bataan Day.

Lee's surrender, 1865.

Astrodome, 1965.

Introductions:

Today is Bataan Day. It does not commemorate a great U.S. victory. It commemorates the surrender of the U.S. and Philippine defenders of the Bataan peninsula, on the island of Luzon, to the Japanese in World War II. It stands as a reminder of gallantry against overwhelming odds—something always very well worth remembering. It is events such as this which sometimes help more than victories to forge the bonds of loyalty and dedication among Americans—and thereby make it possible for us to work together in a common cause.

America's great leaders are generally remembered for their hours of triumph. Today we remember one who was great in defeat. His name was Robert E. Lee, and it was on this day in 1865, at Appomattox Court House in Virginia, that he surrendered his Confederate Army to General U. S. Grant. Lee had been one of the great military leaders of all time. He proved also to be a great leader in peacetime; his living memorial today is Washington and Lee University in his home state of Virginia. In defeat, today was still his shining hour—an anniversary to remind us all to look upward, not down.

When future historians try to figure out when the great American sports explosion really took off, they may start with this day in 1965. That was when the Houston Astrodome opened in Texas—a huge stadium with a roof. It was this idea of making mass spectator sports impervious to the weather that made big time sports an unassailable year-round institution. Now the only challenge remaining is the same one I face here with you today. The physical surroundings are fine. The job is to supply the quality product.

APRIL 10

Patent law, 1790.

ASPCA chartered, 1866.

Buchenwald liberated, 1945.

Introductions:

This is an important day for the man who builds a better mousetrap. On this date, in 1790, the first U.S. patent law was approved. Inventions could now be protected against piracy. Nobody has a patent on honesty, but a property right to the results of human inventiveness and ingenuity is one of the things that has helped build this nation. It is even possible for me to copyright the remarks I am about to make to you here today. Whether I do so is highly moot. It may be determined by your reaction. Don't say you haven't been warned.

The love affair between humans and domestic animals is an old, old one. It is therefore a little surprising to know that only in 1866, on this date, did enlightened New Yorkers get a charter for a new organization called the American Society for Prevention of Cruelty to Animals. But the fact is that mistreatment of animals, particularly cart horses and beasts of burden, was so commonplace that it wasn't even regarded as being particularly cruel. There are those today who believe, and can argue convincingly, that the ultimate cruelty to animals is to breed them, or permit them to breed, irresponsibly and to fail to give them the decent homes that pets need. Cruelty, though outlawed in one form, is apt to surface in another.

Cruelty is not peculiar to one era and absent in another. Three quarters of a century after the birth of the movement to stop cruelty toward animals, the victorious Allies in World War II came upon the horror of the concentration camps run by the Nazis. Today, in 1945, one of the earlier discoveries took place at Buchenwald, Germany. In the concentration camps were found piles of corpses, as well as the living skeletons who survived, crematoria, gas chambers, paraphernalia which made the middle ages look like kindergarten. On this day, civilization discovered that barbarism was more barbaric than ever. We like to think this taught us a lesson. Are we still pleading that we do not know about contemporary cruelties, or that there is nothing we can do about them?

APRIL 11

Jackie Robinson broke the major league color barrier, 1947.

Truman removed MacArthur from Korean War command, 1951.

Introductions:

It was an inter-league exhibition game between the Brooklyn Dodgers and the New York Yankees, in 1947. Ordinarily, exhibition games don't make history, but this one did. On this date, in 1947, Jackie Robinson played for the Dodgers. It was the first time a black baseball player had been a member of a major league team. Jackie Robinson went on not only to break the color barrier but to become one of the legendary competitors of the game. It all began on this day of the year—which makes this a good day to talk about America as a land of opportunity.

There have been enough traumatic events in the conduct of the American presidency to remind us that it is a position of awesome responsibility. It is well described in Harry Truman's phrase: "The buck stops here." On this day, in 1951, the buck stopped with a vengeance. That was the day when President Truman removed General Douglas MacArthur from command in the Korean War. They had been in a dispute about the limits of American action in that war. The civilian President, as commander in chief, removed the popular American hero from his post. MacArthur came back to a hero's welcome, spoke before a joint session of Congress and told the nation that old soldiers never die, they just fade away. But the power of the Presidency did not fade away. And so today brings another reminder that those who are elected, not those who are commissioned, bear the ultimate responsibility of government.

APRIL 12

Civil War began, 1861.

Franklin D. Roosevelt died, 1945.

Salk vaccine declared safe and effective, 1955.

Introductions:

Fort Sumter stands in the harbor of Charleston, South Carolina. A long time ago, on this day in 1861, it was the hub of history. The Confederates fired on the Union garrison in Fort Sumter, and the Civil War began. As we think of that bloody fratricidal conflict, I feel we are all determined that, no matter what the differences among Americans today, violence and war cannot be the answer.

Sadness is not a pleasant state, but it has one redeeming virtue. It seems to bring people together. That was certainly the case on this day in 1945, when President Franklin D. Roosevelt died. FDR was a popular President, but he also had as fierce an opposition public as any Chief Executive of modern times. They never even called him the President. They referred to him as "that man in the White House." But when he died, with World War II still going on, the whole nation mourned. The new President, Harry Truman, came into office on a wave of common dedication to carry on for FDR. It may be that, instead of remembering how we began to bicker at the peak of success, we should approach our present challenges by remembering how we came together in the face of sorrow.

There is one field of human endeavor which has a record of virtually uninterrupted progress. That field is medicine, where we are always learning how to save more lives and heal more wounds. Today is an anniversary in the field of medicine. On this day, in 1955, Dr. Jonas Salk's anti-polio vaccine was declared safe and effective after being tested. One of the most dreaded killers and cripplers of childhood had at last been tamed. Undoubtedly, as I speak here today, other doctors in other places are contributing to the development of new preventives and new cures for other diseases. If we could do as well with the diseases of society as with the physical diseases of humanity, we would be making progress indeed.

APRIL 13

Thomas Jefferson born, 1743.

Metropolitan Museum of Art founded in New York, 1870.

Introductions:

This is a birthday party. It is Thomas Jefferson's birthday, and any time Americans meet freely to hear an uncensored comment by someone exercising the right to speak his mind, we are reaping the rewards for an event which took place in Shadwell, Virginia in 1743. Thomas Jefferson was the principal author of the Declaration of Independence and of the concepts embodied in the Constitution and the Bill of Rights. That is why his birthday is everybody's celebration.

The Metropolitan Museum of Art in New York City is world famous now for the magnificence of its collections and exhibitions. It was founded on this date in 1870, when America was considered an art backwater. The idea that a museum in the United States would turn out to be one of the greatest in the world seemed, at the very least, a bit overambitious in 1870. But it worked. That kind of thing can still happen. My remarks to you today are based on the unalterable conviction that people are not simply at the mercy of whatever happens; people can make things happen.

APRIL 14

Pan American Day.

Lincoln shot, 1865.

S.S. Titanic hit an iceberg, 1912.

Introductions:

Today is Pan American Day. In the context of recent times, perhaps I should make clear that it is not a day to criticize, or pan, Americans. It is a day designed to remind us that we are not the only Americans; that in South, Central and North America there are many nations. Pan American means we are all Americans. On this date, in 1890, nations of the Western Hemisphere joined to found the Pan American Union. We need to be reminded every now and then, it seems, of the spirit of the Good Neighbor, as President Franklin D. Roosevelt put it, or the Alliance for Progress, as John F. Kennedy saw it. Under any title, it is important for us to look North and South, as well as East and West, in our international relations. Pan American Day is a good time to let our camera pan around and remind us of our longtime neighbors.

There are a number of real-life tragedies which have been favorite subjects of drama. Two of those subjects are events which occurred on April 14. In 1865, President Lincoln went to Ford's Theatre for an evening of relaxation as the Civil War was ending. John Wilkes Booth went to the theatre that night too. Need I recall the rest?

Years later, on this same date in 1912, a great new luxury liner, on its maiden trip across the Atlantic from England to New York, struck an iceberg. The ship was the Titanic. There were, of course, many good events that also occurred on this date, but somehow they do not charm our sense of drama in the same way.

President William Howard Taft started the custom of having the Chief Executive throw out the first ball to start the major league baseball season on this date in 1910, little dreaming that the nation's capitol wouldn't even have a team in later years. Tonight, however, I propose to wipe the slate clean; to ignore this date's dubious history, except for the birthday of the Pan American Union, and to share with you an impression of what our current way of life must look like to someone unaware of past history.

APRIL 15

U.S. income tax filing day.

Lincoln died, 1865.

S.S. Titanic sank, with loss of more than 1500 lives, 1912.

Leonardo da Vinci born, 1452.

Introductions:

Some years ago, a gentleman with a penchant for designating special days and weeks announced that April 15 from that point on was to be known as National Hostility Day. Things were bad enough historically for good old April 15 without that designation. After all, it is the day when President Lincoln died of the wound inflicted by assassin John Wilkes Booth in 1865. It is also the day when the Titanic, mortally wounded by an iceberg the previous night, sank with a loss of more than 1500 lives in the icy North Atlantic in 1912. But that was not the whole of it.

It turned out that the reason for dubbing April 15th National Hostility Day was something else. This is the day that your Federal income tax has been coming due for many years. Consequently, it is a day of ill feeling for many taxpayers who feel put upon indeed. Therefore, we have National Hostility Day. There are exceptions, of course; and I sincerely trust that this room is full of people who are *not* observing National Hostility Day and who have all worked things out so as to get a nice fat tax refund.

In case that cheerful prospect is not realistic, I hasten to assure you that April 15 has also had its good things. For example, it is the day on which there was born, in the city of Vinci in Tuscany, a man named Leonardo—Leonardo da Vinci. The world is a great deal richer for having had a versatile man of genius like Leonardo in it. And so today I address you cheerfully. And if you can't do any better, at least give me a Mona Lisa smile.

APRIL 16

Rush-Bagot agreement ratified by Senate, 1818.

Bernard Baruch saw "a cold war," 1947.

Introductions:

This is an interesting day in American history. It is a study in contrasts. In 1818, on this date, the U.S. Senate ratified the Rush-Bagot agreement between the United States and Canada, which was the basis for the creation of an unfortified border between the two nations and the peaceful relationship which has existed ever since. There are all too few peace agreements which work; this one has. It is one of the reasons why our country has grown so notably, and why we have so rarely been afflicted by what has been called the fortress mentality. If every now and then we feel beleaguered, we have the comfort of knowing our longest border is a friendly one.

On this same day that brought the foundations of peace to the north in 1818, another situation entirely was announced in 1947. Bernard M. Baruch, the adviser to Presidents, made a speech on this date in 1947 to the South Carolina legislature in which he said, "Let us not be deceived—we are today in the midst of a cold war." Some have contended that this was not so much a diagnosis as a self-fulfilling prophecy; but my point is that while a peaceful border is one alternative to a shooting war, another alternative in recent times has been what the Baruch phrase so well describes, a cold war. Unfortunately, we have a tendency to attack some of our problems, at all times, as if we were fighting a cold war when we should be fighting a hot one. I am not talking of armed conflicts. I am talking of the vigor and strength with which we face our problems.

APRIL 17

Verrazano Day.

Bay of Pigs adventure ended in Cuba, 1961.

Birthday of J. Pierpont Morgan, 1837, and Nikita Khrushchev, 1894.

Introductions:

I wonder whether many of you are aware of how much this day, April 17, is a day of contrasts. For example, take the subject of harbors. It may seem an unlikely subject, but let me explain. On this day, which is known in parts of the United States as Verrazano Day, Giovanni da Verrazano discovered New York Harbor. That was a happy day, back in 1524. Later on, in 1961, a venture into another harbor area proved less happy. This second area was the Bay of Pigs, in Cuba, where a U.S.-supported invasion force of Cuban exiles was totally defeated by the forces of Fidel Castro. Recalling these contrasting events, I give myself any number of oratorical doorways to proceed through today. I can talk about politics and international relations; I can discuss how much was brought to this country by the flow of people and goods through New York Harbor. Or, of course, I can leave you guessing for a little while longer.

Sometimes birthdays make strange bedfellows. That is certainly true of today, April 17. On this date, in 1837, was born a man who became the archetype of American ruthless wealth and capitalism on the march. His name was J. Pierpont Morgan. On this same date, in 1894, was born a man who led the Communist giant, Soviet Russia, in some of the most spectacular years of the cold war, Nikita Khrushchev. The symbol of Communism and the symbol of capitalism, sharing the same birthday. At least it can be said that April 17 is clearly a good day for strong people.

APRIL 18

Paul Revere Day.

First laundromat, 1934.

San Francisco earthquake, 1906.

Introductions:

Today is known in some parts as Paul Revere Day, thanks to Henry Wadsworth Longfellow. Longfellow didn't name the day, but he certainly embellished the legend. This is the day of what Longfellow described, in his great poem, as Paul Revere's ride with the message to Lexington and Concord that the British were coming in 1775. The fact was that Paul Revere, a distinguished and dedicated leader of the patriots, wasn't a lone star. He and William Dawes both made it to Lexington; Revere was captured by the British on the way to Concord, and Dawes wasn't. Perhaps Longfellow decided that Dawes was a harder name to rhyme than Revere. In any case, I believe that we should, in simple justice on this day, remember—as a symbol of the many Americans whose accomplishments are somehow overlooked—the name of William Dawes, who on a famous night, it's clear, had a longer ride than Paul Revere.

There are sometimes occasions which make a great impact on the life of a nation but remain relatively unnoticed. I would like to remedy one such omission today by saluting the anniversary of the opening, in 1934, of the first laundromat. The great American pastime of literally washing your dirty linen in public automatically was born on this day in 1934 in Fort Worth, Texas. It is indeed a glorious anniversary, and a fitting occasion to talk about cleaning up our problems.

The San Francisco earthquake of 1906 occurred on this date, and was followed immediately by the great San Francisco fire. It was almost as though Mother Nature had decided first to write a movie script and then to do a sequel. California unfortunately has had its share of natural disasters since then, but nevertheless remains, for most Americans, the golden land. Through the years, even the San Francisco earthquake has acquired a certain glamorous cachet—which leads me to the premise that the ingenuity of man is nowhere better demonstrated than in our ability to be fascinated by the unthinkable and to be unthinking about what fascinates us.

APRIL 19

American Revolutionary War started at Battle of Lexington and Concord, Mass., 1775.

General MacArthur's farewell speech to Congress, 1951.

Grace Kelly married Prince Rainier, 1956.

Introductions:

Today, it is often forgotten, is the anniversary of "the shot heard round the world." Forgotten, that is, except in Massachusetts, where the third Monday, rather than this exact date, is observed as Patriot's Day. On Patriot's Day in Boston they hold the annual Boston Marathon, whose connection with the American Revolution is otherwise obscure. It was on this day, in 1775, that the British troops from Boston were met in the square at Lexington by Captain John Parker and his armed farmers. "If they mean to have a war let it begin here," said Captain Parker. Historians now believe that the British did not mean at all to start a war, and that the start of shooting was not only unpremeditated but almost accidental. But men were killed, and the British moved on from Lexington to the Battle of Concord and "the rude bridge that arched the flood," where, as Ralph Waldo Emerson wrote, "once the embattled farmers stood, And fired the shot heard round the world." It is interesting that, on the anniversary of the beginning of the war for American independence, our world is more interdependent than ever.

Today marks two stirring chapters in the military history of America. One was the Battle of Lexington and Concord. The other was an old soldier's farewell. On this date, in 1951, General Douglas MacArthur, removed from his Korean War command by President Truman, addressed a joint session of Congress. He recalled the old song that old soldiers never die, saying, "like the old soldier of that ballad, I now close my military career and just fade away." Douglas MacArthur was a man of brilliance, about whom there was no middle ground. He aroused strong feelings, whether for or against him. His accomplishments were tremendous, but on more than one occasion they were accompanied or followed by controversy. What was indubitable was that he was one of the giants of his time. We do not seem to have many—if any—men of that stature around these days. And we could use some.

Life is not impersonal. We think sometimes in terms of storybook romance, and, on rare occasions, real life is like the storybook. That was the case on this day in 1956, when the glamorous Hollywood star and the royal prince were married. The star was Grace Kelly, the Prince was Rainier of Monaco. They were joined in holy wedlock in Rainier's principality and the whole world relaxed from the cares of the day to see a fairy tale come true. Unfortunately, real life fairy tales are not too plentiful. Instead, we seem to make up our own fairy tales and try to persuade ourselves that they are true. Today I address myself to some of the fairy tales which play important roles in our approach to life's problems.

APRIL 20

Asser Levy and Jacob Barsimson won right as Jews to full citizenship in New Amsterdam, 1657.

Adolf Hitler born, 1889.

Introduction:

History is full of ironies. Today we have one of the more striking contrasts. This was the date, in 1657, when Asser Levy and Jacob Barsimson won for Jews in New Amsterdam the right to full citizenship, one of the earliest victories in America's long battle for religious freedom. We sometimes are led to believe, mistakenly, that all the minority religions of America were Johnny-come-latelies; but the fact is that people of many faiths helped pioneer this land early on. The melting pot was not a nineteenth century invention, even though the pot got a lot more crowded by then. When we celebrate diversity and freedom, we are celebrating what this country has represented for centuries. It is our job to see that those ancient banners remain flying high.

Today, the birthday of freedom for Jews in America, is also the birthday of the worst enemy the Jews or the cause of freedom ever had. That is a broad statement, but when I mention that the birthday was of Adolf Hitler, born in 1889 in Branau, Austria, the irony becomes clear. In the records of history, it is quite possible that Adolf Hitler will turn out to have been responsible for more murders, including millions of Jews, than any other single figure of all time. But was it an accident that Hitler came to power in Germany? Could a country such as ours give rise to a Hitler? Let us not say it couldn't happen here. Let us not ignore the kind of conditions which make a Hitler possible.

APRIL 21

San Jacinto Day.

Projection of motion pictures demonstrated in New York City, 1895.

Introductions:

Today is San Jacinto Day, observed in Texas to commemorate the 1836 victory of Sam Houston's forces over the Mexicans at San Jacinto during the Texas war of independence. That victory came a month and a half after the fall of the Alamo; but I dare say a great many more people remember the Alamo than remember the Battle of San Jacinto. Victory is sweet, but heroism and sacrifice beyond the call of duty are memorable. The human spirit is our most lasting strength. That fact is well to remember, particularly in the dark moments before ultimate victory. If each of us is true to the memory of his or her own particular Alamo, we too shall win the later battles.

When the motion picture was invented, it was a private sort of entertainment. You watched the figures move by peeping into a box where a huge wheel flipped one card after another, in much the same way as the little flip booklets that are still shown. The movies were known as peep shows, not so much because of the subject matter as because that was the way you saw them—by peeping into the machine. On this day, in 1895, it all changed. Woodville Latham demonstrated a process—though not a perfected one—of projecting movies onto a screen, making it possible for a whole group of people to watch the same picture at the same time. That was the key to a great new medium of mass communication. A lot of people had a hand in making modern motion pictures possible. They invented roll film, reliable light sources, and various cameras and so forth. A successful invention is usually made up of several inventions, not just one. And that is as true of inventions in the field of government or social welfare as it is of machines or physical processes. The question must always be, what do we need to make it work. Indeed, that is the question which, in times such as these, we must ask of our whole way of life.

APRIL 22

Army-McCarthy hearings went on television, 1954.

Birthday of Nikolai Lenin, 1870, and Alexander Kerensky, 1881.

Introductions:

The processes of American government have rarely been witnessed live by many of the American people. On this date in 1954, that began to change. The Senate hearings of the dispute between the Army and Senator Joseph R. McCarthy were broadcast on television. This real-life daily drama topped anything contemporary fiction had to offer. It gave the entire nation the opportunity to be eyewitness to history unfolding; and it made the court of public opinion mightier than ever before. It played a great role in the downfall of Senator McCarthy; but perhaps the greatest significance is that it made the politicians aware of how closely they could be watched through television. It gave new interest to the concept of the people's right to know. And it gave a theme for endless remembrance. Be careful—you never can tell how many people are watching. Ask yourself at all times whether you would behave the same way if the unblinking eye of the camera were fixed upon you. Thanks to television, we are not merely watchers of history—we are livers of history.

History, like politics, makes strange bedfellows. Today, for example, is the birthday of two leaders of post-Tsarist Russia. One was Alexander Kerensky, born in 1881, the leader of the moderate democratic government that displaced the Tsar in 1917. The other was Vladimir Ilyitch Ulyanov, better known by his adopted name, Nikolai Lenin, born in 1870, who led the Bolshevik revolution that overthrew the Kerensky moderates. Apparently the only thing these two Russian leaders had in common was their birthday. It is well for us to remember here today that no single man can truly be the personification of a nation. We are all individuals. Being born in the same place makes us no more alike than sharing the same day of the year as a birthday. We must be treated as individuals, not as castings in a mold.

APRIL 23

William Shakespeare born, 1564; died, 1616.

St. George's Day.

Introductions:

This is St. George's Day, honoring the patron saint of England. George was not an Englishman; indeed, there is no indication that he ever set foot in England. He seems to have been, in all likelihood, from the Middle East; it is thought that he died in Palestine around the fourth century. Hundreds of years later, he turned up as a saint whose name was invoked in England before the Norman conquest; and the stories about his slaying of the dragon arose hundreds of years later than that. Thus, there need not be any strong basis of fact to support the logic by which we choose particular figures to regard as our patron saints. Nor does it matter whether St. George was man or myth; he has come to embody an idea, a national heritage. And if we examine our own thoughts, we will find that each of us has our very own St. George. What is important is that, once having chosen a moral preceptor, we at least proceed to live by that preceptor's rules.

If there is one name that comes to mind as the giant of the written word, it is the name of William Shakespeare, who was probably born this date in 1564 and very definitely died on this same date in 1616. Every now and then, life itself manages to live up to Shakespeare's sense of drama and of history; and always, our own lives remind us, "All the world's a stage." Look around you at the heads of state and you see Hamlets, King Lears, Julius Caesars. You see many a comedy of errors and much ado about nothing. Shakespeare, ladies and gentlemen, is excellent training for the realities of life, the realities of life today.

APRIL 24

First regularly issued American newspaper began publication, 1704.

Soda fountain patented, 1833.

Introductions:

If there are any newspaper people present here today, I want to wish them a happy birthday—not for themselves, but for the institution they represent. The first American newspaper issued on a regular basis was the *Boston News Letter* which came out on this date in 1704. Newspapers have always done very well in America and in general they have also done very well by America. They have helped inform us, educate us and wrap our packages. Greater versatility we cannot ask. Naturally, I look forward to having these remarks printed in tomorrow's paper.

Jacob Ebert and George Dulty are not exactly household names. I mention them here and now because, on this very day, in 1833, they received the first patent for a great American institution, the soda fountain. Ours is a soda fountain civilization, whose major advance has been to put the soda in cans and bottles. Did you ever stop to think that soda, or soft drinks, is one of the ways America has colonized—some have said Coca Colonized—the world. In our formative years, when we are too young for beer and too old for just plain milk, it is the soda fountain psychology that shapes our social life and development. In a peculiar way, soda pop is a sort of bottled youth, the elixir of the young masses. But, I wonder what Jacob Ebert and George Dulty, the patenters of the soda fountain, would say of the extent to which soda pop has become a symbol of our times—involved in everything from ecological disputes over bottle and can disposal to arguments about synthetic flavors, dyes and preservatives. The old soda fountain is producing more gas all the time.

APRIL 25

Guglielmo Marconi born, 1864.

U.S. and U.S.S.R. troops met in friendship at the Elbe in Germany in 1945.

United Nations Conference opened in San Francisco, 1945.

Introductions:

This is a particularly appropriate day to be standing up here communicating with you. April 25 has been a high point in recent communications history. Today is the birthday of Guglielmo Marconi, born in 1864 in Bologna, Italy. Marconi made it possible for words to be carried over the air and into space. He was the father of radio, the miraculous transmission, without wires, of a signal from one end of the world to another, or even, these days, to and from outer space. It is no longer at all surprising to realize that what we say may be transmitted into the privacy of homes or across the miles to other communities. What is surprising is that people are still willing to come out and give their time to hear what a speaker has to say. For this I thank you.

It is commonplace to say that America and the countries that don't share our view of life simply don't talk the same language. On this date, in 1945, as World War II was drawing toward a close in Europe, soldiers of the U.S. and the U.S.S.R., whose only bond was that they were both fighting Nazi Germany, met at the Elbe River where the Eastern and Western fronts joined forces. It was a joyous occasion, even though they didn't speak the same language. They needed no common language to know that for that one magic moment they were friends. And that seems to me to prove something that is the theme of my remarks here today. In communicating between people, actions speak louder than words.

On this date, in 1945, an international conference opened in San Francisco for the purpose of creating a United Nations Organization. It took a lot of talk to get that show on the road, and that show has produced a great deal more talk ever since. There are those who feel that what the UN has produced is mainly talk, but talk, as a form of communication, is certainly superior to missiles. Talk, even idle talk, is not futile if it has the effect of postponing or discouraging more active measures. Action speaks louder than words, but also may produce higher casualties. So today I aim to cut through the Gordian knot of choosing between talk and action; instead, I shall talk about the action I think we need to take.

APRIL 26

Confederate Memorial Day.

John James Audubon born, 1785.

Introductions:

For years, this date has been remembered in some Southern states as Confederate Memorial Day, reserved to honor the ultimate heroes of a lost cause. It is one thing to honor all the fallen heroes; it is another to honor those who are our very own. A nation's grief is of almost epic proportions; a state's grief is somehow part of a familial heritage. Today is therefore one of those days on which to suggest that when we consider such sacrifices as may need to be made in our own time, we remember the sacrifices of those who came before us.

John James Audubon, who was born on this day in 1785, made America aware of the magnificence of its birds. He drew them and described them with a master's touch. But some generations later, the Society that bore his name, the Audubon Society, came to be regarded as a rather odd group—people who, in the midst of the greatest industrial surge of all time, were out watching birds, of all things. That attitude, praise be, is now recognized as being—if you will pardon the expression—for the birds. We have come to see that knowledge of and concern for the living things that share our world can help to keep that world healthy. We have come once more to recognize that Nature's children can learn from each other.

APRIL 27

U.S. Social Security System made first benefit payments, 1937.

U. S. Grant born, 1822.

Introductions:

This was a historic day in the United States in 1937, but I don't think many Americans realized how historic it was going to turn out to be. On this day, in 1937, the first payments were made to individuals under the Social Security Act of 1935, which introduced the concept of unemployment and old age insurance. It is difficult to contemplate what would have happened in the ensuing generations if there had been no social security system. Regardless of its problems and defects, it was the first time the United States had committed itself to do something other than provide outright charity for the unemployed and the elderly. On this anniversary day, we are entitled to wonder how we can do more, but only when we recognize how much has already been done.

Today is the birthday of a man who changed his name and went on to fame. He was born Hiram Ulysses Grant in 1822, in Point Pleasant, Ohio. He entered West Point mistakenly listed as Ulysses S. Grant, and he kept that name for the rest of his life. It was he who commanded the winning army in the Civil War and went on in 1868 to be elected President of the United States. History records his Presidency as, to put it kindly, undistinguished. Afterwards, in private life, he was bilked by an investment company and spent the rest of his life writing the memoirs that brought in enough money to pay off his debts and make provision for his family. He was an honest man who reinforced the latent American belief that good generals don't necessarily make good Presidents. It was 66 years before another professional soldier, a man named Eisenhower, again lived in the White House. Grant's birthday reminds us that great men, like smaller ones, can be miscast.

APRIL 28

Rush-Bagot Agreement, 1817.

Mutiny on the *Bounty*, 1789.

Introductions:

It was less than three short years after the end of the War of 1812—which was really the War of 1812, 1813 and 1814—between the U.S. and Great Britain, when the British Minister to the U.S., Charles Bagot, and our Acting Secretary of State, Richard Rush, set down on paper April 28 and 29, 1817, an agreement to limit militarization of the border between the U.S. and Canada. The spirit of that agreement ultimately led to the longest demilitarized and unfortified border between nations in the entire world. As treaties go, it wasn't considered spectacular. It took almost a year for ratification by the Senate; but if you judge treaties by results, this has to be one of the best. It suggests that reasonable people can live next to each other in peace for a long time.

I guess everybody knows the story of the mutiny on the *Bounty*; it is not a story of neighborliness or good will. It was on this day, in 1789, that Fletcher Christian led an uprising of the crew of *H.M.S. Bounty* against the stern Captain Bligh. After that story was transferred from a best selling book to the motion picture screen, the name of Captain Bligh came to mean a sort of sea-going Simon Legree. But that wasn't exactly the way it really was. Captain William Bligh went on, after that mutiny, to become ultimately a vice admiral in the British Navy. When Fletcher Christian set him adrift with 18 others in the Pacific, he sailed the small boat across thousands of miles of open sea to the East Indies. Later he introduced the breadfruit tree to the West Indies. He was harsh and he was tough but he served his country well. I mention this on the anniversary of the mutiny on the *Bounty* as a reminder that things are not always exactly as they may seem; we must take pains to look beyond the surface.

APRIL 29

Coxey's army, 1894.

William Randolph Hearst born, 1863.

Introductions:

If you don't think times have changed, I bring before you today the anniversary of Coxey's army. Jacob S. Coxey was an Ohioan who led a group of unemployed on a march to Washington, D.C. back in 1894; about 400 of them reached the capital on this date. Coxey was arrested for trespassing at the Capitol, and the "army" broke up. The name "Coxey's army" became a symbol for raggedy groups and parades on behalf of lost causes. But let me tell you what Coxey specifically asked for. He wanted the government to finance a public works program of some half a billion dollars to provide work for the unemployed. He thought this could be done simply by issuing that amount of new money. Jacob Coxey may be gone; but proposals similar to his keep popping up—and everyone still seems to look to Uncle Sam for help.

On this day, in 1863, William Randolph Hearst was born in San Francisco. Only a few years after Coxey's army went into history, William Randolph Hearst was helping to raise an Army to fight a war some historians think he helped mightily to start. That was the Spanish American War, which Hearst's newspaper, the *New York Journal*, kept calling for until it was declared. The war was a success for the country and for Hearst. But in later years, the Hearst chain of newspapers began to shrink, and the lands whose liberty from Spain had been won in the Spanish-American War did not prove to be islands of serenity and happiness. The war for circulation between Hearst and Joseph Pulitzer in New York produced a whole era of sensationalist journalism. It was sardonic that this kind of journalism later had one of its greatest field days in reporting the kidnaping and Symbionese Liberation Army days of William Randolph Hearst's granddaughter, Patty Hearst. The world seemed to have come a long way from the time of the grandfather to the time of the grandchild. It makes me wonder with what perspective our grandchildren will look back at what we are doing today.

APRIL 30

George Washington inaugurated as President, 1789.

Adolf Hitler a suicide in Berlin? 1945.

A quotation from Bernard Baruch, 1954.

Introductions:

In a certain sense, this is the birthday of the United States. It is the anniversary of the day in 1789 when, on the balcony of Federal Hall in New York City, George Washington was inaugurated as our first President under the Constitution. In his inaugural address, President Washington said, ". . . the foundation of our national policy will be laid in the pure and immutable principles of private morality . . ." When we consider the state of public morality today, we might do well to heed the words of Washington and look within ourselves.

On or about this date in 1945, many authorities believe, Adolf Hitler killed himself as Berlin was falling to the Russians in World War II. It is interesting that the arch villain of our century should have come to his end as the ruler of a nation on the anniversary of George Washington's inaugural address that planted American policy firmly on the foundation of private morality. People used to say we should have read *Mein Kampf* so we would have known how Hitler's mind worked. Maybe Hitler should have read Washington's speeches, so he could have known that right makes might, not the other way around.

A wise old man named Bernard M. Baruch made a speech at this time of the year back in 1954 to the President's Committee on Employment of the Physically Handicapped. His words are my text for today—and I quote: "There are no such things as incurables; there are only things for which man has not found a cure."

MAY 1

Law Day.

May Day.

Older Americans Month.

Mental Health Month.

Radio Month.

Introductions:

The first day of May traditionally has been a day of celebration. In Europe it has become not merely a day of celebration by the working people, but an occasion for left-wing rallies, most notably in Red Square in Moscow. In our country, it is sometimes observed as Loyalty Day, in direct contrast to the class warfare connotation May Day has elsewhere in the world; but our principal observance is of Law Day, dedicated to the traditional American concept of respect for the law. This American attitude may be the reflection of greater conservatism here than overseas. I prefer to believe, however, that it is simply recognition of better law. Our system is far from perfect, but it is, I believe, the best yet devised for a government of laws and not of men.

The month of May derives its name from Maia, the goddess of spring and fertility. But one of the notable observances of the month is at the opposite pole—the observance of Older Americans Month, in honor of our fellow citizens who are closer to the autumn of their lives than to the spring. Older Americans are the fastest growing segment of our population, thanks to increased life expectancy. Long before we set aside a month in their honor, we were observing Mother's Day in May—and Father's Day in June. But one cannot help wondering about the whole idea of having to set aside a couple of days or even a month to remind us of the older generation. This spurt of solicitude, I suspect, would not be necessary if we were able to provide any kind of viable long-term solution for the problems of the elderly. As we start another Older Americans Month, let us make every effort to do a little more for and with the people who have done so much for and with us.

May is a favorite time for scheduling special weeks and months. I will not attempt even to recite the names of them all, but I do want to make mention of one. Today is the beginning of Mental Health Month. The mind is a powerful vital organ. It can take more punishment than many other parts of the body. But it is also a delicate thing. The human mind is the greatest computer ever invented. It deserves tender loving care. We are solicitous of physical health; we vaccinate and immunize and unguent and salve. Let us be as solicitous of the protection of the mind. Let us try a little more to insulate children from the kind of mental cruelty that leaves scars on their psyches. Let us, above all, try to eliminate that which poisons the mind as surely as cyanide can poison the rest of the body. I refer to that worst of all poisons, hatred and prejudice.

For some years, May has been observed as Radio Month in the United States. We pride ourselves in this country on having a multiplicity of voices heard in the marketplace of ideas. There are more radio stations in the United States than in any other country on earth. They keep us in communication whether we are at home or on the road or out in the woods. In a very real sense, radio provides the feeling of community which is a vitamin for all of us.

It is an example of the degree to which we can find other people whose tastes match our own. And the essential question which radio people worry about is one which is the test of any way of life: Are people listening?

MAY 2

Berlin surrendered to the Russians in World War II, 1945.

First jet airplane passenger service, 1952.

Stan Musial hit five home runs in one day, in two games, 1954.

Introductions:

This is the anniversary of the day the city of Berlin surrendered to the Russians in World War II, in 1945. It is important to remember it because it was a highwater mark of the reversal of history. Russia, which had had so much of its territory invaded and occupied in two World Wars, was now the conqueror of a great Western capital. Only the long perspective of history some decades from now will be able to tell us what this kind of event meant as a lasting influence on Russian international psychology. But it reminds us that even when nations are allied against a common enemy, there is always the desire to be the first to get the job done. There is always what Robert Ardrey has called the "territorial imperative," the desire to stake out a territory as now ours.

We Americans have done so well with new technology that we sometimes like to think it all began here. Therefore, I feel constrained to point out that this very day is the anniversary of the introduction of commercial jet airplane passenger service in 1952—by Great Britain. The age of jet travel began with British service between London and Johannesburg, South Africa. Since then, American manufacturers have built most of the world's jet airplanes. But we know now, more than ever, that progress is basically an international process. America invented the transistor; Japan became its mass producer. Europe invented the ball point pen; America made the ball point revolution. When we look toward the future, we look not merely upward but outward as well.

Not too many baseball players have been able to hit five home runs in a single day. Stan Musial did just that, in a doubleheader, on this day in 1954. In this day of more complicated challenges and problems, it is a pleasure to recall an athletic achievement which, I fear, has largely been forgotten. Stan Musial was not famous as a roisterer or for having an explosive temperament; just for being one of the greatest ball players of all time. It is sardonic that some of the problem children of baseball, or the eccentrics, are better remembered than the good and mighty. And what is true of baseball is true of life in general.

MAY 3

First U.S. medical school, 1765.

Niccolo Machiavelli born, 1469.

Introductions:

Today is the anniversary of the founding of the first medical school in the U.S., at what is now the University of Pennsylvania, in 1765. Our medical system has had its share of problems, but it has long since been established that the education of doctors in this country is as good as or better than that any place on earth. The problems of medical education today are typical of the problems of every kind of education, namely how to provide it for more people without at the same time lowering what the experts believe to be the necessary standards. We have by now tried, more or less, all kinds of methods in various areas of education—open admissions, remedial classes, advanced placement, unstructured study, classrooms without walls and so on and on and on. But one element of progress has been neglected. We still haven't found a commonly accepted way to test and prove out these various methods. We have been able to reach the moon, but we are still trying to find better ways of reaching the minds of students.

On the birthday of Niccolo Machiavelli, who was born in Florence, Italy, on this date in 1469, it is worth noting that his analysis of the ingredients of dictatorship remains as valid today as when he wrote it. Macchiavelli wrote that in politics morality had to yield to power. To him, the reality of politics was that anything goes. Every now and then, we are surprised to find among our own politicians those who agree with him. I don't think politicians should read Machiavelli; voters should. Machiavelli, after all, wrote long before people were allowed to govern themselves. And the only way we can continue to govern ourselves is if we ourselves stand as the guardians of morality and honesty and decency.

Laws are fine, and the Constitution of the United States is just about the finest, but it was one of our great jurists, Charles Evans Hughes, later the Chief Justice of the United States, who said, on this day in 1907, that "The Constitution is what the judges say it is." Justice, in the ends, depends not simply on the law but on the way people construe the law.

MAY 4

Ancient Order of Hibernians founded in New York City, 1836.

Four students killed at Kent State University, 1970.

Al Capone entered Federal Penitentiary, 1932.

Introductions:

America is a land of diverse national origins. Until recently, some of us sought not to be reminded of our antecedents. But one group that has taken a different tack for years is that which, on this day in 1836, provided the constituency for the founding in New York City of the Ancient Order of Hibernians. I expect that if they were founding it today, they might have made it simpler and called it the Ancient Order of the Irish. The Irish, not alone but in mighty numbers, came to this country for freedom of religion and freedom of opportunity that they felt was denied to them while their native land was under foreign rule. They helped mightily to build America, to enliven its politics and its everyday life—and they are still doing it. They furnished the pattern as well for other waves of immigrants. Together, all those different peoples built a mighty nation. They had to conquer prejudice here, after fleeing from prejudice at home. Thank goodness, there is no longer the sign, anywhere, that once was all too familiar in some American cities, saying "No Irish need apply." On the anniversary of the founding of the Ancient Order of Hibernians, I salute what is still and must always be a land of opportunity and of tolerance.

Violence seems always to be with us, some instances are longer remembered than others. One such took place on this day in 1970. When I mention the place it will recall the incident to many. The place was Kent State University in Ohio. The event was the killing of four students by the National Guard. It was a time of student unrest over national policy that was sending young Americans to fight in Vietnam. There had been takeovers of buildings on various campuses, and demonstrations and manifestoes. But Kent State brought the nation up short. Years later, on the ground where the shootings had taken place, there was another confrontation, as demonstrators sought to prevent the construction of a University building on a site they felt should be preserved as a reminder. It is hard to see any social worth in needless killing; but if the memory of what happened at Kent State in 1970 restrains a single similar occurrence in the future, something good will have come out of the tragedy. We must not forget such sad events, nor should we remember them with bitterness. Rather, they should be reminders that there has to be a better way.

Sometimes, direct confrontation is not the most effective way of dealing with a situation. Al Capone was the crime boss of Chicago for years; there seemed to be no way to bring him to book. But there was; when Al Capone entered the Federal Penitentiary in Atlanta on this day in 1932, it was not for any of his principal and obvious crimes. It was, of all things, for income tax evasion. One way or another, lawbreaking can be punished. The moral, for agents of the law and for law abiding citizens, is this: Don't give up. There is more than one way to catch a thief. And there is more than one solution for almost every problem.

MAY 5

Sacco and Vanzetti arrested, 1920.

Denmark Liberation Day.

Karl Marx born, 1818.

Introductions:

In 1977, in a most unusual action, the Governor of Massachusetts held a public ceremony to admit, a half century later, that the prosecution of Nicola Sacco and Bartolomeo Vanzetti had been improperly conducted. Sacco and Vanzetti were executed after having been found guilty of murders committed in the course of a robbery. It was felt by many, at the time, and by more subsequently, that the two Italian immigrants were convicted by a hostile court and jury in an unfair trial because they were anarchists. The Sacco-Vanzetti case became the most widely-known cause celebre in the history of American Justice. It all began on this date in 1920, when the two men were arrested. Today will always be a question mark on the conscience of America.

The conscience of a nation is not always dramatically visible. Today, Liberation Day in Denmark, reminds us of an occasion when national conscience was not only visible but heroic. Liberation Day in Denmark celebrates the end of the Nazi German occupation of that country in 1945. It also recalls the way Denmark behaved under occupation. When the Nazis took over the country, they wanted to force Danish Jews to wear yellow stars of David and be subjected to the same indignities the Nazis had visited on hapless victims in other occupied lands. The Danes refused to go along with this, and ultimately, at the risk of their own lives, succeeded in smuggling every Danish Jew out of the country to neutral Sweden. Yes, under challenge there is such a thing as the exercise of national conscience. It happened there. It has happened here. Indeed, I think it is happening here right now.

Today is the birthday of Karl Marx. He was born in Prussia in 1818. He became the patron saint of the radical left. To half the world his name is one to be revered; for the rest of us, something considerably less. I think that Marx himself could not have foreseen the horrors that would be committed in his name. His life reminds us that it is one thing to fight against evil; it is something else to fight evil with evil. Extremism breeds extremism. We learn that lesson every day.

MAY 6

First postage stamps, 1840.

Roger Bannister broke the four-minute barrier for the mile run, 1954.

Sigmund Freud born, 1856.

Introductions:

Today is the birthday of the postage stamp. The first stamp was the so-called "black penny," issued in 1840 in England. Since then, postage stamps have become big business, not merely for the mailing of letters, but as collectors' items as well. They are still the same small adhesive-backed pieces of paper, but they cost a great deal more than they used to. And, like many ancient and honorable institutions, they are likely to price themselves out of the market—because there are now alternatives. Indeed, the number of different ways to send a message today deserves to be examined.

Humanity seems to be setting goals for itself constantly, and then having to set new ones. For generations, the goal of runners was the four-minute mile run, which it seemed would never be conquered. Then, on this date in 1954, at Oxford, England, Roger Bannister ran the mile in 3:59:4. The barrier had been broken. In the years thereafter, so many runners ran the mile in less than four minutes that it became routine. This is a common attribute of ours. What we once regarded as miraculous becomes routine and commonplace after a while. But life is full of what I suppose we must call routine miracles—including the recurrent birth of life itself. We are surrounded by miracles to which, I suggest, we might pay somewhat more attention.

Sigmund Freud was born on this day in 1856, in Freiberg, Moravia. Few men have opened the kind of new frontier that Dr. Freud explored, the frontier of the subconscious. Like many pioneers, he was himself obsessed and extreme in his views. But without his unyielding efforts, others might not have been impelled to follow his example and explore the workings of the mind. Some people have suggested that the world would be better off if Freud had not started all this. His branch of medicine is certainly one of the less absolute areas; but the fact that such an area of medicine exists, the fact that we are trying to cure the mind as well as the body, is also worth remembering. We need to know what afflicts people; we also need to know why and how.

MAY 7

Lusitania sunk, 1915.

Nazis surrendered to General Eisenhower, effective next day, 1945.

Birthday of Johannes Brahms, 1833, and Peter I. Tchaikovsky, 1840.

Introductions:

The British liner Lusitania was not the first civilian ship sunk by German submarines in the first World War. But it was the first major passenger liner, and when it was torpedoed in the Atlantic on this date in 1915, it played a major role in turning American sympathies toward the Allies and away from Germany. I prefer, on this anniversary, to remember it for the remark of an

American theatrical producer named Charles Frohman, who was aboard the Lusitania. He is reported to have said, as he was going to his Maker, "Why fear death? It is the most beautiful adventure in life." I would hope that we could all go through life with the feeling that the most beautiful adventure remained ahead. The best ingredient for a happy life today is the hope of tomorrow.

VE Day, standing for victory in Europe in World War II, is celebrated on May 8, when the cease-fire went into effect. But the agreement, the surrender of the Nazis to the forces commanded by General Eisenhower, took place on this day, May 7, in Reims, France. I promise not to talk as long as it took that agreement to go into effect.

If we really wanted to enter into what should be the spirit of this day, I shouldn't be speaking to you. We should simply be listening to great music, because two of the world's greatest composers were born on this day— Johannes Brahms in Hamburg, Germany, in 1833 and Peter I. Tchaikovsky in Votkinsk, Russia, in 1840. Brahms and Tchaikovsky—what a birthday pair! It leaves me with no alternative but to hope that at least my words will be music to your ears.

MAY 8

World Red Cross Day.

VE Day.

Harry Truman born, 1884.

Introductions:

Today is World Red Cross Day, observed on the anniversary of the birth of Jean Henri Dunant, founder of the Red Cross, in 1828 in Geneva, Switzerland. Dunant, the co-winner of the first Nobel Peace Prize, helped make sure that mercy became an international language. We have only to look around us to realize that we need more of that international language in the world today.

Today, in 1945, the World War in Europe stopped. World War II began on that continent, almost six years earlier; it still continued for a while in Asia; but the greatest bulk of the conflict was over. As long as the world is even relatively at peace on this anniversary date, I believe I can speak with hope for the human condition.

For Harry S. Truman, President of the United States, his birthday in 1945 was an unforgettable one. He had been President only since April 12, when Franklin D. Roosevelt had died. And on May 8, the war in Europe ended. For Harry Truman, born on this same date in 1884 in Lamar, Missouri, it was quite a day. And, as history developed, the birth of Harry Truman itself proved to make it quite day as well. People have disagreed about Truman's role in history, although he generally receives quite high marks. There is no disagreement, however, about the fact that Harry Truman was the author and the exemplar of the tersest description ever given of the Presidency of the United States. Truman said: "The buck stops here." You and I can stand up and criticize, or applaud, or suggest, or oppose—and I propose to do some of the foregoing on this rostrum here today but it is the President we choose who ultimately has to face up to the fact that the buck stops here.

MAY 9

First flight over North Pole, 1926.

First eye bank, 1944.

John Brown born, 1800.

Introductions:

It took many decades before modern man reached the North Pole. It took only 17 years more for man to fly over the North Pole. That quick capsule tells how the pace of progress quickens. Lt. Commander Richard E. Byrd and Floyd Bennett made that first Polar flight on this date in 1926. Now the same flight is mere routine. In the same way, today we are trying new and risky things that will be routine tomorrow. The only trouble is that, while we are still trying them out, we have no way of knowing whether or how they will work. Consider some of the world's current experiments.

A new kind of bank opened, ushering in a new kind of world, on this day in 1944. It was an eye bank, at New York Hospital, a place where human eye elements could be kept to replace others. Now we are able to transplant other portions of the body, perhaps most notably the kidneys; we have had some relatively successful heart transplants as well. On the anniversary of the first eye bank, I salute the world's greatest mechanics, the doctors who do so well at patching up human beings. The trouble seems to be that we are constantly finding new ways to give them more human beings to patch up.

Right and wrong are relative terms. If they are hard to define at times, it is even harder to define when the goal is worthy but the methods are extreme. That was certainly true in the case of a man born on this date in 1800 in Torrington, Connecticut, a man named John Brown. John Brown fought against slavery. He felt so strongly that he killed to fight it. He helped to make a new land known as bloody Kansas and he met his Waterloo at Harper's Ferry, where a military unit captured him for the trial that led to his execution. The commander of that U.S. unit was a man named Robert E. Lee. Lee went on to command the Confederate Army, and the Union Army marched singing "John Brown's body lies a-moldering in the grave but his soul goes marching on." Yes today is the birthday of John Brown, and I think that his soul still goes marching on.

MAY 10

First transcontinental railroad link completed, 1869.

Nazis burned the books in Germany, 1933.

Winston Churchill became Prime Minister of Great Britain, 1940.

Introductions:

There were big doings at Promontory, Utah, on this date in 1869. They drove a golden spike to complete the first full railroad connection across the American continent. If covered wagons opened up the West, the railroad made it grow up. We aren't too impressed, in the age of jet planes, by railroads; but it was the railroad that sparked the industrial development of the nation. And in some ways the clock is turning back. Confronted with the mass transportation problems of big cities, many are urging not merely the continuance but the expansion of commuter rail service. We may yet see celebrations for the driving of a few more golden spikes.

Human beings are mortal; they don't live forever. But ideas can be immortal. In books and the heritages passed from one generation to the next, ideas can live forever. On this date in 1933, a group of fanatics thought they could change that. On this date in 1933, the Nazis in Germany burned all the books of which they disapproved. It was the book burners' golden hour. And of course it didn't work. The Nazis were ultimately ground into the dust. The message of the books was remembered. There is a lesson for today in this sad anniversary. Book burning is in the same family as censorship, and both are kissing cousins of ruthless conformism. We need the stimulus of the clash of ideas, of argument—decent and civilized, but argument nevertheless. It would be very flattering for me, as your speaker here today, if you agree with everything I said; but it would be far more rewarding if what I said started you thinking about why, perhaps, you disagree.

One of the classic arguments is about whether the times make the men or the men make the times. A man who took office as Prime Minister of Great Britain, on this date in 1940, is a case in point. He had been a brilliantly successful author and lecturer, but more of a gadfly than a success as a political figure. He was 66, an age when most men are already in or close to retirement, when his nation's highest office came to him. His name was Winston Churchill. Did the times, the challenge, make Winston Churchill? Did he inspire England and the free world, or did they inspire him? I suspect the truth is a little, or a lot, of both. Great men do not merely rise to an occasion, they make an occasion. Would England have fought so gallantly in World War II against such overwhelming odds—until America entered the fray—without the eloquence and the bulldog determination of Winston Churchill? We will never know.

What we do know is that, in his democracy and in ours, whenever the times have called for that kind of leadership, that kind of leadership, sooner or later, has emerged. Do we have it now? That is for each of us to answer for ourselves. Will we have it in future? I hope so, because we know now that we will continue to need it. Look around you and see the reasons why.

MAY 11

Irving Berlin born, 1888.

Ottmar Mergenthaler born, 1854.

Introductions:

Today is the birthday of two men, born in Europe, who contributed greatly to the spirit of America.

Every time we sing "God Bless America" or hope melodically for a White Christmas we are paying another tribute to the genius of Irving Berlin. "God Bless America" was written by a man who was born in Temum, Russia, in 1888. The same man wrote "White Christmas" and "In Your Easter Bonnet," lyric celebrations of two great Christian occasions by a Jewish songwriter. Irving Berlin's songs express the hopes, aspirations and attitudes of America, from "Oh, How I Hate to Get Up in the Morning" to "You're Not Sick, You're Just in Love." What is the spirit of America? I submit it is the spirit that welcomes an immigrant boy and makes him its poet laureate. That is the spirit I still see in our nation today. Let me tell you about it.

In the late nineteenth century, this country had an absolute explosion of print. Newspapers flourished; books began a period of growth that continues to this day. All this was largely due to a man born on this date in 1854 in Hachtel, Germany. His name was Ottmar Mergenthaler. He came to the United States when he was 18. As a young man, he invented a machine that set printing type mechanically. It was called the Linotype. In one fell swoop, it changed printing from a hand trade to a great mass production enterprise. It made possible the great mass circulation daily newspapers and mass produced books. We think of America as a very inventive land, which it is. But America is inventive because America is free. It is the place to which inquisitive and inventive people are drawn. Let us hope that this spirit of inventiveness continues. Let us do what we can to insure its continuance.

MAY 12

Soviet land blockade of West Berlin ended, 1949.

Florence Nightingale born, 1820.

Introductions:

Today is the anniversary of a significant victory of the Western world. On this date, in 1949, after 11 months of blockading all the land routes to West Berlin, the U.S.S.R. stopped the blockade. They stopped it not out of any sudden upsurge of conscience or concern, but simply because the Western powers, principally the United States, had made the blockade unworkable by operating the greatest airlift the world had ever seen. That was the victory. It is the kind of victory we can win again. It is victory without shooting, basically the victory of ingenuity over intransigence. We can use more victories like that one.

We use the term Florence Nightingale as a synonym for a kind and ministering angel. The real Florence Nightingale, born on this date in 1820 in Florence, Italy, was an indomitable English lady who changed nursing into a noble profession, contributed greatly to the organization of the modern hospital and changed the whole concept of medical care. On her birthday, the least we can do is to keep alive the kind of progress she worked so hard to achieve.

MAY 13

Jamestown, Virginia, founded, 1607.

Winston Churchill rallies England, 1940.

Introductions:

We meet on the anniversary of the first English settlement in what is now the United States. Jamestown, Virginia, became the first permanent settlement, although other unsuccessful groups preceeded it, on or about this date. We have a tendency, in thinking of our nation's early days, to concentrate on the Puritans in New England, but Virginia was settled first. Pocahontas and Captain John Smith were Virginians. Let us therefore remember that the heritage from our earliest days was broad and even multi-racial, not confined to a single rock-bound coast. As a matter of fact, history records that the Pilgrims themselves were planning to settle in Virginia when they boarded the Mayflower; how and why they changed course has never been explained. Out of such changes of mind come the seeds of a great nation. And on this anniversary date, how far have we come, and how much off course are we since Jamestown?

Winston Churchill, speaking in the House of Commons as Great Britain's new Prime Minister, said on this day in 1940, "I have nothing to offer but blood, toil, tears and sweat." Blood, toil, tears and sweat. That is the human investment. That is the basic investment in our country, or any country of free people. How is our investment doing?

MAY 14

WAAC women's Army unit founded, 1942.

Lewis and Clark expedition began, 1804.

Introductions:

In 1942, on this date, authorization was granted for the establishment of the Women's Auxiliary Army Corps, whose members soon became known as WAACs. This enabled the Army, during World War II, to enlist women in non-combatant units while maintaining the male-only nature of the fighting forces. In later years, women were recognized as regulars rather than auxiliaries, and their career opportunities in the Army and other armed forces were broadened considerably. Back in 1942, as today, the question remained: "Where do we go from here?"

The Lewis and Clark expedition left St. Louis to explore the west on this date in 1804. The expedition returned to St. Louis in September 1806, after mapping much of what was to become the great American west. Lewis and Clark were the pioneers of American government-financed exploration, which began by crossing the Mississippi and, in our time, landed on the moon and reached for the stars. America is founded on the spirit of exploration. We have much to explore not only in outer space, but in the inner space of our own cities, as well as in the secrets of the earth we plow.

MAY 15

Peace Officers Memorial Day.

Nylon stockings went on sale, 1940.

Introductions:

Today is Peace Officers Memorial Day, a reminder that the people who devote their lives to keeping the peace sometimes give their lives as well. American peace officers don't make the laws. They are not a gestapo or a secret police playing by their own rules. They are instruments of the government of the people. Keeping the peace is a high risk occupation; peace officers deserve more than a once-a-year memorial day. Above all, they deserve the cooperation of the public. Any cop will tell you that, in the last analysis, law enforcement depends not so much on how tough the cops are as on how law abiding the people are. Maybe if we all keep that in mind there won't be as much occasion in future for a memorial day of this kind.

On this day, in 1940, the age of synthetics really began when nylon stockings went on sale. Since then, we have had dacron and orlon and pliofilm and any number of other new household words. The only trouble is that as fast as we learn to duplicate or improve upon a natural substance, we start to run into shortages of the raw materials to make the synthetic. Man's ingenuity may be infinite, but we have learned that our resources are very finite.

MAY 16

Impeachment of President Andrew Johnson failed by one vote, 1868.

First Oscars presented, 1929.

William H. Seward born, 1801.

Introductions:

Today is the anniversary of an event chronicled in John F. Kennedy's book "Profiles in Courage," concerning one of Mr. Kennedy's predecessors as President of the United States. In 1968, President Andrew Johnson faced impeachment proceedings as a result of a dispute with Congress. On this date, Senator Ross of Kansas, a man who opposed much of President Johnson's political thinking, stood up and voted his conscience. His was the deciding vote that saved the President. It meant the end of Senator Edmund G. Ross's political career, and he knew it. But he did what he felt was right. Ironically, few people today even know his name. But I hope that in the halls of Congress and across the nation, there are public servants facing the issues today with the same courage and honesty that Edmund G. Ross displayed when the chips were down in 1868.

Today is Oscar's anniversary. Oscar, as if you didn't know, is the annual Award of the Academy of Motion Picture Arts and Sciences, first presented on this date in 1929. It has been imitated everywhere since then. Hardly an art form or an industry does not have its own equivalent of the Oscar—the Emmy, the golden record and so forth. I think Oscar had a good idea. Recognition by one's colleagues is sometimes the sweetest recognition of all. As a matter of fact, I'd like to use this occasion to present a couple of Oscars of my own.

If William H. Seward hadn't been born on this date in Florida, New York, in 1801, the Russians would be a lot richer and the United States would be a lot smaller. Seward was the Secretary of State who negotiated the purchase of Alaska from the Russians in 1867, at a price of $7,200,000. I would like to have Mr. Seward around today doing some negotiating for us.

MAY 17

New York Stock Exchange founded, 1792.

Racial segregation in public schools declared unconstitutional, 1954.

Edward Jenner born, 1749.

Introductions:

Today is the birthday of the New York Stock Exchange, which was founded in 1792. In the course of its long existence, the Exchange has sometimes been castigated as the playground of speculators and stock manipulators—and it has had its share—but its birthday is a good time to be reminded that the idea of stock ownership by the people, through the transactions of the stock exchange, has given a higher percentage of people a "piece of the action" in this country than anywhere else on earth. The idea of stock ownership has made it possible for the small investor to be a significant factor in the economic life of the nation. So, as we look at the major corporations of America, let us remember that we are looking at the investments of millions and millions of small shareholders.

On this date in 1954, in a unanimous decision written by Chief Justice Earl Warren, the U.S. Supreme Court swept away an ancient heritage of racial segregation and declared that "separate educational facilities are inherently unequal." It was the beginning of the dawning of a new age of racial equality in America—an age that still had a long, long way to go. On the anniversary of that historic decision, how far have we come, and how far is the path yet before us?

Edward Jenner was born on this date, in 1749, in Berkeley, England. He grew up to be Dr. Edward Jenner, and every one of us is in his debt. Dr. Jenner developed a new medical idea. It was called vaccination. Thanks to vaccination, smallpox ceased to be a great plague of mankind, and any number of other diseases have been prevented or mitigated by immunization processes based on Dr. Jenner's bright idea. If only for the birth of Edward Jenner, today is a pretty good day in the annals of time.

MAY 18

Napoleon became Emperor of France, 1804.

TVA authorized, 1933.

Introductions:

Napoleon Bonaparte was a Corsican soldier of France who became a general in the First French Republic after the bloody French Revolution. That was not enough for Napoleon. On this date, in 1804, he became the Emperor of France. Under his reign, France sought to conquer Europe and the world—an occupational disease of self-made monarchs and dictators. We should always beware of political or military leaders who talk of the nation's destiny when it is clear that what they have in mind is their own destiny. Somehow the lesson of Napoleon never really seems to sink in. Even here and now, we have too many candidates for Waterloo.

The Tennessee Valley Authority hydroelectric power system was authorized on this date in 1933, over bitter opposition. It can be said, conservatively, to have changed the face of the South. On its anniversary, let us not be afraid of change nor the risks it brings. After all, our country's worth it.

MAY 19

Anne Boleyn beheaded, 1536.

Immigration quotas, 1921.

Introductions:

Over the course of many centuries, a lot of people have lost their heads. Today is the anniversary of one of them. On this date, in 1536, Anne Boleyn, second wife of Henry VIII of England and mother of the princess who was to become Queen Elizabeth I, was beheaded in the Tower of London. In case you want to take the measure of the world's progress, just reflect that if Henry and Anne had a similar falling out today as common folk, it would have been solved by a divorce and Anne would probably have had custody of the child. You may recall that both Henry the Eighth and his queenly daughter had rather nasty ways of disposing of people whose remarks they didn't like. I am therefore very grateful to be appearing to talk today before a group of twentieth century commoners, and I trust that what I am about to say will move you to neither boo nor hiss, and certainly not to shout "Off with his head!"

American hospitality is one of our oldest traditions, but on this date in 1921, Congress decided to limit it somewhat, by establishing national quotas for immigration into the United States. Since then, we have had plenty of continued immigration to the U.S., and some of the discriminations built into the quota system have been given the fate they deserve; but one of the unforeseen results of restrictions on legal immigration has been a tremendous increase in the number of aliens who were illegal immigrants. Maybe we should have remembered that another one of our oldest traditions, along with hospitality, is gate-crashing. For all I know, I may be speaking to a few gate-crashers here today. If so, I can only say I am flattered. I'd rather have you sneak in before I talk than sneak out while I am talking.

MAY 20

Mecklenburg Independence Day.

Lindbergh began flight to Paris, 1927.

First airborne invasion, 1941.

Introductions:

Today is Mecklenburg Independence Day. From the looks on your faces, I gather that some further explanation is in order. Mecklenburg was the name of a county in North Carolina. In 1775, Mecklenburg County was the site of a convention in Charlotte which adopted a declaration of independence from Great Britain on this date and sent words to that effect to the North Carolina delegation at the Continental Congress meeting in Philadelphia. Mecklenburg County was the first to adopt such a declaration. So today is the anniversary of a brave step in the progress of our nation—and therefore a very good time to talk about some other brave steps which seem to be needed these days.

On May 20, 1927, a young American aviator named Charles A. Lindbergh took off from Roosevelt Field, New York and headed for Paris, on a flight that had never before been made. It seemed like an incredible hope to think that he might make it. Hour after hour, the world held its breath and waited, hope rising with news of his progress. He was supposed to land at Le Bourget at 7:30 the following evening. He didn't, but news came that he had been seen over Ireland and then over England. He finally landed shortly after 10 PM, Paris time. What happened thereafter is a story for another day. Today, the anniversary of Lindbergh's historic take-off, serves to remind us that American know-how and American initiative and American success are based on one basic ingredient—the self-confidence that makes Americans willing to take a chance. As a nation, back in 1775 or Lindbergh's time or now, you do not discourage Americans by telling us we're taking a chance. Today I want to talk about a few chances that we should be taking now.

It is a sardonic twist of fate that, on the anniversary of Charles A. Lindbergh's peaceful flight to open new air frontiers across the Atlantic, another aviation first was achieved in the field of warfare. On this same date in 1941, Nazi Germany captured the island of Crete in history's first totally airborne invasion. From that time on, guarding a coastline and patrolling the sea no longer provided sufficient protection. The whole face of warfare—and its costs—changed. The menace of surprise attack became infinitely greater. When we contemplate the cost of national defense these days, or the effect of that cost on other areas of our life, we should remember why, no pun intended, they are sky-high.

MAY 21

American National Red Cross founded, 1881.

Lindbergh landed in Paris after solo flight across the Atlantic, 1927.

Introductions:

Today is the birthday of the American National Red Cross, founded by Clara Barton in Washington, D.C. in 1881. Today the Red Cross may be the world's best known symbol. In America, it is the way good neighbors help each other. It is our national Available Jones. The only people it doesn't help are public speakers who get into trouble by shooting off their mouths; so I will try to avoid any rash statements that may get me in trouble with this distinguished audience here today.

This was the day, in 1927, when Charles A. Lindbergh landed at Le Bourget Airport in Paris after a solo flight of almost a day and a half from New York. There will probably never again be a hero of the worldwide stature of Lindbergh, the Lone Eagle. He was idolized wherever he went, and he went all over, mapping commercial air routes and acting as the ambassador of the world of aviation. The trouble was that he was tempted, later in his career, to get involved with international affairs and political matters, about which his knowledge was less than profound. So Charles Lindbergh ended his life still a hero, one whose personal tragedy in the loss of a kidnapped baby son earned the sympathy of the world, but a man whose politics cast a shadow across his public stature. A public figure, like an actor, is often judged on the basis of something other than his best performance. And this reminds me, as a public speaker, to stick to speaking about what I know best.

MAY 22

National Maritime Day.

"Truman Doctrine" went into effect, 1947.

Richard Wagner born, 1813.

Introductions:

On this day, in 1819, the steamboat Savannah, the first American-built steamboat to cross the Atlantic, started across the ocean from Savannah, Georgia. The anniversary is commemorated every year as National Maritime Day. Somebody said recently that if you don't think the U.S. is still a seagoing nation, how do you explain the way we always find ourselves in deep water. On National Maritime Day, I propose to steam right into my subject, and since we have signalled the engines full speed ahead we don't need a lot of wind.

This is the day when, in 1947, the so-called "Truman Doctrine" went into effect. The Truman Doctrine, as outlined by President Harry S. Truman, was to limit and contain Soviet expansion by providing U.S. aid for countries threatened by the Red giant. On this day in 1947, with the passage of enabling legislation, President Truman approved an initial appropriation of $400 million for aid to Greece and Turkey. In the years since then, historians and revisionist historians have argued over the wisdom and effectiveness of the Truman Doctrine, but nobody has ever doubted that it made absolutely clear the position of the United States in its time. The Truman Doctrine for speakers is a simple one. Stand up to be counted; then count on sitting down. I shall endeavor to tell you where I stand, and trust you will not tell me where to get off.

Richard Wagner, regarded by most as one of a handful of great immortals in the world of composing, was born on this day in 1813. Wagner was a man with definite opinions in many fields besides music. That is true of many of us who don't happen to be musical geniuses like Richard Wagner. Today I propose to speak on a topic which I do not think Wagner covered. And when I am through, I will be happy to face the music.

MAY 23

Benjamin Franklin's bifocals, 1785.

Abie's Irish Rose opened, 1922.

Introductions:

Benjamin Franklin was a man of many talents. One of his inventions is worn every day by millions of people around the world. He first described it in a letter he wrote on this date in 1785, after he had designed and worn it. It was a very simple idea—as are so many great ideas. Franklin, in his later years, like so many of us, needed two pairs of glasses: one pair for reading, one pair for seeing at a distance. Old Ben got tired of switching from one pair to another, so he designed a pair of eyeglasses where the upper portion of the lens was for distance and the lower portion for reading. What he designed was the first pair of bifocals. Our problem ever since, of course, has been to make sure we were looking through the right part of the glass. Today I want to address myself to the bifocal way we look at the world.

I don't know how many of you have ever heard of a play called *Abie's Irish Rose*. The title pretty much tells you the plot. I mention it because the play opened on Broadway on this date in 1922, and the critics gave it a rather unfriendly reception. As a result, it only ran for 2,327 performances and became one of the longest running plays in the history of the theatre. My point in recalling the bad reviews of its premiere is not to throw rocks at the critics. They are entitled to their opinions. What the story of *Abie's Irish Rose* illustrates is something that has happened time and again. The public has an interesting habit of making up its own mind. We are told that, in the age of television and mass circulation periodicals, comments in the press can make or break an artistic offering, or a politician or a product in the supermarket. That seems to me to be a "cop-out." I believe that most products, whether plays, movies, hair tonic or speeches, stand or fall, in the last analysis, on the basis of their own performance. Of course, if I fail to get the reaction I hope for my remarks today, you understand I intend to blame it on the critics.

MAY 24

Samuel F. B. Morse sent first telegraph message, 1844.

Brooklyn Bridge opened, 1883.

Queen Victoria born, 1819.

Introductions:

"What hath God wrought!" When Samuel F. B. Morse sent those words as the first telegraph message between Washington and Baltimore, on this date in 1844, he was being devout and modest, because the telegraph was what Samuel F. B. Morse himself had wrought. I always have the feeling that people who make God the author of their bright ideas are subconsciously hedging—rather like saying, "Now, if it doesn't work out the way we think it will, remember He did it." Nobody had to apologize for the telegraph. It helped knit the nation together as much as the railroad had, and it furnished the basis for one of the first international languages, the language of dot and dash. I mention today as the anniversary of the telegraph because I intend today to practice a virtue first taught to Americans by the fact that telegrams were priced by the word. In the spirit of the telegram, I intend to keep my remarks short and to the point.

This is the day when, in 1883, the Brooklyn Bridge was opened, linking Brooklyn and Manhattan and providing a glorious opportunity for generations of confidence men thereafter. Nobody will ever know how many times the Brooklyn Bridge was sold to a gullible visitor. America has crossed a lot of other bridges since then, but for some reason no other has had quite the cachet of the still impressive span down at the lower end of Manhattan Island. Nobody who ever jumped off a bridge ever won the fame that came to Steve Brodie for supposedly having survived a leap from the Brooklyn Bridge. What this suggests to me is that what a person does, or says, can turn out quite differently, depending on where it is said or done. I am therefore particularly happy to be here with you today, because—if I can paraphrase Steve Brodie—this looks like a pretty good jumping-off point. I appreciate the opportunity to speak to you.

The lady who was to become Queen Victoria, monarch of Great Britain and Empress of India, was born in Kensington, England, on this day in 1819. Few monarchs have reigned as long or been as revered as the doughty dowager of London. Few have left their imprint on a whole way of life or a set of manners as did this lady. It wasn't simply because she was the Queen. It was because she had about her a feeling of integrity that was a reassurance to all her people. She didn't automatically step into this role. She had her downs before her people raised her up. But in the end she prevailed because, first, she stood for something and, second, they liked what she stood for. The lesson is clear. First, above all, stand for something; better still, stand up for something. Right now I am standing up before you; if you can stand me, I intend to stand up for something.

MAY 25

First session of the Constitutional Convention 1787.

Ralph Waldo Emerson born, 1803.

Introductions:

Today is the anniversary of the first session of the U.S. Constitutional Convention in Philadelphia in 1787, the Convention that adopted the Constitution of the United States. I mention it because of one particular point. Today, in 1787, was not supposed to be the first session of the Convention. That was supposed to have been on May 14th. But only the representatives of two states, Virginia and Pennsylvania, were there on time. Not until May 25th was there a quorum. Legislatures seem to have had that same problem ever since, and I am grateful, even though this is not a Constitutional Convention, to see from the few empty chairs here today that, ladies and gentlemen, we seem to have a quorum.

This is Ralph Waldo Emerson's birthday. He was born in Boston on May 25, 1803. It is very hard to make a speech without quoting something from Emerson. It was he who sparked New England's golden age of literature, and I do not intend to let this birthday occasion go by without comment. "Nothing great," said Emerson, "was ever achieved without enthusiasm." I believe we have great things yet to achieve, and I am here to win your enthusiasm for those great things that lie ahead.

MAY 26

Cheops funeral ship found, 1954.

A note about Memorial Day.

Introductions:

The Pharaoh Cheops began the building of the Great Pyramids of Egypt thousands of years ago. When he died, he was buried in a ship especially built for his journey to another world. On this date, in 1954, the funeral ship of Cheops reached another world, when it was uncovered near the Pyramid of Giza. This world of ours is certainly different from that into which the remains of Cheops were supposedly consigned. But I doubt that ours is the world the heirs of Cheops had in mind for their king. It is hard enough to gain your goals in this life, let alone another. So let me speak today about some things we can do with our lives in our time on earth, rather than build funeral ships for an unknown future journey.

There was a time when Memorial Day, the day set aside to honor those who gave their lives for our country, was always May 30. Now, however, in order to assure ourselves of a three-day week-end, it is ordained that Memorial Day is to be the last Monday in May. Therefore, the earliest date for Memorial Day is May 25. These remarks apply, however, with equal force for the last Monday in May whether it is May 26, 27 or any other number through 31. It is not enough to remember the honored casualties of past conflicts. The best thing we can do in their honor is to assure that they will not have died in vain. They died to build or to defend a better world. The least we can do is to live for those same purposes. No matter what a speaker's subject during this last week of May, surely this dedication to the cause for which so many gave their lives deserves to be mentioned. And in the last analysis, the test of anything we say or advocate must be whether and how it makes life better.

MAY 27

Achsah Young hanged as a witch in Massachusetts, 1647.

Amelia Bloomer born, 1818.

Henry Kissinger born, 1923.

Introductions:

Achsah Young is not one of the more famous figures in American history. Let me tell you why. Achsah Young was the first person inscribed in the annals of America for being executed as a witch. It happened on this date in 1647. Some people dispute the identity and the date. Margaret Jones, executed in 1648, is given the dubious honor by some historians. But using Achsah Young's demise as the starting point and today as the anniversary date, I rise to note that we are more civilized today. We don't hang witches; we organize cults around some of them, suggest sanity tests for others. Please notice that I did not say we don't regard people as witches any more. The fact is that we may find other names for witchcraft, but in one way or another, we continue to give it credence, and at times to fear it. Sometimes, indeed, it is easier to say "witchcraft" and to flee than to face up to unpleasant situations. I am not here to blame a single problem on witches. Indeed, some of the things which confront us suggest that so far we have been leading a charmed life. Let me explain.

Amelia Bloomer is remembered in history mainly for an article of feminine clothing which is now so long out of fashion that it may not be remembered in history. But Amelia Bloomer, born on this date in 1818 in Hiram, New York, was one of the early crusaders for women's rights. Incidentally, Bloomer, was her husband's name; she was born Amelia Jenks. Mrs. Bloomer felt that the way women dressed handicapped them, so she began wearing trousers, as well as the garment to which she unwittingly gave her name. A lot of women, including Amelia Bloomer, accepted a lot of ridicule to fight the good fight for equal rights. On her birthday, I salute America's greatest fighting force, the women. Now I'd like to suggest a fight that we can all join—on the same side.

Henry Kissinger was born in Furth, Germany, on this date in 1923. If history had taken a different turn, he would have stayed in Germany and history would have taken a different turn. But, thanks to the need to flee from Nazi oppression, he and his family came to the United States as refugees, and Henry Kissinger grew up to be one of the most celebrated American Secretaries of State. He made history just by becoming Secretary of State, the first of his faith—and the first U.S. Secretary of State to speak with a German accent. But he also made history by breaking away from precedents, by being aware that public opinion was a strong force in the world, and by working about three times as hard as most people. I propose to celebrate his birthday by urging us all to take a leaf or two from that particular Kissinger book.

MAY 28

Dionne quintuplets born, 1934.

Miracle of Dunkirk, 1940.

Introductions:

Most of us are born alone, so to speak; some of us are born twins; fewer of us are born triplets. On this day in 1934, Mrs. Oliva Dionne gave birth to quintuplets. The Dionne Quints were the first of their kind. They were the wonder of the world. Their family doctor became a world celebrity, and they were the most famous children the world had known. Nobody would have dreamed that, thanks to new fertility drugs, multiple births would become so much more numerous in later years. What seems to be a miracle of nature in one generation is a commonplace of science in the next. So let us address ourselves to some of today's miracles which we would like to see become the commonplaces of tomorrow.

I am reminded today of a miracle, one that began on or about this same day in 1940. It was called the Miracle of Dunkirk, when, in a period of about a week, more than 300,000 Allied Forces were evacuated from Dunkirk, France to continue World War II after a bitter defeat by the Nazis on the Continent. The Miracle of Dunkirk did more than bring the fighting men out of what seemed a total trap. It also gave new heart to the people of England. That was in 1940. When I look at the world today, I find it in far better shape than right before the Miracle of Dunkirk. We have a lot of challenges to face, but if we can summon up only a fraction of the spirit of Dunkirk, we will prevail.

MAY 29

Edmund Hillary and Tensing Norkay became first to climb Mount Everest, 1953.

Patrick Henry born, 1736.

John F. Kennedy born, 1917.

Introductions:

Today is a high spot. It represents in some respects the highest point of man on earth. I hope you will not think I am indulging in extravagant language about this gathering. I am talking about this day, May 29th, in the year 1953, when Edmund Hillary and Tensing Norkay climbed higher than any human beings had ever climbed on earth before. This was the day when they became the first men to reach the top of Mount Everest. I find myself wondering what it must be like not just to climb Mount Everest, but then to come back down to normal earth. Today my subject is not up in the clouds, but right down here with the rest of us.

When I began to prepare my remarks for today, I did a bit of research. I found that today was the birthday of both Patrick Henry and John F. Kennedy, two of the finest public speakers this nation has ever produced. It occurred to me that the best thing I could do, on the birthday of these two magnificently eloquent Americans, was simply to practice the three G's—get up, get down to cases and get off. I have done the first; that leaves two G's to go.

MAY 30

Joan of Arc burned at the stake, 1431.

Memorial Day formerly.

Hall of Fame dedicated, 1901.

Introductions:

It is always tempting for a speaker to arise and orate eloquently about his vision of the future. Visions as subject matter are very good because they don't have to be limited by the available facts. But then I realized that today is the anniversary of the burning of Joan of Arc at the stake because she insisted that she heard voices and saw visions. So I decided not to talk about visions and stick to facts instead; like these facts, for example.

Today used to be Memorial Day, defined by date. Memorial Day is now not May 30, necessarily, but rather the last Monday in May. That gives us a three-day week-end, which may or may not add to our memorial to the noble dead but adds somewhat to the pleasure of the moment. Regardless of the uncertain date of Memorial Day in our time, I would like to hope that future memorials will have more of peace to remember than of war. And we can all do something about that.

The Hall of Fame was dedicated on this day in 1901. It is some measure of fame itself that most people now are likely to ask which hall of fame— baseball's, football's, the Cowboy Hall of Fame or what? For the sad fact is that *the* Hall of Fame, dedicated in The Bronx in 1901, is less famous today than some of its namesakes. Fame is indeed fleeting—unless we are interested in keeping it alive. The same is true of progress. It is not automatically self-sustaining. If you like the way things are going, you can't sit back and expect them to keep going on their own; and if you don't like the way things are going, you've got to help change them. If my remarks today make no other point but that one—and make that one clear—then I will be content.

MAY 31

The end of Older Americans Month.

Adolf Eichmann hanged, 1962.

Eisenhower on revolutionists and rebels, 1954.

Introductions:

Today, I must inform you, is the last day of Older Americans Month. It is a sad commentary that in the last quarter of the twentieth century the govern-ment and other groups found it necessary to establish a special month to take notice of older Americans. I trust that the end of this special month does not mean that we now forget about older Americans until next year. And I want to go on record as saying that my remarks today defy Older Americans Month. I am talking today about *all* Americans.

This is the anniversary of the hanging of Adolf Eichmann by the State of Israel. Eichmann was hunted down as the Nazi mass murderer of Jews in the Hitler era in Germany. His hanging wrote a new chapter in international law and scared a lot of fugitive Nazis in various hiding places around the world. But it didn't seem to have a lasting impact. The crime of genocide has not been ended. Let me give you some up-to-date examples.

Dwight D. Eisenhower made a speech on this date in 1954. He spoke at Columbia University's bicentennial, as the President of the United States and the former President of Columbia. I would like to quote what he said, as my text today: "Here in America," he said, "we are descended in blood and in spirit from revolutionists and rebels—men and women who dared to dissent from accepted doctrine. As their heirs, we may never confuse honest dissent with disloyal subversion."

JUNE 1

"Don't give up the ship," 1813.

A midget on J. P. Morgan's lap, 1933.

Brigham Young born, 1801.

Introductions:

Of all the watchwords which have come down through American history, none has been quoted more than the immortal words, "Don't give up the ship." They have been attributed to Captain James Lawrence of the *U.S.S. Chesapeake*, as he lay dying aboard his ship on this day in 1813. Some attribute the quotation to another American captain, James Mugford of the *Franklin* in 1776, also as his dying words. Generally, Captain Lawrence gets the honor and is revered for his ringing call in the annals of American glory. The fact is that Lawrence's command, the *U.S.S. Chesapeake*, was not only roundly defeated by the British vessel *Shannon* but was also boarded and captured. Despite the Captain's fighting words, we did give up the ship. I mention this not to poke holes in an eloquent battle cry, but simply to point out that, while a battle cry is fine, you still need the stuff to back it up. My word to you today is that words simply aren't enough.

The attention of the public is easily diverted. If you doubt this, I refer you to the case of the midget on J. P. Morgan's lap. It was during a Senate hearing on this date in 1933; the man regarded as the mightiest of America's and perhaps the world's financiers, J. Pierpont Morgan, Jr., was sitting in the room waiting to be questioned about current economic problems (it being the depths of the depression). A circus press agent had a lady midget suddenly sit on Mr. Morgan's lap. You won't find much in the history books about that Senate hearing, but you'll find the picture of the midget on J. P. Morgan's lap in one photo history after another. This was certainly a case where one photograph was worth a thousand words. Nothing daunted, however, I shall continue relying on words in my appearance before you today. I will nevertheless keep one eye peeled for a circus press agent with a charming tiny lady in tow.

Today is the birthday of Brigham Young, born in 1801 in Whittingham, Vermont. As the man who led the epochal Mormon trek across the wild continent to Salt Lake City, which he founded, Brigham Young not only believed in miracles, he led one. He had 27 wives and was survived by 47 children; while he lived, the doctrine of plural marriage was accepted Mormon practice. He was both a religious leader and a doer. On the anniversary of his birth, we are reminded that doing and teaching often go hand in hand, and that those who speak with faith in the rightness of their cause are often made more eloquent by their faith. You understand, of course, that I am hoping to persuade you by assuring you that I believe wholeheartedly in what I am about to say.

JUNE 2

First radio patent, 1896.

Marquis de Sade born, 1740.

Introductions:

A long time ago, on this day, June 2, 1896, the first radio patent was awarded to a man named Guglielmo Marconi by Great Britain. It took a fair number of years for the wireless, as it was first called, to be able to transmit and receive anything more than dots and dashes, but today the air is as crowded with radio signals as the New York subway is full of people at rush hour. Radio is not merely a mass entertainment and information medium today; it is the communication line for pilots and police cars and trucks barreling down a lonely road. It talks to and from outer space. And Marconi's invention also furnished the basis for that later refinement, television. The patent that Great Britain granted in 1896 made talk ultimately a great deal more prevalent. Naturally, as I stand here today, I hope it also made listening a lot more prevalent as well.

Today is the birthday of the Marquis de Sade, born in 1740. One need not be a cynic observing contemporary morality, or the lack thereof, to observe that the Marquis de Sade was born before his time. I can't decide whether he would be leading a cult, producing pornographic films or publishing outrageous periodicals today—or doing all three. In his own time, he spent the last decade of his life in a lunatic asylum. If he were around today, he might have thought that the world is an asylum, run by the inmates. I intend, today, to strike a blow against what he preached. Not being a sadist, I shall not attempt cruelty upon this audience by trying your patience and continuing to speak after I have made my point. My point is simply this.

JUNE 3

R.O.T.C. authorized, 1916.

Duke of Windsor married, 1937.

Jefferson Davis born, 1808.

Introductions:

This is the anniversary of the National Defense Act of June 3, 1916. It was neither the first, the last, the biggest budgeted nor the lowest budgeted national defense legislation in our long history; but among its provisions was the establishment of the Reserve Officers Training Corp. The R.O.T.C. has certainly had its ups and downs since 1916, but through it all there has been one idea which I commend to your attention here today. That is the idea of a civilian-officer—the idea that both the Army and the Nation benefit from not having all the officers coming from the military academy. One of our great attributes as a nation has been that we are a nation of laymen; we are not content to leave anything entirely to the experts. Sometimes I think we should establish a reserve training corps for active citizenship, not merely for service in the armed forces. Today, as a matter of fact, I want to talk to you about what we are doing to train our citizens to be good citizens.

When the King of England dramatically abdicated in 1936 to marry the woman he loved, the world gasped and sighed. On this day, in 1937, that historic love story reached its moment of romantic glory. The Duke of Windsor, who had been King Edward VIII, married his love, Mrs. Wallis Warfield Simpson, and they did indeed live happily ever after until his death in 1972. Happiness can be achieved by those who are willing to sacrifice for it. That is the kind of happiness I want to talk about today.

Jefferson Davis is best remembered as the President of the Confederate States of America. It might be well today, which is his birthday, to recall some other facts about this man. Born in Kentucky in 1808, he was a West Pointer who was a brilliant regimental commander in the Mexican War. He served four years in the Senate and later was Secretary of War of the United States—and one of our best such secretaries. Then he went back to the Senate, representing Mississippi. He was not considered an extremist even when he reluctantly followed his state out of the Union. After General Lee's surrender, he tried to continue the war at least until he could get more favorable terms, but he was captured in May, 1865. Held in prison in Virginia, at first he was literally shackled, until public protests put an end to that barbarism. He was indicted for treason in 1866, released on bail the following year and never brought to trial. When he died in 1889, he still had not been given back his citizenship. I have told you all this because I think you should know the story of one American whom many regard as having been a political prisoner. If you see parallels or contrasts with the aftermath of other wars, so be it. On Jefferson Davis's birthday, I think it well that we consider our present in terms of our own past.

JUNE 4

Miracle of Dunkirk, 1940.

Old Maid's Day.

King George III born, 1738.

Introductions:

This is the anniversary of a miracle, an epic of World War II, described at the time and ever since as the Miracle of Dunkirk. It was the amazing evacuation of more than 300,000 Allied soldiers through Dunkirk, France, in the face of the Nazi conquest of the Continent. The Miracle of Dunkirk seemed to be a military impossibility; but it happened. Otherwise the war might have ended with a German victory. Miracles like Dunkirk happen because human beings are determined not to give up; because human beings do more than they ever thought they could do. Today, the Miracle of Dunkirk reminds us that we always have a tendency to underestimate our capabilities, until the chips are down. I believe we underestimate our capabilities today. We simply do not recognize how much we can do. And so today I propose to speak about some important things that we may not think we can do, but that can and must be done.

Today used to be celebrated—if that is the word—as something called Old Maid's Day, originated in 1946. It doesn't get much attention any more, and I think the reason is that we no longer think of people as old maids. This is not a manifestation of a mere alteration in vocabulary to satisfy female militants. It is simply that singleness is not now regarded as a debility. We have come to the belief that people choose, and are entitled to choose, how they wish to live their lives, and contemporary morality no longer equates singleness with loneliness, or necessarily with chastity or virtue. We have finally, I hope, come to regard the individual as the person with the options. In my remarks today, I start with the assumption that the most important thing a person can have is options, choices, the opportunity to choose his or her own path through life. I hope today I can be helpful to some of you in that choice.

The man who became Great Britain's King George III was born on this date, in 1738, in London. It is somewhat thanks to his stubbornness and ill-temper that the colonies first rebelled and then decided to become independent of British rule. Perhaps, therefore, America should celebrate the birthday of King George III; but I do not come here to make that suggestion. I come rather to point out that we should be grateful to the man who could have been our own King George. There were those who urged that role for George Washington. Thank goodness he wanted no part of it. Now we have politicians who must always remember that election day keeps coming round. Without a king—or, as in England, with a monarch shorn of the power that George III had in his time—we need not simply debate national policy. We can influence it. Here is what I have in mind.

JUNE 5

Marshall Plan proposed, 1947.

Adam Smith born, 1723.

General Sherman's historic "no," 1884.

Introductions:

It was in 1947, on this day, that America's senior professional soldier, George Catlett Marshall, having given up his uniform to become the civilian Secretary of State, stood up at Harvard University to propose what soon became known as the Marshall Plan to provide aid for war-impoverished nations. "Our policy," Secretary Marshall said, "is directed not against country or doctrine but against hunger, poverty, desperation and chaos." The European Recovery Plan which was developed from his proposal fulfilled his policy. It healed wounds and rebuilt the hopes of half the world. That is what help from a good neighbor can do. That is what we can do, in many ways and in many places, right now, today. We can start right here in our own home town. One does not need to cross the ocean to find hunger, or poverty, or desperation.

Thomas Carlyle called economics the dismal science. If it is a science at all, we can thank, among others, Adam Smith first and foremost. Adam Smith, born on this day in 1723, in Kirkcaldy, Scotland, was not the first political economist, but his masterpiece, *Inquiry into the Nature of the Causes of the Wealth of Nations*, put the subject all together, so to speak. That was in 1776. We have had a great deal of economic thinking and arguing since then. Economics today is not so much the dismal science as the disputatious one. It may be that I am going to make a contribution to the science today, or perhaps merely to the disputes. So here I go.

William Tecumseh Sherman was a great Civil War general whom some people wanted to nominate for the Presidency. On June 5, 1884, he sent a message which has remained perhaps the most perfect model of total clarity that the English language can produce. It is supposed to have read thus: "If nominated, I will not accept; if elected, I will not serve." Once you accept an invitation, you can't be quite that terse thereafter. So, since I have accepted your kind invitation to talk here today, I shall be saying a few more words than General Sherman.

JUNE 6

D-Day, 1944.

Senator Robert F. Kennedy died of assassin's bullet, 1968.

Nathan Hale born, 1755.

Introductions:

Today is the anniversary of the greatest invasion in recorded history, the landing of the Allied Forces on the shores of the European continent in 1944 on D-Day. We had been told, long before the reality of World War II, that warfare was different now, that the day of the great mass land battle was done. There were no more trenches—we were told. There would be fierce engagements, but no more of the business of waves of infantry following each other into a single battlefield. D-Day was not the only battle of its kind; in the Pacific as well, the infantryman was still fighting by charging and charging again. Will there be another D-Day, after all the fighting we have already known? It would be rash to expect us to find the answer that seems to have eluded so many generations up to now. But I do not mean to strike a pessimistic note on this anniversary of D-Day. If it had not been planned and carried out, I might not be here talking to this group; indeed, there might not be meetings like this. Our side on D-Day was the side of freedom. Things have perhaps grown more complicated since then, but we at least are still on the side of freedom. I propose to use that freedom here today to do some shooting—but I will only be shooting off my mouth.

In war, millions of people have been killed, millions of bullets have found their mark. Yet somehow the bullet which found its mark in one man on a night in June 1968 was more shocking. The man was Robert F. Kennedy, Senator from New York and candidate for the Presidency once held by his martyred brother. Early on the morning of June 6, 1968, he died in Los Angeles after having been shot before midnight. The assassination of Bobby Kennedy is always associated in my mind with a period when somehow we weren't able to talk together. In the same summer we had the Democratic Convention riots in Chicago. The fact that now we can and do talk together, that we have regained the degree of tolerance that seemed lost in the long hot summer of '68, is a comforting one. So let us talk.

Nathan Hale was born on this day, in 1775, in Coventry, Connecticut. He was 21 years old when he was executed as a spy, saying, according to legend as he stood on the gallows, "I regret that I have but one life to lose for my country." These are probably among the most famous last words in the annals of America. Unfortunately for hapless speakers, one can find any number of famous last lines, but not too many equally effective opening lines. Perhaps it will comfort you in the audience today, however, to know that I begin my remarks with such awareness that the ending should be in sight. Nathan Hale's remark, in addition to being eloquent, was brief. I shall try to be the same, though very definitely with a different ending.

JUNE 7

Freedom of the Press Day.

The difference between reverence and prayer, as seen by Henry D. Thoreau, 1841.

Introductions:

Today is Freedom of the Press Day, originated by the Inter-American Press Association for observance throughout the Americas. Freedom of the Press, whether as a special day or as an institution, has not often been observed throughout the Americas. Freedom of the press and freedom of speech must go hand in hand. And, obviously, to a speaker, freedom of speech is a matter of some importance. It is a freedom that I plan to make some use of here and now.

Writing in his Journal on June 7, 1841, Henry D. Thoreau said something worth calling to your attention. On this day, he noted that "Man stands to revere, he kneels to pray." One stands up to man, one kneels to God. Prayer is a noble institution, and I certainly am not here to disparage it. But I am here to say that we should stop confusing reverence and prayer. Reverence is a sign of respect, prayer is the hope of divine intervention. Today I wish to speak about our relationship to our government—a relationship which, I submit, demands respect but should not be confused with prayer. We elect our representatives; we do not anoint them. So let's talk about rendering unto Caesar.

JUNE 8

U.S. forces authorized to go into combat in South Vietnam, 1965.

Frank Lloyd Wright born, 1869.

Eisenhower on protection against big government, 1964.

Introductions:

This was the date, in 1965, when President Lyndon B. Johnson authorized U.S. forces to go into combat against the Vietcong in South Vietnam. It was neither the first nor the last step in the escalation of our role in that terrible conflict, and Lyndon Johnson was neither the first nor the last President to have to deal with our involvement there. With hindsight, we can see that we kept trying, or thinking we could manage, to be just a little bit pregnant. And of course that can't be done. If you are going to end up in something up to your navel, perhaps the best course is either to try to get out of it early or jump in with both feet. I won't get into the argument over which of those courses might have best changed the outcome of events. But I have a speech to make here today on a somewhat different subject and, faced with that challenge, I am about to jump into it with both feet. Otherwise it might take years, or at least hours. So, without further ado, let me say . . .

Not too many architects become national figures, although their distinctive style of architecture may become world famous. One who, to put it mildly, conquered anonymity was Frank Lloyd Wright, born on this day in 1869 in

Richland Center, Wisconsin. Frank Lloyd Wright designed the Imperial Hotel in Tokyo, the Guggenheim Museum in New York, the Johnson Wax Company's modern administration building in Racine, Wisconsin and striking, innovative homes all over the country. He was a pioneer at blending a house into its surroundings. He thought of architecture as a design for living. That is the way we should approach our life on earth today—as something in need of a design for living. To a large extent, we can't count on finding a Frank Lloyd Wright when we want him. So we have to be our own architects, planning for the building of our lives. That is what I want to address myself to here today.

On this day, in 1964, former President Dwight D. Eisenhower delivered an address to the National Governors Conference. He said something which I would like to take as my theme today. He said: "Our best protection against bigger government in Washington is better government in the states." I paraphrase that—or carry it a couple of steps further—by saying that our best protection against government is better governing of ourselves. Repressive measures adopted under the banner of law and order are too often prompted by the excesses of individual citizens and the failure of other citizens to stand together. Let me give you some concrete examples of how we can and should better govern ourselves.

JUNE 9

Jonkers Diamond mailed across the Atlantic for 35¢ postage, 1935.

John Howard Payne born, 1791.

Cole Porter born, 1892.

Introductions:

According to at least one almanac of dates, this is the day when, in 1935, the fabulous Jonkers Diamond, more than 700 carats' worth, was mailed from England to the United States for 35 cents. I bring this matter to your attention not to make us all miserable when we think of what the postage rates are today—although it's a point—but rather to suggest that every time is different. We can recall the past but we cannot live in it. What we can do with the present is to try to make the future better. I have no solution for the postal rates, but I do have some thought on some other matters that I'd like to share with you.

John Howard Payne is the man who wrote the song, "Home Sweet Home." He was born on this date, in 1791, in New York. Today he is remembered practically entirely for "Home Sweet Home," although he was the author of dozens of plays and an actor of some repute. It all goes to show that one success outlives a parade of lesser efforts. Be it ever so humble, there's no place like the top. John Howard Payne didn't get there often, but he made it once, and is remembered for it. There is hope for all of us. That optimistic note is what persuades me to address you here today.

If John Howard Payne is remembered for just one song, another song writer born on this day, but some years later, has quite a different problem. Cole Porter, born in 1893 in Peru, Indiana, was one of our best known popular song writers. His Broadway hits were innumerable, his lyrics sophisticated, his music catchy and clever. Merely reciting the titles of some of his songs provides a selection of themes for my remarks here today: "Anything Goes," "Just One of Those Things," "My Heart Belongs to Daddy," "Don't Fence Me In," "Wake Up and Dream," "You're the Top" and "Let's Do It," to name just a few.

JUNE 10

Italy's two sides, 1940 and 1946.

Lidice wiped out, 1942.

Judy Garland born, 1922.

Introductions:

This is the day of the year when a great nation had both its low and its high point. On this day, in 1940, Italy attacked France as the Nazis were crushing the French. Under the dictator Mussolini, as President Franklin D. Roosevelt put it, " . . . the hand that held the dagger has stuck it into the back of its neighbor." But Italy, given the chance, overthrew Mussolini, and on this day in 1946 exercised its rights to free government by formally becoming a republic. We like to remember the happy events and let them overcome the memory of the unhappy ones. But we can better appreciate our current blessings if we are mindful of how far we have come from the bad days.

Do you recognize the name Lidice? Do you have to stop and think about it? Don't be disturbed if that is the case, because Lidice is not a happy memory. Lidice was a town in Czechoslovakia. On this day, in 1942, after Gestapo leader Reinhard Heydrich was killed, Nazi occupying forces wiped out the town of Lidice. Even in the midst of World War II, it was a shocking event. In the light of what has happened since, would it be as shocking today? I suggest that we ask ourselves whether the vengefulness that destroyed Lidice is a thing of the past. How do we exorcise the spirit of vengefulness today? Are we a non-violent society? Or are we, in our own time and our own land, making our own countless little Lidices of the spirit?

The human spirit is a complicated entity. We are brought up to think that material success is the road to happiness; few have been more successful in their time than Judy Garland, born on this date, in 1922, in Grand Rapids, Minnesota. Few have been more successful in their profession and less happy in their lives. She brought laughter and pleasure to a world which brought her not enough of either. And so perhaps we should be less worried about assuring material success and more concerned with figuring out just how to make people happy. People can create their own unhappiness—their own Lidice—but it is usually because of standards or goals set by other people. How, in the age of group conformism, can we recapture the individualism of the human spirit?

JUNE 11

Climax of U.S.S.R.'s great "purge," 1937.

Ben Hogan's comeback, 1950.

Introductions:

This was the day, in 1937, when the great Russian "purge" reached its climax. After a secret military trial, Marshal Tukhachevski and seven other very high ranking officers were convicted of conspiring with an unfriendly power and sentenced to death. They were shot the next day. Previously, civilian leaders who had fallen out of favor with Communist dictator Josef Stalin, had been convicted and thirteen of them had been executed earlier in the year. With the shooting of the generals, Stalin had managed to terrorize and suppress all opposition, which he branded as Trotskyite or simply traitorous. The unfriendly nation he tied to Tukhachevski and the other generals was Germany, which makes the whole thing a little more interesting because two years later Russia signed a non-aggression treaty—with Germany. Russia was conveniently neutral when Germany started World War II by invading Poland. Now most of this is ancient history for most of this audience; but it is worth recalling because it reminds us of something which every audience should bear in mind. No matter how eloquent the words, actions speak louder than words. The best words, therefore, are those which constitute a call to action, and it is for that purpose I raise my voice here today.

For some reason, heroism in sport seems to be more memorable than heroism in everyday life. That is particularly true when a sports figure comes back after having his career seemingly ruined by an accident. On this day in 1950, a golfer named Ben Hogan thrilled the nation by winning the U.S. Open Golf Championship. Ben Hogan had been a champion long before then, but, more than a year earlier, he had been so seriously hurt in an automobile accident that it didn't seem likely he would ever play again, let alone win. But he was determined to come back. He worked at it. He struggled, he exercised, he gritted his teeth and bore the pain and kept trying. Any number of handicapped people are doing the same thing every day of their lives, and they don't all have the spectacular success that was Ben Hogan's on this day in 1950. Because sports heroes are in the public eye we know about their battles and their courage. For common folk, we who have our health don't always understand how much courage and how much struggle goes into seemingly ordinary achievements sometimes. So today, I ask you to remember Ben Hogan's comeback for what it symbolized, and to rmember also that, for a man who cannot walk, the first step is a giant one. It is easy sometimes to say we simply cannot do this or that. It is much harder to say we can and we will.

JUNE 12

Virginia Declaration of Rights, 1776.

Baseball Hall of Fame opened, 1939.

Introductions:

Today is one of those days which the history books have largely overlooked, and it is a shame, because today is really a red-letter day in American history. It was on this date, in 1776, while the Continental Congress was meeting in Philadelphia, that the Virginia Declaration of Rights, largely written by George Mason, was adopted by the Virginia Convention. Perhaps if I read you a couple of phrases you will see why I attach so much importance to this document, which was adopted almost a month before the Declaration of Independence. Article 1—from which I will omit some words but substitute or add none: Quote: "That all men are by nature equally free and independent and have certain inherent rights . . . the enjoyment of life and liberty . . . and pursuing and obtaining happiness . . . 2. That all power is . . . derived from the people." Unquote. They must have been listening in Philadelphia. But the Virginia Declaration of Rights made some other points as well, like insistence on freedom of the press and freedom of worship. All in all, a remarkable document, whose influence on the Declaration of Independence, the Constitution and the Bill of Rights was obvious. Our great American tradition of freedom has many roots, but one of the greatest is that which was adopted in Virginia on this date in 1776. It is an American privilege to be able to get up and speak your mind. To speak one's mind on this day is particularly appropriate.

Today is the birthday of the Baseball Hall of Fame, opened on this date in 1939 in Cooperstown, New York. Some of you may think a Baseball Hall of Fame is silly, or frivolous. I hail it as an example of something America can use more of—not to plug baseball, but to give more people the pleasure of having their accomplishments recognized and honored. Why not a salesmen's hall of fame, or a pinochle players' or a volunteer fund raisers' hall of fame? I come to you today to speak in favor of more recognition for good people doing good things.

JUNE 13

Alexander the Great died, 323 B.C.

Missile age born, 1944.

First Black Supreme Court Justice nominated, 1967.

Introductions:

This is the day when, in 323 B.C., Alexander the Great was proven right for saying he had no more worlds to conquer. This is the day when the young Emperor died of a fever. He died feeling he had done it all, but just think of how much more has been done since then. There isn't one of us—neither the greatest scientist nor the richest millionaire nor the most successful soldier—who cannot find another hill to climb, another challenge to overcome, another world to conquer. Whether you call it fear or complacency, it is the enemy of progress. This is no time to give up trying for a better world.

One of the ways we are, perhaps even in the literal sense of the words, searching for a better world is through the exploration of the rest of the universe. Today is the anniversary of the modern start of that kind of exploration; and it is a strange anniversary, because the start of this peaceful age of space exploration was the result of the birth of a new weapon of war. On this day, in 1944, the missile age was born as German flying bombs hit England in World War II. That is how rocket propulsion came to the attention of the world. Never underestimate man's ingenuity at taming dangerous tools. When the Bible spoke of turning swords into ploughshares, the world was far away from the jet age. But we are still at it. And there is no lake of opportunity to continue changing the tools of war into the instruments of peace.

This is the anniversary of President Lyndon B. Johnson's nomination of Thurgood Marshall to become the first Black Justice of the Supreme Court. It was a long time in coming, but it came. The genius of America is that what needs doing ultimately gets done. The American way of life is still picking up more polish, more substance. Some things take longer than others, but they get done. And, speaking of some things taking longer than others, I want to assure you that I was not referring to my speech here today. I don't expect my remarks to be short and sweet, but I do expect them to be short.

JUNE 14

Flag Day.

Harriet Beecher Stowe born, 1811.

Eisenhower on the book burners, 1953.

Introductions:

Today is Flag Day. It commemorates the official adoption of the Stars and Stripes on this date, in 1777, by the Continental Congress. The star spangled banner still waves over the land of the free and the home of the brave. It is a very comforting and very inspiring symbol, and it lends itself to graphic representation. We don't take kindly to people who are waving the flag, but we admire those who show the flag. We don't need to have the symbol waved in our faces, but we are comforted to know that what it stands for is still there, still whole, still worth preserving. And one of the things associated with the flag is free speech. The flag stands there for all to see, and the speaker speaks his mind. Here we go.

Today is the birthday of Harriet Beecher Stowe, born in 1811 in Litchfield, Connecticut. Mrs. Stowe wrote a book whose alternate title was *Life Among the Lowly*. You never heard of it? Yes you did. The full title was *Uncle Tom's Cabin or, Life Among the Lowly*. It first appeared in 1852, and it helped greatly in whipping up abolitionist sentiment in the North before the Civil War. Its influence lasted long after the War. When we call someone a Simon Legree today, we are remembering a character from *Uncle Tom's Cabin*; and if Uncle Tom does not mean today what it did to Mrs. Stowe's time, it is still drawn from her book. Not too many authors or speakers can make that much of an impact. But we can still use the symbolism of Harriet Beecher Stowe after all these years. For example, I am relieved that this is a friendly audience; otherwise I would feel like Eliza crossing the ice.

It is interesting that on the birthday of the author of one of the most influential and powerful books ever written, Harriet Beecher Stowe's *Uncle Tom's Cabin*, a President of the United States should have found it appropriate to speak out against the enemies of books. There are those among us who have a fear of books. President Eisenhower had that in mind on this day in 1953 when he said at Dartmouth College, "Don't join the book burners. Don't think you are going to conceal faults by concealing evidence that they ever existed." Speeches, like books, cover a broad range from good to bad. Naturally, I hope my remarks fall in the first category. At least I have the security of knowing that, along with book burning, the hook has been outmoded as a method of dealing with speakers. Thus heartened, I turn to my text for the day.

JUNE 15

Magna Carta signed, 1215.

Franklin's kite, 1752.

Introductions:

There is something contradictory about June 15, the anniversary of the signing of the Magna Carta in 1215 but also the deadline for payment of the second installment of estimated income tax in the U.S. But life is a series of anomalies; not the least is that, on the birthday of the basic document of

Anglo-Saxon law, you should be subjected to the perhaps cruel and unusual punishment of both paying your taxes and having to listen to me. But perhaps I can take your mind off the taxes.

If you want to tell me to go fly a kite, I must tell you that this is a very auspicious day for it. For this is the day when, in 1752, Ben Franklin used a kite to prove that lightning contained electric current. That accomplishment of Ben Franklin's doesn't do me too much good today, but it reminds me of a saying of his which every speaker should remember: A word to the wise is enough, and many words won't fill a bushel. I am not here to fill a bushel.

JUNE 16

John Quincy Adams' three-week speech, 1838.

Abraham Lincoln warns of a house divided, 1858.

Introductions:

History records that on this day in 1838—this very day— a former President of the United States, John Quincy Adams, then serving as a member of the House of Representatives, arose and began a speech opposing the annexation of Texas. The speech, the history books tell us, lasted three weeks. I wish to assure you that my remarks today will be somewhat shorter.

In Springfield, Illinois, the Republican Party, in convention assembled on this date in 1858, was the audience for a man they had just nominated for U.S. Senator. His name was Abraham Lincoln. He lost that particular election, but what he said on this day in 1858 has echoed through the corridors of time. He said, " 'A house divided against itself cannot stand.' I believe this government cannot endure permanently half slave and half free." Those who doubt the power of words would do well to remember these words of Abraham Lincoln, that led to the memorable Lincoln-Douglas debates. Douglas won that election, but the words of Lincoln captured the attention and the imagination of enough people around the country to lead him onward to the Presidential nomination and election in 1860. Unfortunately, a great many speakers since then have used words not quite as well but with similar objectives. Today I stand before you with no illusion of Lincolnian eloquence. But I do share his wish not to see a house divided, and so I will not try your patience today with a long spell of oratory. As Lincoln once said, though not referring to my forthcoming remarks, "People who like this sort of thing will find this the sort of thing they like."

JUNE 17

Bunker Hill Day.

Army-McCarthy televised hearings ended, 1954.

First round-the-world airline service, 1947.

Introductions:

This was the day, in 1774, when an American commander said, "Don't fire till you see the whites of their eyes." It was at the Battle of Bunker Hill in Boston. A wise old speaker told me that the time to stop speaking was when you could no longer see the whites of the audience's eyes, because that meant their eyes were closed. So I want you all to know I shall be watching you closely.

Today is not the anniversary of just one Army battle, however well known the encounter at Bunker Hill. Today is also the anniversary of the Army's televised battle with the late Senator Joseph R. McCarthy. The last broadcast of that epic daytime drama was on June 17, 1954. It ended with the Army clearly ahead. Senator McCarthy had been riding high, but was skidding on his way downhill after a wise old lawyer named Joseph Welch let him talk himself into a box. Lawyers always advise their clients that when they are on the witness stand they should say as little as possible—just answer the questions. I do not plan to take that advice today because I am not on the witness stand and I am not here on advice of counsel. But I will bear in mind the lesson of the day that the art of talking is the art of knowing when to stop.

Listening is on the rise. I can remember the time before portable radios and tape players and canned music when you could walk on the street or ride in a plane without an aural accompaniment. I started to think of this when I discovered that today was the anniversary of the first round-the-world civil airline service, by Pan American Airways from LaGuardia Field in New York. It wasn't 80 days around the world, but it was a lot longer in terms of the time than the same trip in today's jet age. And it was noisy. But the noise was the noise of airplane engines and propellers, not the sound track of a movie or your choice of six channels of taped entertainment programs. Perhaps the time will come when all those of us who are called on to talk before groups such as this will arrive in the form of a video cassette. One advantage for the audience, of course, is that a cassette can be turned off, without giving offense to the speaker, because the speaker isn't really there. But I am here, live and in person, and I shall devote the next few minutes to not turning *you* off.

JUNE 18

Harper's "millions for defense" toast, 1798.

Waterloo, 1815.

Introductions:

I wonder what would happen here today if a speaker spoke the toast that Robert Goodloe Harper, at a dinner honoring John Marshall after Marshall's diplomatic mission to France, uttered on this date in 1798. "Millions for defense," said Harper, "but not a cent for tribute." Of course he would have revised it if he were saying that toast today. It would have to be *billions* for defense or it is not worth mentioning. I have a feeling that with that amendment, his policy would be generally palatable today, even though we are all concerned about the costs of government and taxes. My point is that we are not necessarily as far removed from the days of our nation's youth—in terms of sentiment, at least—as we sometimes think. An interesting sidelight is that Robert Goodloe Harper himself, like some people today, was elected to high public office—in his case the U.S. Senate—but resigned because he couldn't afford it; he did so much better in business and the practice of the law. But, as you can see from the way his words have come down to us, he talked a pretty good case. I shall now endeavor to do the same.

Today is the day when, in 1815, Napoleon met his Waterloo. The Battle of Waterloo smashed his dreams of a renewed empire once and for all. Every man, said Wendell Phillips, meets his Waterloo at last. But Napoleon took a tremendous number of people with him. That brings us to the question asked by Sholom Aleichem's beggar character when the beggar's daily benefactor turned him away, saying "I lost a great deal of money this week" and the beggar replied, "Just because you had a bad week, why should I suffer?" When a poor speaker meets his Waterloo on the public platform, it isn't he who suffers, but the audience. So I have decided not to do battle with you today, but rather to speak in soothing terms.

JUNE 19

Statue of Liberty arrived, 1885.

Black Hole of Calcutta, 1756.

Federal Communications Commission created, 1934.

Introductions:

There is probably no symbol more closely related to everybody's idea of the spirit of America than the Statue of Liberty. Today is the day when the Statue arrived at what was then called Bedloe's Island in New York Harbor in 1885. This noble symbol of America was a gift from France, designed and built on the other side of the Atlantic and then transported here to be put together again. We like to think of our country as the source of all inspiration, but our symbol is an immigrant. It was sent to us as a gift because of the way other people thought of us. What do you think our image is in the world today—if it is a single image? Let me give you some food for thought on that point.

I stand here surveying this room on the anniversary—give or take a day—of a reputed event known as the Black Hole of Calcutta, when some 146 people were supposed to have been confined to a single dungeon so crowded that only 23 survived the night. The date for this event was 1756, but it is not too late to be grateful that your condition is somewhat less crowded here today. I shall be more friendly to my captive audience than Suraj ad Dowlah was to those in the Black Hole.

Back in 1934, on this date, Congress passed a law creating the Federal Communications Commission, which replaced the earlier Federal Radio Commission. That got me to thinking about how communications have expanded since the establishment of the Commission which was to regulate communications. Citizens band radio, television, data transmission, fiber optics—one could go on and on. The fact is that there has been a communications explosion which is still going on. But thank goodness no license is required for me to address you, as long as I do my talking in the old fashioned way—and that is what I plan to do, including the old-fashioned idea of making it short and sweet.

JUNE 20

E pluribus unum, 1782.

Lizzie Borden, 1893.

Introductions:

The Great Seal of the United States, adopted on this very day by Congress back in 1782—before we even had the Constitution—features an eagle holding an olive branch, and the legend, "E Pluribus Unum." One from many. That slogan has numerous meanings today; not just one country made up of many states, but one people, made up of many different strains; or one great freedom made up of many freedoms. "E pluribus unum." I must tell you, however, that it can stand, when utilized by a loquacious speaker, for the kind of speech that gets one small thought out of many words. I will not practice that kind of "E Pluribus Unum" here today. At least I will try not to.

Every generation has its crime of the century. Today we have the anniversary, not of a crime, but of the handing down of a not guilty verdict. This verdict did not put an end to the strangely persistent legend. On this date, in 1893, a young lady in New Bedford, Massachusetts, was acquitted of the charge of having murdered her father and stepmother a year earlier. You may not know that she was acquitted. You are more likely to know that, as a popular doggerel had it: "Lizzie Borden took an axe/And gave her mother forty whacks./And when she saw what she had done/She gave her father forty-one." Thus is folklore born. Well, I am not here to add to the folklore—or to the ledger of crime. I am here, however, to plead a case before you, ladies and gentlemen of the jury.

JUNE 21

Summer.

Long-playing record demonstrated, 1948.

Introductions:

Although the summer solstice isn't always precisely punctual, today, more often that not, is the first day of the summer season. In observance of that occasion, I shall endeavor not to get this audience hot under the collar. When "summer is icumen in," as the poet put it, our major purpose in life is, or should be, to keep cool. At the same time, however, there are issues to which we cannot turn a cold shoulder. I shall therefore try to maintain an even temperature in my remarks today.

It was in 1948, on this date, that the long-playing record was demonstrated by Dr. Peter Goldmark of CBS Laboratories. The long-playing record, with its high fidelity recording and its extended playing time, ushered in a new era in recorded music and launched what has since become the era of the gold and platinum records, the tidal wave of record albums and the wonder on the part of many as to why you need long play and high fidelity for sounds as loud and raucous as some of the popular music of the day. However, I mention the long-playing record merely to point out that if you had brought in a phonograph instead of a live speaker you might be getting a longer and louder—and perhaps funnier—set of remarks than I am about to present to you.

JUNE 22

Civil rights workers slain, 1964.

Judy Garland died, 1969.

Vote for 18-year-olds, 1970.

Introductions:

There is a story about an old vaudevillian whose act was falling flat—so flat that he was yanked off the stage and a local youngster was brought in as an emergency fill-in. The youngster was a smash hit and the next day the local critic wrote that the old vaudevillian's act "had died that others might live." We are inclined to take some martyrs' deaths that lightly. I want to remedy that here today by recalling that on this day, in 1964, three civil rights workers disappeared in Mississippi. Their bodies were discovered two weeks later. They were martyrs in the cause of civil rights for Blacks. Truly, they like so many others through history, died that others might live. Today, I should like to talk about how we can *live* so that others may live.

Judy Garland found success, and then unhappiness, earlier and in larger doses than most of us. On this day, the 22nd day of June, in 1969, Judy Garland died, at the age of 47. With her, some of the youthful spirit of her generation also passed. We do not generally look at ourselves directly; we look at ourselves through our contemporaries. Man is a social animal; we like each other, and all too often we try to be like each other. Let me rise and speak today about the importance of not being like each other—or, more importantly, of not expecting others to be like us.

One reason not all people are alike is that we come in a variety of generations. In 1970, on this day, President Nixon signed into law the bill giving 18 year olds the right to vote in U.S. elections. There were those who saw disaster ahead, in the form of an army of callow adolescents dominating the voting lists. It didn't work out that way. The young people demonstrated just about the same degree of callowness and of sophistication as their parents. None of the generations took sufficient part in the electoral process. And so we discovered once again that young people, like older people, are people of the same generation but otherwise very different among themselves. So today I will not talk about people in general, because people don't come in general. I will talk, instead, about things which affect all of us widely assorted, variable density individuals.

JUNE 23

Luxembourg's birthday.

Peaceful Antarctic treaty, 1961.

Capital letter typewriter patented, 1868.

Introductions:

Won't you join me in wishing a happy birthday to the principality of Luxembourg, founded in this date in 963? The birthday has to be happy because Luxembourg has survived occupations and invasions by more powerful neighbors—and every other country is more powerful than Luxembourg, except in its ability to survive. Good countries, like good speeches, sometimes come in small packages.

It's a long way from the birthday of Luxembourg to an anniversary for Antarctica, but today we commemorate both of the above. On this date, in 1961, an international treaty for scientific cooperation and peaceful use of the Antarctic was signed. It will be a cold day when that treaty ends. Meanwhile, we can benefit from knowing that if a place is cold enough, countries are not as apt to fight over it—until they find buried treasure there. The Antarctic treaty is like my speech today, designed to keep the pot warm and the friendly fire going.

History records that on this date, in 1868, one Christopher Sholes received a patent for a contraption called a "Type-Writer." This particular "typewriter" printed only in capital letters, apparently not having a shift key. I will endeavor today to follow its example. I too plan to take a position from which I shall not shift.

JUNE 24

Flying saucers reported, 1947.

Blockade of Berlin, 1948.

Introductions:

We meet on a historic day. On this day in 1947, the first reports of the sighting of flying saucers were made. The mysterious objects were supposed to have been sighted above Mount Rainier, Washington. That was it. In later years, the reports were considerably more detailed, up to and including accounts of visits by humans inside space ships from other planets, little green creatures and so forth. There is little evidence that the people who offered these reports were deliberately trying to con the public. If they were, they did not succeed, because the general reaction was not a credulous one. What they saw was explained as a mirage of marsh gas, or atmospheric phenomena; and people didn't seem terribly anxious to believe those explanations either. Flying saucers after a while just didn't seem to interest people. Which reminds me of the story of the commander of a flying saucer who came home to his own planet and reported that he had landed on earth and walked into Times Square. "What did you see there," he was asked. "Well," he said, "there were a lot of little creatures moving about and at every corner there was a big creature with red and green eyes bending over and winking at them. I think the big creatures were making speeches." So please consider me today as your resident traffic light, about to signal "go."

It seems hard to believe that in 1948, on this date, Soviet Russia could have thought that by blockading the land and water routes from the West to West Berlin they could starve that city or its Western affiliation into submission. As they learned over the next months, they had forgotten all about going by air. Air is a very good channel for communication. I trust that my remarks today will not be too warm, because I know you don't want hot air.

JUNE 25

Custer's Last Stand, 1876.

Korean War, 1950.

Introductions:

I am mindful as I stand before you today that even a speaker given a cordial greeting should be wary of assuming that the audience has already been won over. Today is the anniversary of Custer's Last Stand, when Colonel George Armstrong Custer and his entire command were wiped out by the Indians at Little Big Horn, Montana, in 1876. Do not misunderstand me. I have no fear that Custer's Last Stand will be repeated here today with me as Custer. It is simply that, remembering Custer's overconfidence as he went into battle, I do not start with any blissful assumption that what I am about to say will automatically win your support. In brief, I am here to sound my own little big horn and to hope that you will find the message to your liking.

Some days in American history are highlighted by warm and peaceful events. Some days, like today, have sterner memories. Long after Custer's Last Stand, on this date in 1876, there was another sad event on this date—the beginning of the Korean War in 1950, when North Korea invaded South Korea. After years of fighting, that war ended with many casualties and the border just about where it had been before; and the battle continued for decades thereafter across opposite sides of a conference table in a border location. One of the aspects of those conferences at the border has been the stream of speeches by the representatives of North Korea. Today, the anniversary of the start of the war of bullets, reminds us that when the bullets stopped, the war of words went on unabated. I am not here to take part in any war of words; I shall not assail your ears with verbal barrages. Instead, I shall speak to you in what I hope will be measured tones for a measured and, I assure you, a limited amount of time, on behalf of a very peaceful cause.

JUNE 26

UN Charter signed, 1945.

Berlin airlift began, 1948.

Abner Doubleday born, 1819.

Introductions:

I come to you as a speaker today on the anniversary of the birth of the greatest gift to speakers the world has yet known, the United Nations. Ever since the UN was established, with the signing of the United Nations charter on this day in 1945, in San Francisco, words have sounded in the international forum unceasingly. I am not sure the United Nations in its various sessions has done much to advance the art of listening, but it has given more people, from more countries, the opportunity to stand up and speak their piece than any other instrument in the history of the spoken word. So, on the anniversary of that invitation to eloquence, I stand before you to carry on the tradition and the theory of the UN—namely that an opportunity to shoot off one's mouth is better than shooting guns.

This is the anniversary of the Berlin Airlift, when the United States and Great Britain began supplying West Berlin by air to overcome the Soviet sea and land blockade in 1948. That Allied response proved what every speaker knows—namely that there is more than one way to skin a cat. Today, we find ourselves forever engaged in searching for alternatives—alternative life styles, alternative courses of action, alternative choices in education. We have not, thus far, however, found an alternative for the ancient art of oratory. Perhaps after I get through today, the search for that alternative may be stepped up.

There are those who claim that the sport which Abner Doubleday is sometimes credited with inventing became the national pastime for a reason other than its athletic challenge. The sport of course is baseball, and Abner Doubleday, born on this day in 1819 in Ballston Spa, New York, is not its inventor; but he played it. Perhaps even in his day, some of its charm may have been the exciting confrontation with the umpire. There is no game more susceptible to disputes over an official's call. After all, every pitch is subjected to the umpire's judgment. Today we find some overtones of baseball in the immediate situation. You, the audience, will be the umpires, making judgment on my every pitch. Shall we play ball?

JUNE 27

Helen Keller born, 1880.

Mormon leaders Joseph and Hyrum Smith murdered by mob, 1844.

FDR's "rendezvous with destiny," 1936.

Introductions:

We generally think of courage in terms of combat—either on the battlefield or on the playing fields of sport. Today we should be thinking of a far greater kind of courage, for today is the birthday of Helen Keller, born in 1880 in Tuscumbia, Alabama. Helen Keller, as most everyone may know, was both blind and deaf. Because she was deaf, she couldn't talk. But she learned to talk; she learned to read lips by touching the lips and throat of the person speaking. She learned to read by touch as well. She became a professional writer and a crusader for education for the better treatment of the blind and deaf. People are courageous when they conquer *one* handicap. Helen Keller conquered many. And I cannot help thinking, as I stand here speaking to you and you sit listening to me, how we take for granted what Helen Keller had to fight so hard to achieve.

The United States prides itself on being a land of religious freedom. It is written in the Constitution. There have been many offenses against it, notably the anti-Catholicism and anti-Semitism of some backward sections of the nation in times past. But there is nothing sectional about religious hatred. I am reminded of this because today is the anniversary of one of its worst examples. Joseph Smith, who founded the Mormon faith, was dragged from jail with his brother Hyrum on this date in 1844 in Carthage, Illinois, by a mob that proceeded to shoot them dead. And this was after the Smiths had been forced to leave one community after another because of their beliefs. It is, as we have found in our history, not enough to have religious tolerance written into the Constitution. It also has to be written into our hearts. We keep telling ourselves that the kinds of things that happened in our country long ago don't happen here any more. That isn't always true, unless we really care.

When Franklin D. Roosevelt was renominated for the Presidency on this day, in 1936, he sounded a rallying call for his time. "This generation," President Roosevelt said, "has a rendezvous with destiny." I don't think that generation of 1936 had a monopoly on such a rendezvous. We too, in our time, can and should have a rendezvous with destiny. The question is: will we recognize it when we get there?

JUNE 28

World War I triggered, 1914.

World War I ended, 1919.

Entebbe, 1976.

Henry VIII born, 1491.

Introductions:

I wonder how many people here know the name of Gavrilo Princip. It is one of the quirks of history that some of the people who kindled the epic flames of history are so little recognized in history. Gavrilo Princip was one—a Serbian revolutionary who, apparently with some knowledge on the part of the Serbian government, planned a blow against Austria-Hungary. On this day, in 1914, Gavrilo Princip assassinated Austria's Archduke Francis Ferdinand in Sarajevo, Bosnia. The killing of the heir to the throne of the Austro-Hungarian Empire was the trigger for World War I. So today we should be mindful that individual events are sometimes part of a larger canvas. It is against the larger canvas of the world rather than the small group assembled here today, that I have prepared my remarks on this occasion.

The fact that the Treaty of Versailles, which ended World War I, was signed on this date in 1919—the same date on which the War had been triggered in 1914—was poetic justice. Not everything can be wrapped up as neatly as that. The United States never ratified the Treaty of Versailles because it contained provisions for the League of Nations; wrapping things up neatly doesn't always make the package palatable. I am encouraged therefore to be less concerned about the packaging of my remarks here today than about the substance.

World War I was set off by an act of violence on this date in 1914. Sixty-two years later another classic instance of terrorism occurred, with far different results. On this date in 1976, terrorist hijackers seized an Air France plane overnight and brought it to the airport at Entebbe, Uganda, holding the passengers, mainly Israeli ones, as hostages. The world was aghast. A week later, a daring Israeli raid freed the hostages and wrote finis to the terrorists' plans. No World War this time. The moral, for speakers as well as doers, is not to overplay your hand. I shall therefore not hold any of you hostage.

Not too many people in this room knew the name of Gavrilo Princip, who triggered World War I. I dare say everybody will recognize the name of a man whose chief claims to fame are the number of women he married, the fight he had with the Church and his gluttonous table manners. His name was Henry VIII, the king who fathered the great Queen Elizabeth I of England. Henry VIII was born in 1491 in Greenwich, England. Henry VIII, as we know him from so many portrayals in drama and from legend, was not a notably lovely character. But he had one attribute which speakers like myself must always envy. No two ways about it. When he spoke, people listened.

JUNE 29

Rubens born, 1577.

Britain passed the Townshend Revenue Act, 1767.

Al Smith nominated for the Presidency, 1928.

Introductions:

One of the clichés of both fact and fiction is the gifted artist starving in a garret—Rembrandt penniless, for example. There are some exceptions and, of the exceptions, none was more exceptional than a man born on this date, in 1577, in Westphalia to a Flemish family. His name was Peter Paul Rubens, and he did very well indeed, not merely in terms of the masterfulness of his paintings but also in terms of the size of his purse. If you visit the Rubens house in Antwerp, you see quite an establishment. Art was very rewarding for Peter Paul Rubens. It is fair to say that, even though so many people have delighted in his work, in a material sense he got a lot more out of it. There is one school of public speaking that operates on the same kind of equation. The speaker gets more out of it than the audience. But I have heard me many times before. What I hope to get out of today's remarks will come to me not from your immediate reaction; rather, it will come from what you say or do afterward.

We are generally familiar with the circumstances surrounding the great Boston Tea Party, when the tea was dumped into Boston Harbor, in 1773, to protest the import tax levied by the British government on the colonies. It is somewhat less well remembered that the whole thing began on this date, June 29, several years earlier, in 1767. That was the date when King George III gave his approval to the Townshend Acts proposed by Chancellor of the Exchequer Charles Townshend, taxing imports to the colonies of glass, paper, lead, paints and tea. The tea tax was retained when the colonists began to boycott importing the other products, and slowly but surely the resentment against "taxation without representation" laid the groundwork for the American Revolution—thanks to Charles Townshend and the Acts he fathered on this day in 1767. As your speaker today, I must be more mindful than he was of taxing people unfairly—so I will be careful not to tax your patience.

It may seem odd to a nation that remembers so vividly the enthusiasm for John Fitzgerald Kennedy, but on this day, 32 years before John F. Kennedy won the Presidency, it was considered almost revolutionary that another Catholic candidate could have won a major party Presidential nomination. In 1924, Alfred E. Smith had been denied the Democratic nomination; such a nomination had never gone to a Catholic. In 1928, he was not to be denied. Another bastion of religious differentiation had been breached. American history, thank goodness, is full of these single steps forward. And so today, on the anniversary of one of those steps forward, I should like to make so bold as to suggest some others.

JUNE 30

Gone with the Wind published, 1936.

Twenty-sixth Amendment gives vote to 18-year-olds, 1971.

Introductions:

The great literature that comes out of most wars appears in the generation after the war. One exception is our own Civil War, which has been spawning great literature for more than a century. Probably the most popular, and some will contend also the greatest, has been Margaret Mitchell's epic *Gone with the Wind*, published on this date in 1936. It was an all-time best seller as a book and a recurrent sensation at the movie box office. Some books are indeed gone with the wind, but not *Gone with the Wind*. It was a very long book, and a very long motion picture too. But do not be alarmed. On its anniversary I will do it homage by making a considerably shorter speech.

The Twenty-sixth Amendment to the Constitution was ratified in 1971 on this date. It completed a job begun on June 22 a year earlier, when the law was enacted that gave U.S. citizens the right to vote at 18. When the Supreme Court ruled that the earlier law could not apply to state and local elections, the

Twenty-sixth Amendment was proposed to extend the franchise all the way to 18-year-olds. On this date, in 1971, it was made part of the Constitution. Whether it has indeed materially affected the character of American politics is something that can be argued morning, noon and night; but I have scheduled a less debatable subject for my remarks here today. That's because to the average person, what you can do at eighteen is only important till you get older. And most of us in this room, I regret to say, have the wisdom of greater years behind us.

JULY 1

Freedom Day.

Battle of Gettysburg, 1863.

Medicare, 1966.

Introductions:

Today is Freedom Day. It was not given that distinction because it is the beginning of the most popular vacation month—July; freedom from the daily grind is fine but the kind of freedom which July represents is somewhat more basic. Today is Freedom Day because it marks the beginning of the month in which so many nations, including our own, gained their freedom. Canada became a self-governing dominion of Great Britain on this day in 1867. France celebrates the anniversary of its first revolution on July 14. Such other nations as Algeria, Argentina, Colombia, Belgium, Peru, Liberia and Venezuela gained self government and freedom during this month. So our theme today is freedom—freedom seen from several points of view: first, how do we keep it and second, what do we do with it. Third, I suggest, how strongly are we committed to it.

Freedom means different things to different people. Today we have a memorable reminder of that sad fact; for today is the anniversary of the beginning of the Battle of Gettysburg in 1863, a battle memorable both for the bravery and dedication of those who fought it and for its role as a turning point in the Civil War. The Battle of Gettysburg, as Abraham Lincoln said a few months later, must be remembered so that from its honored dead "we take increased devotion to that cause for which they gave the last full measure of devotion." In the largest sense, that cause was, again as Lincoln said, "that government of the people, by the people, for the people shall not perish from the earth." It is in that context that I speak to you today.

Medicare—the idea of providing care for those who, by reason of age, are both the most vulnerable to illness and the least able to pay for help—went into effect in the United States on this date in 1966. In the intervening years it has been accused of making a few people rich; it has been credited with making a lot of people able to live healthier and longer lives. Medicare began with the emphasis on its first syllable. Medical help is a vital service for older people. I rise here to say that I believe the time has come to emphasize the third syllable—Medi*care*. We must show that we care. The greatest medicine in the world, for old and young alike, is the knowledge that someone cares. Let us dedicate ourselves, individually and as a nation, to that goal. And to that end, I should like today to call your attention to a number of current opportunities and challenges.

JULY 2

Anniversary of American independence.

Battle of Gettysburg, 1863.

Civil Rights Act, 1964.

Introductions:

Some of you here today are undoubtedly getting ready to celebrate July 4th as the birthday of American independence. I am happy to point out that, since we are gathered here today, we can celebrate right now, because today, July 2, is the real birthday of American independence. It was on this day, not on July 4, that the Continental Congress, meeting in Philadelphia in 1776, adopted the resolution which said that the colonies "are, and of right ought to be free and independent States." John Adams wrote to his wife that—and I quote—"The Second of July, 1776, will be the most memorable epoch in the history of America. I am apt to believe that it will be celebrated by succeeding generations as the great anniversary festival . . . It ought to be so solemnized with pomp and parade, with shows, games and sports, guns, bells, bonfires and illuminations, from one end of this continent to the other, from this time forward, forevermore." And of course we have done just that, but not on July 2. That is because, after passing a resolution of independence, the Continental Congress decided to adopt a much longer and more eloquent full Declaration of Independence on July 4. But we have every right to have a birthday celebration on this earlier occasion, and so I rise with a birthday toast to the past—and the future—of a free nation.

Today is the anniversary of the mid-point in the great Battle of Gettysburg in 1863 in the Civil War. In dedicating a cemetery in Gettysburg some months later, President Abraham Lincoln expressed the hope that the men who died there "shall not have died in vain" and called for this nation to have "a new birth of freedom." It was one of those added touches of history that on July 2, 1964, the anniversary of American freedom, President Lyndon Johnson should have signed into law the Civil Rights Act, which finally extended that freedom to previously neglected segments of our population. So today may well be the anniversay day above all others for the expressions of conscience of free people. It is in that context that I welcome the opportunity to talk to you today.

JULY 3

Battle of Gettysburg, 1863.

George Washington took command of Continental Army, 1775.

George M. Cohan born, 1878.

Introductions:

July 3 is always a day of anticipation and excitement because it is the eve of our greatest national holiday. But it is a pretty exciting day in American history all by itself. The most important battle of the Civil War, the Battle of Gettysburg, was decided on this, its climactic third day, back in 1863. It represented the high tide of the Confederacy. When that tide was beaten back, the tide of history turned. Today we face more peaceful battles, but the stakes, if anything, are even higher; for these are battles of attitudes, states of mind, not of soldiers and of bombs. These are battles where every one of us is a soldier.

Long before Gettysburg, this day was a military anniversary of some considerable importance to our country. It was on this date in 1775, at Cambridge, Massachusetts, that a 43-year-old Virginia country gentleman and soldier assumed command of the Continental Army. His name was George Washington. Although he did not make a particularly spectacular start, George Washington turned out to be a pretty good man for the job in the long run, and went on, as you may recall, to even higher office in the nation he led to freedom. On the anniversary of his assuming command, we might do well to recall the spirit with which he and his troops proceeded to fight against seemingly overwhelming odds. No matter how bleak a situation may look today, the odds are better than those of 1775.

George M. Cohan in his time, and perhaps for all time, was America's number one song and dance man. He was also an unashamed and effervescent flag waver. He wrote "You're A Grand Old Flag" and "I'm a Yankee Doodle Dandy," for example. Now today happens to be the birthday of George M. Cohan, born in Providence, Rhode Island, in 1878. But George M. Cohan's father, with the son's everlasting gratitude thereafter, decided to designate his son's birth date as July 4. So George M. became, in the words of his great song, "a real live nephew of my Uncle Sam, born on the Fourth of July." Let us then give a great entertainer his due and celebrate today as real live nephews and nieces of our Uncle Sam. If it isn't the Fourth of July it's mighty close.

JULY 4

Independence Day.

Three Presidents died and one President was born.

Stephen Foster born, 1826.

Giuseppe Garibaldi born, 1807.

Henry D. Thoreau went to live near Walden Pond, 1845.

Introductions:

Of all the days of the year, none has more glorious starting points for the speaker than today—the anniversary of American independence. Maybe that is why there is even a way of describing a speech as "a real Fourth of July piece of oratory." That means the usual flag waving, tub thumping, chest pounding, pulse beating invocation of the glories of our heritage. Well, one of the glories of our heritage is that we don't always have to be a captive audience to hear once again about the glories of our heritage. Independence Day, after all, is a celebration, a day to enjoy the unalienable right to the pursuit of happiness. So I will not take your time to tell you what you already know about the greatness of the founding fathers or the blessings of our noble land. I will simply ask you to consider those blessings and try to put them to good use. Back in 1776, on this date, the men who signed the Declaration of Independence said, and meant it literally, that "we mutually pledge to each other our lives, our fortunes, and our sacred honor." Think how much less is asked of us today.

Is history a matter of chance or is there some great director guiding its course? When we consider this day, July 4, we find some interesting facts. For example, two of the men who signed the Declaration of Independence, the very two Presidents who participated in the writing of that great Declaration, died years later on the same day. Thomas Jefferson and John Adams, whose careers were intertwined and whose friendship was itself a classic story, died on the fourth of July in 1826, fifty years to the day after they put their signatures on the Declaration of Independence. James Monroe, another President, died on July 4, 1831. And Calvin Coolidge, another President, was born on July 4, 1872, in Plymouth, Vermont. Isn't it interesting that so much Presidential history is associated with Independence Day? Is there some more special meaning to this day than we know? Even if there were not, it is a very special day on facts alone. It should be, for all of us, a day of inspiration and renewal, a day that reminds us that a country is as great as its people.

There are two kinds of national songs—those which are written to celebrate great national ideas or flags or occasions, and those which are written to entertain but somehow capture the essence and spirit of a country. On this day in 1826 in Lawrenceville, Pennsylvania, a man was born whose songs ever since have seemed to mirror the land and the moods and the people of our country. His name was Stephen Foster. Ironically, he died penniless before he was 40, but his songs have lived on. He wrote about the South without having been there but once, and then only briefly. His songs, though, were not regional; they appealed to all America. You have only to list some of the titles— "Oh Susannah," "Old Folks at Home," perhaps better known as "Swanee

River," "'Camptown Races," "Beautiful Dreamer," "My Old Kentucky Home," "Jeanie with the Light Brown Hair." Our country's birthday and Stephen Foster's birthday coincide. Maybe that's why, in addition to always being ready to face the music, we somehow have always managed to be a people with a song in our hearts. Maybe that's why America doesn't spend too much of its time looking back to yesterday, but instead looks forward to tomorrow.

The Fourth of July looms so large in American history that sometimes we forget that it is a day of some significance elsewhere in the world. I am thinking particularly of Italy. July 4, 1807, was the birthday of Giuseppe Garibaldi, the father of Italian independence and unity. He was born in Nice, and later in his life tried, in vain, to incorporate that territory into Italy rather than France. But even for Garibaldi the Fourth of July had other than a birthday meaning. When his fortunes were at a low ebb and his patriotic efforts got him into trouble, Garibaldi found refuge in the country whose Independence Day was his birthday. To some extent, then, Giuseppe Garibaldi was also a "real live nephew" of our Uncle Sam—and the Fourth of July isn't just an American anniversary.

Henry D. Thoreau didn't hold much with the formalities of government or with great civic gatherings. As a matter of fact, he chose July 4, 1845, as the day when he moved to live in a rustic hut in the peace and quiet of Walden Pond, in Concord, Massachusetts. Thoreau, at Walden Pond, produced some of the greatest philosophical writing America has yet seen. If we together can find the peace and inspiration which Henry David Thoreau found in solitude we will be doing pretty well. And we can start by remembering the right, in this country, to do what Thoreau did, to march to a different drummer.

JULY 5

P. T. Barnum born, 1810.

Venezuela becomes South America's first free nation, 1811.

Introductions:

Today is the birthday of Phineas T. Barnum, born in 1810 in Bethel, Connecticut. He is still regarded as America's greatest showman. In much of his life he very adroitly followed the maxim, "There's a sucker born every minute." And he exercised a great deal of ingenuity in not giving the sucker an even break. But he contributed greatly to the vitality and the excitement of American life and even to the education and sophistication of the country. He created the circus that was "the greatest show on earth," he brought soprano Jenny Lind to America, he tried to palm off an African elephant named Jumbo as the last surviving mastodon, and he brought his customers flocking, when he wanted to get rid of them, to a door he had marked "Egress." Only after they had gone through it did they realize that "egress" was just another name for exit. Above all, Barnum put entertainment within reach of the American people. He didn't take life too seriously, and as a result he made a big success of persuading other people not to take it too seriously either. I suspect that wherever Phineas Taylor Barnum is today, he is looking down on us, waiting for me to finish talking and then hoping to convey to all of us his message, "this way to the egress."

On this day in 1811, one day after our own nation's Independence Day celebration, Venezuela became the first South American country to declare its independence. A republic was set up, independent of Spanish rule. The native land of Simon Bolivar had to fight for its freedom, just as we did. And the virus of freedom spread to the rest of the South American continent, uncertain and flickering though the victories were then and ever since. So today, on the anniversary of another nation's declaration of independence, I ask you to remember that we have no monopoly on the tradition of independence and freedom—just a head start.

JULY 6

John Paul Jones born, 1747.

First all-star baseball game, 1933.

Introductions:

If the average American were asked to name our greatest naval heroes, John Paul Jones would be high on the list. Because today is the birthday of John Paul Jones, and because his story is full of surprises, I'd like to begin my remarks to you today with the brief saga of our first great naval hero. To begin with, he was not named Jones. He was born simply as John Paul, in Kirkcudbrightshire, Scotland, on July 6, 1747. As a seaman, he came to America when he was a young man and worked up to a ship of his own. But he flogged a seaman who later died, and John Paul was arrested in Scotland for murder. Cleared of that charge, he later killed the leader of a mutiny at sea, fled to Virginia and changed his name by adding Jones to it. As John Paul Jones, he was commissioned in the infant American Navy in the Revolution and became our most successful seafighter. His high point was probably the epic battle between his ship, the *Bonhomme Richard*, and the British *Serapis*, when he was supposed to have said "I have not yet begun to fight!" He captured the British ship as you may recall. When the American Revolution ended, he was one of the great heroes of the new nation. Then, in 1788, he accepted a commission in the Russian Navy in a war with Turkey. After a short time, he left that post and lived the rest of his life in Paris, dying there in 1792 at the age of 45. Only in 1905 were his remains discovered and brought to a crypt of honor at the U.S. Navel Academy at Annapolis. That, then, is the not always heroic story of one of America's great heroes. Sometimes our heroes have feet of clay, and sometimes we fail to give them their due. Perhaps that is because, however distinguished the past, we all live in the present. Memories of former glory don't pay today's bills or solve today's problems. Yesterday's heroism may have made things easier today, but our eyes are on tomorrow.

Americans pride themselves on being team players. Baseball, basketball and football are all team sports. Therefore, when the first major league baseball all-star game was played on this day in Chicago in 1933, it was regarded as a sort of circus attraction. But as the cult of personality has blossomed in so many areas of human endeavor, so too has the idea of the all-star game. We have such games now in one sport after another. I like to think that it is not only because of the glamor of the big names, but also—and mainly—because Americans want the best. A contest between teams of all-stars, it is thought, will always produce the classic confrontation between champions. It is another form of our striving for the best. I suggest to you here today that this idea, this all-star hope for tomorrow, is worth pursuing.

JULY 7

St. Thomas More executed, 1535.

Commodore Sloat annexed California for U.S., 1846.

Introductions:

Everybody has his or her own definition of a personal Utopia. The original idea of a Utopia—that is to say, the word "utopia" itself—was the inspiration of a man named Thomas More. For most of his life, it seemed that Thomas More had not only coined the phrase Utopia but found one. *Utopia* was the title of a book he wrote, comparing England to a mythical island named—you guessed it—Utopia. The book, which incidentally was written in Latin, did not depict what we would call an ideal land. Thomas More's mythical island was plentiful in creature comforts but not in individual freedom. Indeed, it was written and received as a satire on government and humanity, not as an idealistic vision at all. Real life seemed a lot kinder to Thomas More—Sir Thomas More, as he became. He was a favorite of the King of England, the royal chancellor and a favorite of the people. The trouble turned out to be that the King, who was Henry VIII, got into a fight and left the Catholic Church because he wanted to divorce his wife and marry Anne Boleyn. Sir Thomas stuck to his faith and refused to accept Henry as the supreme head of the church. On July 7, 1535, Thomas More was beheaded. Today, he is remembered by his church as Saint Thomas More. Standing fast on matters of conscience does not bring Utopia to this world; but it does ultimately make this world a better one. With the example of St. Thomas More, let us then examine some matters of our own conscience.

California exerts so much influence on the American scene that it is sometimes surprising to realize that it wasn't always part of us. But we are reminded of that today. On this day in 1846, Commodore John D. Sloat of the U.S. Navy, commanding a force that landed at Monterey, proclaimed California part of the United States. The war with Mexico was on, and there was a good bit of fighting before the annexation was made to stick, but stick it did; when gold was discovered in California less than two years later, it was on American territory and the boom was on. But it is well for us to be reminded today that California just didn't happen to join us; we took it. As we contemplate our place in the world, we should not regard ourselves as plaster saints. We have not always practiced what we sometimes have a tendency to preach. Indeed, I raise the question of whether we should practice what we preach, or preach what we practice.

JULY 8

Liberty Bell Day.

First reading of the Declaration of Independence to the people, 1776.

William Jennings Bryan's "cross of gold" speech, 1896.

Introductions:

When Chief Justice John Marshall died in 1835, it was felt only proper that the historic Liberty Bell in Philadelphia should toll to honor this great American. On July 8, 1835, while tolling in his memory, the Liberty Bell cracked. So today is observed as Liberty Bell Day. Now the Liberty Bell, it seems, must ring only in our hearts. Maybe that's where it should really ring, even if it had no cracks at all. Do we really believe in what it stands for—not merely for ourselves but for others?

We sometimes forget how different our times are from those of the past. Today brings a reminder. The Declaration of Independence was signed in Philadelphia on July 4, 1776, but not until July 8, four days later, was it read publicly to the people of that city. Today is the anniversary of the first public reading of the Declaration to the American people. The delay came because it took two days to prepare copies to be sent to all the colonies, and the carefully prepared Declaration, engrossed on parchment, wasn't finally signed until August. Today, a document of equal importance is broadcast—that is to say its contents are broadcast—usually within minutes after being adopted. We like to think that we move faster and more expeditiously, thanks to our modern communications, than the founding fathers did. But I wonder whether we are not deluding ourselves. The Continental Congress that signed the Declaration of Independence not only put its neck on the line; it kept on doing so. There were not changes of mind; there were no press conferences called to complain of being misquoted. And there were no retakes. What was read to the citizens of Philadelphia on July 8, 1776 was it. We should remember that example. I will today. I will say what I came here to say, and like the readers of the Declaration of Independence to the people of the city of Philadelphia, I will thank you for your attention.

Today is the anniversary of William Jennings Bryan's famous "cross of gold" speech to the Democratic National Convention in 1896. Bryan came to the convention as a delegate from Nebraska. In his speech he said, "You shall not press down upon the brow of labor this crown of thorns; you shall not crucify mankind upon a cross of gold." His oratory electrified the convention. A few days later this 36-year-old Demosthenes was nominated as the Democratic candidate for the Presidency of the United States. I want you to know that I do not expect any similar reaction to my remarks here.

JULY 9

Elias Howe born, 1819.

O. J. Simpson born, 1947.

Millard Fillmore became President, 1850.

Introductions:

Today is the birthday of Elias Howe. In case that makes you feel like asking "how now," let me say a few words about Mr. Howe. You may recognize his name from your school days. He was the man who invented the sewing machine and thereby made possible the great clothing industry of standard sizing and mass production that we have today. Elias Howe was born on this day, in 1819, in Spencer, Massachusetts. He wasn't a comedian, but he has kept us in stitches. On his birthday, as I contemplate the world he was so influential in building, I am moved to observe that we could use his talents once again right now, since so many things seem to be coming apart at the seams.

When you are a great football player and your initials are O.J.S., it is perhaps inevitable that you will become known as "the juice," since that's what O.J. stands for in every fast food emporium in the nation. O. J. Simpson was probably faster than any of the fast food, and a lot more elusive. He was born on this date, in 1947, in San Francisco, and in professional football, in his prime as a running back, he was the most consistent and awesome ground-gainer in the league in his time. But I do not mention him simply because of that. I mention him because in a very real way he symbolizes an aspect of America. O. J. Simpson, as a player, has become one of the highest paid and most expert advertising pitchmen in America. He symbolizes how an American, outstanding in one field, can train, educate and discipline himself—or herself, as the case may be—to move into another field. Adaptability is the word. Carrying talent from one field into another. That can be done more in this country, I suspect, than in any other. We have been, and still are, success oriented people; we can size up a changing environment and adjust to it and achieve new success. That is what America is all about.

Some Presidents of the United States have been more famous than others. One President of the past is so little remembered that a presumably tongue-in-cheek society was organized, bearing his name, to remind the nation of him. I refer to Millard Fillmore, thirteenth President of the United States. Maybe it was the unlucky number that did him in. He acceded to the Presidency, as Vice President, on the death of President Zachary Taylor on this day in 1850. Millard Fillmore decided that the Union must be preserved—this was in the tense years before the Civil War—so, although he was a New Yorker not advocating the continuance of slavery, he supported compromises including the adoption of the Fugitive Slave Act. His own party refused to renominate him. Late in 1852, he did the most memorable thing in his term of office—he sent Commodore Matthew C. Perry to Japan with a fleet to persuade that country to sign a treaty opening up trade with the West. In 1856, he tried to get back into the White House (which he had left after one term) as the candidate of the group known as the Know-Nothings. He lost that election and went back home to Buffalo, where he became a notable civic leader. I don't know why later fame has so thoroughly eluded Millard Fillmore, but I felt that on the anniversary of his accession to the Presidency he could at least be a symbol of all those Americans who contribute their bit to the nation, however unsung their efforts may be.

JULY 10

William Jennings Bryan's third nomination for the Presidency, 1908.

John Calvin born, 1509.

Introductions:

It is hard to discourage Americans. I am reminded of that fact because today is one of the anniversary days of the political convention of 1908 at which, for the third time, William Jennings Bryan became the Democratic nominee for the Presidency of the United States. It turned out, of course, to be "three strikes, you're out." As in 1896 and again in 1900, Bryan did not win the election, but he set some kind of record by his number of nominations. When an American sets his sights on a difficult target, he keeps on trying. And, unlike William Jennings Bryan, we sometimes finally achieve what we have been working so hard for. When we don't, as with Mr. Bryan, we manage to do pretty darned well anyway. So I am here to urge that we continue pushing our eternal struggle for upward mobility.

This is the day on which, in the year 1509, in the French town of Noyon, one of the most influential religious leaders of all time was born. His name was

John Calvin, and, indirectly, he left a tremendous mark upon this country of ours. John Calvin's religious ideas, which bear his name and are known as Calvinism, had the greatest influence on the ethical development of Puritanism—the Protestant work ethic and the concept, which I am here grossly oversimplifying, of congregationalism, small C. Calvin believed in the austerity of life and the founding fathers in this new land lived that way as they built their Puritan heritage. When the chips are down, that heritage remains a bedrock of American strength.

JULY 11

Aaron Burr fatally wounded Alexander Hamilton in duel, 1804.

John Quincy Adams born, 1767.

Robert "The Bruce" born, 1274.

Introductions:

History remembers today as the day in 1804 when, on the bluffs of Weehawken, across the river from Manhattan, Aaron Burr fatally wounded Alexander Hamilton. Because Aaron Burr, both as an individual and in his subsequent public career, was not a favorite of the people, he has been made the villain in this most famous of all American duels. But the fact that Burr had at least some degree of cause is a matter of historical record. Without arguing the merits, we can all be grateful that dueling to the death is no longer a factor in American politics; and on this anniversary day, we can talk together about public affairs while shooting off nothing more deadly than our mouths.

John Quincy Adams, whose birthday is today, was not your usual President of the United States. Born in 1767, in Braintree, Massachusetts, he was the only President who was the son of another President. He served, after he left the White House, as a Representative in Congress for some seventeen years until his death. The Adams family has played a remarkable role in American history, and John Quincy Adams was one of its prime actors. On his birthday, we are reminded that public service very often runs in the family; if we want our children to carry it on, we must furnish them with the examples.

One of the favorite stories of many generations has been the one about Robert the Bruce and the spider. As you may recall, Robert was the king of Scotland who, downhearted by his defeats at the hands of the English, was about to give up the struggle when he saw a spider spinning its web. The spider failed once but went right back and spun and spun until, finally, its web was finished. And Robert said to himself, if a little spider can stick to the fight so long and so courageously, then I can too. So he went back to the fight and ultimately won it. That's the story of Robert the Bruce, who was born on this day, in the year 1274, in Turnberry, Scotland. Now, when we get discouraged and have to be reminded to stick to a challenging task until we can overcome it, we don't have to sit down and watch a spider. We can remember the story of Robert the Bruce.

JULY 12

U.S. Congressional Medal of Honor established, 1862.

Julius Caesar born, 102 B.C.

Henry D. Thoreau born, 1817.

Introductions:

On this day, in 1862, the Congressional Medal of Honor was authorized. Since then, this nation has had no higher form of recognition of valor in the cause of freedom. On the birthday of the Congressional Medal of Honor, I rise to salute those ordinary Americans who, when the chips are down, found that extra measure of devotion that made them heroes of their country. And I should like to take this occasion also to take note of the many more Americans whose heroism is an everyday occurrence, not of the type which wins the Congressional Medal but rather of the kind which enables a land to prosper and its people to grow with it. We do not, I believe, give ourselves enough credit for this kind of contribution to the health of the nation. Today I urge us to look at some of the devotion and energy which are expended every day in maintaining American peace and prosperity—and in defending them.

This is the birthday of two famous people whose lives, almost two thousand years apart, represent two opposite poles of human achievement. Julius Caesar was born on this day in the year 102 B.C. He built imperial Rome, created a new monarchy that lasted for hundreds of years, and in the end fell prey to the same lust for power that had led him to the top. He died in one of the most famous assassinations of all time. His story reminds us that those who use government for their own ends, those who feel that they can disregard the will of the people, often underestimate the resilience and the resistance of the people.

On Julius Caesar's birthday, but many years later, in 1817, a man named Henry David Thoreau was born in Concord, Massachusetts. Thoreau stood for all that was opposite to the ideas of a Caesar. Thoreau not only did not want government to govern him, he did not want to be part of government. Caesar wanted to rule the civilized world; Thoreau wanted to escape from it. Caesar wanted to change the world; Thoreau wanted to watch it as it existed. I mention the contrast between these two men, both born on this day, because it illustrates the essential conflict between the two sides of human nature—not good versus evil, but rather man as an individual and man as a social creature. There is, in every one of us, a little of both. And the challenge is always which side should be on top.

JULY 13

Northwest Ordinance, 1787.

Horace Greeley's comment, 1865.

Introductions:

In 1787, the United States was without a Constitution. We were an infant nation under a loose code known as the Articles of Confederation. But on this date, July 13, 1787, the United States was able to formulate the law which has been basic to our geographical and national growth ever since. It was called the Northwest Ordinance, enacted by Congress to outline how the territory north of the Ohio River should be governed and how it would ultimately evolve into states that would be admitted to the Union. That basic law established the idea of self-governing territories as a way station to statehood and also established the requirement that U.S. territories have freedom of worship, trial by jury and public education. All in all, not a bad day's work. If, on the anniversary of that day, we can contribute however slightly to what they started, we can consider ourselves fortunate.

It is sometimes comforting and sometimes surprising to look back to some of the sages of the past and listen now to what they said so many years ago. On this day, in 1865, a famous editor named Horace Greeley delivered himself of some comments I think you would be interested in hearing. In 1865, he wrote in *The New York Tribune*, "Washington is not a place to live in. The rents are high, the food is bad, the dust is disgusting and the morals are deplorable. Go West, young man, go West and grow up with the country." Have times changed?

JULY 14

Bastille Day.

Sacco and Vanzetti convicted, 1921.

President Gerald Ford born, 1913.

Introductions:

Today is Bastille Day, the French national holiday celebrating the storming of the Bastille prison in Paris during the French Revolution in 1789. I must confess to you that I have never regarded that revolution as having the same constructive impact as our own. It started as a great victory for the rights of man but it also produced the infamous Reign of Terror. Our own revolution produced a nation which has been dedicated unswervingly ever since to the cause of freedom. We have had our struggles along the way—even a bloody

Civil War—but we have given the world a sanctuary for freedom and a symbol of hope. So, on Bastille Day, I rise to say a few words on behalf of an earlier, and I think more lasting, national gift to the world, one that was made and is still being made by the United States of America.

The road to democracy and justice is sometimes a difficult one; one of the reasons is that people differ as to what justice is in a particular situation. A case in point is that of Nicola Sacco and Bartolomeo Vanzetti, convicted on this day, in 1921, in Massachusetts, of the charge of murder in a payroll hold-up. Sacco and Vanzetti were anarchists. That fact shadowed their case. It certainly colored public opinion at the outset against their claims of innocence and their charges of a frame-up. In the long years of their appeals, until their ultimate execution, there was long and anguished public debate as to what was justice in this case. That debate continued; on the fiftieth anniversary of their execution, the Governor of Massachusetts publicly recognized the validity of doubt of the way the case was prosecuted. One wonders now, on the anniversary of their conviction, whether this democratic nation learned something from the case of Sacco and Vanzetti. What we do know of a certainty is that in a free democracy there is, at the very least, a public conscience to which justice can ultimately appeal. The death of Sacco and Vanzetti may indeed prove to have saved the lives of others because of its impact on the public conscience. At the least, it reminds us once again that eternal vigilance is the price of our freedom.

Sometimes, a person's place in history is secured by accident as much as of what he does by design. Today is the birthday of an American President whose place in history is unique. He was a President who came to office in a time of crisis precipitated by an absolutely unprecedented series of events. Simply by becoming President, he wrote a new chapter in our history books. And by his demeanor in the Presidency, he helped to insure further peaceful chapters. His name? Gerald Ford, born on this day in 1913 in Omaha, Nebraska. Gerald Ford was not elected President by the people; he wasn't even elected Vice President. As you may recall, he was the Republican minority leader in the House of Representatives when the then Vice President, Spiro Agnew, pleaded no contest to charges of falsifying tax returns, was fined and resigned his office in October 1973. Two days later, President Nixon nominated Gerald Ford to succeed Agnew, and Mr. Ford was confirmed by both Houses of Congress, taking office as Vice President December 6, 1973. Nine months later, Nixon himself resigned after the Watergate impeachment hearings and Gerald Ford found himself President of the United States. It was quite a shock for the nation—and for Gerald Ford as well. But he kept the country on an even keel. And so today, on Gerald Ford's birthday, we can all take heart from remembering the way one American who found himself unexpectedly in the White House and 220 million Americans who also unexpectedly found him there kept their cool. With those surprises behind us, we should be well prepared for any more surprises ahead.

JULY 15

St. Swithin's Day.

Rembrandt born, 1606.

Introductions:

Today is St. Swithin's Day, when legend has it that if it rains today it will continue to rain for 40 days. If, on the other hand, it remains fair for St. Swithin's, it will rain no more for the next 40 days. Since Saint Swithin himself was the Bishop of Winchester, England, the idea of no rain for 40 days was obviously the expectation of a miracle. No rain for 40 days in England in ordinary times is a veritable impossibility. For us here today I see another significance in St. Swithin's Day. What the old legend says to me, in modern terms, is that we cannot expect the world to change overnight; that what exists today may, and in all likelihood will, be the same next week and the week thereafter, and that changes can sometimes be so subtle as to go unnoticed for a long period of time. We are living in an America quite different from what it was ten years ago; but most of the change has come about in one small step after another. As a matter of fact, if we look at some of those more recent small steps, we can perhaps do our weather forecast not for the next forty days, but for the next decade.

Today is the birthday of a man commonly accepted today as one of the greatest artists of all time. His name was Rembrandt Harmens van Rijn, born on this date, in 1606, in Leyden, Holland. He came of a well-to-do family, and in his time he was highly acclaimed for his paintings; but he outlived his time. He went broke. He kept on working as an artist, producing some of his greatest work; but the public had passed him by. When he died, his greatness seemed to be behind him. Of course it didn't work out that way at all. In the intervening centuries, the greatness of Rembrandt has grown and flourished. And so today I suggest that we remember that our own judgment of our own times may not be the judgment that history will render. Let us try to step back a bit and look at our own world from the broader perspective of history. That is what I propose to try to do here now.

JULY 16

Atom bomb test in New Mexico, 1945.

Apollo 11 blast-off, 1969.

Nixon taping revealed, 1973.

Introductions:

This day is an interesting one. It is the anniversary of two scientific miracles of our time, both probably changing the history of the world, one prompted by war and the other by peace. The first was the test explosion in 1945, of a device called an atom bomb at the proving grounds in New Mexico. Less than a month later, this device was to be demonstrated as the most terrible weapon yet known to man and kill more people and create more destruction than ever before in a single bombing. The threat of nuclear weapons has haunted humanity ever since.

The second anniversary of a scientific miracle on this date carries with it a great deal more hope. On this date, in 1969, three men, Neil Armstrong, Edwin Aldrin, Jr. and Michael Collins, blasted off from Cape Kennedy, Florida in the space ship Apollo 11. Their destination—the moon. Mankind had been reaching for the moon figuratively for centuries. Now we were doing it literally, and a few days later human beings would walk on the moon itself and the rest of us would be able to watch it. It was to be a spectacular, peaceful achievement. But it, too, was the result of wartime weaponry, for the rockets that sent the space ship off to the moon were the lineal descendants of the rockets that carried the buzz bombs to England in World War II. And, similarly, the nuclear fission that was developed to make an atom bomb became one of man's great alternative sources of peaceful energy. Science itself is neither good nor bad; it is a tool. The goodness or the badness comes in the way we use it. Our problem today is to decide what is good and what is bad in the way we use science—not to discourage science itself.

It was on this day, July 16, in the year 1973, that, almost accidentally, the secret existence of tape recordings of President Nixon's White House conversations became known. The President's refusal to surrender those tapes became the crux of the Watergate affair that led to his resignation. Our lives are affected by a series, a chain, of things which link with each other, sometimes for good, sometimes for bad. And so, we must always consider our actions, and our nation's policy, not simply in terms of isolated decisions, but rather with the constant question of what this particular decision or that may lead to. Our national motto should probably be "Where do we go from here?"

JULY 17

Disneyland, 1955.

"Wrong Way" Corrigan, 1938.

Introductions:

Today is the birthday of the original Disneyland, which opened in California, on this date, in 1955. What a glorious opportunity to comment on the way life seems to imitate Disneyland! I shall not let this opportunity pass me by. Disneyland is, of course, a world for children, which the adults seem to enjoy tremendously. It is a simple world, full of mechanical marvels and romance masquerading as nostalgic reality. It is what all of us, I suspect, secretly wish the real world would be. And one reason Disneyland is that way is that they work very hard to keep it that way. That's a lesson from which we can all profit.

Until this day in 1938, Douglas Corrigan was just another American airplane pilot. But on July 17, 1938, Douglas Corrigan took off from New York supposedly to fly to California. The next day he arrived in Dublin, Ireland, after an outstanding job of flying that he insisted had taken him the wrong way. From that point, he became known to history as "Wrong Way" Corrigan, and his name has been symbolic of a total reversal of direction. The world strongly suspected that "Wrong Way" Corrigan had known exactly where he intended to go all along. But only rarely in our public life do we find figures who are willing to reverse themselves and be called "Wrong Way" Corrigans. Consistency, said Emerson, is the hobgoblin of small minds. To be exact, he said a *foolish* consistency was the hobgoblin of *little* minds. The original "Wrong Way" Corrigan was not so bothered. And the world in its time has been advanced by others who did not hesitate to take a sharp turn in a different direction.

JULY 18

Franklin D. Roosevelt nominated for a third term, 1940.

Rome began burning and Nero fiddled, 64 A.D.

Introductions:

There were two times in American history when this nation came closer to having a king than most of us suspect. The first time was in the days of George Washington, who, some people proposed, should be made the king of the United States. Among the people who disapproved most heartily of the idea was George Washington himself. The second time—although his advocates strongly disputed it at the time and ever since—was in 1940, on this day, when a President, who had twice been elected, decided to defy the old American tradition and seek a third term. On this day, in 1940, Franklin D. Roosevelt was nominated for a third term. He was later to be elected to a fourth term in office and to die as President of the U.S. Soon thereafter, a Constitutional amendment was ratified to limit the Presidency for any single incumbent to two elected terms of office. If there is any single tenet of American politics that is an iron rule today, it is the idea that no man or woman is so exceptional as to be entitled to the Presidency for a longer tenure than two elected terms. There is, of course, a provision for a little elasticity when a President dies in office. The Vice President generally is still entitled to two elected terms of his own.

But the installation of a permanently indispensable man or woman in the White House as Chief Executive is now specifically illegal. So we are destined always to be looking for new candidates. That means that higher aspirations are now firmly built into the American dream. Where do we go from here?

We are all familiar with the story of Nero fiddling while Rome burned. This is the anniversary of the day it started, the day in 64 A.D. when Rome began burning. There were those who blamed the fire, which burned for some days and destroyed most of Rome, on the Emperor Nero himself. But Nero picked a new group called Christians as the suspects, and he used the fire as the excuse for persecuting them. Even now, when it seems that some part of the world near or far is always in flames, too many of us keep imitating Nero. First we fiddle, then we look for scapegoats. Let us consider some of our current fires, as cases in point.

JULY 19

First women's rights convention, 1848.

V for victory theme introduced by Winston Churchill, 1941.

Introductions:

The longest battle in the history of the world, some people think, has been the battle for rights for women. Today is a milestone in the story of that battle. On this day in 1848, in the town of Seneca Falls, New York, the first women's rights convention was held. Elizabeth Cady Stanton declared that "man cannot fulfill his destiny alone" and Amelia Bloomer wore the bifurcated garment that was to become known by her name. If there was a single date when the fight for women's rights coalesced and began to get organized, it was at the meeting which began on this date back in 1848. And so today, seeing how far that fight has come, and how steadfastly it continues to be pursued, I believe we can have a feeling of hope and confidence that right ultimately will and does prevail.

Except for national anthems, we do not normally associate a specific musical masterpiece with a specific state of mind; but about this day in 1941, Prime Minister Winston Churchill of Great Britain conceived the idea of using a musical Morse code theme to stand for V for victory. He also symbolized victory by holding two fingers up in a V-sign, but the advantage of a musical V-for-victory theme was that it was recognizable on the air and yet somewhat undetectable because it was a familiar succession of musical notes. It was, in fact, the first four notes of the theme of Beethoven's Fifth Symphony. Ever since, that theme has meant V for victory. It was a radio message of hope to Nazi-occupied Europe in World War II. It is today a reminder that hope is an intangible, and that music and the arts can deal with that kind of intangible. Our support of the arts is part of the hope of tomorrow.

JULY 20

Neil Armstrong walked on the moon, 1969.

Sir Edmund Hillary born, 1919.

Introductions:

This is a day that encourages high hopes and high dreams. On this day, in 1969, a human being set foot on the moon for the first time and walked its surface. That "one small step for man, one giant leap for mankind" was taken by Neil Armstrong after Apollo 11's moon lander touched down on its barren surface. Later, the other U.S. astronaut who landed with him, Edwin Aldrin, Jr., also walked on the moon. Less than a century before, we didn't even have automobiles, but here we were exploring the moon. It was a heady experience not only for the men who did it, but for all of us who watched it on television back here on earth. And it convinced most of us that we were living in a time when the sciences of man could do almost everything—except to understand and control man's own destiny. But it is no longer visionary to speak of reaching for the stars.

It is one of the oddities of this particular day that it is both the anniversary of man reaching the moon, and of the birth of the first man who was to climb to the top of Mount Everest. That man was Edmund Hillary, Sir Edmund Hillary after the Everest conquest. He was born on this day, in 1919, in New Zealand. He and his Sherpa companion, Tensing Norkay, of Nepal, did what no humans had done before when they reached the summit of the world's loftiest mountaintop, Mount Everest, in May, 1953. Others, of course, have climbed that mountain since then. Once a seemingly impossible thing has been done once, it is done again more easily simply because people know now that it *can* be done. That is why there is a special place in history for those who tackled what everybody said couldn't be done—and did it. We still have many Everests defying conquest. But someday they too will be climbed.

JULY 21

Air power demonstrated by sinking a battleship, 1921.

Ernest Hemingway born, 1899.

U.S. Veterans Administration established, 1930.

Introductions:

We are so accustomed to the role of air power in warfare that it sometimes comes as a surprise to recall the fact that, in peacetime, General Billy Mitchell had to sink a battleship to get the military leaders of this country to pay attention. That was on this very day in 1921, when Mitchell, one of our aviation pioneers, took off with some makeshift aerial bombs and sank the former German battleship *Ostfriesland* from the air off Hampton Roads, Virginia. Even that didn't fully persuade military and naval thinkers. When World War II broke out, we saw huge dreadnoughts—and not enough aircraft carriers— regarded as the great weapons. We know now that no single weapon is supreme, but that control of the air is a very decisive factor. Since Billy Mitchell sank the *Ostfriesland*, we have had some even more dramatic weapons demonstrations, particularly in the nuclear area; but the tradition of Colonel Blimpism is a difficult one to erase. Military matters have always been complicated by the disagreements between the visionaries and their proposed new weapons and the play-it-safers with, so to speak, their Maginot lines. We have that same dilemma with us today.

There are successful authors whose world is timeless, and there are others, equally successful, whose achievement is that they capture a world of their own time so effectively. Ernest Hemingway, born on this day, in 1899, in Oak Park, Illinois, was one of those who captured a few great moments and recorded them for all time. His was the world which came of age in World War I, grew disillusioned in the 1920s and 1930s and became an anachronism thereafter. With *A Farwell to Arms*, which was a romance against the background of World War I, and *For Whom the Bell Tolls*, his 1940 classic about the Spanish Civil War, his place in literary history would have been assured, but it was after he wrote *The Old Man and the Sea*, the story of an elderly Cuban fisherman's struggle to catch a giant fish, that he won first the Pulitzer and then the Nobel Prize. What is particularly interesting about Hemingway is that his life became as dramatic an adventure as any of the fiction he wrote. He captured for all time the illusion and disillusionment and the heroism and the frailties of a world that is no longer our world. The human emotions he described seem as real today as when he put them on paper. Events and circumstances change; but Hemingway tells us that people do not. We might remember that when we try to improve the way we live. Human nature is the only constant.

If you were asked what group of citizens has grown the most in our times, you probably would say it was older people, and maybe that's right. But suppose you were asked about a group which has both old and young people in it? What single group encompasses that kind of age spread? The answer, of course, is—veterans. In 1930, on this date, to deal with all the laws involving veterans and the millions of veterans we had, the Veterans Administration was established. That was before World War II, before the Korean War, before Vietnam. If the veterans were a large group in 1930, think what they are today. They may not be as solidly enrolled in the veterans organizations that once played so strong a role—the American Legion, for example, or the VFW—but they are a very large constituency indeed. On this anniversary of the government's recognition of the special needs of veterans, we might give a thought to how we can start making it unnecessary to create a future generation of veterans—not because we don't like veterans; simply because the way you create them in large quantities is through wars.

JULY 22

Pilgrims set out from Holland, 1620.

John Dillinger killed, 1934.

Rose Fitzgerald Kennedy born in Boston, 1890.

Introductions:

Today is the anniversary of the day, in 1620, when the Pilgrims started out from Holland for the New World. They were aboard a vessel called the *Speedwell*. At Plymouth, England, they changed to another ship, named the *Mayflower*, and the rest is history. One wonders what would have happened if they landed where they intended to, which was considerably south of the New England coast and Plymouth Rock. They were originally headed for Virginia. They never should have sighted Cape Cod, but when they did they changed their minds and followed the landfall to the mainland. Interestingly, the day they set sail from Holland was the anniversary of the landing of another group of settlers, in 1587, on Roanoke Island, off North Carolina. When those settlers landed, they expected to be welcomed by a group that preceded them. But there was no one left. And when a third group arrived some years later, the second company had also disappeared. That story is the familiar one of the Lost Colony, still a mystery to this day. But there was no mystery about the Pilgrims—except for what might have happened in American history if they had followed their original plan instead of landing in Massachusetts. History is full of big "ifs." What happens *if* we do this, or *if* we do that? We have some pretty big "ifs" in our immediate horizon.

The fact that today is the anniversary of the end of public enemy number one, John Dillinger, is an interesting sidelight. Dillinger was shot down by the FBI as he left a Chicago movie theater in 1934. It was an event that captured the imagination of the public, largely because of the enthusiasm of the press for the idea of a sort of "hall of fame" listing of public enemies. John Dillinger had been, so to speak, anointed as public enemy number one by being given that ranking on the list. In the strange workings of the human mind, it is possible that being listed as public enemy number one has the wrong effect; it encourages the listee to work hard to maintain his number one position. The dilemma in dealing with crime is that we have to talk about it to deal with it and when we talk about it we invariably glamorize it for people with that turn of mind. This isn't simply the fault of the press. Violence sells newspapers or attracts audiences because it appears to be considered a sort of spectator sport. Instead of just asking what we can do about violence, we ought to ask what we can do about the public's insatiable interest in the subject.

Few people have been as victimized by violence as the matriarch of a great American family, Rose Fitzgerald Kennedy. She was born on this day, in 1890, and on her birthday she deserves to be remembered as a great example of what profound faith in one's family and one's religion can do. We remember that Rose Fitzgerald Kennedy saw her son John rise to the Presidency, only to be shot down by an assassin. Four and a half years later she lost another son, on the road to a Presidential nomination, killed by another assassin. She had lost a son and daughter earlier, dead before their time. But through it all she carried on, and gave inspiration and encouragement to their siblings. On her birthday, this lady from Boston is a symbol of courage, of dedication and of determination. Long after she is gone, her example will remain.

JULY 23

Steve Brodie's jump from the Brooklyn Bridge, 1886.

Ice cream cone, 1904.

Introductions:

One of the legends of American folk history is that on this day, in 1886, a saloon keeper named Steve Brodie jumped off the Brooklyn Bridge and lived to tell the tale. That there is and was a Brooklyn Bridge, that there was a Steve Brodie and that he lived to tell the tale are all established facts. The only uncertainty is whether he ever jumped off the Brooklyn Bridge as he claimed. Whether or not he did, he contributed an expression to American slang. A "brodie" is a blunder or mixup and to "make a Brodie" is to fall down on the job or to make a mistake. That may not have been what Mr. Brodie had in mind when, fished out of the water below the Brooklyn Bridge, he claimed to have survived a jump. It just goes to show that history can be made by taking a dive, or claiming to. Even as I stand here talking to you, the world is full of Steve Brodies, the truth of whose claims we may never be able to find.

The ice cream cone is said to have been invented on this day, in 1904, in St. Louis. As a contribution to the enjoyment of life, it most assuredly deserves a place in history. When you stop and think what the ice cream cone has done for the dairy business and retail trade, not to mention the dispositions of human beings, you've got to regard today's birthday as a blessed event. Let's face it. It's very nice to have something around that is made to take a licking.

JULY 24

Utah Pioneer Day.

Kellogg-Briand Treaty declared in effect, 1929.

Simon Bolivar born, 1783.

Introductions:

This is the day when, in 1847, Brigham Young led his advance party of Mormons into the great Salt Lake Valley of Utah, and chose the site for the city they would build. That was the beginning of Salt Lake City. It was the climax of an epic trek for people determined to practice their faith in peace. It is observed in its own state as Utah Pioneer Day, but I think it is worth being remembered by people of other faiths and in other places. On Utah Pioneer Day, we can all profit from remembering the example of the people who crossed the continent to build a way of life—and succeeded.

Today, only students of history remember or recognize the name of the Kellogg-Briand Treaty. On this day in 1929, President Hoover, at a ceremony in Washington, attended by representatives of more than 40 nations who had signed it, declared the Kellogg-Briand Treaty in effect. Under its terms, the signatory nations renounced war as an instrument of national policy. Is any further comment necessary? If we are a little cynical today, who is to say we don't have good reason?

Simon Bolivar has been called the George Washington of South America. The legislatures of Venezuela, Colombia, Ecuador, Panama, Peru and Bolivia named him officially "Libertador,"—The Liberator—and Bolivia named itself after him. Simon Bolivar, born on this date in 1783, in Caracas, Venezuela, led a continent to independence. You never can tell where, when and how something that will change the course of history will begin.

JULY 25

National Farm Safety Week.

Commonwealth Day in Puerto Rico.

Introductions:

This is the beginning of the last full week of July, observed for many years as National Farm Safety Week. We think back so fondly to the bucolic, rustic charms of the old country farm that we forget the risks. Farming is a risky business and it uses a lot of powerful machinery. But even when farming used horsepower and donkey power it was a physically taxing and dangerous endeavor. There is always an idea among city folk that the city is where the risks are. But cities have no monopoly in this regard. Perhaps it would be helpful to the national interest if we would all remember, at least during National Farm Safety Week, that where the grass is greener it is also apt to be slipperier as well.

On this day, in 1952, the Commonwealth of Puerto Rico came into existence as that territory gained self-government (short of statehood status) in the United States. At the time, it was thought that this would solve the problem of the island's status, but we learned soon enough that the hope was premature. But Commonwealth Day certainly deserves to be considered a noble attempt and a good start. And any day that celebrates a noble attempt and a good start has to be considered a pretty good one.

JULY 26

FBI established, 1908.

Department of Defense established, 1947.

Fidel Castro led a futile attack and was captured in Cuba, 1953.

Introductions:

Today is the birthday of the Federal Bureau of Investigation. It was established by an Attorney General named Charles J. Bonaparte on this date in 1908, and did not acquire its Napoleonic complex until some years later. Today's FBI is a far cry from what it used to be, and, for the most part, I think we can regard the current edition as the best. We can credit the Federal Bureau of Investigation with assuming an important role in modernizing the science and methods of crime prevention, crime detection and law enforcement. On the Bureau's birthday, we have a lot better protection than we might have without it.

In 1947, this was the day that saw the establishment of the United States Department of Defense under the Armed Forces Unification Act. It signaled the recognition that, in an era of the totality of war, there had to be one combined overall military command. Let us hope that the totality of war will not be the ultimate confirmation of the wisdom of the Armed Forces Unification Act now or at any future time.

It has been so long that Fidel Castro reigned in Cuba that today's anniversary seems like an echo from another planet. On this day, in 1953, Fidel Castro was a young revolutionary who led a futile attack on a Cuban Army barracks at Santiago. He was captued and sent to prison. But the adventure on this day gave his movement its name—the July 26th movement—and the next time he struck he was more successful. So today should be a good day to heed the warnings around us. Perhaps, if Cuba had heeded the warning of July 26, history might have been different.

JULY 27

Atlantic cable between England and U.S. completed, 1866.

Korean War armistice signed in Panmunjom, 1953.

Introductions:

We live in the age of communications that really began around the middle of the nineteenth century and has been growing ever since. Today, for example, is the anniversary of the completion of the Atlantic telegraph cable between England and the United States. That made it possible for news to cross the ocean immediately, and that, in turn, speeded up the tempo of events to a pace never before known. Perhaps we were better off when news traveled slower. That, however, is one piece of information we will never know. Meanwhile, we operate now knowing that what we say or do here will—if it makes news—be out in no time.

On this day, in 1953, after more than two years of seemingly endless negotiations, the armistice agreement that ended the Korean War was signed at Panmunjom, on the border between North and South Korea. It was an uneasy truce for decades thereafter, and its anniversary reminds us that a tense peace has only one thing to recommend it, namely that it is better than a hot war. So, in our everyday affairs, we must not always hold out for the ideal if we can settle for a step forward. The hardest part often is trying to decide whether the settlement is really a step forward at all.

JULY 28

Fourteenth Amendment ratified, 1868.

World War I began, 1914.

Bomber crashed into Empire State Building, 1945.

Introductions:

This is the anniversary of the Fourteenth Amendment. That is the Amendment which guarantees due process of law to all. Its ratification was announced on this date in 1868. The Fourteenth Amendment was enacted after the Civil War to extend the federal guarantee of due process to govern state as well as federal matters. It was, therefore, an extension of the supremacy of the federal Constitution and a forerunner of further guarantees and protection of civil rights. It took a long time to move from the Fourteenth Amendment to the civil rights legislation of the 1960s, but the Amendment was a historic step. Its birthday is well worth noting today.

The first World War had seemed well nigh inevitable in the month after a Serbian activist killed the heir to the throne of Austria-Hungary in 1914. On this day, the well-nigh inevitable began to happen. Austria-Hungary declared war on Serbia. Within a week, Germany, Russia, France, Belgium and England were in the war. It was the worst war, up to that time, in all history. On the anniversary of its beginning, we might remember that 25 years later an even worse war began. How much have we learned since then?

In 1945, on this day, as World War II was moving toward its early end, a U.S. bomber crashed into the Empire State Building in New York. The building stood firm. The bomber was destroyed. The crash occurred on a Saturday, killing 13 people. At a busier time, the death toll could have been a lot higher. Scientists had been improving airplanes and skyscrapers for years, but nobody ever imagined that one would crash into the other. And so today, one cannot help wondering what strange, unexpected events lie ahead that nobody, not one of us, has ever dreamed of.

JULY 29

English routed the Spanish Armada, 1588.

Benito Mussolini born, 1883.

Introductions:

Although the Bible, with the story of David and Goliath, encourages us to believe that a little guy can sometimes be more than a match for a big one, we don't usually apply that rule to military encounters. But every time a military machine begins to be too sure of itself and its unconquerable might, it is a good idea to think of the story of the Spanish Armada of 1588, that set out to destroy the British Navy and open England to conquest by imperial Spain. On this day, in 1588, thanks to the indomitable skill and spirit of those led by Sir Francis Drake and company (and thanks also to some very timely help from the weather), the Spanish Armada was totally routed and Britain was saved. The Armada was supposed to have been the mightiest war fleet ever assembled. It turned out to be somewhat less than that. So, even if you are not planning a military engagement, you can take a leaf from the story of the Spanish Armada. It was overpublicized, to the point where its reputation spurred the British on to an unprecedented effort. Please be assured that for your edification today I have not—repeat *not*—assembled any veritable Spanish Armada of fancy words and phrases, or of impossible superlatives. Instead of riding the bridge of a mighty man-of-war, oratorically speaking, I propose to do no more here today than to paddle my canoe.

This is the birthday of Benito Mussolini, the father of modern fascism; a classic demagogue, he was outdone at his own game by his neighbor, Adolf Hitler. Together, they tried to move the world back into the dark ages. Beware of politicians who tell you to beware of politicians; beware of leaders who fall in love with uniforms; beware of those who stand on balconies above the crowd and talk for hours. If Mussolini's birthday means nothing else, I must admit it is a reminder to me that only a dictator can get away with talking too long. In his lifetime, Mussolini was famous for supposedly getting the trains to run on time. Posthumously, his memory will get this speaker, at least, to finish on time.

JULY 30

First representative assembly in America, 1619.

Henry Ford born, 1863.

Thorstein Veblen born, 1857.

C. Northcote Parkinson born, 1909.

Introductions:

We meet here today on the anniversary of the opening of the first legislative assembly in America, which met at Jamestown, Virginia, on this day, in 1619. It was a brief meeting, which in itself makes this legislative session even more unique. I shall, of course, take my inspiration from it today, and get right down to business.

Near Dearborn, Michigan, on this day in 1863, Henry Ford was born. The man who did more than any other single individual to popularize the automobile in America, and to mass produce it, was famous for saying that you could have your car in any color you wanted, as long as it was black. He turned out millions of Model Ts beginning in 1908, and he kept on making the Model T until 1927. When Henry Ford found a good thing, he held on to it. I suggest that we look around at the good things we've got in America today and devote a little bit more of our energy to holding on to them.

I want to say a few words today about Thorstein Veblen. Dr. Veblen was a scholar given to complicated prose and sour views, not the least of which was the "theory of the leisure class." Veblen's theory about the leisure class, if I may oversimplify it, was simply that he was "agin it." Said he, "Conspicuous consumption of valuable goods is a means of reputability to the gentleman of leisure." He wrote that in 1899, and it seems to me that consumption of valuable goods has been becoming more conspicuous every year. Today is Veblen's birthday. He was born in Wisconsin in 1857. In honor of his birthday, I will engage in conspicuous consumption of a portion of your time for a few remarks here today.

Sometimes I wonder where it would all end if C. Northcote Parkinson had not made his remarkable discoveries and given the world that wonderful "Parkinson's Law." I wonder about that particularly on Professor Parkinson's birthday, which happens to be today. 1909 was the year and Durham, England the place. It was in the 1950s that Professor Parkinson brought us up short with his basic law of human behavior, namely that "work expands so as to fill the time available for its completion." Applied to the work of a public speaker, that means said speaker will continue to spout for as long as you let him. Fearful of the workings of Parkinson's Law, I took pains to check beforehand on how much time was to be given me for my remarks here today; I then took pains to plan a shorter speech than that; for if talk, like work, expands to meet the time available, I should have to be more profound in order to find enough words. And if I find enough words I may not find enough audience left and if—but enough! You see the sheer logic of Parkinson's Law. And so, let me be brief.

JULY 31

Apollo 15 astronauts drive a car on the moon, 1971.

Whitney M. Young, Jr. born, 1921.

Introductions:

This is the anniversary of what may well have been the strangest automobile ride in history, part of it with the largest number of back-seat drivers in history and all of it on the most distant straight-away in history. On July 31, 1971, Apollo 15 astronauts David R. Scott and James B. Irwin began three days of exploration on the surface of the moon riding in a specially designed electric car, watched through television transmission by millions of people back on earth. In one respect, the moon's first automobile drivers were like a speaker in front of an audience. Nobody knows in advance exactly where he is going and they can't wait for him to get there. Mindful of this, I shall immediately shift into high gear and get rolling.

If Whitney M. Young, Jr., were to be remembered for nothing else—and there is a great deal for this outstanding Black leader to be remembered—one comment of his alone would be his claim to glory. I am reminded of it particularly today because this is the late Mr. Young's birthday. He was born in 1921 in Lincoln Ridge, Kentucky. In a speech in New York City, in May of 1970, he said something which has given me my theme for my remarks today. "We may have come over in different ships," said he, "but we're all in the same boat now."

AUGUST 1

Swiss Independence Day.

First U.S. Census, 1790.

San Francisco's first cable car, 1873.

Introductions:

Today is Swiss Independence Day. I mention it, not because there is anything novel about the idea of Swiss Independence, but rather, because the reverse is true. Swiss Independence Day marks the founding of the Republic of

Switzerland in the year 1291. That, in turn, makes it the oldest such government still in existence in the world—not a monarchy, but a republic. The Swiss
are not a notoriously talkative people, which may be why they have been able
to keep a government going this long. It may also be long lasting because there
is no hill too high for a Swiss to climb. I plan to keep all this in mind today and
follow the Swiss example. Limit the talk, keep looking up and oh, yes stay
as neutral as possible.

The first U.S. census began, on this day, in 1790. We seem to have been
counting something or other ever since. Mark Twain said there are three kinds
of lies—lies, damned lies and statistics. I will try, therefore, to state my case
here today not with figures, not with statistics, but simply by reminding you of
what you can see and hear for yourselves.

Have you ever stopped to think that, with few exceptions, we use none of
the basic means of transportation today, in our cities, that were in use a
hundred years ago?—except one, in one place in particular. When electricity
and the internal combustion engine replaced the horse, the horsecar disappeared, the steam locomotive was banished from city rights of way, and the
bus, in large measure, displaced the earlier trolley track—except for that one
particular place. Today is the anniversary of the introduction of San Francisco's first cable car, in 1873. And San Francisco's cable cars were still operating
more than a hundred years later. Time after time, the modernists sought to get
rid of them, but the traditionalists—and the tourist trade—won and the cable
cars survived. Why is it that a mechanical contraption seems to have had a
better record of survival than some of our most cherished attitudes toward life
and faith and family? Or do those attitudes live on as museum pieces and
isolated novelties?

AUGUST 2

Warplane anniversary.

Einstein's letter to President Franklin D. Roosevelt, 1939.

Gulf of Tonkin incident, 1964.

Introductions:

On some days, the future shape of the world changes without our even
realizing it. That may well have happened on this day in 1909, when the U.S.
War Department bought the first military airplane from Wilbur and Orville
Wright. Did the airplane's military capabilities speed up aviation's development? Many people think so. On the other hand, the automobile developed
pretty well without any such stimulus. The Bible talked of beating swords into
plowshares; but there are those who dream of having more plowshares and less
swords to begin with. Perhaps we should address ourselves here today to the

basic question, which is not how fast can we get to where we are going, but rather simply where are we going?

Albert Einstein was a gentle man of peace. Today brings a sardonic reminder of how this gentle man of peace not only helped to win a war but also to provide man with the ultimate weapon of destruction—or of progress. It was on this day, in 1939, that Dr. Einstein wrote to President Franklin D. Roosevelt to urge research on atomic energy, which led to the development of the atom bomb. When I consider that, except for his persecution by Nazis, Albert Einstein might never have come here, I am persuaded that there is indeed—or has been—some guiding force which has favored our land. This is a good day to remember that.

In 1964, on this day, as we were told thereafter by President Lyndon B. Johnson and his aides, the North Vietnamese attacked a U.S. destroyer in the international waters of the Gulf of Tonkin. As a result, Congress, a few days later, adopted the Gulf of Tonkin Resolution which gave the President broad powers to use the armed forces without a declaration of war. This, in turn, was followed by deeper U.S. involvement in Vietnam, where over many years the U.S. fought a bloody and ultimately futile war. The U.S. has been urged to remember the Alamo and remember the Maine and remember Pearl Harbor. It might be well for us, on this day at least, also to remember the Gulf of Tonkin. If we occasionally look back, we can look ahead with a much clearer view.

AUGUST 3

Christopher Columbus sailed from Spain, 1492.

Whittaker Chambers accused Alger Hiss, 1948.

Introductions:

On this day, in the year 1492, a sailor named Christopher Columbus set out from the port of Palos, Spain, to look for a sea route across the Atlantic to India. What a glorious failure he had! And how many other discoveries, like that of America, were made by people who were really looking for something else—or maybe not even looking at all. Curiosity, once aroused, is a very driving force. And so I am here not simply to utter a few platitudes but rather to raise a few questions, to give you some information which, I hope, will raise questions in your minds.

Not too long after World War II, when the nation was beginning to be nervous about Communist spies stealing atomic secrets and boring from within, there was a dramatic confrontation in Washington. A confessed former Communist, Whittaker Chambers, accused a former State Department official, Alger Hiss, of having been a Communist agent. Eagerly pursuing the matter was a young California Congressman named Richard Nixon. This was the day in 1948 when Whittaker Chambers made his accusation. Before the case was over, Hiss had gone to jail while his guilt or innocence continued to be debated for the next thirty years, and the young California Congressman had risen to and fallen from the heights like no other before or since. Truth, wherever it may have been in this case, certainly proved to be stranger than fiction. But then, truth often is. Let me give you a few examples.

AUGUST 4

John Peter Zenger acquitted, 1735.

Coast Guard Day.

Bethmann-Hollweg's "scrap of paper," 1914.

Introductions:

One of the great pleasures of American life down through the centuries has been to be able to criticize our government and the people at its head. That right really began on this day, in 1735, when a jury in New York City acquitted a printer named John Peter Zenger of the charge of libeling the royal governor. Zenger's defense had been that what he had printed in his newspaper about the governor was the truth. His acquittal was regarded as a landmark in the evolution of American freedom of expression. The case set no legal precedents, but it helped tremendously in establishing the tradition that public office is a valid subject for public criticism. Thanks to Zenger, we can go in for a zinger now and then. While I do not plan to make that kind of speech here today, it's nice to know that you're not being muffled.

Today is Coast Guard Day, celebrating the founding, in 1790, of the organization that later became the U.S. Coast Guard, an agency known as the Revenue Marine Service. The Coast Guard is not often in the news. It just doesn't have the time, considering the length of coastline it has to patrol. On its birthday, it is nice to note that as of the moment, and let us hope for the future as well, the coast is clear.

When England declared war on Germany on this day in 1914, after Germany had earlier declared war on Russia and on France and had invaded Belgium, the German Chancellor made a statement that has become a classic in the annals of self-righteousness. England was declaring war because of its commitment to its allies and because of Germany's invasion of Belgium. Said German Chancellor Theobald von Bethmann-Hollweg, ". . . just for a scrap of paper, Great Britain is going to make war on a kindred nation . . ." It is the glory of civilization, certainly not excluding Germany, that we do not take our so-called "scraps of paper" lightly. At least we should not.

AUGUST 5

Cornerstone of Statue of Liberty laid, 1884.

Admiral Farragut damns the torpedoes, 1864.

Introductions:

Out in the middle of New York Harbor stands a famous lady, the Statue of Liberty. The statue was a gift from the people of France, and the cornerstone for it was laid at what was then Bedloe's Island, in the harbor, on this day in 1884. Funny thing about that. The Statue itself, as I have said, was a gift from the people of France; but the base, which was a gift from the people of the United States, cost almost as much as the Statue. To me that is rather symbolic. Somebody else can give you liberty, but you've got to establish its base for yourself. Liberty, to be maintained, cannot be just a free ride. We might remember the story of the base of the Statue of Liberty, just as a reminder as we look at where liberty is today.

Most of our battle cries are either appeals to our memory or blunt questions—like "Remember the Alamo!" or "Do you want to live forever?" or even "Who's afraid of the big bad wolf?" One battle cry that was first uttered on this day, however, seems to me to summarize a pretty general American attitude. It was said by Admiral David Glasgow Farragut at the Battle of Mobile Bay in the Civil War in 1864. What he said was: "Damn the torpedoes, full speed ahead!" That is my speech plan for today.

AUGUST 6

Premiere of Warner Bros. talking pictures, 1926.

First atom bomb used, 1945.

Sir Alexander Fleming born, 1881.

Alfred Tennyson born, 1809.

Introductions:

Today was a very big day in 1926. That was when the world discovered that the movies had learned to talk. The Warner Bros. motion picture company presented, in New York, the world premiere of something called Vitaphone in two short films with live sound. People could be heard as well as seen. A great new medium of entertainment and information had been born. All of a sudden, silent screen performers had to be concerned about the way they sounded as well as the way they looked. The movie stars learned what it feels like to be a public speaker. Now if I could only learn what it feels like to be a movie star . . .

Some events in history have been so tremendous, so memorable, that merely mentioning the name of the location recalls the happening. Let me illustrate. Today is the anniversary of Hiroshima. Some pronounce it *Hirah-shima*, some say *Hirosheema*. It makes no difference. You know what event we are referring to. When the first atom bomb was dropped on that city in Japan in 1945, it was more than the shattering premiere of a brand new weapon. It was the ending of one age and the beginning of another. The world did not stand still thereafter. We have made great progress. We now have bombs a thousand times as powerful as the one that destroyed Hiroshima. Well, maybe not a thousand times, but infinitely more awesome. What other progress have we made? Let's talk about that on this atomic anniversary.

Many people know the name of Hiroshima. I wonder how many recognize the name of Sir Alexander Fleming—not because he happened to have been born on this day, in 1881, in Lochfield, Scotland, but because he grew up to discover something which has probably saved many more lives than most other discoveries in the history of the world. Sir Alexander Fleming was the discoverer of penicillin. In a world given to celebrating anniversaries and birthdays of military heroes, statesmen and mechanical geniuses, I think that Alexander Fleming's birthday also deserves a kind word. Having given you that word, I now proceed to subjects for which, alas, there is no penicillin miracle drug.

"Men may come and men may go, But I go on forever." Do not be alarmed. That is not the keynote of my remarks here today. It is a quotation from that gold mine of quotations, Alfred Lord Tennyson. Today I quote him because today is his birthday. The man who became Great Britain's outstanding poet laureate was born in 1809 in Somersby, England. It was Tennyson who had Sir Galahad say, "My strength is as the strength of ten, because my heart is pure" and told the story of the charge of the Light Brigade. But my favorite Tennyson quotation is sort of an all-purpose one, as good for a rousing finish to a speech as for a rousing beginning. I quote: "Some sense of duty, something of a faith,/Some reverence for the laws ourselves have made,/Some patient force to change them when we will,/Some civic manhood firm against the crowd."

AUGUST 7

Whiskey Rebellion anniversary.

Battle of Guadalcanal, 1942.

Gulf of Tonkin Resolution, 1964.

Introductions:

The good old days didn't always seem that good before they were old. As a case in point, I give you today's anniversary, in the form of August 7, 1794, when President George Washington issued a proclamation telling a group of Western Pennsylvania farmers to go back peacefully to their homes and stop what is known to history as the Whiskey Rebellion. A word from Washington was not enough. He issued a second proclamation a month and a half later and sent in some troops to add to the persuasion. It is worth noting that, even though that particular objection to excise taxes on whiskey was taken care of, the revenuers are still engaged in games of wits with some rural whiskey makers. I trust that this brief historical note will put you in good spirits for my remarks here today.

When the U.S. Marines landed at Guadalcanal, on this day in World War II, it was more than merely the beginning of a bitter battle against the Japanese. It was the end of the beginning and the beginning of the end of the war in the Pacific. It was the first time the United States had taken the offensive in that theater of war. So today has built into it a historical reminder that the best defense is a good offense.

I am tempted today to phrase my remarks in the form of questions. If more questions had been asked on this day, in 1964, history might have been different. On this date in that year, Congress passed the so-called Gulf of Tonkin Resolution, as a result of reports it had been given about North Vietnamese attacks on U.S. vessels in international waters. That Gulf of Tonkin Resolution gave the President the broad powers to use the armed forces which, in effect, authorized our getting into a land war in Asia. Yes, it might have been worthwhile to ask some questions. And, while the Gulf of Tonkin is history, we do have some more timely areas to ask questions about. So here we go.

AUGUST 8

Battle of Britain began, 1940.

President Truman's warning, 1950.

President Nixon announced he was resigning, 1974.

Introductions:

The waging of war used to be rather selective. War was conducted by fighting men, while the civilians waited for the results. Over the years, it began to change; but total war, as we know it now, really began on this day, August 8, in 1940, during World War II, with the Battle of Britain. The Battle of Britain was a sustained series of air attacks by the German Air Force against both British home territory and the Royal Air Force. It was a foretaste of what was to come later, when cities were to be main targets, with their civilian populations, for the bombers of both sides. The Battle of Britain had a different ending than anticipated. Not only was the aerial blitz defeated; the British people, finding themselves, so to speak, combatants in the war, responded with a new burst of determination. When you find yourselves in a war, even if you are a civilian who harbors illusions of being a non-combatant, you have not too many alternatives. I mention this by way of introduction to some of the civilian warfronts that confront us in these times of peace.

Citizens have a double-edged relationship with their government. They regard Uncle Sam as a protector and a helping hand, but they want to keep Uncle Sam from intruding too much into their lives. And, above all, they are troubled about where the rights of the individual and the rights of the state part company. President Harry S. Truman gave us one suggestion, when he said, on this date in 1950: "Once a government is committed to silencing the voice of opposition, it has only one way to go, and that is down the path of increasingly repressive measures, until it becomes a source of terror to all its citizens and creates a country where everyone lives in fear." Happily, although we have come closer once or twice than we should, we have never gone down that path. But all around us, all the time, we see other nations going down that path. And every now and then, we have to watch ourselves. I am happy that I can speak to you here today without having to watch *my* step.

It is an odd quirk of fate that exactly 24 years to the day, after President Truman's warning about the consequences of a government silencing the voices of opposition, another President who tried to destroy his opposition should have come to grief. On August 8, 1974, Richard M. Nixon, who had tried to hide information about the Watergate affair, announced that he was resigning as President. It was something new for this country—the resignation of a President, a Chief Executive who was under fire. And, in its own sad way, it reinforced the principle that the public's business is the public's business. Questions, it seems, can and indeed generally should be asked—and answered.

AUGUST 9

Gerald R. Ford succeeded Richard M. Nixon, who resigned, as President, 1974.

Jesse Owens dominated the Olympics, 1936.

Beverly Hills murders for which the Manson "family" was convicted, 1969.

Introductions:

This was the day when, for the first time in our history, a man not chosen even indirectly by the people became the President of the United States. Gerald R. Ford had been named by Richard Nixon and confirmed by the Congress to succeed Spiro Agnew as Vice President when Agnew resigned; when Nixon resigned in the Watergate scandal, Ford became President. I ask you to recall that moment. If ever the United States government could have been brought to a paralyzed halt, that, we feared, could have been the time. But it held firm. The people held firm. I suggest to you here today that the strength of any government, in this country, lies not in those who govern but in the electorate.

Sometimes we are told that government is too big for an individual to fight. Go fight city hall, they say sardonically. Today I want to remind you of just how much an individual can do. My case in point is an American named Jesse Owens, a Black American competing in the Olympic Games hosted by Adolf Hitler in 1936—the Black American competing under the eyes of the world's leading, most virulent advocate of white Aryan superiority. On this day, Jesse Owens, already a great track star, became the first man to win four medals in the Olympic Games. He stood in the winner's platform at the Olympic Stadium, the living proof of the wrongness of Mr. Hitler. Not many of us, of course, have either the ability or the opportunity of a Jesse Owens for that kind of victory. But all of us can do our part to make a better world.

It comes as a shock in the midst of a time of relative civilization to encounter senseless savagery out of nowhere. On this day in 1969, movie actress Sharon Tate and four others were found brutally—incredibly brutally— murdered in her home in Beverly Hills, California. When the case was finally marked closed, it had led to the shocking story of the Manson "family" and of master and slave relationships that seemed to come straight from a book of witchcraft. What brings human beings to that point? We don't always know. And more important, we don't seem to know enough of what we can do about it. We have explored the outer edges of space more than we have the inner recesses of the human psyche.

AUGUST 10

Chicago incorporated as a village, 1833.

Smithsonian Institution established, 1846.

Introductions:

Every great city wears several different faces. When Chicago was incorporated as a village, on this day in 1833, nobody could have foreseen its hectic Prohibition days, its stockyards glory, its anguish at the Democratic convention of 1968, its colorful local politics or its tremendous contribution to American literature. As a matter of fact, I believe that when each of us looks at Chicago today, we see different things in it. A great city is different things to different people. The problems of great cities are different things to different people. The solutions are different, in the view of different people. Today, I propose to try to find some areas of city life about which I hope we can agree.

This is the anniversary of the establishment of the Smithsonian Institution in 1846. The Smithsonian is not a single jewel, but rather a crown of jewels in the nation's capital. Supported by government funds in the main, it teaches a magnificent lesson in the value of the private sector. The Smithsonian was established by an Act of Congress, approved August 10, 1846, under the terms of the will of James Smithson of London, England. It was the money bequeathed by Mr. Smithson that founded the Institution. And since then, units of the Smithsonian have been endowed by other private philanthropists—the Freer Gallery, the Mellon and Kress collections of paintings, the Hirshhorn and many, many others. Public and private funds, working together, have built the Smithsonian. Private initiative started it. Public enthusiasm followed. In doing good, we do not need to wait for the government to take the initiative.

AUGUST 11

Partition of Vietnam, 1954.

Rioting in Watts, 1965.

Introductions:

There is a tale told of Solomon, asked to judge between two women each claiming to be the mother of a certain baby. Solomon suggested that the solution was to cut the baby in half and give half to each woman. The real mother said, "No, let her have the child," and Solomon knew that it was the real mother who cared enough to give of herself to save her child. Partitions of wealth or of land are like the case before King Solomon. Those who agree to such partitions may not be doing so simply out of reasonableness. Today is the anniversary of such a partition. On this day, in 1954, the French withdrawal from what had been French Indochina went into effect and, under the terms of a Geneva agreement, Vietnam was divided into two separate nations. Thereafter, people started voting with their feet, as they said. They left Communist North Vietnam to take refuge in the South. All too soon, there was war—and when it ended, the North ruled all Vietnam. Partition is rarely the final settlement; it is the intermission. We always seem to have an intermission or two someplace.

In modern times, some of the great anguish of history has been told in terms of black and white. On this day in 1965, six days of rioting began in the Black district of Watts in Los Angeles. It came as a surprise to most of the country that idyllic Los Angeles, thought of as the dream factory and the land of the lotus eaters, should have the same social problems as less glamorous cities. It also came as a shock to many in Los Angeles. Ten years later, the same city had a Black mayor—not as a result of the riots, but rather, as an encouraging sign that progress was being made. Progress, it has been said, is the tedious process of taking two steps forward and one step back. As long as the forward steps outnumber the backward ones, that's progress. We can apply that yardstick to many different problems of our society. Let's take a look.

AUGUST 12

Berlin wall, 1961.

Mrs. Kasenkina's jump, 1948.

Julius Rosenwald born, 1862.

Cecil B. DeMille born, 1881.

Introductions:

Dictatorships are sometimes like long-winded speakers. They prefer a captive audience. On this very day, in 1961, Communist East Germany created a literally captive audience. Overnight, they put up a wall sealing off East Berlin from West Berlin. Since very few people were trying to get into Communist East Berlin, the purpose was obviously to keep East Germans from getting out. The wall was not a temporary thing; over the course of years, it was reinforced and—if I may use such a word in this connotation—improved. And of course, it continually raised the question in the West of how long a wall of brick and mortar can stand against the abstract idea of freedom.

Freedom, it has been said, jumps over walls. Not always successfully, I fear. Freedom also has been known to jump through a window. More precisely, a freedom-lover has been known to jump through a window to get it. Today is the anniversary of Mrs. Olga Kasenkina's leap through a window of the Soviet consulate in New York to escape being sent home. She was a schoolteacher, assigned to teach the children of the Russian diplomats in New York. She was ordered home, and was about to be sent back when she broke away and jumped through a consulate window to sanctuary on a free street. This was in 1948, long before the later rage of would-be emigrants became an international embarassment for Soviet Russia. For a closed society, a window on the world can be a difficult thing. For an open society, there have to be windows, if only so that speakers like me can sound again that ancient call, open the windows!

Julius Rosenwald was a great philanthropist, who achieved that role by first being a great businessman. He was the guiding genius behind the fantastic growth of the mail order business, as he built Sears, Roebuck and Company from an enterprise into an institution. Julius Rosenwald was born on this day in 1862, in Springfield, Illinois. His career reminds us that you can do a great deal of good if you do well first. And if you do good, you should keep on doing well. That is part of the theory of corporate good citizenship. It is all around us.

Cecil B. DeMille produced such lavish Hollywood spectacles, many of them built around the Bible, that one captious critic remarked that when the

Golden Age predicted in scripture came to pass, it would have to be known as De Millenium. Cecil B. DeMille was born on this day, in 1881, in Ashfield, Massachusetts. He made the first feature movie ever filmed in Hollywood. Real life has always been hard put to equal the sheer spectacle of a DeMille production. And I sometimes get the impression that life would be a lot more interesting if it could be staged by a Cecil B. DeMille. So today, I would like to talk to you about the spectacle of life and the competition for the role of Moses.

AUGUST 13

The 3,000-mile welcome for Apollo 11 astronauts, 1969.

Alfred Hitchcock born, 1899.

Lucy Stone born, 1818.

Introductions:

Whoever said that you can't be in two places at once must have begun to wonder about that on this day in 1969. On that day, the three Apollo 11 astronauts, Neil Armstrong, Edwin Aldrin and Michael Collins, came pretty close. They attended civic receptions in their honor on the same day in New York, Chicago and Los Angeles, thanks to some high speed aviation transport. And one thing Michael Collins said during the course of the day deserves to be said again now. He said: "We share with you the hope that we citizens of Earth who can solve the problems of leaving the earth can also solve the problems of staying on it."

In life, as in an Alfred Hitchcock movie, there is always a McGoffin, a particular unexpected twist. Life without suspense, without a McGoffin, would be a lot duller. And so would have been our lives without an Alfred Hitchcock, who developed the movie mystery thriller to an art form. Alfred Hitchcock was born on this date, in 1899, in London, England. If he were with us here today, he would have a young and dashing Cary Grant cast as the speaker. But he would also have had the speech interrupted by something bizarre; so perhaps it may be preferable, after all, for me to supply my own McGoffin.

Long ago, before words like "spokesperson" had ever been used and anybody had ever heard of "Ms.," Lucy Stone was born on this day, in 1818, in West Brookfield, Massachusetts. Lucy Stone married a man named Henry Blackwell but she was known as Mrs. Lucy Stone. She was a leader of the women's suffrage movement, but Lucy Stone was also particularly interested in enabling women to keep their maiden names. It was a long hard fight, and when she died in 1893 it was far from won. Today, it is timely to remember that the hardest thing to keep is a good name.

AUGUST 14

Social Security, 1935.

Atlantic Charter, 1941.

VJ Day, 1945.

Introductions:

Today is the birthday of the U.S. Social Security Law, enacted on this date in 1935. Under the provisions of that law, which among other things provided for pensions at age 65 to those eligible, the Social Security Law won't be old enough to retire for some years. But it's old enough to be in need of some geriatric assistance. The whole concept underlying our social security system cries out for some further examination.

When the leaders of two great nations meet at sea and issue a statement of principle, it has to have a certain element of drama. There was more than the usual amount of drama when this happened on today's date in 1941, because the leaders were Franklin D. Roosevelt and Winston Churchill. England was already in what was to become World War II and we were still neutral. Roosevelt and Churchill had a conference aboard the British fighting ship *H.M.S. Prince of Wales* and the U.S. Cruiser *Augusta* from August 9 to 12 and then, on August 14, issued what was known as the Atlantic Charter simultaneously in London and Washington. Let me list the postwar goals it set in its statement of principles; no more territorial aggrandizement; respecting the wishes of the inhabitants of a territory as to territorial changes; recognizing the right of people to decide on their own form of government; easing restrictions on international trade and insuring equal access to raw materials; cooperating to provide better economic security for people all over the world; freedom from want and fear; freedom of the seas; and the ultimate establishment of a permanent structure of peace. Fifteen nations, including Soviet Russia, endorsed the Atlantic Charter in less than two months. Now let's look at the world as it is today.

Today is VJ Day, when in 1945, as somebody put it, peace broke out. Japan. battered by two atom bombs, surrendered, ending World War II. There was a formal surrender in Tokyo Bay on September 2, but this was the day the Japanese stopped fighting and gave up. It was a euphoric day for the winning side. Since then, there seems to have been a long time between euphorias. We have found new battles to fight.

AUGUST 15

Panama Canal opened, 1914.

Napoleon born, 1769.

Introductions:

When the Panama Canal opened, on this date in 1914, it was one of the wonders of the world. A half century later, it wasn't wide enough for some of the larger ships to pass through. Forgetting the political wrangling and maneuvering that centered around the Canal, it became a monument to the rapidity of change. On its anniversary, let us remember that today's superhighway is tomorrow's Route 66.

Today is the birthday of Napoleon Bonaparte, born in 1769 in Ajaccio, Corsica. He was a short man who cast a long shadow. In his honor, I plan to make a short speech and let the shadow shift for itself. A lot of people have imagined themselves to be Napoleon and succeeded only in meeting their Waterloo. As the saying goes, if you want to meet your Waterloo, bite off more than you can chew. My ambition today is considerably more modest.

AUGUST 16

Gold discovered in Klondike, 1896.

George Meany born, 1894.

Introductions:

There is a four-letter word that has inspired more hope in mankind and opened more new lands than any other. I will not keep you in suspense; the word is gold. It started the trek to California by the '49ers, and on this day, in 1896, it rediscovered Alaska. This was the day that they discovered gold on Bonanza Creek in the Canadian Klondike, close to the Alaskan border. It signalled the start of a new gold rush. Thanks to that gold rush, Alaska became a territory and became sufficiently well-known to attract more people. In the 1970's it had another gold rush, this time the black gold of oil. But the key word, from the time Columbus set out to find a new route to the Indies, has been that four-letter one—gold. One way or another, gold is rich and rich is better than poor.

George Meany, who was born on this day in 1894, was the vigorous head of the American Federation of Labor when he was well into his eighties. As a matter of fact, labor seems to have more elder statesmen in its organized leadership than do other walks of life. I know that labor leaders are apt to make more speeches than other people. So, although not a labor leader, I welcome this opportunity to make a speech to you; if it makes me live longer it is a double pleasure. On the other hand, if it just makes things *seem* longer . . .

AUGUST 17

Davy Crockett Day.

Mae West born, 1892.

Introductions:

Various almanacs will tell you that today is Davy Crockett Day, and back in the 1950s any child could have told you who Davy Crockett was. I am not at all sure that the children of today are as well informed. The reason he was well-known in the 1950s was that Davy Crockett was a television star, or rather, the key character in a popular TV series that spawned a generation of small boys wearing squirrel caps and fancying themselves as backwoodsmen. The real Davy Crockett was a somewhat gamier character, whose adept publicizing made him legendary even before he died a hero's death at The Alamo. He was born on this day, in 1786, in the area of Greeneville, Tennesee. In honor of the Davy Crockett in all of us, I should like to talk today about one of his favorite subjects, the frontier. But the frontier to which I address myself is rather different from the untamed southwest of Davy Crockett's time.

Not too many women have given their name to a distinctive article that is worn. In the case of Amelia Bloomer, the name came simply from the lady who wore the article first. In the case of Mae West, it was not that she wore it, but simply that it seemed to remind people of her. The article was an inflatable life preserver, and when it was in wide use in World War II it became known as a Mae West. For Mae West, whose portrayals were considered somewhat raunchy and frank as a movie star in the 1930s, it was a lovely salute. In an era of profanity and vulgar excess, it is interesting to recall that Mae West put more sex into "Come up and see me some time" than most X-rated films. She was born on this day, in 1892 or thereabouts, in Brooklyn, New York. In honor of her birthday, I am here to sound an optimistic note. As long as there's a Mae West keeping us afloat, the world isn't in too bad a shape.

AUGUST 18

Milk condensation process patented, 1853.

Pope Leo's law of history, 1883.

Virginia Dare, 1587.

Introductions:

On this day, in 1853, a man named Gail Borden received a patent for an improved way to condense milk. It ultimately led to the foundation of a great food corporation called, appropriately enough, the Borden Company, but it has also led me to an important decision here tonight. If Gail Borden could condense milk into a more convenient form, there is no reason why I should not condense the three-hour speech I had originally planned for today into a more manageable length. So rest easy; what I am about to give you is the condensed version.

Pope Leo XIII, when he opened the Vatican Archives on this date in 1883, condensed a great deal of morality into a very small package in his remarks. He said, "The first law of history is not to dare to utter falsehood; the second is not to fear to speak the truth." History is not the only arena in which those laws should apply. I do not plan to break them here today.

Today is the birthday of the first child born to English parents in the New World. Her name was Virginia Dare, born on Roanoke Island, North Carolina, in 1587. She, her parents and the whole colony, disappeared from the face of the earth. It is interesting that the history of English-speaking America should start with a lost child. Interesting because one of our abiding problems today, on the anniversary of Virginia Dare's birth, is still the problem of lost children—lost not in the literal sense, as Virginia Dare and her lost colony, but rather in the sense of lost potential, lost chance, lost souls. Let us take a moment to consider what this loss is, in terms of what it means to each of us.

AUGUST 19

National Aviation Day.

Bernard M. Baruch born, 1870.

Introductions:

Since this is National Aviation Day, I may be entitled to try a few flights of fancy—but I shall resist the temptation. It is National Aviation Day not because of any particular or notable flight at all, but simply because Orville Wright, one of the inventors of the airplane, was born on this day, in 1871, in Dayton, Ohio. That reminds me of the fact that when Orville and Wilbur Wright set out to make a heavier-than-air propeller-driven machine fly off the ground, they looked for a place with a big wind. I guess I am to be the wind today.

It is interesting that today is the birthday of a man who put us in the air and also of another man who kept putting us back on solid ground. Bernard M. Baruch, probably America's most notable elder statesman, was born on this day in 1870, in Camden, South Carolina. Bernard Baruch advised every President from Woodrow Wilson to John F. Kennedy. He would sit on a park bench and hold impromptu press conferences as easily as he moved in the inner circles of power. Particularly in his last years, he was hard of hearing and wore a hearing aid, and there was always a suspicion that one of his assets in delicate conversations was that he could decide what he wanted to hear. Selective hearing is a marvelous tactic in negotiations. It isn't quite as marvelous when encountered by a public speaker, in the form of audiences that fall asleep or start talking to each other. I figure that the way to avoid that problem is either (A) to have the sound volume on the public address system turned up so high so that nobody could sleep or (B) to make the speech short and sweet. Since the latter is also a lot easier on the speaker too, you will be relieved to know that I have chosen plan (B).

AUGUST 20

Alaska discovered, 1741.

Benjamin Harrison born, 1833.

Introductions:

Along about this time of the year, in 1741, a Danish explorer named Vitus Bering discovered Alaska. He discovered it while heading a Russian expedition—which is why for more than a hundred years, it was a Russian territory, and eventually was sold to the United States. What intrigues me about this is that it is another of the many instances of people of one nationality exploring on behalf of another. Henry Hudson was an Englishman who explored for the Dutch. John and Sebastian Cabot explored North American waters for the English, but they were Italians; and so was Christopher Columbus, who led Spain's discovery of the New World. If we think the melting pot was a fairly recent innovation, we should take another look at the history of the exploration of America. If ever a continent represented a combined effort, ours is it. We have a long tradition of working together. It's one worth remembering today.

Most Presidents have some particular claim to fame, and I have a particular liking for the uniqueness of the claim of Benjamin Harrison, who was born on this day in 1833, in North Bend, Ohio. He was the grandson of the President who served the shortest time in office, William Henry Harrison. Grandpa Harrison died one month after being sworn in. But that was not the grandson's particular claim to Presidential distinction. It was simply that Benjamin Harrison, who succeeded Grover Cleveland as President, also preceded Grover Cleveland as President. He beat Cleveland in one election, then lost to him the next time around. This can be inspirational if you happen to be Grover Cleveland and rather irritating for a Benjamin Harrison. But it goes to show something that every public speaker should bear in mind. Just because they are on your side when you start, don't think they won't turn on you. I want you to know I will be watching you very carefully.

AUGUST 21

Hawaii statehood, 1959.

German-Russian non-aggression treaty, 1939.

Nuclear submarine anniversary, 1951.

Introductions:

Aloha! That may seem like an odd sort of greeting in this non-tropical setting, but I believe it is timely, because today is the anniversary of the admission of Hawaii as the 50th state—and the first state off the mainland of North America. So I say again, Aloha! It probably would have been nice if, in honor of the occasion, you had been given the opportunity to salute such Hawaiian traditions as hula dancers in grass skirts, or witness a few thrilling demonstrations of surf riding. I guess the only Hawaiian tradition I could emulate would be to lecture you like a missionary, but I feel I would be miscast. So, instead . . .

On this day in 1939, the Soviet Union, which had been claiming to be the only true opponent of Nazism, and Nazi Germany, which had set itself up as the prime enemy of Communism, announced that they had agreed on a ten-year non-aggression treaty, which they signed formally three days later. The so-called non-aggression treaty proved to be the key to the start of World War II, and in no time the Nazis and the Communists were dividing Poland greedily between them. Not too long afterward, they started fighting each other. The moral clearly is that actions speak louder than words. But words can some-times lead to action; and perhaps my words here today may have some con-structive effect in a small way.

It seems hard to realize that it was back in 1951—that long ago—that the U.S. ordered the construction of the first nuclear-powered submarine. But it was way back then, on this day. We got the submarine and many more; but somehow, the rest of the power we expected for peaceful purposes from nu-clear energy hasn't materialized. Why is it that we are willing to accept for weapons use what we do not accept for the uses of peace? Why is war a more powerful motivator than peace? I do not come here today with the answers to those questions. I come, rather, to urge that we renew the search for the answers.

AUGUST 22

America's Cup anniversary.

Genesis of the World Series, 1903.

Introductions:

Yacht racing is not the average mass sport, but a particular yacht race has captured the public fancy over the span of more than a century. It is called the America's Cup. On this day, in 1851, in English waters, a U.S. yacht named the *America* won the race against the British yacht *Aurora* and won the trophy which became known as the America's Cup. It was defended by American sailors and yachts for well over a century thereafter, always remaining in U.S. possession. England's Sir Thomas Lipton tried many times; he lost the races but won the hearts of Americans with his great sportsmanship. The America's Cup races seem, to some people, to be an anachronism in the age of jet travel and mass spectator sports, but some old-fashioned traditions never lose their charm. Today, on the anniversary of the winning of the America's Cup, it is nice to know that there are still those who appreciate how much artfulness can go into the handling of a favorable wind. And now, if you will supply the artfulness, I will supply the wind.

Barney Dreyfuss used to own the Pittsburgh Pirates baseball team. This may not give him a resounding claim to fame, but Barney Dreyfuss also wrote a letter on this day, in 1903, we are told, that does indeed entitle him to be remembered. Writing to an American League club owner, this National Leaguer said, "The time has come for the National and American Leagues to organize a World Series." And indeed, later that year the first World Series was held. Now, of course, we have world series in one sport after another. And if you look at them, you find that most of them are misnamed. Even the original used the name *World* Series when it was actually restricted to one country. We sometimes mistake our world for the entire world. Today I'd like to take a look at some of the ways our world and the rest of the world interrelate.

AUGUST 23

Rudolf Valentino died, 1926.

Execution of Sacco and Vanzetti, 1927.

Introductions:

Today is a day of interesting contrasts, involving what happened to three Italian immigrants a year apart. Two were poor and one was rich and famous. One was Rudolph Valentino; the others were named Nicola Sacco and Bartolomeo Vanzetti.

Rudolph Valentino died on this day, in 1926, in New York, after a short illness. At age 31, he was the great romantic film idol of his time. His passing plunged countless females of all ages into an orgy of public grief. It reminded us, as if we needed any reminder, that people can be just as concerned over actors as over war and peace, and that we have an infinite capacity for hero worship. Before we smile condescendingly at what now appears to be the silliness of the Valentino era, we might take a look at ourselves—not the lunatic fringes and fan club extremists, but the things that grown adults go crazy over.

A year after the Italian film idol, Rudolph Valentino, died in New York, two men, who by then were just about as famous, also died, but not of natural causes. On this day in 1927, Sacco and Vanzetti were finally executed after years of dispute over the fairness of their trial. They were both Italian immigrants and anarchists, and a large body of the public was convinced that they were innocent of the payroll murders for which they died. Fifty years later, the Governor of Massachusetts, where they were tried and executed, officially recognized that their trial might have been unfair. In fifty years, the memory of Valentino was dim and distant, but the memory of Sacco and Vanzetti burned brightly into the consciousness of America and the world. I mention this today to suggest that we ask ourselves not only how the world looks to us today, but how this same world of this year will look to those who are around fifty years from now. Or, to put it another way, how is it going to look for the neighbors? Let me tell you, neighbors, how things look to me—and fifty years from now, why don't you check up on me?

AUGUST 24

Destruction of Pompeii, 79 A.D.

British burned Washington, 1814.

Introductions:

About this time of year, back in 79 A.D., a volcano named Vesuvius began a tremendous eruption; before it was over, two Roman cities, Herculaneum and Pompeii, were wiped out. The ruins of Pompeii remain to this day as a reminder of how suddenly and how thoroughly a living city can cease to exist. Most of the time cities don't go that fast, but they do change. If they don't change, they run the risk of going the way of Pompeii, not through being buried under lava ash, but simply by falling apart. Sometimes I ask myself, if I had a choice of having my home town preserved for all time exactly the way it is now or trying to start it all over, which would I want? The answer, of course, is that neither way is the way things work. Let's talk a little today about the way things do work.

It is an odd coincidence that the destruction of Pompeii by Mount Vesuvius and the burning of Washington by the British in 1814, in the War of 1812, occurred on the same day of the year. The British, of course, were infinitely more selective. They didn't burn the whole city; they concentrated on the White House and other government buildings. Then they went on to try to capture Baltimore, where they were repulsed at the Battle of Fort McHenry and Francis Scott Key was inspired to write "The Star Spangled Banner." Washington was, of course, rebuilt, and the British and the Americans, after a suitable lapse of time, became the best of friends. Indeed, it has been said that the only thing really separating the British and the Americans is their mutual illusion that they speak the same language. Sometimes that is also an illusion for speakers. I hope that today my words will not disguise my meaning, and I must say I have the feeling, which is a nice one as I stand before you, that we do indeed, you and I, speak the same language.

AUGUST 25

National Park Service established, 1916.

Leonard Bernstein born, 1918.

Bret Harte born, 1836.

Introductions:

Today is the birthday of the National Park Service, which was established in 1916. In the course of reviewing what that meant to the nation, I noticed that the first Director of the National Park Service was paid $4,500 a year. That says a lot about inflation; but it also says a lot about how much more popular the national parks are these days. They are getting more crowded all the time, and the job of running them is getting more and more difficult. The wide open spaces just aren't as wide or as open as they used to be. So I guess you might as well resign yourselves to staying here for a while and settling for watching your humble servant go into his Old Faithful act and spout.

Most people, whose work pleases the ears, specialize in one form of audio service—whether it's playing a musical instrument, singing, composing or conducting. One of today's birthdays belongs to a man whose specialty for years was to be a one-man musical wonderland. Leonard Bernstein, born on this date in 1918, in Lawrence, Masssachusetts, was a famous conductor by the age of 25, is the composer of the symphony, "Jeremiah" and made ample use of his spare time by composing ballet music and the score of the musical comedy, *On the Town.* He moved with ease from the classical to the popular side of composing, meanwhile bringing the New York Philharmonic new glory as its conductor. It makes me feel very guilty that all I am here for is to stand and talk to you.

Some people rise like meteors and fall the same way. Others seem to keep on going, shining brighter all the time. One of the meteors was Bret Harte, the writer, who was born on this day, in 1836, in Albany, New York. It was Bret Harte who gave the public its first exciting and grubbily humorous accounts of Western life, including such classics as "The Luck of Roaring Camp" and "The Outcasts of Poker Flat." Within about ten years, he had burned himself out as an author, while friends and colleagues like Mark Twain not only kept on going, but kept on getting better all the time. Bret Harte would probably have a higher reputation today if he had quit while he was ahead. Since his example is one every speaker—as well as writer—should keep in mind, I plan today to keep an eye on you to make sure that I do not hold the podium so long that you end up like the character in one of Bret Harte's works of whom he wrote: " . . . and he smiled a kind of sickly smile, and curled up on the floor,/And the subsequent proceedings interested him no more." So, moving right along . . .

AUGUST 26

Women's suffrage, 1920.

Lee De Forest born, 1873.

Introductions:

In the sad history of women's rights and the righting of women's wrongs—sad because it never seems to get finished—today is a big day. It is hardly a secret that on August 26, 1920, the Nineteenth Amendment to the Constitution was ratified. The Nineteenth Amendment gave women the right to vote. It did not end discrimination against women, but it put into their hands a weapon they had not had before in the United States. Later on, they found out that just as talk hadn't been enough, the vote wasn't enough. Ultimately, they moved into such areas as consciousness raising and awareness sessions. Both, of course, are things treasured by every speaker. So if my remarks today make you more conscious—or even keep you conscious—I will be content. Conscious of what, you may ask? Even if you don't ask, I will tell you.

Lee De Forest was a great American inventor, one of a relatively small group of brilliant men who took Marconi's invention of radio and developed it into the great broadcasting instrument of today, transmitting sight and sound through the air to your home. He was also a pioneer in the development of talking pictures. I think it is safe to say that Lee De Forest was instrumental in giving an awful lot of people a chance to sound off to more people than they could collect in any one place. Today is his birthday. He lived almost 88 years after being born on this day, in 1873, in Council Bluffs, Iowa. Dr. De Forest, wherever you are, thank you. And now a few words for my sponsors.

AUGUST 27

First oil well, 1859.

Hannibal Hamlin born, 1809.

Lyndon B. Johnson born, 1908.

Sam Goldwyn born, 1882.

Introductions:

When Colonel Edwin L. Drake struck oil on this day in 1859, in Pennsylvania, the world had its first oil well. It did a great deal ultimately for the world, but not too much for Colonel Drake, who was broke within 15 years. Oil wasn't quite as precious a commodity in those years before the internal combustion engine as it later became. There's an old saying about striking while the iron is hot. The main concern should be not whether the iron is hot, but rather what you strike. For example, the story is told of the two prospectors on the Western desert who struck it rich. They were looking for gold and they drilled for it and found water. So, with all due respect for Edwin Drake and the anniversary of his drilling of the first oil well, I am not here to offer you the same old oil.

Hannibal Hamlin. Of course you all recognize the name instantly— Hannibal Hamlin. If Lincoln had been assassinated six months earlier, Hannibal Hamlin would have been President. He was the Vice President during Lincoln's first term. And there's an interesting story about that. When the ticket of Lincoln and Hamlin was elected, the two running mates had never even met. Can you imagine that happening today? Today is Hannibal Hamlin's birthday. He was born in 1809, in Paris Hill, Maine and, like another Hannibal many years earlier, he never quite made it all the way to the top. We have a tendency to forget those who, although they climb quite high, never climb high enough. We don't keep our eyes on the stars, but on the one star that happens to be the brightest. I am here to suggest that we spare a little attention for those a little lower on the ladder of fame. Let's talk about us.

President Lyndon B. Johnson, who was born on this day in 1908, in Johnson City, Texas, came to office in the way that Lincoln's first Vice President so narrowly missed. LBJ was the Veep when John F. Kennedy was assassinated. Texas finally was represented in the White House. On Lyndon B. Johnson's birthday, I just want to recall something he once said: "Presidents learn—perhaps sooner than others—that our destiny is fashioned by what all of us do, by the deeds and desires of each citizen, as one tiny drop of water after another ultimately makes a big river." If my words here today can add a few drops to that big river, I will be content.

A Goldfish was born in Warsaw, Poland and I'd like to talk about it. I'd like to talk about this particular Goldfish because today is his birthday. He was a Goldfish in name only; his full name was Samuel Goldfish, and he was born in 1882. When he came here to the United States, he was a successful entrepreneur in the glove business before he became interested in a newfangled enterprise called the movies. He was one of the partners who hired an unknown director named Cecil B. De Mille. Then he joined a producer named Edgar Selwyn and they combined their names to give their company the name Goldwyn. In short order Samuel Goldfish changed his own name. He became

Sam Goldwyn, one of Hollywood's greatest producers and, by all odds, its most famous manipulator of the English language. Among his more quoted lines are such as: "A verbal contract isn't worth the paper it's written on" and "In two words—im..possible," and of course, "Include me out!" He also said of one piece of prose, "I read part of it all the way through." In his honor, I am here to give you part of my thoughts all the way through.

AUGUST 28

Civil rights march, Washington, D.C., 1963.

Demonstrators harass Democratic convention in Chicago, 1968.

Pioneer radio commercial, 1922.

Introductions:

Today is the anniversary of two very different kinds of demonstrations that affected the history of the United States. The first was the great and inspiring civil rights march in Washington, D.C. in 1963, when the Reverend Dr. Martin Luther King, Jr., caught the conscience of the nation with his eloquent "I have a dream" oration. The second was the fighting between radical elements and Chicago police in connection with efforts to influence the Democratic National Convention at which Hubert Humphrey was nominated for the Presidency. The Civil Rights Act was passed, in the emotional aftermath of the assassination of President Kennedy, less than a year after the inspiring march on Washington. The candidacy of Hubert Humphrey missed by a narrow margin, and the Presidency went instead to Richard Nixon less than three months after the violence in Chicago. Taking a lesson from these two events, I have decided to be non-violent in my approach to you today. As Lyndon Johnson would have said, "Let us reason together."

It is recorded in some histories that on this day, in 1922, the commercial message from a sponsor was born, on a station then known as WEAF that was a pioneer radio station in New York. So it is only fitting that I should be here before you today to say—and now, this message.

AUGUST 29

Chop suey, 1896.

Carry Nation vs. John L. Sullivan, 1901.

Introductions:

We like to think that the United States is a pacesetter among the nations of the world, and nowhere is this more apparent than in such great American dishes as—chop suey. It's true: chop suey was first concocted, according to the record books, by a Chinese chef while in New York City, not China, on or about this day in 1896. If I may mix my metaphors, let me say that if America can be the birthplace of a great Chinese dish, then the world is our oyster. Now if I can only handle this speech right, it will be a piece of cake.

It's been a long time since a lady crusader against the evils of alcohol went around the country smashing saloons with her hatchet. I don't know how many people in this audience have heard very much about Carry Nation, who came out of Kansas at the turn of the century determined to break up the bars. On this day, in 1901, she was in New York City and, we are told, decided to pay a visit to a saloon run by John L. Sullivan, the former heavyweight boxing champion. John L. sent a message that he couldn't see her because he was sick in bed. Since I am not carrying a little hatchet and you are not sick in bed, I hope we can have a more meaningful discussion here today.

AUGUST 30

Hot line, 1963.

Thurgood Marshall to Supreme Court, 1967.

Introductions:

This is the anniversary of the establishment, in 1963, of something that has become a favorite of the scenario writers who do screen plays about international crises—the hot line between the White House in Washington and the Kremlin in Moscow. I have no inside information as to when and how that hot line has been used, but I come before you today convinced that I'd much rather talk to you than to the Moscow end of that phone line. The hot line may be technically perfect, but this is a much better connection.

A man named Marshall was the great pioneer of the Supreme Court in the early 1800s. Chief Justice John Marshall was his name. On this day, in 1967, another man named Marshall was the chief actor in a bright new scene for the Court. This time, it was Thurgood Marshall, whose nomination to the Court was approved by the Senate, making him the first Black to sit on the nation's highest tribunal. The march of progress is one marked by a series of victories. As we contemplate all the challenges that lie ahead, it is comforting to know of past progress. Never look back—said Satchel Paige—someone might be gaining on you. I suggest that it's a good idea to look back now and then, if only to see how far we've come. Then we can get a better view of what remains to be done. And that is my purpose here today—to look at some of the victories that are yet to be won.

AUGUST 31

Edison's kinetoscope, 1887.

Lewis and Clark, 1803

Introductions:

In 1887, Thomas Edison invented something called the kinetoscope—or at least he had it patented. This was the day the patent was granted for his device to produce pictures that you watched through a peephole as a length of film ran past a light. The principle was the same as that later employed with a wheel of cards—a series of still pictures which, when viewed rapidly, one after the other, made the pictures seem to move. I come before you today to say that the flip card did not die. As a matter of fact, some speakers on television still use them, only now they contain text rather than pictures, they call them "idiot cards," and the only thing that moves is the mouth of the speaker. I am here without such devices because what I am about to say to you comes from my heart, and doesn't need that kind of stage managing.

When Thomas Jefferson asked Lewis and Clark to explore the vast territory of the uncharted West, it took a bit of doing. On this date, in 1803, they began the preliminary trip that led them down the Ohio River before the expedition proper pushed off the following May from St. Louis. I do not plan to take quite as long in getting started today. But then, what I want to explore with you is not quite as large a subject as the territory from Ohio to the West. After all, Lewis and Clark took several years. So let me not waste any of my precious minutes on further introductions.

SEPTEMBER 1

The Labor Day season.

World War II began.

James J. Corbett born, 1866.

Edgar Rice Burroughs born, 1875.

Introductions:

Along about now, we approach the end of the rites of summer, with the big Labor Day Week-End. Labor Day was intended as a salute to working people. But what it has become principally is a celebration of the end of the formal vacation season and a signal that it's time to go back to work. It has also been a traditional occasion for the kind of oratory that goes with bunting, flags, parades and picnics. Somebody once said that the principal reason for Labor Day speeches was to give the crowd a chance to digest its food quietly. I shall therefore enter into the spirit of the occasion by trying to give you a few modest thoughts to chew over and hope I produce nothing too hard to swallow.

This was the day, in 1939, when Germany invaded Poland, triggering World War II. That event hardly makes for an inspiring jumping-off point for a speech, you may think, but if you compare this September 1 to the one in 1939, you must admit that things have changed. Somehow, slowly and uncertainly, we do seem to learn at least a little from the mistakes of the past. Tomorrow is the heir of yesterday, and today is when we put the estate in shape to be passed on. The world of September 1, 1939 fell apart and had to be put back together again with blood, sweat, toil and tears. What do we have to do with *our* world? That's a broad question, and today I would like to deal with just a few aspects of it.

The name of James J. Corbett probably doesn't mean too much to most people these days. He was the man who beat the legendary John L. Sullivan for the world heavyweight boxing championship. He revolutionized boxing in two ways. First, he was a superb boxer, rather than a slugger or brawler. He was an early, pioneering artist in the manly art of self defense. Second, he was a new kind of professional boxer. He was known, appropriately, as Gentleman Jim. He dressed well and spoke well and moved easily and gracefully in polite society. James J. Corbett, born on this day in 1866, in San Francisco, became a successful lecturer after his pugilistic career ended, and he also appeared on the stage. We have had a succession of fighters since his day who were articulate and accomplished in areas other than the ring, but it was Gentleman Jim who, so to speak, changed the mold. He demonstrated that, man-to-man, science and artfulness could be more than a match for brute force. In speaking to you here today, I am mindful of what his boxing career exemplified—and what is just as true for a public speaker. You don't have to win by a knockout. All you need is to pile up enough points. And so to my first point.

Today is the birthday of the man who created Tarzan of the Apes. Edgar Rice Burroughs, born in Chicago in 1875, first conceived of the character as one who talked far more fluently with animals than with other human beings. Indeed, when portrayed in talking pictures, the apeman had such complicated dialogue as "Me Tarzan, you Jane." Much as we may be fascinated with the idea of conversing with our animal friends, I do believe that we have a lot to learn first as humans about communicating with each other. Of course, if you find areas of disagreement with what I am about to say, you can always decide that my remarks were for the birds.

SEPTEMBER 2

U.S. Treasury Department established, 1789.

Japan's formal surrender, 1945.

Introductions:

The U.S. Treasury Department was established on this day in 1789. The government, under the Constitution, had been operating for five months or so before the Treasury Department came into existence, which shows that our priorities have certainly changed since 1789. Apparently, when this nation started, we were less convinced that money talks. In the beginning, of course, government was not big business; the income tax was more than a century away. People could, and many did, live off the land. The services provided by government were minimal. But times have changed. The U.S. Treasury Department today, thanks to the Internal Revenue Service, has a finger in a lot of pies. As someone remarked, they have so many forms of taxes all over the world these days that they even tax your patience. That, indeed, is a tax on which the government has no monopoly. Today, however, I will defer to Uncle Sam. I am not here to tax your patience. I don't find my appearance before you taxing in the least. And I greatly appreciate the opportunity to share some thoughts with you.

On this day in 1945, aboard the U.S. battleship *Missouri* in Tokyo Bay, Japan signed the documents of surrender in World War II. The War had ended on August 14, but the ceremonies aboard the *Missouri*, staged with care, pomp and dignity, were the formal acknowledgment of Japan's defeat. The photographs of the event are marvelous illustrations in the historical archives. But I find myself wondering whether, in the long view of history, August 14, with no pomp and circumstance, wasn't the really important day—when the War stopped. And I find myself saying that the substance of an event, rather than the staging, is what should concern us. So today I propose not to talk about how things look, but rather, what they mean.

SEPTEMBER 3

Treaty of Paris ended American Revolutionary War, 1783.

Britain and France entered World War II, 1939.

Louis Henri Sullivan born, 1856.

Introductions:

Today is a sort of microcosm of the extremes of mankind—an anniversary of the ending of one war and the igniting of another. On this day, in 1783, the formal end of the American Revolution came when Great Britain and the U.S. signed the Treaty of Paris. And on this same day, in 1939, Britain and France entered the war against Germany, which the Nazis had started by invading Poland. War and peace, humanity at its worst and best, with significant memorials on the same day. What that says to me is that life is a constant choice between alternatives, but we aren't always in a position to make the choice for ourselves. Today I want to talk about a number of choices—not of the absolute

dimensions of war and peace, but choices nevertheless between alternatives—
that we have the opportunity to make. After all, I had to make a decision as to
what I should talk about today; so I think it is only fair to offer you some
decisions also.

In the past century or so, we have changed the face of the earth, the look
of the city and the whole concept of architecture. The man who may have done
the most to bring about this change was an architect named Louis Henri
Sullivan, born on this day in 1856, in Boston. Louis Sullivan built what some
people regard as the first modern skyscraper, back in 1890, in St. Louis. He
trained such disciples as Frank Lloyd Wright and pioneered the idea that the
design of a building should depend on how the building was supposed to function. It is particularly appropriate for a speaker to stand up on Louis Sullivan's
birthday to talk about the shape we are in and the shape of things to come;
while I do not intend to cover that broad a canvas, I hope to deal with a portion
of it.

SEPTEMBER 4

Los Angeles founded, 1781.

Transcontinental live television began, 1951.

Introductions:

I want to start by wishing a happy birthday to El Pueblo de Nuestra
Senora de la Reina de los Angeles de Porcincula, which was founded on this day
in 1781. I also want to thank whoever was responsible for shortening its name
to simply Los Angeles. Because of its spectacular growth in our own time, we
like to think of Los Angeles as a totally modern phenomenon born of the movie
business—a lotusland described variously as "seventeen suburbs in search of a
city" and "an asylum that's run by the inmates" and so forth. But the fact is
that, for most of the United States, Los Angeles, rightly or wrongly, symbolizes the good life. If that is not strictly in accord with the fact that Los
Angelenos, like the rest of us, have to work hard for a living and worry about
water and smog like the rest of us, it doesn't matter. We have to have a symbol
of the good life—and we have one. So on the birthday of Los Angeles, when we
talk about the good life, I'd like to look at life in general and tell you what I find
that really is good about it.

We take instant worldwide communication so for granted these days that
we tend to forget it wasn't ever thus. On this day in 1951, for the first time,
Americans on the East and West Coasts were able simultaneously to see the
same live television picture. The new era began with a broadcast of President
Truman's speech at the Japanese Peace Treaty Conference in San Francisco. I
am happy to tell you that my speech today is on a far less weighty level—and,
of course, presented to a distinctly more selective audience.

SEPTEMBER 5

First Labor Day parade, 1882.

First Continental Congress, 1774.

Introductions:

This is the anniversary of the first Labor Day parade, held in New York in 1882. I do not know whether oratory became a part of the Labor Day celebration earlier—whether the talk came before the walk. In that first labor parade, the line of marchers was replete with banners and slogans, which I will not emulate here today. It is no secret that what labor wants, and what all of us want, is a more rewarding life. One of life's rewards, in a small way, is the chance to sit down and catch your breath. I am happy to give each of you that small reward, by standing here to do all the talking for a few brief moments.

A cynic once remarked that when nobody talks it's a crisis and when everybody talks it's a Congress. Today is the anniversary of a very important series of talks, the start of the first Continental Congress. Americans all know about the Second Continental Congress, which adopted the Declaration of Independence. But the idea of a Continental Congress first flowered on this day in 1774, and it was the first Continental Congress, whose meetings opened on this day in 1774, that fathered the historic gathering the following year. If you look diligently enough, you can find an important anniversary of something good and constructive for most every day of the year. Today is no exception. To those whose attitude is, "what's so good about today?" I should like to say, just listen.

SEPTEMBER 6

First coeducational college, 1837.

Jane Addams born, 1860.

Introductions:

So many of the occasions we commemorate recall the deeds of men only that it is a pleasure to come before you on a day when what happened to women did so much to help the world. Today is the anniversary of the first full admission of women to an American college with men, the birthday of coeducation at the college level. It happened in 1837 at what was then called Oberlin Collegiate Institute, now Oberlin College, in Oberlin, Ohio. Four women and 30 men began their studies together. It was to be a long time until other rights and privileges were extended to the distaff side, but this was a notable beginning. And it makes a pleasant backdrop against which to speak, as I will today, about matters in which women and men have an absolutely equal stake and concern.

There used to be a saying that women's work was never done. I say used to be because the whole idea of women's work, as opposed to man's work, has been outmoded in this age of equal rights and equal opportunities. A good deal of progress has been made by women who went beyond the limits of what used to be regarded as women's work. One of the pioneers was Jane Addams, born on this day in 1860 in Cedarville, Illinois. Jane Addams devoted her life to making a better life for others. She founded Hull House in Chicago, she became a leader in the fight for women's rights and above all in the fight for peace. In 1931, she and Nicholas Murray Butler, the President of Columbia University, were jointly awarded the Nobel Peace Prize. She was the first American woman to receive that honor. Men have their heroes of war or peace; with women, given their chance, peace has predominated. So, given the chance, I rise to say that whether or not my remarks to this audience prove to be educational, I am glad that the audience itself is coeducational.

SEPTEMBER 7

James J. Corbett beat John L. Sullivan, 1892.

Queen Elizabeth I born, 1533.

Introductions:

Today is the anniversary of the first heavyweight championship prize fight in which the contestants used boxing gloves rather than bare knuckles, fought fixed time periods in the form of three-minute rounds and generally observed the new Marquess of Queensberry rules. James J. Corbett, who had a way with words as well as with fisticuffs, beat the reigning champion, John L. Sullivan, by a knockout in the twenty-first round in New Orleans, in 1892. Like boxing, public speaking has changed through the years. They don't have fights that last quite so long, and I hope we don't have too many speeches that last so long either. We do, of course, have occasion to come out swinging and with the gloves off; but today, like a good boxer, my main purpose is not to land a haymaker but rather to make a few good, clean points.

Queen Elizabeth I did not seem to be a very good listener in her time—which began with her birth on this day in 1533 in Greenwich palace, England—but she reigned over a time which made for very good listening. In her reign, William Shakespeare and others made the English language positively sing. I do not expect to do the same here today; but I have borrowed a saying of hers as a theme for my remarks. When Sir Walter Raleigh wrote, "Fain would I climb, yet fear I to fall," Elizabeth added the rhyme: "If thy heart fails thee, climb not at all." Is that where we are today—with hearts that have failed us so we climb not at all? I doubt this greatly. Let me tell you why.

SEPTEMBER 8

King Richard the Lion-Hearted born, 1157.

First permanent European settlement in North America, 1565.

Introductions:

Today is the birthday of King Richard the Lion-Hearted, who was born in Oxford, England in 1157. Richard spent most of his time outside England, and did not quite have the glittering record to go with his reputation in history. Maybe he enjoyed that reputation because he was fond of troubadors and wrote his own lyrics—so the troubadors considered him one of their own. The moral seems to be that if you write your own lyrics maybe history will be good to you. I don't plan to sing for my supper today, but the words you are about to hear are mine, all mine. Maybe that in itself entitles me to be remembered as lion-hearted. Wait till you have heard the words, and then decide for yourself.

This may well be the anniversary of public speaking in America. I say that because it was on this day that the first permanent European settlement in North America took place, in what was then called and has been called ever since St. Augustine, Florida, in 1565. I cannot conceive of a colony being put in place and a community assembled without somebody making a speech about it. So I assume that the anniversary of the first settlement is also the anniversary of the first public speech in America. My remarks will be somewhat different today. To begin with they will be in English. That first settlement was Spanish. Second, what I have to say deals with the known; the New World in 1565 was very much an unknown quantity. Finally, I am going to speak about conditions that simply did not exist in 1565. And now, instead of talking about what I plan to say, let me proceed to say it.

SEPTEMBER 9

California Admission Day.

We became the United States, 1776.

Introductions:

This is the birthday of the state of California, or, more exactly, the anniversary of the admission of California to the U.S. as the 31st state in 1850. Apart from anything else, this was a great service to public speakers, who could now indulge in that extra oratorical flourish of referring to a nation that spread coast to coast—from the rockbound coast of Maine to the sunny shores of California. They had recently struck gold in California when it became a state, and the rush was on. I do not expect to strike gold in my remarks today—although it is possible I may strike a nerve or two. And now, as they say in California, "roll 'em,"

We generally observe the birthday of the United States on July Fourth—and I certainly don't want to make trouble about that. But if you want to be technical, we weren't the United States until this day in the year 1776. It was on September 9 that the Continental Congress decided to change the name of the rebelling group from the United Colonies to the United States. So today is indeed the birthday of the name United States, if not of our independence. Not every name by which we are known requires an act of Congress. As a matter of fact, not every name by which we are known is known to us. People do talk behind our backs as it were. Today I would like to talk, not behind anybody's back, about some of the things that somehow rarely make the news but are nevertheless things people talk about. For example, . . .

SEPTEMBER 10

First coast-to-coast paved U.S. road, 1913.

Commodore Perry's report, 1813.

Arnold Palmer born, 1929.

Introductions:

This may be hard to believe, but today, back in 1913, the first coast-to-coast paved road in the United States was proclaimed open. Up to that time, parts of the highway from the East Coast to California were just dirt roads. They named that 1913 innovation the Lincoln Highway. Of course it made getting from one point to another all across the United States a great deal easier. Getting from one point to another is not always that easy for a speaker. The oratorical highway is sometimes less well paved than the one that the cars roll on. One thing that both the motorist and the speaker have to be concerned about is making sure they don't use up too much gas along the way. And so, now that my engine is warmed up, let me shift into gear and proceed.

The naval history of the United States invites us to look back to epic battles in the two great oceans of the world, the Atlantic and the Pacific. Today, however, is the anniversary of a very important naval battle that was fought on a lake. It was the Battle of Lake Erie, in the War of 1812. On this day in 1813, Commodore Oliver Hazard Perry defeated the British in that battle and Commodore Perry described the day in a succinct message that has been a model for clarity and brevity ever since. I have every intention of keeping it in mind as I address you here today. "We have met the enemy," Commodore Perry said, "and they are ours." Now I don't plan to be quite that brief, but I will try.

Today is the birthday of Arnold Palmer, the great golfer, who was born in 1929 in Youngstown, Pennyslvania. Palmer won an army of admirers, known in fact as Arnie's Army, by the style and efficiency with which he played golf. In speaking to you here today, I plan to emulate conversationally his version of the Palmer method—namely, to tee off properly, aim true and finish with as few strokes as are necessary to do the job.

SEPTEMBER 11

Henry Hudson discovered Manhattan Island, 1609.

O. Henry born, 1862.

Franklin's wise words, 1783.

Introductions:

According to history, it was on or about this time of year in 1609 that Henry Hudson discovered Manhattan Island. One reason there is some uncertainty about the date is that when he first spied that particular body of land, he really couldn't be sure it was an island until he had done some further checking. In that respect, Henry Hudson was no different from many later visitors to Manhattan. The only way to figure out how it works is to be there for a while. The same thing is true of some of the conclusions we reach very logically and very methodically. The only way to reach them is to take them step by step. That is what I propose to do here today—by just giving you the concluding paragraph of my remarks, I would give you every right to wonder how in the world I had gotten there.

Two hundred and fifty three years after Henry Hudson discovered Manhattan Island, William Sydney Porter was born in Greensboro, North Carolina. He grew up to be better known as the writer, O. Henry, who in a literary sense, discovered Manhattan all over again. O. Henry wrote unforgettable short stories about life in the big city. He wrote equally unforgettable short stories about cowboys and about Latin America. But his most famous setting was the city that he called "Bagdad on the subway." O. Henry was particularly famous for the trick endings of his stories, the surprise twists, and it is a great temptation for a speaker to try to pull the same trick on his audience. You'll have to wait until the end to see whether I would do that to you.

Benjamin Franklin was 77 years old when, with John Adams and John Jay, he negotiated the peace settlement with Great Britain, in 1783, that became the Treaty of Paris. On September 11, 1783, shortly after the Treaty was signed, Franklin wrote a letter to a friend in which he said, "There never was a good war or a bad peace." One of Ben Franklin's virtures was that he didn't waste words. I shall try to follow his example here today and not take too much of your time, remembering Ben Franklin's observation that time is money.

SEPTEMBER 12

The Black Crook, 1866.

Nikita Khrushchev to the top in Soviet Russia, 1953.

Introductions:

This was the day, in 1866, when a new era of entertainment in the United States began with the premiere of a show called *The Black Crook* in New York City. *The Black Crook* was the first American presentation to feature beautiful American girls. It was the forerunner of the time when people would go to the musical theatre to hear the show and others would go to see the showgirls. There has been a tendency ever since to, so to speak, bring on the dancing girls as attractive window dressing to help sell a concept or an idea. You can see I am no dancing girl nor do I have any waiting in the wings. I hope that you will find what I have to say worth the price of admission.

Back in 1953, this was the day when Nikita Khrushchev became the First Secretary of the Communist Party of the U.S.S.R., a position which automatically brought him front and center. Khrushchev loved to talk, and in one of his famous public appearances, he brought a new technique to the public forum when he pounded his shoe on the table in the course of a discussion at the United Nations. I trust there are no Khrushchevs in the audience here today. For my part, I plan to rely on the tongue in my mouth and not the one in my footwear.

SEPTEMBER 13

Battle of Quebec, 1759.

First U.S. national election authorized, 1788.

Introductions:

Today is the anniversary of the Battle of Quebec, when the British under General Wolfe defeated the French under General Montcalm in 1759. The battle was a very crucial one in the history of British Canada, but I mention it here today not so much for its tremendous historical importance as for the fact that it was a battle in which both commanding generals were killed. That is not the normal course of events for a military encounter. We have always had some leaders who lead the way and others who simply point the way. The same is true of speakers. We have a choice. We can stand up and say "this is the cause, follow me;" or we can say, far more easily, "this is the situation, now what do we do about it?" One need not have the answers to sound the alarm or raise the question. So I am emboldened to speak to you today without necessarily having any solutions or any panaceas.

When Congress, on this day in 1788, decided that the first national election under the Constitution would be held on the first Wednesday in January, 1789, they were mindful that a lot of people would want to make a lot of speeches, and so they gave them plenty of time. In all the intervening years, we haven't done very much to render speechmaking any less longwinded. Even today, when someone is approached to speak at a public meeting, the first question he or she asks is, "how long shall I talk?" I wonder why neither the speaker nor the chairman of the arrangements committee ever mentions how short the talk should be. Since so many speeches are made to captive audiences, I regard a long speech as cruel and unusual punishment. Being humane, I shall not inflict such punishment upon you here today.

SEPTEMBER 14

Francis Scott Key wrote "The Star Spangled Banner," 1814.

Ivan Pavlov born, 1849.

Margaret Sanger born, 1883.

Introductions:

On this day in 1814—or more exactly, very early in the morning on this day in 1814—the words were written that have been uttered at more meetings in the United States than any other phrases known to man. The words to which I refer are those of "The Star Spangled Banner," which was written by Francis Scott Key in Baltimore Harbor as he watched and waited to see whether the flag would still be there to signal that the United States had turned away the British invaders in the War of 1812. "Oh say can you see, by the dawn's early light," Francis Scott Key asked, whether the Star Spangled Banner still waved. When those lines were written, the British had burned our national capitol in Washington. If they had succeeded in taking Baltimore, that might have been the end of the United States of America. We have a tendency to think that the crises and challenges of our own times are things unique unto us, but I remind you here today that an earlier generation of Americans had good reason to worry whether the flag would still be flying the next morning. Francis Scott Key wrote of the rockets' red glare and bombs bursting in air. In modern times we have learned how to make more murderous bombs and faster, more powerful rockets; but I like to think that we have also learned to communicate a little better, to talk to each other a little more and to express ourselves. It is in that spirit that I stand before you today to discuss a few current aspects of what Francis Scott Key so wisely called "The land of the free and the home of the brave."

Many of the things we do in life are what are called conditioned reflexes. Some people's hearts beat faster when the flag goes marching by. Some people get hungry when they hear the dinner bell ring. Some products have a particular odor deliberately added to them because it triggers a reflex of craving or appreciation. The scientist who pioneered in the study of conditioned reflexes was Ivan Pavlov, born on this day in 1849 in Ryazan, Russia. It was Pavlov who showed how animals could be trained to react in specific ways to specific signals, a dog responding to a particular ring of a bell. The whole course of life conditions us to certain reflexes. There are those among us who immediately become sleepy when the clergyman begins his sermon. Public speakers may have to clear their throats with every sentence—not because of trouble with their vocal chords but rather because, as Winston Churchill once admitted, this form of habitual pause gives one time to collect and organize his thoughts. The most dangerous reflex of all is to close our minds to what we do not wish to hear—or to close our mouths when it would be better to speak. I will make a deal with you. I will open my mouth and talk if you will open your minds and listen.

Margaret Higgins Sanger, who was born on this day in 1883, was trained as a nurse and looked upon herself all her life as one whose first concern was for the health of the individual. She devoted her life to one particular area of conern, birth control, until her death in 1966. When Margaret Sanger began her fight, birth control was a dirty word. Contraceptive information was classified as obscene and barred from the mails and she was arrested on obscenity charges, though the case never went to trial. The dispute over birth control continued even after her death, but the issue was discussed with a freedom that, for many years, was denied to Margaret Sanger. Thanks to her single minded efforts, people are able to speak more freely today. The fact that her ideas became more popular is not the most important testimonial to Margaret Sanger. The most important testimonial is that she helped to make freedom of speech a reality. I do not plan today to test the limits of free speech or try to develop new areas of previously forbidden subject matter. But it is nice to know you and I can speak or hear without being sent to jail.

SEPTEMBER 15

Income tax installment deadline.

William Howard Taft born, 1857.

Introductions:

A speaker who is called upon to address a gathering of Americans on this day always faces a certain psychological hurdle. September 15 is normally the deadline for payment of the third installment of estimated income tax. As such, it is a day which bemuses many of us as Uncle Sam separates us from some of our hard-won income. Look upon me, therefore, as one who steps up today to speak of other things to divert your mind from the tax collector and speak a bit of those wonderful things that money can't buy.

Not too many people in the history of the United States have been chosen as President. Only one also served as the highest judicial officer of the nation.

William Howard Taft, born on this day in 1857, in Cincinnati, was President for four years and Chief Justice of the United States for nine. He was also the head of a distinguished Ohio political family. I thought it might be nice, on his birthday, to start off this modest set of remarks with an appropriate quotation from William Howard Taft. When I consulted the various anthologies of quotations, I discovered that William Howard Taft had another distinction. He wasn't in most of them. Where he was quoted, it was in the weighty words of a judicial decision. You are therefore spared any words from the past and instead I shall endeavor to deal with some subject matter that obviously has arisen since the days of Taft. At the risk of a bad pun, let me say that my speech is without president.

SEPTEMBER 16

Shawmut becomes Boston 1630.

Esperanto goes to college, 1908.

Introductions:

Many people who have come to the United States have chosen new names. On this day in 1630, a community did so. The settlement known as Shawmut, in Massachusetts, changed its name in honor of the town in England from which some of the settlers of the New World had come. It called itself Boston. I wonder whether the language or the history of America would have been the same if Boston had remained Shawmut. Would we be remembering the Shawmut Massacre or the Shawmut Tea Party? Names, like other words, create pictures and impressions. I hope my words here today can be as successful in conveying a message and an impression as the imprint of Boston on the conscience and the panorama of America. That is a difficult act to follow.

Many years ago, a language called Esperanto was devised, to enable different people from different parts of the world to have a common means of communication. On this day in 1908, Esperanto went to college. Clark University, in Worcester, Massachusetts, began a course in what it was hoped, would become the universal language. I don't know how long the course remained in the Clark curriculum, but Esperanto, though still alive, has not been as widely accepted as its sponsors hoped. Indeed, in many areas such as international aviation, the common language is our own English. It is hard enough to communicate in one's own language, as we all know. Let me say that in any language I would be happy to be here.

SEPTEMBER 17

Constitution Week.

Citizenship Day.

Washington's Farewell Address, 1796.

Introductions:

This is Constitution Week, the commemoration of the Constitutional Convention's adoption of the U. S. Constitution in 1787. This was the day when, after weeks of debate, the Constitution was finally approved by the Convention. The anniversary day is called Citizenship Day, and Citizenship Day is observed as a reminder every year of the birth of a great concept of government in this country. Citizenship Day starts Constitution Week—and I must say that if I can start my remarks today under the same happy auguries that came true for the Constitution, I will be very happy.

Constitution Week, which starts today, commemorates more than the adoption of the Constitution by the Constitutional Convention in 1787. That was only the first act. Before the week was over, back in 1787, the proposed Constitution had to be submitted to the Congress. And some people in Congress didn't like the whole idea. They thought the loose Articles of Confederation were all the federal government we needed. So in the week or ten days after the proposed Constitution was submitted to the Congress, there was a lot more talk and a lot more debate. But finally the proposal was sent to the states for ratification. In a very real sense, Constitution Week commemorates a week of talk, talk, talk. I feel that I am celebrating it in a very appropriate manner today—thankfully at considerably less length than might have been the case in 1787—by emulating the example of the Founding Fathers. So let's talk.

Having lived through a number of Presidents' farewell addresses, I always find it difficult to understand one thing about the parting speech of our first President, George Washington. The content of the speech is no problem. The puzzle is that he dated it September 17, but never delivered it as a speech at all. Instead he had it published on September 19, two days later, in 1796. So maybe today is its anniversary—and maybe not. But since we know that Washington never told a lie, I assume it was on this day that he said, "Citizens by birth or choice of a common country, that country has a right to concentrate your affections." We are indeed citizens by birth or choice of a common country, and it is that community of interest that is the basis of my remarks here today.

SEPTEMBER 18

Washington laid the cornerstone of the Capitol, 1793.

Samuel Johnson born, 1709.

Greta Garbo born, 1905.

Introductions:

This is the anniversary of a very solemn and important event in the history of our country—the placing of the cornerstone for the Capitol in Washington,

D.C. by President George Washington in 1793. Unfortunately, the history of our country that I consulted did not report what President Washington said on that momentous occasion, so I can only assume that he expressed pleasure at being present, complimented the assorted dignitaries who were present and so forth. And so, as George Washington may have said . . .

Samuel Johnson, whose birthday we don't seem to be celebrating here today, was nevertheless born on this day in 1709 in Lichfield, England. I mention this because a quotation of Dr. Johnson's is so often in my mind as a warning when I speak in public. Johnson said, about the poet Dryden, "He delighted to tread upon the brink of meaning." I hope today, rather than treading upon the brink, to make my meaning—and the reasons for it—crystal clear.

Greta Garbo was born on this day, in 1905, in Stockholm, Sweden. Apart from the impressiveness of her performances on the screen as a great motion picture star, she was also famous for her constant search for solitude. "I want to be alone," that was supposed to be Greta Garbo's watchword. I have always found that difficult to understand because, frankly, the opportunity not to be alone, the chance to be here addressing a warm and friendly audience, seems to me to be something special. I thank you in advance for your kind attention.

SEPTEMBER 19

Washington's Farewell Address printed, 1796.

Mickey Mouse's debut, 1928.

Introductions:

I don't often have an opportunity to compare myself to George Washington, but today I have my chance. That's because today is the anniversary, in a sense, of a speech that George Washington never made, even though he had it printed. In 1796, on this date, a Philadelphia newspaper published Washington's famous Farewell Address as President of the United States, which was dated September 17, two days earlier. Unlike President Washington, I am not having this speech predated, and I am delivering it in person. But George Washington talked about what *he* wanted to talk about, and I propose to do the same, starting right now.

I suppose that the most well-known character of our time is probably not any real person at all, but the one and only Mickey Mouse—recognized instantly all over the world. Today is Mickey Mouse's birthday. He was born in 1928 in an animated cartoon called "Steamboat Willie" which had its premiere on this day in 1928. Mickey was the first of the Disney characters to speak in a strange and distinctive voice, though not nearly as distinctive as his later sidekick, the irascible Donald Duck. Today I find myself wondering how Mickey and Donald would treat the subjects I am about to discuss. Mickey would laugh and Donald would get mad. But let me state my case, and then you can cast the roles for yourself.

SEPTEMBER 20

Billie Jean King beat Bobby Riggs, 1973.

Truman asked Wallace to resign, 1946.

Introductions:

Back in 1973, this was expected to be a very exciting day. Bobby Riggs, in his fifties, was going to play a tennis match against the outstanding woman player, Billie Jean King. It was being touted up as a main event in the war of the sexes, but of course all it proved was that a great young woman champion could beat a once-great and at least 20-years-over-the-hill male champion. That is rather like some of the less than profound truths that we hear all too often from public speakers. Today, to the best of my ability, I hope that the only deuce I raise is vocally, not on anybody's tennis court, and I will try to serve up a few winners in the process. Today, speaking is my racket.

History records today as the anniversary of some unfortunate consequences of a speech. Secretary of Commerce Henry A. Wallace had made an address on September 12, 1946, that was critical of the U.S. policy toward Russia, and on this day, a little over a week later, the boss of that U.S. policy, President Harry Truman, asked Mr. Wallace to resign. I am quite mindful, therefore, that what I say here today may be held against me. I am also hopeful that what I say may meet with your approval. I guess the only way to find out is to begin.

SEPTEMBER 21

Autumn.

"Yes, Virginia, there is a Santa Claus," 1897.

Introductions:

Although the autumnal equinox sometimes plays games with the calendar and autumn sneaks in a day late or a day early, this is the usual day for welcoming the new season. Autumn, as you know, is apt to bring big winds, and I hope that wasn't why I was asked here today. If that were the case, I would find it a painful blow. So let me abandon that line of dubious speculation and say what I came here to say.

An editorial was published in a now extinct newspaper called *The New York Sun*, on this day in 1897, that said, "Yes, Virginia, there is a Santa

Claus." It was a little early for Christmas, but it is never too early to keep a pleasant thought alive. I am not here today to reaffirm the positive existence of good old Saint Nick, but there are some other jolly thoughts I would like to share with you.

SEPTEMBER 22

Nathan Hale's famous last words, 1776.

U.S. Post Office established, 1789.

Introductions:

Nathan Hale was only 21 years old when'he was captured by the British in the American Revolutionary War. He was hanged as a spy on this day in 1776, and as he went to the gallows he said his last words, ending with the lines, "I only regret that I have but one life to give for my country." Many people since Nathan Hale, regrettably, have given their lives for their country. On the anniversary of his heroic death, I stand here wondering how many of us are willing to dedicate our lives, while still living them, to what this country stands for. Do we have to die for our country to be of service to it? I don't think so. I think that we can serve our country best by the way we live. And so today I want to talk about how we can live better, for ourselves and for our land.

The U.S. Post Office was established on this day in 1789. I was tempted to refer to it as a red letter day, but I will refrain. Delivering the mail in those years was an arduous and uncertain task. I guess this illustrates that every problem is not a brand new one, and that we needn't stand here thinking that our generation is so unique. In fact, as we perfect our means of communication, we seem to have just as much trouble getting the messages through as our forefathers did with horse and buggy technology. Somebody once defined progress as finding new ways to mess things up faster. That is a dismal view which I am prepared to challenge here today. Progress, to me, is the development of alternatives, of choices. And I think we have choices—we have alternatives. Let me elaborate.

SEPTEMBER 23

John Paul Jones' famous words, 1779.

Harvard's first commencement, 1642.

Introductions:

John Paul Jones was in a naval battle on this day in 1779, commanding the *Bonhomme Richard* against the British fighting vessel *Serapis*. The *Bonhomme Richard* was in a bad way, and the British ship captain asked John

Paul Jones to surrender. Jones' answer was the one we all know, "I have not yet begun to fight" or words to that effect. Then he went on to capture the *Serapis.* So, taking a leaf from that story, I stand before you saying, "I have just begun to talk."

The first college commencement in America took place on this day in 1642. It was neither the same month nor the same kind of college commencement that we are partial to these days, but for the students of Harvard College, it was a great event. Whether the event was highlighted by the brilliance of a commencement address I do not know. Whether our events here today will be highlighted by a brilliant address is highly doubtful, since I am your speaker. But, like most commencement remarks, I hope mine will send you away happy.

SEPTEMBER 24

John Marshall born, 1755.

Trial of the "Chicago 8" began, 1969.

Introductions:

This is the birthday of John Marshall, the great Chief Justice who did so much to maintain the Constitution as the supreme law of the land. He was born in Midland, Virginia, on this day in 1755. "The people," Justice Marshall said in a decision in 1821, "made the Constitution, and the people can unmake it. It is the creature of their own will, and lives only by their will." At a time when "Let Joe do it" seems to be all too popular a motto, I quote Chief Justice Marshall in salute to the will of the people. The opposite of the will of the people, as far as I am concerned, is the won't of the people. I am here today to discuss both.

It was more than a year after the disruptions in Chicago, at the Democratic National Convention of 1968, before the leaders of the demonstrations, who had become known meanwhile as "the Chicago 8," went on trial on this day in 1969. About the only thing the trial seemed to prove was that the human tongue can be a blunt instrument. I have made a conscientious effort to make mine smooth around the edges today.

SEPTEMBER 25

Bill of Rights submitted to states, 1789.

First American newspaper, 1690.

Introductions:

The Bill of Rights, which guarantees so many of our basic freedoms, wasn't in the Constitution when the first Congress met, so the Congress did something about it. On this day in 1789, Congress sent to the states twelve proposed Amendments to the Constitution. Ten of those amendments, constituting what has been known ever since as the Bill of Rights, were ratified. It is thanks to the Bill of Rights that we can assemble here, and that I can say what I choose from this rostrum. Now all I have to do is to remember what I came here to say.

The first American newspaper was a rather modest publication of three pages, with a long title. It was called *Public Occurrences, Both Foreign and Domestic*, and it was published on this day in 1690 in Boston. It was never published again, because the Governor didn't like it. In those days what the Governor didn't like was neither published nor speechified. I am happy, therefore, to be making this speech here and now rather than in the good old days. I hope you like it, but in any case I'm glad to know that neither you nor I nor my remarks are in danger of being suppressed. Indeed, the reverse is true. Today, you have to wonder if and how what you say will be reported in the press. Since there is only one way to find out, here goes.

SEPTEMBER 26

First Nixon-Kennedy debate, 1960.

Woodrow Wilson's collapse, 1919.

Introductions:

This is the anniversary of the first of the great Presidential debates, when John F. Kennedy and Richard Nixon wrote a new chapter in national elections with their televised, face-to-face confrontation. The power of words and of the way they are delivered was never more dramatically illustrated. This was a very big day for the spoken word, back in 1960. Perhaps that is a good omen for my remarks here today. At any rate, I am grateful to you for providing a podium but omitting an opponent. It's much better being able to pontificate without having to compete.

Anyone who rises to make a public speech on this day would do well to take it easy—as I plan to do in my remarks here. In 1919, on this day, after Woodrow Wilson had been touring and had made about 40 speeches to persuade the U.S. public to support the Treaty of Versailles, President Wilson collapsed. It was a speaking schedule that proved to be his undoing. It was also a reminder that speaking can sometimes be more of a strain on the speaker than it is on the listener. So today I will try to be easy on you, with very selfish motives.

SEPTEMBER 27

Samuel Adams born, 1722.

Thomas Nast born, 1840.

Introductions:

Today is the birthday of Samuel Adams, who did so much to spark the American Revolution. Sam Adams, who was a second cousin of John Adams, was born in 1722 in Boston. He was the firebrand of his time, the leader of the resistance to the Stamp Act and one of the prime instigators of the Boston Tea Party. When Sam Adams spoke, things seemed to happen; this can be very encouraging to some speakers and very frightening to others. I prefer to steer a middle course, hoping, certainly, that what I say here will have some influence but hoping particularly that it will prove to be right. And always bearing in mind Sam Adams' injunction: "Let us contemplate our forefathers, and posterity, and resolve to maintain the rights bequeathed to us from the former, for the sake of the latter."

Every time you see a donkey symbolizing the Democrats or an elephant symbolizing the Republicans, you are seeing the work of Thomas Nast, the great political cartoonist who flourished in the latter half of the nineteenth century. This is the day Thomas Nast was born, in 1840, in Germany. He came to the U.S. with his family when he was six. Thomas Nast created the Tammany tiger and his cartoons of Boss Tweed did a great deal to harden public opinion against that political potentate. Thomas Nast showed the power of a picture. Today, I have to paint my pictures with words; but word pictures can tell a story too. And there are some stories today that need telling.

SEPTEMBER 28

Friedrich Engels born, 1820.

Betty Ford's mastectomy, 1974.

Introductions:

The name of Karl Marx is known everywhere, and that is largely because of a man whose name is not quite as well known, a man named Friedrich Engels, who was born on this day back in 1820 in Germany. Friedrich Engels wrote the Communist Manifesto with Marx, and edited a considerable portion of Marx's writings. I think it is appropriate, on Engels' birthday, to point out that very few people work alone, and most of life is a collaboration. Today, I seek to enlist you in a collaboration too—not for the writing of a manifesto or the organization of a new "ism," but to do some good that needs doing.

When President Ford was barely in office, little more than a month and a half after the Ford family found itself in the White House, Betty Ford made news in a surprising way. She had a mastectomy and the press was encouraged to make it known. Hers was a courageous decision; for while it is easy in the abstract to agree that showing the public a dramatic instance of confidence in medical wisdom is constructive, it is anything but easy when you are the case in point. If only a few women were persuaded by the example of Betty Ford to have badly needed mastectomies, it was worthwhile. The fact is that all of us, women and men, constantly look to each other for peer models. It is not merely misery that loves company; it is humanity. If what I am about to say here today strikes a familiar chord for some of you, it will not be merely a matter of words, it will be a reinforcement of community. That, at least, is my hope. For what I am going to talk about concerns us all.

SEPTEMBER 29

Admiral Dewey in New York, 1899.

Munich agreement, 1938.

Introductions:

This was a very festive day in 1899. New York City gave a hero's welcome, as it had never before, to Admiral George Dewey on his return from the Spanish American War. Admiral Dewey was famous not only for the great naval victory at Manila Bay, but particularly for saying to his flagship's captain, "You may fire when you are ready, Gridley." Nothing Admiral Dewey said later ever dimmed the fame of that one short sentence. Now I plan to keep my sentences short today, but I don't expect the kind of results that Admiral Dewey got. It is my modest hope that when I am through none of you will be tempted to fire when ready.

Four men met in Munich on this day in 1938 and talked. They were British Prime Minister Chamberlain, French Premier Daladier, Italian Premier Mussolini and German Reichfuehrer Hitler, and what they talked about—and agreed to and announced the next day—was the partitioning of Czechoslovakia. It was not a banner day for talk. I hope that today, this year, will prove somewhat more constructive—or, at the very least, a lot less damaging. With that modest goal, let me proceed.

SEPTEMBER 30

Ether used as anesthetic, 1846.

Porgy and Bess premiere, 1935.

Chamberlain's "peace in our time", 1938.

Hitler's Stalingrad prediction, 1942.

Introductions:

Although ether was introduced as an anesthetic on this day in 1846 by a dentist named William Morton, it has never seemed to be as widely effective as that particular soporific, a long, dull speech. I am therefore very mindful of my obligation, on this anniversary day, not to intrude on ether's territory. In other words, no boring sermon today, folks.

The easiest way to avoid being boring is to startle people by challenging some of their favorite assumptions. Indeed, one of the big hits in the show, *Porgy and Bess*, which had its premiere in Boston on this day in 1935, was a song entitled "It Ain't Necessarily So." A lot of things we assume fall in that category. They "ain't necessarily so." And what "ain't necessarily so" is what I propose to talk about now.

I promise, in my remarks today, to avoid risky predictions. Today has not been a good day in the past for bigtime prophecy. In 1938, fresh from taking part in the carving up of Czechslovakia for the benefit of Nazi Germany, British Prime Minister Chamberlain arrived in England to announce "peace with honor" and "peace in our time." It lasted less than a year. And in 1942 Hitler said that the Nazi conquest of Stalingrad would be "a tremendous success." The Nazis not only never got to Stalingrad but suffered one of their worst defeats there. So much for the September 30 brand of prophecy. Instead of looking into the future, let's take a look at things as they are today.

OCTOBER 1

Model T introduced, 1908.

Winston Churchill's special mystery, 1939.

Introductions:

This is the anniversary of the day in 1908 when Henry Ford introduced the Model T. The Model T, known affectionately as the Tin Lizzie, pulled automobile manufacturing into the era of assembly lines, interchangeable parts and mass production. I want you to know that none of these techniques or ingredients have gone into the preparation of the remarks I am about to make to you. There is a Model T type of speech as well as of automobile, but it takes an awfully long time to get cranked up and it doesn't go very far or very fast these days. So we will leave the Model T's birthday saluted and undisturbed today and devote ourselves to our part of the twentieth century.

The files of history record that Winston Churchill, on this date in 1939, said, "I cannot forecast to you the action of Russia. It is a riddle wrapped in a mystery inside an enigma." A riddle wrapped in a mystery inside an enigma. You can apply that description to a few countries today, to the question of the world's natural resources, to the problem of why people behave as they do. A speaker, as a matter of fact, sometimes looks out on an audience and finds a riddle wrapped in a mystery inside an enigma right out there in front of him.

So, I prefer not to regard myself as a supersleuth trying to figure out that enigma. I do not set myself up to tell you things you never knew till now. Instead, I propose to express some opinions, state some facts, maybe point out some conclusions—but I will leave the solving of riddles to others.

OCTOBER 2

Lost Battalion, 1918.

Mahatma Gandhi born, 1869.

Groucho Marx born, 1890s.

Introductions:

Back in World War I, there was a famous American fighting unit which became known as the Lost Battalion. They were called that because they were trapped in the Argonne Forest, surrounded by the Germans on October 1, 1918, and they held out against unbelievable odds until they were saved on October 8. So, here I am as a standing target up here on the anniversary of the day the Lost Battalion first found itself lost. Let me say to you, therefore, that I intend to speak my way out. And I can ssure you my battle plan is not based on waiting until October 8 for the happy ending. Indeed, since I feel myself surrounded by friends rather than enemies, I thank you for your kind attention. And now to business.

Mohandas Gandhi, better known as Mahatma Gandhi, was the great apostle of civil disobedience and non violence. Those were the tactics he used to lead his native India to independence from British rule. Gandhi was born on this day in 1869. In a strange twist of fate, he himself met a violent death when he was assassinated, in New Delhi, in 1948. But the lesson Mahatma Gandhi taught was that if you speak peacefully and make sense, people will listen and will act on what you say. I plan to speak very peacefully here today, and I hope to make sense. Beyond that, you are on your own.

Groucho Marx was legendary for his wit, and for a time it looked as though he would also be legendary for his age. Like other actors, he listed different years for his birth, at different times in his life. It is definite that he was born in New York City on this day, probably in 1890. It was Groucho who said once that he would never join any club that would accept him as a member. I have known speakers who had a similar attitude; they are not interested in talking to any audience that would sit still to hear them. I have a higher opinion than that of audiences in general and this audience in particular. Indeed, I am greatly impressed with your choice of speaker today. As a matter of fact, as Groucho might say, I can hardly wait to hear me.

OCTOBER 3

Thanksgiving proclamations, 1789 and 1863.

Johns Hopkins University opened, 1876.

Introductions:

It is a little early for Thanksgiving, but this day in history has a very clear connection with that occasion. In 1789, President Washington, on this day, proclaimed the first national Thanksgiving Day, to be observed November 26 of that year in honor of the adoption of the Constitution. And in 1863, President Lincoln, on this same October 3, designated the last Thursday in November as Thanksgiving Day. If Washington and Lincoln considered October 3 a good day to make proclamations to the nation, I am grateful to be speaking on such a well-omened date in the calendar.

This is the anniversary of the opening of Johns Hopkins University in Baltimore in 1876. I don't think there is a University in this country whose name is misstated more often than this one. As a matter of fact, there is a story about a distinguished President of Johns Hopkins University who was asked to speak at an event in Pittsburgh. He was introduced most generously and graciously as the President of John Hopkins University. That's the usual error—no "s" in the first word, which is Johns, not John. So the University President thanked the gentleman who had introduced him and said, as he started his speech, how happy he was to be in "Pittburgh." The moral of this is that the greatest comfort for a speaker is the knowledge, as he rises to deliver his remarks, that he has the last word. And that brings us to my first words.

OCTOBER 4

Sputnik orbited the earth, 1957.

Jet air service across the Atlantic began, 1958.

Rutherford B. Hayes born, 1822.

Introductions:

This is the anniversary of the space age—or at least of one of its key events. On this date, in 1957, the Russians put the first Sputnik in orbit around the earth. It was a startling scientific achivement and it helped jolt the United States into an all-out effort to expand space technology. It also provided a magnificent new topic for speakers—visions of a new era, blue sky dreams—literally. Nowadays, nothing that science does seems to startle us, and speakers are hard put to present visions of miracles that haven't already been talked about.

So I will put the speculation about miracles aside and instead devote myself to topics that are more down to earth.

I find it interesting to look back on what happened on this day in the past. In 1957, the space era began when the Russians orbited the first Sputnik around the earth, and a year later, on the same day, the British began the first jet airplane service across the Atlantic. It is interesting that it took longer to get jet service across the ocean than to put a satellite into orbit. It's rather like how the glib Walter Pitkin—the man who wrote *Life Begins at 40*—answered when asked about the difference between a 200 word article and a 1500 word article on the same subject. He said, "the 1500-word article you can have tomorrow; the 200-word one will take a week." The length or the distance of a subject is not necessarily a measure of its difficulty. That of course is true of speeches as well as articles—or any flights of fancy. I hope that my remarks here today will have the merit of brevity rather than empty glibness.

I also find it worth pointing out that both the space era and the transatlantic jet airplane service began under other than U.S. auspices. We come on fast when we get going, but sometimes it takes a little exhortation to get us going to begin with. Please forgive me if you note a little exhortation here and there as I proceed.

Exhortation is sometimes productive, but it didn't work out too well when Rutherford B. Hayes, who was born on this day in 1822, in Delaware, Ohio, was running against Samuel Tilden for the Presidency. That was the election of 1876, and it wasn't decided until 1877, on the virtual eve of Inauguration Day. The candidates electioneered, the electorate was exhorted, and the result was so close and so much in dispute that it took a special Electoral Commission finally to decide which votes to count and which ones to throw out. We haven't had that kind of situation arise in the Presidency for over a hundred years since then; but I always think of it when I read of a hung jury or a case where the pros and cons seems to be totally balanced. Sooner or later, we have to make a decision. If we don't, somebody else does; and I am here today to argue for keeping "somebody else" out of it. Now here is my "plea to the jury."

OCTOBER 5

First television broadcast by a President from the White House, 1947.

Chester Alan Arthur born, 1830.

Introductions:

Back in 1947, on this day, Harry S. Truman became the first President to speak to the nation from the White House on television. Not too much of the nation had television receivers at the time, and the President's speech was not the hit of the week, particularly since he was asking the nation to save food for

Europe by observing meatless Tuesdays and eggless Thursdays. But after HST broke the ice, the White House became a more popular television setting for one Presidential broadcast after another. It just goes to show that when a rostrum is available, speeches are bound to follow. You are observing the working of this iron rule of oratory here today as I prepare to use the opportunity you have so graciously afforded me.

Chester Alan Arthur was born on this day, in 1830, in Fairfield, Vermont. He was put on the Republican ticket with James A. Garfield, in 1880, as a sop to the old-line spoils-minded wing of the party. When President Garfield was assassinated, everyone thought a new era of crass politics was going to follow automatically. But President Arthur turned out to be something else again. He prosecuted dishonest officials, worked to secure the passage of the Civil Service Act, and did what historians regard as a good job. You can't simply apply past performance as a basis for predicting the future. After all, if history were just past performance repeated over again, we wouldn't have much of a future. So today, I rise to speak on a hopeful note. There may be more Chester Alan Arthurs around than we think. The question is, what should they do?

OCTOBER 6

Edison showed his first motion pictures, 1889.

Al Jolson spoke in "The Jazz Singer," 1927.

The "Amazing" Mets, 1969.

Introductions:

Today is a double movie anniversary. Thomas A. Edison showed his first motion pictures in 1889, in West Orange, New Jersey. And 38 years later, Al Jolson spoke in *The Jazz Singer*, the first talking feature picture, which had its world premiere in 1927 in New York City. We learned to see, via the camera and film, before we learned how to talk in the same medium. We saw before we talked. That is true of us as individuals, as well as of the sequence of invention. A baby sees before it can say a word—or understand a word, for that matter. In school, show comes before tell. And so today, I rise to speak to you about things that we have all seen. Having seen them, we now have to decide what, if anything, to do about them. So let's have the pictures in our minds as I provide the sound track.

In a burst of sheer optimism, I remind you all that on this day, in 1969, a team of perennial also-rans called the New York Mets captured the National League baseball championship and became known for all time as the *"Amazing"* Mets. I said I mentioned this in a burst of sheer optimism. That is because I feel that if it could happen to the Mets maybe it can happen to the rest of us. It is in that spirit—the idea that things can and will get better—that I rise to tell you of my expectations of better days ahead.

OCTOBER 7

Gravity railroad, 1826.

James Whitcomb Riley born, 1849.

Gladstone's comfort, 1881.

Introductions:

This is the birthday of the United States' first railroad, which was a somewhat different kind of railroad when it began operating in 1826. It was powered by a horse and by force of gravity. It was called the Granite Railway and it ran from Quincy to Milton, Massachusetts, carrying granite down to the waterfront. Gravity is a one-way force; it doesn't pull you uphill. And a speech which takes its gravity too seriously ends up going downhill. So, as I think of the Granite Railway, I remind myself that gravity isn't enough, I'd rather work *up* to something than get *down* to it. And today I want you to get worked up with me.

James Whitcomb Riley, the Hoosier poet, was born on this day in 1849, in Greenfield, Indiana. It was he who created "Little Orphant Annie" and warned that the goblins will get you if you don't watch out. Public speakers have been stealing that story line for generations—the goblins will get you if you don't watch out. It is a nice touch of suspense to put the blame on those unidentified, miscellaneous goblins; but remember that Walt Kelly, who created Pogo long after James Whitcomb Riley was dead and buried, pointed the finger a lot closer to home. "We have met the enemy," Pogo said, "and they is us." Today we don't need to worry about the goblins. All we have to do is to look in the mirror. I have looked. Now let me tell you what I see.

Contemplating the sad aspects of our times is an exercise that we didn't dream up. I guess every generation has done the same thing. Back in 1881, on this date, William E. Gladstone, the British political leader, stood up and said, "The resources of civilization are not yet exhausted." They were not exhausted then, and they are not exhausted today. Maybe some of us are, but the resources are not. And so I rise on a note of optimism to speak to you today.

OCTOBER 8

Chicago fire, 1871.

Fire Prevention Week.

Lost Battalion saved, 1918.

John Hay born, 1838.

Introductions:

Let us pause for a moment to remember Mrs. O'Leary's cow. That was the cow who supposedly kicked over a lantern in Mrs. O'Leary's barn on this day in 1871, thereby starting the great Chicago fire. I don't know whether that story libeled an innocent animal. A story, like a fire, is very hard to stop once it gets started. And so is a public speaker.

Fire Prevention Week, traditionally, always includes this day. It is in commemoration of the great Chicago fire which began on this day in 1871. The theory of Fire Prevention Week is that the best way to fight fires is to make sure they don't get started. That's a pretty good policy with regard to most of our problems, not only fires. Make sure they don't get started. Today I want to talk to you about how to do just that with some of the complications that threaten to get started in our everyday life.

One of the great stories of American heroism in World War I was the epic of the Lost Battalion; trapped for many days and surrounded by the enemy, they were urged to surrender. But on this day in 1918, the Lost Battalion was saved. We have Lost Battalions in peace as well as in war. We have some that aren't lost, just overlooked. Today I would like to remedy some of that oversight.

John Hay was born on this day in 1838. He combined a distinguished career as a diplomat with an equally distinguished career as a poet and author. Today I am reminded of some of his more famous maxims. For example, he wrote "Who would succeed in the world should be wise in the use of his pronouns. Utter the you twenty times where you once utter the I." He wrote something else which is very good advice for the public speaker. True luck, he said, consists not in holding the best of the cards at the table; luckiest he who knows just when to rise and go home. I will keep that in mind as I address you here today.

OCTOBER 9

Leif Erikson Day.

Yale's birthday, 1701.

Introductions:

Today is Leif Erikson Day. It was established to commemorate the supposed landing of the Viking explorer on the North American mainland in about 1000 A.D. Who knows how many people discovered America before Columbus, beginning probably with the Indians? It is safe to say that the first Europeans who came upon North America were apparently not greatly impressed. They apparently felt it might be a nice place to visit, but they wouldn't want to live here. I must say that I feel the same way about the speaker's podium. The speaker's platform is a nice place to visit, but I wouldn't want to live here. So I will try to make my visit a brief but happy one.

This is the day of the year in 1701, when the Collegiate School of Connecticut was chartered. The Collegiate School of Connecticut later became Yale University. It has turned out some of America's greatest leaders and, I dare say, turned down some of those who became America's great leaders as well. That is one of the hazards of any process of selection. There are those who deplore this fact of life as it applies to admission to colleges and universities. But no matter what system of education or what system of society exists, every human being is called upon, some more often than others, to be selective, to make a judgment or a choice. For example, I had to select the thoughts I planned to share with you today. You, in turn, will decide whether to accept or reject them. The motto of Yale speaks of "light and truth." We each see the truth in our own light.

OCTOBER 10

The tuxedo is born, 1886.

Giuseppe Verdi born, 1813.

Introductions:

Back in 1886, this date, they had their autumn ball at Tuxedo Park, New York, which was then a very swanky retreat for the rich. Some of the men wore a new garment as a dinner jacket and the garment took its name, or at least its nickname, from the setting. Thus, the birth of the tuxedo. I don't know how thrilled you are by this piece of information, but I regard it as a sort of warning. It tells me that our gathering here may be remembered more for what somebody wore than for anything I say. And so I speak to you today unburdened by any illusions of profundity.

Today is the birthday of Giuseppe Verdi, the great Italian composer, who was born in 1813, in Le Roncole, Italy. Even if you are unfamiliar with *Aida* or the other great operas Giuseppe Verdi wrote, his name is impressive. I keep wondering whether we would be equally impressed if he were known by the English translation of his name. Somehow, I don't think that *Aida*, by Joseph Green, would sound quite the same. We hear a name, or a word, and it puts an idea in our minds. For example, there is a difference being asked to deliver an address or being asked to make a speech or being asked to say a few words. I shall endeavor to live up to the assignment given to me here today and I can only add that I hope I do it so well that other speakers turn Verdi with envy.

OCTOBER 11

General Pulaski Memorial Day.

Pope John XXIII's Ecumenical Council convened, 1962.

Eleanor Roosevelt born, 1884.

Introductions:

Casimir Pulaski was a hero of the fight for Polish independence who came to the United States in 1777. Two years later, he was leading a charge against the British lines in Savannah, Georgia, on this day and was mortally wounded. He died two days later on this day. Brigadier General Casimir Pulaski—the first of many Poles who found America worth fighting for. This is General Pulaski Memorial Day. It is a good day to remember that the freedom we enjoy today came at the cost of blood and tears. We can talk freely as we do here today, because of the sacrifices and the courage of the General Pulaskis and the men they led.

On this day in 1962, future historians may record that a new era began in the world—an era of greater understanding among the various religions. If so, it is because of the Ecumenical Council, convened by Pope John XXIII, which met at the Vatican on October 11, 1962. Pope John's basic message was that if only we would talk to each other, if only we could meet in amity, the world might be a better place. The spirit of ecumenicism is not easy to maintain, particularly when nobody wants to talk or when everybody wants to talk at once. Here we have what I think is the ideal arrangement—I talk and you listen. But I will talk very carefully, for tomorrow *you* may be doing the talking and *I* may have to do the listening.

Today is the birthday of Eleanor Roosevelt. She probably did more to make the role of the First Lady more meaningful in American life than any occupant of the White House before her. Anna Eleanor Roosevelt, who married her cousin Franklin, was born in 1884 in New York City. She was an awkward public speaker all her life; but if I today can be one-tenth as effective as Eleanor Roosevelt was in winning public attention for what she believed to be important, I will be grateful indeed.

OCTOBER 12

Columbus discovered America, 1492.

Lions International founded, 1917.

Introductions:

This is the anniversary of the discovery of America by Christopher Columbus in 1492, so you might logically suppose that this would be Columbus Day. It used to that simple but it isn't any more. Columbus Day is now observed on the second Monday of October. This happened after America discovered the three-day weekend. It is customary, on Columbus Day, to salute his Italian heritage, to spare a fond memory for Queen Isabella of Spain who financed his expedition and perhaps to sympathize with the Indians who were perfectly happy here until Columbus came along. I should like to suggest another form of celebration. I propose that each of us, in his heart, set out to discover America all over again. I have tried to do just that, and I'd like to tell you what I have found.

Today is the birthday of Lions International, which was founded in Dallas, Texas in 1917. For some reason which escapes me, our great fraternal organizations have a tendency to adopt the names of animals—Lions, Moose, Elks being among the most prominent. Having likened ourselves to animals, we proceed to do one thing that animals cannot. We make speeches. And those of us who make speeches always hope that what we are saying is not the same old stuff. So today, in keeping with our love of animal analogies, I hope you will find the present speaker to be a horse of a different color.

OCTOBER 13

George Washington laid the cornerstone of the President's Mansion, 1792.

U.S. Naval Fleet authorized, 1775.

Introductions:

On this day in 1792, President George Washington laid the cornerstone of the Executive Mansion in Washington, D.C. where future presidents were going to live. Like a lot of other people, President Washington began a job but he wasn't around when it was completed. He died in 1799 and John Adams moved in in 1800, toward the end of his single term as President. Life seems to be a process of some people laying down cornerstones for others to build upon. One of the ways that we lay down cornerstones is to stand up on the public platform and pontificate. Some of us have a tendency to lay it on with a trowel a good deal thicker than we need to. I will try to be aware of the obvious hazards as I speak to you here today.

Today is the birthday of the U.S. Navy. On October 13, 1775, the Continental Congress authorized a fleet of two cruisers and on December 22 of the same year, the Continental Navy was officially authorized. In honor of today's anniversary, I shall try to leave the deep water to the Navy and avoid finding myself at sea. And also, in honor of the sailing ships that constituted our first seagoing line of defense, I shall furnish my own wind.

OCTOBER 14

Dwight D. Eisenhower born, 1890.

William Penn born, 1644.

Battle of Hastings, 1066.

Introductions:

Dwight D. Eisenhower, 34th President of the United States and one of our greatest military commanders, was born on this day in 1890. Ike Eisenhower, as he was known, was not regarded as one of his generation's outstanding public speakers, but he used a very eloquent phrase in his speech at the Bicentennial Celebration of Columbia University in 1954. He referred to "the revolutionary doctrine of the divine rights of the common man." I don't think that can be improved upon as a definition of the ideal of modern American life. The divine rights of the common man. Having been through all that nonsense of the divine right of kings, we are now putting the emphasis where it rightfully belongs. And it is that question of what is right for the rights of the common man that I place on the docket here today.

History is sometimes particularly interesting because of the accidents which affect us. I am reminded of that today in the case of William Penn. Today is William Penn's birthday. He was born in London on October 14, 1644. He, of course, founded Pennsylvania and established what he called the City of Brotherly Love, Philadelphia. He made peace with the Indians and established a tradition of brotherhood and decency which is a valued American heritage. The irony is that after he had to go back to England, the people who ran Pennsylvania for him didn't do a very good job. As a matter of fact, he even went to debtor's prison for a while. We are told that he was about to sell Pennsylvania when he suffered a stroke. What would have happened if he had indeed sold Pennsylvania is anybody's guess. The game of "what if" is a fascinating one and we could play it from now to the end of time. Today, I'd rather play another game with you. It's a game called "how come?" I have a considerable degree of puzzlement about why some things are happening now, so I rise to ask some questions.

The Battle of Hastings was fought on this day in the year 1066. That was the battle in which William the Conqueror defeated the English and brought about the Norman Conquest. The Battle of Hastings is regarded as one of the most historic turning points in the development of England, ultimately imposing unity on what had been a divided land, although, in the course of time, divisions bloodily reasserted themselves. And it brought an infusion of Norman culture that ultimately merged with the Anglo-Saxon mainstream to produce a notably rich heritage. In the last analysis, conquest by force of arms is less enduring than conquest by force of Ideas. In our own time, the strength of America is the strength of the American idea. Central to that American idea is the fact that one can stand up and speak one's mind. I thank you for the opportunity you give me to do so here today.

OCTOBER 15

White Cane Safety Day.

P. G. Wodehouse born, 1881.

Introductions:

Some years ago, a Joint Resolution of Congress declared this to be White Cane Safety Day, designed to remind all our citizens that the visually impaired, who get about with the aid of white canes to guide their way, deserve our utmost consideration. This is a sentiment on which there can be no argument. Those of us who are fortunate enough not to need white canes recognize an obligation toward our friends and relatives—and strangers—who cannot see. I find myself wondering why we do not give equal recognition to the needs of others whose handicaps, though not as great perhaps, still put them at a disadvantage in the business of life. Are we helping each other as much as we might? Are we helping ourselves by helping others as much as we might? Take a few areas that might not occur to you, like energy conservation, or volunteer work, for example. Today I want to talk to you about the opportunities we have to help each other.

P. G. Wodehouse was past 90 when he died in the 1970s. He was born on this day in 1881, in an England that passed on long before he did. The scatter-brained Lords and impeccable butlers of Wodehouse's world, particularly the immortal Jeeves, disappeared with World War II; and yet Wodehouse's world entertained millions of readers thereafter. We all have pleasant worlds of the past to remember fondly, even though they are worlds in which we never lived. We think of our parents' and grandparents' times as the good old days, and we imagine those days rather differently than do the people who actually lived through them. Did you ever stop to think how our children will think of the good old days that they are too young to remember? Ask yourself now—or better still, come with me on a stroll through a future memory lane, looking back on the good old days of today. Somebody says, what was good about them? That's the question I am going to answer now.

OCTOBER 16

Noah Webster born, 1758.

Oscar Wilde born, 1854.

The "Amazing" Mets, 1969.

Introductions:

If there is a patron saint of public speakers, he or she must be particularly mindful of this day; for today is the birthday of Noah Webster, of Webster's dictionary fame, Noah the unabridged Webster, born in 1758 in West Hartford, Connecticut. Thanks to him, no speaker can honestly say that he is at a loss for words. I have a fair stock of Mr. Webster's wares that I have assembled for you today. And so to work.

Oscar Fingall O'Flahertie Wilde may have been the most adept user of words in the history of the English language. Born on this day in 1854, he was a great playwright and above all the author of some of the greatest epigrams and pithy sayings the world has ever heard. And if he had been born in 1954 instead of a hundred years earlier, he would now be one of the most honored and lionized figures of his time. But Oscar Wilde was born out of his time. His refusal to abide by the public sexual standards of his time brought him vilification, persecution and total tragedy—for things which weren't thought about twice in the 1970s. Wilde said, in *The Picture of Dorian Gray*, that "the only way to get rid of a temptation is to yield to it." I was tempted to speak to you today, and I am happy to yield to that temptation.

Every now and then a miracle occurs which one does not have to be religious to accept. Today is the anniversary of such a miracle—the World Series triumph of the "Amazing" Mets of New York in 1969. They had literally come up from the bottom to surprise the world of baseball, and on this day, in 1969, they capped the climax. So this must be a day of good omens on the calendar. If the Mets could make it on one October 16, I should be able to talk my way out of trouble on another October 16—and in that spirit of superstitious confidence I make so bold as to proceed.

OCTOBER 17

Albert Einstein came to the U.S., 1933.

Arab oil boycott, 1973.

Introductions:

History moves in interesting chains of events. On this day in 1933, Albert Einstein, the great scientist, came to the United States as a refugee from Nazi

Germany. He had to leave his native country because he was a Jew, and Nazi Germany wanted to get rid of the Jews. This was the same Albert Einstein who, though a pacifist through and through, called to President Franklin Roosevelt's attention the need for research into nuclear energy—a call which led directly to America's development of the atom bomb. If Einstein had remained in Germany, he might have been responsible for giving Germany, rather than America, the secret to nuclear fission—and the history of the world might be a great deal different today. Yes, history moves in strange ways. And we can see some of its strangeness around us now. All over the world we see disadvantaged minorities who came to a new land that was better than the land they left—and now find all too often that the new land isn't good enough. We see a world with people starving in one area and foodland going untilled in another. Let us consider some of the strange contradictions close to us here at home.

In 1973, the Western world suddenly woke up to the realities of an energy shortage when the oil-producing Arab states decided to impose a boycott. Ever since that fortunately short period of time, we have been reminded of the need to conserve our resources and find new ways to produce energy. Have we taken sufficient heed? Have we had so many Cassandras and so many warnings of so many different types of dire calamity that we simply don't pay attention? Let me try to answer these questions.

OCTOBER 18

Mason-Dixon line established, 1767.

Alaska Day.

First American labor organization, 1648.

Introductions:

Today is the birthday of the Mason-Dixon line, the boundary that was later regarded as separating the North and the South. It was adopted on this day, in 1767, as the border between Maryland and Pennsylvania. And that border has remained where they put it, ever since. When you draw a good line, it works. The question always is when and how you decided where to draw the line—not only on a map, but in terms of standards of behavior, for example. Today I should like to help draw a line or two for our own time.

The Russian flag was lowered and in its place were raised the stars and stripes of the United States. That is what happened on this day, in 1867, in Sitka, Alaska, as Russia turned that vast territory over to its new purchaser, the United States. We paid what some people regarded as an exorbitant price—$7 million. Slightly more than 100 years later, for a batch of oil leases, a group of companies forked over almost $1 billion and Alaska still had a lot of room for other investments too. Alaska may not have seemed to be much of an investment for $7 million in 1867, but oh how our perspective has changed.

That's a point worth remembering. Our vision isn't absolute. We see things from a particular perspective—and perspectives change. One year's hemlines look ridiculous a couple of year's later, and yesterday's folly turns out to be today's stroke of genius. Consider, for example, how our own perspective has changed, within our own lifetime, on such matters as nuclear energy, or the nutritive value of whole milk, sugar and lard, or the rights of minorities. Where is the next change coming from, and what will it be? See if you agree with me.

On this day, in 1648, the shoemakers and barrel and tub makers of Boston were given official permission to set up their own organizations, which can probably be regarded as the roots of both trade associations and labor unions in this country. It is interesting to reflect that both trade associations and labor unions had their origins in the guilds of the old world. Not until much later did they go their separate ways. All too often, we tend to forget what they have in common and emphasize their very real differences. But in thinking of this, I am reminded of the illustration Eric Sevareid sometimes used to stress the common interest. It doesn't make much sense, he pointed out, when two people are sitting in a boat, for one of them to point a finger accusingly at the other and say, "Your end of the boat is sinking." Let's not put ourselves in that position now. Let's take a look at both ends of the boat.

OCTOBER 19

Yorktown Day.

Round the world in 18½ days, 1936.

Sir Thomas Browne born, 1605.

Introductions:

Today is Yorktown Day, a fact which not too many people seem to know and a day whose significance even less are aware of. I will pause for a moment while you search your memories. As some of you may have recalled, today is the anniversary of the surrender of Lord Cornwallis at Yorktown, Virginia, in 1781, the surrender that ended the American Revolutionary War. Why isn't that great event better remembered? How in the world does America single out some days like the Fourth of July and forget the day that saved the Fourth of July? Truly, we remember what we want to remember, see what we want to see, hear what we want to hear. Fortunately, we don't all remember, see or hear the same things; and by telling each other of our own perceptions, together we see and hear a little more. So I welcome the opportunity today to share some of my perceptions with you.

It was a big headline story in newspapers all over the world on this day, in 1936, when H. R. Ekins, a reporter for the *New York World Telegram*, completed a round-the-world airline trip in 18½ days, beating out two other competing journalists. Going around the world in 18½ days by commercial scheduled transportation was a rare feat back in 1936. We have certainly speeded up since then. The only thing we may not have speeded up is the art of public speaking. Conscious of that fact, I shall try to go through my subject— not around it—today as quickly as the facts will allow.

This is the birthday of Sir Thomas Browne, the seventeenth century physician and writer who was born in 1605 in London. His name is not very well known today but his thoughts and phrases have lived for centuries. It was he who wrote, "There is no road or ready way to virtue," and "Charity begins at home." I would like to take as my text today another of Sir Thomas Browne's observations: "The whole world was made for man . . ." The whole world was made for us. And what are we doing with it?

OCTOBER 20

Wise words of Washington, 1792.

Wise words of Disraeli, 1867.

The "Saturday night massacre" in Washington, 1973.

Introductions:

In a letter that he wrote about this time of year in 1792, George Washington took a long hard look at the causes of trouble in the world, and came to a conclusion. "Of all the animosities which have existed among mankind," he wrote, "those which are caused by a difference of sentiments in religion appear to be the most inveterate and distressing, and ought to be deprecated." Most disputes in the world are not between abstract good and evil, but between two sides, both of whom are convinced that they are right and that the Lord is on their side—especially when their idea of the Lord is radically different from our own. But the biggest problem arises from those who don't believe there are such abstract concepts as right and wrong—those who think that everything in life is up for grabs. I think it is time we looked at the realities of what people in our nation seem to believe—not the religion expressed in their ideas of the world to come, but what perhaps should be called the ethics of survival. Every year another book about how to survive goes on the best seller list. Let's take a look at the attitude which makes that happen.

Benjamin Disraeli was as clever with words as he was at being the Prime Minister of Great Britain and, at other times, the leader of the loyal Opposition. He lived in a time when great changes were occurring, and a lot of people were afraid of them. Back in 1867, as the late October landscape showed its seasonal alterations, he said that "Change is inevitable in a progressive country. Change is constant." That is the eternal contradiction—change is constant. Once we accept that fact, then we can get on with the business of figuring out what we can do about it. How are things changing and what can we do about it?

In 1973, an event happened on this date which was promptly described as "the Saturday night massacre." It seemed to be a rather lurid description at the time, but later on it turned out not be too far wrong. "The Saturday night massacre" was President Nixon's firing of special Watergate prosecutor Archibald Cox and the accompanying departure of Attorney General Elliot Richardson and Deputy Attorney General William D. Ruckelshaus. To many people, that was the beginning of the end for President Nixon. Certainly, from then on everything went downhill for him until he resigned the following August. It is hard to define what makes a single event the key one in a chain of developments, and we don't always recognize the significance of a particular occurrence at the time. Right now, for example, things are happening all over the world that may hold the key to prosperity or future war or peace, without our even knowing about them. And so we look around us and try to keep informed, and you are patient enough to sit here to listen to what I think is worth noting.

OCTOBER 21

Edison Lamp Day.

Whale Watching Week

Alfred Nobel born, 1833.

Introductions:

Today is Edison Lamp Day, the anniversary of Thomas A. Edison's demonstration of the incandescent electric lamp in 1879. In honor of that bright occasion, I shall endeavor to shed a little light of my own.

For a number of years—perhaps long enough to have become a tradition—an organization based in Honolulu and calling itself the First Society of Whale Watchers ordained today as the start of International Whale Watching Week. Bird-watchers may scoff and girl-watchers may wonder about the charm of whales, but International Whale Watching Week has a very real meaning for public speakers. That is because we and the whale have so much in common. Whale watchers and audiences both come to see the subject spout. In honor of Whale Watching Week, I now rise to the surface to sound off.

Alfred Nobel was born on this day in 1833, in Stockholm, and went on to make his fortune as an inventor and manufacturer of high explosives and detonators. When he died, he left his fortune for the establishment of the Nobel Prizes for the advancement of the peaceful arts and sciences, including the art of peace itself. It is interesting that he is remembered for the prizes and not for the explosives. I guess this proves that last impressions are the most

important, and that in turn suggests that the conclusion of my speech here
today is what you will take away with you; so I hasten toward that end.

OCTOBER 22

Parachute demonstrated, 1797.

Influenza epidemic, 1918.

Introductions:

Andre J. Garnerin is not one of those people whose name rings the bell of
recognition. I doubt that even his countrymen in France have him enshrined in
their hearts. But on this day, in 1797, Andre Garnerin gave his first public
demonstration of a device called a parachute. He jumped from a balloon to show
the way his parachute worked—and it did work, because he went on to demonstrate it in England later. Now this anniversary is particularly important for
speakers. The parachute, you see, was designed to enable people to come down
safely if they wanted to escape from the early balloons. And those early balloons were all filled, literally, with hot air. Since, as you know, speakers are also
filled with hot air, the importance of getting back down to earth cannot be
over-estimated. So, that being understood, let us take off.

At this time, in 1918, a terrible epidemic of influenza was raging in the
United States. For years afterward, we congratulated ourselves that, with the
advances of medical science, that kind of thing could not happen again. Then, in
the 1970s, as you may recall, there was a big government program to inoculate
people against another form of flu, something called swine flu. Not too many
people—if any—died of swine flu, but there was some question about harmful
effects from some batches of the vaccine. That epitomized one of the problems
of our times. Sometimes we really don't know whether the cure is worse than
the disease. We have some miracle drugs whose side effects seem to require
other miracle drugs. We establish welfare programs to take care of needy
people and then we have to set up organizations to ferret out welfare cheats.
And so on far into the night. Today I'd like to take a look, with you, at some of
these contradictions in our way of life.

OCTOBER 23

Swallows leave Capistrano.

Johnny Carson born, 1925.

Introductions:

Today is the day when, according to legend, the swallows fly away from
the Mission of San Juan Capistrano in California. Nature's creatures operate
on a calendar just as rigid as that which we have created for ourselves. Birds of

a feather, however, seem to be a lot better at sticking together than we are. Or is it that we are not quite as much birds of a feather as we think we are? I wonder what happens to a swallow at Capistrano who says, "No, I don't want to leave. It's nice here and I don't want to fly south. I'll just stay here a little longer." Do the birds treat their nonconformists more gently than we do? Or do the birds have a great advantage over us, in that when they decide to leave they don't have to worry about gas for the car, tickets for the plane or rent for a landlord? My topic today, as you can see, is simply: Is this world for the birds?

Although Nebraska claims him as its own, and he has returned the compliment, the fact is that it was in Corning, Iowa, that Johnny Carson was born on this day in 1925. He grew up in Nebraska and aged gracefully and entertainingly in bedrooms all over America as the star of television's "Tonight" show. Johnny Carson's birthday is a comfort to a speaker, because it reminds us that talk, though often accused of putting people to sleep, has also kept thousands—millions—of people awake. I am probably a poor substitute here today for Johnny Carson, but here goes.

OCTOBER 24

National Popcorn Week.

United Nations Day.

Introductions:

For reasons best known to the people who sell popcorn, the last week of October, beginning today, was chosen as the occasion for National Popcorn Week. Since it is also United Nations Day today, commemorating the adoption of the U.N. Charter in 1945, there are those who think it should be known as Pop*off* rather than Popcorn time; but popcorn is part of our precious national heritage, having been introduced to the Pilgrims by the Indians. And National Popcorn Week is literally an event you can take with a few grains of salt. I hope my remarks today will not be taken similarly.

As for United Nations Day, the late Adlai Stevenson remarked on United Nations Day, in 1963, that "The journey of a thousand leagues, we say, begins with a single step. So we must never neglect any work of peace that is within our reach, however small." He went on to say that "Our efforts will be erratic, and the world will remain a dangerous place to live." I have no argument with that reasoning. But I will let the United Nations handle that kind of talk, and concentrate here today on that other world which is more interested in the price of popcorn.

OCTOBER 25

The charge of the Light Brigade, 1854.

St. Crispin's Day.

Introductions:

This was the day in 1854 of the fateful charge of the Light Brigade, when they rode into the valley of death. It's a lot easier to quote Tennyson's poem than to remember the circumstances of the event, which took place in the Battle of Balaclava in the Crimean War. Particulary, we remember lines like "Theirs not to make reply,/Theirs not to reason why,/Theirs but to do and die." Too often, even today, we are asked to do things without being given an opportunity to make reply or to reason why. But if mankind is to continue to move, in Tennyson's words, "half a league, half a league, half a league onward," we had better start asking not only why, but where. I arise here and now to call for a road map.

This is St. Crispin's Day, which for many years was celebrated by shoemakers in honor of their patron saint. We don't seem to do much about St. Crispin's Day anymore, possibly because nobody got around to making him the patron saint of sneakers or plastic boots. But I suspect that the decline of shoe leather, metaphorically speaking, has been a consequence of the automobile age. We simply don't walk as much as we used to. We don't stop and talk along the way as much. So I welcome occasions such as the one for which we are gathered here today. It makes for a welcome stop along the way; and while you rest your weary feet I will exercise my active mouth. Then, with due regard for St. Crispin, we can put our shoes back on and go about our business.

OCTOBER 26

The "roots" of U.S. mules, 1785.

No flying saucers, 1955.

Introductions:

Every now and then, the archives of history turn up an anniversary that has not had its proper due. Today is such a day. On this day, in 1785, we are told, two jackasses arrived at the port of Boston from Spain. These were not ordinary jackasses. They were a gift from the King of Spain to George Washington, and they were sent here so that they could be mated with mares to produce American's first native mules. The roots of American stubbornness and mulishness go back pretty far. But it is at least a comfort to know that jackasses had to be imported to this country and that we didn't start off growing our own. Are we any smarter today? Let's take a good long look at ourselves.

On this day, in 1955, the U.S. Air Force officially proclaimed that flying saucers were a myth and a delusion. But people went right on seeing flying saucers and describing visits with mysterious creatures descended from space. It takes more than an official denial to defeat the power of folklore. As history has shown from the days of the dragons to flying saucers and laetrile, people

belive what they want to believe. And so I come to you today to tell you what I
want to believe, what I do believe, and what I hope I can persuade you to
believe as well.

OCTOBER 27

Teddy Roosevelt born, 1858.

Dylan Thomas born, 1914.

Introductions:

Theodore Roosevelt, born in New York City on this day in 1858, was one
of our stronger Presidents. He was the trust-busting crusader of his time, and
he exemplified the policy he described as speaking softly but carrying a big
stick. He was also the proof of the fact that man proposes and God disposes. He
was a reform Governor of New York whom the political bosses wanted to get
rid of, so they used every power of persuasion to get him to accept the vice
presidential nomination in 1900 as President McKinley's running mate. Within
six months after taking office, Teddy Roosevelt found himself President after
McKinley was assassinated. Good people can't be kept down and good causes
can't be swept under the rug. So, on Teddy Roosevelt's birthday, I'd like to
raise my voice, as he might have done, on behalf of a square deal.

Dylan Thomas, the great Welsh poet, was born on this day in 1914, in
Carmarthenshire, Wales. He is best remembered for the lines, "Do not go
gentle into that good night,/Old age should burn and rave at close of day;/Rage,
rage against the dying of the light." I am not here to discuss the problems of old
age, but I would like to take a leaf from Dylan Thomas and raise my voice to
ask why so many people are willing to "go gentle into that good night," not of
old age but of red tape and sloth and bureaucracy and indifference and all those
things that spread the myth that you can't fight city hall, or you can't fight
Uncle Sam, or you can't fight a computer, or you can't fight big business.
Truisms aren't always true. A generation or two ago, some people found out
that the best way to stand up for their rights was to sit down for them. If you
care enough, you can do enough. So I am here to try to make you care.

OCTOBER 28

St. Jude's day.

Statue of Liberty dedicated, 1886.

Thomas Jefferson's natural aristocracy, 1813.

Introductions:

Today is St. Jude's day. St. Jude, as you know, is the patron saint of the
impossible. I don't know whether that had anything to do with your inviting me

to speak here today. Far from considering these remarks an impossible task, I welcome the opportunity to share with you some thoughts and some reflections—which, with all due respect to St. Jude, I trust you will not find to be impossible.

The Statue of Liberty was dedicated in New York Harbor, on this day, in 1886. The dedicatory speech by President Grover Cleveland said, "We will not forget that Liberty has here made her home; nor shall her chosen altar be neglected." The Statue shows liberty holding aloft a torch and clutching a book. I wonder what the symbolism would be today if a modern sculptor were asked to create a Statue of Liberty. Would it be an abstract geometric figure, perhaps with a Henry Moore hole in it? But don't just try to imagine the artistic concept. Ask yourself what the artist would be trying to convey. Back in 1886, they weren't arguing such concepts of liberty as are embodied in our disputes today over everything from abortion to food additives. Liberty may very likely mean different things to different generations in the same country. Let me cite a few current cases.

Writing on this date in 1813, Thomas Jefferson had a few kind words to say about aristocracy. "I agree with you," he wrote to John Adams, "that there is a natural aristocracy among men. The grounds of this are virtue and talents." America, as the land of opportunity, has done more than any other land to see this aristocracy flower. Today, I should like to salute its current members—the men and women whose virtues and talents epitomize the great strength of our nation.

OCTOBER 29

Sir Walter Raleigh executed, 1618.

Wall Street crash, 1929.

Ingersoll's wise words, 1896.

Introductions:

History remembers Sir Walter Raleigh as the great courtier, the man who spread his coat over the mud so a noble lady's shoes would not be spattered. But Sir Walter Raleigh was a far more adventurous man than a mere courtier. He was one of the pioneer British explorers of the New World and got into enough trouble with the Crown to have settled a lesser man's hash long before it settled his. He was an accomplished writer as well. When he was executed on this day in 1618, he became increasingly popular in memory. That, of course, was small comfort to the late Sir Walter Raleigh. Mindful of the need for immediate rather than long-range approval, I stand before you totally uninterested in the verdict of posterity about the remarks I am about to make. What will it matter years from now if historians say, he made a great speech that day, and my head has already rolled? I do not speak here for the ages, but for the moment.

On October 29, 1929, as the show business paper *Variety* so tersely noted, Wall Street laid an egg. Stock market prices collapsed, signalling the worst economic depression of the twentieth century. Many people believe that the only reason the depression ended was that a World War broke out within a decade. Now everybody who has lived through a great depression spends the rest of his life telling people that no matter how bad things are today they were worse then. And that is often true, because, however glacially, we do make progress in improving the human condition. Let me illustrate.

Robert G. Ingersoll possessed the golden tongue of his time, which was the late nineteenth century. He said many things that challenged established truths, but he also said one thing, on this day in 1896, that has been getting truer all the time. "Few rich men own their property," he said, "the property owns them." Ask yourself how much of what you do today is dictated by what you own, what you have to protect. Are we the property of our property? With every asset, do we buy another liability? And what can we do about it?

OCTOBER 30

Orson Welles' Martian invasion, 1938.

De-Stalinization by body snatching, 1961.

Introductions:

It started out as a radio dramatization by a young actor-director named Orson Welles. He adapted H. G. Wells' story, *The War of the Worlds*, and put it on the air on this evening, in 1938, over a coast-to-coast network. It was so realistic that even though it had been announced as a piece of fiction, people all over the country actually thought that Martians had landed in New Jersey. Telephone lines were jammed in the panic and it took a long time to persuade people that it was all a work of the imagination. We are always ready, it seems, to believe the strangest things. Man is the most credulous beast on the face of the earth. For some speakers, this is a great comfort. For others, like myself, it is a warning. My speech today, I must assure you, will not be a work of fiction. It will be, to the best of my ability, a work of fact.

We usually think of the past not so much in terms of events as in terms of people. The American Revolution is George Washington and Thomas Jefferson. The Civil War is Abraham Lincoln and U.S. Grant and Stonewall Jackson and Robert E. Lee. In Russia, Communism was first Lenin and then Stalin. And when Nikita Khrushchev wanted to emphasize his regime's break with Stalinism he chose a very simple way. He ordered Stalin's name taken out of the books and, on this day in 1961, also ordered that the body of Josef Stalin be removed from its tomb in Red Square. We may laugh at this kind of thing when it happens elsewhere, but all of us have a tendency to be diverted from the real issues through arguments over where the bodies are buried, who should be credited with this or that, was Truman a great President, what about Richard Nixon and so forth. I am not here today to empty tombs or to remove names from the history books. Instead, I would like to look at our current world in terms of some of its current people.

OCTOBER 31

Hallowe'en.

Reformation Day.

National UNICEF Day.

Introductions:

Today is Hallowe'en, and I hope that my appearance here was not arranged as part of a Trick or Treat exercise. There are probably more superstitions about Hallowe'en than about any other day of the year, and the witches floating around on their brooms probably need an air traffic controller today. So, with all due deference to the occasion, I will try to keep you all in good spirtis while the goblins roam.

When Martin Luther posted his 95 Theses on the church door in Wittenberg, Germany, on this day in 1517, he had no cue sheet that told him he was starting the Protestant Reformation; but that, in fact, was what he was doing. Reformation Day. History does not provide for retakes. We will never know whether a little less intransigence might have prevented—or delayed for centuries—the schism between Catholicism and Protestantism. What we do know is that those who are unwilling to accept the status quo often change it more than they started out to do. The one unchanging rule of life, it has been said, is change. We see it all around us. Nature changes; beaches erode or build; cold lands become colder—or warmer. And people change. We are people in a condition of change today. But we don't have to post theses on church doors. Thanks to kind audiences like you, we can propound our theses and describe our changes in words, not manifestoes. I thank you for the opportunity to do so here today.

This is National Unicef Day, observed on behalf of the United Nations Children's Fund. Children speak a language of their own. Before they can talk, they can communicate with you. They are direct, uninhibited, single-minded. In many ways, the job of a speaker is to think like a child. Decide what you want, tell the audience what you're after and wait for somebody else to do something about it. I have just given you the structure of my speech. Now for the details.

NOVEMBER 1

Religion in American Life Month.

Weather Bureau's first observations, 1870.

H-bomb era began for U.S., 1952.

Introductions:

November traditionally is Religion in American Life Month. It is the month of Thanksgiving, the month when we start selling Christmas Seals, the month when a worldwide Bible reading observance gets under way. But for a month of spiritual remembrance, it has some rather surprising anniversaries. On this very day when the month begins, we have the anniversary of the attempt by a group of Puerto Rican nationalists to assassinate President Truman in 1950, the anniversary of our nation's test explosion of an H-bomb and the beginning of the Algerian revolution against the French. Counterbalancing these violent items is the anniversary of the Armistice that ended World War I on November 11, 1918. The message of Religion in American Life Month—at least for the speaker—is that a faith worth keeping is worth fighting for. And that, in turn, brings us back to the essential teaching of every religion, which is, broadly speaking, "keep the faith."

This is the day when, in 1870, the United States Weather Bureau made its first observations. It wasn't called the weather bureau then, because it was a service of the Signal Corps of the U.S. Army. On this day, in 1870, reports were telegraphed from 24 places around the U.S. and the national weather service was born. Unfortunately, the history sources at my disposal do not indicate how accurate those early reports proved to be, and weather forecasts only seem to be remembered when they are spectacularly wrong. Most of the time, they are neither spectacular nor wrong. So, most of the time the work of the weather people goes relatively unappreciated. They are not alone in this respect. Bad work, like bad news, usually gets more attention than good. That always provides a temptation for the speaker to stand up and talk about bad news and bad people—because audiences react to that sort of thing; but today my news is good, my words are kind and my audience—I hope—will be of good cheer.

In 1952, the United States conducted a test explosion of a hydrogen bomb at Eniwetok island in the Pacific that began a new era of military power for the U.S. It was an awesome test, so awesome that it probably strengthened the resolve of sensible people everywhere never to come to the point of having to employ such a weapon. And later developments reminded us that we were not a chosen people in the hydrogen age, because other nations with other ways of life also discovered the secret of the ultimate atomic weapon. So, today's anniversary is a reminder that, in the last analysis, it is not our weapons but our spirit that sustains us. And today, as I look around me, I find much sustenance for the spirit of America.

NOVEMBER 2

Marie Antoinette born, 1755.

Radio reported Harding-Cox election results, 1920.

Warren G. Harding elected President on his birthday, 1920.

Introductions:

Marie Antoinette was an Austrian princess who married the crown prince of France in 1770, became Queen of France when he succeeded to the throne in 1774 and was guillotined during the French Revolution in 1793. She was born in Vienna on this day, in 1755, and is remembered not so much for any of the events I have recited, as for a line she is supposed to have said when told that the people had no bread. "Let them eat cake," Marie Antoinette replied, according to the legend. The fact is that long before Marie Antoinette was born, "Let them eat bread" was a wisecrack of the same sort as "Tell them to go into the garden and eat worms." And the "Let them eat cake" remark was also attributed to a French queen of a previous century. I mention this because it shows how people can be remembered in history for the wrong reason. How do you think our time and we ourselves will be remembered in history? Will we be remembered at all, and if so for what reason? Let me tell you how I see us being described by some future historian.

In 1920, a small minority of American homes had a newfangled contraption called a radio. On this night in 1920, people with radios, particularly in the Pittsburgh area of pioneer station KDKA and a few other places, were able to follow the results of the Presidential election by listening to the radio in their own homes. It was the beginning of modern radio news reporting. It was the beginning of a new public interest in and awareness of the political processes of the nation. Not enough people as yet participate actively in the process by going to the polls and casting their votes. But in the age of broadcasting, public business has become the public's business—and it all began on this day back in 1920. Today, in recognition of that anniversary, there are a few pieces of public business that I would like to broadcast to you here and now.

The 1920 election had one rather unusual aspect. Warren G. Harding, the Republican candidate, was celebrating his birthday. He was born on that very day back in 1865, in Corsica, Ohio. On his 55th birthday, the people of the United States went to the polls and elected him President. I think the verdict of history is that it was a far better birthday present for Warren G. Harding than for the people of the United States. During his Presidency the Teapot

Dome scandal broke, and when he died and was succeeded by Vice President Calvin Coolidge, few people felt the nation was the loser. Harding was the nominee whose selection was described as having taken place in "a smoke-filled room" by a group of political bosses. Now it may seem very strange for a speaker to be recalling all these less than inspiring memories about a past figure whose big day happened to be a past November 2; but I hope it will suggest to you, as it has to me, that we can look forward to doing better than we did in the past. On this November 2, I turn my eyes resolutely forward, and I will tell you why.

NOVEMBER 3

LBJ's record triumph, 1964.

Karl Baedeker born, 1801.

Introductions:

On this day in 1964, Lyndon B. Johnson, who had become President the year before, on the assassination of John F. Kennedy, won the Presidential election over Barry Goldwater by the largest popular vote plurality in the history of the United States up to that time. Four years later, LBJ faced up to the facts and announced he would not run for re-election. If he had run, he might easily have been defeated, as was his chosen successor, Hubert Humphrey. From the most popular President ever, in 1964, to one whose chances of re-election were doubtful, to say the least, is quite a change. It doesn't make public opinion seem particularly stable. And it reminds us that opinions are triggered by events. The event in the years between 1964 and 1968 was the war in Vietnam. As to the events that affect the ebbs and flows of the tides of public opinion today, let me give you my own first-person-singular assessment.

Karl Baedeker was a man who didn't rely very much on public opinion. He made a career of selling his own opinion. Born on this day in 1801, in Essen, Germany, he was the pioneer writer and publisher of international travel guides. Indeed, his name became synonymous with guide book. Today, I'd like to give you my own Baedeker for portions of the world we live in.

NOVEMBER 4

Will Rogers born, 1879.

Walter Cronkite born, 1916.

Cash register patented, 1879.

Introductions:

Today is the birthday of Will Rogers, a man whose name is probably unknown to many in this audience, but a man who was responsible for much of the political freedom of contemporary humor. Will Rogers, born in Oolagah, Oklahoma, in 1879, began as a vaudeville trick rope artist, discovered that audiences liked to hear him talk, and went on to a brilliant career as a monologist, lecturer, newspaper columnist and movie actor. He made government and politics his targets. One of his most famous cracks, for example, was about Congress. When they make a joke, he said, it's a law, and when they make a law it's a joke. He also said, "I do not belong to any organized party. I am a Democrat." At first, particularly when he said this kind of thing on network radio in the 1930s, people were shocked. But, thanks to his good-humored and brilliant delivery, the needling of sacred institutions became popular mass entertainment—and we can see the results all around us today. We take government seriously but not solemnly. At least, that is the spirit with which I propose to look at some of the workings of our way of life today.

Walter Cronkite was by no means the first television news broadcaster; he was, however, the first to become a national institution. When Walter Cronkite told his audience that that was the way things were, they believed him. During his vintage years, television became the prime news medium for millions upon millions of Americans. When Walter Cronkite was born on this day in 1916, in St. Joseph, Missouri, broadcast news was something for the future. Now it is our window on the world. I have been looking through that window rather closely lately, and I'd like to tell you what I see.

Today is the anniversary of the granting of a patent for a device called a cash register, in 1879. It was a long time between the cash register and the computer, but I think that the triumph of the machine probably began on this day in 1879, when we started punching keys instead of writing out receipts. The trouble is that the age of the machine, instead of reducing human error, seems to have carried ahead the capacity to enlarge and compound human error. I am not standing up here to suggest that we destroy the machines. But I am standing up to suggest that we might create a new balance between the amount of attention we devote to making machines think better and the amount we devote to showing humans how to think better.

NOVEMBER 5

Guy Fawkes Day,

First U.S. automobile patent, 1895.

Eugene V. Debs born, 1855.

Introductions:

Today is Guy Fawkes Day, occasionally the basis for lighthearted celebration although the event it commemorates, known as the Gunpowder Plot, was anything but lighthearted. Guy Fawkes was captured, on this day in 1605, as he was about to blow up the House of Lords in Great Britain. He and a number of other conspirators were executed. Over the course of centuries, the event seems to have diminished in serious memory, at least in this country, and become a piece of whimsy. That does happen to serious history sometimes, and I cannot help but wonder whether many of the things we take so seriously are not, in point of fact, rather whimsical to begin with. Like professional sports, or high fashion, for example. Are we not taking too seriously the outrageousness of some current levels of taste? Let me give you some examples.

The first U.S. patent for an automobile was issued on this date, in 1895, to George B. Selden. He had actually invented his auto much earlier but held off getting the patent while he tried to raise money. He still hadn't gotten either the money or the patent when other people started making motor cars. His patent did bring him money from various manufacturers but Henry Ford and some others refused to pay him, claiming that their cars were not based on his design, and, in the end, a lot of other people made a lot more money than George Selden made out of the idea of the automobile. The moral, I guess, is that if you have a good idea, you shouldn't hide it while you're looking for backers. You get going with it as fast as you can. So, keeping the case of George Selden in mind, I shall try to get my ideas out to you as quickly as I can.

The name of Eugene V. Debs is not too well known today. In the early days of the century, it was a name that was honored by some and reviled by many more. Eugene V. Debs, born on this day in 1855, in Terre Haute, Indiana, was a labor leader who became a Socialist and ran for the Presidency of the United States many times on the Socialist ticket. In his time, Socialism was originally regarded as the most leftist of left-wing movements—Communism not yet being on the scene. And it was also regarded as a foreign idea that was absolutely treasonous in this country. Eugene Debs was particularly reviled because he was not a foreign agitator, but a native American; not an intellectual, but a man of the working class. In other words, a walking contradiction of the popular mythology about Socialism. Although he became, in his last years, a figure of considerable veneration to liberal and distinctly non-Socialist portions of the population, he died long before some of his ideas became incorporated in the political realities of modern state ownership. On his birthday, I rise to remind myself and you that people of good will may differ as to the road to a better day, but that such differences need not, today, create the kind of ill will and passion which needlessly made Eugene V. Debs a martyr in his own time.

NOVEMBER 6

Abraham Lincoln elected President, 1860.

First intercollegiate football game, 1869.

John Philip Sousa born, 1854.

Introductions:

In 1860, the candidate of a young new political party was elected President of the United States, on this sixth day of November. The standard-bearer of the Republican Party, Abraham Lincoln of Illinois, was chosen to lead a nation that was standing on the brink of the Civil War. As we consider our present fortunes, we may not see another Lincoln on the horizon, but even if we don't, we see a nation less divided, stronger and a great deal larger than the one that Lincoln knew. Did you know that two days after the election of 1860, Lincoln wrote to the man elected as his Vice President, Hannibal Hamlin, suggesting that it might be a good idea if they met. The two running mates were elected without ever having been introduced to each other. Yes, we have made progress since Abraham Lincoln's time. Please be mindful of that as we view the contemporary scene together in my remarks here today.

On this day in 1869, Rutgers University and Princeton played the first intercollegiate game of football, in New Brunswick, New Jersey. It was the dawn of a new era not only for sports in America but also for higher education. We hear a lot about the evils of college football, but the fact is that it has been the great democratizer of college education in America. It has financed expansion of student bodies and facilities, given college educations to young men who would never have been able to get them otherwise, and even inspired a great deal of loyalty to many an alma mater. Today, on the anniversary of college football, I would like to address myself to a question about which college football coaches and college faculties alike grow more and more concerned: What, in the face of the changing American population demographics, is the future of higher education in America?

One of the by-products of college football has been the great American marching band. Marching bands and march music in America owe a great deal to a man who was born on this day in 1854, a man named John Philip Sousa. He was called the "March King" because he wrote so many of the great pieces of marching music, and he led some of the greatest bands of his or any other time. His most famous composition was undoubtedly "The Stars and Stripes Forever." I challenge any American not to be moved by the music of John Philip Sousa. And on his birthday, I intend to march right on into my topic for today. So here I go, ready to face the music.

NOVEMBER 7

Nixon reelected, 1972.

Bolshevik revolution in Russia, 1917.

Billy Graham born, 1918.

(See also item on Elijah P. Lovejoy, November 9.)

Introductions:

On this date in 1972, more than four months after the break-in at Watergate, Richard M. Nixon was reelected President of the United States, by the people of the United States. There had already been reports of a far greater degree of involvement than merely a break-in at the Democratic campaign offices, but the electorate found it hard to believe that the involvement was as deep as it turned out to be, and chose Mr. Nixon over Senator George McGovern. But not long after, both President Nixon and Vice President Agnew were fated to resign under fire. It takes a long time to convince Americans of things they would rather not believe. I hope that in my remarks today I will not have to take a long time to convince you—because I don't have a long time to talk. So let me get started.

On this day, the seventh of November, 1917, the Bolshevik party in Russia led a revolution against the provisional democratic government to establish a Communist dictatorship. The Russian Revolution did not begin as a Communist movement; the Tsar was overthrown and replaced by a democratic coalition. When a free election was held later on November 25, 1917, the Communists lost; so they just threw out the election. On this day in 1917, the Communists opted for armed force as the weapon of change. And ever since, the world has wondered whether this particular leopard can change its spots. As I address you here today, the memory of November 7, 1917 is very green—or should I say very red—and it colors many a view of the world. Indeed, it affects the views I am about to give you. For one cannot discuss the realities of life today without being aware of the realities of the Communist tradition that remains the dominant rival to our way of life.

Billy Graham came a long way in the world from Charlotte, North Carolina, where he was born on this day in 1918. As the greatest evangelist of his time, he became a friend of Presidents and a missionary to the world. The results seem to have been mutually rewarding. Those who find religion are usually willing to put their money where their mouths are, and so evangelism is one of the most consistently self-sustaining efforts in the world today. I commend it to you as an example of the basic truth: if we believe in something, we should be prepared to *do* something for what we believe in. And so I come to you today with a call to believe, and a call to act.

NOVEMBER 8

Hitler's beer hall putsch, 1923.

Franklin D. Roosevelt elected President, 1932.

Invasion of North Africa, 1942.

Introductions:

November 8, 1923, Adolf Hitler and a group of followers generally regarded as semi-lunatics broke into a Munich beer hall in Germany and proclaimed a new government. They had some thousands of adherents, but they miscalculated the attitude of the government and of the people. Not only did the so-called beer hall putsch fail, but a few days later Hitler fled, only to be arrested and sent to prison. Some people thought that was the end of Adolf

Hitler. I am here to say to you today that we cannot stop ideas—even the worst of them—by imprisonment. We can only stop ideas with better ideas. As to what are the better ideas—that is my subject for today.

Franklin D. Roosevelt was first elected President of the United States on this day in 1932. He was elected again and again and again—four times in all—the only President to have that kind of record of public approval. It seems fair to rate him, therefore, as one of our greatest political figures. Whether liked or disliked, he was universally regarded as the politician par excellence. No American politician was ever more successful than he at convincing the American people that theirs was the generation that, in his words, had "a rendezvous with destiny." It's been a long rendezvous, ladies and gentlemen, and today I would like to tell you why I think it is still going on.

On this day, in 1942, U.S. and British forces invaded Nazi-held North Africa. It was the biggest invasion thus far in World War II, although even greater ones were to come. But it was more important because it marked the beginning of the turning of the tide, with the Allies turning from the defensive to the offensive. It is very important in life not merely to be on the defensive, reacting to events, but to take the initiative and help shape the events. You and I can do that—and today I'd like to give you a few examples.

NOVEMBER 9

New York's first blackout, 1965.

Elijah P. Lovejoy born, 1802.

Introductions:

Back in 1965, on this day—or, more exactly, this night—most of the northeastern United States, and New York City in particular, was blacked out in a massive electrical power failure. It was a night that nobody wanted to have happen again, even though it proved to be a night of peace and great public cooperation. Twelve years later, in the middle of the long, hot summer of 1977, New York City had another power blackout, and that time the looters had a field day. Was it because people had changed, or because the weather was different, or because times were harder? We will never really know. We do know that things are much better in the light than in the dark, and so I am here to try to shed a little light on some items that I hope you will find of interest.

Elijah P. Lovejoy was in the business of trying to shed some light. He was a newspaper editor. He was also a fiery abolitionist during the days of slavery. Born on this day in 1802, in Albion, Maine, he established a newspaper in Alton, Illinois. His coverage of the abolitionist movement irritated some of the people in the town, and his presses were destroyed many times. On November 7, 1837, he was murdered by a mob while trying to defend his newspaper. It is comforting to realize that times have changed. Newspaper editing and public

speaking are both somewhat less hazardous today. And so, with consummate
~~bravery, I leap into the fray.~~

NOVEMBER 10

Marine Corps established, 1775.

Stanley found Livingstone, 1871.

Introductions:

Today is the birthday of the U.S. Marine Corps, established by the Continental Congress in 1775. Since then, the Marines have seen plenty of action and
succeeded in getting many a situation—in their phrase— "well in hand." There
are many things which we know are in good hands when the Marines get the
assignment. But today, I plan to tell you many things which do not fall into that
popular category of "Tell it to the Marines." By the way, did you know that the
expression originated with Sir Walter Scott. He had a character say, in *Red-
gauntlet*, "Tell that to the marines—the sailors won't believe it." So, fellow
civilians . .

This is the anniversary of the day, in 1871, when reporter Henry M.
Stanley found David Livingstone, a missionary who had gone into the wilds of
Africa. I have always thought that when Stanley spoke his famous line, "Dr.
Livingstone, I presume," the good doctor probably should have answered, "You
certainly do presume." For Dr. Livingstone, far from being lost or in need of
rescue, remained in Africa while Stanley returned to civilization and glory. I
want to assure you that I am not here to play Stanley to your Dr. Livingstone.
I do not believe you are lost or need me to find the way. But perhaps I can put
up a signpost or two.

NOVEMBER 11

Armistice in World War I, 1918.

"God Bless America" has a delayed debut, 1939.

Introductions:

On this day in 1918, the worst war in the history of mankind up to that
time came to an end. The guns went silent in World War I. The silence,
unfortunately, did not last as long the world hoped. Twenty years later came
World War II. Today, as we remember those who died in the war that was to
"make the world safe for democracy," we might give some thought as to how
we can make democracy safe for the world.

Today, "God Bless America" is so well-known as a sort of semi-offical
national anthem, that it may come as a surprise to you to learn that the song

was 22 years old before it was heard in public. Irving Berlin wrote it during World War I, but it was not sung in public until this day in 1939, when Kate Smith introduced it on a radio broadcast. As you may recall, the last line of the song refers to our land as "home, sweet home." Today I propose that we examine what we can do to keep our land that way.

NOVEMBER 12

Elizabeth Cady Stanton Day.

Princess Grace of Monaco born—Grace Kelly.

Introductions:

Elizabeth Cady Stanton, who was born in Johnstown, New York, on this day in 1815, isn't too well-known in our own time, but few women have had a greater influence. She was in some respects the greatest of the early feminist leaders. She wrote the historic Declaration of Sentiments at the first Women's Rights Convention in 1848 and she spearheaded the successful efforts to give women in New York State joint guardianship of their children, the right to own property and the right to sue in court. Just listing the rights she did so much to win is an indication of how bad things were for women before she came along. She did not live long enough to see women win the right to vote, but on her birthday she deserves to be saluted by women and men alike for the way she fought for equality and justice. Today I want to talk to you about some things which I think Mrs. Stanton would be fighting for if she were alive today— things far broader than sex discrimination or the franchise.

I don't know how many American girls these days dream of growing up and becoming royal princesses. It's an old fashioned idea, but it happened in our own time to lovely Grace Kelly, the Philadelphia girl who became first a movie star and then the wife of a reigning prince. When she married Prince Rainier, she became Princess Grace of Monaco—a world away from her birth on this day in 1929 in Philadelphia. Dreams sometimes do come true—and so today I would like to talk about some other dreams of some other Americans.

NOVEMBER 13

Holland Tunnel opened, 1927.

Vietnam Moratorium demonstrations, 1969.

Introductions:

On this day in 1927, the Holland Tunnel was opened under the Hudson River between New York and New Jersey. Up to then, the only way to get to Manhattan from New Jersey in an automobile had been to take a ferry. There was an earlier railroad tunnel, but the bridges were yet to come. I must confess that I have never understood why the tunnels under the Hudson preceded the bridges over the Hudson, but I assume that there is some irrefutable logic to it. Perhaps the moral is that if you want to go straight to a point, you get right into the deep water—or under it—rather than trying to stay above it. In that belief, I shall proceed immediately to head for the deep water in my remarks to you here today.

Over a three-day period that began on November 13, 1969, hundreds of thousands of people throughout the U.S. participated in what became known as the Vietnam Moratorium demonstrations. Despite fears of violence, the demonstrations were peaceful, and hence far more impressive. We are a proud people; we do not like to be threatened into doing things; peaceful persuasion is more to American taste. Even the best of causes suffers in America when it is advocated violently. I don't know whether what I am about to advocate is the best of causes, but I think you will find it a lot better if I simply talk about it than if I try to hit you over the head with a heavy placard. In that hope I now proceed.

NOVEMBER 14

Nellie Bly set out to go around the world in 80 days, 1889.

Moby Dick, 1851.

Introductions:

On this day, in 1889, a newspaper reporter who called herself Nellie Bly was sent off by *The New York World* to try to travel around the world in less than 80 days. She made it in 72. There is so much to see in the world that I have never understood why people want to keep on going around it faster and faster, thereby seeing less and less of it in less and less time. Fortunately, the same spirit has not yet invaded the speaker's platform. I will try to get to my subject, not around it, and while I do not plan to tarry I am not trying to set a speed record here today. Now, if you are ready for takeoff, so am I.

Herman Melville had written five books before the one which was published on this day in 1851. But if the book whose anniversary today had been his only work, he would still rate as one of our greater authors. The book, as you may have guessed, was *Moby Dick*. It begins with the words, "Call me Ishmael" and goes on to say, "I love to sail forbidden seas, and land on barbarous coasts." There is much other imagery in *Moby Dick*—the great white whale itself, Captain Ahab's grim pursuit and all the rest—but today it is the world of Ishmael that gives me my theme. The world is full of Ishmaels, disenchanted with what is around them and seeking forbidden seas and barbarous coasts. It is that state of mind, that human condition, that I wish to address here today.

NOVEMBER 15

Articles of Confederation adopted by Congress, 1777.

Pike's Peak sighted, 1806.

Introductions:

This country of ours has many birthdays. It may come as a surprise to know that today is one of them. On this day, in 1777, the Continental Congress, facing up to the fact that 13 separate colonies were engaged in the war with England, adopted the Articles of Confederation, which were sent two days later to the various states for ratification. The Articles, numbering 13 in all, were not completely ratified until 1781, but they did provide a governmental framework for a united group of states. It took a while, as we know from the history books, to work out the kinks, but, once united, the states stayed that way. Today, I rise to suggest that we consider as individuals, a set of Articles of Confederation of our own, not as a charter of government but rather as a declaration of mutual interdependence. How are we mutually interdependent? I'm glad you asked.

This was the day, in 1806, when Zebulon Montgomery Pike, a young Army officer on an exploration expedition in the West, sighted a high mountain and decided to try to climb it. Before he could do so, he was taken prisoner by the Spanish authorities for trespassing on Spanish territory. He didn't climb the mountain, but it bears his name. It is Pike's Peak, in Colorado. I like to think of the story of Pike's Peak as pointing a moral. The person who reaches for the heights doesn't always get there, but he helps to identify the goal. Maybe that is a mixed or confused metaphor, and perhaps my remarks here today can undo the confusion. For what I am here to say is that by looking to the heights, we spur ourselves and our colleagues to higher levels of achievement. Let me be specific about some of the heights toward which we—you and I—can and should be looking today.

NOVEMBER 16

U.S. and U.S.S.R. established diplomatic relations, 1933.

Sherman's march to the sea, 1864.

Introductions:

Back in 1933, this was the day when the United States and Soviet Russia established diplomatic relations. What it meant was that they finally agreed to start talking to each other. I am happy to establish diplomatic relations with this audience today, and I hope to be a little more diplomatic about it than our friends across the water.

Probably no wartime event in American history left a greater residue of bitterness than Sherman's march from Atlanta to the sea in the Civil War. It began on this day, in 1864, and it left a broad scar of ruin and destruction for hundreds of miles. For generations the South remembered. But, unlike some of the bitter memories of other lands, this one finally began to fade, and when a Georgian named Jimmy Carter was elected President the South had indeed risen again. It is important that we remember some of the events of history— and it is also important that some of the more bitter memories be permitted to fade. Today I speak to you in the spirit of looking forward and of putting the past where it belongs, behind us. Let us remember, but let us not live, in the past.

NOVEMBER 17

John Peter Zenger arrested for libel, 1734.

SALT talks began in Helsinki, 1969.

Introductions:

A lot of Americans, particularly those involved in journalism, remember John Peter Zenger's victory when he was jailed for libeling the Royal Governor of New York. The date that sticks in their minds is the date when Zenger was acquitted, because it was a victory for freedom of the press. Today, however, is the anniversary of the day he went to jail on libel charges, in 1734. Not until the following summer did he come to trial, and meanwhile, he remained in prison. A great many of the victories of principle are won at a considerable sacrifice, and this was one of them. It is very easy to make a speech invoking noble traditions and glorious high ideas, but it is sometimes not quite that easy to put them into practice. So, if you don't mind, I will not be talking today in lofty philosophical terms. Instead, let's get down to cases.

On this day, in 1969, the United States and Soviet Russia began talks on strategic arms limitation. SALT, standing for strategic arms limitation talks, proved to be a smashing success in one sense. They were still talking eight years later. Perhaps they should have considered having strategic talk limitation talks. At any rate, I am imposing my own talk limitation here today. This is not an open end discussion and I shall limit the extent to which it is an open mouth one.

NOVEMBER 18

Standard Time adopted in U.S., 1883.

L. J. M. Daguerre born, 1789.

W. S. Gilbert born, 1836.

Introductions:

Today is the anniversary of something most of us probably think was there all the time. On this date in 1883, Standard Time was adopted in the U.S. Up to then, every locality set its own time preference. My time, prior to 1883, was not your time, necessarily. Thereafter, a system of time zones made life a lot simpler. Now we have time in common, and I will try to be careful of your time as I proceed to use mine.

Most of us have an ancient photograph or two of one of our forebears, and virtually all of us have cameras to record ourselves for posterity. All of this traces back to a man who was born on this day, in 1789, in Cormeilles, France. His name was Louis Daguerre, and he gave his name to the early photographs that were called daguerrotypes. It was Louis Daguerre who popularized photography and first proved that one picture was worth a thousand words. But I was not asked here today to take your picture; so I will offer you a thousand words, more or less.

On the birthday of W. S. Gilbert—of Gilbert and Sullivan—a speaker can be forgiven, I think, for treating his or her assignment a bit lightly. W. S. Gilbert, born on this day in 1836, in London, treated life lightly in the marvelous operettas he wrote with Sir Arthur Sullivan. Today I should like to recall some of W. S. Gilbert's immortal observations, such as: "When everyone is somebody, then no one's anybody," and "Things are seldom what they seem, skim milk masquerades as cream," and "The Law is the true embodiment of everything that's excellent; it has no kind of fault or flaw, and I, my lords, embody the Law." I have no such gems of philosophy to offer here today, but now that W. S. Gilbert has set the facts straight I shall proceed.

NOVEMBER 19

The Mayflower arrived off Cape Cod, 1620.

Lord Chesterfield's advice, 1745.

Lincoln's Gettysburg Address, 1863.

Introductions:

On this day, in 1620, the Mayflower arrived off Cape Cod. I imagine that the Pilgrims aboard the Mayflower at that point had somewhat the same feeling as the audience here today about now—sitting there wondering why they got into this and what in the world was going to come up next. I don't think I have any great surprises for you, but I do have a few thoughts and observations which I hope you will find of interest.

The Earl of Chesterfield was a fountainhead of good advice for his son, and most of his suggestions were incorporated in a book. On this date in 1745 the fatherly advice was this: "Be wiser than other people if you can, but do not tell them so." Never were wiser words put in the mind of a speaker. I speak to you today with absolutely no illusions of superior wisdom on my part— and the hope that my audience feels the same.

On this day in 1863, Abraham Lincoln dedicated a national cemetery with a few brief remarks. The cemetery was at Gettysburg, Pennsylvania, and the few brief remarks turned out to be the Gettysburg Address. I am planning to make a few brief remarks myself here today—but I assure you in advance, there is no further resemblance between what I am about to say and the Gettysburg Address. And I am sure that we are all equally delighted to be here on an occasion other than the dedication of a cemetery to fallen heroes. On the anniversary of the Gettysburg Address, we have the opportunity to dedicate ourselves, and I hope that what I have to say can provide a target or two.

NOVEMBER 20

Robert F. Kennedy born, 1925.

International War Crimes Tribunal trials began, 1945.

Introductions:

Today is the birthday of Robert F. Kennedy, who was born in 1925, in Brookline, Massachusetts. At the memorial service after his tragic murder, his brother, Senator Edward Kennedy, recalled that Bobby had said, "Some people see things as they are, and say why. I dream things that never were and say, why not." Today I propose to speak of things that could be, and say, why not?

After World War II, an International War Crimes Tribunal was set up to put suspected war criminals on trial. On this day, in 1945, the trial of Nazi leaders in Nuremberg, Germany, began. The trial process was not endless and the verdicts were prompt; but many decades later, in our own country and elsewhere, people accused as war criminals were still being sought, fighting extradition or simply hiding. And there had been several wars in between. The war crimes of World War II had been followed by the war crimes of later struggles and it was time to wonder what had been learned. That, indeed, is my subject today. What, in terms of human justice, have we learned in our time?

NOVEMBER 21

Vanity and the first balloon, 1783.

Mayflower Compact, 1620.

Voltaire born, 1694.

Introductions:

The fact that today is the anniversary of the first human flight in a free balloon, back in 1783, is of passing interest, but what I find of much more interest is the story of the two men who flew in that historic journey. Their names were Jean Pilatre de Rozier and the Marquis d'Arlandes. The balloon had been designed by two brothers named Montgolfier, and had aroused the interest of the king of France. When he decided to approve of sending human beings up in a balloon, de Rozier and the Marquis, who had had absolutely nothing to do with the original idea, thought it would bring them some attention in history and so they asked the King to let them go aboard. I wonder how many other times it has been as naked a hunger for glory that has sparked a new human accomplishment. I also hasten to add that I am not only the passenger in my own hot air balloon here today—the design and the hot air are all my own.

Self-government goes a long way back in this country. It began in deep water aboard the Mayflower off the New England coast on this day in 1620, when the Pilgrims signed the Mayflower Compact for what they called "a civil body politic." Self-government, I am happy to say, is not in deep water these days. And I have a few suggestions to offer to keep the waters calm.

Francois-Marie Arouet was born on this day, in 1694, in Paris. This fact becomes a little more meaningful when I add that Francois-Marie Arouet adopted a pen name; he called himself Voltaire. Among his wise observations was his remark that "The way to be a bore is to say everything." Since I do not want to bore you here today, I will try not to say everything. That will make both our tasks—mine of talking and yours of listening—somewhat more bearable.

NOVEMBER 22

John F. Kennedy assassinated, 1963.

SOS adopted as international distress signal, 1906.

Introductions:

November 22 is a date that will always be remembered, by everyone who lived through it, as the day, in 1963, when a young President was struck down in a brutal assassination. So much of what transpired thereafter was seen on the television screen, that the event is vividly engraved on the memories of millions of people. And questions about it have persisted ever since. It is the nature of human beings to ask questions, to wonder, to be skeptical. It was the nature of John F. Kennedy to stand back and look at himself, and sometimes to be amused at what he saw in himself. I would like to think that in this regard he was typical of America; that, while we are serious in our purposes, we don't always take ourselves too seriously. John Kennedy said, in the year he died,

". . . if we cannot end now our differences, at least we can make the world safe for diversity." So if you find you disagree with what I am about to say, remember the Kennedy injunction and together we will make the world safe for diversity.

We don't have very much luck in the world as different peoples attempt to talk to each other, but there is one phrase at least that is universal. Ever since this day in 1906, the letters SOS, spelled out in wireless code, have been the international distress signal. I wonder why we can have an international distress signal that everybody understands and still not be able to convey happy news to each other just as easily. I have no SOS to signal to you today. Instead, I am here to speak in calmer terms of happier things.

NOVEMBER 23

Abigail Smith Adams born, 1744.

Repudiation Day in Maryland.

First women's medical society, 1848.

Introductions:

When Abigail Smith was born in Weymouth, Massachusetts, in 1744, she never dreamed that she would celebrate her birthday in 1800 as the First Lady of a new nation in a brand new Executive Mansion. Abigail Smith married John Adams; she became the wife of one President and the mother of another, which is a pretty good record, I would say. She also became about the first major spokeswoman for the cause of women's rights in the infant nation. After the Declaration of Independence was signed, she wrote to her husband, "In the new code of laws which I now assume will be needed, please give a thought to the ladies and see to it that it is put beyond the power of the vicious and lawless . . . to treat us with cruelty and indignity with impunity. Don't forget that all men would be tyrants if they could." On Abigail Adams' birthday today, I think it is only fair to point out that the amazing contributions of the Adams family were not those of men alone. American men and women make an unbeatable combination, and it is that combination whose common efforts I salute today.

Today is Repudiation Day in Maryland, commemorating Frederick County's repudiation of the British Stamp Act in 1765. The seeds of revolution were sown in this country long before the Declaration of Independence. Things that seem to happen suddenly often have spent years developing. One of the challenges to a speaker is to find and call to the audience's attention some of the developing trends before they burst upon a surprised world, and that is what I propose to try to do today. There are so many currents in contemporary life that one would have to spread oneself exceedingly thin to try to cover them all; but perhaps my remarks may illuminate one or two areas that deserve to be recognized.

According to at least one major reference book, today is the anniversary of the founding of the first women's medical society in America, an organization called the Female Medical Educational Society of Boston, in 1848. What I found interesting in reading about this group was that the officers of the Female Medical Educational Society were all men! I want to talk today about our changing times, and times have certainly changed since the men organized the Female Medical Educational Society.

NOVEMBER 24

Lee Harvey Oswald killed, 1963.

Warren's wise words, 1963.

Introductions:

Probably no homicide in the history of the world has ever been witnessed by more people than the killing of Lee Harvey Oswald, accused assassin of President John F. Kennedy. Oswald was in front of the television cameras in the basement of the Dallas jail when he was shot by Jack Ruby, on this day, in 1963. The whole world saw it happen; but we have yet to fully understand how and why. When things which we have all seen with our own eyes defy our comprehension, then abstract ideas must certainly be more difficult to comprehend. Yet we live in a nation whose ideals, whose abstract principles and traditions, are not at all hard to comprehend. Our job is not to comprehend them but to live up to them. That is the basis of my remarks here today.

Chief Justice Earl Warren spoke some wise words at the memorial tribute to President Kennedy two days after the President was killed in 1963. I can think of no better way to begin my remarks here today than to quote Justice Warren's words: "If we really love this country, if we truly love justice and mercy, if we fervently want to make this nation better for those who are to follow us, we can at least abjure the hatred that consumes people, the false accusations that divide us and the bitterness that begets violence." In peace and good will, my friends, I humbly raise my voice.

NOVEMBER 25

St. Catherine's Day.

Russia's last free election, 1917.

Disraeli describes his times, 1864.

Introductions:

Today, in Paris, according to tradition, is St. Catherine's Day, when the young seamstresses are supposed to go out on a carnival manhunt. Some young

American men say this is an anachronism, because young women in America do not need a St. Catherine's Day—and neither do the young men. But I am not here to tell you things about American men and women that, I trust, you already know. Rather, I am here to take a look at some other matters that good old St. Catherine could never have encountered.

On this day, in 1917, there was a free election in Russia. It was for the purpose of electing a constituent assembly; and the Russian voters chose an assembly in which less than a third of the deputies were Communists. So naturally, the Bolsheviks suppressed the assembly when it convened the following January. Since I am going to be talking today about some of the problems of life in America, I thought it might be helpful to remember that we solve our problems a little differently than do some other places on this earth. To live and speak in a climate of freedom, I remind you, makes every problem just a little smaller.

Benjamin Disraeli was one of the most sophisticated men of his time and he viewed his time with a critical eye. On this day, in 1864, he noted that "The characteristic of the present age is craving credulity." That was over a hundred years ago, and in another country, Great Britain; but I suspect that if Disraeli were alive today, he would say the same thing. "Craving credulity," the ardent eagerness to find things to believe in, is one of the problems of our time. Young people—and older ones—follow false prophets and waste their substance on false illusions. Will this change? Is it a phenomenon of our times or of all times? Today I want to share with you some thoughts about what people are looking for—and where.

NOVEMBER 26

First lion exhibited in America, 1716.

Thanksgiving, 1789.

Introductions:

Among the more obscure annals of American history is the saga of the first lion ever seen on these shores. It was announced for exhibition in Boston on this day in 1716. I feel somewhat as that lion must have felt, standing up here trying to gauge your mood as you, in turn, wait expectantly for me to roar. I hope you won't mind if I speak somewhat more quietly than the lion's roar. I may not be as loud as the king of beasts, but I hope to demonstrate that I have a few more words in my vocabulary.

The first Thanksgiving ever proclaimed by a President of the United States was observed on this day in 1789. It was proclaimed by President Washington as a day of gratitude for the adoption of the Constitution. That is not a bad reason for our Thanksgiving celebrations two centuries later either. In the season of national thankfulness, I rise to express what should certainly be a general sense of appreciation for a way of life that, despite all its faults, has given this country the best the world can devise. I rise also to exercise a right of free speech which is also a glorious part of the American heritage.

NOVEMBER 27

Army War College authorized, 1901.

Chaim Weizmann born, 1874.

Introductions:

Today is the anniversary of the establishment of an institution of higher education not quite like most such others in this country. On this day, in 1901, the Army War College was authorized. It was a form of recognition that the art of warfare was becoming more complicated. If they thought it was complicated in 1901, what must they think today! Now, more than ever, the most important weapon of offense or defense is not hardware, but knowledge. Admittedly, some of that knowledge today is the knowledge of how to use the hardware. But what lies in the human mind is the most potent instrument of all. And so today, I would like to explore what lies in the mind of America, the attitudes with which we approach the world in which we live.

Back in World War I, an emigré scientist from Russia was director of the British Admiralty laboratories. His name was Chaim Weizmann, born on this day in 1874, in Russian Poland. He was a brilliant scientist who helped synthesize some of the ingredients for vitally needed explosives in World War I. He was also an active enthusiast for the idea of a homeland for the Jews in Palestine, being himself Jewish. Years later, when that Jewish homeland became a reality, Chaim Weizmann was elected the first President of Israel, and today a great scientific institute of worldwide fame bears his name. His birthday reminds us that there is no Berlin wall isolating scientists, that scientists can also be political animals and that positions of leadership today are not the exclusive domain of politicians. I don't know how you feel about these facts, but I find them very encouraging. Let me tell you why I think that public life today needs all the talent it can get.

NOVEMBER 28

Ferdinand Magellan reached the Pacific Ocean from the Atlantic, 1520.

Richard E. Byrd starts flight over the South Pole, 1929.

Communist China loses a UN admission vote, 1967.

Introductions:

Down at the tail end of South America is a rough body of water known as the Straits of Magellan. The Straits were discovered by Ferdinand Magellan, in 1520, as he was trying to find a way to get to the Moluccan Islands in the Pacific. On this day in 1520, Magellan reached the Pacific. I think it is fair to say that he did it the hard way. Today my goal is not the Pacific, but rather something specific, and I shall try not to circumnavigate the globe to get there.

When Ferdinand Magellan went through the Straits that now bear his name he must have thought he was at the bottom of the world. But 409 years later, Commander Richard E. Byrd went somewhat further, just about as close to the bottom as one can get. On this day, in 1929, Commander Byrd—he wasn't an Admiral yet—took off with Bernt Balchen and a flight crew from their base in Little America to try to fly over the South Pole. That, I guess, is the course of life; we keep trying to outdo previous generations. And on the whole, we seem to succeed. Take a look at today's world with me, my friends.

In 1967, the United Nations voted on the question of admitting Red China. For the 18th time, the Communist government was turned down. This sounds like ancient history, now, because the People's Republic of China has been a member of the UN for quite a few years. I mention it to emphasize that times change, and we change with them. We are changing right now. May I give you some examples?

NOVEMBER 29

Richard E. Byrd flew over South Pole, 1929.

First Army-Navy football game, 1890.

Karl Marx on "The Star Spangled Banner," 1865.

Introductions:

This is the day that human beings first flew over the South Pole. It happened in 1919, and Richard E. Byrd was the commander of the plane that did it. What it meant basically was that there was now virtually no place on the face of the earth that we couldn't reach, if not on foot, then through the air. And if we ran out of places on earth, we could start looking elsewhere, as we have. But at this late juncture, it seems appropriate to wonder whether we have indeed found all the poles on earth, or whether we have a bit more exploring to do. Let me talk to you about where we go from here.

This is the anniversary of a continuing bitter battle between our two major senior armed forces, the Army and the Navy. It is a battle that began on this day in 1890, and I see no sign of its ending. What I am talking about, of course, is the annual Army-Navy football game. In other countries, the Armed Forces get caught up in rival juntas and cabals, competing with each other for control of the government. I find it comforting that our military's power plays and deceits occur on the playing field. And now, it is only fitting that we go into a huddle to discuss the nation's next move.

In the course of researching some material for this day, I came across a quotation from a letter dated November 29, 1865 and supposedly sent to Abraham Lincoln. The year is obviously wrong, because Lincoln died in April 1865. But if the text of the letter is accurate, it is rather interesting. The letter said, "From the commencement of the titanic struggle in America, the working men of Europe felt instinctively that the Star Spangled Banner carried the destiny of their class." I say this purported letter is rather interesting not only because of its content but also because of its signature. The letter, we are told, was sent by a man named Karl Marx. We have come a long way from the days when the United States was considered the hope of radicalism, but it may put things in a little better context to stop and realize that the American concept of freedom was pretty radical back in 1865 and, indeed, is pretty radical today in some quarters, including those lands where Marxism is the dominant political philosophy. I begin my remarks today, therefore, with the premise that we here in America, in a free society, represent the wave of the future. Now let's see how it works.

NOVEMBER 30

Winston Churchill born, 1874.

Mark Twain born, 1835.

U.S.S.R. invaded Finland, 1939.

Introductions:

On this day, in 1874, Winston Leonard Spencer Churchill was born in Oxfordshire, England. He had a distinguished career as a writer and politician until he reached the normal retirement age of 65. But by then, he had embarked on a new job, as Prime Minister of the United Kingdom, when the Kingdom was fighting for its life in World War II. Winston Churchill's words rallied the nation and what was left of the free world. And on his 80th birthday, in 1954, Churchill for the first time fudged a bit. The War was long since over by then, when he said, "I have never accepted what many people have kindly said, namely that I inspired the nation. It was the nation . . . that had the lion heart. I had the luck to be called upon to give the roar." Winston Churchill certainly gave the roar, but in his case it wasn't just luck. As I can tell you from my present assignment, it takes somebody else to give you the chance to sound off, but the sound is strictly up to you. I thank you for the opportunity you have given me here today; now let's see what I do with it.

Samuel L. Clemens was born on this day in Florida, Missouri, back in 1835. When he grew up, he was better known as Mark Twain. Among his many words of wit and wisdom, one sentence seems particularly appropriate as advice to me today. "Thunder is good," he wrote, "thunder is impressive; but it is lightning that does the work." Taking that to heart, I have decided that, in my comments to you here today, I will not thunder, and my capacity to provide lightning is considerably limited. But perhaps I can shed a little light, quiet though it may be. At least, I can try.

A lot of people tried to find excuses for Soviet Russia when that nation signed a treaty with Nazi Germany in 1938. When the Soviet Union invaded little Finland on this day in 1939, it was hard to find excuses. And when Finland proceeded to hold out for three months, the world cheered. Ultimately, of course, mighty Russia imposed its own peace on Finland, but in the process it had cast itself as an imperialist nation, once and for all. Today, I ask—or remind— you to judge people and nations not by what they say but by what they do. Of course, in my case what I do is stand up here and talk to you today. And now is when I start.

DECEMBER 1

National Indigestion Season.

Boys Town founded, 1917.

Skywriting introduced, 1922.

Introductions:

Some years ago a company that manufactured bicarbonate of soda designated the period betweeen Thanksgiving and Christmas as National Indigestion Season. Naturally they had a remedy for it, but I take that with a grain of salt. I prefer—as I am sure you do—to deal today with the pleasures and inspirations of the holiday season, and let the heartburn fend for itself.

In 1917, a priest in Omaha, Nebraska, named Father Edward Flanagan founded a unique institution on this day. It was called Boys Town, and its basic concept was centered in Father Flanagan's firm belief that, in his words, "There is no such thing as a bad boy." Father Flanagan was no starry-eyed dreamer. He defined the problem; it wasn't bad boys; it was the conditions that created their problems. So he tried to put friendless boys into an environment where they could have a chance to grow up as good citizens. That isn't a bad idea for the rest of us. Today, I'd like to address myself to what we can do to bring out the good in people.

Back in biblical days, there was some miraculous handwriting on the wall. In our own day, the writing is sometimes a good deal larger, if a lot less profound. I refer to that modern lofty form of communication called skywriting. We first saw it in this country, I am told, on this day in 1922, when a pilot flew over New York and released a trail of white smoke that spelled out the friendly word "hello." Since then, skywriting has been used on behalf of soft drinks and other familiar products. But the most dramatic language in the skies has been the vapor trail of a jet and the fiery thrust of a rocket as it leaves the earth. Maybe that is part of the communications explosion of our times. We no sooner look up at the sky than we start looking beyond it. And all the time we overlook things right here on earth. Today, I take the occasion to suggest a few careful looks at things fairly close to home.

DECEMBER 2

Monroe Doctrine, 1823.

Atomic age born, 1942.

Senator McCarthy censured by Senate, 1954.

Introductions:

In 1823, on this day, President Monroe told the European powers to stay out of the Western Hemisphere. We remember that as the Monroe Doctrine, but perhaps we don't remember quite as well the other side of the coin, as stated in the same document. "In the wars of the European powers, in matters relating to themselves, we have never taken part, nor does it comport with our policy to do so," said President Monroe. We, like all other human beings of other nationalities, like to protect what we regard as our territory. And of course we think of it in global terms. Today, I rise to suggest that we view our territory close-up, not merely in terms of what is happening in the hemisphere but in terms of what is happening—or failing to happen—in our own home towns and in our own homes. Christmas, like charity, starts at home, and I have a few suggestions for the season.

Some years ago, a small plaque was placed on the wall of an old stadium at the University of Chicago. It read, "On December 2, 1942, man achieved here the first self-sustaining chain reaction and thereby initiated the controlled release of nuclear energy." In a secret laboratory below the football stadium, they had figured out how to get a chain reaction from uranium; not until 1945 did it explode upon the public consciousness—and we have not solved the ensuing problems yet. What other scientific miracles are being born in other laboratories today? I don't have the answer; but I have a few hopes that I would like to share with you—a few miracles that are badly needed.

On this day, in 1954, the Senate did something it very rarely has done. It censured a member. The member was Senator Joseph R. McCarthy, who had risen on the strength of his campaign against alleged Communists and had, in the opinion of a majority of his Senate colleagues, ultimately gone too far.

Censure is not a major sanction—as, Lord knows, has been proven time and again in the United Nations. But, among one's colleagues it can lead to a serious loss of face. Today I want to look at *our* face. How do we rate with ourselves—one generation to another? How do we rate with each other?

DECEMBER 3

John Paul Jones hoists first seagoing American flag, 1775.

First human heart transplant, 1967.

Introductions:

On this day, in 1775, a young lieutenant named John Paul Jones raised an American flag aboard the *Alfred*, the flagship of the brand new Continental Navy. It was the so-called Grand Union flag—13 stripes and the British Union Jack. John Paul Jones's days of glory were still ahead of him; but when he showed the flag for the first time, he made a glorious beginning. I have shown the flag today in a somewhat more modest way by showing up here on the speaker's platform. So now let's weigh anchor and get under way.

Dr. Christiaan Barnard did something on this day, in 1967, that had never been done before. He transplanted a human heart. The patient survived for 18 days, in Capetown, South Africa. It was a short beginning for a major new era of progress in medicine. Today I am using another short beginning, to get quickly into my remarks. I offer no prospects for heart transplants, but if I can transplant some of my own sentiments into this gathering here today, I will consider the operation a success.

DECEMBER 4

First Thanksgiving, 1619.

Phonograph born, 1877.

Introductions:

When we think of our national holidays, one of the first that comes to mind is Thanksgiving, with the Pilgrims sitting down to a groaning board. But the Pilgrims weren't even at the first Thanksgiving in America. It was celebrated, on this day, at Berkeley Plantation in Virginia, a year before the Pilgrims landed further up north in Massachusetts. The year of that first Thanksgiving was 1619. That's a long span of years till now, and Thanksgiving and Christmas are also a little further apart these days. But the spirit of thankfulness should be timeless and calendarless. And since this is the season of the year for timeless and calendarless sentiments, I am happy to have so pleasant an occasion to speak to you.

The story is that on the night of December 4, 1877, some of the people in Thomas A. Edison's laboratory at Menlo Park, New Jersey, sat up all night playing with a new device whose first model had just been completed. The device was the phonograph, and Edison and his assistant weren't really playing; they were checking out a recording for a public demonstration a few days later. History does not record how early in the game they had trouble with a stuck needle. But I take the occasion of the anniversary of the phonograph today to raise my voice in person—this is not a recording—and to hope that you do not find yourselves subjected to a broken record.

DECEMBER 5

Repeal, 1933.

Walt Disney born, 1901.

Introductions:

On this day in, 1933, the dam broke. The dam in this case was Prohibition; and it broke with the ratification of the 21st Amendment, repealing the 18th Amendment and making liquor legal again. As we found later with other substances, prohibition did not stop people from drinking; it just made it illegal and spawned a whole new era of crime. Repeal may not have solved any problems, but it stopped creating new ones. If my speech can do the same here today, I will consider it a success.

Today is Walt Disney's birthday. The man who gave us Mickey Mouse and Donald Duck and Sneezy and Dopey and so many other unforgettable characters was born in Chicago in 1901. We think of his contribution in terms of animated cartoons, but it went a lot deeper. Did you ever hear the song, "Who's afraid of the big bad wolf?" That came to us courtesy of Walt Disney. Above all, he found a way to show us the funny, the whimsical, the sentimental side of life. I could not try to be angry before you today without reminding myself of the comic fury of Donald Duck; so I will approach my subject as Disney might have—not to scare you, not to depress you, but perhaps to make us all feel a little bit better.

DECEMBER 6

St. Nicholas Day.

Gerald Ford became Vice President, 1973.

Introductions:

Today is St. Nicholas Day, always a pleasant prelude to the Christmas season. St. Nick was a bishop in Asia Minor and is the patron saint of children and sailors. As such, he helps to provide smooth sailing for the young ones and is a personification of kindness and good will for all of us. St. Nicholas, or Santa Claus, lived in the fourth century. More importantly, he lives in the hearts and minds of most people today. And on St. Nicholas Day, I'd like to deliver, here and now, an open letter to Santa Claus.

It is very rare that people remember the name of a past vice president and even rarer to have any particular memory of his inauguration. But the swearing in of Gerald R. Ford as Vice President of the United States on this day in 1973 was like no other in our history, and so I think it will be remembered more than most. To begin with, Ford was not the winner of a popular election. He had been named to the post by the President, Richard M. Nixon, after Vice President Spiro Agnew resigned. Ford had been confirmed by both Houses of Congress, and the nation breathed a sigh of relief to have a new successor available should anything happen to the man in the White House. And something was already beginning to happen to the man in the White House. The Watergate mystery simply was not going away. There was a feeling that maybe Ford was being chosen for something more than a token post—although, as yet, nobody could envision that within the year he would be moving up. On the anniversary of Mr. Ford's assumption of the office of Vice President, I think it is both timely and comforting to reflect on the ability of the structure of government in the United States to meet the crises that occasionally confront it. Our system is unique in its separation of powers and its various checks and balances. Today I ask you to join me in considering how we can make this system work even better.

DECEMBER 7

Delaware Day.

Pearl Harbor Day.

Introductions:

One of the ironies of human memory is that we tend to remember the spectacularly bad over the unspectacularly good. That is certainly the case in our perception of December 7 in American history. How many remember this as Delaware Day? Outside of Delaware, that is. Well, Delaware Day was the beginning of the ratification of the United States Constitution. On this day, in 1787, Delaware became the first state to approve the basic document under which our nation is still governed. In my book that makes today a pretty significant day—and in particular, a day on which we can take pride in the good things about our country. So I speak to you out of that pride and with a sense of optimism.

For most Americans, December 7 is remembered as Pearl Harbor Day—if it is remembered at all. It is the day when, in 1941, a sneak attack on our military and naval base in Hawaii brought the U.S. into World War II. "Remember Pearl Harbor" was the battle cry of that War in the Pacific. But, when the War ended, Americans were happy to resume a close and peaceful relationship with the nation that had attacked Pearl Harbor. Today we have proven that it is possible to forgive and forget among the most bitter of enemies. Now all we have to do is the same thing among friends. And so I rise to speak on behalf of an era of peace and goodwill among near neighbors as well as far ones.

DECEMBER 8

American Federation of Labor founded, 1886.

Horace born, 65 B.C.

Introductions:

Today is the birthday of two great institutions, one a collective and the other an individual. On this day, in 1886, a group of labor unions meeting in Columbus, Ohio, organized the American Federation of Labor. It wasn't the first combination of labor unions, but it proved to be the one that worked for many generations. There has been much dispute about the power of labor unions, but there is no dispute that, before unionism gained its stength, the lot of the average working person was a good deal harder. History is a sort of pendulum; when it swings too far in one direction it reaches a point where it is pushed to swing back in the other direction, and ultimately to reach its own gentle balance. The AFL has been part of that delicate balance for a long time. On its birthday, I rise to salute the idea of decent pay for honest work, and to suggest how we can insure more of the same.

The other birthday of a great institution that we take note of today involves one person—a person who has long since become an institution to countless generations that have had occasion to study his work. Not so many students are doing so these days, but Horace, the great Latin poet, is still an institution. He was born in Venusia in the Roman Empire on this day in 65 B.C. Today I will not quote from his greatest works, but I will quote one line which seems appropriate. He wrote, "Brevis esse laboro, Obscurus fio." Translation: "It is when I am struggling to be brief that I become unintelligible." So today I will speak just a bit longer.

DECEMBER 9

John Milton born, 1608.

First sermon in New England, 1621.

Introductions:

Today is the birthday of a poet who wrote many famous lines in his lifetime, which began in London, on this day, in the year 1608. His name was John Milton, and I have culled a few of his bits of wisdom, any one of which could be the basis of my talk here today. "Peace hath her victories," he wrote, "no less renowned than war." "Give me the liberty to know," he wrote, "to utter, and to argue freely according to conscience, above all liberties." He also said, "With thee conversing I forget all time," but let me reassure you. I will not abuse my welcome here today with lengthy oratory. For I am acutely conscious—again to quote John Milton—that "They also serve who only stand and wait." While you are sitting, not standing, I do not wish to keep you waiting overlong. So let us go immediately into our subject for the day.

We know that the first sermon in New England that was published was delivered on this day at Plymouth, Massachusetts, in 1621, a year after the Pilgrims arrived. It was described on the occasion of a reprinting as the first sermon ever preached in New England; but what I find most interesting about it was not its being the first so much as the topic that preacher Robert Cushman picked. The title of the sermon was "The Sin and Danger of Self-Love." Now that is a very appropriate reminder for a speaker, particularly after a generous introduction. The sin and danger of self-love can lead a speaker into deluding himself that the audience is hanging on his every word, whereas in fact his every word may be hanging him with the audience. I hope, of course, that neither you nor I find ourselves in that predicament. So I speak to you today in thoughtful humility.

DECEMBER 10

UN Human Rights Day.

Nobel Prizes.

Wyoming Day.

Introductions:

Today is Human Rights Day, United Nations Human Rights Day, commemorating the adoption of the United Nations Declaration of Human Rights in 1948. Among other things, that Declaration says that "All human beings are born free and equal in dignity and rights . . . Everyone has the right to freedom of thought . . . Everyone has the right to freedom of opinion and expression." To which I can only add, as your speaker here today, try and stop me,

There is no day of the year when great achievements are more notably recognized than today, the day when, according to the will of Alfred Nobel, the Nobel Prizes are presented for achievements in peace and in the literature and sciences of the world. I must say, contemplating the stature of those who receive the Nobel awards, I have the feeling that while Oslo and Norway drew the winners today, you good people found yourselves with the booby prize! But I will do my best.

Today is Wyoming Day, and if you think it celebrates some exciting event you are absolutely right; but not too many people seem to know what that event was. On this day, in 1869, the Territory of Wyoming became the first government virtually anywhere to adopt women's suffrage and give the distaff side the right to vote. Out in the West, where the men were men, they were half a century ahead of the rest of the country and the rest of the world, for that matter, in rights for women. On Wyoming Day, I rise to express the hope that we can be as farseeing and wise in our time as the Territory of Wyoming was in 1869.

DECEMBER 11

Edward VIII abdicated, 1936.

Alexander Solzhenitsyn born, 1918.

The tower atop the Empire State Building, 1929.

Introductions:

We are supposed to be living in a time when old-fashioned romance has gone out of style, but there are those among us who can recall a romance that took place in real life but would probably never have been believed if told as fiction. On this day, in 1936, the King who reigned over the empire of what was then truly Great Britain, Edward VIII, abdicated to marry the divorcée he loved. Love, my friends, can still conquer all. And so today, I would like to talk to you of a couple of kinds of love—love of country, love of justice, to be specific.

Today is the birthday of Alexander Solzhenitsyn, born in 1918 in Rostov, Russia. Solzhenitsyn grew up to become the most eloquent protester against the inhumanity of the Soviet system. He proved that one voice, raised in protest and in truth, can start a chorus, and that words can be a mighty weapon. I regret that, as regards that weapon, I do not come as heavily armed as Solzhenitsyn, but I welcome the opportunity to raise my voice here today.

The Empire State Building was a long way from completion when an announcement about it was issued, on this day in 1929, by the sponsors of the building. The announcement said that, because it seemed likely that there would be regular worldwide Zeppelin service in a short time, a dirigible mooring tower would be built on top of the Empire State Building—and it was. I believe one blimp did actually tie up briefly, but the major effect of the mooring tower was that it gave the building a good deal more height, and another observation deck. The moral, I guess, is that if you aim high you are bound to stand taller, and that there are better things to do than latching on to a large bag of air. So I will try not to be a large bag of air today.

DECEMBER 12

Ford Foundation's half-billion dollar gift, 1955.

Golf tee patented, 1899.

Introductions:

I did not realize how modest an offering I was bringing to you in my remarks today until I checked on what notable events had happened on this day in the past. I found that in 1955 the Ford Foundation gave the largest set of philanthropic contributions ever put together—a full half a billion dollars for U.S. colleges and universities. I don't know what my words of wisdom today are worth, but it certainly doesn't come within hailing distance of the wisdom of the 12th of December 1955. But, of course, my friends, money isn't everything. So I stand before you to offer something else.

There are unsung events in the history of mankind which leave a mark on their times. One such occurred on this day in 1899, when a patent was issued to one George F. Grant of Boston for a wooden golf tee. Can you imagine the state of the world without golf tees? Do not laugh, my friends. Without golf tees, the game might have been replaced by croquet, and then what would have happened to the country club grounds and the golf club business? I could go on, but you see the point. For want of a tee, the game could be lost. Now a speech, like a golf game, has to tee off somewhere, and what you have just heard was my opening drive. Now if I can only stay out of the rough, we will be on our way.

DECEMBER 13

Dartmouth College chartered, 1769.

Robert E. Lee's wise words, 1862.

Introductions:

When Dartmouth College was chartered, along about now in 1769, it was the successor to Moor's Indian Charity School, and the founder of that school, Eleazar Wheelock, became the founding father of the new college—a fact duly celebrated in Dartmouth song and story. Some years ago, there was a brouhaha over the fact that Dartmouth athletic teams were nicknamed the Indians—the successors of the constituency of Moor's Indian School. The brouhaha was based on the complaint that the Dartmouth teams weren't really Indians and neither was the Dartmouth student body. Now I am not here to analyze the logic or the justice of college nicknames, but I recall this story for one particular reason. We live in times when things that have existed unchallenged for generations are suddenly being challenged. And the challenges are often expressions of much broader concerns than the seemingly minor thing that triggers them. Today I should like to talk about some of these minor things that I regard as symptoms.

Robert E. Lee said many wise things in his distinguished career, but perhaps none wiser than a remark he made on this day in 1862. Contemplating the Battle of Fredericksburg, he said, "It is well that war is so terrible, or we should grow too fond of it." The same is true of various kinds of wars—those fought by soldiers in uniforms, those fought in courts of law, those fought with broadside after broadside in the public press. Contention and competition often spur the adrenalin and stimulate progress, but there can be a cost. Today I am here to say a few words for peace and quiet—and how we can keep them.

DECEMBER 14

Amundsen discovered the South Pole, 1911.

Nostradamus born, 1503.

Introductions:

Back in 1911, Roald Amundsen of Norway became the first human—so far as we know—to reach the South Pole. That was the ultimate, I suppose, in getting to the bottom of things. Today, on the anniversary of Amundsen's accomplishment, we still have a few poles to reach. Perhaps it would be more correct to say that too much of the world is still poles apart. And when you stop to think of it, the North Pole and the South Pole, however far apart, have a lot in common. Today I would like to put up my soapbox on some of the common ground that keeps us from being poles apart.

On December 14, 1503, a man named Michel de Notredame was born in Provence. He became a doctor and then published a book, not about medicine, but about future events. He used a pen name. It was Nostradamus. Getting up to deliver a speech on the birthday of Nostradamus is a powerful temptation to try to be a prophet—and if I could be as vague or ambiguous as some of the prophets of the past, I would take the chance. But since being that vague or ambiguous is itself a high art, I shall have to settle for present truths, as I understand them.

DECEMBER 15

Bill of Rights Day.

Nero born, 37 A.D.

Introductions:

Today is Bill of Rights Day, marking the anniversary of the ratification of the first ten Amendments to the Constitution, the Bill of Rights. The first of those Amendments provides for freedom of speech, of religion, of the press and of the right to assemble or petition the government. No matter how you look at it, we are meeting here today and I am speaking to you thanks to the Bill of Rights. I am mindful that audiences have another right—the right not to listen, so I will not trespass unduly on your time or patience.

On any list of bad kings, the name of Nero would probably be prominent. The man who fiddled while Rome burned was born on this day in 37 A.D. in Antium. Four years after Rome went up in flames, Nero went down in disgrace, branded by the Senate as a public enemy. He committed suicide, which may have been the only thing he really did well. I am tempted to say, on Nero's birthday, that I did not come here to set the world on fire—but I will refrain. I have found that when the speaker fiddles around, the audience burns. So let us leave ancient Nero and get on with the business at hand.

DECEMBER 16

Boston Tea Party, 1773.

Battle of the Bulge, 1944.

Beethoven born, 1770.

Noel Coward born, 1899.

Introductions:

We meet here today on the anniversary of the most memorable tea party in history, a very select event that took place in Boston Harbor in 1773. The Boston Tea Party was, as those who remember their history will recall, a protest against British taxation. It was a picturesque demonstration, but we had to do a good bit more to get rid of British taxation in this country. Today, I remind you of the Boston Tea Party to make the point that tea parties rarely solve anything. What they accomplish, and what perhaps I can accomplish here today, is to get people talking—and thinking—about matters of mutual interest.

I dare say that when I mention the Battle of the Bulge, some of the people here today will think I am talking about waistlines. But the Battle of the Bulge was one of the critical battles of World War II, and it began on this day in 1944, when a German counter-attack in Belgium against U.S. troops created a dangerous bulge in the battle line. It was an epic battle, and it was stubborn courage that ultimately stopped the German threat. Whether the bulge is a battle line or a waistline, it calls for prompt and strong measures. There is also a sense in which a speaker and an audience also take part in a battle of the bulge. If there is too much fat in a speech—or in the speaker's head—that is the bulge that loses the battle, and loses the audience as well. So I will try to keep my lines lean and battleready here today.

Ludwig van Beethoven was probably born on this day, in 1770, in Bonn, Germany. It has been said that what Shakespeare was to drama Beethoven was to music. Beethoven himself said that "true art is selfish and perverse—it will not submit to the mold of flattery." In that sense, my friends, I regard you collectively and severally as true artists—not for selfishness or perversity, I hasten to add, but because as thinking people you will long, in Beethoven's words, "not submit to the mold of flattery." So I will skip the sugar coating, if I may, and get to the substance of my remarks.

There is an old tradition that the show must go on. It goes back for many generations. But Noel Coward, who was born on this day in 1899, in Teddington, England, and became one of the great playwrights, actors and songwriters of his time, once wrote a song entitled "Why Must the Show Go On?" He pointed out that if one packed up one's talent, there was plenty more to step into the breach. There are times when a speaker echoes Noel Coward's question and wonders why must the show go on. And there are times when the speaker doesn't ask the question but the audience does. Today I will therefore try not to prompt the question, but perhaps to answer it. I think I know why this particular show must go on, and I would like to share that information with you.

DECEMBER 17

Wright brothers' first flight, 1903.

No UFOs, 1969.

Introductions:

This is a good day for flights of fancy and for airy promises. That's because today is the anniversary of the Wright brothers' first powered airplane flights at Kitty Hawk, North Carolina, when we learned how to take off into the wild blue yonder. The first takeoffs and flights by Wilbur and Orville Wright were short and not too high, and I shall endeavor to make my remarks here today follow that same pattern.

This seems to be a day to look upward. The Air Force did just that over a period of 21 years ending on this day in 1969, when they announced that, after checking over 12,000 reports of Unidentified Flying Objects, they had found no ships from outer space and no tangible threat to the security of the nation. Now if you think that was the end of tales of UFOs, you have another think coming. Legends die hard. But let me assure you that I am not here on behalf of any unidentified flying objects. I have some other objects in mind.

DECEMBER 18

Voice from space, 1958.

First commercial nuclear power plant in U.S. began, 1957.

Edwin Armstrong born, 1890.

Introductions:

For the first time, a voice from space was heard on this day in 1958. Well, it was a voice from space, but it was a very human voice sent from earth out into space and then transmitted back to us via communications satellite. It was the voice of President Eisenhower, with a Christmas message for the world. Today, I have no such elaborate hook-up to send my words to you. I hope you will forgive the absence of satellites and transmissions from outer space as I proceed on my simple way.

The first commercial nuclear power plant in the United States began supplying electricity in Shippingport, Pennsylvania, in 1957, on this day, as a sort of pre-Christmas present. Electricity, as you know, comes with two poles, a positive and a negative, and the long dispute over nuclear energy produced a lot of both, positives and negatives. We have a great tendency to be positive even when we are being negative. Today I would like to remove the electricity from the air and talk of calmer things.

Edwin Armstrong, who was born on this day, the 18th of December, in 1890 in New York City, was a great inventor in the field of radio. His greatest invention was probably what we know as FM, or frequency modulation, which eliminated the static from radio. In honor of his birthday, I will make every effort also to remove any static from my remarks to you today. Besides, we are at the Christmas season, which I trust will be static free for all.

DECEMBER 19

Thomas Paine's "The American Crisis," 1776.

Valley Forge, 1777.

Introductions:

"These are the times that try men's souls." Thomas Paine published those words on this day in 1776 in the first of his essays on "The American Crisis" in *The Pennsylvania Journal.* He went on to say, "The summer soldier and the sunshine patriot will, in this crisis, shrink from the service of his country; but he that stands it now, deserves the love and thanks of man and woman." And he added, "Those who expect to reap the blessings of freedom, must, like men, undergo the fatigue of supporting it." In all fairness, I don't think I can improve on that brief presentation of patriotism, so I won't try. Instead, I will speak to you today, in the season of peace and goodwill, about the blessings only. It is, I think, a good time to count our blessings.

A year after Thomas Paine announced "the times that try men's souls," the times got a lot worse. On this day in 1777, General George Washington led the Continental Army into winter quarters at Valley Forge, Pennsylvania. It was not exactly a winter resort. Now if the Continental Army could endure Valley Forge, even listening to me speak shouldn't be too bad.

DECEMBER 20

Pneumatic tire patented, 1892.

Electric lights on Broadway, 1880.

Introductions:

This is the day when, back in 1892, the pneumatic tire was patented. It demonstrated that an air-filled hollow surface could provide a cushioned ride. Apparently, I was selected to commemorate the anniversary by providing some hot air of my own. I will endeavor to do so without running the risk of overinflation.

In 1880, electric lights came to the theatrical section of Broadway on this day, to be followed shortly by the saying that "there's a broken heart for every light on Broadway." We do a great many more things with electric lights today than we did in 1880—and we have a great many more kinds of lights to do things with, such as laser beams. Light, we have found, is not simply a source of illumination. It also has a cutting edge. It also has the ability to burn and even to obscure. If you shine a light that's very bright, it can blind. So, if today I attempt to shed a little light on a few areas, I will try to make it neither cutting nor blinding nor burning. Let us say that it will be light, but not heavy.

DECEMBER 21

Forefathers Day.

Snow White and the Seven Dwarfs, 1937.

Introductions:

Today is Forefathers Day, the annual commemoration of the landing of the Pilgrims at Plymouth in 1620. I am reminded of the remark that the late Whitney M. Young, Jr., made. He said, "We may have come over on different ships, but we're all in the same boat now." We may have had different sets of forefathers but we're all in the same family now. And at today's family gathering I rise to talk about some matters of general interest.

Back in 1937, Walt Disney premiered a new animated cartoon feature picture called *Snow White and the Seven Dwarfs*. It was based on the famous fairy tale, but Disney, in his own inimitable way, had added some touches of his own. I do not recall that the brothers Grimm gave the seven dwarfs individual names or personalities, but Disney certainly did. There were Doc and Happy and Grumpy and Sneezy and Sleepy and Bashful and Dopey—a sort of cartoon profile of humanity. Dopey never talked—which may have made him, in the long run, less dopey than the others. I am here to talk, which may mean that I am Doc or Happy or Grumpy or one of the others. You'll have to decide that for yourselves after you hear what I have to say.

DECEMBER 22

"Nuts," 1944.

Continental Navy, 1775.

Introductions:

In the winter of 1944 in the town of Bastogne, Belgium, the Battle of the Bulge had come to a major crisis. The U.S. 101st Airborne Division was completely surrounded. On this day, its acting Commander, Major General Anthony McAuliffe, was called upon by the Germans to surrender. His answer, brief though it was, became a rallying cry for the rest of World War II. "Nuts," said General McAuliffe. The 101st Airborne held out and survived and the bulge was ultimately pushed back. Now, on the anniversary of an occasion when one simple four-letter word meant so much, I cannot in all conscience be quite that terse and concise, but as I speak here today, I shall keep in mind the lesson of General McAuliffe. You don't have to talk a long time to make your point.

On this day, in 1775, a new naval fighting force came into being as Esek Hopkins took command of the Continental fleet. The American Navy consisted of seven fighting ships. It has grown somewhat since then, and its commanders have been greatly distinguished, although Esek Hopkins turned out to be a center of controversy and was suspended from command early in 1777. On this particular day of Navy anniversary, I am delighted to have the opportunity to weigh anchor and see where my wind carries me.

DECEMBER 23

Transistor invented, 1947.

Maryland gave land for District of Columbia, 1788.

Introductions:

Today is the anniversary of the invention of one of the great keys to the modern technological revolution. On this day, in 1947, John Bardeen, Walter H. Brattain and William Shockley saw the fruition of their work at the Bell Telephone Laboratories in New Jersey when the first transistor came into being. The transistor not only made possible the miniaturization of all kinds of equipment, it produced a whole new world of electronic miracles. Its inventors won the Nobel Prize and great new industries grew up on the basis of their work. But we have not yet transistorized—or miniaturized—the basic process of human communication. It still consists of such things as a speaker standing on a rostrum and an audience gathered to listen. Perhaps some form of transistor one day will summarize a speaker's comments in one tiny capsule and deliver them to the audience like a gum drop; or conversely, perhaps the audience will be delivered to the speaker that way. But meanwhile, old-fashioned though it is, I am delighted to have this opportunity to come before you and speak my mind.

In 1788, on this day, the state of Maryland gave ten square miles of its territory to the United States for the establishment of a Federal city to be the capital of the new nation. Congress finally got around to voting to put the capital there in 1790. The pace of government in those days was rather leisurely. But times have changed. Over the past half century or so, government has become just about our largest growth industry. Since government is in large part a process of talking things over, talk also seems to have become a very large growth industry—one, however, to which I do not wish to make any undue contribution. I am here to talk to you, and I appreciate the opportunity. At the same time, I shall keep in mind the advice of the poet, James Russell Lowell, who said, "No, never say nothin' without you're compelled tu,/An' then don't say nothin' that you can be held tu."

DECEMBER 24

Christmas Eve.

Howard Hughes born, 1905.

Introductions:

I cannot think of any speech made on this day in the Western world that did not draw at least some of its inspiration from the fact that tonight is Christmas Eve. I do not speak of Christmas Eve in a sectarian religious sense but rather with the knowledge that it is a time when faith and the love of peace, however hidden during the year, are manifested once again by millions upon millions of people throughout the earth. At such a time, every speaker knows that there is an opportunity to speak to people's consciences and to people's hearts. I thank you for that opportunity.

On this day in 1905, in Houston, Texas, there was born a man whose life would fascinate and mystify the world. His name was Howard Hughes. His career raised many questions that remain unanswered. The tangle he left behind him proved once again that real life has a plot a lot more complicated than fiction. One of the things Howard Hughes managed to avoid all his life was making speeches. That wasn't too difficult, since he also avoided making public appearances. Those of us who have less of an aversion to such chores have always been puzzled by the Hughes type of shyness. I regard speaking to you here today as both a privilege and a pleasure and I thank you for your attention.

DECEMBER 25

Christmas.

Washington crossed the Delaware, 1776.

Sir Isaac Newton born, 1642.

Introductions:

On Christmas Day, the greatest speeches are those found in the books of prayer and the hearts of the people. But when one is called upon to deliver an address on this day, the temptation merely to quote from prayers is best resisted. Few of us can improve on the prayers of the ages; what we can do, and what I propose to do here today, is to move from prayer to pragmatism. We have thought today of how the world should be. Let us not meanwhile forget how the world is—and here is how I see it.

It was on Christmas night, back in 1776, that George Washington led his troops across the Delaware to attack the British the next day in New Jersey. For all the calm solemnity of Christmas day, the world is still with us on Christmas and we are still of this world, perhaps a little better for having paused to catch our breath. Most of us still have our own Delawares to cross. Perhaps, if we remember the example of Washington, we will be inspired today to get moving. My own particular Delaware is the assignment to speak here today, and so I am ready for the river. Shall we cast off?

Sir Isaac Newton, who was born on this day in 1642, in Woolsthorpe, England, was the man who discovered the law of gravity. For today, I would like to repeal the law of gravity and impose the law of levity in its place. There is a time for our hearts to be light, and I would like this to be such a time. So I speak of pleasant, happy things.

DECEMBER 26

Mao Tse-tung born, 1893.

Boxing Day.

Introductions:

Today is the birthday of Mao Tse-tung, the godfather of Chinese Communism. Even more than Lenin, Mao Tse-tung became a sort of Biblical prophet to his people. The sayings of Chairman Mao became gospel. It seems to me that we are fortunate not to have a similar national cult here. Our founding fathers are venerated for their views and deeds, but no one man has been enshrined—thank goodness. More importantly, our founding fathers didn't always agree, so we can usually find support for almost any kind of view from at least one of them. Today, however, we live in a world that the founding fathers could hardly have imagined, a world toward which Mao Tse-tung sought to raise his people. We live on the threshhold of the future as well as on the edge of the past. Today, I choose to look to the future, and I invite you to come along with me.

In Britain, the day after Christmas is known as Boxing Day; it is a holiday elsewhere simply named the Day After Christmas. The story is that it became known as Boxing Day because it was the day when presents were given in boxes to the postmen, retainers and so forth. It is nice to remember that the giving or receiving of presents need not end with Christmas. It is nice also to have a day off to recover from an excess of the Christmas festivities. On the day after Christmas, I rise to celebrate with you a new coming of peace, the end of the Christmas shopping season.

DECEMBER 27

Flushing Remonstrance, 1657.

Louis Pasteur born, 1822.

"Sweet Adeline," 1903.

Introductions:

Back in 1657, Peter Stuyvesant was the governor of the Dutch colony of New Amsterdam. He ordered the people of Flushing, Long Island, not to extend their hospitality to Quakers. On this day, the people of that town sent a petition to Governor Stuyvesant. It is known to history as The Flushing Remonstrance, and it said, "we are bounde by the law of God and men to doe goode until all men and evil to noe one." More than 300 years later, I believe the reminder is still in order. We are bound to do good to all and evil to none. The big question, of course, is how. I come here with no sensational new panaceas, but perhaps a suggestion or two.

Louis Pasteur is one of those figures in history whose name has been incorporated into the language. But pasteurization was far from his only contribution. Louis Pasteur, born on this day in 1822, in Dole, France, discovered that disease can be produced by various bacteria; thereby, he laid the groundwork for the whole modern idea of antisepsis, sterilization of surgical instruments and prevention of infections. On Louis Pasteur's birthday, I find myself concerned with devising a better kind of antisepsis against a different kind of infection. I speak here today of the problem of infection of the mind, of the hates and lunacies that afflict the world. What can we do about these?

The first public performance of a song called "Sweet Adeline" was on this very day in 1903, in New York City. "Sweet Adeline" has been the flower of the heart of every barbershop quartet ever since. It is an interesting thing that a barbershop quartet can perform the same song in the same way year after year to the delight of the crowd, but a speaker has to keep his text up with the times. There are occasions, I must admit, when I would rather be up here singing "Sweet Adeline" than pontificating. Today, however, I can reassure you. I will neither sing nor pontificate. What I have to say is not meant to be profound. I hope you will find it of interest.

DECEMBER 28

Chewing gum patented, 1869.

The great bathtub hoax, 1917.

Introductions:

Today is the anniversary of a major addition to American life and to the habits of the world. On this day, in 1869, William F. Semple of Mount Vernon, Ohio, received a patent for chewing gum. We had had gums of various kinds before then, but Mr. Semple's patent covered "the combination of rubber with other articles" for "an acceptable chewing gum." I don't know that there are any gums extant that are made with real rubber, although it sometimes seems that way, but I regard this day as the anniversary of the idea of additives in food. The virtue of chewing gum is that it is still there when you finish—which is what suggests a rubber additive. The problem is that it sticks around. The same problems can exist with that other form of chin exercise known as public speaking. It can be rubbery and elastic, stretched to meet a time frame; it is hard to get rid of for a captive audience; and it can get very sticky. I shall keep those dangers in mind as I invite you to chew over a few thoughts with me.

Back on December 28, 1917, H. L. Mencken published an article in *The New York Evening Mail* describing the origin of the great American bathtub, how it was first installed in a mansion in Cincinnati by one Adam Thompson in 1842, and how various cities and states passed laws to regulate or tax it. The article was a pure hoax; Mencken never intended it to be taken seriously, but it was. To this day, you can probably find articles relaying as fact the items of Mencken's imagination. The great American bathtub hoax reminds us all to be skeptical. I hope that, while you will take me seriously in my remarks here today, you will nevertheless remember that saying something is so does not make it so.

DECEMBER 29

Texas joined U.S., 1845.

Battle of Wounded Knee, 1890.

Introductions:

The history books say that on this day, in 1845, Texas joined the United States as the 28th state. Considering the size, riches and political wiliness of the Lone Star State, people have, from time to time, reversed the phrase and said that the U.S. joined Texas. In any case, the combination proved to be a rewarding and stimulating one. On this anniversary, I hope that our coming together here today will also prove productive. Or, at the least, like Texas, provide some entertaining moments.

What has been described as the battle of Wounded Knee occurred on this day, in 1890. When it was over, 25 U.S. cavalrymen were dead, and so were about 150 Indians. Later it was referred to as the massacre at Wounded Knee. It was the last major engagement between the Indians and the Army, and it aroused the conscience of Americans then and even more later on. Perspectives being what they are, it is understandable that what one view sees as a battle, another view sees as a massacre. Our perspectives sometimes vary with our distance from an event, sometimes with our sympathies. The important thing always, of course, is to recognize that we do speak from perspective and not from absolute divine revelation. It is in that spirit, that awareness that I have no patent on total truth, that I rise to give you my view here today.

DECEMBER 30

Gadsden Purchase, 1853.

Kiss Me, Kate opened, 1948.

Frank Sinatra had them swooning, 1942.

Introductions:

Now that we are mercifully past the Christmas shopping season, I find we are assembled on the anniversary of one of our better shopping expeditions. On this day in 1853, James Gadsden, on behalf of the U.S., signed an agreement with the Republic of Mexico whereby we purchased the southern portion of Arizona and New Mexico for $10 million. That was by no means our biggest land purchase. There was the Louisiana Territory and there would be Alaska and, much later, that tropical archipelago, the Virgin Islands. It is interesting how much of what is now the United States was purchased from other nations. We may not have the world's best record around the conference table, but we seem to do very well over the counter. America's greatest success has been in the peaceful marketplace—and not the least of that success has been in the marketplace of ideas. In the marketplace of ideas, you put your concepts on the counter and take your chances that they will be bought. So here I go, putting an idea or two on the counter.

On December 30, 1948, William Shakespeare found some new colleagues named Bella and Samuel Spewack and Cole Porter, when *Kiss Me Kate*, freely adapted from *The Taming of the Shrew*, opened on Broadway. In 1948, this essentially anti-feminist classic became a bigger hit than ever, thanks in large measure, of course, to Cole Porter's music. Looking back on it, and also looking back on the year we are about to end, I find myself wondering what would happen if *Kiss Me Kate* burst upon the scene as a brand new Broadway presentation for the first time today. How much have our concepts changed since 1948? What is new in the relationships between men and women, in the views of human rights, even in the idea of what is funny? History tells us that all these things evolve and change, that they operate in a sort of cycle, but it is always hard to determine where in that historic cycle we may be at the particular moment. Today, I rise to try to get our bearings, to try to figure out where we are in the field of human relations and human rights.

Not all the events which are chronicled in history deal with war or great political movements or revolutionary new inventions. One of the entries for this day is the notation that in 1942, Frank Sinatra began a singing engagement at the Paramount Theatre. The police reserves in New York City had to be called out to cope with the public swooning, crush and enthusiasm of the hordes of teen-age girls who flocked to see and hear their idol. The offspring of that generation did the same thing for another generation of singers, but with considerably more abandon, in the Woodstock era, and it seems to happen regularly in the preservation of the species. Each time also seems, to its elders, to be worse than the times before. I find myself wondering how the next generation will report the year we are now concluding. Let me make a few guesses.

DECEMBER 31

New Year's Eve.

Edison's lamp demonstrated, 1879.

Introductions:

Well, we made it. We got ourselves through another year and have arrived at its last rites. Tomorrow we will look toward the future. Today, we look back to see how far we have come and what the year meant to us. I will not presume to intrude upon anyone's personal memories, but I find a very easy way to measure what the year has brought. All it involves is thinking back to last year at this same time. Do you remember last year at this time, and the shape we were in? Let me refresh your memory.

They say that moths flock to the light. Not only moths. Human beings too. That's why crowds go to the Great White Way. And I guess it was why, on this last day of the year, in 1879, hordes of people crowded special trains to get to Menlo Park, New Jersey, to see the first public demonstrations of Thomas A.

Edison's new incandescent electric light. I suppose that at this time of year, when we have fewer hours of daylight, the fascination with artificial light is at its height. "Give the people light," says the saying, "and they will find their way." Today, though neither an Edison nor a prophet who can stop the sun, I shall endeavor in my own small way to generate a bit of light, which I hope will brighten a portion of our path.

Volume 4

The
Special
Occasion
Book

Introduction

For each of the occasions covered in the following pages, there are a number of paragraphs which can either be used in sequence as the outline of a full speech or as separate introductions for a speech on the subject.

The paragraphs are all of a general nature. That is, they deal with the particular subject in general terms, leading into the special information or acknowledgments the speaker wishes to include.

Some of the subjects have a certain degree of overlap. If you are making a speech of acceptance for a nomination, you may find something suitable not only under the category Acceptance, but also under Acknowledgment or Responses.

Please be sure, therefore; to consult the list of subjects that follows to locate all the categories that may apply to what you want to talk about.

List of Subjects

Acceptance speeches
Acknowledgment of honor
Appreciation
Armed Forces Day
Armistice Day
Artist's unveiling
Award presentation
Bachelor party
Birthday
Bon voyage
Candidacy announcement
Christmas party
Columbus Day
Commencement
Cornerstone laying
Easter
Election Day
Father's Day
Fund-raising
Funeral
Graduation
Greeting
Groundbreaking
Inauguration
Independence Day
Induction of new members
Introduction
Invocation
Jubilee

Keynote address
Labor Day
Lincoln's Birthday
Long service
Membership meeting
Memorial ceremony
Memorial Day
Moderator
Mother's Day
New Year's Party
Opening
Political campaign
Promotional event
Recruitment
Responses
Retirement
Reunion
St. Patrick's Day
Sales meeting
Self-introduction
Statement of position
Testimonial
Toastmaster
Veterans Day
Washington's Birthday
Wedding
Wedding anniversary
Welcome

ACCEPTANCE (of gift, nomination, etc.)

(See also Acknowledgment; Responses)

I am delighted to be in the presence of so blessed a company. We have it on very good authority that it is more blessed to give than to receive. Since you have been kind enough to give so notably, and to make me the recipient of your favorable attention, you must be greatly blessed for your generosity. I can only regard myself as being honored to be the subject of your generous attention.

They tell the story of the graduation at which the mothers of several of the students were sitting together, when a third student was singled out to be saluted as the finest all-around member of the class. The speaker recited the student's feats of scholarship, deeds on the athletic field and notable achievements as the leader of the class. As the trophy was being presented, one of the mothers leaned over to another—neither being the parent of the student being honored—and whispered, "That's all very fine, but what do you think is the real reason that they chose him?" Only the most immodest of recipients of an honor is free from wondering that same thing.

Your recital of the reasons for this occasion has been flattering and convincing, but nevertheless, in all modesty, I recall the comment often made about feats of legerdemain: "There's less to this than meets the eye." Your citation is most kind, and I would be happy to accept it as total truth. But I must add that in reciting my qualifications you have given me a goal for the future and for that in particular I thank you.

Through the centuries, people have been selected for various kinds of designations on many different standards of judgment. Some are based on the drawing of straws, some based on purity, even virginity, some the result of knowing the right people—or the wrong people. We have all seen the choices that emerged from smoke-filled rooms, or draft lottery fishbowls or a sort of game of blind man's buff. I prefer, of course, to regard your choice of me here today as either divine inspiration or the reward of virtue.

The fact is that some things come to the man who waits, some things come to the man who seeks them, some things seek the man. If a person of political bent in New York City goes on a trip to what has been called the political Three I League—Ireland, Italy and Israel—it is not unlikely that said person is planning to run for office in New York City. If a manufacturer subtly scents his product to attract the ladies, the chances are that it is a case of the reward seeking the customer. And if the gift comes in the form of a a Trojan Horse, we must beware of those bearing the gift. The late Groucho Marx, not the most gracious recipient of honors, once said "I don't want to belong to any club that will accept me as a member." Suffice it for me to say, then, that I am not here as a product of any political Three I league, nor as the result of the blandishments of a well wrapped package, nor as a sucker falling for a Trojan Horse and finally and most important, I am perfectly content to be accepted by this club and present company.

I have looked the gift horse you have presented me straight in the mouth, and I pronounce it a thoroughbred. I thank you for your kindness. I appreciate the honor you have paid me and the graciousness which accompanied it.

Thank you very much.

ACKNOWLEDGMENT (of honor)

(See also Acceptance, Responses)

On occasions such as this, I am reminded of the old story about the man who was being tarred and feathered and ridden out of town on a rail. He was asked how he felt about it and he said, "If it wasn't for the honor of the thing, I'd just as soon walk." I certainly don't feel that I am being tarred and feathered or ridden out of town on a rail here today, but I must tell you that I am walking—on air. The honor you have done me is one I shall long remember and prize.

It was Yogi Berra, you may recall, who, upon being honored at a special night in the baseball park for his distinguished career, responded to the acclaim and tribute of the crowd by saying, "I want to thank everybody who made this night necessary," or words to that effect. I will not presume to define this happy occasion as necessary, but it is most certainly one which I find memorable and rewarding.

There are some who react to honors in the same way as the psychologist who, upon being greeted in most friendly fashion by a longtime colleague, started muttering to himself, "What did he mean by that?" I will not search for ulterior motives for the way you have received me here today. If my presence is in any way supportive of the objectives and/or needs of this group, suffice it to say that it is not a coincidence nor an ulterior aspect. If my participation in this event aids the cause, I can only say I am grateful for the opportunity.

There is a saying—or should be—that the greater the gratitude, the shorter the speech of thanks. If that were the rule on this occasion, I must confess I would by now have completed my remarks, because words cannot convey the fullness of my appreciation. So I shall not take up your time with a long litany. Suffice it to say that I shall endeavor to justify your vote of confidence.

In listening to the remarks preceding mine, I sometimes had difficulty in realizing that some of the references were to me. You have portrayed me, I think, with all the warts removed and the rough edges smoothed over. It is a portrait that not only touched me—I fear it retouched me. That, as much as the honor itself, is what makes this occasion so moving for me.

Robert Benchley unsed to tell the story of the temperamental actress who was complimented by a child performer on the set in the studio. "My," said the child, "you look so beautiful today." The actress said, ungraciously, "What am I supposed to say to that?" And the child, as sweet as ever, said. "You're supposed to say thank you." Nobody needs to prompt me on that line. Thank you—very much.

APPRECIATION (of contribution, service etc.)

There are three basic reasons that bring people together—other, of course, than the reasons that bring two people together. In larger groups, the three reasons that bring people together are (1) To take note of something that has already happened—either to celebrate it or to deplore it, but in any case to do so en masse; (2) to take note of something that hasn't happened—either to try to make it happen or to prevent it from happening, and (3) to salute someone we hold responsible for any of the above. And that is the nicest kind of get-together. It is why this occasion today is so special.

Celebrating events can be a very joyous time, but it is always even better when we celebrate the people who are responsible for the events. Today, then, is a doubly gratifying occasion because we are saluting someone as well as something. We are saying thanks and well done and congratulations. Our presence here is the beginning of that salute. We are here not because we *had* to come but because we wanted to come, and we wanted to come because we wanted to be part of this occasion.

For many years, at historic Cooper Union in New York, there was a series of free lectures, followed by questions from the audience. Every night, no matter what the subject, the same little man would show up and sit listening closely while the lecturer talked; and when the question period came, every night, the same little man would raise his hand to ask a question. No matter what the subject, the question he asked was always the same. "What you have spoken about tonight," he would say, "is it good or bad for the workingman?" There was no doubt in his mind of what life's goal should be. And I suspect, from the wonderful record of the person we are honoring here tonight, that there is something of that same single-minded attention to a single all-important goal too.

We are here to honor one who has made a success and been an inspiration in a chosen field. Eddie Cantor once said that it takes twenty years to make an overnight success, and Nathan Bedford Forrest, the Confederate general, said it was simply a matter of "git thar fustest with the mostest men." Perhaps Booker T. Washington was wiser still when he wrote that "success is to be measured not so much by the position that one has reached in life as by the obstacles which he has overcome while trying to succeed." Success, indeed, comes in different forms at different times for different people. But it is sweetest when it comes with the approval, the applause, the rewards freely given by the people. And that is why we are here today.

In the spirit of the occasion, I am reminded of the story of the professional toastmaster who came to preside over the ceremonies honoring a local celebrity, and was given a piece of paper with the honoree's name on it so that he could pretend to know the man. Well, as luck would have it, the little slip of paper fell through a crack on the rostrum just as the guest toastmaster arose to introduce the guest of honor. Without a moment's hesitation, the toastmaster said, "And now it is a pleasure to present our guest of honor, a man whose name is on everyone's lips, just as his accomplishments are on our minds today."

And so today, I ask you to join me in honoring what's-his-name.

ARMED FORCES DAY

Rudyard Kipling wrote a salute to the professional soldier, many years ago, which deserves to be recalled as we observe Armed Forces Day. Kipling wrote of the British enlisted man, better know as Tommy Atkins, and he wrote in an era of simpler times—no airplanes, no tanks, no nuclear bombs. But what he said is, I believe, as true today as it was then. He wrote: "For it's Tommy this, an' Tommy that, an' 'Chuck him out, the brute!'/But it's 'Saviour of 'is country' when the guns begin to shoot."

There are great divisions of opinion in peacetime about the level of armament, the size of the armed forces, the pay and perquisites of the soldiers and sailors and air force and marines. But should the nation be attacked, our priorities, of course, would be rearranged and there would be no doubt that the armed forces would be at the top of the list. Wouldn't it be wonderful if we could achieve that form of patriotic pride without having somebody shooting at us?

Our armed forces are unique in the world—unique in their tradition, unique in their relationship to the government and the people. They are the lineal descendants of the citizen soldiers and sailors who fought the American Revolutionary War, led by a Virginia planter named George Washington. The officers of our armed forces come through great educational institutions to which they are admitted on merit, not by privilege of birth. And the command of our armed forces rests at the top with the Chief Executive elected by the people. The funds that maintain the armed forces are voted annually by the people's representatives in Congress assembled. We are not a nation where the armed forces are one camp and the rest of the nation another. It is not a case of "them" and "us." They are part of us.

The armed forces are like insurance. No matter how much you have, some salesman insists you need more; and, on the other hand, no matter how much you have, if the occasion comes to use it, you always need more. That is why, whichever side of that equation you happen to find yourself on, it is comforting on Armed Forces Day to salute the conscientious men and women who represent our first line of insurance.

What is the secret weapon of our armed forces? Or perhaps it might be wiser to ask, what is the invisible weapon shared by our Army; Navy, Air Force and Marines? I am not giving away any deep dark military secret when I answer that question, because the invisible weapon of our armed forces is a very simple one. It is nothing more than the confidence of the free citizens of a free nation. It is the fact that our armed forces are the servants, not the masters of the nation. It is the fact that we recognize the soldier, the sailor, the air force man or woman and the marine as people, citizens, not as peculiar animals. On Armed Forces Day, it is fine to take pride in the machinery of defense, but I salute, first and foremost, the *people* of the armed forces.

I have a particular suggestion to make on Armed Forces Day to the people of the armed forces. Today I suggest we extend to them a special courtesy. I propose that we salute them—and they don't have to salute back.

ARMISTICE DAY

(see also Veterans Day)

Some of you may remember a headline which appeared on a momentous day years ago in the *New York Daily News* and was reproduced elsewhere because it said something so profound and yet so succinct. It came at the end of World War II, and it read, very simply, "Peace Breaks Out." Not simply peace, but rather peace breaks out. It was particularly appropriate because peace is precisely that—a break-out, or a break-away, from the grinding horror of war. On Armistice Day, which recalls the cease-fire in what until then had been the most terrible war of all time, World War I in 1918, we remember all those occasions when the shooting stopped and the bombing ceased.

Wars sometimes end with a whimper, sometimes with a bang; sometimes with an unconditional surrender, sometimes with a cease-fire painfully negotiated over a bargaining table. The important thing about Armistice Day is not how the fighting ended, but simply the fact that it ended at all. We have yet to see the time when an armistice proved total and eternal. And when we celebrate Armistice Day we always express the hope that no further anniversaries of this kind will be created—or that, if fighting rages anywhere as we meet, it too will reach an Armistice Day of its own.

Benjamin Franklin, at the end of the American Revolution, was a wise old man who had labored long and hard in the struggle for our nation's independence. He wrote, in 1783, that "There never was a good war or a bad peace." I don't believe he meant totally to condemn the violent struggle for independence, in which he himself had played so great a role. What he meant, I believe, was that at its best war is nothing more than a necessary evil, and that mankind was meant to live in peace. Armistice Day reminds us that man at peace is better than man at war, that the silencing of the guns of war is the true victory.

On this day, we remember—whether from having taken part or from the history books—the struggle which was carried on to preserve our world. We remember the joy of finding the nation at peace. We remember the people who made that possible. And we remember, also, how brief, in the long march of time, was the particular Armistice we commemorate today. Less than 25 years after Armistice Day 1918, the world was aflame again with weapons of destruction far more terrible than those of World War I. The dictionary defines an armistice as a temporary suspension of hostilities by mutual agreement.

Perhaps one day, instead of celebrating an Armistice Day, we shall truly celebrate a Peace Day, when the suspension of hostilities is permanent, not merely temporary.

As yet, nobody has found a way to arrange a lasting armistice in the cold war, the ideological conflict that underlies so much of the politics of the world today. As yet, nobody has found a way to turn all the world's swords into plowshares. Armistice Day is a day which reminds us not to give up trying, not to give up that fight—the fight for lasting peace.

"The mere absence of war," said John F. Kennedy in the year he died, "is not peace." And John Milton, hundreds of years earlier, gave us the true meaning, the true significance of Armistice Day when he wrote, "Peace hath her victories, no less renowned than war." And so today we celebrate the best of victories.

ARTIST'S UNVEILING

There is probably no torture ever devised by the ingenious mind of man more excruciating than what a painter or a sculptor is subjected to when he does his work out in the open. An idler passes and asks, "What are you making?" The artist is distracted; if he tries to reply, he will probably be further distracted by the reaction of the questioner who, as often as not, will say something like "What do you want to do that for?" or "It sure doesn't look like any such thing." The torment of prejudgment by amateurs has driven many an artist bonkers. It is bad enough to go through the anxiety of revealing a completed work to an uncertain public, without having that public looking over your shoulder and breathing down your neck while the work is being done.

It has always seemed to me, therefore, that the artist whose talent was reserved for himself or herself alone was in many ways the wisest. He or she alone knows to the full what the creation was conceived to be and what has gone into it. To share that finished product with the world is—in some cases—an act of courage and in every case an act of generosity. For, no matter what the material rewards for a work of art, that work of art is essentially a giving of oneself, a personal confession by the artist, a deliberate invitation to the judgment of strangers.

We here today are not merely spectators. Art essentially is a form of expression, a type of communication, a means of establishing a rapport between artist and audience. Some people are artists with words, some with clay, some with cameras, some with paint, some with rock or mortar or with seeds and soil. All, no matter what the medium, come to that point when what they have done is brought to the moment of harvest, of fruition, of unveiling.

The time has now come to draw back the curtain, to unwrap the package, to exchange the joy of anticipation for the pleasure of perception. Some things, such as a hooded harbinger of hate, are best left veiled because when they are unmasked they turn out to be far less than meets the eye. But a work of art calls for the public eye. Its unveiling is, in one sense, the beginning of its life. It is in that spirit, with that feeling of welcoming a new addition to the vast family of the arts, that we now open this work to public view.

I believe it was Sam Goldwyn, years ago, who said he had found the perfect formula for commenting on a new work without necessarily committing himself. He would simply say, "What a picture!"—leaving the interpretation to the imagination of whoever heard him. I remind you, however, that what you say about a work of art is not necessarily as important as what you take away with you after seeing that work. Art does not grow on people; people grow on art. With that thought in mind, I am happy to declare this exhibit open.

AWARD PRESENTATION

Many years ago, there was a summer camp for boys which found itself unhappy with the competitive aspects of camp activity. Awards were given for proficiency in various sports, and inevitably, some campers who were natural athletes won batches of medals and others won none at all. The director of the camp tried to solve this by creating new categories for awards—skills in various arts and crafts, for example. But even this failed to achieve his goal of finding at least one award for every camper. Finally, for every age group, he established a new medal. It was called the Improvement Medal, and it always went to a camper who had no other claim to glory. The result, infortunately, was not quite what the camp director had intended. The winner of the improvement medal, and the whole camp, knew that he had been singled out as the saddest apple in the basket. His award was in fact a consolation prize that didn't console at all, but instead aggravated the injury. Today, I am happy to say we are presenting no improvement medals, no backhanded consolation prizes.

Today's award presentation is very simple in its concept. It is meant to be, and is, formal recognition of excellence, as determined by a process of selection that reflects the accomplishments of outstanding people. I want to make that clear, because we live in a time of so many award presentations that one can sometimes be entitled to a healthy dose of skepticism about the whole idea. I recall, for example, the story of the famous writer who was called upon one day by the head of a literary organization, Mr. Jones. Said Mr. Jones, "Your work is so distinguished, your influence on the literature of our times has been so profound, and your reputation throughout the world is so unique, that our society has decided to have you as our guest of honor and award winner at our annual dinner two months from today." The great writer thanked him but said he would be unable to attend on that day since he would be out of the country. "In that case," said Mr. Jones, "do you know any other writer that might fit the qualifications and be able to attend?" Suffice it to say that today's awards were not determined by the honoree's ability to attend.

Virtue may be its own reward, but we believe that virtuosity deserves some more concrete and tangible form of recognition. From the time of the laurel wreath awarded by the ancient Greeks, we have recognized that in every field of endeavor some people are outstanding in their particular work, and some people are outstanding simply as people. Very often, in saluting these outstanding people, we do more than merely honor them; we help them to set standards for emulation from this time forth.

When the Academy of Motion Picture Arts and Sciences began giving out what came to be known as the Oscars, they were relatively unique. Since then we have had Emmies and Edgars and so many Halls of Fame that fame itself has become commonplace. But there is nothing commonplace about the people we are honoring today or about the reasons for their selection. So let me get down to particulars.

BACHELOR PARTY

We are here tonight in honor of what Benjamin Franklin called "an incomplete animal." Yes, that was the way old Ben defined a bachelor. "A single man," Franklin wrote, "has not nearly the value he would have in state of union. He is an incomplete animal. He resembles the odd half of a pair of scissors." Now it is rather unusual for half a pair of scissors to spend the night cutting a few capers, but that is the agenda for tonight.

It is traditional to have a very special party on the night before the end of bachelorhood. It is traditional in the same way as making sure that the condemned man eats a hearty meal. The purpose in both cases is to make sure the man of the hour knows what pleasures he is about to give up.

You've heard of trial by fire and trial by ordeal. Tonight it's a case of trial by association. Anybody who brings out this kind of crowd is clearly going to have to change his ways. But that change, of course, won't come until tomorrow. And meanwhile, the night is young.

Years ago, tradition had us believing that before the wedding, the groom spent his last waking hours carousing and the bride spent them blushing. Actually, both of them—if they are like most normal human beings—are probably wondering what they have gotten themselves into and worrying about it. The bachelor party, if the truth be known, has, as its true purpose, the idea of getting the future bridegroom's mind away from the worries of the morrow. We call it one last fling, but the flinging is usually more on the part of the people who are throwing the party. And the future groom is the party of the first part.

So tonight I call upon all and sundry present to join in saluting one who is doing his best to bring a small truce to that most ancient of conflicts—the war between the sexes. One small segment of that war, you see, is due to end tomorrow in mutual surrender. But in the meantime, the instructions are simple—come out swinging.

Tonight we are celebrating what Ralph Waldo Emerson and Montaigne saw as a very contradictory institution, the state of matrimony. Matrimony is what those outside want to get into and those inside want to get out of. For our guest of honor tonight, I commend the wisdom of Emerson and Montaigne. You are about to enter a new state, which I am reliably informed is the result of a temporary madness called love. I refer to this as a temporary madness because I am told that it rarely lasts more than 50 or 60 years. Or is it that it just seems like 50 or 60 years?

On the night before the wedding, a man and his friends are soon partied. Eat, drink and be merry—not necessarily in that order—for tomorrow is somebody else's turn. And remember the wise words of that ancient seer who said, "Keep your eyes wide open before marriage and half shut afterwards."

BIRTHDAY

Mark Twain, who sometimes had a rather sombre view of life, said that we rejoice at a birth (and grieve at a funeral) because "we are not the person involved." Others have noted that, in the course of a person's life, he or she is always being congratulated for the one thing he or she did not do for themselves—a birthday. But that is not totally correct. For a birthday is also celebrated as a feat of survival, and that each of us can view as a very individual accomplishment.

Thoroughbred horses at the racetrack all grow a year older on January 1; they don't have individual birthdays. For people, birthdays have sometimes been far more complicated than they are today. George Washington, for example, was born on February 11, 1732. In his early manhood, the old-style calendar was abandoned, making his birthday February 22. For most of his life, however, he continued to observe the 11th as his birthday. Then February 22 became the accepted date, for about a century and a half, until somebody got the bright idea of celebrating Washington's Birthday on a Monday to give us all a three-day weekend. For most of us ordinary people nowadays, however, the day we were born is the birthday we keep for the rest of our lives. Sometimes we are tempted to try to fuzzy up the exact year, but we don't generally fiddle around with the day of the month. And there are always people around, of course, to remind us what day it is. Sometimes they are friends; sometimes they are enemies. You'll have to decide which is which or who is who today.

On the average, about 11 million people have their birthdays on any given day of the year; if they decided to celebrate together, they'd have to have a birthday *country*. We prefer, of course, to concentrate on a somewhat smaller and more modest constituency. Rather than wishing happy birthday to 11 million people, we have decided to single out our own birthday star.

No matter how we celebrate birthdays today, it is better than it used to be. You may recall the stories of the aborigines who, when adults reach a certain age, push them out in the jungle to stop cluttering up the village. You may also recall the savage initiation ceremonies for younger individuals at various ages, the tests of strength and so forth. Now all we require is that you keep smiling on your birthday while you endure the same old jokes about your age and the reminders that you're not as young as you used to be.

It is appropriate to remind this gathering, on this day, of the words of *I Timothy 6:7*, "For we brought nothing into this world, and it is certain we can carry nothing out." Birthday parties are designed to take care of that gap between coming into the world with nothing and going out the same way. In between, your friends and admirers take pleasure in loading you down—or is it loading you up—with expressions of their esteem.

On some birthdays, it has been said, you take the day off; on others, you take a year off. As far as your friends are concerned, it's okay either way.

BON VOYAGE

In the ancient days of mankind, travel was usually a hard necessity, not a pleasure. Instead of wishing the traveler bon voyage, the people who stayed behind were more likely to be the ones who forced the traveler to move on. But time have changed. Today we speed the parting guest or the prodigal son with good wishes and good cheer.

A bon voyage occasion, however, is one of the more ambiguous kinds of tribute. We wish bon voyage to people we like, in the hope that they will enjoy the trip; but we also wish bon voyage to people that we are glad to see the last of for a while. So, just as travel itself carries the excitement of uncertainty about what the traveler will find, a bon voyage party carries the uncertainty of the motive. Is the purpose of wishing a bon voyage to make sure the traveler actually leaves?

In the old days, wishing a traveler bon voyage was a very serious expression of hope and good will in a truly uncertain world. Caravans were apt to be raided, ships sailed sometimes unknown and always dangerous seas; wherever you were going, the natives were apt to be unfriendly. The people who set out on such trips faced, at the very least, sudden storms and lots of surprises.

Things are different for the modern traveler than in the old days—or are they? Today's tourist may not have to worry about sudden storms; instead he has to worry about sudden transport strikes or overbookings. Instead of possibly losing his way, he has to beware of losing his luggage. So travelers now, as in the past, go with those age-old good wishes—safe journey and happy return!

Probably no nations have been more travel-minded or mobile than the English-speaking ones. All the modern means of transportation except the railroad virtually began in the United States—the airplane, the steamship, the automobile. We commute greater distances to work—or to play—than any other people since the dawn of time; and our British cousins, in their time, traveled and ruled the four corners of the earth. But when we wish the traveler well, we use a French term, not our own English language. That is because the language of international relations and diplomacy, until our own time, was French. When important people were traveling to or from foreign climes, they received good wishes in the language of diplomacy—the French bon voyage.

But today, bon voyage crosses all language barriers. It isn't just French. It is universal.

Somehow, it sounds more festive than the simple "have a good trip" and it is considerably shorter than that ancient and lovely Irish blessing, "May the wind be at your back and the sun light the paths ahead."

No matter how you say it, the message is the same: "A safe and happy journey be yours." Sometimes we urge the traveler not to eat the food and not to drink the water, but of course that too is part of our expressing the hope that nothing will interfere with an enjoyable trip. In other words, "Bon voyage!"

CANDIDACY ANNOUNCEMENT

The act of running for office in the United States is one that is surrounded with symbolism. You throw your hat in the ring, or you dicker in "a smoke-filled room" or you coyly let yourself be "drafted" in response to popular demand. All the terminology—and the accompanying circumstances—cannot alter the basic single fact that a candidate, in the cold language of the dictionary, is one who seeks or aspires to be elected or appointed to an office, or is put forward by others. What not too many candidates are willing to recognize is that the word itself—candidate—means "clothed in white," from the old Roman custom of wearing a white toga to signify the seeking of office.

I am fresh out of white togas, so I should like to signify my quest for popular support by simply announcing that I am a candidate for the office of —————. I am neither a "favorite son" candidate nor a "dark horse" candidate nor, at this early juncture, "the people's choice." I submit myself to popular consideration in great confidence that, when they come to choose, I will indeed be the people's choice. But that comes at the end, the climax of the campaign, not at this early juncture.

A candidate, in this country, runs for election; in England, he stands for election. Either way, he runs or stands on a platform. A platform is designed to let you know how the candidate proposes to use the office he wants you to choose him for. In announcing my candidacy here today, I assume the immediate obligation to make public, before the election, how I propose to carry out the duties of the office for which I am running, and why I believe my candidacy deserves your support. In the course of this effort, I propose to talk about positive principles and programs. I remember, and I am sure you do too, the story of the candidate who swore that he wouldn't base his campaign on his opponents' shortcomings but instead would try to make his case on his own. Well, I am not going to maintain that I am that rarest of species, the candidate wholly without shortcomings. I am sure that I need not dwell on them because others will. So I will confine myself to trying to acquaint you with my positive qualifications, which I think—and trust—you will find outweigh by far any other considerations.

It has been written that some people pretend to see the light when what has really happened is that they felt the heat. My candidacy is neither the result of my suddenly seeing the light or suddenly feeling the heat. It is neither a sudden decision nor one undertaken recklessly. Nor is it the other type of candidacy—the one prompted by the candidate's spouse's desire to get said mate out of the house. I am committed to this candidacy simply because I think I can do the job and I would like to do it. I don't believe in drafted candidates. Someone who has to be coaxed or cajoled into running simply doesn't bring to the office the enthusiasm and the confidence which any office requires if it is to be done well. So I am here with my own enthusiasm, my own confidence and my own candidacy, eager for the campaign and ready for action.

CHRISTMAS PARTY

One of the things which makes a Christmas party so delightful is that it is everybody's party. Most other parties are in honor of some friend, relative or colleague. We celebrate and salute the guest of honor's great new achievement or anniversary. We come together to congratulate a particular individual for a notable accomplishment. But Christmas is something else.

Christmas, of course, *is* a birthday party, but it is an idea, a symbol and above all a spirit of fellowship. At the same time, a Christmas party has another unique attribute we cannot ignore. Christmas is a gift-giving occasion—and gift-giving and gift-receiving are times when most of us have more reason than elsewhere in the year to feel happy, to feel friendly toward our companions, perhaps even to be wallowing in the milk of human kindness.

I think it is only fitting to remember that Saint Nicholas, who is more celebrated at this time of year as Santa Claus, is not only the patron saint of children and of sailors but also of pawnbrokers, suggesting that it is all right to go into hock at Christmastime. But prudence argues as strongly against that course as against overestimating one's capacity for Yuletide wassail. Think before you drink and take stock before you hock.

A great many of the things we accept as ancient Christmas customs are a lot younger than we think. It was little more than a hundred years ago that Americans began sending each other Christmas cards. The night before Christmas was a fine time for the kids long before Clement Moore wrote a poem about it in 1822. The Christmas tree, however, is a good deal older, and so is the Christmas party. George Washington won a great victory over the British in the American Revolution when he surprised Hessian troops who were sleeping off their Christmas revelry.

Christmas, of course, is the time for strange gifts, and the day after Christmas is the time for many happy returns. As far as commercial enterprise is concerned, Christmas starts around Thanksgiving—or seems to —and when it finally ends on Twelfth Night the milk of human kindness is apt to have become a bit skimmed. So we must cherish the high points and weather the low ones. That is the Christmas spirit.

I can't think of a more thankless task for a speaker than trying to talk when the audience either wants to get down to exchanging gifts, toasting the season or singing carols. Even Santa Claus is not expected to make a speech at Christmastime. All he does is say what I am about to end my remarks saying: "Merry Christmas to all, and to all a good night!"

To this I can only add the sage advice an old friend gave me many Christmases ago. "Don't shoot off your mouth, because you can never tell whether you're loaded."

COLUMBUS DAY

On a Monday close to October 12, Americans celebrate the discovery of the New World by Christopher Columbus. There are those who contend that the Norse Vikings or Irish missionaries or the ten lost tribes of Israel somehow discovered America before Columbus did; but the fact is that Columbus alone got back to the old world and spread the word. He also gave history something good to say about 1492, which otherwise would have been remembered mainly for the flowering of the Spanish Inquisition.

In recent years, Columbus Day has become a very special day of celebration for those of Italian derivation, because Columbus, although in the service of Spain, was an Italian himself. Just as St. Patrick's Day has a very special meaning for those of Irish heritage, Columbus Day is an Italian-American tradition. But it may surprise you to know that a man named William Mooney founded an organization called the Society of St. Tammany that had what is generally regarded as the first American celebration of Columbus Day back in 1792. Later on, of course, Tammany turned to other things and this celebration became more closely involved with an organization aptly named the Knights of Columbus. Columbus Day owes a great deal to the Knights.

It is one of the sardonic jests of history that the world Christopher Columbus discovered does not bear his name, but rather is named after Amerigo Vespucci. The basis for calling it America was that Vespucci claimed to have been the first to reach the continental mainland—in 1497 to be exact—about eight days before Sebastian Cabot, another Italian who was in the service of the English crown. No matter who deserves the credit, he was an Italian. But if Vespucci got the continent, history has certainly made it up to Christopher Columbus. And how many cities in the U.S. are named Vespucci?

The celebration of Columbus Day seems to me to be far more significant for what Columbus symbolized than for how the credit was distributed for his discovery. He refused to be diverted from his goal by the conventional wisdom of his time. He was gifted with courage, and with the patience to stick to the course he had laid out for himself. "Every ship that comes to America," Ralph Waldo Emerson wrote, "got its chart from Columbus." I go further. It seems to me that every American, everyone who is the beneficiary of the great discovery of Christopher Columbus, got his chart—or hers—from that dedicated sailor.

In the words of Joaquin Miller's memorable poem "What shall we do when hope is gone?/The words leapt like a leaping sword/"Sail on! sail on! sail on! and on!" There are always new dimensions to be explored, new worlds to be discovered. On Columbus Day, we honor his memory by remembering to sail on, with our eyes alert for the far horizon.

COMMENCEMENT

(See also Graduation)

A commencement address is usually delivered by someone who commenced a long long time ago, and whose audience waits hopefully for the finish. It is supposed to offer sage words of wisdom or inspiration to young people about to commence their next phase of mortal existence. With the shape the world keeps getting itself into, however, the thought keeps occurring that the new generation might do best to work up its own helping of conventional wisdom.

But, despite the tremendous advances in education, and the genetic improvements which make this, I truly believe, the finest generation yet, I must carry to you the perhaps sad word that you are all doomed to have more schooling—this time in the school of experience. They used to call it the school of hard knocks, but it doesn't always live up to that billing these days. As a graduate of the school of experience, I am called upon here and now to welcome the commencement of a new class.

Although what we celebrate here is a commencement, it is also an ending, the climax of years of education. Some of you may feel a real glow of accomplishment, some an equally satisfying sense of relief, and some of you may even be a bit uncertain about what lies ahead. That all goes with the territory. I am a good bit older, and I must confess that I begin each day much that same way—remembering good things from the past, relieved to have gotten through some of the not-so-good things and wondering what's coming next.

That legendary old baseball pitcher, Satchel Paige, once counseled his public in these words: "Don't look back; someone might be gaining on you." I would like to amend that advice somewhat. Don't be afraid to look back; but try to look ahead with the advantage of past experience. That, rather than to see whether anybody is gaining on you, is why man was designed to be able to turn around and look in any direction.

Above all, as you move on, remember that human attribute: the ability to turn around and look in any direction. Blinders are for horses, not for people. If education has any single goal, it is to encourage people to know how to ask questions and to know how to go about getting the answers. It is not enough in life to be a listener, a passive member of the audience. It is not enough to look straight ahead and never look around. It is not enough to breathe a sigh and figure that your learning days are over. The lucky individual is the individual who never stops learning until he or she stops breathing.

This is your Commencement Day. And it is only fitting to say to you, as we salute you for your accomplishments, that, truly, this is only the beginning.

And I conclude with this final observation. One of the greatest achievements of graduation is sitting through the commencement exercises.

CORNERSTONE LAYING

I have it on the hallowed authority of the Encyclopaedia Britannica that a cornerstone today need not be what it originally was, "a support, a corner or a key part of the foundation of a building." All it needs is a message—sometimes carved on it, sometimes ceremoniously placed inside it—entrusted to stone for the information or possible amazement of a future generation. My function here today is probably first to make sure we all know where the cornerstone is, second to tell you the message we are asking this stone to convey to those who pass this way in future times, and third, and perhaps most important, to give us another good reason to finish the building.

One thing that always worries me about the kind of cornerstone inside which documents and mementoes are placed, is the question of whether, when, how and why the documents will ever be seen again. If a date for having the stone opened is specified at the time we have the cornerstone laying ceremony, how do we know the stone will be around for the unveiling on that specific date? How do we know the building will still be around?

We don't know—we hope. And in modern times we have been able to add some new twists as forms of insurance. We take pictures of the cornerstone; we keep copies of the messages and/or mementoes of the occasion.

Cornerstones are almost as old as the oldest buildings known to man. They existed even in buildings that didn't have corners. They signified offerings to the gods, prayers, threats to deter people from disturbing the building and sometimes simply identification of the builder or owner of the establishment.

Cornerstones can be dedicated, troweled, prayed over, inscribed, sprinkled, used as the setting and occasion for human sacrifices. Even these days, a nervous speaker at a cornerstone ceremony every now and then gets the strange feeling of being a human sacrifice himself. That occurs when a cornerstone dedication has been known to bring a train of unfriendly stones as well.

Today, however, the occasion is friendly, the timing is salubrious and the cornerstone has, in a figurative sense, a real point. Any building, or every building, represents the flowering of an idea, the collaborative effort of many people. This building represents something more, in terms of what it means to the community.

In dedicating this cornerstone, I hope it will be a symbol of permanence and of strength in this community. For this cornerstone, we all know, represents more than meets the eye.

I am honored to be invited to participate in this ceremony. It is always gratifying to be in on the start of something new, and particularly so when what you are taking part in is the challenge of building for the future.

EASTER

Easter is, of course, a profoundly religious occasion, but it is also associated with so many different customs and traditions that an Eastertime speaker has a wide range of topics from which to choose the subject of discourse. For the fashion-minded there is the life and times of the Easter parade, or whatever happened to the Easter bonnet? For the artistic there is the decorated egg; for the competitive, the egg roll; for animal lovers, the Easter rabbit. As you can see, people have been observing Easter in lots of ways.

Easter derives its name, it is believed, from an ancient Teutonic deity, the goddess Eostre. A festival in honor of the goddess Eostre was celebrated every Spring, and when the Resurrection of Christ became a movable Christian celebration, it seems to have taken the popular title of an established seasonal occasion. But, by any name, it is a time to rediscover the miraculous joy of life.

This is the time of the year when the lifegiving breath of Spring begins to cause the grass to grow and the leaves to bloom and the buds to blossom. "All the veneration of Spring," said Emerson, "connects itself with love." It is a lovely sentiment, and an ideal to which we all aspire.

It is customary, at Christmas, to exchange gifts, and at New Year's to exchange resolutions. Easter seems to be the season of hope and good wishes and moral communion—in many ways the most spiritual of the year's many traditional occasions. And so it seems appropriate for me today to speak of some of the difficult moral issues of our time.

Perhaps one of the most important is faith. I speak not of faith in the formal religious sense nor in terms of the relationship between mankind and its Maker, but rather of the kind of faith on which the greatest of human progress has always been based—faith in one's fellow man. It is so easy to contemplate the things which divide us—the prejudices, the distrusts, the suspicions, the isolation—that we are apt to lose sight of the extent to which humanity means compassion, love, brotherhood, sympathy, a helping hand.

Look around you. Examples of that kind of faith are not hard to find—or to emulate and honor. Easter, like the Jewish Passover from which it arose, reminds us that, however difficult things may seem, faith will be rewarded.

The truth shall rise again.

ELECTION DAY

The trouble with a speaking engagement near Election Day is that whatever you say is likely to be regarded as at least subtly partisan. In a time of picking sides, the burning question too often is "whose side are you on?" I am here to make a few frankly political statements, but they are concerned with the election process itself and not with who is to be elected.

First and foremost, I am here to say there are very clearly two opposite sides on the question of voting, and I am an unabashed partisan. The two opposite sides are those citizens who exercise their right to vote—and indeed regard it not merely as a right but as a duty—and those who choose not to be represented in our representative government. It is guaranteed in the Constitution that one has the right of free speech and free assembly and all the other basic freedoms; how sad it is that so many millions of Americans, enjoying the blessings of liberty, have opted out of the fundamental process of free democracy in a free republic. "Let Joe do it" is never much of a policy, but leaving the voting to Joe or Josephine, and failing to cast your own ballot, certainly does not get my vote.

Election time is also an appropriate occasion for speaking out about the sad fact that so many people of outstanding attainments and great qualities of leadership avoid elective office like the plague. Such public office used to be a great achievement and honor. But the risk and discomfiture of running for office have discouraged all too many good people. There is a great contradiction between our increasing recognition of the right of privacy and our increasing and understandable curiosity about the personal and private business and life of candidates. This, as much as greater income opportunities for outstanding people in the business and professional world, has created for our times a problem which previous generations did not have to face—the problem of persuading more people to try for public office. I have no easy solution to offer; but I believe it is something about which we all might do some thinking.

Lest I seem to be using this occasion to view things through dark glasses, let me say a few words in praise of an ancient and honorable American election tradition—the tradition of the good loser and the gracious winner. There are so many places in the world where peaceful elections are virtually impossible, that it is only fair to salute the good temper, good faith and good judgment of our local winners and losers alike. We have a great respect in this country for the voice of the people—even when we may think the voice has been wrong.

Henry D. Thoreau said that "Even *voting* for the right is *doing* nothing for it," and Franklin D. Roosevelt said "Nobody will ever deprive the American people of the right to vote except the American people themselves." So, while everyone who votes deserves credit for keeping the breath of life in our way of life, everyone who abides by the decision of the voters is making a further contribution. After all, reflect on what might happen if we held an election and nobody came.

FATHER'S DAY

You may recall that ancient saying that every dog has his day. Father's Day is of somewhat more recent vintage—and so, in all fairness, is Mother's Day as well. In bygone times, the idea of setting aside a day to honor your father and your mother would have seemed to be a feckless dilution of the ancient Commandment. As I recall, it said "Honor thy father and thy mother," not "set aside one day a year to honor one or the other."

So I prefer to think that the real purpose of Father's Day is to do in public, so to speak, what we do in our hearts all year long. And in that spirit, I am here to celebrate the idea of fatherhood in general and one father in particular.

There are two maxims—or two sides of one maxim—that make a very important point about fatherhood in general. It's a wise father who knows his own child, and a wise child who knows his own father. As babies, we begin with the assumption that father knows everything; as teenagers we are apt to lean more to the theory that father knows nothing; as adults we finally come to the point where we know our father, what makes him tick, how much he means to us—and how much he has put up with in the process of our growing up.

Kids find it easy to excuse their own mistakes because every next step in life is still new to them. But fathering is also an experience where every step as the children are growing up is also a new one for good old Dad. In a family relationship, part of what makes it memorable is the process of learning together—the joy of a father suddenly realizing that somehow or other he has helped to bring up somebody of whom he can be proud, and/or fond—and who is proud of and concerned about him.

Fatherhood basically is a long battle to make a dependent independent. It is a steady battle to keep the next generation from making the last generation's mistakes and to change the generation gap into a generation bond. Today, I am happy to salute one of the winners—I hesitate to use the word survivors because the process of fatherhood, while trying, is not fatal. The song says "What's the matter with father? He's all right!" and that's the truth. All of us are children, many of us in our time become parents and grandparents, and some of us have the happy occasion to salute or be saluted by another generation along the way. Some of us are chips off the old block and some of us are regarded more as splinters. But all of us can join in saluting fatherhood. It's a dadgummed good idea!

FUND-RAISING

Years ago, the famous publisher, M. Lincoln Schuster, attended the planning session for a big fund drive in behalf of a distinguished educational institution. One of the campaign planners said that, although he recognized that big business should not take part in the management of education, he felt it would be productive to invite major corporations to take part in running the fund drive. "In other words," said Mr. Schuster, "you want to drive the money changers back into the temple."

Almost every fund-raising campaign these days has a little of that spirit in it. That's almost inevitable, because the hard fact of life today is that before a campaign can do good, it has to do well. The business of raising money, even for charitable and public purposes, is precisely that—a business, not merely because there are professional experts who make a living by running fund campaigns but because a successful campaign today, whether run by amateur volunteers or by a professional organization, still has to be run along basic business lines. You are dealing with "customers" when you seek contributions just as much as when you sell goods across the counter. Before a contributor makes a gift, he or she has to be convinced that the donation is worthwhile, the cause praiseworthy and the administering organization deserving of trust and confidence.

Some people think that these considerations only apply if you are asking for and receiving a multi-figure contribution from the aforementioned "customer." But that is not necessarily the case. Any of you who have been stuck with the responsibility for selling charity raffle tickets for a mere pittance or for getting the neighbors to chip in a buck apiece for a local health society can probably testify to the fact—noted in one of Parkinson's laws as a matter of fact—that people are sometimes even more persnickety about small expenditures for which they are responsible than for huge ones. No matter what the size of the gift, nobody likes to feel it is being thrown away.

Anyone who sets out to raise funds without believing in the cause, but simply as a matter of duty, is giving himself a doubly difficult task. It is hard enough to get people to open up their hearts and their pocketbooks when you are talking to them with all your heart and soul. When you are simply going through the motions, it just doesn't work. So I ask you to remember that when a dedicated campaign worker asks for your charitable "investment" in a worthy cause, that campaign worker is already committed to what is usually a larger investment of time and effort and commitment.

I have always felt that the gift of money—while forever needed—cannot tell the whole story. The most precious gift, always, is the message that you care. There are, in practical terms, only two ways of showing how much you care for a particular cause. One is the amount of work you do for it; the other is the amount of your substance you give to it.

We live in times when, thanks both to the complications of modern life and the generosity of the human spirit, the number of worthy causes seeking contributions grows with every passing day. Very few, if any of us, can afford to give to a great many of these worthy causes. That is why the concept of the United Way became popular, to enable the individual giver to let somebody else divide the gift among the various needs. But virtually every non-profit organization also needs primary funding of its own, and virtually every such organization needs to know that it can depend on the steady interest and support of a specific constituency.

One of the nicer aspects of personal giving in the United States is that a substantial portion of what you give turns out to be somebody else's money. Depending on your income tax bracket, you save a varying percentage of the taxes you would otherwise have to pay Uncle Sam, because contributions up to a rather substantial proportion of your income are tax-deductible. If you don't make contributions, you may have to pay more in taxes; so it is Uncle Sam's money, as well as yours, that you are donating.

I hope for the help that will enable this campaign to do well. Only then can the money do good.

FUNERAL

When we assemble to note the passing of one who, until so recently, lived among us, we do not mourn for the deceased. Indeed, most religions regard death as passing on to another reward and those without religion see death simply as a mortal's final chapter. We mourn *our* loss; we sympathize with the sorrow of the bereaved. We search for the good things to remember as solace. If we understand the nature of the occasion, it may serve to give us comfort.

Traditionally, a memorial address searches out and takes not of the good and noble things in the life we are remembering. It is this remembrance that remains when the curtain falls. But each of us, in our own life, is the sum total of many memories. Each of us learns from what we remember fondly. Each of us, in some measure, looks back to the departed and chooses that which is worth remembering. Even in the act of remembering, we are moved somewhat to emulate—or to avoid, depending on the memory. Generally, what we choose to remember is the best of the past life—and the best is always a model, which we try to emulate.

"No man is an island," John Donne wrote. But we do not simply share the tolling of the bell. We share a learning process, a degree of inspiration, a lasting lesson of friendship for some, love for others. And when we say that something of the departed remains with us we are not speaking allegorically. We are speaking of part of the experience of our own lives.

One of the things which always deserves to be said to those who come to extend their last respects is that they are not your last respects to————. You have remembered; and forever filed away in your spirit is the memory of whatever it was that linked you with (him) (her.) You have also come to be part of the community of mourners—to add to the mutual comfort that arises from knowing that grief is shared and understood.

Most of the richness of the human experience is in what is handed down from one life to the next—not simply things of mortar and stone, but memories of what this one did or that one said or this one felt. That is why we remember the good things—because they are worth remembering, and because we, the living, have a need to remember. And we have much to remember about————.

The departed never wholly leave us. We never wholly leave each other. And we remember.

GRADUATION

(see also Commencement)

The word "graduation" has several meanings. The primary meaning is the state of being arranged in steps or degrees. It is worth pondering that an inanimate thing, as well as a human being, is subject to graduation. Anything which comes in an orderly progression is a process of graduation. We graduate from one phase of life to another, because life is a series of progressions.

Some of the young people taking part in today's ceremony may therefore be saying to themselves, "Wouldn't I have graduated to the next phase of life without going to school? Wouldn't I graduate from being a child to being an adult when I get old enough without having to earn a diploma or take tests?" The answer, of course, is that growing up is a series of graduations—some simply the result of your physical growth over the course of years, which is not usually at all under your own control; and part the result of your studying and learning, which is aided by teachers and parents but is principally your own accomplishment. What we are here to celebrate today is what you have accomplished—what came about not simply because you grew older but because you learned.

Today is generally thought of as a vacation from learning, a day of freedom from books and memorizing and homework. If that is what you think is the sum total of learning—books and classes and memorizing and homework and tests—then you still have a lot to learn. As a matter of fact, human beings, if they are lucky, keep on learning until the day they die. They learn from what they read and what they see and what they hear and what they do. The hope is that your schooling and your teachers have been able to help you to know how to keep on learning for yourself.

The graduation ceremony and the diploma you receive tell the world that you are ready to go ahead to the next step in your lives. You have passed through an important part of the learning process. If it has been completely successful, the main thing it has taught you is how much more there is to learn. An American writer of the nineteenth century said something very wise about this whole subject. His name was Bayard Taylor, and what he said was this: "Learn to live, and live to learn."

Every time you graduate, you go on into a bigger world, where there are more people to know, more difficult jobs to do, more experiences to have than you have yet gone through. One of the things which graduation says is that you are now ready to get more out of life. When you learn to read, a whole new world opens up. When you learn to understand the way a machine works or a government works or why a plant thrives in the sunlight, other worlds open up to you. We always speak of people growing up; we don't simply mean that they get taller. We also mean that they move higher in the world, like climbing up a mountain so you can see more and further.

You have climbed up the mountain. It was easier for some of you than for others. But for all of you, it is an accomplishment which your parents and friends applaud. We congratulate you. You have completed an important phase of your education. Use it well.

GREETING

I rise to express the spirit of this occasion, to greet and welcome you. It has been said that human beings are the only living creatures who ever ask themselves, "Why are we meeting here like this?" Even though, in common with all the other inhabitants of the planet, we have the usual herd instincts, we also have more personal and more uplifting motivations—friendship, affection, appreciation, a sense of justice, a sense of beauty.

It is particularly pleasant to meet to share any of these rewards. Happiness is one of those things which seems to grow when it is shared. For that matter, even misery loves company.

My function here today is rather like that of the orchestral overture, to let you know that what you come for is about to start—and also to begin to get you in the appropriate mood. It isn't a difficult job, because you all know very well why you came here and the purpose of the gathering. In that sense, no overture is needed.

If I may paraphrase a much quoted remark of Yogi Berra's, which he is supposed to have made when he was the guest of honor at a civic celebration, "I want to thank everybody who made this occasion necessary." It is a pleasure to greet you.

Of course there are many ways of extending greetings, salutes and hospitality. Sometimes, there is that strange symbol known as the key to the city. Sometimes there is a toast; sometimes there is a commemorative monument. Always, and this is my function at this juncture, there are the words of welcome and the official starter who says, as I do now, "it's time to settle down to the pleasant business of the day."

GROUNDBREAKING

I suspect that there is some rather ambiguous symbolism in the fact that, when we launch a great new building project, the two tools we use are a shovel and a speech. If your comment when this is over is that this was a ceremony where we really "shoveled it," there will always be a certain element of doubt as to what the comment really meant to say. Or look at it another way, life is a process of digging a hole and then building your way out of it.

Groundbreaking as a ceremonial event goes back to the early roots of man. It goes back to tilling the soil and to the time when the idea of digging, of interfering with the natural order of things, seemed terribly daring—a sort of defiance of the gods. So when we dug—which was then about our only civil engineering—we thought it wise also to say a few appropriate words of veneration for the gods, to be sure they knew we were not defying them.

We went to the point of asking for their blessing on our enterprise. And, if you stop to think about it, that's what we still are doing today. A groundbreaking ceremony is designed to celebrate the start of a project which we think deserves to be smiled upon by the Supreme Power. The ceremonial turning over of the soil is our signal of hope for a new enterprise.

It also reminds us that nothing is stronger, nothing is firmer than the ground on which it is built, and I suppose that where you choose to build is as important as what you choose to build.

Finally, we should remember that the ceremony of breaking ground is also the signal that it is time to go to work, to prepare the land for whatever we are hoping to do with it. Being asked to preside at a ground breaking ceremony, like being chosen to throw out the first ball at the start of the baseball season, is a great honor; but to me it has always seemed that it was also a means of doing honor to the worthiness of a project. Baseball didn't get the President to throw out the first ball until long after it had been accepted as an American national game. In a certain sense, building new constructions is also an American national game. From the quonset hut to the skyscraper, we have been originators and doers in the field of construction. We attach a spirit of good citizenship to the idea of building. Breaking ground is thought of as a sign of progress. So I am happy to have the privilege of being part of this ceremony.

And as we press our tool into the earth to break the ground, we should remember that for all the countless centuries that we have taken sustenance from the soil, we have also built upon it. The land is good and, Fate willing, we shall use it well.

INAUGURATION

For as long as there have been leaders among mankind, there have been formal procedures for installing new office holders. Everything from human sacrifice to majestic coronation rites has been used to celebrate the advent of a new regime. I am happy to note that we are going to be somewhat between those two extremes of human sacrifice and majestic coronation here today.

In the old days, loyal subjects used to prostrate themselves as a sign of allegiance to the new top brass. Then, when democracy came along, there was a certain fear that candidates for the top brass would prostrate themselves before the electorate, reversing the old custom in search for votes. In the old days, the big day was highlighted by the show that was put on for the new official—the parade, the dancing girls, the gifts from far places. That got turned around too. The big show, for example, in the case of U.S. Presidential inaugurations, has been the speech made by the new Chief Executive. And some of those speeches have been most memorable. President Franklin D. Roosevelt said "we have nothing to fear but fear itself." John F. Kennedy suggested that we "ask not what your country can do for you; ask what you can do for your country." Lincoln reminded us that "This country, with its institutions, belongs to the people who inhabit it."

It has been said that, in this country, people who run for office to win a seat in the government often win in a walk because of their popular stand, and spend a good part of their term riding high. That last is certainly the hope as we inaugurate today's standard bearer. I remind you of the words of *Matthew*, 22:14: "For many are called, but few are chosen." To be chosen is a rare honor, and in this case we all feel that the rarity was well done.

One of the great problems in a democracy is that some of the people who help select the people's choice like to try to exercise a shopper's prerogative and demand a lifetime guarantee. Even though we all expect a superb performance from our new office-holder(s), we can't help remembering the old adage that first the man holds the office and then, if he isn't careful, the office holds the man. We like to think there will be no holding our new office-holder(s), and that today we are seeing the start of better things to come.

Al Jolson, the greatest performer of his time, used to say to the audience when they cheered him, "You ain't seen nothing yet." The grammar may leave something to be desired, but the message is crystal-clear, and I believe it furnishes a fitting theme for this inaugural occasion. With the kind of good wishes which accompany this taking of office, with the kind of person on whom the mantle of responsibility now rests, with the kind of need and the kind of challenge and the kind of opportunity that loom before us today, it is fair to say that "You ain't seen nothing yet."

And now, the time has come to install our new officer(s). Or, as it is sometimes put, "batter up!"

INDEPENDENCE DAY

(See also July 4th in Volume 3)

If Independence Day did not exist, a holiday on or about the Fourth of July would probably have been invented. It is the natural start of the vacation season—the bridge between spring and summer, the traditional half-way point of the major league baseball season. But the Fourth of July, Independence Day, is something more than just another holiday. It is the birthday of a great idea—not merely the idea of independence, not merely the idea of the rights of man, but a profoundly idealistic and profoundly influential charter of liberty.

The revolution which was signalled by the adoption of the Declaration of Independence in Philadelphia on July 4, 1776, laid down the principles which have been the foundation-stones of human progress ever since—the truths which the Continental Congress declared to be self-evident, although, some- how, most of the world had failed to take notice of them. The Declaration established, and the world steadily followed the statement, "that all men are created equal and that they are endowed with such unalienable rights as life, liberty and the pursuit of happiness. Also that government derives its just powers from the consent of the governed."

Ask yourself in how many parts of the world today, more than two cen- turies after the men of the Continental Congress pledged their lives, their fortunes, and their sacred honor, in how many parts of the world today the very utterance of the words of the Declaration of Independence would still be regarded as sedition or revolution. Then, on the other hand, consider the explosion of recognition for the rights of man which followed, all over the world, in the wake of the Declaration of Independence.

The Declaration of Independence did not merely signal the birth of American freedom and American self-government. It marked the birth of freedom as an international idea. It was the inspiration for democratic movements on other continents. It raised the torch of liberty and kindled an undying flame.

Back in 1857, Abraham Lincoln, in a truly prophetic observation, noted that the mention in the Declaration of Independence that "all men are created equal" was—and I quote—"a stumbling block to all those who in after times might seek to turn a free people back into the hateful paths of despotism".

It is sometimes suggested that the world now needs a Declaration of Interdependence. But a careful reading of what was presented to the Founding Fathers by Thomas Jefferson, John Adams, Benjamin Franklin, Roger Sherman and Robert Livingston, in 1776, contains all the ideas a peaceful, just and democratic world needs to live by.

And a quotation from the preamble to the Declaration of Independence makes another point worth noting. It is the phrase which mentions "a decent respect to the opinions of mankind . . ." No nation, any more than any man, is an island. We were the first nation to be concerned about a decent respect for the opinions of mankind. Indeed, even more than 200 years later, we seem to be the people most anxious to be liked. Even when we have waged war, we have ended up working to be liked by our erstwhile enemies. A decent respect for the opinions of mankind—just one more example of the almost universal application of the document whose birthday we celebrate today.

INDUCTION OF NEW MEMBERS

One of the traditions of human society, going back as far as the early tribes, is the rite of passage—that's rite, R I T E, which in this case is the opposite of R I G H T. The rite of passage is the ceremony of admitting new members to an already established group. And, as you know, every already established group likes to regard itself as the best judge of whom it wants to add. So it is particularly pleasurable to add you all to the most wanted list and to welcome you as new members of this notable group.

We have come a long way, of course, since the first youth was sent out into the jungle to prove that he belonged with the men instead of the boys. We have also come a long way from the tradition of the Heidelberg dueling scars or the college hazing. We have come a long way toward recognizing that it is much nicer for all concerned to welcome people than to devise trial by ordeal, or to think up hazardous initiation stunts.

There is always a certain conflict with regard to new members. Some of the older members feel very strongly that the organization—any organization—can always use new blood. Sometimes other members, however, seem to be truly out for blood, determined to keep a good thing to themselves. In this case, I am happy to say that the prevailing wisdom is simply that a good thing is worth sharing.

It is said that an organization can be judged by its members and an individual can be judged by his organizations. What this adds up to is simply the fact that now we are all in this together.

A familiar phenomenon in connection with many ceremonies is the fact that the ceremony itself sometimes seems to overshadow the significance of the event. That's why I counsel you to regard today's event simply as the opening of a door, not the summit achievement of your lifetime. You have, of course, every right to feel gratified that you are going through this new doorway. All who have already entered before you know, as you will soon also come to know, that this is the beginning of further opportunities, not the climax.

They tell the story of the young man who was very anxious to become a member of a very exclusive key club. He sought out everyone he knew who might be a member. He heard that they favored people with low golf scores, so he took lessons to improve his game. He did everything he could to wangle an invitation to join, and finally he got his membership and his key. He came to the club, opened the door, went in and sat down. And as he looked around, he suddenly realized that after all his effort, he was now a member of a club in whose activities he wasn't really interested; all he had wanted was to know that he could get in. I hope that none of you here today are or will be similarly afflicted. We welcome you as active members, colleagues, friends.

Incidentally, there are more than 16,000 regional or national associations in the United States, plus many times that number of local groups. There is still a lot of the feeling of togetherness left in the land. Congratulations and best wishes for a long and happy association.

INTRODUCTION

Once upon a time, there was a magnificent public speaker who was asked to introduce the guest of honor and principal orator at an important public dinner. Gazing out at the distinguished audience, which came to a respectful silence as the introducer cleared his throat, he launched into a magnificent discourse, which described the sterling qualities of the guest of honor beginning in early childhood. The introducer spoke and spoke and spoke and suddenly realized that he had used more time than the guest of honor was to have for the speech of the evening. Trying to recover, the introducer said to the guest of honor, "You'll have to forgive me, because I see I have used up most of your time. I hope you will understand that I was simply carried away." The guest of honor looked at him and said, "You should be."

I do not want to be carried away today, because I am looking forward, as you are, to hearing from the person it is my privilege to introduce. The easy way out, of course, would be to say simply that our honored guest here today needs no introduction. But if he/she needs no introduction, why am I here? Let us say, rather, that our guest deserves to be introduced in terms which convey the interest and appreciation we feel for the opportunity to have so notable a guest among us.

There are several standard methods of introduction. There is the "one who" style, in which you don't mention the name of the person you are introducing until the end, as if the identification is the climax of a mystery. But our guest today is too well known for me to play that kind of game. Then there is the "Who's Who" school of introduction, the dull recital of a canned biography, which always sounds as if it were snipped from a directory. I will not lead you down the road in that direction either. Let me rather confine myself to a few salient facts about our guest and about this occasion as well.

As you can readily understand from the facts I have mentioned, we are most fortunate to have _____ here to speak to this gathering. We are also fortunate that I have come to the end of my allotted time, and I now close by introducing this audience to our honored speaker (name of speaker). As the peanut butter said to the two pieces of bread in the peanut butter sandwich, I have brought you together, and now you are on your own.

INVOCATION

We thank Divine Providence for having given us the opportunity to meet together here today, and we ask most humbly for the blessing of our gathering. It is written that "While the earth remaineth, seedtime and harvest, and cold and heat, and summer and winter, and day and night shall not cease." And while the earth remaineth, so shall the children of earth be grateful for the guidance of the Lord.

Brighten our eyes with greater understanding, enrich our hearts with compassion and with courage, receive our gratitude for the feasts of fellowship and the fellowship of breaking bread together.

For the knowledge that there is hope, for the hope that there is more knowledge yet ahead, for the gifts of the Lord's devising that we enjoy today, and for the vision of tomorrow, we offer a thankful prayer.

As the ancient psalmist David said thousands of years ago, "Lead me to the rock that is higher than I." "Thy word is a lamp into my feet and a light unto my path."

So is it still today. And so today, as in ancient days, we thank Thee, oh Lord, for all thy blessings, and let us say Amen.

(Lighter Material)

In recognition of the hour, this invocation will be brief, though not quite as brief as what I call the hungry grace, which is simply: "Good food, good meat, Good God, let's eat." Let me say rather, "Oh Lord, bless our gathering and our going forth; let us see the light without being blinded by it."

When Cardinal Cushing was delivering the invocation at the inauguration of President Kennedy, a mishap in the vicinity of the podium caused smoke to rise. One of the correspondents seated nearby turned to a colleague and said, "When the Cardinal is hot he's really hot."

Martin Luther said, "The fewer words, the better prayer." We invoke thy blessing, oh Lord, on this day and in this place, for what we now prepare to face. And lest we seem to plead again, we humbly all now say Amen.

The story is told of the long-winded man of the cloth who, when invited to deliver an invocation, spoke so long that they had to cut the rest of the program short. When one participant complained about the shortened program, a colleague differed. "I thought the invocation was more successful than most," he said. "Any time the average speaking program is shortened, it's a blessing."

Or, to put it another way, a brief invocation is a real blessing.

JUBILEE

There are two sources for the idea of a jubilee. One is the Latin word jubilar, which litterally means to make sounds of joy. The other source is the ancient Hebrew word "yobel," which refers to the trumpet that was sounded to call upon the people of Israel to celebrate every fiftieth year, in the words of the *Book of Leviticus*, Chapter 24, when "it shall be a jubilee unto you." In the jubilee year, it was ordained, and again I quote the *Book of Leviticus* in the *Bible*, "Proclaim liberty throughout the land unto all the inhabitants thereof." That, as you know, is the inscription on the American Liberty Bell. The year of jubilee was very real in meaning at another time in American history too. In the period of our Civil War, as you may recall, there was a popular song about "the year of Kingdom coming, the year of Jubilo." Jubilo, more properly jubilee, recalled the fact that in the Biblical year of celebration the slaves were to be freed and joy was to be the happy lot of all.

That is always the purpose of a jubilee—joy for all concerned, a time for celebrating, an occasion for looking back with satisfaction and with pride. For what we are celebrating here is not merely the passage of time; not merely the very special birthday that a jubilee represents. We are celebrating a notable accomplishment. We live in times when it sometimes seems that merely surviving is an accomplishment, but what we celebrate here is far more positive. It is recognition of an example of enduring worthiness. And like the Biblical year of jubilee, it isn't a private matter. It is a happiness which lots of people share.

But there are all kinds of jubilees these days. If you look in the *World Almanac*, under the heading of anniversaries, you will find that after 25 years a married couple celebrates their silver wedding; and a king 25 years on the throne has a silver jubilee. The fiftieth anniversary is a golden jubilee year, and as the life of mortals is measured, a diamond jubilee after 75 years is about as far as we go with most individuals. But for nations, for institutions, for ideas, time offers less limitations—and if diamonds are for a 75th anniversary, we will simply have to find yet more precious stones or metals to denote the added years.

Go beyond the immediate occasion for this jubilee and ask yourself what we are celebrating. Ask yourself how much went into the building of what we are celebrating here today. Ask yourself what made it work. And join me in saluting those who made this jubilee possible.

So let us, in the spirit of the Latin jubilar, make sounds of joy. Let us, in the tradition of the celebration of the Biblical jubilee, be grateful to have been privileged to be brought to this time and this happy occasion. And let us say to all who have been part of the events which made this occasion possible, congratulations.

KEYNOTE ADDRESS

Most of us can remember being led in song at an elementary school assembly by a teacher who came out and either blew a pitchpipe or hit a key on the piano to give us the starting tone. I feel somewhat like that teacher here today—not quite certain how close my key note will be to yours, hopeful I have not pitched my sounding-off too high or too low.

We all recall the story of the commander who stood off to the side as his troops rushed forward. "What are you doing back here?" he was asked. He replied, "I am waiting to see which way they go, so I can lead them." The function of a keynoter is to see in advance which way his audience is going, so he can get there ahead of them or lay out the path; but it is also sometimes the function of a keynoter to constitute himself as a scouting party to explore alternative paths.

One thing, however, is always in order. That is the duty to present, as clearly, concisely and cogently as I can, a statement of the facts as they exist today, the conditions which underlie this meeting, the common concerns and objectives which bring us together.

Above all, we must remember what has brought us together. We must be aware of the challenge, the need, the opportunity we have before us. We can make harmonious music—if we heed each other's voices—or we can produce a cacophony and a dissonance that end up making us not part of the solution, but rather part of the problem.

As the sages have said, all human effort can be reduced to three questions: Where are we, how did we get here and what can we do about it? Let me deal with those basic questions. First, where are we?

Now, as to how we got to this point, I remind you of the familiar Rashomon syndrome. Five people may all have undergone the same experience to get to the same place, but you'd never know it to hear each one tell it his way. Or, for another example, there is the familiar story of the blind men examining an elephant by touching it. Result: one blind man felt the trunk and said an elephant was like a snake. Another blind man felt a leg and said an elephant was like a tree trunk. A third blind man felt the elephant's tusk and said there was no question about it; an elephant was like a long thin rock. How did we get here? We each have our own ideas on the subject. We each had our own experience along the way. We meet here to have the mutual benefit of all that experience, all that differing perspective.

And, of course, we meet here also to decide what we can do about what brought us together. First we consider the choices available to us, and then we make our choice. Let me list what I believe our options are.

Life has been described as one door after another. I hope that our meeting will choose to open the right doors, to walk the right paths and to come to the right ultimate position. For myself, I can only try in this keynote speech to find the right key.

LABOR DAY

A long time ago, a wise and cynical man named Voltaire said that "work saves us from three evils: boredom, dissipation and want." Today we have a better cure for boredom. It is the great Labor Day holiday, a time to rest from our labors by working hard to have a good time. Labor Day began as a parade on September 5, 1882 in New York City. It became a national celebration in 1894. It became much more than a parade long before then—a patriotic celebration, a picnic, a big day at the airport and the bus station. Most important, it is everybody's end of summer celebration, everybody's salute to the work ethic.

There has been some extraordinary eloquence heard on this day, and also a considerable range of sentiments. President Franklin D. Roosevelt said, "Labor Day symbolizes our determination to achieve an economic freedom for the average man which will give his political freedom reality." Fiorello LaGuardia, the Mayor of New York, called Labor Day "America's Day" and said "it is typically American because American labor, whenever it gathers, does so with love for its flag and country and loyalty to its government." And John L. Lewis, on the eve of the Labor Day weekend in 1937, as his C.I.O. faced bitter times, proclaimed that "Labor, like Israel, has many sorrows." President Theodore Roosevelt, in 1903, found Labor Day the occasion to observe that "No man needs sympathy because he has to work . . . . Far and away the best prize that life offers is the chance to work hard at work worth doing."

Peter J. McGuire, who was a leader in the Knights of Labor back in 1882, proposed Labor Day as the occasion for a parade to be followed by a picnic, a holiday described as being "representative of the industrial spirit, the great vital force of the nation." He chose a date more or less halfway between Independence Day and Thanksgiving Day, and who is to say his choice was not a perfect one? For many, Labor Day became the dividing line between vacation time and back to work season. For all, it has been the signal to get back to business, to start the new entertainment season, get ready for the new year and so forth. It has been suggested that Labor Day should make a better time for new resolutions than New Year's Day, but that's one tradition that not even the Labor Day weekend has been able to challenge.

There have been suggestions that, in view of the way we celebrate Labor Day, the holiday should be followed, rather than preceded, by a day off. But we might reflect on the fact that in the 1880s, when Labor Day began, child labor was lawful, the 12-hour day and the six-day working week were commonplace and the idea of a labor union was considered by many people to be revolutionary. What labor has achieved in this country deserves all the celebrating it can get.

The United States and U.S. labor have indeed come a long, long way together. And, it is safe to say, they still have a long way to go. But Labor Day is not just Labor's Day. It is a celebration of an all-American accomplishment and an all-American concept. In most other countries, labor's day is intertwined with the political overtone of May Day. Here, the dignity of labor is not a matter of partisan politics. It is a matter of civic pride and public recognition—and a good time is had by all.

LINCOLN'S BIRTHDAY

Even if February 12th were not Lincoln's birthday, it would be a notable day in history for America and for the world. But the memory of Abraham Lincoln makes the day even more meaningful.

On the 100th birthday of Abraham Lincoln, Henry Cabot Lodge said, and I quote, "That nation has not lived in vain which has given the world Washington and Lincoln, the best great men and the greatest good men whom history can show." We can say, too, that that nation has not lived in vain which on this same day of the year saw the birth of so many people who have played an important role in the history of America; Thaddeus Kosciusko, the Polish patriot who fought in the American Revolutionary War; General Omar N. Bradley, the famous GI's general of World War II; labor leader John L. Lewis—all share Lincoln's birthday.

One of the problems of the speaker who is called upon to talk on Lincoln's birthday is that it is so challenging to try to wax eloquent about a man commonly regarded as perhaps the most eloquent American who ever lived. Long before the nation celebrated Lincoln's birthday, he himself made a speech on February 12, 1861—the day he observed his 52nd birthday—which expressed many of the sentiments that caused him to be so greatly venerated in later times. Speaking in Cincinnati, he said; "I hold that while man exists, it is his duty to improve not only his own condition, but to assist in ameliorating mankind . . . It is not my nature, when I see a people borne down by the weight of their shackles—the oppression of tyranny—to make their life more bitter by heaping upon them greater burdens; but rather would I do all in my power to raise the yoke than to add anything that would tend to crush them."

Lincoln was the first of our martyred Presidents. After him there came Garfield, McKinley and Kennedy. It is no disrespect to their honored memories, however, to say that the tall man the people called "Father Abraham" towers in the annals of our land.

Why is this so? Why is it that, so long after his own time, Abraham Lincoln is, as his Secretary of War, Edwin M. Stanton, said of him, a man who "belongs to the ages"? I think the poet and biographer Carl Sandburg captured the secret when he said, on Lincoln's 150th birthday in 1959, that "the well assured and most enduring memorial to Lincoln is invisibly there, today, tomorrow and for a long time yet to come in the hearts of lovers of liberty, men and women who understand that wherever there is freedom there have been those who fought, toiled and sacrificed for it."

When Lincoln delivered his great address at Gettysburg he said, "The world will little note nor long remember what we say here." He was wrong. The world has greatly noted and continues long to remember the man of the poeple who so eloquently reminded us that "government of the people, by the people and for the people shall not perish from the earth."

Lincoln was a rail splitter once, a hair splitter never. He said "the ballot is stronger than the bullet." And so, too, is the memory of a great man, whom not even an assassin's bullet could diminish in the long view of history.

LONG SERVICE

It has been said that of all the arts of man the most difficult is that of survival. Those who do more than merely survive, those who distinguish themselves not only by the duration but by the quality of their service, are to be doubly saluted. Today we salute a notable combination of seniority and service.

One of the strange contradictions of modern attitudes is that we no longer seem to venerate age, but we have great respect for endurance. It is a contradiction in our thinking because nobody these days grows older without a great deal of endurance. Staying power, like experience, cannot be taught. You develop it—and it develops you. And it is not contagious. You do not hand it on like a condition of the human anatomy. You help create it in others by a good example. That is the method of teaching which, in the real sense, has been the backbone of humanity through countless generations. Today we honor someone with staying power, with experience and with a long and distinguished record of being a good example to colleagues, contemporaries, disciples and even to competitors.

In recent times we have lived in an increasingly mobile world. There has developed a new type of human being known as a job hopper. The idea of making a long career with one organization is not as orthodox as it used to be. So I must say to our guest of honor here today that we are honoring one who, by a distinguished record of long service, has done honor over the course of years to this organization by ignoring the blandishments of other organizations and by stalwart adherence to the principle that the grass is not always greener on the other side.

There are all sorts of recognition of long service—the stripes on a uniform sleeve, the special lapel pin or the timepiece that commemorates the years by keeping track of the hours—but it has always seemed to me that the truest recognition is that which comes from the hearts of friends and fellow workers. It is people turning out that should truly turn you on.

One thing that is particularly important to note is that this is not a retirement occasion. We are not saluting the end of a career, but rather the contributions to this date of one who is still contributing, competing, doing. It is fine to have applause at the end of a performance, when all the applaudee can do is bow and thank you. How much better, however, to have that electric reaction of approval while the performance is still going on! And the performance of our guest of honor is most assuredly still going on. Indeed, there are those who claim it is an Academy Award performance.

They say that you can judge a man by the company he keeps; I think it is just as true that you can judge a company by the people it keeps. The company that has kept our guest of honor for lo these many years is entitled, I believe, to a round of applause for the company *it* keeps.

Above all, we owe to our guest of honor a great debt of gratitude for showing us that the right person doing the right job in the right way stays among the very young in heart.

MEMBERSHIP MEETING

It is a pleasure to welcome you to this meeting. The most important thing at a meeting of a membership organization is that the privileges of membership be exercised by as many members as possible. The voice of this group is most effective when it is the voice of many. In the new dictatorships that arose after World War II, many who couldn't raise their voices chose to flee. This was described as voting with their feet. I am happy that so many of you have chosen rather to vote in person here today.

The democratic meeting is an ancient and honorable tradition in America. We have lived for hundreds of years under the principle that ours is a participatory philosophy, that we have a right to ask questions and to offer answers, to speak for or to speak against, to listen and think and pick sides and stand up or sit down for what we believe in. What we don't have, of course, is the right, after refusing to participate, to object to the actions of the other people who chose to be present and accounted for. So your presence here gives each of you an expanded franchise to sound off later, as well as in the course of our meeting.

In a poem written for the fiftieth anniversary of his college class, Henry Wadsworth Longfellow talked of "The joy of meeting not unmixed with pain." The playwright Nicholas Rowe, sometime earlier, said, "The joys of meeting pay the pangs of absence." I congratulate you all on being spared the pangs of absence on this occasion.

We all know that it is easier to have a meeting of members than to have a meeting of minds, and we also know that the members have to meet first to get the meeting of the minds. As we proceed with the business of this gathering, let us go about it with the conviction that what brings us together is more important than where we differ, that consensus is better than "nonsensus" and that we can do a lot more together than any of us can do alone. Now let's get down to business.

The first step for any meeting in getting down to business is to make sure everybody knows the rules of the game. I do not plan to bore you at this point with a long recital of Robert's Rules of Order or a lecture on parliamentary procedure. Our approach is very simple. We operate on the principle that membership means participation, the right to be heard and the obligation to let other members be heard as well. Therefore, your cooperation and attention will both be appreciated.

MEMORIAL CEREMONY

"Memory," said Cicero, "is the treasury and guardian of all things." "Praising what is lost," said Shakespeare, "makes the remembrance dear." We meet here today in that spirit. We are gathered to treasure and praise one who has been lost to us, and thereby to make the memory even more meaningful.

Different peoples have different ways to memorialize and remember those who have preceded us to the ultimate reward. Some build monuments of stone or statuary; some erect shrines; some keep the shrines in their hearts. In ancient times the Pharaohs built their own memorials, which to us today seems a strange and morbid thing to do. Pyramids and tombs, for all their awesome grandeur, are totally impersonal. But every human being leaves another memorial of his or her own building. It is the impact of one life on those lives that fellow.

The function of this gathering is to renew the memory of the impact on our lives of (one) (those) whose journey through life preceded ours. We are reminded here of what that journey left behind.

What distinguishes humanity from the beasts of the field is not the construction of monuments nor the composition of epitaphs, but rather the privilege of memory. Memorials can be found in many places and many times, but principally in our hearts.

In some ways a memorial service is a transfer—a transfer of the impression and impact of a human being from what used to be a physical presence to a remembrance, a part of our own inner being. Each of us is a storehouse of memories, from which we draw examples, inspirations, lessons in living. As today we remember _____ , each of us draws from that remembrance an idea that lives. The virtues and the contributions that we remember have a personal meaning in our own lives.

We have not come together here today, however, just to reinforce our individual memories of one so well worth remembering. We came also for the very real purpose of trying to show those nearest and dearest to (him) (her) that their deep sense of loss is shared. We hope that in some way, by showing our own sense of loss and fond remembrance, we can help further the sense of a life well lived, a time on earth well spent, a heritage of lasting meaning.

Traditionally, the occasion of a bereavement, or the anniversary of a bereavement, is a time when friends gather with the bereaved to say, "You are not alone in this loss; you are not alone in remembering; you are not alone in holding onto the memory of a good human being and in recollecting the ways in which he made his mark." As we come together and share that process of remembering, the remembrance becomes clearer, stronger, better for us all.

The epitaph of Christopher Wren in St. Paul's in London, the cathedral he designed, reads, in translation from the Latin, "If you would see his monument, look around." Let me paraphrase that here today. If you would see the real monument to the human being we memorialize today, look around. It is in your faces and your hearts.

MEMORIAL DAY

The memory of fallen heroes is, unfortunately, as old as the hills, because, as long as the hills have stood, mankind has gone off to battle and soldiers have fallen in the fight. In our own country, we had fought four or five wars before the idea of a Memorial Day became a reality.

For the first time, in 1868, a national memorial occasion was observed. It began with the Grand Army of the Republic, the organization of veterans of the Union Army, doing on a nationwide scale what Southern women in several Dixie cities had been doing as a local Spring ceremony—remembering the Civil War dead by placing flowers on their graves. The Grand Army of the Republic asked its members to do the same on May 30, 1868, wherever its fallen comrades lay interred. General James A. Garfield, who was later to become one of our martyred Presidents, spoke at this first Memorial Day observance on the hallowed ground of Arlington National Cemetery. The cemetery had been established only four years earlier; its graves were those of the recent dead, the casualties of a recent war. General Garfield said, "We do not know one promise these men made, one pledge they gave, one word they spoke; but we do know they summed up and perfected, by one supreme act, the highest virtues of men and citizens. For love of country they accepted death, and thus resolved all doubts, and made immortal their patriotism and virtue."

Today, those who laid the flowers on those fresh graves of the Civil War are themselves long gone. And we have seen other generations caught in the savagery of too many other wars. What began as the memorial to the fallen heroes of one war is now our day to honor the memory of the casualties of all our wars.

This is not a time for statistics, but there is one figure that deserves to be remembered. More than half a million Americans have died in battle since the beginning of the Civil War in 1861, and more than half those dead were killed since 1940. That may be why the observance of Memorial Day has become so major an American occasion.

In the beginning, it was more popularly known as Decoration Day, because it was observed by decorating the graves with flowers or flags. That tradition of leaving a symbol of our remembrance is still a strong one; but our emphasis today is and must be mainly on remembering the nature of the supreme sacrifice so many made in the service of our country. And the function of a Memorial Day speaker now, as in generations past, must be not merely to remind his audience of past sacrifices. Rather, the occasion is to be used to inspire us to appreciate what we have in times of peace and how willing our predecessors were to risk their lives to protect this heritage.

The words of General John A. Logan, the Commander of the Grand Army of the Republic, in his first call for the observance of Memorial Day, in 1868, are as eloquent and meaningful today, perhaps even more so: "Let no ravages of time testify to coming generations that we have forgotten as a people the cost of a free and undivided Republic." And, the words of Lincoln, spoken at another but related occasion, express our feelings today: "That we here highly resolve that these dead shall not have died in vain." We can do them no greater honor than to keep alive that which they gave their lives to preserve; love of country, duty, honor and defense of the right as it is given to us to see the right.

MODERATOR

Somebody once described the role of the moderator as being the one to say "Let's you and him fight." On the other hand, when "you and him" fight, it is the job of the moderator to keep things civil and cool. As the monitor of the middle, so to speak, I shall try to state the subjects and questions of the evening as concisely as possible, so as to elicit the full measure of the wisdom and the zeal of our distinguished participants.

I recall the story of the moderator who kept droning on and on, reciting the conditions, rules and regulations under which the discussion was to proceed. At long last he turned to the first panelist and said, "I'm sure you understand why I wanted to be so thorough and precise. It is very important to understand the ground rules." And the panelist replied, "I've never been so thoroughly grounded in my life, when I had hoped to be flying high." I hope that our speakers tonight will fly high with no fear of grounding.

Essentially, the role of the moderator is precisely what appears in the dictionary definition: to serve as the presiding officer, which means to be your timekeeper, clock-watcher, referee, bailiff and master of ceremonies; also the traffic cop, as far as questions from the floor are concerned. Please hold your questions until you are recognized.

With regard to questions from the floor, I would ask that they be precisely that—questions, not speeches. A wise counselor once told me you can make more points more clearly with questions than with declaratory sentences and the burden of proof remains with the questionee. I will, however, step in if it seems that the question is too loaded such as "Have you stopped beating your wife?"

We are here, let us remember, to generate light rather than heat. Such heat as may develop will, I trust, illuminate the subject rather than fry it to a crisp. And I would remind all participants that we have a lot of things to discuss tonight, so that we should all bear in mind the observation made by Edgar Allan Poe. "In one case out of a hundred," he said, "a point is excessively discussed because it is obscure; in the ninety-nine remaining it is obscure because it is excessively discussed."

Let us now proceed to consider what has brought us together on this occasion. I invite your careful attention to our distinguished speakers as we consider the subject of _____.

MOTHER'S DAY

Somebody once said, or should have, that "Years of toil turn mothers gray, for every year they get a day." Mother's Day is a twentieth century invention to honor an eternal institution.

The Reverend Henry Ward Beecher said that "The mother's heart is the child's schoolroom." Motherhood is so universally well regarded that I must confess I am totally baffled at how differently we regard mothers-in-law. We have, I believe, outgrown the era of Philip Wylie's observation, in *A Generation of Vipers*, that "megaloid momworship has got completely out of hand."

I am happy to be able to tell you that Mother's Day was not dreamed up by a mother. It was the brainchild of a loving daughter, Miss Anna M. Jarvis of Philadelphia. The Encyclopaedia Britannica insists that Mother's Day traces back to mother worship in the pagan world, and cites the rites that were conducted to Rhea, the Great Mother of the Gods, also sometimes known as Cybele, long before the Christian era. But, with all due respect for the ancient Greeks, it is a fact that Anna Jarvis, back in 1907, thought it might be nice to have a special service in church for sons and daughters to honor their mothers. She thought it would dramatize the occasion if every son or daughter wore a white carnation to church on that special Spring day.

Since then, I fear, a great deal more attention has been paid to the merchandise of Mother's Day than to the simplicity of the basic idea. It has become a merchandiser's holiday; there is no limit to the hardware, software, rolling stock and common stock that, we are assured, is the gift to tell mom you love her. But the simple fact is that generally the best gift of all is the love itself, particularly since you cannot possibly give back to her as much as she has given you since before you were even able to recognize it.

What is a mother? Let me tell you a story. It is about the mother of an eight-year-old boy. They were staying at a fashionable resort and every day the youngster couldn't wait to go swimming in the lake. One day he went in the water and disregarded the warning ropes and swam way out into the lake. His mother couldn't swim, but she sat watching him and suddenly screamed. "He's in trouble," she cried to the lifeguard. The lifeguard looked out and called to the boy, "You're out too far; come on in." But the boy didn't seem to hear. Then his head couldn't be seen, and the lifeguard went plunging into the water. It took him a long time to come back, and before he found the boy he had to go under water a few times looking for him. The boy was lifeless when they came to shore, and the lifeguard, even though he worked many minutes, couldn't revive him. The mother refused to let the lifeguard stop and finally the boy stirred, spat up some water, opened his eyes and came back to life, to be grabbed to his mother's bosom. The lifeguard waited a moment and then said gently to the boy, "I hope that'll teach you not to go out in the deep water." The mother looked at the lifeguard and said, not "thank you for saving his life" but rather, "he also had a hat."

The moral is that, as far as a mother is concerned, nobody does enough for her child, on any occasion any day of the year. So it is only fair that on this one day of the year, nobody does enough for mother.

NEW YEAR'S PARTY

It is always a treat to be so situated that you can see in two directions at once. A New Year's party doesn't give you quite that ability, but at this time of year we all have our choice of what to celebrate—the year that is just ending, the year that is just beginning, or both of the above. If you think the old year was a great one, it deserves a rousing send-off. If you think it was a bad one, you deserve to celebrate the fact that it is over. If you have high hopes that the new year will be a big improvement, then you ought to give it a warm welcome. And if you are pessimistic about what lies ahead, I suppose the best idea is to enjoy yourself now while you can.

What the coming of January adds up to is a time for looking for good tidings, good fortune and good cheer. January gets its name from the Roman god Janus, who had two faces. He could look in two directions at once— forward and backward. And while two-faced people are not normally a social asset, the ability to simultaneously take comfort from the past and hope in the future is the very heart of the human experience. So, old year and new year, here's looking at you!

Of course, in a realistic sense, we have many different new year occasions, and January is only one of the claimants. The school year, for example, begins shortly after Labor Day; the U.S. fiscal year began on July 1st for a long time and then moved to October 1st. But not too many people, other than some harried parents, celebrate the beginning of another school year, and a fiscal year is not exactly a moving occasion. When all is said and done, there's nothing quite like the time when good old anno domini changes numbers, new office holders take up their jobs, old terms of office end and we all resolve to do better this time.

This is a time for turning over a new leaf. We don't just try to do that with New Year's resolutions. We do it with matters of state as well. On New Year's Day in 1863 President Lincoln issued the Emancipation Proclamation freeing the slaves. On New Year's Day in 1898 the great and historic City of Brooklyn finally merged into the City of New York—and if you don't think that was something of a new leaf being turned you've got another think coming. On New Year's Day in 1902 the Rose Bowl began the epidemic of football bowl games. There is probably no date in ancient or modern history more tied to the introduction of new ideas, serious and frivolous alike, than the time that signals the arrival of still another year.

Everybody resolves, at this time of year, to make some good resolutions and keep them. I have found it safest to resolve never to make any more New Year resolutions. But Alfred Tennyson wrote a few words on the subject that are worth quoting:

> "Ring out the old, ring in the new,
>   Ring, happy bells, across the snow;
>   The year is going, let him go;
> Ring out the false, ring in the true."

And as we look forward to a happy New Year for all, let us also remember the advice of Bobby Burns and "tak' a cup of kindness yet for auld lang syne."

OPENING

(see also Cornerstone Laying, Groundbreaking)

Anybody who is asked to say a few words at the opening of a new attraction faces an immediate challenge. That challenge is to sum up in comparatively few words the attractiveness or significance or sheer challenge of what you are about to see and hear and to get out of the way fast to let you see and hear and judge for yourselves. The challenge lies in the fact that it is very hard to decide how much to say and how much to leave, at least momentarily, to your imaginations.

There is a familiar exercise in psychology that points the way. If you set up a table on the street to sell some baubles, it is very likely that, in the rush of pedestrian traffic, few if any will stop to look at your wares. But if one or two do stop to inspect your exhibit, the chances are that any number of others will then crowd around it. We all want to get a chance to see what every else wants to see. That, ladies and gentlemen, is why we are here today.

One of the most difficult things in these times of feverish communication is to keep a secret. Every time there is an ambitious endeavor in the world of the arts there is a stream of advance reports, most of them usually tinged with but not overladen with accuracy. Even on that rare occasion when nobody knows anything at all in advance, there is an advance diagnosis. One whisperer says, "I haven't heard much about it at all; it must be pretty bad," and another says "They are keeping it quiet because it is a real blockbuster." The fact of the matter, of course, is, that all this, whether seemingly flattering or destructive for the particular project, fades into insignificance when, at long last, the new entry appears for itself. The preliminaries are now over and the main event is about to start.

A hard-boiled publicist has been known to say, give me three weeks, four searchlights and five famous people in the audience and I will give you a grand opening even for a can of sardines. Indeed, part of the fun of an opening is the hoopla, the excitement, the rubbernecking even by the notables who, being human, like to see what other notables are present. I would be refusing to face facts if I did not admit that your presence here is indeed part of the show.

Someone viewing a play by Shakespeare, a sculpture by Michelangelo or hearing a sonata by Beethoven all alone may be transfixed, but how much more so when the experience is to be shared with people by your side.

So here today we are assembled for what I suppose I can call a collective experience—one to which we are all looking forward and one which will proceed as soon as I get out of the way. Let me then give you the essential advance billing and credits for what you are about to enjoy for yourselves.

And now, ladies and gentlemen, the curtain rises.

POLITICAL CAMPAIGN

(See also Candidacy Announcement)

Politics is a matter of opinion. One is moved to take a political position either through ambition for public office or because of firm conviction or both. In either case, the decision of the voters is an expression of opinion, and a political campaign is an effort to persuade public opinion.

"Politics," as President Kennedy observed, at a dinner of the National Football Foundation back in 1961, "is an astonishing profession." "It has enabled me," he said, "to go from an obscure member of the junior varsity at Harvard to being an honorary member of the Football Hall of Fame."

The campaign which I want to discuss with you here today is not an attempt to promote a candidacy for office or for any Hall of Fame so much as to persuade the electorate. I am here to seek your support for specific governmental action on specific public issues, which, I hope to convince you, require your clear and prompt mandate. I am here particularly to do what I can to get rid of mugwumpism. In case you are not familiar with the term mugwump, let me define it. For the past 100 years or so of American politics, a mugwump has been defined as a person who has his mug on one side of the political fence and his wump on the other.

I propose to put the mug and the wump on the same side of the fence. Otto von Bismarck, who was known as the Iron Chancellor of Germany, said that politics was the art of the possible, and Ambrose Bierce, the cynic, defined politics as "the conduct of public affairs for private advantage." That, indeed, is what it will be if the electorate does not stand up to be counted for specific positions on specific issues. I am not going to talk to you about compromise proposals which are merely the art of the possible. I am not going to talk to you about proposals to conduct public affairs for private advantage. I am here to talk about positions and actions which I hope to convince you are in the best interest of all the good people of this (community, state, nation.)

We do not, as individuals, as professionals or business people or families, all have absolutely the same interests. But we all have the same stake in healthy, prospering, civilized and peaceful existence. We are all dedicated, or should be, to those simple goals—life, liberty and the pursuit of happiness. The campaign about which I speak today is not unique in claiming it is in the spirit of those goals. Every political campaign makes that claim. But a great many campaigns, in an effort to be all things to all people, straddle the issues and ask you to vote for compromise positions. I prefer to state what I believe to be right, as God gives me and you the power to see the right. I ask your support for that which is needed, not merely for that which is the minimum, the compromise, the so-called "possible."

Does this mean I am advocating extremism, fanaticism, all-or-nothingism? No, emphatically no. It means, it represents the belief, that a political campaign which begins by compromising, by giving ground on matters of principle, is a disservice to the electorate. I believe voters are entitled to clear confrontation of the issues, to forthright proposals which, in their wisdom, they can accept or reject. In that spirit, let us proceed.

PROMOTION

It is always a pleasure to announce good news, and the occasion for my remarks here today is good news for our organization. I am happy to report to you that _____ is our new (title of position).

On this kind of occasion it is customary to say that we did not take this step lightly. I must tell you that we did indeed take it lightly, if by lightly you mean with pleasure. We regard _____ as being the right person in the right spot at the right time, and I am saying this right out in public as bluntly as I have said it privately.

Anyone assuming a new task deserves to be given the confidence and support of all of his or her colleagues, regardless of whether they report to him, he to them or all are on the same level of responsibility. In this case, I must tell you that if we had not had the confidence in him before the fact, we would not have made the appointment. It was, in that respect, an easy decision. The appointment was both earned and deserved.

Part of the strength of this organization, or of any organization, lies in its upward mobility, its capacity for bringing new leadership up the ladder. Elbert Hubbard wrote that "Some men succeed by what they know; some by what they do; and a few by what they are." Knowledge, energy and identity. _____ has all three. It is a pleasure to welcome him to his new post for his knowledge, for his accomplishments thus far and for himself as a person.

A very successful business executive once observed that he had encountered two kinds of good people in his move up the ladder. He called them shakers and caretakers. The shakers, he explained, were people who were always looking for a better way or a greater level of accomplishment at their jobs; the caretakers were more concerned with not ruffling the waters or disturbing a satisfactory operation. Another successful man made a different distinction. He said some people just want to be fat cats and others have fire in their bellies. What both these executives were saying comes down to this: it isn't enough to keep things running smoothly, though that is often hard enough; the people who get things done are the people who always want to get things done better. That is what we look for, and that is what I think we have in _____.

He has the experience and background to know the history of the new assignment. He has not been asked to repeat that history but rather to write his own chapter. I will be disappointed if he does not give us a few surprises—all good ones, I am sure. Progress, after all, is a succession of surprises.

But there is nothing that should be surprising about his promotion to his new post. He has earned it. On behalf of all his colleagues, it is a pleasure to wish him every success.

RECRUITMENT

The familiar story of recruitment is that of the Army sergeant who lined up his company and said, "I need three volunteers," pointed his finger at three hapless privates and roared, "You, you and you!" If only I had that power here today!

I am here to recruit you. I will tell you of what I believe are the temptations, the advantages and the attractions that may motivate you to join up. I cannot pretend to be non-partisan in this presentation because, after all, I myself have been recruited on the basis of being convinced of the temptations, the advantages and the attractions that I am about to explain to you.

Let me start by saying to you what I hope is clearly understood. I came here to talk to you because you are what we are looking for—you in particular. Only beggars can't be choosers. We are choosers, with a vengeance. We are out looking for people who have both the qualifications and the motivation to join us. First we choose you, then we hope that you will choose us.

This isn't simply a case of "come on in, the water's fine" and "the more the merrier." If it were that kind of deal, my job would be a lot easier, or maybe even non-existent. But we truly have only a limited number of opportunities and we want to fill them with the best possible people. Let me tell you a little more about us and the way we operate, and I think you will understand why meetings like this are so important to us.

We know we are up against some pretty strong competition in coming to you. There are many good organizations which, like us, are constantly engaged in trying to bring in the best people. Those of you who are outstanding may have some very difficult decisions to make—just as we do in considering admissions to our ranks. Recently it was suggested that history had been wrong in calling the tribes of Israel the chosen people and might more accurately have said they were, to begin with, the choosing people, because they chose to worship the single God. If I can apply that comparison here and now, I would say that before you can be chosen you have to make a positive choice for yourselves. We have chosen to invite you to choose us. There is another element of choice now that belongs to you.

I want to thank you for the opportunity to present our case, and, as the fiddle said to the bass viol, "Maybe if we pull a few strings we can make beautiful music together."

RESPONSES

(To an Introduction)

Thank you very much. I am reminded of the story of a speaker who, at the conclusion of his splendiferous oration, was congratulated by the gentleman who had introduced him. In turn, he congratulated the introducer for the eloquence of the introduction—to which the introducer replied, "It really was nothing. I had a much simpler subject." As the simple subject of the introduction just concluded, I thank you for your kind words and gracious reception.

In television there is a function called the warm-up, when a very skilled speaker or entertainer comes out to get the audience into the mood for the entertainment that is to come. You did such a good warm-up just now that I find myself waiting with great anticipation for the act that is to follow—until I realize in consternation that *I* am the act that is to follow. So I had better get right to it.

I cannot listen to an introduction as gracious and flattering as yours without thinking of the story of the distinguished English statesman who was to be the speaker of the evening. The man who was to introduce him whispered a question to him before the program began, saying, "Shall we let them enjoy themselves out there a little longer or shall I introduce you now?" I thank you today for being somewhat more gracious.

(To a Presentation)

Thank you very much. There are times when the words, the spirit which accompanies a presentation, are the greatest gift of all. I am more than doubly honored here today—for the spirit, the words and the item you have chosen to convey to me are all so meaningful that they will have a very special place in my memories. The most precious thing in the world, for anyone, is the esteem of one's friends. Today you have made me very rich, and I thank you.

It has been said that it is more blessed to give than to receive. If so, then you today must be greatly blessed indeed, for you have given me so much. What you have done is so gratifying to me, and so greatly appreciated. Thank you very, very much.

I used to go to a camp which operated on the principle that every child had to win at least one medal before the season was over. When all else failed, the camp would present what was officially described as an "improvement medal." And, of course, the recipient of an "improvement medal" was expected to march up proudly to receive the award along with the gold medalist for track, the winner of the best camper cup and so forth. I can only say to you, in accepting this wonderful presentation, that I do not regard it as an "improvement medal." or a consolation prize.

(To a Toast)

You have had a tremendous effect on me. Indeed, I may go so far as to say you have driven me to drink. And now, as the prairie dog says when he ducks back into his hole, "bottoms up."

Some people will find any excuse for a drink. And I am one of those people who likes the dish you have just served me, toast well buttered up. Thank you very much.

RETIREMENT

(By the Retiree)

I guess you spend a good part of your working career looking forward to the day when you can look back on it. And as you approach retirement you keep looking back and wonder what's gaining on you. But most of all, you look around and you see the wonderful friends you've had and, if you're lucky, the way what you have been working at has grown and prospered.

But there is no point in retiring unless you look forward also; and so today I'd like to tell you what I am looking forward to.

I start by agreeing with Oliver Wendell Holmes, who wrote that "It is very grand to 'die in harness,' but it is pleasant to have the tight straps unbuckled and the heavy collar lifted from the neck and shoulders." I hesitate to say this to so many people who are still in harness, but it is pleasant somehow to contemplate other people running for the money while you are already nestled in green pastures. The trouble always is, of course, that there is never enough of the long green in the pastures, but that's what keeps us on our toes, isn't it?

These days there is a great enthusiasm for early retirement. As a matter of fact, we seem to have some people who retire before they even start work. I want you to know, however, that it took a lot of work to get me here today. And once you get in the habit of working, it's hard to take the cure. So I expect to go on working—even if I only work at taking things easy.

When I started work we didn't have all these modern labor-saving devices. I was well along in my career before society discovered the easiest way to do the work of 50 men—hire 50 women.

I feel somewhat like the man who was tarred and feathered and ridden out of town on a rail. They asked him how he liked it and he said, "If it wasn't for the honor of the thing, I'd just as soon walk." There is, at least to my way of thinking, a lot of honor in the thing that's happening here today, and to say I am honored and touched by your presence here is putting it mildly, but I frankly will miss you all so much that I have very mixed emotions. I could speak for more time than you've got, just reminiscing with so many of you, one by one. It's been a pleasure working with you, and it will be a pleasure remembering that pleasure.

It is very difficult to say goodbye when you know it is really goodbye, not just *au revoir* or *auf wiedersehen*. So let me just say that when I walk out of here I'll keep remembering when—I'll think of you and think of this, until we meet again. Thank you very much.

(By Master of Ceremonies)

In the immortal words of that sage of the ballpark, Yogi Berra, I want to thank our guest of honor for making this occasion necessary. It is always difficult to define the nature of a retirement party, because whether you are celebrating the fact that we are finally getting rid of an ancient mariner or coming to tell our guest how sorry you are to see him go, the fact is that we are all here because of our guest's magnificent staying power.

(Name of guest), has given years to this company, and now he is going to get them back. He is going to have the time to do what he wants to do, and I dare say there are a few people here who envy him that privilege. It was earned the hard way, over the course of a long time.

I would like to remind our guest of honor of a few simple precepts that deserve to be called to his attention at this turning point in his life. Remember that you are not losing your friends, just your expense account. Remember that the years in your life are less important than the life in your years. And above all remember the wise words of Henry Wadsworth Longfellow, namely, "Age is opportunity no less/Than Youth itself, though in another dress."

So we have some advice to give you as you enter this new age of opportunity. First, whatever you do, enjoy yourself. Second, don't write us off your list. You may be leaving the active payroll, but you are not leaving our thoughts. Third, remember that no matter how well the company does hereafter, it's because of the way you helped the company heretofore. And of course, if the company doesn't do as well hereafter, it may prove that a certain human asset is hard to replace.

But let us not dwell on the Company's prospects, and turn rather to your own. It is our earnest hope that in your time here you have learned a little and are now prepared to leave the bosom of your workaday family for the big outside world in your time here we have learned a lot from you.

And as you go forth I cite for you the immortal words first uttered by Jerome K. Jerome many years ago: "I like work: it fascinates me. I can sit and look at it for hours." Or is that what you've been doing all along?

We have a few parting shots—excuse me, I mean parting gifts—to present to you now. I can only say that we are giving you a great deal less than you are taking from us with your departure. We wish you success and happiness now and always.

REUNION

When the lower animals have a reunion, they all lie down together. When the reunion involves human beings, lying is an occupational hazard. You don't think so? Ask yourself how many times you have said to someone you hardly recognized, "Gee, you haven't changed a bit."

The real test of whether a reunion is worthwhile is not how you look, but how the meeting makes you feel. I know that this reunion makes me feel happy—happy not merely to see old friends, but also to bring those friendships up to date, and to discover new things I never knew before about people I did know before.

Let's face it. Part of any reunion is sort of an informal exercise in comparison shopping. How did I do in the intervening years compared to so-and-so? Does so-and-so's life seem better than mine, or happier? How many of us have done what we set out to do? Who has turned out entirely different from what we expected? For the answers to these and many other questions, circulate, friends, circulate and fraternize. That's the only way to find out.

As a matter of fact, there is a very real dividend that comes out of a reunion such as this. We all have a common frame of reference. We all started with that common frame of reference and from that start we have all gone our separate ways. So, for each of us, today offers a perspective on that old subject, how am I doing. Not a competitive perspective, I hasten to add, but rather an overall assessment of whether life has treated us all kindly, or differently.

The times have changed quite a bit since we all first met. If you don't think so, let me read these excerpts from an old (yearbook), (class newspaper). They will remind you all of some old memories.

I found something interesting when I did some research for this occasion. I went to the quotation books to find some bright epigram or clever saying about reunions. I couldn't find any. In the key word index to *Bartlett's Familiar Quotations*, the word reunion doesn't even appear, nor in the *Oxford Dictionary of Quotations*—at least not in the second edition. I guess the answer is that, while a great many people have enjoyed reunions, not very many have said anything worth preserving on the subject. As you can see, I am following in that glorious tradition.

There was at least one distinguished man of letters, however, who tried to provide some words. Henry Wadsworth Longfellow wrote a poem for the fiftieth reunion of the Class of 1825 of Bowdoin College, and he read it to his classmates in 1875. It was entitled "Morituri Salutamus," which, as you may know, means "we who are about to die salute you," the cry of the gladiators in the old Roman arenas. He wrote: "Whatever time or space may intervene,/ I will not be a stranger in this scene./ Here every doubt, all indecision, ends;/ Hail, my companions, comrades, classmates, friends!" You don't have to be as old as Longfellow was, to appreciate the unique feeling of being back with the people who knew you when.

ST. PATRICK'S DAY

This is one day of the year when we truly see the greening of America. It commemorates the patron saint of the Emerald Isle, the missionary who is supposed to have driven the snakes out of Ireland. In his honor, I hesitate to calculate the number of potions prescribed for snake bite that have been im-

bibed over the course of what has sometimes been referred to as time immemorial.

The writer Myra Waldo once noted that, while other people speak in black and white, the Irish speak in Technicolor. I am here to say that, while there are some other people who celebrate in black and white, the Irish celebrate in gorgeous living color. We live in a land where some of those most prominent in the wearing of the green have been born to the purple, in the pink of condition—and have even been known to drink orange juice.

It is easy and customary for a St. Patrick's Day speaker to discourse on the accomplishments, the charm and the special circumstances of the Irish— the Irish in America, the Irish in Ireland. Today I would rather discourse about what, for want of a better term, I must describe as the Irish in all of us, regardless of our surnames or our antecedents. What exactly is the Irish in all of us? Let me tell you. The ability to hold your head up high no matter how oppressed—there's a lot of Irish in that. The willingness, even the eagerness to fight for what we believe to be right—there's a lot of Irish in that. The ability to charm and to defy and to take pride in your lineage—there's a lot of Irish in all that.

It is also characteristic of any occasion involving the Irish that there is joyous laughter and good humor in great supply. The Irish firmly believe that they have a very special approach to life, as witness the story of the public school classroom with a characteristically mixed group of students. The teacher asked one student, "If you were not of Italian descent, what would you like to be?" and the student answered, "Maybe French." Another student was asked, "If you were not of German descent, what would you like to be?" and he answered "I think I'd like to be an Arab prince." Then the teacher asked a third student, "If you were not of Irish descent, what would you be?" and the student answered, "If I were not Irish I'd be ashamed of myself." I sense no wave of shame here today.

It is indeed a privilege to be Irish, although today practically the whole world is Irish by adoption. The wearing of the green is number one on today's hit parade and the shamrock is luckier today than its cousin, the four-leaf clover.

We Americans take pride in what America has given to the world. How then should an Irishman, whose homeland is so small a nation, feel about what Ireland has given to the world—the songs, the literature, the leaders, the patriots, the fighting men, the builders. St. Patrick brought a great heritage to Ireland and the Irish in turn have given a great heritage to the world. Today, remember and salute both the people and the heritage. Today there isn't a little bit of Ireland everywhere. There's a whole lot of Ireland everywhere, and I am happy to join with you in that God-given heritage.

SELF-INTRODUCTION

It is my function here today, first of all to introduce your speaker. That is to say, to introduce myself. My name is _____ and I am here for the purpose of _____.

I hasten to introduce myself because I imagine that everybody shares the same need to know whom they are listening to. You've probably all had the experience of one of those strange telephone conversations where the phone is picked up and the caller starts by saying, "Hello—who am I speaking to?" and the party at the other end says, "Who's calling?" and both sides spar around a bit verbally because we all are a little bit reluctant to identify ourselves till we know whom we are talking to. Now that we have gotten that introduction out of the way, let me proceed to the business of the day.

It is always difficult for a person to introduce himself from the rostrum. It is much easier to introduce someone else. When you say something complimentary about someone else, it is regarded as a nice, friendly gesture and very probably true. When you start telling things about yourself, to establish your credentials so to speak, it is rather awkward. I hope you will forgive that awkwardness and permit me, very briefly, to indicate my relationship to the matter that has brought us together.

There is one advantage to having a speaker introduce himself, of course. He gets to the point quicker. At least that is the hope of the person introducing the speaker today. So let me get right to the point.

SELLING

Let me start by telling you that I am here to sell you something. I say that to you at the outset because, in point of fact, nothing really sells itself. It has to be demonstrated, described or otherwise impressed upon your consciousness. A good salesman's job is not to sell you a bad product. If he sells you a bad product, he isn't a good salesman at all; he's a skilled salesman, and they don't necessarily go together.

I am here to sell you something I believe in. I believe in it because I have seen it work and I know what it can do. I think I know what it can do for you. It has a price tag. One way or another, anything worthwhile has a price tag—not always in the coin of the realm, but never something for nothing. Part of my job here today is to convince you that what I have is worth the price. You have the last word, of course. I can only try to tell you what it's worth in general terms. What it's worth to you is your own decision.

I ask you to consider the claims of every product most carefully—including what I am selling. In that connection, remember the story of the famous singer who endorsed a cigarette by saying it had never given him hoarseness or throat discomfort. Someone who knew him said, "It was ridiculous for you to endorse that cigarette. You don't smoke." "That's true," said the singer, "but read the ad carefully. I said the cigarette had never made me hoarse or irritated my throat. I never said I smoked the cigarette." You will find no such tricky usage of words in my approach to you here today. What you see and what you hear is what you get.

I want you to consider what I am trying to sell you neither as a pessimist nor as an optimist. The pessimist looks at the bottle and says it is half empty.

The optimist looks at the same bottle and says it's half full. But then there is the person who looks at that same bottle and says simply it's half a bottle's worth. That person is a realist. Today, don't render judgment as an optimist; don't render judgment as a pessimist. Be a realist. What I have to offer is a real, real bargain. And here it is.

In the days of the old medicine man/pitch man shows, they would have some free entertainment to collect a crowd before the silver-tongued spieler let his imagination run riot in describing the virtues of his particular brand of snake oil. The pitches are apt to be somewhat subtler these days, but there is still plenty of snake oil around. One thing worth remembering, however, is that the snake oil salesman operates as a sort of hit and run artist. My appearance here today is not a hit and run operation, and my product is anything but snake oil. My own good name and reputation are invested in what I am here to sell. It is on that basis that I am offering my wares.

STATEMENT OF POSITION

In a world of ambiguity and equivocation, we tend to describe people's attitudes on the issues of the day in terms of physical position. We say this person is a fence sitter, not committed to either side, or that person is sitting on his hands, meaning he applauds neither side, or this other person is sitting it out or lying low. I am here today, however, to stand up in plain view with what I hope is a clear, forthright statement of position. I want you to know exactly where I stand.

When George Romney was the Governor of Michigan, he had a news conference back in 1965 at which he said, "I'm as conservative as the Constitution, as liberal as Lincoln, and as progressive as Theodore Roosevelt." Today I propose to be neither conservative nor liberal nor progressive nor classifiable under any overall rubric. I will speak of specific issues and how they should, in my view, be dealt with. If you want, thereafter, to decide whether a particular label fits, whether it be conservative, liberal, radical, reactionary, crackpot, visionary or any other catchall category, you are welcome to your own judgment. My own feeling is that the time has come to discuss substantive solutions to real questions of policy and of conscience, and the substance is more important than any label.

There is a strong conviction among us, as a peace-loving people, that differences in a democratic society are easily resolved if the various sides are willing to meet half-way, as the saying goes. I should like to stress that the positions I will enunciate here are not bargaining points. I do not have hidden lines of concession. I am not playing poker at this point or trying to bluff. I am not exaggerating or extremizing to leave myself room for compromise. What I *am* doing is trying to tell you, as simply as I can, where I stand, what I advocate, what I believe.

Bernard M. Baruch once was quoted as advising people to "Vote for the man who promises least; he'll be the least disappointing." I have another piece of advice along the same line. Vote for positions, not promises. A promise that isn't backed by a carefully enunciated and reasoned position is like Samuel Goldwyn's famous remark about a verbal contract. A verbal contract, Goldwyn said, isn't worth the paper it's written on. I offer premises rather than promises; firm beliefs rather than expediency and, I hope, clarity rather than fuzziness.

In stating my position here today, I begin by asking each of you to do what I think must come first. Establish the goal—the end result you seek. Then figure out the best way of achieving that result. So, as I tell you of my goals, think of whether they agree with yours. If we are not going in the same direction, how we choose to travel there is pointless. I hope you agree with my goals; then we can proceed to examine the specific positions designed to make those goals possible.

TESTIMONIAL

It has been said that a man is judged by the company he keeps. A person is also judged by the company that keeps him—or her. But the best judgment of all is the judgment of one's peers. The company that has been assembled here does honor, by its presence, and by its deliberate purpose, to a person of distinction, a person who has few peers but many admirers and much to be admired for.

John F. Kennedy once said, "A nation reveals itself not only by the men it produces, but also by the men it honors, the men it remembers." Were President Kennedy alive today, I am sure that he would have changed the word "men" to the word "people," but otherwise there is no change in the basic thesis, namely that we reveal ourselves in the people we choose to honor and in determining what achievements, positions or sacrifices to single out for such distinction. And so sometimes we honor people not only for what they have brought out in themselves but also for what they have brought out in others. Today we are here as a testimonial to our honored guest and friend. A testimonial is, literally, the bearing of witness. We are here to bear witness to the contribution of our guest of honor.

We have a tendency to honor people for doing the seemingly impossible. We have gathered to honor one who has successfully bitten off more than the rest of us could or would chew. Some will say we are honoring accomplishment and others will say that the essential element we are saluting is sheer bravery above and beyond the call of duty. But in fact, we are not honoring abstract ideas; we are here to express our respect, appreciation and faith in an outstanding individual.

At the outset, I should like to apologize to our guest of honor for what is about to happen. We are going to talk about him to his face; and we may even find ourselves saying some of the things that have been said about him behind his back. In fact, I am sure we will be saying some of those same things, because they are very nice things. Let me give you a few samples.

There are many people who do good deeds. But there are differences in the way the deeds are done. There is, for example, the story of the man who passed a most attractive-looking restaurant, walked in, ordered a steak and found the food so marvelous that he returned the next night, found a cozy table in the back and ordered steak again; but this time it was so small and scrawny that he called the waiter. "How come," he asked, "that I had such a big juicy steak here last night and tonight you brought me such a small scrawny one?" "Simple," said the waiter; "last night you were sitting in the front window." Some people do good deeds when they are sitting in the front window. Our guest of honor does good deeds out of the spotlight as well as in front of it. And what you see of his good works is only the front window of his tremendous accomplishments.

It is a pleasure now to ask one who has stood up for so many worthy purposes to stand up now for himself and be recognized.

TOASTMASTER

I am your toastmaster. That is to say I am here to bridge the gap between the food and the feature attractions. My function is somewhat like that of the person who does the warm-up at a television studio. It is a role based on several established facts. The first is that a full stomach takes some blood away from the brain and therefore there has to be some time to digest the food before you are given anything else to digest. The second is that any important presentation comes with an overture.

The first wish of any toastmaster is a simple one. He prays beforehand that a funny thing will happen to him on the way over. Failing that, he recalls the story of the man who was asked to introduce Senator Spooner of Wisconsin. The man said, "I have been asked to introduce the Honorable Senator Spooner, who will make a speech. I have done so; now he will do so." But our program today requires a bit of mood and a bit of stage setting, and that would not be the way to introduce it.

The late Ed Sullivan was a toastmaster in a class alone. In fact, that was probably how he got into show business—as an introducer. He was a working newspaperman who knew entertainers and could inveigle them into taking part in benefits. It was sometimes said that they liked being introduced by the man who became known as the Great Stone Face because he made them all look good. But of course he did a great more than introduce the acts. He set the stage, he bridged between, he timed the acts. There's a famous story about that last—about the occasion when he told a lion tamer a moment before a broadcast that the lion act would have to be cut to three minutes. "That's fine with me," said the trainer, "but who's going to tell the lion?" I am happy to announce that we don't have that problem here today.

(Closing)

I feel like a cheerleader who came too late. Nothing I can say can match the eloquence or the warmth of that applause or the effectiveness of what was being applauded. On behalf of those on the dais, our thanks for the kindness of your reception. On behalf of the audience, our thanks for the excellence of the presentation. We stand adjourned.

VETERANS DAY
(see also Armistice Day)

Today we pause to remember those who were called upon to put their lives on the line for their country. We think of those who died in the service of the nation. Let us remember not only those who died, but those who lived; for while the giving of one's life is, as Abraham Lincoln said, "the last full measure of devotion," those who came home from the wars also deserve not merely the grateful thanks but also the salute of their fellow countrymen.

Those who have known war, up close, do not forget it. They have forged a fellowship while facing the fire. They have had more occasion than the rest of us to ask themselves what is worth fighting for, to wonder what are the real values that must be defended. In the history of the United States—and of other nations as well—the most remarkable thing about veterans in general is that they come home as motivated in peace as they were in war. Calvin Coolidge once said that "The nation which forgets its defenders will be itself forgotten." I would like to revise and update that remark a bit. The nation whose defenders forget it will cease to be a nation.

Many a veteran will tell you that, second only to the fear of death, the most difficult aspect of wartime service in the armed forces is the boredom. It is not merely a sort of state of suspended animation; it is the feeling of being in limbo far away from home, the dread of receiving bad news and being unable to do anything about it, the weight of loneliness in the midst of other lonely people. That is part of the alienation of war. And for Americans, used to the freedom of civilian life, military discipline, however it has changed over the years, is still a far more rigid structure than the give and take of peace at home. Yet the veterans of every war have come home and brought new vigor to their interrupted lives. They have not withdrawn; they have not constituted themselves a separate class. They have continued to give of themselves as good citizens. Today we salute them.

In 1950, 37 percent of the male population 18 years and over were veterans. By 1975, thanks to a couple of newer wars, the figure had risen to 41.8 percent. And of course, as women have served in greater numbers in the armed forces, the percentage of female veterans has also grown. In the twentieth century, we have had all too many occasions to create new veterans. We have had all too many occasions to ask our young people—for it is mainly the young who are called upon—to risk that "last full measure of devotion." Perhaps the greatest honor we can pay our veterans, living and dead, is best expressed in another quotation from that most eloquent of American presidents, Abraham Lincoln: "It is for us, the living . . . to be dedicated here to the unfinished work that they have thus far so nobly advanced . . . that we here highly resolve that these dead shall not have died in vain; that this nation, under God, shall have a new birth of freedom, and that government of the people, by the people, for the people shall not perish from the earth."

Lincoln spoke those words on November 19, 1863. For some reason, November is a particular month of remembrance, the time when we give thanks as a people, when we commemorate the end of the first World War, when we go to the polls to exercise the rights in defense of which so many veterans have worn the uniform, carried the flag, fought the good fight. But behind every veteran in the front lines there stood an anxious, gallant and sacrificing family at home. The veteran has never been a separate entity here, perhaps because so many of us are veterans. In paying tribute to our veterans, we are in fact paying tribute to the great heritage that we all share.

WASHINGTON'S BIRTHDAY

It is fitting, in a peculiar way, that the date of observance of George Washington's birthday has varied so through the years. At first, the celebration was on February 11, because when Washington was born, in 1732, we were still using the old calendar. Not until the new calendar was in general use did he himself adjust the date to February 22. It remained at February 22 for not quite two centuries and then, in order to give us a three-day holiday, was moved to a permanent Monday in February. All along, many Americans have felt that the date was less important than the spirit. Indeed, Washington is memorialized in so many ways in the hearts and heritage of his countrymen that setting aside a single day in his honor is almost a contradiction in terms.

If you stop to look back at his role in the creation of the United States of America you can see not one but several historic decisions, made by Washington, that shaped the nation for all time. Perhaps the most dramatic was the one symbolized by Valley Forge—the decision to continue to lead what must have seemed to most a totally hopeless struggle against the British for independence. It was a decision particularly sacrificial for George Washington, patrician planter and pillar of the Virginia establishment, a man with more than most to lose should the Revolution fail and leave him branded traitor to the crown. As we remember what Washington accomplished, we should also remember what he risked.

One of Washington's great decisions came after Cornwallis surrendered and before the Continental Army disbanded. A group of his officers had a plan to get rid of the Continental Congress and make Washington the king of the new nation. He squelched that quickly and thoroughly, and, when the peace treaty was signed, he went back home to lead the life of a quiet civilian. He was then past 50; he had served his nation long and well. But when he was asked to come back as the unanimous choice to be our first President, he again gave of himself, and he set the new country on a firm course.

Not many people remember that George Washington was asked to serve a third term. He could have been President for life; he rejected that proposition as firmly as the idea of being King; a century and a half later, a Constitutional Amendment wrote into law the two-term limitation on Presidential tenure which Washington had insisted upon. He was not merely first in war, first in peace and first in the hearts of his countrymen. He was, first and last, a selfless patriot and a man of principle.

One of his successors had this to say of him, though hardly aware at the time that he would follow in Washington's footsteps: "Washington is the mightiest in moral reformation. On that name no eulogy is expected. It cannot be. To add brightness to the sun or glory to the name of Washington alike is impossible. Let none attempt it. In solemn awe pronounce the name, and in its naked deathless splendor leave it shining on." Those somewhat fulsome words were spoken on the 110th birthday of George Washington by a young Illinois lawyer named Abraham Lincoln.

He was not considered an eloquent man, this George Washington, but few documents in our history have spoken more eloquently of the principles of our nation than his acknowledgment of the language and spirit of his correspondence with the Hebrew Congregation of Newport, Rhode Island, in 1790. "For happily," he wrote, confirming some of the words of the Congregation's message to him, "the Government of the United States, which gives to bigotry no sanction, to persecution no assistance, requires only that those who live under its protection should demean themselves as good citizens, in giving it, on all occasions, their effectual support."

"Every post is honorable in which a man can serve his country," George Washington wrote in 1775, and he lived by that unswerving principle. His example proved more effective, however, than those particular words; for he said them to a man named Benedict Arnold. And in that contrast we can see still further the greatness of George Washington.

WEDDING

We are here to welcome two new recruits into an old institution. They are now citizens of the state of matrimony. The wedding is the swearing-in ceremony, at which the bride and groom have a large supporting cast. The rest is up to them.

To a starry-eyed young couple, love is a wonderful miracle. The wedding seems equally miraculous to all the fond relatives who still think of the newlyweds as junior members of the family. But just think of all the hard work that went into what has just happened here. The simple chore of deciding whom to invite, for example. The task of tracking down at least one long-lost relative—

because it is always the long-lost one who complains if he or she isn't invited. Sometimes I think the bride and groom don't really know what they are letting the rest of us in for.

I know that it is usually the function of the person who performs the marriage ceremony to deliver a discourse to the newlyweds on what lies ahead. But there are some important facts that always seem to be left out in those ceremonial messages, so I would like, on behalf of this experienced group of veterans of the marriage game, to set the stage for today's featured couple. To begin with, you are starting off with a number of serious problems. These problems are called wedding gifts. There never was a set of wedding gifts yet which didn't include things you wouldn't let into your house, items whose nature you can't even figure out and stuff in boxes from fancy stores that, when you bring them back to said fancy stores, turn out to have been purchased elsewhere. You are going to have to make some very difficult decisions. You are going to have to keep things you don't want, and even display them on appropriate occasions, to avoid blood feuds with the people who gave them to you. You are going to have to lie like Trojans in some of your thank you notes. And that's only the beginning.

The state of matrimony, like the state of the nation, requires a certain modicum of what are best described as unofficial sacraments. One such is the sweating out of how to address your in-laws. If you don't know whom to call Uncle or just plain Joe, or if you can't bring yourself to call your spouse's mother "Mom," just take consolation in the fact that Uncle Joe and Mom aren't sure either.

There are a number of romantic myths that have been seducing people since the dawn of time. I think this is an appropriate occasion to state, emphatically, that two cannot live as cheaply as one; two's company but three is not always a crowd; absence does not necessarily make the heart grow fonder; one man's mate is another man's poison; a good marriage, like a good brandy, is apt to grow better with age; if courtship isn't a part of marriage, then court is apt to be.

The time has come to toast two fine people as they embark on their life together. So here's to the bride and here's to the groom and here's to marriage in full bloom; here's to a long and happy life for a brand new, grand new husband and wife!

WEDDING ANNIVERSARY

The almanacs regularly carry a list of anniversaries. The first wedding anniversary is the paper anniversary, followed in successive years by cotton, leather, linen or silk, wood, iron, wool or copper (strange alternatives for the seventh anniversary), bronze and pottery or china. A tenth anniversary is tin or aluminum, the eleventh is steel and so on. I find it interesting that between the eleventh anniversary and the 25th or silver anniversary, there are none that conduct electricity.

The electricity in the marriage we are remembering here today has never failed, and the current has been strong and steady. From the silver 25th anniversary on we symbolize the passing years of marriage with ever more precious themes—pearl, coral, jade, ruby, sapphire and then the golden 50th, the emerald 55th, the diamond 60th and the super diamond 75th. Few of us indeed ever reach that pinnacle of married life; but each step along the way is itself an occasion to be saluted and to be cherished.

Marriage is often described as a partnership; but it is a partnership which dissolves over the course of time into a sense of unity and mutuality unlike anything else known to humanity. It is not merely the passage of time. In our own days, we have recognized that it is at least as easy for a marriage to break up as to survive. So when we congratulate a couple on their wedding anniversary, we are hailing something far more happy and far more significant than mere survival. We are recognizing a very positive and very triumphant achievement.

One reason the celebration of a wedding anniversary by friends or relatives is so joyous an occasion is that it shows the rest of us that lasting happiness is indeed attainable, and that it does indeed become the good fortune of some very nice people. I guess we all also cherish the hope that it is contagious.

A marriage is like an individual. It starts off very young, then grows into maturity, and gains in wisdom, in understanding. If it is a healthy marriage, it gets better with age. This marriage certainly has. If you could sell the secret, you would have no lack of buyers.

George Bernard Shaw said that "marriage is popular because it combines the maximum of temptation with the maximum of opportunity." To this I must add that marriage is also popular because, as our guests here today so happily demonstrate, it can work so well.

In the traditional wedding service the participants are asked whether they "take" each other as lawful wedded wife and husband. I submit that the taking is far less important than the giving. We are here today to give our congratulations and our affectionate greeting to a fine couple. But they have given, and continue to give, each other the real happiness. For this above all we honor them today.

WELCOME

There is a Scottish saying that "welcome's the best dish in the kitchen." It is certainly the warmest, at this moment, as we take advantage most happily of the opportunity to greet you. You are indeed most welcome here and now.

We are honored by your presence among us. It gives us the occasion to show you, face to face, the friendship and the appreciation felt for you here. We pride ourselves on being an open and friendly community. That is an easy reputation to maintain when the visitor is one who, like you, has already established a basis for the cordiality and the hospitality of this greeting.

You need no key to the city; all doors are open to you, all hands outstretched in welcoming greeting, all hearts the happier that you have come to be our guest.

Sam Levenson tells the story of how his mother coped with the problem of the family larder when a guest showed up at the dinner table. She would take some of the children aside and tell them that when the main course was served they should say, "Please don't give me much, because I'm not really hungry." That way there would be enough to go around. But what happened was that when the dessert was served and the children reached for it, mama would say "If you weren't hungry for the main course, you don't need dessert." I am delighted to assure our guest that no such situation applies here. Rather, your coming means a very special gala time for all of us. It is a red letter day and we have the stuff to prove it.

We have killed the fatted calf, put the icing on the cake, polished the windows and put the welcome sign on brightly. Our house is your house.

You are "well come." I mean to say, it is well that you have come. We have been looking forward to your visit. And I am sure we will long remember it. I hope that we can make it worth your remembering as well. As the hot dog said to the mustard, it means a lot to have you around.

Index

NOTE: This Index covers Volumes 1, 3 and 4. Volume 2, **Apt Comparisons**, is not indexed. Roman numerals are used to indicate the Volume numbers.